PLAYFAIR

To Paul, with
Best Wishes

22 MAR 2018

Excerpt from William Playfair's proposal for his counterfeiting operation against France:

"Having already in a Pamphlet which was published in the beginning of the month of February bearing for title, A General View of the Resources of France etc etc I declared in a Public Manner that it was my opinion that the best & most effectual method of attacking the French Nation would be to destroy their credit by falsifying their Assignats, which pamphlet has met with a pretty general approbation, I have resolved for that and for other reasons to falsify the Assignats myself. …"

Playfair

The True Story OF THE British Secret Agent
Who Changed How We See THE World

Bruce Berkowitz

George Mason
University Press
Fairfax, Virginia

George Mason University Press
Fairfax, Virginia

ISBN: 978-1-942695-04-2   (cloth)
ISBN: 978-1-942695-05-9   (ebook)

First edition

Library of Congress Cataloging-in-Publication data is available.

Printed in the United States of America

Jacket and book design: John W. Warren

Jacket illustration credits, front cover (clockwise from top left): 1) Bar chart, from William Playfair, *The Commercial and Political Atlas*, 2nd ed., 1786, via Wikimedia Commons; 2) Line chart from William Playfair, *The Commercial and Political Atlas* 2nd ed., 1786, via Wikimedia Commons; 3) Pie chart, from William Playfair, *Statistical Breviary*, 1801, via Wikimedia Commons; 4) (bottom of page) Playfair's proposal, from The William Playfair Correspondence Collection, Special Collections Research Center, Temple University Libraries, reproduced with permission (also used in frontispiece); 5) Pie chart, from William Playfair, *Statistical Breviary*, 1801, Thomas Fisher Rare Book Library, University of Toronto, reproduced with permission; 6) Assignat image courtesy Le Catalogue Général des Assignats Français.
Front flap: Line chart from William Playfair, *The Commercial and Political Atlas* 2nd ed., 1786, via Wikimedia Commons
Back flap: Line chart from William Playfair, "Linear Chronology," 1824, via Wikimedia Commons
Back cover: William Playfair, *The Commercial and Political Atlas*, 2nd ed., 1786, via Wikimedia Commons

To Rachael and T.G.

Contents

List of Figures

Explanatory and Acknowledgments

It took about ten years to piece together William Playfair's story, mainly because he was so good at covering his tracks and hiding his connections. It was as much detective case as history project, and required travels to England, Scotland, France, and Canada, as well as across the United States. The project would never have been possible without the help of many friends, colleagues, and professional acquaintances.

So I'm glad to have a chance to thank James Adams; Thomas Behling; Antony Braithwaite; Jane Braithwaite; John Browne-Swinburne; Susan Browne-Swinburne; Bruce Bueno de Mesquita; Richard Buel, Jr.; T. R. Bird; John Clayson; Rob Collins; Patricia Costigan; Ikumi Crocoll; Robert Darnton; Darryl Davis; Jean-François Dunyach; Christine Engels; Henrietta C. Evans; Paula Davis Fair; Randall Fort; Adam Garfinkle; Michael Geary; Audrey Glasgow; Mary Haegert; Graham Hodges; Benjamin Hoffmann; Les Hull; Josue Hurtado; Tutti Jackson; Wendy Keller; David Levy; Stafford Linsley; Kylea Little; Ralph McLean; Carol Morgan; Jennifer Mori; Bette W. Oliver; Jaclyn Penny; Hugh Playfair; Debra Playfair; Munro Price; David M. Riches; Alison Rosie; James Sack; Jonathan Sachs; Linda Showalter; J. David Singer; Ian Spence; Peter Stearns; Eric Stockdale; Edward Tufte; Howard Wainer; David Wright; and Mary Yakush. I would like to thank from the George Mason University Press and the University Libraries: Emily Cole, Wally Grotophorst, John Warren, and John Zenelis. The usual caveats apply; I am responsible for the content and conclusions. Special thanks are owed to Kelley and, once again, Bob.

I particularly appreciated John Playfair, Stephen Stigler, and the Earl of Home providing documents from their family papers and personal collections. Peter Bower provided unique information and several images from his decades of research on currency and banks notes; and Suzanne Desan graciously shared notes from her own research on the French Revolution. In addition to providing notes and material, Jocelyne Zanelli was kind enough to provide comments and to help track down several original documents in France, as well as Playfair's old haunts in Paris.

Also, it would have been impossible to have completed the project without the invaluable support of archivists, curators, and staff at the following institutions: American Antiquarian Society; Archives nationales; British Library; Library of Birmingham; Cincinnati History Library and Archives at the Cincinnati Museum Center; Discovery Museum at Newcastle-up-on-Tyne; John Hay Library, Brown University; Library of Congress; London Metropolitan Archives; Houghton Library, Harvard University; JSTOR; Manchester Central Library; National Archives (US); National Archives of Scotland; National Library of Scotland; New York Historical Society; Northumberland Archives at Woodhorn; Ohio History Connection; and Temple University Libraries, Special Collections Research Center. Archivists are the frontline soldiers in the process of writing history, and I truly appreciate both their aid and their patience.

In quoting documents from all these sources, I've presented them in their original form and dialect, complete with any lapses in grammar, spelling, and syntax. Also provided are smatterings of bravely, if imperfectly, translated French. This note is offered lest some readers suspect—to paraphrase Mark Twain—that all the characters were trying to speak in a common tongue but not succeeding.

Who's Who in the World of William Playfair

Henry Addington, 1st Viscount Sidmouth (30 May 1757–15 February 1844): British Chancellor of the Exchequer (1801–1804), Prime Minister (1801–1804), and Home Secretary (1812–1822).

Charles Alexandre, vicomte de Calonne (20 January 1734–30 October 1802): Finance minister to Louis XVI before falling out of favor, later involved with the émigré community in London and the royalist resistance.

Samuel Arnold (10 August 1740–22 October 1802): Songwriter, Playfair's partner in *The Tomahawk!*

Prince Frederick Augustus, Duke of York and Albany (16 August 1763–5 January 1827): Second son of George III, Commander-in-Chief of the British Army (1795–1809). Reportedly worked with Playfair on counterfeiting project.

Joel Barlow (24 March 1754–26 December 1812): Playfair's partner in the Compagnie du Scioto, later U.S. diplomat.

Jean-Joseph de Barth (1726–1793): counselor to King Louis XVI, member of the Society of the Twenty-Four; traveled to America with the Scioto settlers.

Henry Bathurst, 3rd Earl Bathurst (22 May 1762–27 July 1834): British Foreign Secretary (1809) and, later, Secretary of State for War and the Colonies (1812–1827).

Jean, Baron de Batz (26 January 1754–10 January 1822): French dealmaker and businessman, Playfair's friend and business partner, and, after the Revolution, member of the royalist resistance.

Jeremy Bentham (15 February 1748–6 June 1832): Philosopher, political writer, and protégé of the Marquess of Lansdowne.

Samuel Blackden (DOB/DOD unknown): American Revolution veteran from Massachusetts, traveled to Europe to generate business for American investors; introduced Playfair to Joel Barlow.

Alexander Blair (DOB/DOD unknown): Former British army officer, friend and business partner of James Keir.

Matthew Boulton (3 September 1728–17 August 1809): Birmingham industrial magnate, business partner and friend to James Watt.

Antoine-Constant de Brancas (16 October 1764–21 May 1809): French soldier and political activist; member of an aristocratic family who nevertheless joined the Republicans.

Louis Charles Auguste le Tonnelier de Breteuil (7 March 1730–2 November 1807): Minister of the King's household under Louis XVI; with the king's grant of authority, effectively became head of the royalist government in exile.

Jacques-Pierre Brissot (15 January 1754–31 October 1793): French lawyer, writer, editor, and politician; later became a leader of the Girondins during the Revolution.

Thomas Byerley (DOB unknown–1826): British essayist and editor; published the *Literary Chronicle* and other works.

Abbé Jacques-Ladislas-Joseph de Calonne (9 April 1743–16 October 1822): Brother of Charles-Alexandre, also involved in the royalist resistance.

George Canning (11 April 1770–8 August 1827): Tory writer and politician, editor of the *Anti-Jacobin*. Later held numerous positions, including Under-Secretary of State for Foreign Affairs (1795–1799), Ambassador (1814–1816), Foreign Secretary (1822–1827), Chancellor of the Exchequer (1827), and Prime Minister (1827).

Claude-Louis de La Châtre (30 September 1745–13 July 1824): French army officer, veteran of Quiberon; later ambassador representing the restored royalist government in London.

Étienne Clavière (27 January 1735–8 December 1793): Genovese banker, sometime French Finance Minister, business partner to Batz, friend and benefactor to Brissot.

William Cobbett (9 March 1763–18 June 1835): Brilliant but mercurial British soldier, pamphleteer, publisher, and politician; originally aligned with conservatives, later aligned with reformers.

Henry Colburn (c. 1784–16 August 1855): British bookseller, editor, and publisher.

Patrick Colquhoun (14 March 1745–25 April 1820): Merchant in Glasgow and London; statistician and friend of Playfair; later founder of the London Metropolitan Police.

Thomas Cooper (22 October 1759–11 May 1839): Friend of James Watt, Junior; member, Manchester Constitutional Society; in Paris during the October 1792 insurrection; later emigrated to United States and entered politics.

William Cope (DOB unknown–1815): Dublin merchant, British intelligence source against Irish nationalists; occasionally joined in proposed business ventures with Playfair.

Andrew Craigie (22 February 1754–18 September 1819): Boston financier, Apothecary General during the American Revolution; partnered with William Duer in the Scioto speculation.

Manasseh Cutler (May 13, 1742–July 28, 1823): Massachusetts clergyman and polymath; chaplain during the American Revolution; co-founder of the Ohio Company.

Thomas Dale (1729–21 February 1816): U.S.-born British physician, co-founder of the Literary Fund.

Archibald James Edward Douglas, 1st Baron Douglas (10 July 1748–26 December 1827): British nobleman benefitting from the resolution of the Douglas Cause.

Charles Douglas, 3rd Baron Douglas (26 October 1775–10 September 1848): Son of Archibald, student at Oxford.

William Duer (March 18, 1743–May 7, 1799): British-born New York financier, member of the Continental Congress; Secretary of the Board of the Treasury under the Articles of Confederation; engineer of the Scioto speculation.

Guillaume-Michel Dufay (1765?–1 January 1834): Veteran of Napoleon's army, beneficiary of the confiscation of the Saint-Morys estate; killed Charles-Étienne de Saint-Morys in duel.

Henry Dundas, 1st Viscount Melville (28 April 1742–28 May 1811): Friend and ally of William Pitt, served as Home Secretary (1791–1794), Secretary of State for War (1794–1801), and other positions.

Jean-Jacques Duval d'Eprémesnil (5 December 1745–22 April 1794): French magistrate, instigated opposition to Louis XVI in the Paris parlement; friend to Playfair and partner in the Scioto project; later a figure in the royalist resistance.

Royal Flint (12 January 1754–17 October 1797): Connecticut-born, Massachusetts-based speculator, Duer's partner in the Scioto Company.

Charles James Fox (24 January 1749–13 September 1806): British Whig politician; flamboyant supporter of electoral and social reform; Secretary of State for Foreign Affairs (1806).

Giovanni Antonio Galignani (1757–20 January 1821): Italian born, London-based bookseller and newspaper publisher, later known for his circulating library in Paris.

William Garrow (13 April 1760–24 September 1840): British lawyer, politician, Solicitor General (1812–1813), and Attorney General (1813–1817); known for his courtroom skills and legal mind.

(First name unknown) Gérentet (DOB/DOD unknown): French *mécanicien*; Playfair's acquaintance from Birmingham, later his business partner in Paris.

Sir Vicary Gibbs (27 October 1751–8 February 1820): British attorney, politician, Solicitor General (1805–1806), Attorney General (1807–1812), and judge (1812–1818).

Charles Gravier, comte de Vergennes (20 December 1717–13 February 1787): French official and diplomat; Minister of Foreign Affairs (1774–1787) during the American Revolution.

William Wyndham Grenville, 1st Baron Grenville (25 October 1759–12 January 1834): British Tory (until 1801) turned Whig (after 1801) politician;

served as Foreign Secretary (1791–1801), Home Secretary (1789–1791), and Prime Minister (1806–1807).

(First name unknown) Guillaume: (DOB/DOD unknown): Paris lawyer, partner in the Maison de Secours.

James Harris, 1st Earl of Malmesbury (21 April 1746–21 November 1820): British politician and diplomat, conducted missions to Spain, Prussia, and Russia; worked to keep support of German states during the wars with revolutionary France.

Jan Casper Hartsinck (13 August 1755–23 October 1835): One-time partner in the Hope & Company banking house; became Playfair's "moneyed partner" in the Original Security Bank

Logan Henderson (DOB/DOD unknown): Former marine and Boulton & Watt employee from 1776 to 1783, contributing to the design of The Counter.

John Charles Herries (November 1778–24 April 1855): British financier and politician; held several positions in the Treasury before becoming Chancellor of the Exchequer (1827–1828).

Louis Lazare Hoche (24 June 1768–19 September 1797): General commanding republican French forces at Quiberon and planned invasion of Britain.

John Baker Holroyd, 1st Earl of Sheffield (21 December 1735–30 May 1821): soldier/merchant/agrarian, noted for friendship with Edward Gibbon and mustering defenses during the 1780 Gordon Riots.

Rev. Julius Hutchinson (16 December 1750–11 May 1811): Playfair's partner in the Original Security Bank.

Thomas Jefferson (13 April 1743–4 July 1826): U.S. Minister to France (1785–1789), later Secretary of State (1790–1793), Vice President (1797–1801), and President (1801–1809).

James Keir (20 September 1735–11 October 1820): Former army officer, chemist, assistant to Joseph Priestley, manager of engineering at Boulton & Watt.

Brackley Kennett: (DOB/DOD unknown): Brother of Robert Kennett; co-defendant in criminal case with Playfair.

Henry Kennett (1789?–DOD unknown): Son of Robert Kennett; co-defendant in criminal case with Playfair.

Robert Kennett (DOB unknown–16 June 1813): London upholsterer and Playfair's partner in a gun carriage business, later tried for fraudulent actions in a bankruptcy case; executed for forgery.

Lloyd Kenyon, 1st Baron Kenyon (5 October 1732–4 April 1802): British politician, barrister, and judge; served as Attorney General (1783–1784), Master of the Rolls (1785–1788), and Lord Chief Justice (1788–1802).

Edward Law, 1st Baron Ellenborough (16 November 1750–13 December 1818): British politician, judge, Attorney General (1801–1802), Chancellor of the Exchequer (1806), and Lord Chief Justice (1802–1818).

George Leveson-Gower, 1st Duke of Sutherland (9 January 1758–19 July 1833): Member of Parliament and British Minister to France (1790–1792) at the time of the 10 August insurrection.

Marquis Claude-François de Lezay-Marnésia (25 August 1735–9 November 1800): Partner in the Society of the Twenty-Four, friend of Jean-Jacques Duval d'Eprémesnil.

John Lightly (DOB/DOD unknown): London stationer around 1794–1803.

Paul Lukyn (1756?–21 September 1799): London stationer, defendant in *Strongitharm v. Lukyn* (1795).

Andrew Meikle (5 May 1719–27 November 1811): Scottish millwright and inventor; master of Playfair and John Rennie.

Joshua Montefiore (10 August 1762–26 June 1843): London-born adventurer, military officer, writer, and lawyer; published several legal texts; later emigrated to the United States.

Abbé André Morellet (7 March 1727–12 January 1819): French economist and writer; friend of Benjamin Franklin and Lord Shelburne, facilitating the Treaty of Paris.

John Philip "Jack" Morier (9 November 1776–20 August 1853): British diplomat to the Middle East and the Americas; later served in the Foreign Office in London and various postings in Europe.

Gouverneur Morris (January 31, 1752–November 6, 1816): American statesman, diplomat, and speculator; Minister Plenipotentiary to France (1792-1794) contributed to the drafting of the U.S. Constitution.

William Murdoch (21 August 1754–15 November 1839): Scottish engineer and inventor; longtime employee of Boulton & Watt.

Jacques Necker (30 September 1732–9 April 1804): Genovese banker, Controller-General of Finances to Louis XVI (1777–1781, 1788–1789).

Daniel Parker: (DOB/DOD unknown) New York City businessman; served as a commissary officer during the American Revolution; afterwards pursued business in Europe.

Spencer Perceval (1 November 1762–11 May 1812): British politician; Chancellor of the Exchequer (1807–1812), Prime Minister (1809–1812); only British Prime Minister to have been assassinated.

William Petty, 2nd Earl of Shelburne (2 May 1737–7 May 1805), later Marquess of Lansdowne; member of Parliament and Prime Minister (1782–1783); instrumental in ending the American Revolution, later patron to several economic thinkers.

Sir Richard Phillips (13 December 1767–2 April 1840): British author, editor, and publisher; founder of *The Monthly Magazine*.

William Pitt (28 May 1759–23 January 1806): British Prime Minister (1783–1801, 1804–1806).

Rev. James Playfair (6 November 1712–28 May 1772): William Playfair's father; served as chaplain on Shetland before being appointed to parish of Benvie; also assumed responsibility for Liff in 1758.

James Playfair (5 August 1755–23 February 1794): William Playfair's architect brother.

John Playfair (10 March 1748–20 July 1819): William Playfair's eldest brother, initially assumed father's position at parish of Benvie and Liff, later became a respected and beloved professor at University of Edinburgh.

(First name unknown) Protot (DOB/DOD unknown): Paris businessman, partner in the Maison de Secours.

Joseph-Geneviève, comte de Puisaye (6 March 1755–13 September 1827): French aristocrat, aligned with the Girondins before joining the royalist resistance; promoted and led the invasion at Quiberon.

John Rennie (7 June 1761–4 October 1821): Renowned Scottish civil engineer, apprenticed with Andrew Meikle, worked for Boulton & Watt, went on to design numerous public works.

David Ricardo (18 April 1772–11 September 1823): British entrepreneur and, later, economist influential in promoting free trade.

John Scott, 1st Earl of Eldon (4 June 1751–13 January 1838): British politician, barrister, Solicitor General (1788–1793) and Lord Chancellor.

Richard Brinsley Sheridan (30 October 1751–7 July 1816): Playwright, impresario, popular Member of Commons, known for his floor speeches and wit.

John Gordon Sinclair (DOB/DOD unknown): British army officer, supported efforts to assist royalist forces despite continuing conflicts with the Calonne brothers.

Robert Small (12 December 1732–23 August 1808): Scottish minister, neighbor and friend of Rev. James Playfair; recommended William Playfair for employment at Boulton & Watt.

William Small (13 October 1734–25 February 1775): Scottish physician, educator, and entrepreneur; friend and teacher of Thomas Jefferson at the College of William and Mary; became advisor to Matthew Boulton, introducing him to James Watt.

William Smith (11 April 1751-13 September 1825): Owner of Haughton Castle and its paper mill at the time of the counterfeiting operation; a sea captain, occasionally known as "The Buccaneer."

John Southern (c. 1758–1815): Engineer at Boulton & Watt, becoming Watt's assistant after Playfair left; co-invented The Indicator with Watt to monitor steam engine performance.

Dugald Stewart (22 November 1753–11 June 1828): Professor at University of Edinburgh, colleague and friend of John Playfair.

John Strongitharm (1772–1839): London-based printer and engraver, plaintiff in *Strongitharm v. Lukyn* (1795).

Sir John Edward Swinburne (6 March 1762–26 September 1860); Master of Capheaton, one-time Whig Member of Parliament, witness to counterfeiting at Haughton Castle mill.

Peter Isaac Thellusson, 1st Baron Rendlesham (13 October 1761–16 September 1808): British financier; Director of the Bank of England; cited as responsible for arranging payment for "French paper" at Haughton Castle.

Charles-Etienne Bourgevin de Vialart, comte de Saint-Morys (17 January 1772–21 July 1817): Royalist army aid de camp; killed in duel with Dufay.

Charles-Paul-Jean-Baptiste de Bourgevin de Vialart, comte de Saint-Morys (11 July 1743–15 August 1795): Art collector, royalist officer.

Marie-Anne-Charlotte de Valicourt, comtesse de Saint-Morys (DOB/DOD unknown): Widow of Charles-Etienne Bourgevin de Vialart; charged Playfair with libel.

Alexandre-Théophile Vandermonde (28 February 1735–1 January 1796): French mathematician and scientist, member of the *Académie des sciences,* befriended Playfair after his arrival in Paris.

Jacques-Anne-Joseph Le Prestre de Vauban (10 March 1754–20 April 1816): French army officer; aid de camp to Rochambeau during the American Revolution, fought for royalists at Quiberon and in other actions during the French Revolution.

Benjamin Vaughan (19 April 1751–8 December 1835): British merchant and political activist, became friends with Benjamin Franklin, Dugald Stewart, and Lord Shelburne.

Benjamin Walker (1753–January 13, 1818): English-born American merchant; later aide to George Washington, customs officer, and Member of the U.S. House of Representatives.

Thomas Walker (3 April 1749–2 February 1817): Manchester fabric merchant and political activist; co-founder of the Manchester Constitutional Society.

Brook Watson (7 February 1735–2 October 1807): English merchant, Lord Mayor of London (1796-1797); Director, Bank of England.

Anne McGregor Watt (1738–25 August 1832): Second wife of James Watt, daughter of Glasgow dyer.

James Watt (30 January 1736– 25 August 1819): Scottish engineer and inventor; developed the improved steam engine, utilizing a condenser; entered into partnership with Matthew Boulton.

James Watt, Junior (5 February 1769–2 June 1848): Son of James Watt, assumed responsibilities at Boulton & Watt after several years as a political activist in Manchester and, later, France.

Rev. David Williams (1738–29 June 1816): Dissenting minister and educator, leading force behind the founding of the Literary Fund.

William Wilson (DOB/DOD unknown): Modeler and designer at Boulton & Watt; left with Playfair in 1782 to form partnership in London; dissolved partnership in 1785.

William Windham (14 May 1750–4 June 1810): Strongly anti-radical Whig politician and patron to Playfair; aligned with Pitt; served as Secretary at War (1794–1801) and Secretary of State for War and the Colonies (1806–1807).

Key Dates in the French Revolution and Age of Napoleon

It can be a challenge to keep track of who was governing France between 1789 and 1815, and this is often important for understanding what William Playfair was doing and why. Here is a simplified guide:

5 May 1789: Louis XVI convenes the **Estates General**, seeking a solution to France's financial problems.

17 June 1789: When the Estates General reaches impasse, members of the Third Estate (commoners) declare themselves to be the **National Assembly** of France.

9 July 1789: National Assembly renames itself as the **National Constituent Assembly**; Louis approves members of the First Estate (clergy) and Second Estate (nobles) joining the Third.

14 July 1789: Storming of the Bastille demonstrates Louis is unable or unwilling to crush the Revolution with force.

30 September 1991: Under the constitution accepted by Louis XVI, the new **Legislative Assembly** replaces the National Constituent Assembly.

10 August 1792: Insurrection topples Louis XVI; the **National Convention** replaces Legislative Assembly on 20 September.

21 January 1793: Execution of Louis XVI.

6 April 1793: National Convention establishes the **Committee of Public Safety**, which effectively becomes the governing executive body of France.

27 July 1794: Robespierre ousted and executed in the Thermidorian Reaction.

31 October 1795: The National Convention replaces the Committee of Public Safety with the **Directory**, a five-member executive body.

9 November 1799: Napoleon and allies seize control in the Coup of Brumaire and replace the Directory with the three-member **Consulate.**

2 December 1804: Napoleon crowns himself as ruler of the French **Empire**

11 April 1814: French Empire ends with the abdication of Napoleon and exile to Elba; **First Restoration** begins as Louis XVIII, brother of Louis XVI, is installed as King.

26 February 1815: Napoleon escapes from Elba, re-assumes rule as Emperor during the **Hundred Days**.

8 July 1815: Napoleon is defeated at Waterloo and exiled to St. Helens; Louis XVIII re-assumes throne in the **Second Restoration.**

Where there is no danger there is neither gain nor glory.

Satisfied with my motives which I explain before I begin, I hope that should I succeed my country shall gain, and my own will be the consequence; and that should I fail I can only blame myself.

William Playfair
20 March 1793

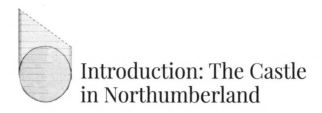

Introduction: The Castle in Northumberland

One morning in the summer of 1793, Sir John Edward Swinburne rode over the rolling green hills of Northumberland. Sir John was making the journey from the Swinburne family seat at Capheaton Hall to Haughton Castle, three or four hours distant. He had heard rumors of suspicious activities there and decided to investigate.

Haughton Castle overlooked a bend of the North Tyne, six miles from Hexham Abbey and just a short hike from Hadrian's Wall. It dated from 1250, when Ranulf de Haughton built a tower house at the site. Owners added fortifications during the Civil Wars when Northumberland became a sort of no man's land between England and Scotland. Distant from London, Edinburgh, or any other authority, the region was prey to Border Reivers— rustlers, highwayman, and feuding clans.[1]

Things settled down by the eighteenth century, but the castle was still a long ride into the moorlands. Swinburne, just thirty-one years old, was the picture of a North Country gentleman. He had a keen interest in science and literature, and spent his time riding horses, expanding and improving Capheaton, and supporting the local antiquarian society. He also had a political bent and served in Parliament for two sessions.[2]

Many events might have occupied Swinburne's mind that morning. Britain and France were at war again. They had fought over territory and trade for centuries. The wars were incredibly expensive. The Seven Year's War and the American Revolution nearly doubled the Britain's debt, and its economy was straining. Yet France had gone even deeper in the red fighting Britain.

That debt triggered the French Revolution.

When King Louis XVI tried to levy new taxes, his magistrates refused to enact the edict. Louis was forced to convene the Estates General, the closest thing France had to a legislative body. It had not met since 1614. Deputies representing the First, Second, and Third "estates"—the clergy, nobles, and commoners, respectively—assembled at Versailles on 5 May 1789.

After a six-week impasse on voting procedures, the Third Estate deputies convened their own meeting on in a vacant tennis court on 20 June. In the "Tennis Court Oath," they declared themselves the National Assembly of France, and demanded Louis accept a constitution granting them new powers and limiting his own. Louis gave in, and ordered the clergy and nobles to participate.

By then Paris was swamped by demonstrations and riots. The storming of the Bastille by a combination of mobs and local militia on 14 July proved the king was unwilling—or unable—to quash an insurrection. He agreed to the new constitution in September 1791, and it looked as though France would evolve into a constitutional monarchy similar to what England established almost a hundred years earlier. Most Britons were optimistic about how events would play out.

They would be disappointed.

The new regime in France feared the old European monarchies would try to snuff out their revolution. On 20 April 1792 French legislators declared war on Austria and Prussia. Louis, hoping to survive, went along, or at least pretended to. The French army invaded the Austrian Netherlands, triggering what would later be called the War of the First Coalition. It would be followed over the next twenty years by the wars of the Second, Third, Fourth, Fifth, Sixth, and, at Waterloo, Seventh Coalitions.

Surprisingly, the well-born Swinburne had some sympathy for the revolutionaries. He supported reform in Britain, too—political, economic, and social. In short, Swinburne was a Whig. It may have been the influence of the liberal Benedictines who tutored him in France as a teenager.

The Whigs' champion was the boisterous Charles James Fox, a huge man with an ego and personal life to match. Fox's womanizing and gambling were matched only by his drinking. King George III couldn't stand him, but his followers cut him slack because few were more passionate when it came to issues like popular rule and abolishing the slave trade.[3]

Naturally, a larger-than-life figure like Fox needed a nemesis that was a perfect opposite. He did: The slim-statured, reserved, and ever-calculating William Pitt.

Born into a political family, "Pitt the Younger" was just twenty-four when George invited him to form a government in 1783—even today, he's the youngest man ever to serve as Prime Minister. These days many would call Pitt an early Tory, though he was really a pragmatist to his core. If Pitt had any ideology, it was simply to keep Britain stable, secure, and wealthy.[4]

That was a challenge. Britain had no shortage of foreign rivals, and it had its own ready-to-fracture fault lines. Whigs wanted to make voting more fair. The aristocracy wanted to keep everything as it was. Dissenters wanted to worship outside the Church of England. The Irish wanted independence. Mechanization was pushing tenant farmers off their land, while industrialization was taking off in cities like London, Birmingham, and Manchester—all homes for "Constitutional Societies" pushing radical change. Some corresponded with counterparts abroad—like the Jacobin Club in France.

In short, the last thing Britain needed was another expensive war. Soon, however, it would have no choice.

In France the radical wing of the Revolution wanted to abolish the monarchy completely. They plotted, and on 10 August 1792 mobs stormed the Tuileries Palace. The new regime executed the King—now "Citizen Louis Capet"—on the guillotine on 21 January 1793. That soured whatever was left of civil relations between France and Britain. The French declared war on 1 February; the British reciprocated eleven days later.

Yet on this particular morning, Sir John wasn't concerned about war; he was concerned about crime. He was investigating a forgery ring.

Forgery was a huge deal at the time—a capital offense, in fact. London authorities were known to hang forgers outside Newgate Prison a dozen at a time. Respectable men thought forgery was just about the most despicable, scurrilous crime imaginable. Bogus paper could kill commerce and credit— the foundation supporting Great Britain's power.[5]

So when Sir John heard rumors of a forgery operation going on at Haughton Castle, he had to know more. "I applied to a Gentleman that lives at Humshaugh of the name of Richmond," he wrote, "who informed me that it was true."

That was Henry Richmond. He was a freeholder in Humshaugh, a village about a mile from the Castle.[6] Richmond wrote Sir John that he had indeed heard about "paper with the French watermark" being made there. France was financing its government and its wars with "assignats," currency backed by confiscated Church lands. The watermark was supposed to identify a note as genuine.

Swinburne and Richmond decided to see what was going on. The path from Humshaugh passes a cottage marking the edge of the estate, crosses a brook, and turns east through the fields before leading around the Castle and down a hill to the paper mill on the bank of the Tyne.

William Smith bought Haughton Castle sometime around 1769. He was known as "The Buccaneer" for his years as a sea captain and kept a sundial in his yard inscribed with the names of ports he had visited. Smith built the paper mill, a two-story factory in the Georgian style of architecture, in 1788.[7]

FIGURE 1: Haughton Castle, a key site in Playfair's counterfeiting operation. The paper mill is the low building at top center left, half hidden behind the trees, on the near side bank of the River Tyne. Source: courtesy Antony Braithwaite; reproduced with permission.

When the two men arrived, the mill was busy at work. The rumors were true. Indeed, the foreman, John Magnay, told Sir John that the mill had been making nothing but "French paper" for months. It was turning out *ninety reams* a week, Magnay said, and shipping it to Smith's partner in London, Brook Watson, by mail coach—the fastest, most expensive transport available.[8]

Sir John could scarcely believe it. Smith was reasonably well known, but Watson was positively famous. Brook Watson was the peg-legged Chairman of Lloyds of London. He also served as a director of the Bank of England—and a Member of Parliament, firmly in Pitt's camp.

It was clear: The government was running a forgery operation. "I believe little doubt will exist," Sir John wrote, "of the share ministers had in this scandalous business." He thought it outrageous. "So fatal an example, in a commercial country whose existence depends on good faith!"

Bad enough, Swinburne thought, that gentlemen like Smith and Watson would be involved in such a sordid activity. But he saved his greatest venom for another individual.

"If these people were not employed by government," Sir John asked rhetorically, "how come they connected with so notorious a hireling as Mr Playfair?"

That's what the opposition called writers on Pitt's payroll—"hirelings." It was an epithet reeking with upper class disdain; gentlemen did not write for money. Playfair, Sir John recalled, was the author of the "notorious pamphlet" proposing that the Allies not only defeat France, but also partition it as well so it was no longer a threat. It was bound to infuriate a Whig like Swinburne.[9]

Magnay told Sir John that Smith had met Playfair in London after they were caught using a tax dodge. The government taxed paper by the sheet. Since paper used for correspondence was taxed at a much lower rate than paper used for banker bills, the mill had been passing off its bogus blank notes as stationary.

The exciseman at Hexham had gone along with the ruse for a while, but when he balked, Smith and Playfair tried straighten things out. The clerk at warehouse in London where the paper was delivered, a man named Lightly, joined them. Apparently Playfair agreed to eat the added cost, for when Smith returned, the Hexham exciseman began stamping the paper at the higher rate.

In Sir John's account Playfair was the operation's "fixer" and government link. Swinburne thought the whole operation at Haughton Castle outrageous and summarized what he had witnessed in a four-page, hand-written memorandum—which is how we know about it today. He also alerted his former Whig colleagues in Westminster.

"I wrote to Mr. Grey about it, & I believe Mr. Sheridan once alluded to my Letter in the House of Commons," Swinburne recalled. That was Charles Grey, the 29-year-old reformer (and later Prime Minister) representing Northumberland; and Richard Sheridan, the Member from Stafford.

Who was this man Playfair that Sir John knew, and apparently loathed? An even better question is: What kind of man could have proposed, planned, and carried out such an ingenious covert operation—a Great Op—the first designed to destroy the economy of a rival nation?

§ § §

The "Mr Playfair" to whom Sir John referred was William Playfair, and, to understand who he was and all he accomplished, it helps to begin at the end—his death in London's Covent Garden district, a few blocks from the banks of the Thames.

Today, Covent Garden is a gentrified neighborhood of shops and theaters—the Transportation Museum is especially worth seeing—but originally it was exactly what the name implies: a convent's garden. It belonged to Westminster Abbey, which lies about a mile to the south. Henry VIII seized the land sometime around 1550 when he broke with the Roman Catholic Church.

About eighty years later the Earl of Bedford bought the tract and commissioned architect Inigo Jones to design a public square resembling an Italian piazza. It became the largest market in Britain and a favorite of Londoners. Then urban decay set in, business fell off and the wealthier residents moved on. By the 1700s Covent Garden had earned a decidedly different reputation.

It was the city's red light district.

Indeed, those readers who have taken the time to explore the full breadth of eighteenth century English literature will recognize Covent Garden as the fictional home of Fanny Hill. In real life, sailors from ships moored at the nearby docks called a trip to the brothels their "cruise to Covent Garden." By 1776 the neighborhood's reputation was so well established that London magistrate Sir John Fielding famously referred to the piazza as "the great square of Venus."[10]

The Theatre Royale in Drury Lane—one of two venues in London licensed to stage live performances—was just a few blocks from the piazza. Covent Garden had become the kind of bohemian neighborhood that was a natural magnet for marginally employed actors, artists—and political writers.[11]

It was where William Playfair resided when he died on 11 February 1823, at the age of sixty-four. He was living in a four-story walk-up at 43 Bedford Street with Mary, hiw wife of forty-four years—broke,, in failing health, and unable to walk.

You can find references to Playfair if you look hard enough. They are usually in books and articles about statistical graphics—pie charts, bar charts, trend lines, and the like. Playfair invented all of them, and that, today, is his main claim to fame.

The more diplomatic writers say that Playfair had a "questionable reputation." Others describe him as "colorful." Some get right to the point, and simply call him a fraudster and extortionist. When *The Economist* ran an article about current uses of statistical graphics, it called Playfair "a scoundrel" who "was convicted of libel in England and swindling in France."[12]

(Actually, it was the other way around; he was convicted of libel in France and swindling in England, but we'll soon get to that.)

And those are just writers today. Nearer to his own era, he was famous enough—or notorious enough—to merit an entry in the *Dictionary of National Biography*, the Victorian era reference book.[13] It's a portrait of a ne'er-do-well, or, at best, a might-have-been. It takes just a page to capture his entire life:

William Playfair was born in 1759. His father was James Playfair, a clergyman in Dundee, Scotland. Reverend Playfair died when William was thirteen. The *Dictionary* recalls that, "In 1780 Playfair became a draughtsman at Boulton and Watt." So young William had opportunities. But things went awry.

The *Dictionary* says Playfair went into business in London but failed. He moved to Paris. Then he got involved in an American land deal that went sour. He fled France because his "plain-speaking" got him in trouble with "the revolutionists."

The *Dictionary* recounts that Playfair once heard an émigré describe France's telegraph system, and later "claimed to have introduced the semaphore into England"—a polite way of saying that he stole the idea. The *Dictionary* helpfully corrects the record, noting that, "both its invention and adoption in the United Kingdom properly belongs to Richard Lovell Edgeworth," the Oxford-educated Lunar Society attendee.

Then, the bio says Playfair started a bank that also failed, got involved in some kind of odd episode where he claimed to have warned of Napoleon's return from Elba, and returned to France to edit a newspaper. But Playfair was on the lam just four years later after he lost a libel suit and fled France (again!) to dodge a three-month sentence in a Paris jail. He then returned to England and died in poverty.

§ § §

From the cash in your wallet, to your 401(k) statement online, you could not get through the day without the inventions of William Playfair. Indeed, the way you see the world and talk about trade, economics, money, and national power all depend on ideas directly traceable to Playfair. He developed basic concepts in each that are still used today. He was an ingenious inventor and serial entrepreneur.

He was also a secret agent for the British government.

Indeed, Playfair performed all the major functions of modern intelligence that are familiar today, and pioneered several. He produced all-source analysis, conducted espionage—both technical and human—and carried out covert operations. France was funding its government by printing paper money. Inflation was rampant. Playfair's analysis said that it would take just little more to push it over the edge, and he devised the plan to provide that extra nudge.

To make it happen, Playfair needed a theorist's understanding of what makes nations grow, and, by extension, the factors that can make them collapse. He needed a practical knowledge of business and finance. He needed a network of senior officials, industry barons, foreign contacts—and an assortment of knaves, corruptible pigeons, and dupes. And he needed to be able to keep a secret.

Which is the main reason Playfair is so misunderstood.

If anyone could keep a secret, it was William Playfair. He took the knowledge of the covert operation to his grave, even after his government abandoned him to complete, utter poverty. He never published his story. He did not mention the operation even in his private, unpublished memoirs.

It is only by piecing together fragmentary letters and forensic evidence that we can link Playfair to the operation. But the evidence is ironclad and the case is bulletproof. What's more, when you discover the depth of Playfair's secret relations to British officials, you begin to see the rest of his life—and, perhaps, the history of the French Revolution, modern economics, and the development of strategic analysis—in a different light.

Besides, it's a great story. You wouldn't believe it if it were not true.

1 Inventing William Playfair

Sometime in late December 1781 a twenty-two-year-old Scottish engineer made his way south on the road from Birmingham to London. William Playfair had just left his job at Boulton & Watt and was traveling to the city to live with his brother James while he started a new business.

Playfair—a fair-complexioned man with brown hair, blue eyes, and strong features—wasn't bad looking, but wasn't the kind of man who would stand out in a crowd, either. At five-eight, he was just a little taller than average for the time.[1]

Family histories say Playfairs have lived in central Scotland since the 1400s. Some argue Playfairs are English who migrated north; others say they are Norsemen who sailed west and south. In either case, "Playfair" (or Playfere, or Playfeir) comes from the Middle English *playfere*, meaning "playmate,"—that is, a companion.[2]

The Rev. James Playfair died on 28 May 1772. His eldest son, John, twenty-four, became the head of the family. He would assume his father's parish at Benvie and go on to be a professor at the University of Edinburgh. The daughters, Rachel and Margaret, would eventually marry. Robert, the second son, was twenty-three and already practicing law. James, seventeen, was about to become an architect.[3]

That left the youngest brother—William, thirteen.

John—parish minister, philosopher, mathematician, and amateur meteorologist—took over William's education. The boy had a mechanical bent, so John found him an apprenticeship in East Linton with Andrew Meikle.

Today Meikle is best known for inventing the threshing machine, but his neighbors knew him mainly as a millwright.

Millwrights were essential to preindustrial Britain. About the only alternative to manpower or beast-power was falling water. Meikle had a reputation for designing elegant combinations of flues, ponds, and waterwheels that got the job done.[4]

Working for Meikle taught Playfair a trade—and shaped his character. Forty years later, Playfair touted apprenticeships for building both good craftsmen and good men. Without apprenticeships, he said, a youth would have too little supervision and too much money. The result, warned Playfair, would be *indolence*, about the closest he came to an epithet. A young buck would seek the "society of other youths who are in a similar situation, and the means of gratifying the passions." Without a master, before long he "changes his place of work, becomes ashamed of himself, and most probably turns out forever to be a bad member of society."[5]

In early 1777 Playfair had finished his apprenticeship and was ready for a job. Robert Small, a family friend, helped him to find one.

Small was a minister in the neighboring parish of Carmyllie—about twenty miles from Benvie. Robert's brother, William Small, two years younger, had left Scotland to teach at the College and William and Mary in Virginia. One of his closest friends was a student named Thomas Jefferson.[6] Young Small had hoped to be named president of the college, but its Board of Visitors had other ideas. So when Small went back to Britain to buy scientific instruments for the school, he didn't return. Instead he settled in Birmingham—thanks to Benjamin Franklin.[7]

Franklin had met Matthew Boulton, a young, hard-driving Birmingham entrepreneur while touring the English Midlands in 1759. When Franklin visited William and Mary four years later, he was impressed with William Small and gave him an introduction to Boulton. The two hit it off, and Small joined Boulton as an all-around advisor and confidant.[8]

Birmingham had long specialized in making "toys"—buckles, buttons, hooks and the like. Boulton's big idea was to make them more efficiently by dividing the process into steps and putting all his workers together in a single big building—a precursor to the assembly line. The result was the Soho Manufactory, built in 1766 a few miles outside town. (Birmingham's Soho district got its name from the call—Soho! Soho!—that rabbit hunters shouted when the neighborhood was still open fields.)[9]

Boulton became rich and famous, and the Manufactory became a "must see" for travelers. William Small was always ready to provide a tour, even to a semi-employed surveyor on his way back from dealing with licensing problems in London. That was how Boulton met James Watt, which led to Boulton & Watt, which led to William Playfair becoming a steam engine erector.

§ § §

To understand what Playfair was about to get himself into, you need to understand something about steam engines. And, to understand steam engines, you need to understand mines.

Mines constantly collect water. If you can't remove the water, the mine eventually floods. Until the early 1700s the only solutions were hand pumps and buckets. Then ironmonger Thomas Newcomen designed a primitive steam engine.

Basically, it was just a piston-and-cylinder assembly fitted to the top of a boiler. The boiler produced steam, which pressurized the cylinder, which raised the piston, which worked a pump. When the piston reached the top of its stroke, a valve opened, injecting a jet of water that cooled the cylinder, allowing atmospheric pressure to return the piston to its starting point. Newcomen engines were notoriously inefficient, requiring a lot of coal to remove not much water. But it was better than carrying a bucket up a ladder.

Then James Watt came along.

Watt was born in 1736 in Greenock, about thirty miles from Glasgow. He was a quiet boy, remarkably bright, but rarely in good health. After spending a year doing odd jobs for professors at Glasgow College, Watt went to London to learn to be an instrument maker. He returned a year later and set up shop in an apartment off the college quadrangle. He was twenty years old.[10]

One day a science professor brought Watt a malfunctioning model steam engine. It was a Newcomen. Watt realized intuitively that the engine was inefficient, even when it worked. Cooling the cylinder after each cycle and then reheating it wasted energy. His new idea: leave the cylinder hot, vent the steam into a separate vessel, and *then* cool it. In other words, he added a condenser.

That was the improvement behind Watt's "improved steam engine." It used just a third of the coal of a Newcomen. But money was tight, and Watt had to work a second job as a surveyor. He had little time to experiment with his steam engine idea, so development went slowly.

Watt was in the middle of plotting a planned canal in 1867 when its builders decided to change the route. He had to go to London to have the permits revised. On the return Watt passed through Birmingham and stopped by the water wheel-powered Soho Manufactory. He happened to meet William Small—who quickly saw the potential of steam power. Watt wound up staying two weeks.

Small and Watt began to correspond. Small advised Watt on everything from cylinder materials to patent applications.[11] On 5 January 1769 Watt received Patent No. 913 for his "New Invented Method of Lessoning the Consumption of Steam & Fuel in Fire Engines."[12] Boulton and Watt founded Boulton & Watt on 1 June 1775.[13]

The two men were Mutt and Jeff. Boulton was tallish, handsome, and totally self-confident. He mixed easily.[14] Watt was short, slight, and frail. He hated crowds and always seemed deep in thought.[15] Naturally, the two became best friends. Soon after they signed their partnership, Watt, widowed three years earlier, married Ann McGregor, the daughter of a Glasgow dyer. They moved to Soho in 1775 with Watt's two-year-old daughter Margaret, and his six-year-old son, James Watt, Junior.

Unfortunately, it was all too late for William Small, the man who set everything in motion. Boulton and Watt had planned to give him a share of the new business, but he passed away just five months before the company was set up. It snows in much of Virginia during the winter, but the coast is in the Plasmodium zone. Small contracted malaria while he was teaching at William and Mary. It killed him fifteen years later. He was only forty.

§ § §

Robert Small stayed close to Boulton & Watt after his brother died. In 1777 he wrote to James Keir, a chemist friend who had joined the company as its manager. Small told Keir that when he was last at Birmingham he had discussed the new steam engine with Boulton, who said "he might have use for some ingenious young man that might go to distant places & superintend the Erection of them."

"There is a young man here with whom I am exceedingly pleased," Small wrote, "and who I think might be very serviceable to Mr Boulton in that business or in various other ones."

"His name is Playfair & his age 18 or 19," Small continued. "I have a very great opinion of his capacity & ingenuity, having seen many curious inventions & models of his, & his drawings are in my opinion remarkably good also." Small added that, "If you can find out by means of Mr Boulton or Mr Watt any proper employment for him I shall think myself greatly obliged to you."

Small closed: "And I think I can answer for the goodness of his heart, as much as for the honourableness of his principles and the goodness of his understanding."[16]

When Boulton & Watt sold a steam engine, it really just granted a license to the buyer and supplied some key parts: a cylinder, a piston, and the all-important condenser. Then a Boulton & Watt "erector" would journey to the buyer's designated site to execute what was, in effect, a major construction project. This is what Boulton had in mind when he asked Robert Small for a young man to "go to distant places."[17]

Erecting an early steam engine was a close cousin to building a watermill. One had to survey the land, lay out the location of major components, and design mechanical linkages so everything worked together. You can get a sense of the work Playfair was doing by visiting the British Science Museum at South Kensington.

The Museum reassembled several steam engines from across Britain in its main gallery to show how the technology evolved over the eighteenth and nineteenth centuries. Each is two or three stories tall, extending below the exhibit hall floor and above the mezzanine. It's a mélange of huge boilers, rocking beams, spinning flywheels, and reciprocating pistons, with everything connected by hissing pipes and clanking linkages.

Now, imagine you're a young William Playfair, erecting one of these contraptions at a coal mine in a far corner of England.

The main challenge is that you have to build Industrial Age machinery using pre-Industrial Age infrastructure. Even if there is a decent road—rare in those days—just getting components to, say, John Wilkinson's iron works at nearby Snedshill is a two-day adventure in a horse-drawn wagon. Travel to a Cornwall copper mine takes weeks.

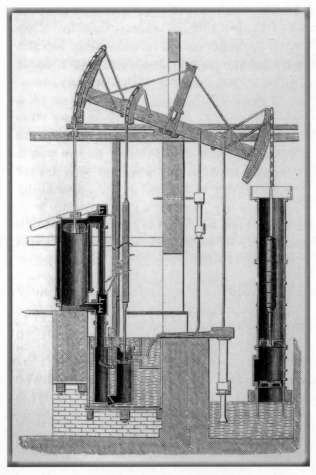

FIGURE 2: A Boulton & Watt pumping engine from the late 1780s for draining mines. Playfair erected engines like this one during his early years at the company. The piston-and-cylinder assembly is at left; it operates the pump at right via the rocking beam. Watt's key improvement—the condenser—is at bottom left center. Later, as Watt's assistant, Playfair made drawings for specific installations, or for modifications that Watt developed. Source: Samuel Smiles, *Lives of Boulton and Watt* (London: John Murray, 1865), 236. Source: University of California Libraries, via The Internet Archive.

You also have to deal with a civil society that is often hardly civil and barely a society. Highwaymen try to rob you along the way. Press gangs try to steal your men. You "better take care of any young hands that he might send down," a co-worker wrote Playfair, telling him that he had been stopped by a gang in Okehampton.[18]

That was your basic job description at Boulton & Watt: designer, drafts-man, logistician, mechanic, and occasional tough guy staring down outlaws and dodging the Royal Navy.

Company records have Playfair on the road as early as May 1777, on the Wilkinson job.[19] It was the Industrial Revolution and Playfair was in the middle of it. Working for Boulton & Watt got him comfortable planning big projects in faraway places, figuring out solutions, developing plans, and dealing with all kinds of people.

Playfair had been at the company just a year when Watt and Boulton began giving him more responsibility. Watt made Playfair his personal assis-tant and clerk, keeping the books in the company counting house; by then Watt worked mainly at home, and Playfair went to see him each afternoon.[20] Later, when Watt started a new company with Keir to sell copying machines they had invented (it made press copies, as sort of an early version of carbon paper) he hired Playfair for the venture, too.[21]

Then, in October 1781, Keir wrote Watt, "Mr Playfair tells me he wrote to you acquainting you of his intention of leaving us & settling in London."[22] Boulton had already sensed that Playfair's "mind seems to be absent from our business."[23]

You get the feeling the separation wasn't acrimonious, but may have been untidy. Boulton wrote Watt that, "I think he should have been open to with us & said what business he was going to follow." Playfair had not told him of "any other of his views or new plans."[24]

Why did Playfair leave?

James Watt was a contradiction: radical inventor, conservative developer. Once he had a design that worked, he was loath to change it. He once told Boulton, "Let us go on executing the things we understand and leave the rest to younger men, who have neither money nor character to lose."[25]

Playfair, on the other hand, was an incurable risk-taker. You can sense he chafed under his master when he recalled almost forty years later, "Mr. Watt was an enemy to all new schemes." Playfair said Watt needed Boulton to "push" and "excite" him. Boulton "was ambitious of being the first engineer and well as the first of Birmingham manufacturers." Watt, Playfair said, was not.[26]

Playfair had ambitions. Boulton & Watt paid well for the time, but few employees got rich; even fewer gained fame or influence.

If Playfair had stayed, he might have done as well as John Southern, the quiet, diligent engineer who replaced him as Watt's assistant. Southern waited eighteen years before Boulton and Watt gave him a percentage of the steam engine profits. It took almost three decades for them to make him a partner in the firm, in 1810. He died five years later.[27]

At best, Playfair might have done as well as William Murdoch, a Boulton & Watt lifer. Murdoch was so important to the company that he's often called the "Third Man." When Birmingham memorialized the city's favorite sons, the larger-than-life bronze statue outside the old Register Office on Broad Street portrayed *three* figures: Boulton, Watt…and Murdoch.[28]

Murdoch, five years older than Playfair, joined the company at about the same time, starting in 1777 as a pattern maker earning fifteen shillings a week. He became an engine erector around 1779 and moved to Cornwall to oversee operations there; by then he was earning twenty-one shillings a week. Boulton wanted to pay him more, but Watt said "an example of that kind would ruin us by stimulating every other man to make similar demands."[29]

No one worked harder than William Murdoch. No one was more loyal. Murdoch was the kind of man who would punch out a Cornish miner who gave the company trouble.[30] Or drive off French privateers at gunpoint when they tried to steal engine parts waiting in harbor for shipment.[31] It was Murdoch who kept pushing new ideas on the ever-cautious Watt, like gas lighting—even steam locomotives.[32]

Boulton & Watt did pay Murdoch a bonus for his gas lighting idea. And Murdoch made partner in 1810, the same year as Southern. But by then the company—now Boulton, Watt & Sons—was mature. The upside was limited. Murdoch chose a straight salary rather than profit sharing. It was good pay for the time—£1,000 per year.[33] So good, in fact, that James Watt, Junior sacked Murdoch soon after he and Matthew Robinson Boulton (Matthew Boulton's son) took over the company, feeling they could no longer afford him.[34]

And Murdoch was the exception. John Rennie followed Playfair from Andrew Meikle's mill to work for Boulton & Watt. Watt wanted to keep Rennie, whose reputation as a superb civil engineer was growing. But Watt insisted Rennie sign an agreement never to build steam engines; he didn't want a potential competitor. Rennie refused and, like Playfair, went off on his own.[35]

Playfair understood the lay of the land. He was ambitious. He was a risk taker. He was bound to bail eventually. Yet his immediate reason for leaving was simply that Watt's copying machine business was struggling.

"The copying business does not go on so well," Playfair wrote Boulton in September 1780, "there are not many more than 200 sent off from hence, not half that number delivered, still fewer payed for." So, while "that business is not quite dead," as Playfair said, it was being "carried on with no spirit."[36] Keir agreed; Playfair later told Boulton, Keir thought "the manufacturing of them should be stopped till the stock on hand was a little decreased."[37]

Playfair thought he might be laid off. Writing Boulton to apologize for not seeing him before leaving for London, he explained, "one reason for my turning my Eyes to other employment" was that "I don't think the copying business would for this sometime at least pay for my attending it."[38]

Playfair told Boulton he planned to "engage in a business here with the assistance of my brothers." Playfair said he regretted "the end of a connection" that he said was "a very useful and agreeable one to me," adding that, "if I can ever be of any use to you in business, believe me you cannot easily oblige me more than by giving me an opportunity of being so."[39]

But if Playfair's mind wasn't on Boulton & Watt that final year, what *was* it on? Just follow the patent trail. Playfair had a plan to make money in metalworking.

Keir, who told Boulton he "was very sorry" when Playfair gave notice, said the young engineer had a vision and "could not be easy without making a trial of it."[40] Just weeks after leaving, Playfair received the first of four patents Britain's Great Seal Patent Office would award him over the next three years. Patent No. 1308, issued on 29 December 1781, was for a new kind of rolling mill.[41]

Rolling mills work exactly like the pasta makers you'll find in kitchens today: a crank turns a set of rollers, which draw in a metal plate and press it into a thin, smooth sheet. The basic idea had been around for centuries; Leonardo da Vinci drew exquisite diagrams of imaginary rolling mills in 1486. But no one seems to have actually built one until the 1600s. Water or beasts provided power.[42]

Playfair's idea was to mount the rollers in a cast housing with a single screw that allowed the operator to adjust their position and pressure precisely.[43] You can see small versions of Playfair's rolling machine in high school shop classes today, and huge ones in steel plants. He still gets credit for the basic idea in the technical literature; usually the writers don't know anything else about him.[44]

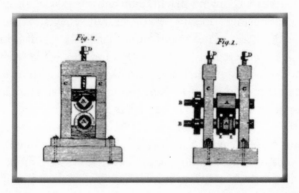

FIGURE 3: Playfair's rolling mill, as illustrated in Patent No. 1773, May 1783. Source: Literary and Philosophical Society, Newcastle upon Tyne, and reproduced in H. J. Louw, "The Rise of the Metal Window in the Early Industrial Period in Britain, c. 1750–1830." *Construction History*, Volume 3 (1987), 34. Source: National Heritage Ironwork Group, courtesy Department of Architecture, University of Cambridge.

In May 1783 Playfair received a second patent, No. 1373, for another rolling mill innovation. Just as pasta makers have special rollers and fixtures for cranking out fettuccine, linguine, or cavatappi, Playfair's new mill had rollers and fixtures to make steel channels, ornamental borders, or horseshoes—in the last case, at the rate of ten per minute.[45]

A few months after that Playfair registered Patent No. 1408. This one was for a tool for "cutting or dividing pieces of metal, and giving them a cylindrical or other uniform shape through their whole length, or making them taper regularly for the formation of bars, bolts, wires."[46]

In all, it was quite an accomplishment—and risk—for a young man; the typical patent could cost £100.[47]

Technology in hand, Playfair began to assemble his new business. His partner was William Wilson, a Boulton & Watt co-worker. The two opened for business as "Playfair, Wilson & Co." with offices at 2 Portland Place and registered their hallmark—WP over WW—as silversmiths on 16 May, selling spoons, tongs, and other utensils.[48]

FIGURE 4: The hallmark Playfair and William Wilson registered with the London Assay Office. Source: SilverSugarTongs.com, courtesy of Graham Hodges.

Playfair wrote Boulton on 9 March 1782 to tell him Wilson "intends to leave your service and join in the Business that I am engaged in."[49] Boulton complained to Watt three days later that Playfair had poached his only "diesinker, draughtsman and modellor."[50] Playfair had tried to put the best face on the situation, writing Boulton that, "I do not wish to do any thing in an underhanded way to a person who has behaved in a manner that will always preserve my respect and Esteem."[51]

But business was business.

Playfair hoped to continue his relationship with Boulton. Nine months later, he wrote from London, "It often happens that people who are at different places can be of service to each other without inconveniency to themselves." He passed along some leads for potential work, adding, "if any thing occurs where you think I can be of use to you here I shall be happy to do it if I can."[52]

Around this time Playfair also began working with James Keir and Alexander Blair. Keir and Blair had bonded in the West Indies, serving in the British army. It was the kind of friendship that comes out of surviving a hellhole together. Keir almost died of yellow fever; Blair took care of him.

Returning to Britain, Keir set up a chemist shop specializing in glass. He abandoned his start-up to join Boulton & Watt in 1778.[53] He expected to be a partner. Then he got a look at the company's books. Recently married, he decided he couldn't take the risk.[54] Some say Boulton and Watt played Keir to his disadvantage.[55]

But again, business was business.

Keir thought highly of Playfair—which is why he passed along that golden recommendation from Robert Small to Boulton. Keir was a close friend of John Playfair, too; by now John was a professor at the University of Edinburgh, and the two had formed their own business in 1794.[56]

After William settled in London, he apparently partnered with Keir and Blair in a company formally established as William Playfair and Company, but also doing business as the "Eldorado Manufactory." An ad in *The Times* announced the Manufactory offered silver tableware and buckles, in addition to windows and skylights. If you found yourself in dire need of a spoon (or a skylight) some evening, it was "Open from Eight in the Morning until Nine at Night."[57]

Why "Eldorado"?

That was the name many used for a new alloy Keir had patented.[58] Playfair apparently used the metal in some of his products. Eldorado combined copper, zinc, and iron in specific ratios to produce a lustrous, gold-colored metal that, according to the patent, could be "forged hot or cold, for making bolts, nails, and for other purposes."[59]

It's just a coincidence, but the Great Seal Patent Office index lists the patent Keir received for his alloy immediately above the patent Playfair received for his metalworking processes. If you read them in sequence, you get a snapshot of the Eldorado Manufactory's business plan: using new kinds of machinery to shape new kinds of alloy into new kinds of products.[60]

On 26 January 1785 Playfair submitted an application for another patent. This one was for "certain new Methods" for "covering the Surfaces of Copper and other Metals with Silver, Gold or Mixtures of Silver or Gold with other Metals which Operation is commonly called Plating."[61] He received his patent, No. 1466, a month later.[62]

Buckles were big business, and silver buckles were high fashion. Playfair's plating process resembled how a plumber "sweats" a pipe joint. Instead of melting silver or gold in a crucible and dipping a buckle in it, Playfair covered the buckle with a leaf of precious metal, and then heated the assembly in a furnace. The hot buckle melted the leaf; capillary action worked its wonders, and the result was a thin, tightly adhering coating.[63]

"A careful survey of the available evidence," an article in the *Journal of the Institute of Metals* reports, "leaves little doubt that the possibility of making gold plating by the sweating process, as used for the manufacture of silver plating, was first conceived by William Playfair."[64] Today we're more likely to use electroplating, but in 1785 Patent No. 1466 was cutting-edge.[65]

Yet Playfair's businesses hit hard on the rocks just two years after he set up shop. The first sign of trouble was an advertisement in *The Times* on 1 April:

> William Playfair and Co offer 'A complete Assortment of BUCKLES as well as the PLATED GOODS and JEWEL-LERY' at their manufactory, London-Street, Tottenham-Court Road.[66]

No mention of Wilson. The breakup was official by mid-summer. The two men put a notice on the front page of the 25 June issue of the *London Gazette*:[67]

> Notice is hereby given, that the Partnership lately carried out between William Playfair and William Wilson under the firm of Playfair and Wilson, London-Street, Tortenham-court-road, is this Day, by mutual Consent; dissolved; and the Business carried on there as usual by William Playfair only
> William Playfair,
William Wilson

Wilson entered his own hallmark a few weeks later.[68] At about the same time Playfair, Keir, and Blair jointly announced they were parting as well. A notice in the *London Gazette* announced:[69]

> THE Partnership lately carried on under the Firm of William Playfair and Company, of London-streets Tottenham Court-road, in the County of Middlesex, was, by mutual Consent, this Day dissolved. All Persons indebted to the said Partnership, are desired to pay such Debts to the undersigned James Keir, or to whom he shall appoint; and all Persons who have any Demands on the said Partnership, are requested to send an Account thereof to the said James Keir at the Manufactory late belonging to the said Company, in London-street aforesaid. Witness our Hands this 26th of April, 1785
> William Playfair
James Keir
Alex Blair

What happened?

The 1896 *Dictionary of National Biography* says Playfair left for Paris after "not succeeding in this business."[70] The *Gazette*, however, never carried a bankruptcy notice.

More recently, the 2004 *Oxford Dictionary of National Biography* (a modern counterpart to the original *Dictionary*) says the partnership ended in "an acrimonious breach" when Keir discovered "his own ideas had been appropriated." But if you track down the source it cites—a rare, century-old reference book—you find it's been misquoted. There's no mention of any breach.[71]

You have to spend some time in the Birmingham archives to get the full story. Keir didn't accuse Playfair of stealing ideas. Quite the opposite—Keir and Playfair had their disagreements, but Keir thought highly of Playfair.

Keir, remember, was the one who gave Boulton that golden recommendation for Playfair from Robert Small: *"I can answer for the goodness of his heart, as much as for the honourableness of his principles and the goodness of his understanding."* Keir endorsed Small's assessment by copying it, word for word, in his own hand, and sending it to Boulton.[72]

And when Keir informed Watt that Playfair planned to leave Boulton & Watt, Keir was not only sorry to see him go; he knew enough about Playfair's plans that he agreed to partner in the company.[73] Keir trusted Playfair enough that let his best friend join them—Alexander Blair. How could Playfair steal an idea that Keir and Blair knew was going to be part of their business?

If you track down the original documents, it becomes clear the disagreement wasn't over anything as glamorous as intellectual property theft. The squabbling was over much more mundane matters. It seems to have simply boiled down to the price of soap—or, more precisely, alkali.

Playfair gave his side of the story in a letter to Watt on 20 September 1785. "I have had a very disagreeable difference with your friend Mr. Keir," Playfair wrote Watt.

"I foresaw a quarrel as soon as I found I could no longer be of his opinion about the Price of Alkali," Playfair told Watt. "Mr. Blair's hopes depended on that and certainly that alkali would not bear nor could not be sold at £30." It sounds like Blair was selling raw materials to the partnership, and Keir wanted Playfair to pay Blair, his friend, more than Playfair thought he should.

There was other friction, too. "Mr Keir," Playfair wrote, "lets his men persuade him of whatever they please his mind I managed by constant want of success & impending ruin prevents all attack on but to his displeasure."

Playfair continued, accusing Keir of telling others he wasn't paying his bills. Playfair's defense: "My present straits for money are a Proof I never wronged Blair." He accused Keir of maintaining on his books a debt Playfair owed as a means to "destroy" him, and vowed he would respond in kind.[74]

Playfair's syntax (and handwriting) is sometimes close to indecipherable, but Watt seemed to understand what he meant. In a letter to Anne five days later, Watt inserted an afterthought squeezed vertically along the margin. Watt told Anne that Playfair "complains of injurious and unjust treatment from Mr. K and imputes it in part to K's being chagrined by constant want of success in all his schemes, and impending ruin staring him the face."

Watt scribbled further in the margin that Playfair accused Keir of maneuvering to destroy him, and that Playfair planned to retaliate, tit for tat. As Watt put it to Anne (you can imagine the sigh and his eyes rolling), Playfair was thinking "of imitating him in that, by way of fighting him with his own weapons—What a rascal!"[75]

Watt waited almost three weeks before he wrote back to Playfair. In a 10 October letter, he gave Playfair fatherly advice: "I am sorry to observe so wide a breach between Mr. K & you. As in such cases one is apt to at times to say what they afterwards wish unsaid, I have not shown your letter to any body and as I do not wish to be the projector of any thinking which may tend to increase discord, I shall return it to you if you desire it."[76]

One of Keir's great regrets—the "constant want in all his schemes," as Watt put it, paraphrasing Playfair —was that he couldn't convince the Royal Navy to use his alloy. Keir thought he had a solution to a problem mariners had faced since antiquity: Wooden hulls don't do well in seawater. Bottoms get fouled with barnacles, ruining speed and handling. Teredoes—shipworms—bore into timbers, potentially wrecking a vessel in just a few years.

Shipbuilders had tried to prevent all this by sheathing their hulls with copper plates. The challenge was finding a workable fastener. Copper is too soft to use as a bolt. Iron bolts, on the other hand, quickly corrode. (Combine a copper plate with an iron bolt and place them in seawater, and you've effectively constructed an electric battery; the resulting charge causes the iron to oxidize.)

Keir's new alloy—similar to the Eldorado window sash material—was comprised of 100 parts copper, 75 parts zinc, and 10 parts iron. It was soft enough to be drawn through a die when cold, hard enough to use as a bolt, and resistant to corrosion. But the Navy Board rejected it in favor of another alloy. Keir then proposed his metal for the sheathing itself. The Navy rejected that proposal, too.[77]

So the new alloy was used only for window sashes. Even then it wasn't clear who deserved credit—the developer of the alloy (Keir) or the designer of the tool for shaping the alloy (Playfair). Playfair's obituary said his Eldorado sashes were used in windows at Carlton House and the doors of the British Museum.[78] Keir got credit for the Carlton House sashes, too, and those installed in Windsor Castle.[79]

It was a convoluted mix of friendships, partnerships, and rivalries. Just about everyone in the Birmingham family revered Watt. They admired Boulton. And most of the associates who Boulton and Watt kept around for any length of time were able men in their own right.

Yet just about everyone could claim a grievance of some kind.

Watt was stingy when paying employees, and he wouldn't share equity. Keir, who gave up his glass business and bought a house in Soho to work for Boulton & Watt, believed the company had been less than forthcoming about its finances; he once vented to Boulton in a letter reflecting on their rocky relationship.[80]

Meanwhile Boulton had his own beef; he wanted credit for Keir's Metal, or Eldorado, or whatever anyone preferred to call it. Keir even admitted that the alloy came out of his joint experiments with Boulton.[81] While all this was going on, Keir stewed over the Royal Navy's repeated rejections. And Boulton was disgruntled that Playfair and Wilson planned their business on his time, while Playfair feared being left in the cold if the copying machine company failed.

None of this would shock anyone with experience in the business world. Colleagues—especially those working at close quarters—bicker all the time. Partners and competitors can be friends and enemies simultaneously. It's nothing new, and the only thing that really counts—literally—in business is, "What's the bottom line?"

Historian Robert Stuart summed it up this way in his 1829 account of the early steam engine and British industry: Playfair's "adventure" needed "only a little perseverance and attention" to become "a permanently lucrative one." But, Stuart claimed, the business "did not make returns fast enough to satisfy Playfair's restless activity."

Meanwhile, Stuart wrote, Playfair was driven by a "writing mania." So, "in an evil hour" he "essayed to become a political advocate."[82]

§ § §

Playfair's earliest known publication is a 122-page monograph: *The Increase of Manufactures, Commerce, and Finance, with the Extension of Civil Liberty, Proposed in the Regulations for the Interest of Money*.[83] He wrote it while designing rolling mills and setting up his silversmith shop in London.

It was two years after Britain lost the American War of Independence— and its colonies—and people were asking: How could Great Britain remain great?

Playfair's answer: Manufacturing, banking, and trade.

That wasn't conventional thinking at the time; territory (and the people and resources that went with it) had always been the measure of power. Yet Playfair had seen the coal mines, steam engines, and blast furnaces of the Midlands. Manufacturing made land less important. The new measure of power was industrial output.

How then to expand industry? The main lever at hand, Playfair said, was "by a new and proper REGULATION of the INTEREST OF MONEY." (The emphasis is Playfair's; he was very sure of himself.) Investors needed capital, and they wouldn't get it unless Britain got rid of its antiquated usury laws—that is, interest ceilings.

Interest caps often had unintended consequences, Playfair argued, and they were almost always bad. He showed how commerce suffered under Edward VI, when borrowing was "free" (meaning interest was banned) but flourished under Elizabeth, when borrowing was expensive (meaning the Crown allowed up to fourteen percent interest).

All usury laws achieved, Playfair claimed, was to keep businesses from getting the capital that they needed. Interest controls were price controls, and price controls always had the same effect: shortages. No interest, no money. No money, no expansion.

Playfair wanted the market to allocate capital, allowing it to flow to investors who wanted it most and were willing to pay for it. Their investments, in turn, would make the economy grow. Just "as the rate of insurance varies with the risk that is run by the insurer," he wrote, "so, undoubtedly, the rate of interest ought to vary, according to the risk that is run by the lender of the money."[84]

One reader who saw *Increase of Manufacturers* read it with particular interest. He worried about being scooped. That was Jeremy Bentham.

Best known today for his theory of "utilitarianism"—the idea that the best solutions offer the greatest good for the greatest number of people—Bentham was a well-known philosopher even in 1787. Born into wealth, he was by all accounts a brilliant student. He graduated from The Queen's College at the age of fifteen, and basically spent the rest of his life thinking and writing.

When Playfair's *Increase of Manufactures* appeared, Bentham was working on his own book, which also happened also to be a defense of usury; it was titled, aptly enough, *A Defense of Usury.* We know from his correspondence that Bentham was eager to get his book out.

We also know that he had read Playfair's *Increase of Manufacturers.*

Bentham had a friend he often used as a sounding board: Manchester entrepreneur George Wilson. Bentham was circulating drafts of *A Defense of Usury* and asked Wilson to give it a hard look. "Abuse it and keep it, or abuse it and print it, as to your wisdom may seem meet," Bentham wrote Wilson in May 1787. "Don't let any very flagrant absurdities go for want of correction or erasure."[85]

Bentham couldn't wait to get his book published. "If you do print it," he wrote Wilson, "send it to the press quickly, that it may begin sooner to lay in a little stock of reputation for me against I get home." Then he sized up the competition.

"There is one Playfair who published," Bentham wrote, "a trumpery book in 4to, called the Interest of Money Considered. Nine-tenths of it is bad writation about the origin of society and so forth; the other tenth is a perfectly vague and shapeless proposal for relaxing the rigour of the anti-usurious laws in favor of projectors; yet without any argument in it, or any other idea, but that vague one thrown out in almost as general and vague a way as I have stated it in."

"I understand," Bentham sniffed, "it has been well enough spoken of by several people."

A bit of translation: "Trumpery" means "showy but worthless." "4to" was shorthand for "quarto," a medium-sized, cost-saving binding method.

"Projectors" were financiers who funded projects—what we call "venture capitalists" today for early-stage projects and "investment bankers" for more mature enterprises. Bentham was likening Playfair's book to costume jewelry, and dismissing it as a screed for money-lending sharks with a venal interest in uncapped interest.[86]

But he *had* read it.

Playfair wasn't "perfectly vague." He was just approaching economics like a millwright: Create a reservoir of money by relaxing usury laws—like a mill-pond. Establish an institution to direct the money to industry—like a financial flume. Regulate the financiers to prevent risky loans that could overstress the system—like a sluicegate.

Playfair believed investors were gamblers. They put money on the line hoping they would get back more—and ideally, *much* more. Or, as Playfair put it, "ALL projecting partakes of the nature of gaming, in a very considerable degree; the risque incurred is of the same nature, and the effect produced on the mind of those concerned is often the same."

Playfair added, "PREVIOUS to engaging in any new thing, it is customary to reckon the advantage that will arise from success even among the most sanguine, and to consider what may be the expence of a trial." This calculation was based, he said, on "the chance of gain; the risqué of loss; the probable amount of gain; and the probable extent of loss."[87]

An investor, Playfair said, works through that calculation and decides if, on net, he will make money. Today economists, game theorists, and math mavens describe the calculation as an "expected value." They use symbols instead of words, but the idea is the same:

$$E(X) = p_1(x_1) + p_2(x_2) + \ldots p_n(x_n)$$

where "n" is the total range of possible outcomes, "x" is the cost or benefit of each outcome, and "p" is the probability of each. If $E(X)$ is greater than zero, a rational investor commits the funds. He places his bet.

Besides explaining decisions in Wall Street and Las Vegas, there's often an expected value calculation lurking in the background when companies budget for product safety—and when insurance companies write policies to cover companies budgeting for product safety.[88] Expected value as a model can also help explain decisions in negotiations,[89] deterrence,[90] and war making.[91]

This was new thinking. Adam Smith never could square his idea of how incentives drive investment with his idea of "moral sentiments." Jeremy Bentham could not get beyond justifying usury as the greatest good for the greatest number. Playfair, on the other hand, described financial decisions the way analysts describe them today—impersonal outcomes resulting from hard-nosed calculations.

Described that way, it's clear why economic growth depended on usury. Cap interest, and there will likely be someone with a high-risk, big-payoff idea who won't get the funding he needs. Boulton demanded two-thirds ownership of Boulton & Watt for his investment in Watt's engine. That usurious deal powered the Industrial Revolution.[92] It's the common wisdom today, but Playfair's thinking was a radical breakthrough in the eighteenth century. Not bad for a twenty-five-year-old mechanic with little formal education.

The obituary writers had it all wrong. Playfair might have done reasonably well had he persevered with his metalworking businesses. But it was his writing that would open doors—and lead to the opportunity to render his greatest service to Britain.

2   A Dundee Scot In King Louis' Court

On the morning of 22 March 1780 two men stood twelve paces apart in London's Hyde Park: William Fullarton, a wealthy young Scot who claimed his honor had been questioned; and William Petty, 2nd Earl of Shelburne, the man who allegedly questioned it.[1]

Fullarton represented Plymouth Erie in the House of Commons. He was also a lieutenant colonel in the British army, and that's where the trouble began. By his own admission, Fullarton had little or no military experience; for him, the army was a business proposition. He had bought a commission, raised two regiments, and fronted the costs for an expedition to raid Spanish holdings on Mexico's Pacific coast. Since commanders could take booty, there was profit to be made, assuming he didn't get himself killed.

That rubbed Shelburne the wrong way. Shelburne fought for Britain in France and Germany. He had won promotions for bravery. He was the real deal. In his eyes, Fullarton was a mere *poseur*, whose foreign experience amounted to the Grand Tour and a political appointment as personal secretary to the British ambassador to France.

Unfortunately, Shelburne made his views known while speaking in the House of Lords. To be sure, he probably wasn't even thinking of Fullarton when he took the floor; he was raising a largely unrelated and entirely forgotten matter—two county militia officers who had been dismissed for allegedly expressing political views. Shelburne just had a habit of meandering as he spoke, a habit unfortunately mated to a remarkable talent for sarcasm. Once unholstered, that talent was largely unaimed.[2]

Shelburne began by defending the two officers. Then, according to reports, he "entered into a detail of the rise and power of lord-lieutenants of counties." After that Shelburne "averted to the establishment and power of the militia" before veering off to a discussion of "the alarming influence of the crown" in appointing outsiders to "occasional rank."

That's where Fullarton caught fire. Shelburne called such appointments a "destructive, humiliating" practice that undermined the military profession. He used Fullarton as proof, describing him as a mere "clerk" who won his rank "by ministerial caprice," leaping ahead of more worthy officers.[3]

Shelburne, intentionally or not, put Fullarton's honor at stake. He also put at risk the seventy or eighty thousand pounds his friends had put up for those two regiments.[4] Fullarton responded with a letter in the *Public Advertiser* questioning Shelburne's own character. He accused Shelburne of corresponding with one Benjamin Franklin, a leader of the American Revolution (true), thus aiding the enemy (possibly, though not necessarily; the two friends might just as easily have been writing about their shared interest in fossils).[5]

Formal letters were exchanged. A time was set. And now the two men prepared to shoot it out in Hyde Park.

The supporting entourage was suitably distinguished. Fullarton's second was Alexander Lindsay, 6th Earl of Balcarres. Shelburne's second was Field Marshal Lord Frederick Cavendish, who served with Shelburne in Germany. At approximately five-thirty, the two principals faced off. Each was armed with a pistol.

They aimed. They fired. They missed.

This actually happened fairly often, given the accuracy of smoothbore flintlocks; otherwise, the carnage resulting from late eighteenth century dueling would have been even greater. Each man drew a second pistol. Fullarton fired again. This time he hit Shelburne in the groin. Reports later said Shelburne was only "slightly" wounded.

Shelburne stood his ground and fired his weapon—straight up into the air. At that point the seconds performed their true function—keeping the participants from killing each other—and intervened, agreeing that the matter was settled and that the honor of all parties had been preserved. Each went his separate way.

Such was William Petty—Playfair's earliest sponsor to the high circles of British politics. Shelburne would, in turn, open doors for Playfair in France, which, in turn, would put him in business, and, in turn provide another step on Playfair's path to becoming a British secret agent.

§ § §

As 1785 began, Playfair was a busy man. He had just published *Increase in Manufacturers*. Between April and June, he dissolved his partnerships with Wilson and Keir. In the middle of all this, he was putting together an entirely new project: *The Commercial and Political Atlas*, the first book ever to portray numbers with pictures.

Think about the various ways you visualize numbers. The graphs in your bank statement, the charts in the latest government report, and the *Wall Street Journal* financial section are obvious. But what about the "charge remaining" and "signal strength" indicators on your smart phone? They're bar charts. Would you really prefer a number? Or prose? ("Sir, you have the lesser part of an hour left to complete your call.")

The speedometer in your car is probably a round gauge or an electronic simulation of one—that is, a pie chart. Numerical displays are great for matching your speed to a posted limit, nearly worthless to tell you how much of the allowed limit you've consumed. In fact, your instrument panel is itself a statistical graphic: well-designed cockpits have all their gauges pointing in the same direction when everything is normal. It instantly tells you, "All OK." Anything else says, "Something's wrong!"

Your brain likes graphics because, instinctively, humans are more comfortable making comparisons than trying to comprehend absolute quantities. *Which* tiger do you need to fear more? *Which* woolly mammoth will make the bigger meal? Or, in today's less primal society: *Which* fund is performing well? *Which* fund is lagging the average? Have you allocated more to stocks than you thought? Maybe you need to trade into bonds.

Cognitive psychologists say the process of comprehension we take for granted is, in reality, quite complex. Visual perception and mental cognition occur in a series of discrete steps, with each step collecting, selecting, and integrating data. Graphics—forms varying in shape and size—can facilitate the process.

This process begins in the eye itself, since the receptors in our retinas are each sensitive to some wavelengths and not others, and because different parts of the retina have different combinations and densities of receptors.

This acts as a filtering mechanism. There is also a "data overwrite" phenome-non. If a receptor is re-stimulated a millisecond before an initial impulse has a chance to reach the brain, you only "see" the second signal. Perception is shaped by the basic fact that some data get registered, and other data do not.[6]

Additional processing takes place after a neural signal arrives at the brain; how much depends on the complexity of what you are looking at. Simple objects require little attention; more detailed processing involves concentra-tion, reaching back to longer-term memory to find a match or counterexam-ple from past experience.[7]

Even word recognition is largely a process of recognizing *forms*—length, distinctive letters, frequently occurring fragments, and so on. Indeed, you can comprehend the essence of a message through shape and pattern recognition even when the literal details of words are ambiguous or imprecise. A couple of memes that bounced around the Internet in recent years shows how this works:[8]

> It deson't mttaer in waht oredr the ltteers in a wrod aepapr, the olny iprmoatnt tihng is taht the frist and lsat ltteer are in the rghit pcale. The rset can be a toatl mses and you can sitll raed it wouthit pobelrm.

> S1M1L4RLY, Y0UR M1ND 15 R34D1NG 7H15 4U70M471C4LLY W17H0U7 3V3N 7H1NK1NG 4B0U7 17.

Paragraph structure plays a role in comprehension, and shorter jumbled words are easier to recognize than longer ones. A lot depends on context and what a person expects to see.[9]

The point is, there's nothing like a good, hard, accurate number—perhaps with three or four decimal points—when you really require precision and have time to ponder and calculate. On the other hand, if you want to make comparisons, need an overview, or act fast, go with the graphic. It's how our brains work.

Playfair didn't know about cognitive psychology—that didn't come along until the last half of the twentieth century—but he intuitively understood the principles.[10] Using a geography analogy, he explained, "A map of the river Thames, or of a large town, expressed in figures, would give a very imperfect notion of either, though they may be perfectly exact in every dimension; most men would prefer *representations*, though very indifferent ones, to such a mode of painting."[11]

The *Atlas* has forty plates. It's a small book—158 pages, landscape format, about eight inches tall and a foot across. If you set it on a coffee table today and removed two hundred years of patina it might pass for a World Bank publication. Twenty-five charts analyzed England's imports and exports between 1700 and 1782. Ten depict "Public Accounts"—changes in national debt, military spending, and interest. Five provide Irish budget trends; Playfair got these data by corresponding with James Corry, an aide to the speaker of the Irish House of Commons, John Foster.

Simply publishing the *Atlas* was quite a challenge in 1785, as there were only two methods for printing graphics: etching and engraving. Both required a good amount of work. In etching, you pour wax over a soft metal sheet—usually copper—and then transfer the drawing into the wax with a stylus. Dunk the sheet into acid to "bite" the drawing into the metal, melt off the wax, and you can then use the plate to make a few hundred prints. The *Atlas* used copperplate charts.

The other method was engraving, where an artist inscribed the figure directly into a hard metal plate—usually steel. This was more challenging, as it required a master's deft hand and correcting mistakes was much harder. (With copperplate, if you catch a mistake before the acid dip, you just pour wax over the bad spot and try again.) But engraving allows more intricate, detailed, nuanced pictures. And the plate lasts longer, and can make thousands of impressions.

That's why engraving is used to print money.

The idea of describing numbers with pictures was so new Playfair gave readers step-by-step instructions for reading his charts. The first chart in the *Atlas* depicted annual changes in England's balance of trade during the preceding eighty-two years. "Observe where the line of exports passes the line marked at the bottom, 1750," he explained, "and by looking at the right hand margin, you will find it 12,650,000."[12]

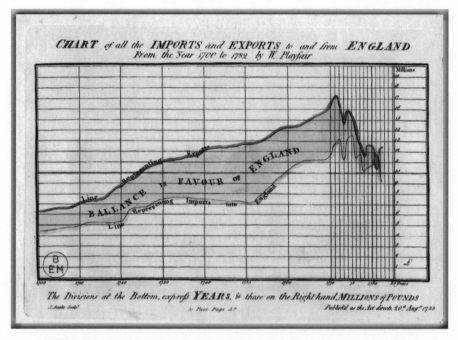

FIGURE 5: Possibly the first graphic ever published measuring an economic variable over time—"Chart of all the Imports and Exports to and from England from the Year 1700 to 1782." Source: William Playfair, *The Commercial and Political Atlas,* 2nd ed. (London: John Stockdale, 1787) via Wikimedia Commons.

A reviewer at the time called it "Mr. Playfair's ingenious contrivance for denoting the increase or decrease in numbers by geometrical line." The reviewer understood it well enough to provide some background. Playfair, he said, was building on a technique Joseph Priestley introduced a few years earlier. His "charts of biography" showed how one notable person's life overlapped with others and were pegged to significant dates. They were quite popular in the mid-1700s.[13]

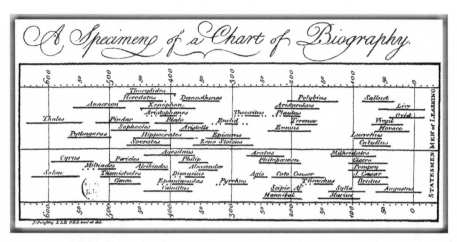

FIGURE 6: "Specimen of a Chart of Biography." Priestley had the basic idea of a metric indicating time on a horizontal axis; Playfair measured variables over time by adding a vertical axis. Source: Joseph Priestley, *History of Electricity* (London: J. Dodsley, 1767) via Wikimedia Commons.

Unlike Priestley's charts, Playfair's charts aimed to make points about British policy, like the one alerting readers to the growth in government borrowing. The line measuring national debt seems to approach escape velocity as it rockets to the top right hand corner of the graph. A reader half expects it to fly off the page.[14]

Graphics mavens, incidentally, loathe this chart. They say Playfair unfairly compressed the horizontal metric for "years" and stretched the vertical metric for "pounds," sending a subliminal message the data don't support, objectively speaking. An entire subculture exists where said mavens debate whether scales selected for an "X" and "Y" axis are intended to be fair or to distort.[15]

They're missing the point. Playfair may have been exaggerating the rate of increase. It might have even been intentional. But his main message is clear, and about as subliminal as a dope slap: *War Increases Debt*. It's right there, in black and white: each step increase in debt coincides with a war.

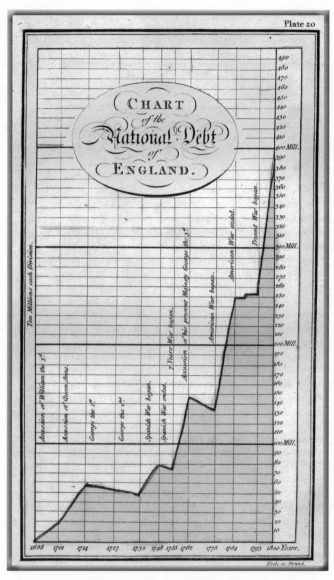

FIGURE 7: "Chart of the National Debt of Britain from the Revolution to the End of the War with America." One can quibble over Playfair's selection of vertical and horizontal scales; some say it distorts the rate of change. But it's hard to make a plainer argument that *war increases debt,* the point Playfair was trying to make. Source: William Playfair, *The Commercial and Political Atlas* 2nd ed. (London: John Stockdale, 1787) via Wikimedia Commons.

Playfair also published what is likely the first bar chart, depicting Scottish exports to seventeen different foreign jurisdictions. He may have used this approach because he had data for only a single year; all he said was that "the limits of this work do not admit of representing the trade of Scotland for a series of years." But this kind of chart offered an attractive feature: It showed, at a glance, Scotland's "portfolio" of trading partners—and the significance of each.

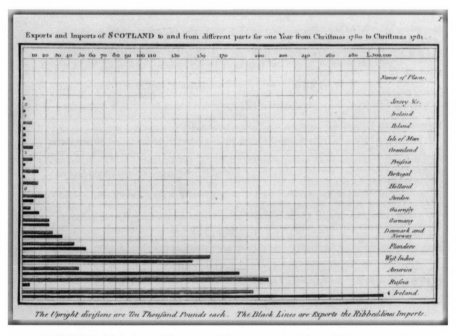

FIGURE 8: "Exports and Imports of Scotland to and from different parts for one Year from Christmas 1780 to Christmas 1781." Playfair may have used a bar chart instead of a line chart to portray Scotland's trade with other countries because he had data for only a single year. By putting all of its trading partners on a single graphic, however, Playfair also was able to present Scotland's "portfolio" of partners; comparing the importance of one to another was simple. Source: William Playfair, *The Commercial and Political Atlas*, 2nd ed. (London: John Stockdale, 1787) via Wikimedia Commons.

Playfair sent his old master James Watt a copy of an early version of the *Atlas* in September 1785, along with a note. (This was the same letter in which he complained about Keir.)

"I have taken the liberty of sending and requesting your acceptance of the 1st number if a work which I mean to continue from time to time," Playfair wrote. He asked Watt "as a particular favor your remarks on this specimen and farther also any thing that you think might make an improvement upon it either in the Execution or the Plan."[16]

Watt replied three weeks later. (This was the same note in which he advised Playfair to chill out about Keir.)

"I can think of nothing in addition to your plan," he wrote, "except that it might be proper to give the tables from which the Charts have been constructed, something in the manner Ld. Sheffield has done, for the charts now seem to rest on your own authority, and it will naturally be enquired from whence you have derived your intelligence."[17]

Playfair would later write of Watt, "I have seldom seen a more ingenious, and never a more pains-taking accurate man than him."[18] Playfair added the tables. But Watt may have been missing the point.

You had to read between the lines—literally—to see what was really on Playfair's mind. The space between the two trend lines depicting trade between England and another country were labeled to indicate whether the balance was in "*favour* of England" or "*against* England." Playfair was providing a way to keep score—because he wanted Britain to win.

The "Ld Sheffield" Watt mentioned was Lord John Baker Holroyd, 1st Earl of Sheffield, a farming expert with an interest in finance. Sheffield was also the friend, editor, and, later, literary executor of Edward Gibbon, then working on his six-volume *The History of the Decline and Fall of the Roman Empire.*[19]

Playfair apparently took Watt's advice to heart. He not only added the tables "in the manner of Ld Sheffield;" he was determined to meet Sheffield. He reached out to Patrick Colquhoun for an introduction.

Colquhoun was a fellow Scot who also had a bent for writing and statistics. He and Playfair seem to have been close; Playfair signed the copy of *Increase of Manufactures* gave Colquhoun a few years earlier, "To Patrick Colquhoun, Esq., with the respectful compliments of his obliged Friend & obtnt svt."[20]

Now Colquhoun was promoting Playfair's new book. "I thank you very much for the copy of the Political Atlas which you had the goodness to send me," Colquhoun wrote. "I have pleased and gratified many of my friends by the perusal of it," adding, "I am glad the Sale has exceeded your expectations."

"I called at the Bookseller the other day but I did not find that he had received the 6 dozen Copies you had ordered down," Colquhoun continued. "When I know they are in the Shop I shall take care that they do not remain unnoticed."[21]

After fighting for the British in the American Revolution, Colquhoun returned to Glasgow, did well in the fabric trade, and got into in politics before moving to London in 1785. There he made his mark with a proposal to solve the city's crime problem—thieves were targeting merchants selling Scottish cloth. Colquhoun led the establishment of the Thames River Police, Britain's first constabulary.[22] (Jeremy Bentham collaborated; interconnections did run thick in eighteenth-century Britain.)[23]

Colquhoun gave Playfair a letter of introduction to his "invaluable friend Lord Sheffield." He wrote Playfair, "I am sure the longer you know that worthy man the more you will be pleased and gratified with his society," adding, "Adieu, Mrs. Colquhoun joins in complements."[24]

Colquhoun could not know how prophetic he would be. One day Playfair would need Sheffield's help to put food on his table.

§ § §

William Petty made a reputation fighting the French in places like Minden and Kloster Kamp during the Seven Years' War. He caught the attention of King George III, and that, in turn, got Petty into politics and elected to the House of Commons in 1760. But his father died a few months later, so Petty instead took the family's seat in the House of Lords. During most of his political life Petty was known as Lord Shelburne.[25]

Shelburne was a passionate, forceful, if somewhat unfocused orator (See: "Duel with Fullarton"). He had many strong beliefs; one was free trade.

To hear Shelburne tell the story, his conversion was like Peter on the road to Damascus. Except in Shelburne's case the road was between Edinburgh and London, and the voice he heard wasn't that of any Deity, but rather that of his traveling companion, Adam Smith. By journey's end Shelburne believed in the efficacy of capitalism, the efficiency of markets, and the wisdom of the Invisible Hand.[26]

Today free trade is about eliminating complex tariff schedules or discriminatory regulations. In Playfair's day, free trade was about eliminating state-chartered monopolies, like the British East India Company, and reducing barriers to trade with colonies. Free traders like Shelburne said colonies—and colonial wars—were expensive. That's why, when the Americans rebelled against British taxation, his response was: Let them go. Britain didn't need to *own* the colonies, just the opportunity to trade with them. Besides, the war was costing Britain fifteen million pounds a year.

Prime Minister Lord North was more inclined to beat the Americans into submission. End result: On 22 March 1782—after more than six years of war—North became the first British Prime Minister to lose a vote of no confidence. The king turned to opposition leader Lord Rockingham to form a new government. Rockingham was determined to end the American War. Shelburne joined his cabinet. A few weeks later Rockingham caught the flu and died. Shelburne became Prime Minister.

The Treaty of Paris was signed in September 1783, but by then Shelburne was gone. His blunt style was great for fighting at Kloster Kamp, less so for managing a coalition at Westminster. North and Fox set aside their differences just long enough to form the most unlikely of alliances to force Shelburne out of office. William Pitt became Prime Minister in December. Shelburne was created the Marquess of Lansdowne. In effect, he got kicked upstairs at the age of forty-six.

Shelburne—Lansdowne after 1784—retired to Bowood, his estate a hundred miles west of London. But he still had influence. He had his seat in the House of Lords. He had his contacts across Britain, the Continent, and the former colonies. And he could set a table.

Lansdowne held court for young men with new ideas about economics, sociology, politics, and how the world ought to work in general. It became known as the "Bowood Circle," a sort of informal think tank. He subsidized some attendees, like Étienne Dumont, hiring them as tutors for his kids. Wealthier members, like Jeremy Bentham, stayed as guests.[27] Lansdowne invited Playfair to visit him at Bowood in 1787.[28]

So how did Lansdowne come to know Playfair?

Increase of Manufactures might have caught his eye. Lansdowne's guru, Adam Smith, said supply and demand ought to set the price of goods; Playfair simply applied the idea to the price of money. Bentham might have mentioned Playfair to Lansdowne—we know Bentham read *Increase of Manufactures* because he gossiped about it. No matter whether he praised it or dissed it, it was buzz either way and Lansdowne would have heard.

Or it may have been another connection: Dugald Stewart.

Stewart was John Playfair's colleague, friend, and dining partner at the University of Edinburgh. John took Stewart's chair at the University as professor of mathematics when Stewart was given a newly created chair as professor of moral philosophy.[29]

William didn't get to Edinburgh often, but he did apparently did visit in the winter of 1785–1786. Stewart had a chance to meet William and apparently was quite taken with the young man.[30]

As it happened, Stewart was also a friend of Benjamin Vaughan, the wealthy son of a London merchant. Vaughn met Stewart at Edinburgh after Vaughn left the University of Cambridge; Vaughn was a Unitarian, and since Cambridge did not graduate Dissenters at the time, he moved on. But before Vaughn arrived at Edinburgh, he befriended...William Petty, 2nd Earl of Shelburne.[31]

Vaughan and Shelburne met through Benjamin Horne, another member of the Whig/reformer/merchant network. They shared several interests: political reform, free trade, and horticulture (both were fond of strawberries).[32]

Vaughan was young enough to be a protégé of Shelburne, but rich enough to be more of a peer, class-wise. They got along well, and Shelburne made Vaughan his private secretary. When Shelburne became Prime Minister, Vaughan helped him secure the treaty that got Britain out of its American War. After that Vaughan served Shelburne informally as a Bowood talent scout.

For whatever reason, Vaughan asked Stewart for his opinion of William in 1786, shortly after Playfair published the *Commercial and Political Atlas*.

"Mr Playfair about whom you make enquiry in your last letter," Stewart wrote, "was originally destined for the profession of a civil engineer." He admitted, "I am not acquainted with the particulars of his history in England, but I know in general that he has been unfortunate in business."

"Of his principles and dispositions I have a very favorable opinion," Stewart continued, "and I know that he possesses a great deal both of mathematical & mechanical information." He said Playfair has "turned his attention to the study of commercial politics, & so far as I am able to judge he is well fitted for such speculations as he has strong natural abilities, and has acquired a considerable stock of facts both from books and from his own observation."

Recalling William's visit, Stewart added, "During the last winter he made a short stay at Edinburgh and I found his conversation extremely instructive.

Indeed I know few who have been more attentive & intelligent observers both of men & things."[33]

So that's how Playfair met Lansdowne: William Playfair was John Playfair's brother; John was best friends with Dugald Stewart; Stewart and Benjamin Vaughan became friends when Vaughn attended Edinburgh; and Vaughan was on the lookout for promising thinkers for Lansdowne after the two collaborated on the Treaty of Paris. A circuitous connection, yes, but there's good evidence for all of the links.[34]

In 1786 Playfair was working on a new pamphlet Lansdowne was bound to find interesting: *An Essay on the National Debt*. Lansdowne and Playfair both worried about the debt. In the new pamphlet, Playfair proposed a "sinking fund," money earmarked to pay it off. It would cost more than simply rolling over bonds in the short run, but it would save money in the long run.

It wasn't a new idea; indeed, Britain already had a sinking fund. The problem was that officials were continually raiding it. Lansdowne thought that was a huge mistake, and Playfair's charts gave him intellectual ammunition— visual arguments to put in front of British officials, who still listened to him, not withstanding his forced retirement.[35]

When Playfair visited Bowood, Lansdowne invited Isaac Barré, to join them. Barré had been his political ally and perhaps his closest friend. Like Lansdowne, Barré had Irish roots and had been a soldier. Like Lansdowne, Barré had opposed the American War.[36]

The two men scrutinized Playfair's draft and parsed his arguments. Years later Playfair described his encounter with Barré, recalling "I never found any person who approved more completely of the manner I had invented of representing the progress of revenue and expenditure by lines in a divided surface."

That was all the more remarkable because Barré was blind.

Barré had taken a shot in the face at the siege of Quebec during the French and Indian War. It cost him the use of his right eye. By the time he and Playfair met his left eye had failed, too.[37]

Lansdowne agreed to endorse the pamphlet; Playfair thanked him in the dedication: "Your Lordship's unremitting attention to the good of your country, and profound knowledge of what constitutes her best interests," Playfair wrote, led him to solicit "your Lordship's unprejudiced patronage, that protection to the following Essay, which I could not expect to receive under the wings of any party."

"The marks of approbation with which it has pleased your Lordship to distinguish my endeavours to illustrate Political Subjects by Lineal Arithmetic," Playfair continued, "will, I hope, be the means of their obtainting at least a candid attention from the Public; At any rate, I shall always consider them as an high honour on to their Author."[38]

Playfair and Lansdowne would continue their friendship. At least, they would until the French Revolution put them on opposite sides of British politics.[39]

§ § §

Playfair wrote another book in 1787—anonymously. It was titled *Joseph and Benjamin in Conversation*. There was no reason for anyone to have suspected he was the author until after he died, when his obituary listed it among his publications.[40]

It's a curious work. The "Joseph" in the title is Joseph II, the Habsburg ruler of the Holy Roman Empire who personified enlightened despotism—totally monopolizing power while simultaneously pushing social reforms like religious tolerance and press freedom. The "Benjamin" is Benjamin Franklin—inventor, writer, businessmen, philosopher and probably the best-known American of his era.

Joseph and Benjamin claims to be a transcript, translated from French, of a secret meeting between the two when Franklin was the American ambassador to France. In reality, the book is a made-up fantasy. It's Playfair's own views about free trade and constitutional monarchy put in the mouths of two well-known figures.

Many of the ideas—even the phrasings—appear in his later writings. "Franklin" says, for example, that he was constantly telling Americans "to attend to husbandry, breeding cattle, and manufacturing those coarse materials which are necessary to the lower class."[41] That's actually Playfair saying nations should concentrate their efforts in sectors where they enjoy a "comparative advantage." If they did, they would all be wealthier and less apt to fight over markets, trade routes, and resources.

The book was a flop.

Merely "the effusion of some inexperienced writer," one reviewer said.[42] Another, more charitable, got into the spirit and called it "the work altogether of an innocent and harmless nature." But he couldn't resist correcting Play-fair's grammar and Scottish idioms.

"Some expressions, such as *learned* for *taught*, &c. seem to indicate that it may have travelled from beyond the Tweed," the reviewer observed. "We take notice of it to put young writers on their guard with respect to purity of language." Pay attention! [43]

True, the dialogue in *Joseph and Benjamin* does sometimes read like a sophomore composition assignment. But there's a twist to the story. Playfair was more knowledgeable of world affairs than his reviewers suspected. He probably had more inside information, too.

You see, Joseph and Benjamin really *did* schedule a secret meeting.

It happened when Franklin was ambassador to France. The story did not emerge until forty years later, when Franklin's grandson, William Temple Franklin, published a memoir of the great man. He had been Franklin's secretary in France when Franklin tried to pitch Joseph.

Franklin was up to his elbows in secret diplomacy, espionage, and clandestine operations during the American Revolution. [44] He hoped to keep the British-leaning Holy Roman Empire neutral. Franklin's private notes recall he learned Joseph was traveling through France that spring under his pseudonym, "Count Falkenstein." Franklin said he planned "to give the Emperor an opportunity of an interview with me that should appear accidental." [45]

Abbé Niccoli, minister of the Grand Duke of Tuscany, agreed to have Franklin "accidentally" stop by his apartment for chocolate at nine o'clock on Wednesday morning, 28 May. The Abbé also invited Anne-Robert-Jacques Turgot, the liberal minded, recently resigned French finance minister. Franklin wanted witnesses "to prevent or contradict false reports."

Alas, the Emperor was a no-show. The Abbé told Franklin that Joseph heard the meeting wasn't a one-on-one and it spooked him off. Joseph did come by later, but by then Franklin was gone. [46]

How would Playfair have known about an obscure, clandestine encounter planned ten years earlier between two top diplomats that never came off? Playfair was just a twenty-eight-year-old underemployed engineer trying to break into writing. He hadn't even traveled abroad.

Here's one possibility: Joseph's sojourn to Paris was known among top diplomats. Lansdowne would have heard about it. He might have shared the behind-the-scene story with Playfair during that visit to Bowood. It does help make sense of *Joseph and Benjamin*. And it suggests Playfair was getting a taste of high-level secret diplomacy and off-the-books operations.

One other thing: There is a passage buried deep inside *Joseph and Benjamin* that never gets anyone's notice but reveals one of Playfair's big ideas—a project he would keep in the back of his mind for years. Playfair's "Franklin" described a fictional secret weapon that France kept in a closet—literally:[47]

> A book is kept in one of the most secret parts of a Royal Build-ing in Paris, in which book each nation in Europe has a place assigned for itself; something in the manner of a merchant's ledger. France is first, Spain next, then England, Holland, the German Empire, Prussia, Russia, Portugal, Sweden, and Den-mark. These are all the nations on the list, and to the best of my recollection that is the order in which they follow. Perhaps if the book were to be arranged now, the order might be a little different; but it is a very considerable number of years (though I do not know how many) since it was begun.

> There are a number of excellent maps kept in the same apart-ment, to which they have a reference; and every circumstance that affects in any degree, the political importance of either of these nations, is registered under the proper head as soon as possible; and with as much accuracy as possible. The circum-stance upon which the importance of each country depends, are minutely described; and in another part of the same book is the plan of the French Monarch; that is to say, the out-lines of a plan, by which France must be raised above her neighbors,

> This book may, I think, be called the POLITICAL BIBLE of France, and it is preserved in the Sanctum Sanctorum, with all due care and secrecy. The people concerned in the compilation are men of first rank and fortune, and it is death as well as confiscation of property and degradation of family, ever to mention the exis-tence of this work. The King of France, I have been told has often spent three hours at a time consulting this oracle; and though he has not I believe, ever actually projected any import-ant measures himself, yet he has become so much master of the

subject, as to be able to judge of the expediency, and enter with proper interest into the undertaking of his Court.

Playfair already possessed a penchant for intelligence. He was inventing the regularly updated, all-source estimate—so sensitive it had to be kept in a secure facility and its drafters had to swear to secrecy before they could work on it.

"Political Bible"? A better name might be "Political Breviary." Or maybe "Statistical Breviary." One thing's certain: no minister or general who really believed knowledge is power would want to be without it.

§ § §

On 16 June 1787, about a month after arriving in Paris, Playfair climbed six flights of stairs to an apartment in one of the more imposing buildings on rue St. Honoré. He rang the bell; no one answered. He rang again. Finally, a man with a sour look on his face opened the door. A maid was just behind him, vainly trying to reach the door first, a couple of steps too late.

The man gave Playfair a cursory glance, motioned him in, turned, and proceeded to unleash a verbal volley of Gaelic abuse at the maid. Playfair could make out only a word or two, but the gestures needed no translation. The maid trembled. Playfair made a mental note: His host had a hair trigger temper and, clearly, a lot of practice exercising it—especially on underlings.

The man with the temper was Abbé André Morellet, one of Lansdowne's close friends. The two had met in 1771 when Lansdowne (then Shelburne) was traveling through France. Morellet visited Bowood the following year; Benjamin Franklin joined them. The three had corresponded ever since, and Morellet helped facilitate the Treaty of Paris. Later Lansdowne convinced Louis XVI to reward Morellet with a four thousand-livre pension.[48]

Morellet may have been Lansdowne's friend, but first impressions count, and Playfair took an instant dislike to him. It was not a happy meeting. Communication was definitely part of the problem.

Playfair thought Morellet "spoke as bad English as I did French." Morellet, on the other hand, didn't think Playfair spoke French at all. He invited Playfair to return if he ever had something in writing that he wanted to share. He even offered to introduce Playfair to his friends. But Playfair loathed the man so much that he never went near him again.[49]

France was swarming with Brits looking for business, a result of the new Commercial Treaty. Lansdowne and Vergennes were rivals, but both wanted to end the wars Europe had been fighting for centuries. Both believed free trade might do the trick. They made sure the treaty ending the American War also committed Britain and France to negotiate an agreement encouraging imports and exports between the two countries. The Commercial Treaty was signed on 26 September 1786, going into effect the following March.[50]

Playfair arrived a few months later. Lansdowne gave him several letters of introduction, like the one to Morellet. Playfair did not think they helped much. "When a friend gives an introduction, it is not so much because the person to whom one introduced is likely to be serviceable," he recalled. "It is done from friendship or politeness." He reckoned that "an invitation to dinner and some civilities are all the fruits of such acquaintances."[51]

It was the *Commercial and Political Atlas* that made connections for Playfair. Lansdowne sent copies to his friends in France. It was hit or miss. One copy went to Abbé Morellet. He was utterly unimpressed. "When you communicate, you need numbers," Morellet wrote Lansdowne. "Playfair's chart is useless." That was a miss.

Several copies went to Vergennes. That was a hit—by the narrowest of margins.

Vergennes died on 13 February 1787. Reportedly the king, devastated, cried at hearing the news, saying Vergennes was "the one minister who never deceived me."[52] But before he passed, Vergennes gave Louis a copy of the *Atlas* Lansdowne had sent him.

You might not be reading this had he died just a few weeks earlier.

§ § §

The first Sunday after Playfair arrived in Paris, he and his wife Mary took a walk to check out the city. Just like tourists today, they strolled down the Champs-Élysées and took in the Tuileries Gardens.[53] They walked through the Place Louis XV. Today it's the Place de la Concorde. In between it would be the Place de la Révolution, when authorities replaced the statute of the Sun King with a guillotine.

But that was three years in the future. For now, William and Mary Playfair were enjoying Paris in the springtime.

About two months later Playfair ran into a fellow Brit and began talking business. A local happened to overhear them. Fluent in English, the Frenchman introduced himself as Chevalier d'Ajeux. He was accompanying Henry Cecil, a British noble traveling with his young family. He was also glib, entertaining—a player. If Playfair was looking for business, d'Ajeux wanted to know about it—and get in on a piece of the action.[54]

A French acquaintance that Playfair knew from his Birmingham days, a M. Gérentet, was also in Paris and had set up a manufactory. He told Playfair that "a rolling mill was greatly wanted in Paris"—exactly what Playfair, rolling mill patentee, wanted to hear. The chevalier offered to introduce him to the officials who could make it happen. Nothing could be done without them, he warned.[55]

So Playfair drafted a business plan, as he put it, "in the French manner": forty shares were reserved for the founders, thirty-six to be sold to raise capital, and six more to be dispensed as bribes.

Plan in hand, d'Ajeux set up a meeting with Jean-Claude Richard, the Abbé Saint Non.[56] The Abbé, a painter and man of the cloth, would arrange a meeting with the Baron de Batz, a young gentleman. As Playfair put it, Batz would "get the business done" with Louis Charles Auguste le Tonnelier de Breteuil, the minister of the King's household—gatekeeper for favors from the Crown.[57]

Fans of historical thrillers and pulp romances might recognize Jean, Baron de Batz, as a character in several period novels—most notably, Emma Orczy's *The Scarlet Pimpernel*, the first action hero franchise.

In the Pimpernel storyline, Sir Percy Blakeney, a foppish English noble (think Bruce Wayne) adopts a secret identity as the Scarlet Pimpernel, an adventuring swordsman (á la Batman). The Pimpernel rescues French aristocrats before they get their heads lopped off by the guillotine during the Reign of Terror. Orczy created the Scarlet Pimpernel in 1905 as a character in a play, and spun him into a series of novels later adapted to film.

It gets a little confusing because Blakeney—the Scarlet Pimpernel—resembles the real-life Batz, but Orczy also inserted a character named Baron de Batz in her stories. The fictional Batz is the Pimpernel's rival in *El Dorado*, the book on which most of the films are based. In the novel, the Baron works for Austria and competes with the Pimpernel to rescue Louis-Charles, heir to the Bourbon throne.[58]

Orczy never broke character and scoffed when asked if her Pimpernel was based on Batz. The Baron was a mere Gascon, she said, a rube from the French Pyrenees, "who never justified either his own ambitions or even his existence." The Scarlet Pimpernel, in contrast, "was a personality of whom an entire nation"—meaning England—"might justly be proud."[59]

Nationalism was running at full tilt during the early 1900s.

In real life, Jean de Batz was a well-connected financier and one of the least likely of individuals to be picked out of a lineup as an action hero. He was a slight, small-statured man—good looking, if you believed his passport description. Batz supported the Revolution at first but joined the royalist opposition when the radicals seized power. His exploits—combined with his enigmatic background—would make him the go-to scapegoat whenever the regime encountered contretemps or scandal.[60]

But that was in the future; for now, Batz was a master of the inside business deal in pre-Revolution France. Playfair took a liking to him almost as immediately as he took a loathing to Morellet. The Baron was straightforward, he thought, and worked hard to understand the rolling mill project. While collaborating on their plan, Playfair lent Batz a copy of the *Atlas* as a token of friendship. Two days later he received an invitation to Batz's house for dinner.[61]

When he arrived Playfair discovered Batz had also asked Étienne Clavière, a Swiss financier, to join them. Clavière had fled Geneva in 1782 along with other bankers when Catholic France allied with Savoy and Berne to crack down on the Calvinist reformers. Clavière settled first in England and then in Ireland, before moving to France when the political atmosphere improved in the mid-1780s. Along the way he made a fortune through speculations.

Clavière spoke excellent English and played interpreter. As the evening progressed, Clavière told Playfair that he, too, owned a copy of the *Atlas*. And, he said, he had heard that, before he died, Vergennes had given a copy to Louis XVI. And, Clavière added, the King liked it—a lot.[62]

As Playfair later told the story, this all came as a pleasant surprise to the Baron. What had started as just another job of greasing a deal for a likable businessman had turned into a partnership with one of the King's favorites—a real coup in a country where royal favor meant everything. Playfair respected Batz all the more because the two men had bonded before the Baron knew about his royal endorsement.[63]

Twenty years later Playfair would write that he had been "particularly intimate with the Baron de Batz"—the eighteenth century term of art for someone you liked and trusted.[64] In his never-published memoir he would recall, "our friendship was mutual and remained while I staid in France."[65]

On 5 April 1788 the Société Gérentet et Playfair—the company set up by Playfair and his Birmingham acquaintance who got the ball rolling—secured permission from Louis to build a rolling mill. It helped that when the partners presented the rolling mill proposal, they made a point of saying that it was "for the inventor of the Linear Charts." The King even threw in the land for the factory as a bonus.[66]

Now Playfair had cash flow. He had political allies. He was in business.

3 Accidental Revolutionaries

The magistrate cried out, pointing to a picture of Christ on the wall of the *Grand Chambre du Parlement*. "Would you crucify Him a second time?" It came natural to Jean-Jacques Duval d'Eprémesnil. He was prone to dramatics—as everyone in the chamber knew.

It was 19 January 1788. The Parlement of Paris was in a standoff with Louis XVI. The King had issued a decree that would grant non-Catholics the right to pray and marry. France lived on borrowed money, and many of its loans came from Protestant bankers; this was a modest reform to improve relations. But d'Eprémesnil thought even that went too far; hence the dramatics.

In the end, it didn't matter. The King enacted the edict unilaterally, and even d'Eprémesnil's fellow magistrates abandoned him. Just seventeen colleagues voted with him against registering the edict into the statute books. It was typical d'Eprémesnil: much rhetoric, mixed results.[1]

Jean-Jacques Duval d'Eprémesnil was born in 1745 in the French trading enclave of Pondicherry, on the east coast of India. Son of a trading family from Le Havre, his father was a French East India Company director. Young d'Eprémesnil arrived in France at the age of five. He later studied law and went on to become a *counseiller* in the parlement, where he won a reputation as a firebrand—a passionate, occasionally effective speaker with a nose for publicity.[2]

For d'Eprémesnil, a devout Catholic, the French monarchy was a holy compact among king, clergy, nobles, and commoners, all for the good of man, all ordained by God. He was determined to protect the role of parlement in this arrangement; monarchy needed checks and balances. It was a cause grounded on logic and principle.[3]

But some of d'Eprémesnil's other causes could be, let us say, a little less grounded, a little more eccentric, and a lot more opportunistic—like his obsession with mesmerism.[4]

It all started when Franz Anton Mesmer, a Viennese physician, arrived in Paris in 1784. Mesmer claimed he could cure the sick and make crazy people sane by channeling the invisible magnetic fluid that supposedly circulated around and through them. He called this fluid "animal magnetism," as opposed to "mineral magnetism," the more familiar kind generated by magnets.

Mesmer would put a patient in a tub lined with colored glass. Then he and other participants would hold electrodes bolted to the tub. This would supposedly direct their animal magnetism through the subject. Sometimes the assembled were told to hold each other's hands to pool their collective energy.

The urgent need to relieve the suffering of an ailing patient thus offered young Parisian men a socially acceptable opportunity to hold the hand of a pretty woman in public. After all, it was all in the name of science.

Mesmer would then utter some incantations. The subject would convulse. Men would gasp. Women would swoon. The subject would step out of the tub—cured! It was remarkable what collective hysteria combined with the power of suggestion could achieve.

The French popular press was filled with accounts of Mesmer's miracles. Soon mesmerists were holding sessions in cafés and salons all across Paris. Mesmer was raking in the livres. It was all junk science and the sessions were tent shows—but that was precisely its appeal to d'Eprémesnil.

In the Old Regime, science was synonymous with the state. Serious researchers taught at established institutions like *L'Université de Paris* and were members of the royal *Académie*. Dallying in mesmerist hoodoo was one way to question the regime's authority. Which made mesmerism a *cause célèbre*. Which made it irresistible to d'Eprémesnil. He joined other devotees to form the *Société de l'Harmonie Universelle* ("Society of Universal Harmony").

The Society was part therapy group, part cult, part upper-class debating society, and part cash cow for Mesmer, who sold treatments and lessons in the art of magnetic healing. It broke up sometime around 1787 when the members more interested in politics than therapeutic magnetism went their own way. The breakup revealed how the Society had been a proxy for political reform—and a holding tank for soon-to-be-leaders of the French Revolution.

Most Americans would likely recognize at least one of them: The Marquis de Lafayette, soon to be a leader of the pro-constitution, keep-the-monarchy wing of the Revolution. Another was Jean-Paul Marat, physician, pamphleteer, and, thanks to Jacques-Louis David's painting of his bathtub murder, icon of the revolution's radical wing.[5]

Jacques-Pierre Brissot joined, too. Brissot was a journalist; later he would be a member of the National Convention. He vacillated on whether to keep the king, and, later, whether to execute him; his more important role, however, would pressing for war against the monarchies of Europe.[6]

One of Brissot's closest friends also joined: Étienne Clavière, the Swiss banker who played interpreter when Baron de Batz invited Playfair to dinner. He would go on to become finance minister—and an architect of the plan to finance the revolution with paper money. The two had sat across the table from each other.[7]

§ § §

To understand how d'Eprémesnil accidentally triggered the French Revolution—and became intertwined with Playfair—one must first understand France finance in the late eighteenth century.

France's biggest problem was not just its corruption (which was pervasive), its record keeping (which was opaque), or its debt (which was huge). Its most pressing problem was *liquidity*. France was wealthy, but struggled to pay its day-to-day bills because it lacked a functioning tax system.[8]

France's class-based society was divided into three "estates." The First Estate comprised the nation's 10,000 or so clergy members. The Second Estate consisted of 400,000 or so nobles: *ducs, princes, comtes,* and *marquis,* who also officered the French army and navy. The Third Estate was everyone else—about 25 million people, mainly peasants, but also merchants, craftsmen, and a small but growing number of entrepreneurs.[9]

The saying went, "The clergy prays for France, the nobility bleeds for France, and the commoners pay for France." The First and Second Estates were excused from most taxes. That left the Third Estate with most of the burden.

And those taxes were endless: a head tax (the *taille*), a salt tax (the *gabelle*), a tobacco and drink tax (the *aide*)—plus a tax to the Church (the *tithe*) and forced labor for road repair that commoners had to perform (the *corvée royale*). Yet while commoners felt their taxes were too high, nobles resented having to any pay taxes at all.

Which explains how d'Eprémesnil, Paris Parlement magistrate, triggered the French Revolution.

The thirteen French parlements were one of the few constraints on the King's rule by Divine Right. Their members—magistrates, or *parlementaires*—were supposed to apply the king's edicts. Strictly speaking, magistrates weren't nobles; they were more like a self-perpetuating legal bureaucracy. Even so, they enjoyed many of the privileges of nobles, hung in the same circles, and identified with them.[10]

The magistrates had leverage—not much, but some. A parlement had to register an edict into statute before the magistrates could apply it. If they objected to an edict, they could respond with a remonstrance to the king, stating their concerns and requesting he clarify his intent. If they *really* had problems with it, they could repeat the process—sort of like a filibuster.

The king could always convene a *lit de justice* and simply command a parlement to register an edict. But that risked conflict with the nobles; besides commanding his army they also controlled the largest share of France's land (and, thus, its wealth). The result was a constrained tug-of-war, with the king asserting absolute supremacy, and the parlements, sort of representing the nobility, resisting.[11]

By the mid-1780s, French finances were dire; the parlements resisted raising taxes or taking out new loans. Louis decided to stop their obstruction once and for all. In early May 1788 his ministers secretly began to prepare edicts transferring the parlements' responsibilities to a new court—rendering the magistrates irrelevant. It would, in effect, be a royal coup.

When d'Eprémesnil learned of the plans, he and fellow magistrate, Anne Louis Marie Françoise Goislard, compte de Monsabert, convinced the president of the Paris Parlement to call an emergency session. The parlementaires dug in their heels and preempted the king by voting for a "Statement of Rights."[12] This had never happened before in France.

The revolt of the French nobles echoed English nobles forcing Magna Carta on their own king five centuries earlier. It, too, was written by nobles to protect their privileges, as a step toward replacing the unlimited, arbitrary rule of kings with the rule of law. Had events played out a little differently, the Paris Parlement's Statement of Rights might have done the same in France.

That's one of history's great "what ifs"; the reality was that the Statement was sedition, and d'Eprémesnil and Goislard were at the head of it. The next evening soldiers went to arrest them at their homes. Word got out and the two escaped, disguised, over the rooftops of Paris, making it to the parlement's chambers at the Palais de la Cité, where the magistrates voted to give them sanctuary.[13]

A battalion of royal troops surrounded the Palais. Crowds gathered. The captain of the guard, the Marquis d'Agoust, entered the grand chamber. He read the king's arrest order for d'Eprémesnil and Goislard. After a thirty-hour standoff, the magistrates realized it was hopeless and surrendered.[14]

The inevitable *lit de justice* came two days later. Louis banned the parlements from meeting. But he still had to deal with his budget crisis. The king had already promised to convene deputies representing the Estates General no later than 1792. To mollify the nobles he now moved that to May 1789.[15]

For his part, d'Eprémesnil landed in the prison on the Île Sainte-Marguerite off France's southern coast. When the king moved up the date for the Estates General, he also released d'Eprémesnil, who left jail a hero. He was the toast of French, British, and American circles favoring France incrementally evolving into a constitutional monarchy. Crowds cheered him as he traveled north, through Toulon, Marseilles, and Lyon to Paris. He would never be so popular again.[16]

§ § §

By mid-1788 Playfair was busy wheeling, dealing, and making the rounds in Paris. It was a productive period for Playfair in more ways than just business and politics. He and Mary already had a son and daughter, John and Elizabeth. While in France they had two more children: Louise died young, Andrew William was born in 1790. (Their youngest daughter, Zenobia, would arrive in 1795.)[17]

Another one of Playfair's friends was Alexandre-Théophile Vandermonde, the musician-turned-mathematician best known for his contributions to matrix algebra. Vandermonde likely saw a link between his matrices and Playfair's charts; both provide shorthand for a numerical array.

In any case, Vandermonde thought enough of Playfair to introduce him at a session of the Académie Royale des Sciences. He sat him next to the president, and Playfair received a standing invitation to attend Académie sessions—quite a coup; the top minds of France met at the Académie. Playfair and Vandermonde grew close.[18]

"I frequently dined with him on Sundays," Playfair recalled.[19]

Unfortunately, Vandermonde was becoming a certifiable political junkie. With the convocation of the Estates General scheduled, new ideas about freedom and democracy were bouncing all around Paris, and Vandermonde was like a kid on Christmas morning trying out all his new toys. He just could not stop talking politics.

At first Vandermonde was captivated by the elegance of the unwritten British constitution. But that was a mere fling. Soon he was flirting with the American approach—better, he thought, to have principles spelled out in a formal, negotiated document. Then he discovered democratic renewal, insisting, "Nothing would do but a constitution that was either Terminable at the will of the nation, or at some fixed and near period that people might again to return to first principles."

The problem with the British constitution, Vandermonde complained, was that "there is no legal mode of insurrection." Playfair thought Vandermonde might be a brilliant mathematician, but was bonkers when it came to politics. "Insurrection and revolt" might necessary for the new French Government, Playfair mused, but for England it was "a ridiculous and most dangerous idea."

Playfair's problem wasn't just that he disagreed with Vandermonde; the problem was that he didn't live and breathe politics like his friend did. Vandermonde was determined to discuss every point with Playfair. It was a hazard of the time for those digesting Voltaire, Montesquieu, Hume, Rousseau, and the rest of the *philosophes*. Vandermonde "began on them with me at every opportunity," he recalled, and so "by degrees I withdrew myself from his society."

Playfair may have thought Vandermonde's model of perpetual revolution was a loser, but he agreed the French government was hopeless and had to go. It didn't matter that he was getting rich off the king's patronage. In fact, it was Playfair's first-hand experience that convinced him the Old Regime was doomed, and none too soon.

"The court of justice in France were also corrupted to such a point that justice could not be obtained by fair means," Playfair later recalled. "It was a common custom to solicit openly the judges." He even confessed, "I have done it myself in a process depending before the Parliament of Paris."

"I did it at the express instigation of my friends," Playfair added, "who told me that if I did not the members would consider it as an insolent neglect and that I should lose my cause." A magistrate wasn't offended at the offer of a bribe; he was offended if you didn't offer one.[20]

Case in point: The Machine de Marly, the pumping station that supplied the towering geysers and flowing ponds at Versailles. The Machine was probably the largest industrial power plant built up to then. It was huge. Some called it a "forest of iron and wood." It consisted of fourteen water wheels, each 11.5 meters in diameter, geared together to drive some two hundred-odd pumps. Andrew Meikle would have been impressed.[21]

With that kind of complexity, though, the Machine was constantly breaking down. Even in the best of times required a crew of sixty to keep it running. Matthew Boulton and James Watt had gone to France in 1786 as royal guests to explore how to replace the Machine with one of their steam engines; like Playfair's rolling mill later two years later, it was part of the king's effort to modernize French industry.

Boulton and Watt met with Charles Alexandre de Calonne, the Comptroller General, and his brother, Abbé Jacques-Ladislas-Joseph de Calonne. They were close to an agreement when Louis dismissed Charles Alexandre after he failed to get the nobles to agree to a tax hike. It had nothing to do with the Machine, but in France's patronage-based system, when Charles Alexandre was gone, so was the deal.[22]

Playfair and Gérentet decided to have a go. They also proposed replacing the Machine with a steam engine, but agreed to accept the old plant in payment; they planned to sell the parts for £38,000.

"This project was relished," Playfair later recalled. The only catch was that they would have to give a third of the profit to the brother of Louis-Léon, duc de Brancas. Jean de Batz, Playfair's facilitator, was a protectee of the House of Brancas.[23]

French nobility was like the Mafia, with patrons and entourages and families and dons. Each had his own turf and each boss got his "taste." Everything depended on privilege, and privilege flowed from the King, down each tier—sort of like the water pumped into the Versailles reservoirs by the Machine de Marly.

The Brancas connection may have been an exploitive relationship, but at least it was a relationship. It would later save Playfair's life.

§§§

Though Playfair knew the Old Regime was hopelessly corrupt, the Revolution worried him even more. Its leaders were too theoretical, he thought—too sure they could design a perfect society if they could just find the perfectly phrased constitution. Playfair believed they should concentrate on practical matters—like making sure people were safe walking down the street.

France was growing more violent. Playfair never did build his rolling mill or replace the Machine de Marly. He would later recall how "the ordinary course of industry was stopped." As the French political crisis grew "nobody thought of building, planting, or improving, in a country a prey to disorder."[24]

They had heard what happened to the Réveillon wallpaper factory.

For the *nouveau riche* with large but limited wallets, wallpaper was the affordable alternative to tapestry. Jean-Baptiste Réveillon was famous for his remarkable ability to simulate the depth and texture of cloth. With around 350 workers, he was one of the largest employers in Paris.[25] Réveillon built his factory and adjacent mansion in Faubourg Saint-Antoine, near an old fort that guarded the eastern approach to the city—the Bastille.[26]

Paris in 1789 bore little resemblance to the city we know today. The broad boulevards and elegant apartments did not come along until Georges-Eugène Haussmann's massive 1853–1870 reconstruction under Napoleon III. Save for a few churches, official buildings, and the royal palaces, Paris was a dark, smelly town of narrow streets and hovels. It was filled with squalor, disease, and about 600,000 people, about a third dirt poor.[27]

At a meeting to elect deputies to the Estates General, Réveillon was heard—or rather, misheard—saying something like, "a working-man with a wife and children could live on fifteen sous a day." Since the typical Paris laborer earned about twenty-five sous, some took this to mean that he favored cutting wages.[28]

In reality, Réveillon was a generous employer. But word of his alleged excursion in labor statistics swept through Faubourg Saint-Antoine like wildfire, igniting tempers along the way. By Saturday, 27 April, hundreds of angry residents were gathered outside the Bastille. They remained through Sunday—loud, but peaceful.

That changed on Monday when thousands of protesters arrived from across the city. They burned Réveillon in effigy and headed to his factory and mansion, only to find fifty cavalrymen waiting. So instead they ransacked the home of his neighbor.

The next day an even larger mob gathered. That evening they over-whelmed Réveillon's guards, broke into his factory, and smashed the wooden vats and paper molds inside. Throwing the pieces out the windows and into the street, they used wallpaper as tinder and built bonfires with the wreckage, illuminating the neighborhood.

The mob then moved on to Réveillon's mansion, gutting the house. They even chopped down the trees in his garden. By the following morning, the house and factory were smoldering ruins. Depending on whom you believed, between twenty-five and several hundred people were dead.[29]

The Réveillon Riot was a turning point. Paris was dangerous, no doubt about it. But it was hard to tell which was the greatest threat: The demonstrators? The gangs—"brigands"—roaming the streets? The king's troops? In the summer of 1789, the average Parisian did not lack for opportunities to be shot, beaten, or skewered.

§ § §

Meanwhile, another player arrived in Paris.

Joel Barlow wasn't a sailor; he was a 34-year old Yalie poet who had never been to sea. But on 25 May 1788—two weeks after d'Eprémesnil's confrontation at the Palais de la Cité—Barlow boarded a French packet sailing from New York for Le Havre. No one knows the ship's name. Someone told him it was a British frigate the French had captured in one of their recent wars.

It was a rough crossing and Barlow got seasick as soon as the ship left sight of shore. Violently seasick. So incredibly and memorably seasick, in fact, that his diary account of being seasick was published in the *Yale Journal of Biology and Medicine* as part of an article titled—naturally—"Joel Barlow and Seasickness."[30] Barlow was still wobbling as he walked six days after landing in Le Havre. His innards continued to churn. Rooms swayed as though he were still at sea. It helped if he lay flat and closed his eyes. So he did.[31]

Barlow was going to see Paris thanks to an insider deal between William Duer and Manasseh Cutler. Duer was a well-connected New York City financier. Cutler was the polymath pastor of a Congregational church in Ipswich, Massachusetts.

During the American Revolution the Continentals Congress often paid its soldiers with IOUs—"Continentals." With no real backing and the shaky foundation of the new federal government, the script depreciated to pennies on the dollar and fluctuated month to month, depending on the prevailing sentiment as to whether the Americans would get their act together.

Cutler and his partners hoped the federal government would redeem the paper for land in the Northwest Territory; Britain, wanting to limit French influence and expand trade with America, had given the land to the new United States in the Treaty of Paris. The partners, who had set up the Ohio Company to settle the region, pooled the soldiers' money, and proposed to buy a million acres.[32]

Cutler set out for New York, reaching Manhattan early in July 1787. Congress, still operating under the Articles of Confederation, was holding its sessions in the City Hall (today's Federal Hall). Unfortunately, the legislators proved to be a hard sell. Perhaps it seemed too sweet a deal. Or Southern legislators might have known Cutler was an abolitionist, and they feared creating new free states in the Territories. Northern legislators may themselves have feared that creating any states would dilute their vote in Congress. Whatever the reason, after two weeks Cutler was ready to ride back to Ipswich.[33]

Then William Duer approached him.

Duer was born in England in 1747, attended Eton, joined the army, and served in India, seeing little action. He moved to America in 1768, where he became friends with Alexander Hamilton and others in the growing New York business community.[34] He served in the Continental Congress during the American Revolution; after the war he pulled strings to become secretary of the treasury board under the Confederation Congress. That's where he heard about Cutler's proposal.[35]

Duer offered to help—for a price. The two men met at a dinner at Duer's Manhattan townhouse on 20 July 1787. Cutler noted in his diary that Duer lived "in the style of a nobleman."[36] Duer may have been putting on a show; he had a knack for obscuring his true net worth.[37]

Duer had Cutler modify his plan. The Ohio Company would buy "pre-emptive rights" to an additional three million acres—that is, rights to buy at a set price. Duer would get the deal through Congress, and Cutler would assign the rights to a new firm Duer quietly set up—the Scioto Company.[38] To seal the deal, Duer advanced the Ohio Company $143,000 for its first payments for the land it was buying outright.[39]

The legislation passed. Duer told Cutler to keep the deal "a profound secret."[40]

Duer's co-conspirators—okay, associates, if you insist—included Royal Flint and Andrew Craigie.[41] Like Duer, Flint had been a commissary officer during the war.[42] Craigie had been Apothecary General of the Continental Army.[43]

The Scioto Company barely existed. It had no staff, organization, or facilities. In their correspondence Duer and the others sometimes called it the "Company Formed for Land Speculation."[44] The agreement with the Ohio Company referred only to "William Duer of the State of New York for himself and others his associates."[45] When required to act together, the associates signed themselves as "Trustees for the Scioto Purchasers."[46]

Today Wall Street analysts would call the Scioto Company a "shell" and Duer's preemption rights an "option," or a wager on whether the price of some commodity will go up or down. One *could* exercise the preemption and buy the land, just like one *could* exercise an option for orange juice concentrate and have fifteen thousand pounds of frozen OJ delivered to your door. But it wouldn't be smart, and it wasn't the objective. Duer planned to flip his preemption rights, selling them for a quick profit to an institutional investor.

And he had a good idea where he might find one.

§ § §

European banks were awash in Continentals; the American War was financed mainly with IOUs. Duer thought the banks might be willing to trade bad paper for an option on good land, especially if Congress would let buyers pay with their devalued notes at face value. He just needed someone willing to go to Europe and knock on doors.[47]

That would be Barlow. At first Duer wanted to send Flint. Then Flint fell ill. Cutler proposed Barlow. Barlow was willing; it seemed like a great way to see Europe! Duer was skeptical. But he had no better alternative. So it was agreed: Barlow would go.[48]

Joel Barlow was the kind of earnest, likable up-and-comer that important men recommend to other important men. It didn't matter that his singular achievement up to then was writing *The Vision of Columbus*, a 15,000-word poem portraying the creation of the United States with suggestions of Divine intervention.

Vision of Columbus was the kind of work that was bought much more often than it was read.* But its mere existence—and the fact that someone would write it—struck a chord with veterans and patriots. Washington would order twenty copies. Lafayette ordered ten. Benjamin Franklin ordered six. Alexander Hamilton ordered a copy. So did Aaron Burr.[49]

The result: Barlow had buzz. People had great expectations for him. And Barlow had great expectations for himself, too. The only problem was that he did not have anything like a plan.

Barlow had lollygagged through the American Revolution as a chaplain. "My duty is extremely easy and is not disagreeable," he wrote home. Barlow divided his time between funerals, weddings, sermons, and working on his poems. By his own admission, he was an uninspiring preacher; it took Benedict Arnold to get him going.[50]

Barlow wrote a fiery sermon condemning the traitor—so fiery that soon soldiers across the army were talking about it. Word got passed, bivouac to bivouac, campfire to campfire—all the way to George Washington, who invited Barlow to dinner at his headquarters at Passaic Falls.[51]

It was the only time the two would ever meet face-to-face.[52] Washington's adjutants seated him at the general's right hand. Barlow did make an impression, and struck a friendship with David Humphreys, Washington's aid de camp. Humphreys, a fellow Yalie, also dabbled in poetry. They began to correspond.[53]

---

* A sample, describing Christopher Columbus pondering his voyage to the New World:

> *Long had the Sage, the first who dared to brave*
> *The unknown dangers of the western wave,*
> *Who taught mankind where future empires lay*
> *In these fair confines of descending day,*
> *With cares o'erwhelm'd, in life's distressing gloom,*
> *Wish'd from a thankless world a peaceful tomb;*
> *While kings and nations, envious of his name,*
> *Enjoy'd his toils and triumph'd o'er his fame,*
> *And gave the chief, from promised empire hurl'd,*
> *Chains for a crown, a prison for a world.*

With these connections, Barlow asked Washington for letters of introduction to use when he went to Europe for the Scioto Company. Washington was glad to oblige. His letter to Lafayette, his wartime friend, was rhapsodic.

"Mr. Barlow," the usually restrained Washington wrote, "is considered by those who are good Judges to be a genius of the first magnitude; and to be one of those Bards who hold the keys of the gate by which Patriots, Sages and Heroes are admitted to immortality."[54]

Barlow got his legs back after resting a few days in Le Havre and caught a carriage to Paris. Navigating France was a challenge; he noted in his diary, "I speak the language so badly that I could get but little information except from the eye."[55]

Arriving on 3 July, he checked into a hotel and sent his letter of introduction to Thomas Jefferson, then the American Minister to France. Jefferson invited Barlow to visit, and they celebrated the Fourth of July together. A few days later Barlow paid a call on Lafayette. Then he turned to business.[56]

Duer had arranged for Barlow to contact Daniel Parker, another of his circle of New York investors. Like Duer, Parker had profited on army contracts during the Revolution. After the war he fled to Europe to avoid creditors. Duer did not fully trust Parker, but the two had stayed on good enough terms that Duer was willing to have him help with business on the Continent. Barlow and Parker caught a packet across the Channel to England.[57]

Barlow's diary is more travelogue than business record; it says almost nothing about meeting potential investors. He does describe buildings and gardens, a constituency election, and a string of meetings with various men of letters, like John Trumbull, the painter famous for his portraits of George Washington.[58] He also attended a Sunday service in the royal chapel—open to the public, if you knew whom to ask. George III caught his eye across the pews. Suddenly Barlow found himself in a staring contest with the King of Great Britain. He lost.[59]

And Barlow paid a visit to the Marques of Lansdowne at his town house in Berkeley Square. The man who made the introduction: Benjamin Vaughan.

Lansdowne may have been a war hero, former Prime Minister, engineer of the Treaty of Paris, and sponsor of promising economic thinkers, but Barlow was not impressed. He wrote in his diary that Lansdowne was "not a man of great abilities or influence," though, he observed, his house was "one of the best in London, price 30,000 guineas."[60]

From his journal, it sounds like Barlow was having a grand time. He was also making zero progress selling Duer's land options. So Barlow and Parker left London in early September, crossed the Channel again, and traveled to the Low Countries to meet Nicolas and Jacobus Van Staphorst.[61]

The Staphorst brothers had loaned money to the Continental Congress as well as to individual colonies, and held millions in (depreciated) American securities.[62] They had no interest in Duer's speculation. By the end of the month Barlow was back in Paris. There was no interest there, either; the French economy was risky enough, thank you.

Ensconced in Paris, winter approaching, Barlow settled in. He continued to keep his diary, and continued to socialize with Jefferson, Lafayette, and the small circle of Americans there. At least one of them was also keeping a diary—Gouverneur Morris.

Morris was not only unimpressed with Barlow; he loathed him. Morris, from New York, was two years older than Barlow—close enough in age and ambition that the two inevitably became rivals.

Morris had been Washington's ally in the Continental Congress and later a delegate to the Constitutional Convention; he wrote much of the final document. He originally came to Europe as George Washington's special envoy on a secret mission to re-establish relations with Great Britain.[63]

Morris combined diplomacy with business; it helped pay the bills, it was good cover, and, besides, that's just what diplomats did in the 1790s. Among the "business" activities Morris was tasked to perform was to buy a gold watch for Washington. The President instructed his envoy: "Not a small, trifling nor a finical, ornamental one, but a watch well executed in point of workmanship, large, flat, and with a plain, handsome key."[64]

Even if Barlow and Morris had they not been rivals, they were bound to clash. Personality-wise, they were polar opposites. Barlow was a near-radical republican; Morris was virtually a monarchist. Barlow was the too-serious ex-chaplain, deferential to would-be patrons, insecure under a veneer of bravado; Morris had a reputation as a financial *wunderkind*, bender of social conventions, and a ladies' man, despite having lost a leg in a carriage accident (it wasn't a handicap; it was part of his persona).

Morris watched as Barlow faltered. By April 1789 Barlow was running out of options—and money. Just as he was hitting bottom and thinking of returning to America, Barlow met another American in Paris: Samuel Blackden, a war veteran from Massachusetts.

Blackden introduced Barlow to a British businessman he had met: William Playfair.

Playfair had learned to speak French fluently in a little less than two years—not bad, considering that when he arrived, Abbé Morellet did not think he spoke the language at all.[65] Barlow thought Playfair might yet save the project. Playfair, however, thought Barlow did not have the foggiest idea of what he was doing. Barlow asked if he might want part of the venture; Playfair passed.[66]

§ § §

On 3 May 1789—just as the Estates General were about to convene at Versailles—Paris financier Étienne Delessert invited Playfair to his home for dinner.[67] They had friends in common. Delessert's son, Benjamin was studying in Britain; John Playfair was one of his professors at Edinburgh, and the young man visited James Watt, Playfair's ex-boss, in Birmingham.[68] Delessert's wife, in turn, helped the Boultons find a tutor in Paris for their own son, Matthew Robinson.[69]

Delessert was part of the same network of reform-minded Calvinist bankers that included Étienne Clavière.[70] Delessert had a broad view of the banking business; he was funding the demonstrators. (He later claimed his house was an arms factory, too.)[71] Arnaud Berquin, the well-known children's author, joined them. Playfair had a tie to him, too; they shared the same publisher in London, John Stockdale.[72]

Everyone was anticipating the Estates General. The three men talked about "the approaching change from despotism to liberty," Playfair recalled. But it wasn't a happy conversation.

Berquin insisted "the possession of liberty" would grant Frenchmen "new lights instantly." At first Playfair thought Berquin was being sarcastic, parodying "the hot headed Democrats." But, no, he was serious—"dogmatical," even, as Playfair recalled.[73]

Playfair scoffed. He could not fathom how anyone could believe that merely "being in possession of a new and very complicated right," also carried "the knowledge and modernization necessary to the making a proper use of them."

The conversation went downhill from there. "Though I exposed myself merely as doubting the sudden conversion, M. Berquin was inclined to be offended," Playfair said. "Yet still he could not explain how it was to happen though he attempted it various ways."

Two days later some twelve hundred delegates assembled for the Estates General. The First Estate clergy filled the left side of the floor, wearing their red vestments. The Second Estate nobles sat on the right; they wore finery, usually knee britches and silk stockings. The representatives of the Third Estate—commoners, with a heavy proportion of lawyers—dressed in black and sat in the rear.[74]

Jacques Necker, the just-reappointed, Geneva-born Comptroller General, was set to speak after the king. Necker was popular; France prospered when he held the post a decade earlier. Also, Necker had made a big show of transparency; he published France's financial records for the first time. The deputies and spectators had high expectations. Many hoped to hear a deal that would break the fiscal impasse.

Didn't happen. The opening session was a bust. Necker—who spoke with a nasally drone even in the best circumstances—delivered a three-hour, shift-in-your-seat, when-is-this-ever-going-to-end analysis of the French economy.

Playfair wasn't surprised; he never thought Necker was as good as his reputation. France had been living beyond its means in Necker's previous term; the economy had been fueled with borrowed money. What's more, Necker's so-called transparency was a sham; the books had been cooked. He was really just hiding France's debt.

If France needed someone to hose out the corruption, Playfair said, Necker wasn't the solution; he was part of the problem. Playfair claimed Necker "acquired his fortune by stock-jobbing," gambling on "artificial rises and fall." Playfair wasn't fooled. "Those who know the banking business," he said, speaking from experience, "know that though it is a good one, it is not possible to rise so quickly by the fair line."[75]

Necker really cared only about his image, Playfair claimed. He was a phony, posing as an "able financier, honest man, and philosopher" while "ruining the French nation." By Playfair's reckoning, Necker was "one of the principal causes of the revolution in breaking out when it did and in the manner it did."[76]

It was after Necker spoke that the Estates General got stuck on how to count votes. Historically it had voted "by order," with each Estate having one vote. That gave the First and Second Estates a two-to-one majority. Members of the Third Estate wanted to vote "by head," which would give them a majority once a few clergy and nobles joined them. They held out for weeks.

The clergy and nobles would not budge, either—including one well-known Second Estate delegate, Jean-Jacques Duval d'Eprémesnil. He had no reluctance to express his views, either; d'Eprémesnil *believed* in privilege. It defined hierarchy, and he could not imagine how France could function without it. As word got out, his popularity plummeted.[77]

Then, on 17 June, Third Estate deputies unilaterally declared themselves the National Assembly—a legislature to rule France. The king retaliated, barring them from the chambers. The new Assembly convened in a tennis court and vowed not to adjourn until the king recognized its authority. The king relented on 27 June, ordering the First and Second Estate deputies to join the Assembly.

"It was," Playfair would later say, "a half-measure; for an arbitrary monarch it was too much, and for a free people too little."[78] The looting and demonstrations continued. On Saturday 11 July reports reached Paris that the king had dismissed Necker. Many in the mob concluded that Louis had given up on reform and would crack down instead. The rioting got worse; no one seemed in control.

On Sunday mobs and royal troops faced each other at the Tuileries Gardens. Some French National Guardsmen fired on the King's cavalry. Inmates were escaping from prisons or set free by the demonstrators. Those jailed for political crimes now could join the demonstrators. Those jailed for real crimes were free to loot and pillage.[79]

Playfair was in the middle of the chaos.

"From this time," he recalled, "the revolt obtained a physical existence; and the greater force was on the side of the revolted." According to Playfair, "the undecided individual knew, by embracing their cause, he had least to fear." He called it "the Rubicon of revolutions." The calculation is "realized in an instant," Playfair said, and "force lies where it is thought to lie, as the greater number are determined only by the simple feelings of fear and of hope."[80]

As the violence increased, the new National Assembly passed a resolution directing neighborhoods to raise forces for their own protection.[81] About half the districts created to elect deputies to the Estates General regrouped to form "bourgeois militia"—including the Petit Sainte-Antoine district, where Playfair lived. According to its records, 1,192 residents reported on 13 July.[82]

Playfair later recalled that a report "circulated that Paris was to be attacked, the Assembly dissolved, and perhaps the members massacred." Meanwhile, "ill commanded" and "corrupted and debauched" royal troops marched toward the city. Now "self defense was the word, and in the midst of panick fear all ranks took up arms not only in Paris," but "all through the khingdom."[83]

The situation was dire. The violence continued through the night. Abbé Morellet later wrote of spending "a great part of the night of the 13th at my widows, watching the scum of the population armed with muskets, pikes, and skewers, as they forced open the doors of the houses and got themselves food and drink, money and arms."[84]

Monday morning, Playfair recalled, "found all the inhabitants of Paris either armed or assembled." Each neighborhood "assumed the appearance of so many federal states, having the town-house for its center, to which deputies from the different sections were sent." Playfair wrote that the, "whole of the Monday was thus spent in securing Paris against the attack supposed to be meditated by the troops."[85]

Meanwhile, Versailles seemed paralyzed. The government did nothing. "Not one effort was made either to seize the ringleaders of the people," Playfair said, "nor to dispatch messengers to explain the affair to the distant provinces."[86] In Paris, authorities closed the city gates, but that had exactly the opposite of the intended effect. Instead of quieting the situation, people were stuck either inside or out. It also cut off communications. The court in Versailles was clueless about the situation in Paris, and the mobs in Paris were apt to think the worst.

Militia members, not knowing what to expect, prepared to defend themselves against whatever came. Everyone "set to work in Paris," Playfair recalled, "safety rather than revolt being the common object." and thus "the morning of the memorable Tuesday, the 14th of July, began by a more regular plan of operations." The militia and hangers-on had taken arms from L'Hôtel des Invalides; now they were searching for gunpowder. Word was it could be found in the Bastille.[87]

Thomas Jefferson, still in Paris as the American minister, recalled in a report to Secretary of Foreign Affairs John Jay five days later that "The people now armed themselves with such weapons as they could find in Armourer's shops and private houses, and with bludgeons, and were roaming all night through all parts of the city without any decided and practicable object."[88]

The London Gazette, reporting just a week later, said a "general Consternation prevailed throughout the Town." Tension grew, and "All the Shops were shut; all public and private Employments at a Stand, and scarcely a Person to be seen in the Streets, except the armed Burghers." The "Burghers"—that is, militiamen—"acted as a temporary Police for the Protection of private Property, to replace the established one, which had no longer any Influence."[89]

Playfair later recalled that the mob—militia, brigands, and hangers-on—marched toward the Bastille. Royal troops who had encamped nearby scattered. Their officers had no orders, and so they took no action.

FIGURE 9: Storming of the Bastille, 14 July 1789, as depicted by Jean-Pierre Houël in *Prise de la Bastille*. Playfair remarked how the city had grown around the old fort and the mob was able to crowd against its walls. Source: Bibliothèque nationale de France, via Wikimedia Commons.

"The party that went against the Bastile," Playfair said, met "with some difficulty from the nature of the building." The problem, he said, was that "it was impossible to walk straight into it, as it was built with all the precautions of an ancient fortress," but, "without any advanced works, and the embrasures of the cannons (of a small calibre) seventy feet from the ground, those who, might attack the drawbridge and the gate, run but little risk."[90]

The Bastille was built around 1380 to defend the Porte St. Antoine, the old eastern gate to the city. Playfair was saying it looked formidable, but was really ill suited to this kind of attack. It lacked trenches or earthworks to keep mobs away from the foot of its walls. The mob grew larger.

The reporter for the *Gazette* claimed the fuse was lit for the final attack when "a Detachment with Two Pieces of Cannon went to the Bastile, to demand the Ammunition deposited there." The party advanced under a white flag, but "nevertheless, the Governor (the Marquis de Launay) ordered the Guard to fire, and several were killed." As a result, the "Populace, enraged at this Proceeding, rushed forward to the Assault."[91]

The "Governor" was Bernard-René de Launay. He had bought his position (as was typical) and had little military experience. Playfair thought that the Bastille might have held out if Launay had prepared for a siege and waited for reinforcements. But the jail keeper was caught flat-footed; his food stores totaled two sacks of flour. The attackers cut off the fort's water; Launay had no reserves.[92] A few years after the event, Playfair described how the situation unfolded:[93]

> The state of the Bastile only permitting a negative defence, the proper way would have been to have kept the gate shut, and to have waited, without any offensive act: but de Lawnay, the governor, lost whatever presence of mind he had; a few random shot, which went to a distance, were fired from the cannon on the top, and some musketry discharged from the narrow windows that are to be seen in most old fortifications, for the purpose of using small arms.

Faubourg Saint-Antoine had grown over the years. By 1789 it was a tightly packed neighborhood, with houses almost abutting the Bastille. Mobs could quickly gather around the fort, but could not easily disperse. Any shot the defenders fired was apt to hit a shop, a house—or a person. Playfair continued:[94]

> This only exasperated the mob, which from its numbers, and the situation of the streets, could not retreat, as the crowds which

were out of all danger would not make way for those who were foremost, and who run some little risk.

This tumultuous attack was continued from eleven o'clock in the morning till about four in the afternoon, at which time the gates were opened, upon a promise from those who directed the people at the town-house, of mercy to the governor and garrison.

By the time Playfair published his recollection of the attack on the Bastille he had soured on the revolution and wasn't about to credit anyone for anything smart or heroic. But take his account for what it is:[95]

All the accounts of bravery on one side, and resistance on the other, which were spread abroad with industry, were not merely exaggerated, they were absolutely without foundation, though they were far from being without utility to the popular side.

On a pretence of treason, the governor and the sub-governor were carried to the Place de Greve, before the town-house (with all manner of blows and ill-usage on the road) where their brains were blown out, and, shortly after, their heads cut off. Two private invalids were hanged to the lamp iron, opposite the town-house, and were the first sacrificed by that mode, which was for some time so popular and so highly in vogue amongst the mob in all the towns in France.

The attack on the Bastille may have been rag-tag tactics, but it was a strategic success. The *Gazette* said, "In the course of the same Evening, the whole of the *Gardes Françaises* joined the Bourgeoisie, with all their Cannon, Arms, and Ammunition." Under the *Ancien Régime*, the French Guard formed part of the King's Military Household. The balance of forces shifted—both in material and in morale. Playfair again:

The taking of the Bastile furnished the people of Paris with an ample subject for boasting, and admiration, as well as with materials for inflaming the minds of the people, as they got possession of a large collection of printed books and manuscripts that had been suppressed by government, and, besides these, of the registers of that famous prison.[96]

Playfair—a writer, after all—believed the books and manuscripts were as potent as any arms and gunpowder the mob might have found. He continued:[97]

> There was now a complete change on the countenances and in the minds of the inhabitants; the consternation of the two preceding days gave place to a joyful triumph. Their own bravery was celebrated by themselves, and magnified without difficulty on account of the confusion and general enthusiasm. They thought that they had taken the Bastile by storm and irresistible effort.

So public sentiment and the strategic situation had been turned over completely. But for Playfair, it was no "storming." A naïve jailer just "opened the door, and let the conquerors walk in."

The important thing was this: When the troops around Paris did not respond, everyone realized the king was unwilling to fight. Perhaps he feared civil war in the middle of Paris. Or perhaps he doubted his troops would obey. Either way, it showed he could not hold on to power by force. That meant that the Old Regime was finished.

Playfair was always coy about where he was and what he was doing on that day. His name is not on the list of the 954 *vainqueurs de la Bastille* who received a medal a year later. But Playfair dismissed that as just a political document, and by then he was so disillusioned with the Revolution he probably would not want to be included in any case. His role would not emerge until ninety-two years later as the centennial of the Revolution approached, official documents were released, and French writer Georges Lecocq published many of them in his book, *La prise de la Bastille.* .[98]

Records show that, at eleven o'clock on the morning of 13 July 1789, local residents met in the church of Petit Saint-Antoine to organize their militia. It would be at the forefront of the attack the next day. Officials kept minutes and took roll, recording names, occupations, and addresses as each signed up. There, on page 270 was…"*William Playfair, ingénieur anglais, petit hôtel de Lamoignon rue Couture Sainte Catherine.*"[99]

By November the Bastille was gone. The new city authorities had it dismantled, stone by stone. "I shall always remember with pleasures the agreeable sensation," Playfair recalled, "which I felt on seeing these same battlements thrown down by a justly enraged people. "

If only, he said, "they had known where to stop."[100]

The revolutionaries brought down a government but had nothing to replace it. Playfair said mayhem filled the vacuum as the "fabric of feudal rights was destroyed throughout the largest kingdom in Europe." Gangs roamed the countryside as "the licentious and idle formed themselves into regular bands, for the purpose of burning and plundering, without paying any attention to whom the property belonged."[101]

They called it *la Grande Peur*: "The Great Fear."[102] As French society came apart, Playfair began to reconsider Barlow's Scioto speculation.

§ § §

Meanwhile, in England a young man was having trouble paying his bills. Fortunately, James Watt, Junior, knew Matthew Boulton had a soft spot. Writing to Boulton in December, he lamented how his father had "only allowed me £70 for all expenses this year."

Junior scoffed, "This has proved totally inadequate to my necessary wants." The problem, he said, was that his father simply did not understand. Apparently, "never having been a young man himself he is unacquainted with the inevitable expenses which attend my time of life."

Actually, when Watt was Junior's age he was laboring in his repair shop off the Glasgow quad, sweating to make ends meet. In any case, Junior appealed to Boulton for a loan. "I assure it required great exertion before I could come to the resolution of soliciting even your assistance," Junior wrote. But the bottom line was that "The sum I would wish to borrow from you is £50."[103]

Junior's connection to Playfair? Playfair was Junior's tutor.

When Playfair was twenty and Junior was ten, James Keir told Boulton he had devised "a scheme" to have Junior and Matthew Robinson "come every day to Mr Playfair's counting house during the holidays for a couple of hours to reckon and draw under the care of Messrs. Henderson, Playfair, etc."[104]

"Reckon and draw" meant Playfair was teaching the boys mathematics and drafting. The lives of Playfair and Junior would intersect again and again over the next forty years, though about the only thing Playfair and Junior had in common was a deep affection for James Watt.

Take the word of those who knew them.

When Robert Small recommended young Playfair to James Keir, he cited "the goodness of his heart." When Watt wrote to Junior's teacher, he complained Junior was falling into "insolence sauciness and disobedience"—so bad that he had to be brought home for "a severe correction." Watt even questioned the boy's "word of Honour."[105] Junior was a liar.

Watt pondered packing Junior off to a boarding school in Shifnal, thirty miles away, telling the headmaster that "a strict attention" needed to be paid "to his manners and morals." That was "the prevailing reason with me to remove him from a public school."[106] Yet Junior was quite intelligent, and Watt had plans for him. "You know my intention," he wrote Junior, "has been to breed you to the business of an Engineer if you should possess that Ingenuity and attention to mechanical pursuits that I did at your time of life."[107]

When Junior turned fifteen, Watt sent him eighty miles away to John Wilkinson's ironworks in Bersham to learn bookkeeping, mathematics, and carpentry.[108] A few months later Junior left for Europe. Arriving in Geneva just before Christmas 1785, to broaden his education further, James Watt, Junior, met up with Joseph Priestley, Junior—son of the famous scientist. Then he moved on to Stadtfeld.[109]

Watt kept a close eye on Junior from across the Channel. Be sure your "memorandums be made in clear and orderly method so that by an Index you may easily refer to them," Watt told him, and "keep your letters, and other loose paper, regularly folded up and docketed." Watt complained about Junior's handwriting, and scolded him for using an entire piece of letterhead when a half-sheet would do.[110]

Junior learned a lot in Europe. He had a knack for chemistry, and picked up local languages so well that Watt had to tell him not to use German for "any parts of your letters which require to be well understood by me."[111]

And he was becoming a dandy.

Anne Watt complained, "I have seen Mr. Priestley," comparing Junior to Joseph Priestley's son. "No long bills to barbers and hairdressers for powder and perfumes was in his charges," she fumed.[112] Junior would become known for his morning visits to the barber.[113] Meanwhile James questioned why Junior would "charge two watch chains in the space of a month" when "one has lasted me these six years and I do not remember having had above 3 in my whole life."[114]

Watt was missing the whole point. Dandyism was conspicuous consumption combined with studied insouciance, masquerading as petty rebellion—like zoot suits in the 1940s, Teddy Boy fashions in the 1950s, and L.A. Raider gangsta gear in the 1990s.

Junior's early "macaroni" phase meant chains, fobs, and a minimum of two watches were *de rigueur* ("Why do I wear two watches?" the dandy would say. "One is to tell what time it is and the other is to tell what time it is not.") As fashion shifted a few years later, Junior gravitated to the high collars and enormous cravats iconified by George Bryan "Beau" Brummell, which is how Junior appears in his portrait.[115]

Playfair couldn't stand that sort of thing, or most other fashion affectations for that matter. He made fun of Parisian men who dressed in military regalia, with the boots and spurs and formidable mustaches French officers favored. As for the English dandies, "Ridicule cannot make the dandy ashamed," he wrote.[116]

In October 1787 Junior returned to Birmingham. The bickering resumed. After one clash with Anne, his father scolded him, saying he had a "dogmatical and positive manner of speaking on many subjects and a rather rude way of arguing with those who are older than yourself."[117]

Junior was out of the house within a year. Matthew Robinson Boulton wrote his father that had learned that one of Junior's tutors in Europe had "received a letter from Mr Watt junior, his situation is indeed one of the most unhappy." Matthew Robinson pitied Junior, observing that, "to be forced to quit the paternal dwelling, to abandon that pure joy resulting from the company of a Father is truly a rigorous fate."[118]

Junior took an apprenticeship with a fabric maker in Manchester.[119] It gave him a chance to apply the chemistry he had learned in Germany to dye making—and it put eighty-six miles between him and Anne.[120] After Junior completed his apprenticeship, he went to work in the countinghouse at Thomas and Richard Walker, textile merchants.

Watt hoped his son would grow up by moving out of the house to learn a trade. No way.

"I am very disappointed in you for exceeding your allowance & continuing debts, the very thing I expressly cautioned you against," Watt wrote Junior in December 1788. "When I fixed the allowance at £40 a year you told me it was amply sufficient and I know that it was so & yet you have contrived to make it run short by throwing it away upon objects that not only were of no use to you but prejudicial such as Tavern meals and plays."

Watt was on a tear. He continued, "Your shoemaker's bill was more than 4 times as much as mine, partly because you would not be troubled to wear serviceable shoes, but would have them made so as little good as possible following a nonsensical fashion but do not answer tradesmen."

"I beg you will never bring yourself into such difficulties again for such paltry gratifications as may well be dispensed with. Once I know the full extent of your debts, I shall make you a remittance. Learn to live within your income and remember you cannot always have a father to protect or direct you."[121]

Even so, Manchester did develop Junior in other ways.

Britain wasn't quite the tinderbox that France was, but it did have its potential flashpoints—like Parliamentary representation. Peerages in the House of Lords were inherited. Even in the House of Commons a rich man could buy a "rotten borough" like Old Sarum (population: zero) and get a seat in Commons thrown in with the deal. Meanwhile a city like Manchester (population: 100,000 or so) might not have any representation at all.

Another issue: the Church of England. Today it's difficult to appreciate how important a church was in day-to-day eighteenth-century life. A parish was the local government. Parishes kept birth records and issued death notices. Parishes officiated weddings.

In other words, the Church of England gave the government in Westminster control at a very personal level; Dissenters wanted more freedom. Add a few other issues like trade policy, tax policy, labor policy, farm policy, and foreign policy, and there was more than enough subject matter to support a population of restive young men looking for a cause. That was Manchester.

It was Thomas Walker who drew Junior into politics.[122] The young man hadn't much interest in it before; Junior may have acted like a rebel, but he was mainly rebelling against his father, his headmaster, and his stepmother. Junior was basically a likable fop—and a hothead, unable to hold his tongue and lucky enough to have the money and connections to get away with it. If he had a view on constituency reform, the British East India Company, or the Anglican Communion, he had not bothered to articulate it.[123]

Thomas Walker, on the other hand, was a true believer—a genuine, committed activist. (One's tempted to call him a dyed-in-the-wool radical, but that's too obvious.) As president of the Manchester Constitutional Society, Walker pushed for ending the slave trade, eliminating those rotten boroughs, extending suffrage, and curtailing the Church of England's favored status. Walker recruited Junior to the Society, where he met Thomas Cooper, a lawyer from London about ten years his senior.[124]

The Society was part political action group, lobbying for reforms in Britain; and part revolutionary cell, corresponding with like-minded organizations abroad—like the Jacobin Club.[125]

After the Estates General, the Tennis Court Oath, the merging of the estates, and the storming of the Bastille, France seemed on its way to a democratic constitutional monarchy. As in any democracy, factions began to coalesce.

Royalists like d'Eprémesnil wanted to keep the old system pretty much as it was, but less corrupt and cruel. Monarchists like Lafayette wanted a British-style system, with an executive king constrained by a constitution and an aristocratic legislature.

Republicans, on the other hand, wanted full, direct democracy. Many were connected at one time or another with the *Société des amis de la Constitution*, or the Society of the Friends of the Constitution. It was better known as the *Club des Jacobin*—Jacobin Club—after the monastery on rue Sainte Jacques it used for meetings.

Playfair tended to call all republicans "Jacobins," but they really came in different flavors. The Girondins were dominant early on; Brissot emerged as their unofficial leader. They got their name from their opponents in the Legislative Assembly, who referred to many of them by their home region, the Gironde in southern France. The Girondins favored a republic, but became better known as the war party because they urged striking Austria and Prussia, fearing they would try to crush the Revolution.

The more radical—and ruthless—Jacobins made eliminating the French monarchy a higher priority; they wanted the king gone, quickly and completely. They also favored reforms like the revolutionary calendar (1792=Year One), decimalization (the ten-month calendar's gone; the metric system remains) and income redistribution (Playfair called it "leveling"). Many of them took seats in the top tier of the Assembly, and thus became known as Montagnards (literally, "mountain people"). Maximilien Robespierre, a lawyer, emerged as their leader.

Georges-Jacques Danton (like Robespierre, a lawyer) and journalist Camille Desmoulins also frequented the Jacobin Club. They initially aligned with the Montagnards. But had their own base, the less genteel *Société des Amis des Doritos de l'Homme et du Citoyen*—the Cordeliers. They were also named for their meeting place, a former Cordelier convent.

(Robespierre and Desmoulins, incidentally, were childhood friends. That's typical of civil wars, and the French Revolution in particular: Everyone seems to know everyone else—and their goals, their strengths, and especially their vulnerabilities. That's one reason why they often become so vicious.)

Royalists and monarchists organized clubs, too. Jean-Jacques d'Eprémesnil and his wife hosted one in their salon. They would regret it.

And then there were the *sans-culottes*—the laborers and tradesmen who wore pants rather than the knee britches favored by the wealthy, augmented by less-oppressed-but-sympathetic shopkeepers and merchants who dressed the part. Playfair described the *sans-culottes* as "about sixteen to thirty years of age, cloathed in rags, and covered with dirt." They were "the street," incited, if not led, by pamphleteers like Jean-Paul Marat and broadsheet publishers like Jacques Hébert.[126]

As Playfair taught Junior to "reckon and draw" in Soho twelve years earlier, doubtlessly neither dreamed they would one day find themselves meeting in Paris in the middle of a revolution.

 **4** Feudal France on the Banks of the Ohio

I t was shaping up be a sunny spring day on 3 May 1790 when Alexandria dockhands spotted a vessel making its way up the Potomac River. Before steam power and radio, ships simply arrived whenever they arrived—if they arrived at all, that is. The main way anyone knew a ship was lost at sea was, well, if it was never seen again.[1]

This time, though, passengers and crew aboard the French merchantman *Patriot* were fortunate. It was a rough voyage, but the ship arrived at the mouth of the Potomac seventy-three days after clearing the channel at Le Havre. It fired a three-gun salute as it passed George Washington's plantation at the bend around Mt. Vernon, and soon Alexandria was the unexpected host to its 149 passengers.

They were an unusual assortment. Few spoke English. Most were in their twenties. About a third came from Paris. They included a painter; two sculptors; a counselor to the King; a mathematician; two tailors; two restaurateurs; a surgeon; a cook; a fruit vendor; a student of law; a perfumer; a hatter; a wig maker; and nine persons identified only as "commoners," along with their spouses and children.[2]

At first the Alexandrians had no idea of what was going on. The quay became a scene of friendly confusion as the travelers disembarked. It was evident that the new arrivals were settlers of some kind. But no one was there to greet them. The Alexandrians thought the French were exotic. The nobles among them played their part to the hilt, acting with stately reserve.[3]

Twelve days later a second ship, the *Liberty,* arrived with 121 passengers.[4] Then word came from New Jersey that an English merchantman had landed with the survivors of a third ship that had sunk in route.[5] That vessel, ironically named *Recovery,* was an old boat whose seams had simply given way. The crew and passengers pumped, bailed—and prayed. It turned out that they were part of some kind of Catholic community bound for the New World to escape the French Revolution. The Brits spotted the ship just as it was about to founder.[6]

Over the next several weeks more ships arrived: *Discovery, Lady Washington, Union, Mary, Citizens of Paris.*[7] The size of the operation was becoming clear; it was huge. But who sold the settlers the land? And why hadn't anyone had been sent to greet them?

One of the new arrivals had a brochure he received in Paris that sort of explained the situation: *PROSPECTUS POUR L'ÉTABLISSEMENT SUR LES RIVIERES D'OHIO ET DE SCIOTO IN AMÉRIQUE.* The "Prospectus for an Establishment on the Ohio and Scioto Rivers in America" began:[8]

> The United States assembled in Congress having sold five million acres of land, located on the Ohio & Scioto rivers, in America, to a number of people who have formed a company with the intention of cultivating and populating this land; and this company, finding that two million acres are enough to be well exploited, proposes to sell the other three million acres, which compose the western part of this territory, a part of which is contiguous to the one already under cultivation.

The Alexandrians knew the land described in the brochure—knew it well, in fact. The Northwest Ordinance of 1787 set the Ohio River as the boundary between Virginia and the newly organized Northwest Territory—America's next frontier. You had to cross the Appalachians to get there, but once you reached Pittsburgh, where the Alleghany and Monongahela converge, the Ohio River provided a throughway into the new lands.

American settlers were working their way down the river, northeast toward southwest. The Ohio Company—Manasseh Cutler and his partners—had already founded Marietta, the first settlement in the Northwest Territory, in 1788, at the point where the Muskingum River flows into the Ohio from the north. The next major fork is about seventy miles downriver at

Point Pleasant, where the Great Kanawha River enters from the south. The Scioto River, flowing from the north, is about fifty miles beyond that. The Scioto is not especially large, but its broad floodplain—a product of Ice Age glaciers—was said to be some of the best farmland in the Territory.

The French were surprised when the Alexandrians told them that it took months to get to the Scioto. Somehow they had it in their heads they could reach their land in just a few days. One, a merchant named Jean-Baptist Parmentier, had what he claimed was a deed for a hundred-acre tract in the Scioto basin.[9] It looked legitimate; it had the seal of M. Fermain, the French notary, and two signatures by representatives of the "Compagnie du Scioto."

One of the signatures was "M. de Soissons, Attorney, Member of Parlement." The other was "William Playfair, engineer, Englishman."[10]

The Scioto Affair—the first great scandal of American politics, incidentally—would maroon hundreds of French settlers in the Ohio wilderness; ruin several Wall Street financiers; and involve a host of American Revolution war veterans, several nobles, a future leader of the French Republic, and, along the way, Thomas Jefferson, Alexander Hamilton, and even George Washington.

Untangling the affair—and Playfair's role in it—is like watching *Rashômon*, the classic Akira Kurosawa film. Witnesses to a crime offer different accounts. Each account touches on the same facts. But the accounts are inconsistent, each with a different set of heroes and villains. You have to wait until the final scene when someone comes in with the facts that pull the threads of the story together.

§ § §

The first version of the Scioto Affair was written in 1794 because Congress—now meeting in Philadelphia—received a petition from a few dozen French settlers marooned in the Northwest Territory. They claimed to have purchased land from the Paris branch of the Scioto Company, an American firm. The titles turned out to be bogus, and now they were stuck on the frontier, landless and luckless.[11]

The emigrants hoped Congress might bail them out. When the petition got hung up in the Senate, a settler who signed himself "John Rome" wrote to George Washington, asking the President himself if he would help.[12]

John Rome—Jean-Baptiste de Rome until a few years earlier—was a noble from the southern French province of Languedoc and one of the settlers who had arrived in Alexandria. The petition said the Scioto Company's agent, Joel Barlow, had published "vast Numbers of Maps, pamphlets and Handbills" throughout France advertising prime land in the Ohio Territory. Around twelve hundred Frenchmen—"industrious Men from almost every Class of the Society"—bit at the offer.[13]

Rome was one of them; he bought fifty acres. Or at least he thought he had.[14] When the settlers arrived in Alexandria, no one was there to greet them, and no one knew anything about a Scioto land offering. William Duer, the "Superintendent of the Scioto Company," sent word from New York promising he'd get them to their new homes. Eventually they made it, naming their new settlement "Gallipolis"—the City of the French. (The village still exists in Ohio today, surrounded by the French-settled Gallia County.) The land, however, was nothing like what they had been promised.

The settlers "struggled against Obstacles of every kind," the petition said. Many died. Some were killed clearing the forest—though they had been promised their land would be ready to farm. Yellow fever took others—though they had been told Scioto had a mild, healthy climate. "Savage War" snared some, too—no one told them they'd be landing smack in the middle of hostile Indian territory. Only about four hundred remained, and they had "almost exhausted all their Resources."

Yet the settlers' biggest problem was simply that they could not get legal title to their land. Rome claimed that they had been told their plots were actually "the Property of another Company" that "threatens to dispossess Your Petitioners." That was the Ohio Company. It turned out the Scioto Company had sold them land that was in a tract Congress had sold to one Manasseh Cutler and his partners. It was a confusing situation. So the Senate directed William Bradford, the Attorney General, to figure out what had happened and assess the various claims. Yet another year passed. The settlers were in dire straits, and that was why they were asking President Washington to step in.

Bradford delivered his report on 24 March 1794. It was a classic legal "finding of fact." Like any good lawyer, Bradford followed the paper trail—the Ohio Company's contract with Congress, the Scioto Company's contract with the Ohio Company, Barlow's agreement with the Scioto Company, and so on. He noted gaps in the record—Bradford found nothing on Barlow's activities in Europe—and described in terse Joe Friday language who had done what.[15]

The Attorney General began: The Confederation Congress passed a statute in July 1787 authorizing the Treasury Board to sell land within a tract "bounded by the Scioto, the Ohio River, the western boundary of the seventh range townships, and the northern boundary of the tenth township, continued due west to the Scioto." It had been impossible to calculate precisely how much land this encompassed. It was on the edge of the American frontier and the official surveyors had not yet made it that far west. The location of each of the main geographical points that defined the tract was known, but not much else.

Bradford then said that the Treasury Board signed two contracts on 27 October 1787. The first contract was with the Ohio Company for the sale of a million and a half acres within the tract. The second contract, also with the Ohio Company, was for preemption rights on what they termed the "residue"—everything within the tract that the Ohio Company didn't buy outright.

But, Bradford said, there was something odd about this second contract. Though the contract said it was between the Treasury Board and the Ohio Company, parts of the contract and "the subsequent conduct of the parties" suggested "other persons" were involved—William Duer and his associates.

Bradford then explained how Cutler signed over the Ohio Company's preemption rights to the second tract to Duer, how Duer set up the speculation, and how Barlow went to Europe. Yet, Bradford said, none of that mattered. As far as the U.S. government was concerned, its agreement was with the Ohio Company. Legally speaking, Duer, Barlow, and anyone else involved were just Ohio Company subagents.

As a result, the French settlers who thought they had bought land from the Scioto Company were instead squatters. The Ohio Company *could* have bought the land under its preemption rights with the government. But it didn't, and if that made the settlers' deeds worthless—well, the government did not have a canine in that conflict. The settlers and the Ohio Company would have to sort things out. Each individual settler would need to sue the Ohio Company to get relief.

Bradford conceded the French would suffer "great inconveniences" in pursuing their claims. He admitted that the settlers were "by no means able to prosecute at law the authors of their misery." And he acknowledged that the settlers were accommodating. They had, Bradford confirmed, offered to "cede to the United States all their rights and pretensions" if the government would just give them what they thought was their land.

What to do? Truth be told, the United States needed to fill all of that empty land west of the Appalachians, vast territories that Britain, France, and Spain all still coveted. If the U.S. government simply told the French emigrants *pas de chance*, it would be hard to get others to follow.

So a deal was struck: Congress set aside a "donation tract." Any male settler who had stuck it out could get a free plot. Or, if he wanted to keep the land he had already cleared, the Ohio Company said it would sell it to him—for just a $1.25 an acre. A few settlers moved to what came to be called the "French Grant"; most bought the plots they were already working and got on with their lives.[16]

Thus was written the "Official Version" of the Scioto Affair. Transcribed in 8-point font from a clerk's original longhand, the entire report fits on a page and a half. No one came out looking good: Duer was duplicitous, Barlow was inept, Cutler was callous. But by the time everything was sorted out, Duer was in debtor's prison; he went bankrupt in March 1792. Barlow, meanwhile, had moved on to other ventures and was *en route* to Hamburg.[17]

One interesting thing about Bradford's report: It never mentions William Playfair.

§ § §

For nearly a hundred years that was the official account: American land speculators gazumped hundreds of Frenchmen, leaving them marooned in the wilds of southern Ohio. Historians like John Bach McMaster judged the Scioto Affair "one of the earliest and most shameful pieces of land-jobbery that has ever disgraced our country."[18] It might have remained both the official story and common wisdom had Rufus King not received an invitation sometime around 1896 to write a history of Ohio.

Houghton Mifflin was planning to publish a collection of authoritative histories for each of the United States. (This was the late 1800s, when it was actually conceivable that anyone might deem any history "authoritative," and that a commercial press might actually believe that anyone would buy it.)

Horace Scudder, editor of *The Atlantic Monthly*, was overseeing the project. His working title: *The American Commonwealths*. King was a natural choice to write the volume on Ohio. He had chaired the State Bar. He had been dean of the Cincinnati Law School and served as president of the University of Cincinnati. And he had lived in the state almost his entire life.[19]

Lawyer that he was, King used Attorney General Bradford's report for his basic storyline when he got to the section on Scioto. He added some color, describing how in 1790 General Arthur St. Clair, Governor of the Northwest Territories, had come upon a settlement of "refugees from France" while returning from an inspection of the territory's western defenses. The Frenchmen, King wrote, had "been trapped by sharpers"—taken in by swindlers—"who pretended under the name and title of the Scioto Company." King titled his book *Ohio: First Fruits of the Ordinance of 1787.*[20]

True to Bradford's report, King's account stuck Duer and Barlow with most of the responsibility for the settlers' plight. Cutler also got some blame because he had a piece of the original speculation. And the Ohio Company wasn't pure, either; it got the money it needed to make its first payments to the government from Duer. In any event, King agreed with McMaster: Scioto was a "disgrace upon the American character."[21]

This was when Playfair first appeared in the Scioto narrative. According to King, he was Barlow's "assistant" in Paris. King knew enough about Playfair to say he was the brother of "the distinguished mathematician at Edinburgh" and that he had a "conspicuous hand in the destruction of the Bastille."

Ephraim C. Dawes didn't buy any of it, and that's how the "Revised Version" of the Scioto Affair came to be. Soon after King's book appeared, Dawes published his own article in the *Magazine of American History* to "correct some of the many erroneous statements" in the *American Commonwealth* volume, "as well as in other histories."[22]

Dawes came from an old Massachusetts family that had helped settle Marietta. His grandfather was William Dawes, the "other rider" who warned Bostonians that the British were coming in 1775. Dawes himself had been a Union officer in the Civil War; after a Confederate round shot off much of his lower jaw during Sherman's march through Georgia, he survived an agonizing, daylong ride in the back of a wagon to reach a hospital.

A mere mangled jaw, however, would not stop Ephraim C. Dawes. He got fitted with a prosthetic, grew a full beard to hide the scars, married, moved to Cincinnati, and made a fortune in railroads—which he subsequently lost in the Panic of 1873. He made another fortune in coal, and still found time to write about American history.[23]

Dawes gave much of the credit for his information to his friend John Marshall Newton.[24] Newton had his own colorful history. His family could trace its roots to the *Mayflower*. He traveled west to take part in the California Gold Rush before settling down in Cincinnati and taking a position at the Young Men's Mercantile Library. There he spent years collecting papers about the Scioto Affair.[25]

Newton's files—the "Gallipolis Papers"—are our main source on the American side of the affair even today. They're preserved at the Cincinnati Museum Center, a massive Art Deco building converted from a railroad terminal on the west side of town. Newton used his network of friends and colleagues to find records that had been passed down from generation to generation. Once he discovered a document of interest, Newton would either borrow it or arrange to have someone transcribe it, verbatim, in longhand. The project was a tremendous effort.[26]

Newton was planning to write a book about the Scioto Affair when he died at his desk on 19 December 1897. After eighteen years at the Library, he simply slumped over in his chair one day.[27] His friend and colleague, Eugene Bliss, who had been helping Newton with translation and organization, gathered the documents and filed them in three enormous albums. Bliss, a modest man, said that he was merely doing the task of a "mechanic" and didn't think he could possibly complete the story Newton planned. That would be left to others—like Dawes.[28]

Dawes' version of the Scioto Affair, with just a few detail variations, would be the storyline American scholars accepted as fact for the next hundred years.[29] It was full of new information—to be expected, considering all the material Newton had collected over the years. This is how it went:

The Scioto Affair began when the Ohio Company's Manasseh Cutler and Winthrop Sargent contracted with the Continental Congress to buy two tracts of land. The Company planned to sell lots in the first tract—1,500,000 acres—to American Revolution was veterans. It transferred half of its rights to the second tract—over 4,000,000 acres—to William Duer, a New York financier.

Dawes didn't mention that Duer was secretary of the treasury board—that it was an inside deal. He also skipped over how Duer piggybacked on the Ohio Company's legislation, thus getting his land speculation for free. He simply said Duer sent Joel Barlow, a poet, to Europe to sell the preemption rights.

Barlow, Dawes said, had no success until "he made the acquaintance of William Playfair, an Englishman then residing in Paris." The two organized a company Dawes called the "Society of the Scioto" to sell small lots to individual Frenchmen (For consistency, let's call it the Compagnie du Scioto; it's the same.) Barlow signed over most of the preemption rights to the Compagnie, and the Compagnie agreed to pay Barlow as it sold the lots.[30]

In Dawes' account, Duer learned of the Compagnie when Barlow wrote him from Paris in November 1789. Barlow told Duer to send him bank drafts totaling 220,000 livres, which he would cash, using the proceeds from the sales in France. Duer could then pay Congress. There was some confusion over the precise location of the plots Barlow had sold, and they could not issue titles until they paid for all the land. But everyone believed they could finesse these issues and agreed to proceed after meeting at Duer's house on 27 February 1790.[31]

The emigrants began to arrive in May—about two months later than expected. The Scioto Company's agent, thinking they might have strayed off course, left to search for the settlers at ports up the Atlantic seaboard. That's why no one had been there to meet them.[32]

With the confusion in Alexandria, the settlers sent some of their "leading men" to New York—like "Count de Barth," and "Marquis Lezay-Marnésia"—to meet Duer and make sure everything was on track. They also met with Treasury Secretary Hamilton and several congressmen. President Washington and Secretary of War Knox agreed to station troops near the mouth of the Great Kanawha for protection.[33]

The delegation returned to Alexandria. The Scioto associates sent John Burnham to lead forty-six New England woodsmen to clear land and build huts at the site of what would come to become Gallipolis. Burnham had served as a major in the Revolution and was said to have been present at every major battle from Bunker Hill to Yorktown. The settlers began the trek in June and in mid-October began to arrive in Ohio. Everyone was playing catch-up, but Duer seemed to have the situation under control.[34]

Then the trouble began. When Duer sent his drafts to Paris, Barlow returned them unpaid—without explanation. Dawes said Barlow had "left the management of the whole affair" to Playfair and his fellow "sub-agent," Jean-Antoine Chais de Soissons. Then Playfair "refused to provide" for the drafts. In other words, Barlow told Duer to write several big checks that bounced when Playfair withheld the company's funds.[35]

This left Duer and his partners unable to pay the government for the land they were putting the settlers on. Naturally, the settlers, now unable to get title to the lands they thought they had bought, refused to pay the balance they owed the Compagnie. This stretched Duer even further. And now he had to pay to feed, house, and transport hundreds of French emigrants. The bills were mounting.

In mid-summer more bad news arrived. For some reason, Barlow had sold the Compagnie to a new company comprised of several French nobles, along with Barlow. From what Duer could learn, Barlow had given away the Compagnie for a pittance, put the Scioto associates at the end of the line for getting paid, and gave the new French owners any windfall if land prices fell or American securities strengthened. And for some reason Barlow kept Playfair as a partner in the new company. And there was still no word on the whereabouts of the money Barlow promised and Duer desperately needed.[36]

One could imagine Duer's reaction; the term "ballistic" comes to mind.

Dawes said Duer wrote Barlow a letter "upbraiding him in the severest terms."[37] He and his associates agreed to have Benjamin Walker, an officer who had served in the American Revolution, to go to France to figure out what was going on. They gave Walker letters authorizing him to review the Compagnie's files—and to either fire Barlow or work with Barlow, depending on what he found.[38]

Yet, Dawes said, Barlow was *relieved* when Walker arrived. It turned out he was broke. Walker advanced him money. Then he met with Playfair. Dawes reported Playfair sandbagged Walker on the Compagnie's finances. He did not elaborate—just that Walker's "most diligent effort failed to secure either money or property." So Walker took out advertisements advising the public not to buy lands from Playfair, "who meantime disappeared."[39]

Walker, Dawes claimed, "exonerated" Barlow from "intentional wrong-doing."Walker tried to salvage the project by setting up a new company with Étienne Rochefontaine, a French officer who had also served in the American Revolution and had bought some Scioto land, and General Louis Lebègue de Presle Duportail, who had been named to head the French war ministry. But soon they were themselves fleeing the country as French politics got more lethal. And that, Dawes said, was the end of the Scioto venture.[40]

Meanwhile, back in Ohio the French settlers found themselves in the middle of an Indian war. Anyone venturing far from the stockade was liable to get killed or kidnapped, which made it exceptionally challenging to grow anything. That picked up the story at the point where Rufus King had begun—with General St. Clair discovering hundreds of marooned Frenchmen in a failed and beleaguered settlement.

Dawes said that the Ohio Company eventually reached a settlement with the federal government for its land, paying $350,000 for 750,000 acres. It was—alas—just under half the land they had wanted, for—alas—just under half of what government had planned to receive.[41] The Scioto Company—alas—was defunct. Congress agreed to donate 100,000 acres to the French settlers. The donation tract—alas—did not include Gallipolis, despite the "earnest effort" of the Ohio Company to see that it did. So the settlers had no alternative—alas—but to pay the Ohio Company if they wanted to remain on their plots.[42]

The way Dawes told it, the Scioto Affair was just a business deal gone really, really, bad. It was an ambitious, and admittedly complex project. It might have worked. But Barlow just let things get away from him. No one really knew what happened to all that money the French settlers had paid—only that Playfair was the last person to have his hands on it.

Thus was written the Revised Version of the Scioto Affair. A sad tale, true that. But by the time Dawes finished telling it, one thing was for sure: No one could blame Manasseh Cutler for anything. The facts showed Manasseh Cutler made the best of a difficult situation. The evidence proved Manasseh Cutler had acted in good faith.

All of which all made perfect sense. Ephraim C. Dawes rarely used his middle name. He didn't have to. Everyone knew he was the son of Sarah Cutler Dawes—and probably the last man in the world who would question the honorable intentions of his great grandfather.

§ § §

That version sat until 1903, when Theodore Thomas Belote received a $300 grant from the Society of Colonial Dames to write a scholarly account of the Scioto Affair. Belote was born in 1881 and grew up on Virginia's Eastern Shore. He graduated from the University of Richmond, toured Europe, studied in Germany, and returned to America to earn a master's degree in history at Harvard.[43] His Fellowship in Ohio Valley History gave him a year to study at the University of Cincinnati.[44]

Belote used the same information as Ephraim Dawes—the Gallipolis Papers. So it's natural that his monograph, *The Scioto Speculation and the French Settlement at Gallipolis*, resembles a longer version of Dawes's article, with an academic's footnotes—and one important twist: Belote made Playfair the heavy.[45]

In Belote's telling, ten months after arriving in France, Barlow "was out his time, his trouble, and five hundred pounds sterling." He had sold nothing and was thinking of going back to America, accepting failure. Then, "a chance acquaintance changed the whole face of affairs."[46]

Belote said Barlow happened to meet Samuel Blackden, an American trying to sell Kentucky lands in Europe. Blackden introduced Barlow to one of his own acquaintances—an Englishman named William Playfair. Then, Belote said, Blackden "disappears from the scene almost as soon as he had stepped on."[47]

According to Belote it was Barlow who came up with the idea for the Compagnie du Scioto. Barlow knew he needed an organization that could raise the money to pay for the land up front; only then could he sell off individual lots. It was by combining "Barlow's ideas and Playfair's efforts" Belote wrote, that the Compagnie du Scioto came to be.[48]

Unfortunately, Belote wrote, Barlow was "cruelly disappointed" by his partner.[49] "It is a pretty well established fact," Belote wrote—without offering a scintilla of evidence—"that Playfair put into his own pocket the greater bulk of the money received by him as subagent for the Scioto associates."[50] That was why, he said, Barlow couldn't pay Duer's drafts, which was why the venture failed.

After Walker arrived and gave him money to tide him over, Belote said, Barlow "seems to have taken no further part in the affair." Like Dawes, Belote said that Walker "exonerated" Barlow, and Playfair "disappeared."[51]

Dawes merely said that Playfair confounded his partners with opaque accounting, and "failed to turn over the proceeds" Duer needed to pay Congress and cover his expenses.[52] It was Belote who turned Playfair into an outright crook. His monograph then became the accepted reference on Scioto.

There's no telling why Belote had it in for Playfair, but here's a hypothesis—or, if you insist, a speculation: Playfair was British.

American attitudes toward Britain in 1903 were very different than today. For a historian like Belote, the American Revolution was a rebellion against the *British*. The National Anthem was about a battle against the *British*.

During the Civil War, the Confederates got support from the *British*. The great US-UK alliance that would set the course of the twentieth century was far in the future; in Belote's era, if an American were conjuring up a villain with a foreign accent, that accent would very likely be British.

In any case, the characterization of William Playfair as an embezzling English schemer stuck. That's how the Library of Congress describes him even today—citing Belote.[53] As does Ohio's State Historical Society.[54] Invariably, Barlow's biographers do the same.[55] Along with business and finance historians.[56] Articles about Playfair and the development of statistical graphics often toss in his malfeasance as an interesting aside.[57]

After his Colonial Dames fellowship, the Smithsonian Institution hired Belote as an assistant curator. He worked there for the next forty-two years. Swords, medals, and flags especially fascinated him.[58] When the Smithsonian spun off the History Division from its Department of Anthropology in 1919, Belote was a natural choice to head it. He can claim much of the credit for organizing the collection that sits today in the National Museum of American History.[59]

But as far as anyone can tell, Theodore Thomas Belote never published another word about Scioto, Barlow, Duer, Cutler, or William Playfair.

§ § §

You can find Playfair's side of the Scioto Affair—if you know where to look. It's buried in a footnote in a book Playfair published in 1813: *Political Portraits for the New Æra*. When the market for pamphleteering dried up, Playfair created a new vehicle, combining current biography with political commentary. It sold for £1 4s in boards, ready to be bound. It included a profile of Joel Barlow.[60]

Partners from failed business ventures often sound like spouses from failed marriages: lots of recriminations, and neither would likely use the other for a character reference. In Playfair's telling, Barlow had been adrift in Paris, "unable to speak French and ignorant of business"—a "taciturn and selfish" man who took "great pains to give an idea to others that he was a profound genius."[61]

(Barlow's opinions of Playfair veered all over the place. His December 1790 letter to Walker introduced Playfair as "an Englishman of bold and enterprising spirit and a good imagination."[62] Five months later Barlow was telling Walker that Playfair was "a most imprudent & unfit man to have any authority in a business of this kind."[63] Sort it out for yourself.)

In any case, Playfair recalled that Barlow, having failed to sell any of Duer's preemption rights, had given up. Then "another person"—that's Playfair, referring to himself, *sotto voce*—offered an idea: Exercise the options and sell individual lots, each with a mortgage. Buyers would pay off the mortgage as they worked the land. Playfair said the plan failed only because Barlow, "though his avarice, and that of his employers, stopped the sales when 150,000 acres were sold."[64] He did not elaborate.

There's also another place to find Playfair's account. Thomas Byerley published an article about Scioto in an 1817 issue of the *Colonial Journal*, a short-lived quarterly specializing in articles about Britain's expanding empire.[65] Byerley said he got his information from "the immediate authority of the principle mover of the undertaking." In other words, Playfair.[66]

So who was Thomas Byerley?

To the degree he is remembered at all, Thomas Byerley is known as the editor of the *Literary Chronicle and Weekly Review*, a journal published from 1819 to 1828, specializing in essays and poetry, along with literature, music, and theater reviews.[67] He was also Playfair's collaborator—and, as we shall see, occasional co-conspirator. Probably no one knew him better. Byerley wrote the obituary of Playfair the *Literary Chronicle* published four weeks after he died. Virtually all biographers of Playfair are using that sketch as a starting point, even if they don't realize it.[68]

In any case, the *Colonial Journal* article looks legit. It gets the basic facts correct, and it's consistent with accounts Playfair gave Duer and Walker. According to Byerley—that is, Playfair—Barlow met Playfair in early 1789 through a mutual acquaintance, a "Col. Blagdon"—which is how Blackden's name was sometimes rendered, or how Byerley might spell it after hearing the story told in Playfair's Scottish brogue.

Barlow asked Playfair to partner with him to sell the preemption rights. But Playfair turned him down. He considered it a "visionary" project—an understated way of saying "half baked."

Byerley said Playfair changed his mind after the storming of the Bastille, realizing "extensive emigration to some other country would be the natural consequence"—an understated way of saying nobles might want to get out of France before they lost everything, including, possibly, their lives.

So, in September, Byerley said, "Mr. Barlow and Mr. Playfair, having continued their acquaintance and friendly intercourse," agreed to do business. Playfair still doubted anyone would buy 500,000-acre tracts that Barlow's partners didn't own. But he thought one might be able to exercise the preemption rights, buy the land, and then sell it in individual lots—if the U.S. government agreed and offered financing for half the cost.

It all depended on whether the U.S. Minister to France, would "approve of the plan and give sanction and authority to the transaction." The minister: Thomas Jefferson. They approached Jefferson. He agreed to the deal. Playfair and Barlow were in business.

According to Byerley, Playfair would receive a ten percent commission on each lot, and pay all the Compagnie's expenses in France. Barlow would send the remainder of the money to America. Maps, prospectus, and plans were ready in November, and in two months the new company sold more than 50,000 acres. The Compagnie chartered two vessels in January 1790.

Once sales got going, wealthier buyers joined in. Byerley—remember, that's Playfair—said some kind of consortium of nobles bought 180,000 acres early in 1790 and sailed in March. Two more vessels followed in May. The only reason the project collapsed, Byerley wrote, was because of the "impatience and avarice of Mr. Barlow's constituents at New York, to realize the great fortunes they had planned for themselves." He did not elaborate, either.

Is Playfair's account credible? Yes; there's proof.

Diligent as he was, John Marshall Newton missed a key document about the Scioto Affair. It puts the relationship between Playfair and Barlow in a different light—very different.

In 1901 William Sibley, a Gallipolis newspaper editor, published *The French Five Hundred*, what he called a "historiette" of the Scioto Affair.[69] Sibley was no Playfair fan; he labeled him a "villain." But in his historiette, Sibley happened to include a transcript of a letter Playfair sent to Duer from Paris on 20 November 1790—just before Playfair's encounter with Walker.

Sibley said he got the document from Charles Slack, an Ohio businessman who collected autograph letters. Slack donated his collection to Marietta College, which sold most of it in the 1990s. The original letter disappeared, most likely into the files of a private collector.[70]

Sibley's transcript, however, looks genuine. It has Playfair's idiosyncratic misspellings and casual grammar. Also, in the Gallipolis Papers there is another letter from Playfair to Duer dated 27 December 1790—an original, in Playfair's handwriting. In this one, Playfair opens: "Since I had the honor of writing to you last month at such great length…."

Sibley's transcribed letter was dated 20 November 1790 and is two thousand words long. It's indubitably the letter Playfair was referring to.[71]

The clincher proving Sibley's transcribed letter is genuine is a passage in which Playfair tells Duer to route correspondence to him though "I. Playfair" at "Russel Place" in London to avoid interception by French authorities. The transcriber (possibly Sibley himself) misread James Playfair's first initial—easy to do, with William's handwriting. Yet he got the address correct—the two brothers often shared a house on Russell Street. No newspaper editor in Gallipolis, Ohio would have known that. It means Sibley's transcription is authentic.[72]

It also means Barlow lied.

Barlow claimed later that he distrusted Playfair and didn't know what happened to the settlers' money. But that's not what the letter says: the Compagnie had "*as Mr. Barlow very wisely proposed,*" placed the settlers' deposits "with Mr. Grand the Banker." So Barlow knew exactly where any money was; it was his idea to deposit it with Grand.

Yet the most important item in the transcribed 20 November letter is a notation at the bottom: "*I have read this letter and approve generally of the facts & the reasoning therein contained—J. Barlow.*" Barlow countersigned it.

Sibley even described the signatures: Playfair's is "bold;" Barlow's is "cramped"—a fair description of how they appear elsewhere. The letter proves Playfair and Barlow were working as one, right up to the moment Walker came through their door. Barlow would never have co-signed a letter telling Duer all was well if he thought Playfair was stealing from him.

Why then did Barlow let Duer's drafts bounce?

"The Bill of 100,000 francs which was returned," Playfair wrote Duer, "arrived here at a Moment when all was in a State of Stagnation"—that is, no sales—"occasioned by the bad news received from Alexandria." He was referring to the disorganization and lack of anyone to meet the settlers. That killed sales, and their cash flow.

Even worse, "there were 8 persons returned." The Compagnie had to reimburse them. Playfair and Barlow feared more would return, demanding their money, too. So the Compagnie had to keep money in reserve—and Barlow couldn't pay Duer's drafts.

How did Belote miss this letter? Sibley lived just a hundred and fifty miles away—a two-dollar train fare.

It's an example of how time and technology can change the entire picture; a hundred fifty miles was a long way in 1903. And two dollars was a lot of money for a recent graduate on a $300 stipend that had to last an entire year. Belote was depending almost wholly on the Gallipolis Papers, and John Marshall Newton died before Sibley published *The French Five Hundred*. So Playfair's 20 November letter never made it into the Gallipolis Papers—or into Belote's research.

§ § §

The full story of Playfair, Barlow, Duer, and the Scioto Affair had to wait another hundred years. It came from an unexpected source: Jocelyne Moreau, a schoolteacher at a lyceum near Orleans, about two hours south of Paris. Moreau grew up not far away and enjoyed studying history, but never wanted a university position; she didn't care for the old boy politics of the higher academic scene.

Moreau was looking for a new topic to study as the French Revolution's bicentennial approached. She had heard of the French effort to settle Ohio (that's how you see it if you're from France) and got interested in Scioto and Joel Barlow. There was bit of nationalism motivating her, too; American scholars portrayed French settlers as wig-wearing urbanites dancing in the wilderness to the sound of violins. "The French have never proven very successful as colonists. The best they ever accomplished in America was as explorers and trappers," Belote claimed.[73]

Moreau (who published as Moreau-Zanelli and now generally goes by her married name, Zanelli) was perfect for unraveling the Scioto Affair as no one had before. She didn't just teach in a lyceum; she taught English, and she had the idiomatic fluency of a native in both languages. She also had a sense of adventure; in her earlier years she lived in Britain, doing odd jobs.

Moreau not only could *translate* English to French or French to English; she could *do analysis* in both languages. There's a big difference.

Hard-core historical research depends on reading between the lines, finding obscure sources, and seeing the patterns among persons, places, and events. You can't do that if you have to translate each website, page, or document. It's too hard and takes too much time; you also miss subtle connections, the meaning of jargon, and figures of speech. That kind of analysis requires native fluency—and, if you have that kind of fluency, you don't bother to translate, you just do the analysis. That's doing analysis in a foreign language.

Because Moreau could navigate in both French and English, she could piece together old newspapers, notary records, ship manifests—and the family papers of Jean-Jacques Duval d'Eprémesnil.[74] She could maneuver through the files at the Archives nationales—and the Cincinnati Museum Center. Moreau completed her thesis in 1996.[75] It was published as a book in 2000, but it was never translated, so it did not receive the attention it might have.[76]

That was unfortunate, since it provides the key pieces of the story. More elements became available in the years after Moreau published her thesis, when many American archives went online. With all this in mind, here's what really happened in our *Rashômon* tale of Scioto.

§ § §

As January 1790 arrived Joel Barlow could breathe a sigh of relief. "The year 1789 of all the years of my life has been the most tedious, the most filled with anxiety and distress," a homesick Barlow told his wife Ruth in a letter on New Year's Day. "You never can know the difficulties I have encountered, arising from an infinity of indefensible circumstances attendant on this business."

All year Barlow had been homesick and depressed. He missed his wife. "While my careless and indefensible associates at home conceive me to be rioting in the luxuries of Europe, I should be infinitely more happy to be locked in prison in America, where I might hear the cheering voice of my Ruthy through the grate, saying good morning to my love."[77]

Worst of all, Barlow could not escape the sad, hard fact that he had failed. He had sold none of Duer's preemption rights. That had always been his greatest fear—going home a failure. His father-in-law had opposed his daughter's marriage to him, his stint as a schoolmaster was unremarkable, his law career was undistinguished, and he had never truly wanted to be a minister. *The Vision of Columbus* got buzz, but he lived in the shadow of his brother-in-law, Abraham Baldwin—delegate to the Constitutional Convention, founding president of the University of Georgia, and, now, U.S. congressman.[78]

But that chance meeting with the Englishman Playfair had turned things around. That meeting saved him. No need to worry about sulking back to Connecticut now. Scioto was on its way to success. On 29 November 1789,

Barlow wrote Duer to share the good news: He had just set up a land company in Paris and hundreds of settlers were now on their way from France.[79]

Probably the last thing William Duer wanted to hear was that Joel Barlow had set up a land company in Paris and that hundreds of settlers were now on their way from France.

The key to understanding the whole, sordid Scioto Affair is to always, always, always remind yourself: *Duer never planned to settle Ohio.* Everything follows from that. William Bradford, Rufus King, Ephraim Dawes, and Theodore Belote were all trying to explain a settlement that failed, a land deal that went off the rails, or a misbegotten corporation. But Duer never planned a settlement, land deal, or corporation.[80]

The Scioto speculation was always supposed to be just that—*a speculation*. A paper transaction. A flip. Easy money. Nothing more. Duer never dreamt Barlow would actually try to colonize the land. And surely it had never occurred to him that Barlow would partner with a British engineer who had friends hoping to recreate feudal France on the banks of the Ohio River.

You couldn't have written a better tale of someone being hoisted with his own petard if you hired O. Henry to do it himself. Duer left Barlow hanging for months in Europe. He gave him no guidance from America. But Duer's original commission authorized Barlow to dispose of the preemption rights any way he saw fit. That's why you appointed an agent in the telecommunications-free eighteenth century. Without such a commission, an agent like Barlow could not do business. With it, Barlow could do pretty much anything he wanted. Which he did.

When we left Playfair at the storming of the Bastille, bread riots, demonstrations, and crime were spreading across France like never before. As France looked more and more dangerous, America looked more and more attractive. That's when Playfair reconsidered Barlow's offer. Just as Belote reported, Barlow and Playfair met through a mutual acquaintance, Samuel Blackden.

So who was Samuel Blackden?

Blackden wasn't just a Kentucky land dealer, and, no matter what Belote may have thought, he didn't "disappear from the scene." Records show that Lieutenant Colonel Samuel Blackden served in the Continental Army during the American Revolution, and if ever there was a solid, reliable officer, it was "Blackie." He fought in both New England and the Carolinas.[81] George Washington knew Blackden better than he knew Barlow; Washington was

Blackden's commander. He trusted Blackden enough to preside over the court martial and execution of a deserter.[82]

Washington stayed in touch when Blackden went to Europe after the war to do business.[83] And Washington wasn't alone. Henry Knox—soon to be Secretary of War—used Blackden to follow developments in Britain.[84] Jefferson used him as an unofficial envoy and intelligence source.[85] Even John Paul Jones was a friend; Blackden cared for the ailing Jones in the weeks before his death.[86]

American leaders trusted Blackden. He would never have recommended a rogue or a knave to a fellow patriot like Barlow. Indeed, Blackden remained a good friend of both Joel and Ruth Barlow for many years; they were neighbors in Paris a few years later, residing at the Maison Bretagne. Certainly there's no sign Barlow thought Blackden had given him a bum steer with Playfair and the Scioto opportunity.[87]

Playfair was unimpressed with Barlow but he maintained his "friendly intercourse." After the Bastille storming, Playfair realized Frenchmen might be looking for a safer neighborhood. That's when he—not Barlow—set up the Compagnie. Barlow gave Playfair a thirtieth of his stock up front for his services because Barlow couldn't do the job himself and was willing to pay for Playfair's assistance.[88]

One partner Playfair brought to the table was Claude Odille Joseph Baroud—in Belote's telling, a "Paris merchant."[89] Baroud was actually a well-known financial writer and jurist—*and* Batz's banker, *and* a partner in Étienne Clavière's insurance company, *and* one of the first persons to greet d'Eprémesnil upon his return from Saint Martinique.[90]

Playfair called Clavière "a man of knowledge in several lines, but of a cruel and vindictive temper."[91] But he would do business with him, and the two occasionally crossed paths.[92] Playfair's "intimate" friend Batz led to Clavière, and Clavière and Batz led to Baroud.

Pull on a few more threads, and you begin to appreciate how intertwined and tangled the French side of the affair really was. Besides his links to Batz, Clavière was also both a business partner and a close friend of Jacques Pierre Brissot. Brissot was Clavière's ghostwriter; Clavière had rescued Brissot from poverty by cutting him in on business deals.[93]

So Brissot had ties to Clavière, and Clavière had ties to Batz, and Batz was Playfair's friend and business partner. But when it came to Scioto, Brissot and Playfair were competitors. That's because Brissot had his own hopes for building an American settlement.

Brissot's newspaper, *Le Patriote français*, touted his plan, saying it "does not at all resemble the one proposed by the Scioto du Compagnie." Brissot couched the venture as a means for Frenchmen to find opportunity in America, while keeping their ties to France—indeed, *Le Patriote* said, it would serve France by bolstering ties to the new United States.[94]

To complicate matters further, Brissot had been working with…William Duer.[95]

Brissot had met Duer through Daniel Parker, Duer's man in Europe—and, later, Barlow's chaperone.[96] Duer, in turn, introduced Brissot as a friend of the United States to George Washington. Duer wrote Washington saying that he was communicating in behalf of Hamilton—Washington's protégé.[97] Brissot visited Washington and Hamilton (as well as James Madison, Benjamin Franklin, and other notables) while touring America in 1788.[98]

In other words, these men all knew each other well. Indeed, sometimes they were even rubbing elbows.

The Compagnie du Scioto set up its office at 162 rue Neuve des Petits Champs, just down the street from the Palais Royale, and today part of rue Danielle Casanova. Baroud was already conducting business there—as were Clavière, Batz, and Brissot.[99] The building is still standing; it now has a nineteenth century façade, but the rough-hewn timbers inside betray its eighteenth-century origins.[100]

Yet Scioto wasn't just Playfair's inside ballgame with French elites; it soon became a social phenomenon—a mania, in fact.

Once the Compagnie opened its office, prospective buyers could stop by and browse through a sales package: copies of the Northwest Ordinance of 1787 (which made the sales legal), regional maps, and *Letters from an American Farmer,* a popular account of life in the Colonies by Hector Saint-John de Crèvecoeur. Jefferson's endorsement was available for inspection, too.[101]

And then there was the company brochure. *Prospectus pour l'établissement sur les rivières d'Ohio et de Scioto en Amérique.*[102] Playfair usually gets credit for the brochure—or blame. Some say it was singularly responsible for making hundreds of Frenchmen suddenly decide lemming-like to emigrate to America.[103]

In reality, the information came from a pamphlet Manasseh Cutler drafted two years earlier when he and his partners set up the Ohio Company.[104] Cutler mainly wanted to show the Ohio Valley was fertile and had access to New Orleans via the Mississippi. The maps and descriptions were good enough for Thomas Hutchins, Geographer of the United States to endorse as "judicious, just, and true." Barlow took copies with him to Paris.[105]

The *Prospectus* hyped the case for Scioto a bit, but for the most part it reads like, well…a prospectus. It's basically a business plan explaining terms and conditions of the land sale, describing the nature of the farm business one would set up, and projecting costs and revenues. (Main income streams: tobacco, cotton, and hogs; one might also hunt game for pelts.)[106]

Sure, the *Prospectus* went overboard when it asserted Scioto was at the center of the new country, and thus likely to become the nation's capital. And it did offer some anecdotes about the lands that were, let us say, optimistic. But you have to get into the mind of a Frenchman in 1789.

America had a mystical image in France—a peaceful, happy place, beyond the seas, free of hunger, corruption, and unfairness. Jean-Jacques Rousseau—an icon at the time—based his entire philosophy on man's yearning to be back in the state of nature. Scioto was certainly that. All the Compagnie needed was a plausible case for success, and that's what the brochure provided.[107]

In any event, the reaction was electric. They called it *Sciotomanie*—a craving for an ideal land no one had seen. Not even mesmerism could match it. One young Parisian, writing under the pseudonym "d'Allemagne" described the obsession, with a bit of *ennui*:[108]

> At night I dreamt of nothing any more except Scioto, during the day I thought of nothing but Scioto. I cared nothing about the rest of the world. Paris had no charm any more; France…was nothing beside Scioto. Happiness was to be found only there. Boredom took hold of me.… I neglected my duties; my business seemed foreign to me. Only Scioto had the power to hold me.

All d'Allemagne needed was a smoldering Gauloise to finger as he told his tale.[109] Sales were brisk. Most buyers in November and December were craftsmen and traders, purchasing lots of fifty to seven hundred acres. In the first weeks they were almost all from Paris, but soon about a quarter were from the provinces. Only a few were farmers. Many were luxury service providers, craftsmen, and tradesmen—merchants whose customers would disappear after the nobility lost its wealth and privileges.

By mid-January the notaries were processing five, six, and even occasionally eight sales each day. Then a new kind of buyer began appearing in the records.[110]

The lynching of Joseph-Françoise Foullon de Doué, a wealthy *fermier générale*—tax collector—on 22 July 1789 made many nobles rethink their view of the Revolution. When a mob threatened Foullon and his son in law, Paris officials took them into City Hall and put them under protection. The mob forced its way in, dragged both men into the street, hanged Foullon from a lamppost, cut out his heart, and—just in case anyone missed the point—returned it to the city officials in their chambers.[111]

Foullon had been a deputy in the Paris parlement. When the Compagnie du Scioto set up shop, one of his colleagues took notice—Jean-Jacques Duval d'Eprémesnil, another notable doing business at 162 rue Neuve des Petits Champs.[112]

After his triumphant return from St. Marguerite, d'Eprémesnil had hoped to represent a Normandy constituency in the Third Estate.[113] But, the Revolution had passed him by; there was no way now that commoners would accept a noble as their representative. So d'Eprémesnil attended the Estates General as a deputy of the Second. When the chambers merged, he took a seat in the National Assembly.

By spring 1789, d'Eprémesnil was sorry he had any part the Revolution at all.[114] When moderates and radicals organized political clubs, d'Eprémesnil began to organize his fellow nobles. He hoped he could preserve rank and hierarchy—the vital structures he thought society needed to function.[115] It was a lost cause. On the evening of August 4, 1789, the Assembly voted to abolish all the privileges nobles enjoyed in one fell swoop.[116]

The seigniorial system was dead in France. But perhaps, d'Eprémesnil hoped, perhaps it had a future in the United States. America was open to all kinds of new ideas—even new *old* ideas. For months d'Eprémesnil had been talking with his friend, Marquis Claude-François de Lezay-Marnésia, about leaving the country and setting up a colony of their own. With the Compagnie du Scioto offering vast lands at great prices, they decided to act.

D'Eprémesnil and Lezay-Marnésia were as odd a couple as Boulton and Watt. D'Eprémesnil was the classic urban noble. He reveled in the cosmopolitan Paris lifestyle, and lived for the intrigue and tussle of Versailles. He couldn't bear to be out of the game.[117]

Lezay-Marnésia, in contrast, was the classic country noble—big thinker, a little eccentric, man of letters, and an agricultural experimenter. For him, the world was just one enormous laboratory. The Revolution might make France temporarily inhospitable—but what an opportunity for adventure! If it meant traveling across an ocean and pioneering in the American wilderness, so much the better.[118]

Dawes and Belote knew the Scioto settlers included some aristocrats. In Belote's telling, they didn't mix with the other settlers waiting in Alexandria and had no reluctance to take complaints directly to Duer. In other words, they acted like nobles. Belote said that when they reached Scioto they made a "tour of exploration" and were "charmed" by the countryside, but ultimately abandoned their plans for "a city with a magnificent cathedral."[119]

There's more to the story than that.

After the fall of the Bastille, the murder of Foullon, and the announcement of the Compagnie du Scioto, d'Eprémesnil and Lezay-Marnésia decided to act. They met at the end of January 1790 with twenty-two other men of substance to form a company they called, logically enough, the *Société des Vingt-Quatres*, or the Society of the Twenty-Four.[120] Within weeks, the members purchased almost 70,000 acres from the Compagnie—about 100 square miles, or the size of the original District of Columbia.[121]

Who introduced Playfair and d'Eprémesnil? The likely candidate is Batz, Playfair's "particularly intimate" friend—and business partner.

Batz and d'Eprémesnil had ties going back to when Batz was a young man determined to become an army officer. One had to be a noble for promotion beyond colonel under the Old Regime, and Bernard Chérin, France's official genealogist, nitpicked every irregularity in the papers Batz offered to establish his lineage. D'Eprémesnil used his influence, and Batz got certified in 1780.[122]

The two would remain friends and thoroughly intertwined as the Revolution unfolded. They even became in-laws when Batz married d'Eprémesnil's stepdaughter, Augustine Michelle Désirée Thilorier. Later, when Batz became a counterrevolutionary, d'Eprémesnil's wife, Françoise-Augustine, was accused of being his accomplice (the royalist meetings in her salon in the early years of the National Assembly were widely known). It would have been natural for Batz to steer d'Eprémesnil to Playfair.[123]

§ § §

The irony was exquisite: at the same time the Compagnie du Scioto was pitching Ohio as a land where French commoners could escape the oppression of the Old Regime, d'Eprémesnil and his Société des Vingt-Quatres were pitching Ohio as a land where nobles could recreate constitutional monarchy, perfected.

It would be "a new State, in the bosom of the United States," as Lezay-Marnésia put it.[124] He touted the Société, saying it offered their new country "the most energetic, tested, and perfected Frenchmen, who would bring further riches: their industry, knowledge, arts, constancy, courage, and sociability."[125]

The Société members agreed to pledge allegiance to their new country. For the nobles, it wasn't much different from pledging fealty to a monarch.[126]

D'Eprémesnil put enormous effort into his plans. He envisioned a 10,000 acre estate (between fifteen and sixteen square miles) that he planned to administer himself, organized around a village of 432 acres with just under half the land reserved for streets, squares, common buildings, and walkways. Twelve families would make homes on the estate, each receiving six acres. He also planned to bring forty tenant farmers, plus masons, carpenters, and various tradesmen—a total of about one hundred fifty settlers.[127]

The Church was to be at the center of the new colony, and d'Eprémesnil lobbied the Vatican to assign a bishop to Scioto. Lezay-Marnésia and Barth also petitioned the Priests of the Christian Doctrine to send clergy.[128] In June d'Eprémesnil sent Playfair "a plan to establish in America the convents and religious houses being abolished in France"[129] Playfair replied the next day, saying he thought that "America would allow people in a religious society to follow their old habits" and that America could offer "an asylum" for those who could no longer practice their religion in France.[130]

Playfair asked his brother James to design what they began to call the "American City." (Lezay-Marnésia dubbed it "Aigle-Lys," with a coat of arms combining the American eagle and the French fleur-de-lis.)[131] James had practiced architecture in London since 1787, developing a distinctive neoclassical style using traditional elements—columns, porticos, and rotundas—while avoiding Rococo excess. He exhibited work at the Royal Academy and had just begun his masterpiece, Cairness, a country house for Charles Gordon in Aberdeenshire.[132]

On 8 August James duly listed a job in his journal to design the American City for "Wm. Playfair." It took him about a week. His journal did not indicate a fee. It did list the main components of the city, which more or less followed the plans in d'Eprémesnil's notes: town center, public square, government buildings, churches, courts, and a prison.[133]

§ § §

Reports that d'Eprémesnil and his partners had established their company propelled *Sciotomanie* to new levels. It became a proxy for the fissures splitting France; the various sides fought it out in the Paris newspapers. Sciotophiles—mainly monarchists hoping to shepherd the old system to safety in the New World—depicted Scioto as the Promised Land. *Annales patriotiques et littéraire de la France* reported d'Eprémesnil was leaving with his family "to champion feudalism, magnetism, mesmerism, martinism, theosophy, and parliamentarism."[134]

Meanwhile, Sciotophobes—largely anti-aristocratic republicans eager to paint the monarchists as spineless wimps unable to deal with change and ready to abandon their nation—described d'Eprémesnil's settlers as passengers on a "ship of fools."[135] *Le Fouet national* opined how the emigration of twenty-four noble families "provides further evidence of the state of decay in which France has fallen."[136]

No matter; d'Eprémesnil began to hear from eager recruits all across France.[137] One young man wrote of the "secret anxiety that makes me want to travel," and how "the apparent impossibility of finding a permanent situation" made him "turn my eyes towards the New World." Another claimed his "good constitution, strong and robust" qualified him. A third, perhaps less qualified, cited his talents as a "good calculator" with a hand that "draws and paints nice miniatures." There were also divorcées, widows, and other unmarried women seeking a new start under a new set of rules.[138]

Lezay-Marnésia was on one of the first ships. So were Jean-Joseph de Barth and his son, François Joseph Barth Meinard Bourogne, and Charles Antoine Louis Thiebaut, all members of the Société. After the meeting with Duer in New York, the plans gelled. There would be two cities. One for the tradesmen, farmers, and other commoners who had bought individual plots; that became Gallipolis. The other—Aigle-Lys—would be the seat of government, culture, and education that d'Eprémesnil had planned.[139]

By January 1790 the aristocrats were the Compagnie's biggest customers. When Lezay-Marnésia and Barth said they were dissatisfied with the site originally staked out for them, Duer offered to select an alternative. Lezay-Marnésia never did find a suitable location. Instead, he settled near Pittsburgh. He stayed long enough to avoid the Terror, and eventually returned to France. Meanwhile, Barth went his own way—with George Washington.

5 The First Great Scandal of American Politics

In addition to forgery, statistical graphics, and new processes for metal plating, William Playfair has a credible claim for making significant contributions to another innovation: the high-level American political scandal, along with its ancillary technologies, the official cover-up and the federally funded bailout.

Since Duer never expected to be in the land settlement business, he had made no preparations. None. So when the Scioto project crashed, the American officials who facilitated it—you will recognize all of them—had to fix it, and wipe their fingerprints from the wreckage.

Communications technology—or lack thereof—paced the unfolding events. A packet ship required four weeks to carry a letter from France across the Atlantic—at best. Six was more likely. Ten was not unusual. The letter Barlow wrote on 29 November 1789 telling Duer settlers would soon be arriving in Virginia had not even made it as far as Bermuda when he sent a follow-up letter on 8 December informing Duer that the settlers were at that very moment en route from Paris to Le Havre.[1]

Barlow's letters dribbled into New York. A 29 December letter said the first ship had embarked. There were around sixty settlers on board. Within weeks they would be landing. There was nothing Duer could do about it. Now he was in the colonization business, like it or not.[2]

Meanwhile, an insider deal that was supposedly "a profound secret," was becoming less and less secret all the time. None of the chroniclers of the

Scioto Affair—Bradford, King, Dawes, let alone Belote—ever mentioned it, but top U.S. officials knew all about the plan to settle Scioto almost from the very beginning. Indeed, several had a personal interest in it—beginning with George Washington.

The soon-to-be-President of the United States had put his reputation behind Barlow, the Scioto Company's agent. He vouched for the "genius of the first magnitude" in his letters to the American Minister to France (Jefferson) and the commander of the French National Guard (Lafayette).

With such endorsements, it was only natural that Barlow would want to tell Washington how things were going. And, sure enough, on 24 April 1790 Barlow wrote President Washington (by now sworn in) to inform him that the Scioto settlers were on their way.

Barlow wanted the new President to be aware of one traveler in particular: Claude-François de Lezay-Marnésia. "He & many others are transferring their property to the United States, and are going to settle themselves on the Ohio near the Scioto," Barlow wrote Washington. Lezay-Marnésia "requests me to take the liberty to announce to your Excellency their intentions, & to solicit for them your countenance & protection."

Barlow added, "I think it a fortunate circumstance for the interest of the United States that an agent for the sale of lands happened to be here at the time of this revolution in France." Determined as ever to mark his place in history, Barlow was referring to... Barlow.[3]

Washington, however, had already heard the news—from his old friend from the War for Independence, Duportail, now France's War Minister. The French general wrote Washington on 10 February to tell him about the Société des Vingt-Quatres, which he had joined. He told Washington he saw the Ohio project as "a kind of experiment," which, if successful, would "be followed by a much greater one, so that a large French Colony may rise florishing in a few years."[4]

Duportail wrote that, unfortunately, he could not leave at that moment, as "the critical situation in our affairs at home does not permit it." But he hoped to visit the colony in the future. It would "be a great pleasure for me to see our people live in an abondance and happiness which they could never hope in this country." In the meantime, "two members of our society, mr. bart and mr. thiebaut are the vanguard, they go to America immediately and are to land in alessandria."[5] (Duportail apologized for his spelling and grammar.)

Barth carried a letter authorizing him to mark out the 2,000 acres Duportail bought; Barlow countersigned.[6]

When the *Patriot* landed in Alexandria and found only confusion, the settlers wrote the President requesting assistance. Washington was seriously ill at the time—feverish and bed-ridden with an abscess in his thigh—and did not reply until four weeks later.[7] When he did, he assured them not to worry; the situation was in hand.[8] By then Lezay-Marnésia, Barth, Bourogne, Thiebaut, and the rest of the "leading men" had met with Duer in New York. Soon the *Virginia Gazette and Alexandria Advertiser* reported the French settlers "are on their Way to the Western Country, and that a much larger Number may be hourly expected."[9]

Yet Washington would soon have a connection to Scioto beyond his endorsement of Barlow and his assurances to the settlers. None of the New York associates—Duer, Flint and Craigie—had ever even *seen* Scioto. Neither had Barlow. Neither, of course, had Playfair. Even Manasseh Cutler apparently never made it further down the Ohio than Marietta.

But Washington had.

Washington made his name fighting up and down the Ohio Valley as an officer in the Virginia militia during the French and Indian War. He started speculating in land while a young man. Washington had a vision: a nearly all-water route that tied the country together. He could see a day when, starting from Alexandria, near his home at Mount Vernon, one could navigate up the Potomac to Cumberland, make a short portage across to the Ohio, and then continue down the Mississippi to New Orleans. Or the other way around, from the American heartland down to the Atlantic. A settlement at Scioto would be a major transportation hub.[10]

When Washington went off to war, he kept an eye out for investment properties. He bought many, using cash and warrants he received for his military service. As a result, Washington owned nearly 10,000 acres of land on the southern bank of the Ohio… just up the river from where John Burnham and his New England woodsmen were building Gallipolis. He owned an additional 23,000 acres across the river in Virginia, extending along forty-three continuous miles on the Great Kanawha.[11]

Besides his journeys into the Ohio watershed in 1753, 1754, 1755, and 1758, Washington traveled to the region in autumn 1770, surveying the lands he would later buy. He planned a return trip but Indian raids made travel too risky. Then the American Revolution put a hold on everything. After the war he made another trek to the Ohio, reaching Pittsburgh in 1784.[12]

So when John Rome wrote him in 1794 about the situation of the hapless settlers in far-away Scioto, Washington knew as much about the land as anyone in America. After all, he had seen it—and he owned a lot of it.[13]

And that's how George Washington went from being a spectator of the Scioto Affair to being a participant. When the Compagnie's lands failed to meet his expectations, Barth turned to another land dealer—who now happened to be President of the United States.[14] Barth bought Washington's lands along the Ohio and Great Kanawha for 65,000 French crowns.[15] Washington thought it a good deal; he told George Clendinen, his agent, that he had been trying to sell the tract for "a considerable time."[16]

(Louis-Guillaume Otto, the French chargé d'affaires in New York followed all of this, step by step. He had heard about the hundred French survivors from the *Recovery*, and that twelve thousand more settlers were on their way.[17] He also knew about Washington's land holdings; he reported to his Foreign Ministry that his sources told him the project would double their value.)[18]

In short, Washington knew all about Scioto. As did his Secretary of the Treasury, Alexander Hamilton.

When Duer had to resign his position at the Treasury Department in April 1790—the conflicts of interest were too great, even by eighteenth century standards—Hamilton sent heartfelt regrets. "I count with confidence on your future friendship, as you may on mine," he wrote, concluding, "Adieu— God bless you, and give you the success for which you will always have the warmest wishes of Your affectionate, A. Hamilton."[19]

Hamilton continued to correspond with Duer about Scioto even after Duer left the government.[20] Friendship aside, Hamilton needed to know what was going on because he was responsible for the settlers. The entire Executive Branch had only three departments—State, Treasury, and War— and administering the Northwest Territory came under Treasury.

On 19 May Hamilton wrote Governor St. Clair to make sure he understood how important the Scioto settlers were to the nation's future. "The truth is, humanity and policy both demand our best efforts to countenance and protect them," Hamilton wrote.

"There is a Western Country. It <u>will</u> be settled," he insisted. The only question was whether it would be "settled from abroad rather than at the entire expence of the Atlantic population." Hamilton didn't want easterners to move west; he wanted immigrants, and told St. Clair to "lay hold of the affections of the settlers and attach them from the beginning to the Government of the Nation."

"If these emigrants render a favourable account," Hamilton wrote, "there is no saying in what numbers they may be followed." He directed St. Clair to work with War Secretary Knox to make sure they were protected from Indian attack.[21]

Hamilton had plenty of sources to keep him informed about Scioto. Daniel Parker and Andrew Craigie—Duer's partners—were part of Hamilton's New York City network.[22] He also had official dispatches; William Short, Jefferson's personal secretary in Paris, had written him about the project.[23]

Then there was Thomas Jefferson.

Jefferson knew about Barlow's interest in Scioto even before Barlow arrived in France. One of Jefferson's sources was...Parker, Barlow's chaperone-to-be. The two had a history of correspondence.[24]

After Barlow arrived in Paris he effectively became Jefferson's protégé.[25] So it was no surprise Jefferson endorsed the project in behalf of the U.S. government. Playfair recalled that when he and Barlow presented their plan for the Compagnie, Jefferson "readily agreed to sanction the transaction, without waiting for instructions from his government."[26]

Jefferson followed the project as the settlers gathered at Le Havre; Lafayette asked him to assist a friend.[27] Gouverneur Morris alerted Jefferson from London in December 1790 that Barlow and Blackden had been "promising freely what in the Nature of Things could never be performed."[28] Later, relatives sought out Jefferson for help after months passed with no word from the settlers.[29]

And, Jefferson, like Washington, tried to piggyback on the Scioto ploy, pitching some of his own lands to Jean-Joseph de Barth. Writing from Philadelphia in March 1792, as the Scioto project was imploding, Jefferson asked Barth if any of his friends might be interested in buying a tract he owned in middle Virginia. It offered great hunting, beautiful views, and was already cleared. Besides, Jefferson observed, in Virginia one could own slaves.[30]

So Jefferson knew about the project in detail, too, from start to finish.

Jefferson also knew Playfair. They already had a distant link through the Small brothers before they met face-to-face in March 1789, soon after Playfair arrived in Paris—months before the Scioto project was even conceived.

Playfair gave Jefferson a copy of the just-published French translation of *The Commercial and Political Atlas* (Jefferson knew about the book and had already planned to buy a copy.) They were never close, but, as we shall see, Jefferson thought highly of Playfair's work and followed it for many years to come.[31]

In short, Scioto wasn't just an obscure land deal gone bad, as Bradford reported. General St. Clair did not just happen to find those settlers, as King wrote. It wasn't just a matter between Duer, Barlow, and Playfair, as Dawes and Belote suggested. The affair involved Washington, Jefferson, and Hamilton from the very beginning. The President, the Secretary of State, and the Secretary of the Treasury all knew about it and, in one way or another, had all endorsed it. And in doing so, they put the reputation of their new nation behind it.

This may explain why in 1795 the U.S. government was willing to give 100,000 acres of prime Ohio farmland to a bunch of bedraggled Frenchmen whose only distinction seemed to be extraordinarily bad judgment in their selection of a real estate agent. In any case, by the time Rome wrote Washington for help, it would have been hard to find anyone at the senior levels of the U.S. government who did *not* know about the Scioto land deal and the settlement on the banks of the Ohio.

Sort of ironic for a project that was supposed to be a "profound secret."

§ § §

What really killed the Scioto Company? Cash flow. William Duer had to pull the plug on it before it bankrupted him. He almost made it. Almost.

Barlow's original letter led Duer to believe he had found a buyer for the land: "I now have the pleasure to inform you that the contract was completed on the 3d of this month. It is for the sale of 3 millions of acres—the price of six livres the acre." A reasonable man would conclude the Compagnie had taken in eighteen million livres.

In reality, all the Compagnie had, and all it would ever have, was the settlers' deposits. Under the Compagnie's scheme—endorsed by Jefferson—the settlers put down half the cost of their land. The rest was due in two years. There was no other money. As Rochefontaine later told Lezay-Marnésia, "these gentlemen have no other funds to fulfill their engagements."[32]

With no other income, those deposits had to cover all the Compagnie's expenses: renting the office on rue Neuve des Petits Champs, chartering the ships, tending to hundreds of settlers assembling at Le Havre, and everything else. As the schedule slipped, the tab grew.

Meanwhile, in America the Scioto Company, or associates, or whatever they chose to call themselves, had to pay to house the settlers as they arrived in Virginia. They had to pay to transport them to Ohio. They had to pay John Burnham and his Massachusetts woodsman to clear the forest and build huts. And, of course, they had to pay Congress for the land.

Dawes claimed Duer, Flint, and Craigie agreed to be jointly responsible for the project's expenses.[33] But Craigie's letters say he assumed Duer would cover the costs.[34] Back in France, under his agreement with Barlow, Playfair was obligated to fund the Compagnie's expenses in Europe.[35] This all meant Duer was at the end of a long line of potential payees, and he wasn't going to get any money until both the French and the American arms of the company broke even.

The question was, how deep were his pockets, and long could he stand to be underwater? Barlow and Playfair apparently believed Duer's pockets reached to his ankles and that he could hold his breath like an Ama pearl diver. And why not? No one really knew how much money Duer had, and he flaunted what he could. Recall Cutler thought Duer lived "in the style of a nobleman."

Duer gave the Ohio Company a $143,000 advance so it could make its first payment to Congress for its land.[36] Couldn't he write a similar check for the Scioto Company to tide it over? Once news from Ohio put the emigration into overdrive, funds would begin pouring in. That's what Barlow seems to have assumed. He told Walker later that, "I had good reason to expect news from emigrants on the lands by the month of June which I was sure would enable me to pay Mr. Duer's drafts."[37]

Barlow knew cash would be tight; that's why he implored Duer on 25 January 1790, "Dont for God's sake fail to raise money enough to put the people in possession—make any sacrifice rather than fail in this essential object." He insisted, "You can certainly among all your Connexions raise one or two thousand dollars for a few months." In other words, Barlow wanted Duer to support the project with a bridge loan until it broke even. But Duer had never signed up for that.

Barlow also knew buyer confidence was critical. He had warned Duer that cash flow would "depend almost entirely on the accounts written back by the first people that arrive."[38] Bad news from America could kill sales—and the Compagnie.

That's exactly what happened.

D'Allemagne, the young Parisian who couldn't get Scioto off his mind, was one of the passengers arriving on the *Patriot*. He was, let us say, surprised by what he found in Alexandria when he landed.[39] He later recalled,

> The Paris Company had assured us that from Alexandria to Scioto was no more than forty leagues, all by water. But we learned that it was three hundred forty-two leagues of which one hundred twenty-two were by water and the rest over land. We found out further that Scioto is nothing but a wilderness which means that all provisions must be carried in. In addition, we were informed that one is exposed to fierce beasts: tigers, bears, and flying serpents, and that it takes five months to get there through the forest and across the swamps and mountains. And finally, once there... one will be welcomed by savages who number more than eighty thousand.[40]

The Alexandrians were exaggerating, but only a little. Three hundred forty-two leagues equal about a thousand miles. The journey required three, maybe four months, but not five. There were no flying serpents. And the "savages"—to be precise, Western Confederacy Native Americans, mainly of the Shawnee Nation—numbered no more than ten thousand. The problem was, when Britain gave the Northwest Territory to the colonies under the Treaty of Paris, no one bothered to consult the Indians. Little wonder they were hostile; the Brits gave away their land.

The Alexandrians were definitely right about one thing, though: Scioto was indeed a wilderness. The settlers were starting from scratch.

D'Allemagne sized up the situation. On 26 May he and seven others boarded a Dutch vessel, the *Confidence*—the eight passengers Playfair cited in his 20 November letter to Duer that Sibley quoted.

Duer's men arrived just as they were ready to set sail. They pleaded with the Frenchmen not to leave. But it was too late. Their bags were stowed and they were ready to go. As one Alexandria reporter put it, "having been weaned from the object they had in view in coming to America, their minds were so strongly fixed on HOME, that they could not be prevailed on to relinquish the idea of it."[41]

The *Confidence* and the returnees were like a slow-moving torpedo aimed across the ocean.[42] It would take a few weeks for the voyage back to Le Havre, and from there it was a few days to Paris. That would be enough to sink the Compagnie de Scioto. "In the month of July," Playfair would later tell Duer, "the affair was reduced to nothing by the return of the emigrants."[43]

When the Compagnie's sales cratered, its cash flow disappeared. That's when Playfair and Barlow started looking for an angel. That month they sold most of the potential profit of the company to a consortium led by Barth; his son, who had returned to France, handled the negotiations. Theodore Belote said Barlow's selling the Compagnie to Barth and his partners was "inexplicable."[44]

Hardly.

Barlow's reasoning is perfectly clear in a letter he wrote for Benjamin Walker on 21 December 1790 to explain the fiasco after Walker arrived in London; indeed, Belote published the letter with his monograph. Barlow said he worried sales would fall short and that he wouldn't be able to cover the European costs, the American costs, and the payments to Congress. He needed help, and turned to Barth, one of the Compagnie's biggest customers.

"I shall only say that the treaty out of which the transaction grew"—that is, the sale of the Compagnie—"was begun in March soon after the departure of the first ships," Barlow told Walker. "I feared the funds would not come from the direct sales so fast as would be requisite for the Engagements we might be under in America."

Barlow was panicking. The poet called it "a train of indescribable events which filled my mind with horror." So, he said, "In this state of doubt and anxiety" he looked for "a company who could advance some immediate funds to take and fulfill our engagements to the public and allow us a sure profit though a small one compared with what had been before calculated."[45]

Barlow had other reasons for "doubt and anxiety." Because the Compagnie couldn't pay Congress, the settlers couldn't get titles to their land. The settlers—and their families back home—did not take it well. The Revolution had made Frenchmen somewhat blasé when it came to violence. Barlow told Walker he was "many times threatened with assassination."[46]

And to complete his troubles, banks did not take it well when Barlow refused to honor the notes he had authorized Duer to send. Gouverneur

Morris noted in his diary that he had discovered Barlow had an outstanding bill of 100,000 pounds at the house of Phyn, Ellices, and Inglis.[47] Five days later Morris wrote that Inglis himself had complained.[48] In August, Morris's banking partner, William Constable, showed him a letter from another house, Le Couteulx et Cie; Barlow wasn't honoring bills drawn on him, either.[49] Word was getting around.

Morris's reaction: "This is vexatious."[50]

When Barlow saw him in November, Morris could tell the pressure was taking its toll. He wrote in his diary that Barlow called on him and, after a "lame stammering conversation," confessed that he had "no Means at Command to retire the Bill upon him," only saying something about an "Expectation to make future Sales."

Morris's reaction: "This Scioto Business will turn out very badly."[51]

Meanwhile, Duer was hearing these complaints on his side of the Atlantic. On 15 August 1790 Rochefontaine wrote him from Paris. The French officer, ever the diplomat, urged Duer to send "a gentleman from America more acquainted with business than Mr. Barlow to be ajoined to him & with Mr. Playfair." (Rochefontaine wanted to supplant Barlow *post haste*, but wanted Playfair to remain).[52]

Debt collectors and disgruntled returnees were chasing Playfair, too, though he had a somewhat different approach for dealing with them. The records of his encounters aren't in Morris's diary; they're in Paris police reports.

By the time he left Paris, Playfair would have more than a passing acquaintance with local law enforcement organizations. One report has a man and wife getting into a scuffle with Playfair and his servant, Étienne Lacroix, on the stairwell of his apartment. Playfair didn't dispute he owed the couple money; he just wasn't prepared to pay, at least not all, or at least not now. The parties resolved to arbitrate the dispute with *un gros bâton*.[53]

Lacroix denied trying to throw the couple off the stairs. Nevertheless, "big stick" was a common element in more than one of the reports. It's what two men said they encountered a few weeks later when they went to Playfair's apartment, hoping to serve papers—only to be met by a *bâton*-wielding Mary Playfair. They pounded on the door until the police arrived with additional officials in tow.[54]

The Compagnie was clearly a mess, and when Duer learned Barlow had sold off the profits from his speculation—the only reason Duer ever had any interest at all in the unsurveyed, unexplored wilderness in Ohio—it was the last straw. That's when the Scioto associates turned to Walker.

So who was Benjamin Walker?

Colonel Benjamin Walker was the consummate military staff officer. Born in England, he was within a few months of Barlow's age, five years older than Playfair. Walker emigrated to New York, went into business, and joined the Continental Army when the American Revolution began. Promoted rapidly, Walker eventually served under Major General Friedrich Wilhelm von Steuben, best known for making ragtag American soldiers drill like their European counterparts

Walker then became an aide-de-camp to George Washington, joining Washington's "military family," the youngish aides the childless Washington often treated as sons (Hamilton was also a member). Walker served Washington for almost two years, from January 1782 to December 1783, just after Yorktown, when Washington was laboring to hold his army together as peace talks dragged on. The idle soldiers were restless. Washington was a demanding boss. It was a tough job.[55]

About a third of Washington's military family went on to a senior command or political office; Walker was later elected to Congress. But that was in the future. In 1791 he was the Naval Officer for the Port of New York City. (The United States did not yet have a navy, so an Army colonel in the Revenue Cutter Service—predecessor to today's Coast Guard—directed the city's defenses against smugglers and raiders.)[56]

Duer needed someone to fix the mess in Paris; Walker was perfect. He was no-nonsense, orderly, and trustworthy. And he spoke French. But he was also a serving Army officer. So he needed approval from his chain of command to leave his post. Fortunately, his chain of command was remarkably short—and remarkably familiar with Scioto.

Walker's chain of command went as follows: Secretary of the Treasury, President of the United States.

The Scioto Company may have been a private venture—for that matter, the Compagnie du Scioto was a *foreign* private venture—but Hamilton and Washington apparently both thought fixing that mess in Paris was really important. If you've gotten this far, that would be no surprise, because you know that both had had a stake in the fiasco.

Washington acquiesced. His secretary, Tobias Lear, told Hamilton that Walker could go, noting for the record that "it is contrary to the general sentiment and wish of the President that any officers under the general government and particularly one of such importance as the naval officer of New York, shou'd be long absent from their trusts."[57] The new government might be only two years old, but officials had learned the art of covering their hindquarters.

Hamilton passed the word to Walker; he had twelve months.[58] And that was how Colonel Benjamin Walker, U.S. Army went to Paris.

But meanwhile Duer needed to vent. On 4 November he composed a letter to Barlow.

"I have received your several letter of the 23d June & July & 15th of August," Duer wrote. "The astonishment I am under from their contents can only be equaled by the distress you have subjected me to by the violation of your faith pledged to me as an honest man." For months Duer had been pressing Barlow to honor his drafts.

Duer went on. "The Reason you assign for not accepting, or paying the Bill you authorized to be drawn on you are by no means satisfactory." He told Barlow "it was certainly your duty to do in the most accurate manner" to tell him "what had been received previous to the arrival of the Bills, and how it had been disbursed." Furthermore, "general explanations & apologies are not sufficient." Duer was telling Barlow he was dishonest, incompetent or both.

"You desire me not to blame you for what you have done. This is impossible," Duer wrote. "I have staked the welfare of myself and a numerous family to support you in the enterprise you have undertaken." Duer claimed Barlow had pushed him to the "brink of ruin." He said Barlow had "always represented to me that the monies received on account of the sales were under your control," and, if "they were not they ought to have been."

As to the new partners he had brought in? Duer said, "I neither know Mr Playfair or any of the new Directors, in the business entrusted to you."[59]

This was the letter "upbraiding" Barlow that Dawes had mentioned. It's hard to understand why Belote did not include it in the selection of Gallipolis Papers he published. It's an exceptional specimen of late eighteenth century vituperation, and you won't find a more explicit statement on Barlow and the Scioto Affair by the usually reticent Duer.

Walker arrived sometime in early December. It seems to have gone pretty much as Dawes and Belote described: Barlow was relieved to see Walker; Walker found Barlow at wit's end and broke.[60]

Walker gave Barlow some money to tide him over, and had him write a statement documenting what had happened over the preceding two years. That was the 21 December letter in which Barlow cited "a train of indescribable events which filled my mind with horror" as his reason for selling the Compagnie.

Reading the letter, you get the feeling Barlow was like a suspect writing out a statement en route to a plea bargain. In his own hand, he admitted his failings, adding justifications and qualifications where possible to reduce the stain. Once that was on the record, Walker showed mercy, relieved him of responsibility, and put him on an allowance. Barlow glommed onto Walker—a financial lifeline who would ultimately front him a hundred guineas.[61]

As for Playfair: At first he was glad Walker arrived, telling Duer in his letter of 27 December that it was a "very lucky circumstance."[62] His view changed after he met the man. Playfair later described the encounter to Jefferson, saying that Walker "acted in the strangest Manner that Ever any man did," telling him that, as far as the Scioto project was concerned, "whether it fell or not was alike to him." Walker was prepared to shut the whole thing down.[63]

The worst part, Playfair told Jefferson, was that Walker "would not shew his Powers." Playfair wanted to see papers proving Walker was who he said he was and authorized to act. Walker blew him off. Playfair sent a similar account to Alexander Hamilton ten days later, recalling that Walker "Refused to shew his power of attorney or procuration" and would not "Enter with any degree of frankness or Candor into the Nature of the affair."[64]

Walker was playing it by the numbers, exactly as a good staff officer would. He had the papers Playfair wanted to see; he just felt no obligation to share them.[65]

You can imagine how Playfair saw the situation: Hostile American stranger—a serving U.S. Army officer and recent enemy combatant, no less—appears unannounced. He claims to represent Duer. He won't show his credentials. He demands information about the Compagnie. He says he doesn't care if the project lives or dies.

Playfair's French partners—including Jean-Jacques d'Eprémesnil—had entrusted thousands of livres with him. If Walker was unwilling to tell Playfair anything about what was going on in America, it's little wonder that Playfair was unwilling to tell Walker what was going on in France.

Walker, of course, had a different take. After meeting Barlow and Playfair he wrote Hamilton, saying that their affairs were "in so embarrassed a situation as to require my utmost exertions to save them from ruin." He thought the Compagnie—or at least the project—might still be saved, and was determined to give it a try. He told Hamilton that, "tho my leave of absence expires in March I will not desert their business till I have endeavoured to rescue it.[66]

Walker's worry was that the "honor and interest of the United States" was at stake, and that the government would "never get a farthing unless I can rescue the business from the miserable situation it is in." Yet, oddly, he was coming around to Playfair's thinking: There was no way a buyer would give an enormous lump sum to Congress for the land, so the only feasible approach was to sell it plot by plot, Frenchman by Frenchman.

Walker told Hamilton, "I cannot help thinking that Congress will find it their Interest to agree to some new arrangement in which the Company shall be bound to pay for the land only as they want it." Walker was even optimistic that, "Under such an arrangement I have no doubt great quantities may be well disposed off and thousands of Emigrants be sent over."[67]

But money wasn't the only problem; the Compagnie was in legal trouble, too. In January 1791 French authorities filed a judgment against Playfair and Barlow with the American consulate.[68] Walker spoke with Gouverneur Morris, who in a few months would replace Jefferson as minister. Morris claimed he had no advice to offer, "not knowing sufficiently all the facts."[69]

Morris was being, let us say, disingenuous. He had been following Barlow's adventure, step by step, for months. Would-be settlers came to him for advice—which he gave. He had even seen the plans for the Compagnie.[70]

"They shew me the *Projet*," Morris wrote in his diary, "and I am sorry to observe that those who embark will have too much Reason to complain of the Delusion." He resolved to "Say as little as possible on this Subject, but enough to save those who have asked my Advice, for that is certainly a Duty to them."[71]

Yet, contrary to what Dawes and Belote claimed, after the Scioto project went south, Playfair did not "disappear" from Paris. But Joel Barlow did.

There was a second letter that Newton did not find. Today it's in the Ohio Historical Society archives in Columbus. (This collection is entirely separate from the one at the Cincinnati Museum Center). The letter is in Playfair's handwriting; it's dated 18 March 1791.

The letter is from Playfair to Walker. The two men quarreled, but they continued to deal. Playfair told Walker that he had left a package at his lodgings with Ruth Barlow, who had come to France to join her husband.

Playfair said the package included a new letter that had arrived from Scioto. The letter said the settlement was doing well. If similar letters arrived—and Playfair thought they would—then they could resuscitate the project, using a "new system of billing" that would satisfy Walker, Duer, and the other associates. If that happened, Playfair wrote, it would be "necessary that Mr. Barlow returns, whether he acts in the affair or not."[72]

Apparently three Frenchmen were dunning Barlow. Playfair said he would "undertake to Retire the bills before he returns so that he will not have them to fear." Barlow's return was essential because "it must not be said," as Playfair put it, "that Mr. Wm. Duer's & the Company's agent has run away clandestinely to avoid paying a debt."[73]

This clarifies Playfair's comments to Jefferson and Hamilton the following week, when he told them "Mr. Barlow has gone off Privately in debt without telling any one." It also helps explain a comment in the letter Rochefontaine sent to Duer several months earlier. Rochefontaine warned Duer that Barlow—against his advice—was trying to raise funds "according to his own ideas," in a scheme that would cut Playfair out of the deal.

Rochefontaine thought Barlow's maneuvers were unfair and ill advised. Playfair "has been attached to Mr. Barlow's affairs from the beginning," he wrote, and was "exceeding good to carry on the details of the sales" and "extremely well acquainted with the usages of France and Paris."[74]

Whatever the specifics, it sounds like people were after Barlow, and it sounds like they were looking for their money.

There's no telling where Barlow might have been. According to the letter he sent Walker on 10 April, Barlow said his "personal situation" was "more distressing" than anything he had experienced before. But it has no return address.[75]

We do know that Barlow was somewhere in Paris on 3 May because a letter he sent Walker that day did have the city as the return address. Barlow recommended that Walker "suggest to the Secretary of the Treasury" that the government take over the project and sell the lands directly. This was the letter where he judged Playfair "imprudent & unfit."

Barlow told Walker that for "more than a year" he had distrusted Playfair and had been "determined to get rid of him in the best manner possible"—a claim completely at odds with letter he countersigned with Playfair six months earlier, assuring Duer the project was on course and the money under control. At least it was consistent with Rochefontaine's report to Duer that Barlow had been trying to squeeze out Playfair.[76]

The same day, Barlow also wrote Abraham Baldwin, his brother-in-law, complaining that he thought his letters were being intercepted: "Those same wicked folks who used to open my letters have taken upon them of late to stop them." That would have been no surprise; Barlow was a foreigner in the middle of a revolution, with creditors looking for him.

"The delays & inattentions in America have ruined, or at least fatally suspended the operations here for a long time," Barlow told Baldwin. "Whether they will ever recommence or not I cannot tell—if they do I shall have nothing to do with them," he wrote. "We shall soon go to England, wifey & I, & go to America if possible this summer."[77] By October Barlow was writing Baldwin from London.[78]

Walker posted notices across France saying Playfair was no longer authorized to sell Scioto land.[79] By then Duer had soured on Playfair; he wrote Walker that "what he had long feared appears to be realized" and that Barlow had allowed Playfair to take control of the money, and his "character is not to be trusted."[80]

Playfair countered Walker's handbills with his own.[81] Walker tried to restart the project with Rochefontaine and Duportail, cutting out Playfair; in his letter to Hamilton, Playfair cried foul and threatened to sue, saying he would "make my appeal to the Public & defend myself in the tribunals at the same time."[82]

It didn't matter. The venture was finished. Within months the Revolution would take an even more violent turn.

§ § §

The question historians invariably ask about the Scioto Affair is, "Where did the money go?"

Most likely the money "went" nowhere. There was no money; it was spent. The Compagnie was broke. The reason was right there in Barlow's report to Walker. As he deftly put it, it was the *increase of expenses* and the *diminution of sales.*[83]

The Compagnie had to house and feed the settlers while they were waiting to sail. The weather turned bad, delaying them several weeks. Costs mounted. Between the discounts and the expenses, the coffers were bare.

What's more, the government of the United States knew this. Playfair told the Secretary of the Treasury—Hamilton—that he had "contracted debts to support the thing." If the American insisted on killing the project, Playfair planned to use any Scioto money still sloshing around in Paris to pay his creditors—and the fee Barlow promised.[84]

It was all over—except for William Duer. Even today experts debate whether it was Scioto that put him over the edge.[85] Some believe Duer went bankrupt because of a classic bubble: a dip in stock prices caused a dip in Duer's net worth, so, as he put it to Hamilton, he "skipt payment" to his investors.[86]

Andrew Craigie, however, believed it was Scioto that broke the camel's back. Craigie (who also went bankrupt) wrote Walker in November 1790 after Barlow returned Duer's drafts unpaid. He told Walker that "Mr Duer is extremely mortified at having his Bills protested—indeed I don't know how he can manage to prevent the ruinous consequences of the disappointment."[87]

This would explain Duer's urgency in sending Walker to Paris. Craigie claimed in his letter to Walker that Duer "made very heavy advances on the strength of Mr Barlow's assurances." Whatever the trigger, and coincidence or not, when Duer went bust, New York banks began to fail.

Thus Playfair had a hand in sparking the Panic of 1792—the first American recession.

Everything began to unravel. Recall the Enron implosion of 2001 or the Lehman Brothers failure in 2008 and you get the picture. There was no shortage of investors ready to file suit. Then Duer's problem multiplied; the Comptroller of the Treasury was considering whether to prosecute him for misuse of government funds.[88]

Duer knew he had to get to Philadelphia to patch things together. He reached out to Hamilton for help. "For Heavens sake, Use for once your influence to defer this till my Arrival," Duer wrote on 1 March. He insisted, "My Public Transactions are not blended with my private affairs. Every Farthing will be Immediately accounted for. Of this I pledge my Honor."

"If a Suit should be bought on the Part of the Public," he pleaded, "under my present distrest Circumstances, My Ruin is complete."[89]

Three weeks later he was writing Hamilton from New York to say, "Your Letter of the 14th has been a Balm to my Soul, in the Midst of my affliction." He then turned fatalistic. "Whatever may happen, you shall never blush to Call me your Friend. Of this no more!"[90]

To his credit, Duer tried to take care of the Scioto settlers. He feared his erstwhile Ohio Company partners would put them off the land they thought they had bought. Or that the Indians would overrun them. He asked Hamilton to ensure "protection" for the "Flourishing Colony of Gallipolis." It was only fair, he pleaded. After all, Marietta—the Ohio Company's settlement—"Experienced Constantly the fostering Care of Government, as far as our military Force will admit of."[91]

Duer landed in debtor's prison two days later. His last act in the Scioto Affair was on 30 May, writing to Hamilton again, this time to ask him to look after the Scioto settlers' property claims. Duer saw how negotiations in Congress were shaping up. He feared the proposed donation tract would not include Gallipolis, leaving the settlers at the tender mercies of the Ohio Company. The only thing that could save them, Duer told Hamilton, was direct intervention by the President.

"If you think any thing which I under my present Circumstances can say, will have any Effect to defeat the Artful Designs of the Ohio Directors, let me know—and I will write such a Letter, as you may judge adviseable," he wrote. It didn't help; the settlers got land, but not the land they had settled.[92] Duer died seven years later in 1799, still in debtor's prison.

Eventually the settlers petitioned Congress for relief—resulting in the letter John Rome wrote to George Washington on 6 March 1793. Washington had Tobias Lear send a note to Jefferson that same day.[93]

The President—who had endorsed Barlow—asked the Secretary of State—who had endorsed the project—to "consider the enclosed letter, written in behalf of the French settlers at Gallipolis, and return an answer to the writer as favourable as circumstances can warrant." Duer was starting to make noises from debtor's prison, and Jefferson told his friend James Madison that, "if he is not relieved by certain persons, he will lay open to the world such a scene of villainy as will strike it with astonishment."[94]

And that swept the first great American political scandal under the rug for the next hundred years.

§ § §

Barlow's take on all this? He observed in his 17 October 1791 letter from London to Baldwin, "The purity of my intentions I believe will never be doubted by my acquaintances, & I expect no great difficulty in convincing them of the rational combination of the plan." He conceded, "How far others will trouble themselves to judge of it, I cannot tell."

"I have done with all ideas of pushing Scioto any farther," Barlow wrote, walking away from the effort—and a few hundred French emigrants who had been counting on him. He blamed the failure on logistics and weather.

"The delay of six months in getting to the land (which considering the season was the same as a year) may be considered as the sole cause of failure of the whole project," he wrote. "All the difficulties in Europe had their origin in that. Perhaps it could not have been avoided." In the mind of the ex-chaplain, the failure was an Act of God.

He closed, speculating where he might land: "Hamilton talked last year of establishing a land Office. I'll be hanged if they will find a better fellow to put at the head of it."[95]

Samuel Blackden tried to help Barlow after he quit the project. He wrote to Jefferson in May 1791, diplomatically telling Jefferson what he already knew. "Our inestimable friend Mr. Barlow," he wrote, "came to Europe upon a speculation which has not altogether succeeded." So, Blackden said, "he is at liberty to pursue any other object that presents."[96]

Blackden still believed in his friend, telling Jefferson that he had lived under the same roof with Barlow and that "a more worthy man does not exist." Blackden thought Barlow would be best suited to writing a history of the American Revolution.[97]

At one level, Barlow and Playfair look remarkably alike. Both were would-be writers, would-be entrepreneurs, and ambitious young men with prominent patrons. Both were partly driven by the same goal: bragging rights.

"I had raised the expectations of my friends as well as my own," Barlow said when he wrote Baldwin with his post mortem, "not so much on account of the expected profit as the pleasure of having accomplished a thing that I thought clever both on account of the difficulty & utility that hung about it."[98] Playfair was of the same mind; in his old age he told friends he would be remembered for the Scioto project long after his political writings were forgotten. He didn't realize how prophetic he would be.[99]

But at another level the two young men could not have been more different. It shows in their letters. Barlow was whiny, self-possessed, self-justifying, and self-indulgent. And once Walker arrived to shut down the project—and paid Barlow's bills—Barlow never lifted a finger for the settlers. He just sat down, wrote his confession, thanked Walker for not blaming him, and moved on.

Belote said Playfair wanted to "fill his pockets with French gold."[100] But the plan Playfair proposed to Jefferson, Hamilton, and Walker in March 1791 would have given all profits to the U.S. government. Even after it was clear there was no money to be made, even after Barlow bailed, and even after knocking heads with Walker, Playfair hung in there.

The main thing driving Playfair, it seems, was simply the challenge. When writers don't label him as an engineer, writer, or scoundrel, they sometimes call him an "adventurer." That seems accurate; his motivation, as often as not, was just the chance to do a big, audacious project—a Great Op.

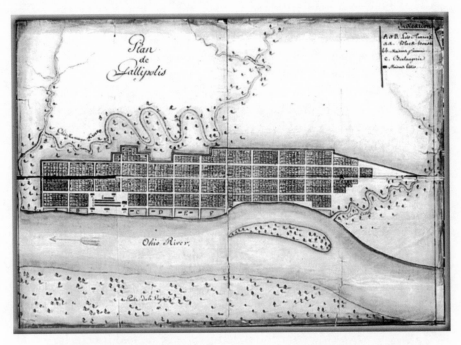

FIGURE 10: Plan of Gallipolis. D'Eprémesnil had great plans for the settlement on the Ohio. No maps or drawings seem to exist for Aigle-Lys, the seat for nobles that William and his brother James called "the American City." But this map of Gallipolis, the settlement for farmers and tradesmen, is from d'Eprémesnil's papers. Source: Archives nationales 158AP/12, reproduced with permission.

Meanwhile, Jean-Jacques d'Eprémesnil never gave up on his dream. In a folder among the d'Eprémesnil family papers at the Archives nationales, there is a color map depicting the "Plan de Gallipolis."[101] It shows neatly laid out lots along the bank of the Ohio, each with its own number. At one end is a town square. The project never ended; it just faded away. D'Eprémesnil was still receiving letters from would-be settlers years later.

It wouldn't have mattered. Lezay-Marnésia, settled for the time being in nearby Pittsburgh, wrote to d'Eprémesnil, pleading with him to flee "the horrible convulsions that inflict the agony on their dying homeland."[102] But d'Eprémesnil could never bear to leave Paris, let alone France. He stayed behind. Fortunately for him, so did Playfair.

6 Turning Point

William Playfair had left for Paris in June 1787. Twenty-two years later, in April 1809, he was back in London, with a prosecutor in the Court of King's Bench hot to put him in Newgate Prison. Supposedly Playfair was party to a swindle. Actually, he just got sucked into a scam that was already underway and didn't get clear quick enough. But splitting hairs was not going to help.

Even the threat of incarceration in nineteenth-century England could make a brave man tremble. Indeed, Newgate was specifically designed to scare the bejeezus out of anyone unfortunate enough to face the prospect of spending time there. A classic example of *L'Architecture Terrible* school of design, it combined narrow slit windows with massive brick walls, topped with ornamental touches portraying chains and irons.

About the only thing the facility lacked was Dantean signage over the entrance recommending an attitude adjustment by all those who entered. Today connoisseurs say the *Terrible* style aimed for "a sense of grandeur combined with strength, immensity, and terror."[1] It worked. Newgate was synonymous with the squalor of the imprisoned, the wails of the condemned, and the stench of the dead.

Playfair scrambled to find a rescuer. He sent a note on 10 April to Spencer Perceval "on a personal matter."[2] Perceval was Britain's Chancellor of the Exchequer. Six months later he would be Prime Minister.

John Charles Herries, Perceval's private secretary (and himself a future Chancellor of the Exchequer), responded the very next day. "I have just received your letter," he wrote from Downing Street, "and have lost no time in following Mr. Perceval's directions." Playfair liked young Herries; he thought he gave "great satisfaction to those with whom he transacts business."[3]

The Chancellor of the Exchequer, alas, couldn't help; apparently this needed to be handled lawyer-to-lawyer. "I am sorry that the answer which I am instructed to convey to you is not satisfactory to your wishes," Herries apologized. He advised Playfair to go to the Attorney General.[4]

So Playfair sent a note to the Attorney General. Sir Vicary Gibbs was known as "Vinegar Gibbs" for his acidic sense of humor, but Playfair thought highly of him as well—he called Gibbs "a profound and acute professional man." Gibbs and Perceval's solicitor at Treasury, H.C. Litchfield, both weighed in.[5]

But time was short. So Playfair wrote back to Herries to make sure everything was on track. His message for the Chancellor was curious. He underscored some phrases, as though he was trying to get Perceval to read between the lines. It went like this:[6]

> Sir,
>
> As tomorrow is the day I am to appear in Court and as I can only apply to it <u>by affidavit</u> in which it would be improper to allude to any service I have rendered to Government. I am taking the liberty of marking this circumstance hoping that it may by some means be made to operate in my Favour. <u>Tomorrow is the day</u>.
>
> I have the honour to be
>
>
>
> Sir
> Your obliged
> & obedient humble svt
> William Playfair
>
>

Playfair needed help, and fast. But why would it have been improper for him to allude to his government service? Something made him reluctant to explain the relationship in an affidavit—that is, in writing. For the record.

His allies came through. Gibbs and Litchfield vouched for him. The fix was in. But the deal went off the rails. One of the prosecution's attorneys spoke out at sentencing, insisting Playfair was guilty. He swayed the judge, who hit Playfair with a three-month sentence for "certain conspiracies and misdemeanors." Playfair was off to Newgate.[7]

Now writing from prison, Playfair sent another note to Perceval the next day.[8] He apologized that "I am compelled once more to trouble you."

"'Tho the Attorney General and Mr. Litchfield," Playfair wrote, "acted in a way for which I shall always be thankful," the plan had failed. As a result, he said, "relief now lies with His Majesty's ministers & I confess I expect it." Playfair reminded Perceval "I did not introduce into my affidavit the nature of the service I did last year else I shall have been I so suppose better treated."

Playfair went on, telling Perceval that "Lord Liverpool is the person I should regularly apply to I know & if you will not have the goodness to interfere I must apply to his Lordship for this is a horrible place." He also needed a doctor, "which I cannot have here."

Lord Liverpool was Robert Banks Jenkinson, the Home Secretary. Jenkinson would become Prime Minister three years later when a dissatisfied petitioner shot Perceval dead in the lobby of the House of Commons. Playfair and Liverpool also had a connection from two decades earlier: Jenkinson had witnessed the storming of the Bastille too, and like Playfair, the Revolution left him loathing the Jacobins.[9]

"I hope" Playfair repeated, "my attachment to government will operate in my favor. Had the Judge saw the case as the Attorney General did it would have been otherwise; & my condition as to health—the state of my affairs is miserable."

He added a postscript at the bottom: "A Release as Soon as Possible is My Request."

Playfair wrote Herries at the same time[10]—and again, four days later.[11] He told Herries said that he had also approached the Prince of Wales, "to whom I was well known." That was Prince Frederick Augustus, who would be named regent in 1811 after dementia left his father, King George III, unable to function. In 1820 he would be crowned George IV.

"I confess that I prefer owing the obligation to you, but," he wrote, "it is necessary I do what I can." Playfair was clearly having a bad time. "I shall take it as a great favor that my relief might be as early as possible as my health is bad I want need of a surgeon & there is no conveniency in this miserable place."[12]

A week later Playfair was still in Newgate. On 13 May he gave Herries a prison travelogue and a report on his health. (Remember, this is the private secretary to the Chancellor of the Exchequer of Great Britain.)

Playfair told Herries "the best appointments here are occupied by persons under sentence of Death and Transportation." Apparently prisoners were entitled to a few last rights before they received last rites. And, Playfair said, he was now having so much trouble with his legs he "cannot walk in the Court Yard." "I am in a situation that is really distressing," he said and that, while "I do not expect on that account to that I am to meet relief but I hope you will be so good as mention my case to his Lordship."[13]

It's not clear whether Playfair served out his full three-month sentence. Nevertheless the whole exchange begs a few questions.

How did a millwright-turned-mechanic-turned-speculator-turned-writer come full circle to land in Newgate?

Why would he expect the senior-most leaders of Great Britain—the Chancellor of the Exchequer, the Attorney General, the Home Secretary, never mind the Prince of Wales—to spring him?

What was this "attachment to government" that Playfair kept talking about? What was "the nature of the service?" And what was so sensitive about it that he couldn't describe it in writing?

Playfair could have cited quite a few things he did for the British government had he been less discrete. Here's a letter he sent to the Home Office four years earlier, on 28 October 1805:[14]

Sir:

The enclosed information may probably be of use—you may in consequence of it get some of the agents of government to watch at Hamburg & prevent the mischief from falling with full force. A Frenchman that was long in this country is the chief man & I believe they are at work in Holland—300,000 Florins were to be expended if necessary & there is no idea of passing the notes for gain.

I can tell you how I came to know this if it is thought a matter
worth attention.

I am sir,
Your obdt
& most humble servant
William Playfair

Hamburg was a neutral city in 1805 and a favored hangout for agents and
operators. Florins—Florentine gold coins—were still a common currency
unit on the Continent; today 300,000 florins would equal approximately forty
million dollars, depending on the current price of the metal. Playfair's enclosure, *Information Concerning a Plan Formed Against the Credit of the Bank of
England & Other Banks in Britain* read as follows: [15]

> The French Government has employed an agent who has pur-
> chased a bank note of every size under 500£ (& great numbers
> of small ones) together with a few notes of Each Private Banker
> in the Great Towne the Scotch Banker & with an Intention
> to copy them all as well as possible neither sparing pains nor
> Expence. When the notes are made they are not be negotiated
> by Private Channels as usual in cases of Forgery but they are
> to be Remitted over in letters to every commercial house to be
> dropt in the streets by agents sent over in that they are to be
> well initiated & every method taken to disperse them in order
> to occasion such a mistrust that the paper of this country may
> no longer serve as specie. The quantity intended to be made is
> immense & nothing of it is intended to be seen till it all comes
> at once or nearly at once by every means that can be devised.
>
> It will probably be two months or more before this attempt can
> be made & it will be partly by way of Hamburgh.

Playfair knew his tradecraft; he kept the sensitive information separate, in
a no-name, blind memo. After all, he had been assisting British leaders in
a variety of covert and clandestine operations for more than a decade. On
24 October 1795, for example, he delivered a package to William Windham, Britain's Secretary at War. In his cover letter, Playfair wrote that he had

enclosed "the printed prospectus of the periodical work of which I spoke to you and which you desired me to send when I had the honor of seeing you."

The "periodical" was black propaganda—a publication without attribution, or at least without acknowledgement that the government was bankrolling it. The cover said only that "This work is compiled and collected by several Gentlemen, who (having resided long on the Continent of Europe) have established a very extensive correspondence, and who have the means of receiving the most authentic information on every occasion." The page proofs give a flavor of its message:[16]

> THE REVOLUTIONARY MAGAZINE will contain many very curious and interesting Anecdotes and Details of the Treatment of Prisoners—of the *Wives and Daughters of accused Persons—Gallantries and Cruelties of the National Commissioners in the several Departments of France;* many strange facts relative to *the Revolution, the Revolutionary Army,* &c. &c.

By eighteenth century standards, this bordered on the lurid. But that's how information operations work. First you get the target's attention, and then you slip in the message. As Playfair put it in his proposal:[17]

> To act upon the minds of the people at large a work must be Entertaining, Periodical, & Cheap. Men are found to read with great eagerness & avidity relations of what is cruel or criminal, so that by giving them every with something of this sort with very little reasoning or argument but now & then with observations on the immediate & necessary connection between mistaken principles & the unhappy consequences it might be expected that a universal hatres & fear of revolutions would be inspired into the people in both Town & Country.

Playfair went on to explain how he planned to produce, distribute, and promote the magazine and how much it would cost. Then, in his cover letter, Playfair shifted gears from black propaganda to espionage. He told Windham about a new intelligence source he planned to meet, and provided contact information for a member of the royalist resistance:[18]

Mons. Messin from Paris (of whom I spoke to you) is still I
believe in town tho' I have not seen him. He is to be heard of at
the House of Mademoiselle Berthia, milliner to the Queen of
France. If I can meet with him and pass an Evening I will, for
he can really give more information about Paris than any person
who has resided there as a stranger, or not in trade. He has seen
all [parties?] and spoke to all by keeping a large [unintelligible]
in and is himself an intelligent and clever man.

The Abbe de Calonne lives at 112 Sloan Street near Chelsea
under the name of M Montague.

> I have the honor to be with request for
> Your obedient and very humble servant,
> William Playfair

"Mons. Messin" was most likely Jean-Pierre Messin, jeweler and long-time
collaborator in haute couture to Marie-Jeanne Rose Bertin—"Mademoiselle Berthia"—France's celebrity dressmaker. Besides Marie Antoinette,
Bertin also dressed the queens of three or four other courts and dozens of
lesser ladies, traveling across Europe. For Playfair, Messin was a conduit for
information from denied territory; his note doesn't say whether Messin was
witting.[19]

Meanwhile, if the Abbé de Calonne sounds familiar, he should; he was
the court insider Boulton and Watt hoped would wire their deal to replace
the Machine de Marly with a steam engine. He left France after his brother's falling out with Louis XVI in 1787. By 1789 both were living in exile in
England. Playfair apparently knew where the Abbé could be reached—and
his pseudonym.

One other thing about the Abbé de Calonne: today he is known as a
grand fabricateur de faux assignats for counterfeiting French currency after he
fled to Coblentz, the ancient city on the Rhine that became a royalist base on
the Continent.[20]

Another letter from Playfair appears in Windham's files dated three
months later. Britain feared a slave rebellion in Grenada almost as much as
France feared a slave rebellion in Saint-Domingue—today, Haiti. The two
sugar colonies produced fortunes feeding Europe's sweet tooth. Naturally,

each tried to stir up unrest in the other's turf. Playfair offered to bring a contact with firsthand knowledge of the region to the secretary's chambers:[21]

Sir,

I have with this taken the liberty of sending you a Book but little known written by a Mr. Turnbull of Grenada who is now in London and is going out there again in a month or two.

As he has grown old in that Island & from several conversation I have had with him seemed to have good news about the method of preventing the slaves from being led to revolt by the acclamations of the French it occurred to me that perhaps you might wish to speak with such a man before his return. If so I shall bring him to visit on you when you please.

As tomorrow is the End of the week if I am not favoured by hearing from you I shall take the liberty of calling.

I am with respect
Sir your most obedn't and obliged
Humble servant
William Playfair.
Friday 22 January 1796

Apparently Playfair could just stop by Windham's office. The two men had a friendly relationship, at least within the formality and class-consciousness of Georgian England. Playfair later wrote Windham, "I confess your conduct towards me has been such that I am inclined to let no occasion slip of shewing my gratitude." Both had initially favored the French Revolution; both were alarmed and disgusted when it degenerated into mob violence.[22]

Playfair was close enough to Windham to join in private meetings in his office with French émigré leaders. "I met Cazalès there the other morning," he recounted in a March 1796 letter to a British colonel.[23]

That was Jacques Antoine Marie de Cazalès, a noble from southern France. He was part of Britain's clandestine connections on the Continent. About Playfair's age, Cazalès served in the French army as a cavalry officer and represented the Second Estate at the Estates General. He later won election to the National Constituent Assembly and worked closely with his fellow royalists like—Jean-Jacques Duval d'Eprémesnil and Jean de Batz.[24]

Cazalès had traveled often to Britain and was well connected. He was especially close to Edmund Burke; the two met through Burke's son, Richard. He got out of Paris in time to miss the Reign of Terror and set himself up in England, using his knowledge of France to assist the British in war planning. Cazalès later moved to Spain to run agents for the British from Madrid, then moved to Switzerland, before finally returning to France in 1803.[25]

Cazalès, like Batz, would later be accused as a British "spy," though technically they were both more like "liaisons" representing the royalists' intelligence organizations. Both had their own networks, both had their own objectives, and both cooperated with the British—as it served their interests.

Playfair sized up the relationships. He worried that Windham might get carried away with the cloak-and-dagger game. "I believe he is misinformed & misled by the emigrants," he told the colonel, observing that Cazalès' "warmth & energy added to that of Mr. W is like throwing oil on fire."[26]

§ § §

In addition to being an engineer, inventor, entrepreneur, economist, and writer, William Playfair was an intelligence officer. Or at least he would have been if such a position had existed at the time. But that would have meant Britain had an intelligence service, which it did not.

One of the great myths of Western civilization is that of a British secret service dating from the time of Queen Elizabeth. According to this myth, Sir Francis Walsingham founded the service, which expanded in size and influence step-by-secret-step with the Empire. For centuries, it ensured British interests were served by deftly shaping world events. It was so deft that it was nigh impossible to find any evidence it existed.

That's precisely because it was *only* a myth. In 2002 Britain's Security Service (better known as MI5) gave University of Cambridge professor Christopher Andrew access to its archives to write an authorized history. According his book, *Defend the Realm,* the British government did not establish MI5 until 1909, along with its foreign intelligence counterpart, the Secret Intelligence Service (otherwise known as MI6) at about the same time.[27]

Some scholars—justly respected scholars, mind you—say this is a crock. They document all the reporting, clandestine operations, skullduggery, and espionage that Britain carried out for centuries before that. If it had no intelligence service, they ask, who was doing all that stuff?[28]

That's the point. In eighteenth-century Britain the term "secret service" meant literally that: a service provided to His Majesty's government, secretly. Ministers had funds for such operations, which were almost entirely ad hoc.[29] The United States used a similar arrangement; upon taking office, President Washington established a line for secret services that comprised about ten percent of the total federal budget. Thomas Jefferson drew on it a few years later as President to pay for one of America's first covert operations—an émigré army tasked with toppling the regime in Tripoli.[30]

British intelligence in the late 1700s wasn't just piecemeal and spur of the moment; it was temporary and disposable. Britain stood up operations as needed and wound them down when finished.[31] Britain's "clandestine services" were in actuality just the military officers, diplomats, and game civilians who left their regular jobs for a while, did their duty, and then faded back into their lives after it was all over. With any luck, their jobs would still be there and their patrons would remember their service. Unfortunately, it did not always work out that way.

For example: William Wickham.

Wickham was perhaps the most successful intelligence officer Britain had at the time. The son of an army colonel, he attended Harrow and Oxford, and became friends with Charles Abbot and William Wyndham Grenville (not to be confused with William Windham, his cousin). Abbott would become a barrister and judge; Grenville would inherit his family's peerage as Lord Grenville and serve as Home Secretary, Foreign Secretary, and, later, Prime Minister.

After Oxford, Wickham studied law in Geneva. Since he was well connected and knew Switzerland, it was natural for Grenville to ask him in 1793 to serve as a diplomat to Berne. But that was only a cover. Wickham's real mission was to organize a secret network of "foreign correspondents"—that is, intelligence assets.[32] (Today a "foreign correspondent" is a news reporter, a splendid linguistic link that illustrates the historical overlap—and tension—between intelligence and journalism.)

Wickham eventually became ambassador to Switzerland, all while functioning as spymaster. He was so successful that the French government pressured the Swiss to send him home in 1798. Wickham held various home-based assignments, did another mission on the Continent from 1799 to 1801, and then returned to London. He resigned, exhausted, in 1804.[33]

Expecting a pension of £1,800 a year, Wickham was surprised when he was told he was due just £1,200. At least it was better than the £600 the government offered him after the Swiss had declared him *persona non grata* and booted him out of Berne.

Why did the government stiff Wickham? Mainly it was the doings of lower-level bureaucracy, compounded by administrative glitch. As he moved from one post to another—partly to maintain cover, partly because there was no official billet designated for espionage—he fell between the organizational cracks.

"I have been treated unkindly and unhandsomely by a government which I have served faithfully, zealously, and with affection," he wrote Abbott. "I shall do my best so as to manage matters as that I might not be exposed to a similar disappointment in the future," he declared, with some bitterness.[34]

Wickham should have seen it coming; "I can never become a rich man by honest means," he had once told another classmate, and therefore it would be necessary for him "to live and die poor."[35] Wickham served a few unsatisfying years in Parliament, and then quietly lived out his remaining three decades. (At least that's what they say; you never know what you never know.)[36]

An especially valuable officer might receive a sinecure for some especially valuable service. But that took an act of Parliament, or, at least a cabinet decision. Playfair had an acquaintance who found that path to wealth and security: William Cope.[37]

Around 1791 Irish nationalists, inspired by the American and French revolutions, formed the Society of United Irishmen, sort of an Irish version of the Sons of Liberty. When the French Revolution turned radical and France declared war, British leaders cracked down and the society went underground. By the end of the decade it was ready to launch a revolt. It hoped to seize Dublin and then push out to the countryside.

Cope, a well-known Dublin merchant, favored union with Britain, but kept his views to himself. Thomas Reynolds, a clothier, was a long-time acquaintance. He had dabbled with the United Irishman in its early days and still knew many of its members. In February 1798, Cope and Reynolds took a business trip together to Ardglass. Cope chatted him up. Then he went to the authorities and offered to recruit Reynolds as a spy.[38]

Cope played Reynolds brilliantly. First he compromised him with loans he could not afford. Then Cope offered to excuse the loans in exchange for information on the United Irishmen. Reynolds balked; the authorities put him in prison as a debtor. Reynolds then agreed to cooperate. Reynolds and Cope both received rewards, pensions, and, in Reynolds' case, relocation to England. The British crushed the rebels; it was a grisly affair and forms part of Irish lore even today.[39]

Playfair recalled Cope received an annual pension of £1,000 for his espionage work because "his information was correct and his conduct honourable."[40] Adjusted for inflation and currency conversion, today that would be somewhere in the neighborhood of $40,000 a year.[41] Playfair wished he had done so well. His friends would tell obituary writers Playfair echoed Wickham's complaints in his last years.

Managing an intelligence career in the late 1700s was nearly as risky as running an operation. An officer had to navigate bureaucratic whitewater and political crosscurrents. If his patrons lost office, lost interest, or died, he could be left high and dry.

§ § §

France's perennial problem was its debt. After Louis accepted the National Constituent Assembly in the summer of 1789, it became the Assembly's problem, too. Charles Maurice de Talleyrand-Périgord thought he had the solution.

Talleyrand, son of a noble family, entered the priesthood instead of the army after a childhood fall left him crippled. He represented the First Estate when the Estates General convened, but sat with the Third Estate when its delegates declared themselves the National Assembly.[42]

Talleyrand proposed to seize ecclesiastical properties and sell them off to pay the nation's debt. (This was one of several deeds that got Talleyrand excommunicated.) The Catholic Church owned about six percent of all the land in France—about 2.5 billion livres worth. On 2 November 1789 the Assembly adopted the proposal and issued the required decree.[43]

Now the question was, how to tap the land's value? Some Assembly members offered a plan: issue notes "assigned" to the confiscated land—*assignats*. Payees could hold the notes, trade the notes, or cash them in for land. As the notes were cashed, the government would destroy them, and everything would balance.[44]

One member pushing the idea was…Jean de Batz, advised by Étienne Clavière. Batz had got himself elected as a deputy representing the Second Estate, and became a member of the National Assembly after the estates merged. When the Assembly turned to dealing with the debt, Batz won an appointment to its Liquidation Committee, tasked with raising funds by selling off government assets.[45]

Batz took to politics like a natural; he was in his element. Most nobles knew only the genteel give-and-take of soft salon conversation; the earthier Gascon businessman understood the cutthroat sarcasm, couched innuendo, and feigned outrage that defined debate in the Assembly. He trained his fellow nobles for legislative combat. He had them rehearse in front of him, sparring like boxers, practicing to remain cool when attacked, and rally with counterargument.[46]

Batz's background in finance make him a logical choice for the Liquidation Committee. After all, he traveled to London, had friends like Clavière, and had got rich playing the Paris Bourse. The future of the constitutional monarchy seemed to depend on his success in selling national assets and arranging loans. His colleagues were apt to overlook the details.[47]

One detail was… a slush fund for the king.

When Batz negotiated financing for the debt, he added provisions to skim part of the cash flow. He also built personal relationships with foreign officials across Europe. The slush fund and those relationships would serve Batz later.[48]

Clavière and Batz had a complex relationship, and it became even more complex as the Revolution unfolded. Batz had opened doors in the Old Regime for Clavière, and Clavière and Batz had made mountains of money together. When Clavière became finance minister, he provided Batz the passports he needed to travel abroad.[49]

But Clavière was a staunch Swiss Protestant republican; Batz was a faithful French Catholic royalist. Within three years, the king would be dead— with Clavière signing the death warrant and loaning his carriage to take Louis to the scaffold. Batz, on the other hand, would support Breteuil in the royalist opposition—secretly, even as he continued to work with Clavière to get loans from foreign bankers.[50]

That was in the future. For now Batz and Clavière had a more straight-forward task: Set up the plan for the assignats, and sell the idea to the French public. It was a tough one; France had experience with paper currency—most of it bad. Seven decades earlier Scottish financier had John Law convinced French officials to issue notes backed by its colonial holdings along the Mississippi River. The ensuing land bubble and bust vaporized the savings of thousands.

Enter William Playfair.

At about the time he was assembling the Scioto settlers at Le Havre, Playfair was also writing a seventeen-page pamphlet to support the proposal to issue assignats: *Qu'est-ce que le papier-monnoie?* In "What Is Paper Money?" Playfair argued French officials had no alternative, and the scheme could work if they kept to their plan: limit the number of notes issued, and destroy them when holders exchanged them for land.[51]

They did neither.

It started off well enough. In January 1790 French authorities issued 800 million livres in large denomination, investment-style notes. But Frenchmen then began hoarding silver and gold—as people often do when facing riots, war, and political chaos. So merchants started accepting assignats; they had no alternative.

In April the Assembly, bowing to reality, decreed assignats "legal tender between all persons in all parts of the kingdom." By September authorities were issuing assignats in smaller denominations and no longer paying interest. That made the notes a true currency, not just tradable bonds.[52]

France had created—without intending, let alone planning—the first national system for fiat money. Its notes possessed value purely because the government said so; it could increase or shrink the money supply at will, by either destroying notes or simply letting the printing presses run for a bit longer.

Playfair still thought it could work, and penned a follow-up pamphlet: *Lettre II d'un Anglais a un Français sur les assignats.* In *Letter II from an Englishman to a Frenchman about the Assignats,* Playfair doubled down on his earlier argument: France needed the assignats to keep its economy running. "If there is no trade," he wrote, "no taxes will be paid." And if the economy failed, so would the government.[53]

Yet issues remained, he said.

FIGURE 11: An early five hundred-livre assignat, issued under the April and December 1790 decrees. This one's real. Source: Bank of France via Wikimedia Commons.

The Assembly had authorized assignats in smaller denominations, easier for the average shopper to use. That worried Playfair. If workers and the poor began to depend on small notes and they lost value, the "results could take a very serious turn."[54] Indeed.

Better, Playfair said, to leave the issuance of small notes to municipalities; people knew their local officials. Or leave it to trusted individuals in the community.

He had a plan.

§ § §

Sometime in early 1791 Playfair's chief clerk, Soissons, brought him a prospectus from two young Frenchmen hoping to set up a trading company: a "M. Protot" and a "M. Guillaume." Playfair still had his hands full with Benjamin Walker, Scioto returnees, irate families whose relatives had disappeared into the Ohio wilderness, and the Paris police. But he was willing to give the proposal a look.[55]

Playfair had never heard of the pair, and apparently neither had anyone else. They planned to raise four million francs in working capital, purchase a shipment of goods, auction them off, and then divide the profits with their investors. Playfair had seen such trading companies in London and was sure it was easy money. So when Protot and Guillaume announced a meeting inviting potential investors, Playfair made a point to attend.

But when he arrived the only person he recognized was Étienne Delessert. He settled into the bench his friend had staked out and began to make conversation. Delessert thought the two entrepreneurs had a good plan, but in France, what you knew was a lot less important than whom you knew. All business depended on connections.

"Men in credit would find persons to advance money on the most empty schemes provided they were in any way plausible," Delessert said, but even the best plans in "bad hands" failed. Within a year Delessert would be foreign minister, hectored by Brissot for opposing his war with Europe.[56]

Protot came off as a full-of-himself businessman; Guillaume was a lawyer. Playfair thought they talked a good game. So he offered some friendly advice: They were asking for twenty times the money they really needed. If they were serious, he said, ask investors for less, get the venture off the ground, and, if they needed more, go back to the investors and hit them up again.

The two admitted they were talking big bucks (or large livres) mainly to show they were serious. "In Paris, it was necessary to make appearances and to talk millions," Playfair later recalled. Otherwise "you could not get men who had money to embark on a business."

Playfair didn't disagree; he just thought Protot and Guillaume were overdoing it. One the other hand, he didn't think it was his business to tell them how to run their business, either. He told the two to get back to him when they were ready to launch. If they looked like they were going to make a go of it, he'd take a tranche.

Protot and Guillaume occasionally stopped by, though nothing came of the visits. Then, in March 1791 Playfair was out for dinner and decided on the spur of the moment to check in the two. He found Protot in his office; the young man was desolate. It turned out his braggadocio had been a facade. Now he had a meeting with a potential prospect but didn't even have the money to hire a carriage to get there.[57]

Playfair took pity on the young man—with the kind of help a Sand Hill Road venture capitalist might offer to a cash-strapped Silicon Valley entre-preneur today—and loaned him one hundred Louis in exchange for twenty-five shares in the venture. It's not clear exactly what that amounted to, but Playfair described it as a "usurious bargain," and since he wrote the book on usury—literally—one can assume he spoke with some authority.[58]

Then Protot and Guillaume disappeared. A few months later Playfair heard the two had founded a bank and were making money hand over fist. Playfair tracked down Protot to demand his payout; Protot told him to pound sand. Playfair went to the notary who had certified the deal; he backed Play-fair—after Playfair threatened to go public and expose everyone involved. Playfair managed to salvage 8,000 livres, a third of the return he was due, and everyone went their own way.

It wasn't until three years later that Playfair, back in London, happened to run into Guillaume. Then he learned what had really happened.

Protot and Guillaume didn't buy merchandise with the hundred Louis that Playfair loaned them. Instead, they rented a cabriolet—which they then drove to a tailor. The tailor, assuming anyone riding in such a fine carriage must be creditworthy, outfitted the two on spec. Now sporting the clothes and accessories of gentlemen, they wrangled money to lease space in Paris's high-rent district. They were in business.

Of course, they still needed to capitalize their trading company. They solved that problem with the simple expedient of removing the mirrors in their new offices, telling anyone who asked that they were remodeling. Then they sold the mirrors, used the proceeds to buy their merchandise, and held their auction.

The bank was an accident. Assignats still came only in large denominations, and no one in his right mind would make change with coin; the notes were already losing value. Besides, as assignats depreciated, everyone began hoarding their gold and silver. So Protot and Guillaume began giving customers promissory notes—IOUs—as change.

At first they drafted the IOUs by hand. That proved tedious, however, so they had decks of chits printed with an amount owed. People began exchanging the chits like money; they were desperate for some kind of currency to use, and the notes fit the bill (so to speak).

The demand for the notes grew—and grew. So Protot and Guillaume printed more—and more. The two literally *were* making money hand over fist.

Before they knew it, Protot and Guillaume were in the banking business. Playfair claimed that within nine months they were employing two hundred clerks. On an average day they were exchanging 72,000 livres in assignats for their homebrew currency.

Playfair said the scheme collapsed in May 1792 when a third associate stole somewhere around two million livres from the bank and fled to Germany. Guillaume told Playfair that he and Protot landed in jail because they made the mistake of reporting their partner to the local authorities instead of just swallowing the loss.

When word of the embezzlement got out, depositors got worried they wouldn't be able to redeem their notes. That threatened a "public commotion," as Playfair put it. The "municipality was "obliged to step in" and take charge. At least, that's the story Playfair recalled years later in his never-published memoirs.

The tale sounds fantastical. But it's true, or at least mainly true, and there's proof: It turns out you can find some of those promissory notes even today, signed "Protot, Administrateur" and "Guillaume, Directeur." Here's a picture of one:[59]

FIGURE 12: One of the notes Protot and Guillaume issued from their *Maison de Secours*. Assignats came only in large denominations, so the two young entrepreneurs began to write individual IOUs to make change. Later they printed notes indicating the amount owed—like this one, for forty sols. Soon enough they found themselves in the banking business. Playfair thought it was a great idea—and later adopted the scheme for his own Bank of Assignats, which led to other things. Source: Delcampe, reproduced with permission.

Yet though it's a true story, Guillaume wasn't telling Playfair the whole story. Records show that the bank Guillaume set up with Protot, the *Maison de Secours*, or "House of Relief," imploded after issuing notes totaling 23 million livres.[60]

There was little financial regulation in France. There were no reserve requirements. Customers didn't care; they just wanted the convenience of small change. So Protot and Guillaume were free to print as many notes as they wished—which they did. There were some suspicions; in October, posters appeared in Paris: *Qu'est-ce que la Maison de Secours, rue des Filles-Saint-Thomas, et de qui elle composee?*[61] No matter; as long as everyone accepted the chits and no one asked to redeem them, everything was fine.

Inevitably, something (no one knows what, and it doesn't matter) led someone (no one knows who, and that doesn't matter, either) to cash his notes. Or, more precisely, to try to cash them.

With little real money on hand, Protot and Guillaume were stuck. Word got out that the Maison might have trouble honoring withdrawal requests. That, in turn, triggered a full-scale bank run. Customers of the House of Relief began demanding real relief, and authorities had to pony up millions of livres to cover depositors' losses—which explains what happened to Protot and Guillaume. They got tossed in the clink for fraud.

Prison in Paris was an especially bad place to be when the September Massacres broke out a few months later. After overthrowing the king in August, the republicans rounded up clergymen who refused to swear allegiance to the new constitution, along with all the royalist sympathizers they could find. They threw them in jail. Then they turned the *sans-culottes* on them.

Historians say the *sans-culottes* feared the prisoners might form a fifth column; the Prussians had just defeated the French army at Verdun and little stood between them and Paris except rolling hills and open road. But it might have been simply that those who did not wear knee britches considered it open season on those who did. The mobs killed over a thousand prisoners. Protot died. Guillaume escaped.[62]

Protot and Guillaume may have had a bad sense of timing, but Playfair must have thought they were on to something, because it was around this time he opened his own Bank of Assignats. Records are even scantier than for the *Maison de Secours*, but it seems Playfair was offering the same deal: exchange assignats in livres for his own one-franc, half-franc, and quarter-franc notes.[63]

Others soon followed suit. "The creation of assignats having in a very short space of time driven all gold and silver coin out of the ordinary circulation," Playfair later wrote, "several public bodies and some private Compagnie had circulated promissory notes for small sums, which notes were in fact found admirably to answer the purpose." He didn't mention he was running one of them.[64]

These "public bodies and private Compagnie" caught the attention of the government, which, always desperate for money, wanted the business for its own. The Assembly thus "declared such emissions unlawful, forbid their continuance, and authorised the civil magistrates to sequestrate for the public security the properties for such compagnies."[65]

But the plan backfired. Playfair recalled the "first consequence of this arbitrary and rash proceeding was that one of these banks stop't payment two days after; and the Assembly, in order to avoid an insurrection, was obliged to grant three million livres of the public money to pay the bills in circulation." In France, printing money was a really lucrative business.[66]

So Playfair was a participant in France's paper money scheme from the beginning. Playfair's Bank of Assignats gave him first-hand experience in French finance. It also happened to give him first-hand experience in making banknotes.

§ § §

At about the time Playfair was learning how to be a banker, a few blocks away James Watt, Junior was taking toddler steps as a revolutionary. On 16 April 1792 he delivered a speech to the Jacobin Club. "We feel a sincere satisfaction," Junior said, "in communicating to you the resolution by which our Brethren of the Constitutional Society of Manchester have appointed us their Deputies to the Patriotic Societies of France."

"Men who feel strongly interblend in your cause," Junior said, as it is "the cause not merely of the French, but of all Mankind." Thus he proposed "an amicable communication and correspondence" with his hosts leading to a "federation amongst the Patriotic Societies of Europe, having for its object the fraternal union of all Men."[67]

Thomas Cooper composed the speech; Junior charged him for the translation and printing. They distributed a thousand copies.[68]

Junior had arrived in Paris the month before with Cooper, a Manchester lawyer about his age. Cooper later insisted Junior was in Paris merely to sell fabrics for the Walker brothers. He, Cooper, was accompanying him "as a relaxation from a long-continued application to business." Cooper denied they had a "purpose of establishing any political Correspondence whatever."[69]

That was a lie.

Weeks after arriving in Paris, Junior wrote his father privately, "it was upon the motion of Mr. Walker that I was appointed delegate" of the Manchester Constitutional Society, "and therefore without some strong reason I ought not to have refused it."

Yes, Junior had legitimate business in Paris: collecting payments for the Walkers and selling James Watt's copying machines. But Junior and Cooper were so deeply enmeshed in the Manchester Constitutional Society that they could not have avoided politics even if they had wanted—and they did not.[70]

"We knew very well that the measures we were about to take would not be agreeable either to the Ministry or to Opposition," Junior admitted to his father. But, Junior went on, "our intention was not to please any Party." Indeed, they were "equally indifferent about their anger or approbation" because they were serving a higher purpose, "laying the foundation of a general alliance amongst the patriotic Societies of Europe to fix a barrier against the intrigues of Ministers & Kings and to establish the peace & happiness of nations."[71]

A few weeks later, on 30 April 1792, Edmund Burke denounced both Junior and Cooper in the House of Commons. He read quotes from their speech.[72]

And Junior's reaction? He reveled in the attention. "I have seen Burke's sortie against Mr. Cooper, Mr. Walker, & myself," he wrote his father, and for giving "a degree of publicity to our actions, which we could never have otherwise attained I thank them."[73]

Nonetheless, Junior was putting his father in a tough spot. Boulton & Watt was in a bitter patent fight with its competitors; the company needed all the support it could get in Parliament.

No problem, Junior said. "Bad as my opinion of governments & ministers in general is," he wrote his father on 5 May, "I can scarcely think them so depraved as to revenge the sins of the Child upon the Father." He assured his father, "They will find that I act independent of you and am connected with Mr. Walker," and that "alone will be sufficient to exculpate you."[74]

You can imagine Watt's reaction when he read that one. Naïve. Legalistic. Clueless. Whatever your descriptor, Junior was admitting, in his own hand, that he was indeed on a political mission. Keep in mind British authorities intercepted Channel mail—precisely because they were watching for radicals and subversives.[75]

The Jacobin Club ought to look familiar; it was a forerunner of today's transnational political parties and activist organizations. Inside the Assembly, the Jacobin Club pushed legislation. Outside the Assembly, it mobilized to win elections. On the street, it organized demonstrations.

"As these clubs were therefore so numerous, and carried on a very active and vigorous correspondence; and as they consisted of members actuated with one spirit, there was no difficulty of regulating almost all public affairs," Playfair observed, duly impressed.

"The club in Paris," Playfair estimated, "corresponded directly with eleven hundred, and upwards, of these societies," each of which had "circles of clubs in inferior towns and villages." And, "when they could not regulate, they could counteract any measure," and "whom they could not counteract they could denounce."[76]

Playfair was also getting drawn into the Revolution—but on the other side. A month after Junior addressed the Jacobins, he tried to explain the situation in France to his fellow Englishmen. In May 1792 Playfair—still in Paris, still trying to save the Scioto project, and still wheeling and dealing —he somehow found time to publish *A Letter to the People of England on the Revolution in France*.

Playfair, like many Britons, favored the French Revolution at first, but was disappointed. He wanted reform—just not the kind of reform he was seeing. He thought the French Revolution went too fast, too far, and off course. If only "they had known where to stop," he wrote.[77]

The Jacobins alarmed Playfair. It was their grand designs and pretentions toward perfection. Ideally, he said, a nation's constitution "consists of a few immutable truths."[78] The National Assembly drafted one that was "philo-sophical" and "abstract." Its goal was equality, so "a foundation was laid for endless error."[79] The French, he claimed, were attempting too "great an experiment at the risqué and expenses of their fellow citizens."[80]

The Jacobin Club is "not only inconsistent with, but diametrically oppo-site to a free Government," Playfair said, because "it enables the minority to control and guide the majority."[81] The Jacobins, furthermore, "aim at nothing else than the destruction of the peace, prosperity, & political importance of other Nations."[82]

He added, taking aim at the likes of Cooper and Junior, that anyone "who by their writing or their clubs endevour to spread the French system in England" or "associate for the purpose either directly or indirectly changing the English Government," are but "*traitors to their country.*"[83]

§§§

In June 1791, Louis and the royal family were caught trying to flee to the Austrian Netherlands—what became known as the "Flight to Varennes." The king never really accepted reform, and hoped his fellow monarchs would quash the Revolution. Now he was exposed; his popularity never recovered. A month later republicans organized a rally on the Champ de Mars. The demand of their petition: abolish the monarchy. City authorities called in the National Guard when the gathering became disorderly (just how disorderly has been debated for two hundred years).

La Garde nationale evolved from the militia Parisians organized during the weeks before the storming of the Bastille. Unlike the army, which was manned largely with German and Swiss mercenaries, the National Guard drew on French shopkeepers, tradesman, and, as the Assembly put it, "active citizens." Lafayette assumed command.

It was the National Guard that first began wearing tricolor cockades; Lafayette added royal white to the red-and-blue colors of Paris; it lives on today in the French national flag. For able Frenchmen of a patriotic bent, the National Guard was an opportunity to wear a uniform and knock some heads in the name of civil order.[84]

The rally on the Champ de Mars was partly genuine reaction to Louis' betrayal, and partly provocation that Danton and fellow republicans engineered to marginalize the monarchists. When Lafayette and the Guard marched on the demonstrators, the demonstrators threw stones. The guardsmen responded by firing a volley over their heads. More stones and taunts followed; the guardsmen fired another volley. Except this time it wasn't over their heads.

Many guardsmen joined precisely because they feared—and were fed up with—the mounting violence. Whatever the cause, the impact of that volley went far beyond the thirty to fifty demonstrators killed. The Revolution was ratcheted up another notch.

Paris authorities began arresting hundreds of suspects. The National Assembly pushed through the new constitution, and the King signed it.[85] But now the monarchists were under a cloud. Lafayette was discredited. Danton and other radicals who had gone underground gradually resurfaced to take control of the Paris Commune, the city's government after the storming of the Bastille. It became their power center, as they organized supporters in the city's sections.

As traditional authority broke down further into the summer of 1792, more and more of the *sans-culottes* took to roaming the streets to enforce their own brand of justice. They were on the lookout for anyone who had the dress of a businessman or the bearing of an aristocrat.[86]

Both of which pretty much described Jean-Jacques Duval d'Eprémesnil.

It was inevitable that d'Eprémesnil would become a target. He had managed to put himself on the wrong side of just about every issue since returning from Saint Martinique. When Frenchmen demanded democracy, d'Eprémesnil supported a strong king. When Frenchmen favored voting by head, he supported voting by Estate. When Frenchmen favored equality, he endorsed privilege.

And, d'Eprémesnil was not just well known; he was easily recognized.

Antoine Beauvilliers ran the *Taverne Anglaise* in the Palais Royale, just a short way down the rue Sainte-Honoré from the Tuileries Garden. Today many gastronomes consider it the world's first true restaurant: a destination where friends meet and cooking is an art. It was the sort of place Playfair, by now a five-year resident of Paris, would appreciate.[87]

On 17 July Playfair was just leaving the Taverne when he heard a commotion outside. He saw a crowd on the far side of the Garden. People were running from the scene, saying a mob had attacked Duval d'Eprémesnil and were preparing to cut off his head. A *sans-culotte* had spotted d'Eprémesnil walking across the garden and cold-cocked him. In an instant, he was being attacked from all sides. The mob began beating him and ripping off his clothes.

(The *sans-culottes* were more likely venting anger at d'Eprémesnil's status than trying to humiliate him. Clothes indicated social class. It was hard to fake upward—unless you hoodwinked a tailor with fast talk and a borrowed cabriolet.).

Playfair recalled later d'Eprémesnil had momentarily broken free and had made it as far as the Palais Royale, where he collapsed, dazed and exhausted. By the time Playfair got to him he had sixteen sabre wounds and his body was one continuous bruise. The mob looked about to finish him off.

All Playfair could think was that he had to get Duval out of there. "Had I not, for some years, been personally acquainted with M. d'Eprémesnil," Playfair later explained, "I should not have exposed myself to this danger."[88]

Playfair dove in. People began shouting at him, demanding to know who he was and where he was from. The crowd kept growing as more people stopped to watch—or join in. Playfair tried to get to d'Eprémesnil. The mob shoved him aside. He tried again; again the attackers pushed him away. He tried a third time; same result.

Now he was surrounded. When the fighting began, all the shops closed their doors and shutters. Parisians had learned to take cover when they heard rioting. They remembered Réveillon: in Revolutionary Paris, there was no one to make you whole after the dust settled and fires burned themselves out. There was nowhere to go, and no one to call for help.

Just when Playfair and d'Eprémesnil looked like goners, a man wearing a National Guard uniform passed by. Seeing what was happening, he dove in, too, reaching Playfair's side. Then a half-dozen more guardsmen, hearing the shouting, joined in.

Some of the thugs continued to wrestle with Playfair, wanting to get to d'Eprémesnil. One guardsman, an older man, came to Playfair's aid; together they grabbed d'Eprémesnil's arms and started to drag him away down to rue Neuve des Petits Champs, Playfair thinking they could reach his hotel. But by then the mob had grown even larger and had circled around the Garden, blocking their path.

They changed course and pushed their way across the street with d'Eprémesnil to the gates of the Royal Treasury. They shouted to be let in—only to be faced by fifty or so more guardsmen inside. The soldiers took Playfair for an aristocrat. They had no use for a member of the Second Estate, either, and started to throw Playfair back into the street.

Playfair had to think fast. By "means of good words and bad ones," as he put it, he convinced the guardsmen to let him stay. He appealed to their honor, telling them to kill him there, as he would rather die at the hands of men wearing the National Guard uniform, since all Frenchmen knew the

Guard could do no wrong. That unlikely line of argumentation did the trick; the soldiers relented.

The mob continued to grow, surrounding the Treasury, all the while shouting for d'Eprémesnil's head. The guardsmen laid d'Eprémesnil on some straw. Bruised and bloody himself, Playfair found a bed to lie under. Hours went by. Then, as the sun was setting, Jérôme Pétion de Villenorthneuve arrived, leading some fifteen hundred soldiers.[89]

Pétion, mayor of Paris, had been a deputy of the Second Estate. Thomas Carlyle, writing his epic history of the Revolution, would later mangle the storyline and give him credit for rescuing d'Eprémesnil. He and the troops made their way to the Treasury. Pétion saw d'Eprémesnil. He recognized his fellow deputy. He saw the state he was in. He fainted.[90]

Accounts differ on what happened next. Some say Pétion had d'Eprémesnil carried away in the mayor's carriage to protective custody. Others say Pétion told the mob he was putting d'Eprémesnil in jail to be tried by a tribunal as a traitor. Yet others claim Pétion, fearing the mob, fled and left d'Eprémesnil with members of the Paris Commune. Whatever the truth, he was now in the prison at the Abbey of Saint-Germain-des-Prés.[91]

Playfair took stock. It had been hours since he had left the Taverne. His adrenaline was gone. Now he was ravenous. He saw a boy, either a bootblack or messenger, and asked him where one might find some wine. The boy said he knew of a Swiss vendor; Playfair sent him off. The boy came back with a dozen bottles. Playfair recalled, "It was the best I ever tasted"—no surprise, considering the circumstances.

So he sent the boy to fetch another two-dozen bottles. He offered to share them with the guardsmen. The soldiers contributed some onion soup and they all had a feast. They toasted the king of England. But the guardsmen declined to drink to the king of France. It was a weathervane foretelling events soon to come—the National Guard was responsible for the safety of Louis XVI.

§ § §

At half past nine on the evening of 9 August, Playfair met his three partners at the Bank of Assignats on rue des Bons Enfants. When they were all assembled, he locked the door.

Playfair's sources had told him the Jacobins would put their forces in the street in the morning. He told his partners a riot was likely, and when the violence broke loose the mobs would sack every bank and shop in sight. He offered a proposal: count their assets, set aside enough to cover ten days' withdrawals, and divide the rest among themselves. If the coup fizzled, they could pick up where they left off. If not, the more they saved, the better.[92]

In his memoirs, Playfair said he had three partners—one named Moore and two others, best described as "dullards." The dullards offered what Playfair called "stupid common place objections," giving every reason not to act. Playfair told them he wasn't leaving without his share of the money. He turned to Moore and gave him a look. Moore looked back, agreeing with Playfair. Then Moore drew a pair of pistols and set them on the table.[93]

We don't even know who "Moore" was—Playfair never said, and records from the Bank of Assignats haven't survived. They may have gone up in smoke when the second Paris Commune took over the city during the Franco-Prussian War in May 1871 and torched many of the public buildings.[94]

We do know, however, that the scene was so fixed in Playfair's mind that three decades later he could still describe the events in detail. He knew the dullards would be indecisive. He knew they would freeze. That's why he and Moore had rehearsed their little drama beforehand.

The dullards looked at each other. They looked at the pistols. They came around.

Playfair recalled the four men splitting the bank's assets. First they divided 60,000 livres in assignats. Then the divided the gold coin: about 800 Louis. Finally, they divided the bullion: about 100,000 livres. They assembled a parcel for each man. Playfair and Moore left to find dinner at a coffeehouse. Then Playfair went to his hotel to sleep.[95]

As I said, Playfair never revealed who was bankrolling him through all his adventures. His London businesses ran in the red. His early books and pamphlets sold well, but not nearly well enough to have paid for the travels he described. There was cash flow from the Compagnie du Scioto, but that was stretched thin just taking care of the embarking settlers. The Machine de Marly was a barter deal; it wouldn't produce revenue until Playfair sold off the old machinery. The rolling mill never got underway.

It's truly a mystery. Playfair certainly knew men with money—Colquhoun, Lansdowne, Delessert, Batz, d'Eprémesnil, and the other Scioto investors. Perhaps they were fronting him. Or perhaps we have the dates wrong about when British ministers began to support Playfair's ventures. Playfair later recalled that "ever since the year 1792" he had been a "volunteer" supporting "the main and general plan of opposition to French principles." Most likely Playfair got by through a combination of ad hoc schemes and his innate ability to ride the float, roll over debt, and talk his way out of a fix.[96]

One thing is for sure: money was flowing in Paris—Playfair's bank was evidence of that. But the average Parisian was hurting.

A few weeks earlier, Playfair had been sitting at dinner with the National Guardsman who had come to his aid when he was rescuing d'Eprémesnil from the mob. His "agreeable and handsome daughters" joined them. Playfair could tell the house had seen better days. Still, there was plenty of food, and everyone had a good time.

Dinner completed, the daughters took their leave and Playfair and the soldier proceeded to "drink in the English fashion," as Playfair put it. The soldier was soon well lubricated and, after a few rounds, began to tell his story.

It turned out that he had been a horse dealer. The Revolution had ruined him. When the nobility lost their privileges and income, the first to feel the pinch were the wig-makers, poets, valets, painters of miniatures, and ladies in waiting. And horse dealers. The soldier was so stretched that he had hocked his uniform to pay for the dinner.

Yet he still supported the Revolution. He was even a member of the Jacobin Club. And d'Eprémesnil? The soldier saved him because, well, it was a matter of principle. The fact that d'Eprémesnil represented everything that he was trying to change? Didn't matter.

Playfair puzzled over the disconnect; if ever there was a nation utterly unsuited to rational discourse and self-government, he thought, it had to be France. But he could not help but like the French. Playfair never saw the soldier again.[97]

Events began to accelerate. On 30 July the Marseillaise mobilized.

When France declared war on Austria, many men volunteering to defend the Revolution came from its raucous port on the Mediterranean. Paris was teeming with the soldiers—which explains the French national anthem. It's about *citoyens* from Marseille forming *bataillons* to *marchons, marchons* for the Revolution, soaking the fields of France with the impure blood of foreign soldiers. The soldiers could be Austrians at Wissembourg, Prussians at Valmy— or Swiss, guarding the Tuileries.

Playfair called the Marseillaise "banditti" and recalled their "open murder" and "assassinations." He claimed they never numbered more than four hundred and was amazed such a small force could overwhelm the king's Swiss Guard. He also insisted that the Marseillaise fired first. (That was a sticking point at the time; just about everyone writing about the Revolution was trying to assign blame for starting the violence.)[98]

In the early hours of the morning of 10 August bells rang throughout Paris. The radicals had forced the selection of new representatives in the city sections. Now they were taking power. Playfair, already up at six-thirty, heard his neighbor knocking on his door. Then he heard the sounds of a distant crowd. The Place du Carrousel, the park across from the Louvre, was packed with people from the faubourgs outside the city gates.[99]

Playfair downed a fast cup of coffee, rushed out the door, and crossed the Palais Royale. As he headed down rue St. Honoré, a mob approached from the opposite direction. Two scruffy men seemed to lead it, each carrying something in their hands. Playfair felt sick when he realized what they were: human heads, freshly severed, still oozing blood. He turned and started back to his apartment.[100]

Playfair's sources were right: the radicals had made their move and were preparing to take down the king. By the end of the day, he thought, one side would win, the other lose.[101]

At the Tuileries, the king went out to the Court of Princes, on the south side of the palace, along the river. He hoped to rally support. At first all looked good. Soldiers and civilians chanted, "*Vive le roi, vive le roi!*"

Then, as if cued by signal, the chant changed to "*Vive la nation, vive la nation!*" Louis got the message; a nation can live without a king. Sensing danger, he backtracked, left the Tuileries from the north side, and headed for the National Assembly, a few blocks to the west. He hoped the legislators would shelter him.[102]

At eight o'clock, as Louis was making his escape, the demonstrations turned into the riot Playfair had anticipated. Prisoners arrested the night before for various reasons were held in a guardhouse near the Assembly. Playfair recalled the mob marched one out, a writer named Souleau, and cut off his head; apparently he had been too friendly to the royalty. Another prisoner was guilty simply of looking too handsome; they killed him, too. Soon the mob had murdered seven prisoners and were parading their heads on pikes through the streets.[103]

He had to find out what was going on, Playfair thought. So he headed for his bank on rue des Bons Enfants. His three partners were already there—thankful that they had squared away their business the night before. Playfair told the clerks to carry on as usual, and gave them the money they had set aside for ten days' business.

Playfair turned to leave. As he was walking out the door, a man rushed in, exclaiming that the Tuileries was under attack. Playfair heard cannons and musket firing in the distance. It was ten o'clock.[104]

The streets were suddenly filled with people fleeing the mayhem at the palace, crowds so dense Playfair could hardly move. Clinging to building walls, he was able to inch along until he reached his hotel. The porter recognized him, cracked open the door, and let him in.

Playfair could see both the street and the Palace Royale from his room. He saw the battle unfolding in front of him. He knew that some of the king's entourage stayed in his hotel. That made it a likely target.

As a precaution Playfair had rented a second flat in the nearby Hotel Garni and sent his belongings there a few days before. As he made his way out of the building, he invited an old woman to walk with him. She was protection. They began to head to his redoubt.

Returning to the street, Playfair soon heard sounds of victory. But he could not tell who had won. People were saying the Tuileries had been sacked (true) and the king had been taken prisoner (not quite true, yet).

Playfair heard later that the king took some of the guardsmen with him when he fled the Tuileries for the Assembly. Most of those who remained joined forces with the Marseilles when they rushed the garden. That left the Swiss Guard—outnumbered. They refused to surrender.

Playfair estimated around six hundred Swiss died in the battle that followed inside the palace.[105] "The Swiss, after a defense of fifteen or twenty minutes, were either taken or murdered one by one," Playfair recalled. They were "hunted down by the people like wild beasts," Playfair recalled. "It was thought a glorious act to give any of these ill-fated men a blow with a stick, a sabre, or a bayonet, and still more so to shoot him through the head."[106]

The Assembly voted that evening to suspend the monarchy. On 13 August the new rulers of France put the king and his family in the Temple, an old monastery at the east end of town that doubled as a fort. They were now prisoners.

The night after the insurrection and throughout the next day Playfair walked the neighborhood to "see all I could and get the best information I was able." Playfair discovered the radicals had stopped "all communications that are unfavourable to their cause," and "suspended the departure of all foreign couriers." They wanted time to issue their own account.[107]

Reflecting, Playfair decided the attack could not have been just a spontaneous demonstration that got out of hand. It was a planned operation. The attackers worked as a group, and seemed to know just where to go and which positions to take.[108]

He was correct. The coup had been in the works since June, when the *sans-culottes* and other protesters had forced their way into the Tuileries. It had demonstrated that the king might be unwilling to accommodate the republicans' demands, but he wouldn't unleash his mercenaries on them, either. It also showed that the palace was vulnerable. And it proved the republicans could get their people into the streets.[109]

A few days later Playfair received a message from Antoine-Constant de Brancas, a recently commissioned French army officer. He said he wanted to speak with Playfair. The two found a quiet alley to talk.

Antoine-Constant was the twenty-nine-year-old half-brother of Luis Alberto de Brancas, Playfair's shotgun partner on the Machine de Marly project—and, so, part of the network that included Batz. Antoine-Constant was one of four out-of-wedlock children his father, Louis Léon de Brancas, had with his mistress, Sophie Arnould, a remarkably attractive actress and singer.

Near-noble birth notwithstanding, the young Brancas was a devoted republican—a Jacobin Club member, even. Two months later the second lieutenant would distinguish himself in combat against the Austrians at the Battle of Jemappes. In 1809 he would die in combat against the Austrians at the Battle of Aspern-Essling.[110]

Antoine-Constant was making good on a Brancas family commitment. He had heard from his republican sources Playfair was a marked man. He was going out of his way to warn Playfair he needed to get out of Paris—now.

Playfair had compiled a remarkable tally of "accomplishments" during his five years in Paris: partnerships with nobles like Batz; a patronage from the King; Scioto; the venture with Protot and Guillaume; the Bank of Assignats. Any one of these might have got Playfair chased out of France, assuming he wasn't strung up from a lamp iron first. But according to young Brancas, it was

Playfair's pamphlets and the riot he triggered when rescuing d'Eprémesnil that got him on the wrong side of Bertrand Barère.

Barère, a journalist, first gained notoriety when he was included in Jacques-Louis David's famous depiction of the deputies taking the Tennis Court Oath. (Barère is at left center, legs crossed, taking notes.) An agile political player, he started as a Girondin, but realigned with the Montagnards. Danton invited him to join the government after the 10 August coup; the following year he became a member of the Committee of Public Safety, the junta that took control soon after Louis was toppled.[111]

What got Barère on Playfair's case? Barère despised all things British, but it was most likely Playfair's pamphlet, *Letter to the People of England on the Revolution in France* that really set him off. Printed in Paris, published in London, it was widely available on both sides of the Channel.[112]

Letter to the People of England didn't just criticize French policy. It criticized the architects of the new government—like Barère—for their hubris and recklessness. It was personal. "I reproach them for the inhumanity," Playfair wrote, "of making so great an experiment at the risqué and expences of their fellow citizens."

Also, Playfair wrapped up the pamphlet with a firsthand analysis of French finance—especially the weakness of the assignat. In effect, Playfair was cranking out propaganda and intelligence from his apartment a few blocks from the Legislative Assembly. No wonder Barère wanted him gone.[113]

As he was putting his affairs in order, Playfair ran into his old friend Vandermonde on the street. He had not seen him for almost a year. The mathematician could barely speak. Still obsessed with politics, he had shouted himself hoarse attending public meetings. The attendees were, as Playfair put it, "instructing each other" endlessly.

How, Playfair wondered, could such an "honest, well-intentioned" man of science like Vandermonde "be led astray by the absurdities propagated by a set of villains who laboured for their own advantage?" You couldn't really fault him, Playfair thought. The man's only failing was that he was "extravagantly democratical."[114]

Playfair had seen people impaled, beheaded, and torn apart —"scenes of rage and horror, which I shall never forget," as he put it.[115] And, though, "I can neither complain of weaker nerves, nor boast of stronger feelings than the generality of men," he said, "the impression which I have on those occasions felt will never be effaced from my memory."[116]

Yet, though Playfair's thinking was shaped by the violence he witnessed, he was just as repulsed—maybe more—by the self-styled intellectuals who rationalized the brutality. "I do not consider virtue to consist in the simple manners and republican phrases of a Brissot," he said, "and I have told him so to his face."[117]

It explains why Playfair—draftsman, inventor, economist, writer, and entrepreneur—decided to become an agent for His Majesty's government. For the rest of his life he would often think back to what he had seen that summer. He loathed the Jacobins, and defeating them became his obsession.

7 The British Agent

The key to counterfeiting currency is mainly in the paper. Many competent engravers can duplicate the swirls, cross-hatching, and hidden details printed on a bank note. Duplicating the security features built into the paper, on the other hand—the color, texture, and, in particular, the watermark—is much harder. You need to know what the features are, and replicating them essentially requires recreating the entire papermaking process the issuer used.[1]

But, as Samuel Johnson once observed, forgery is based on the axiom that what one man can do, another man can do.[2] It was the paper that enabled the British to carry out the first large-scale covert operation to collapse an enemy's economy. And it is the paper that absolutely, positively links William Playfair to the operation.

§ § §

In the 1790s all paper was made by hand, one sheet at a time. The main ingredient was rag—discarded cloth. Occasionally you'll read that papermakers got their rag from the undergarments of the recently dead, but that's an old wives tale. The rag trade was a major industry; British papermakers consumed about a quarter million pounds each year—clothing, rope, sailcloth, sacking, whatever. The only real constraint was weeding out wool; any fiber that came off an animal was unusable.[3]

To make paper, you needed a vat man, a coucher, and a crew of several assistants. First the crew sorted the rag by weight—removing buttons, buckles, and hooks along the way—and cut the rag into small squares. They then dumped the pieces into a water-filled "hollander."

Before the Dutch invented the mechanical rag beater in the 1600s, papermakers pulverized rag by hand with hammers. A waterwheel powered the hollander; that, plus the need for prodigious amounts of clean water for the paper itself, was why paper mills were usually built along a river—like the one at Haughton Castle, next to the River Tyne.

FIGURE 13: The Houghton Castle mill today. The exterior looks much as it did in 1794, though the second-floor slats that allowed air to circulate through the drying lofts have been replaced with windows. Source: Les Hull; reproduced with permission.

After the hollander beat the rag into mush, the crew transferred the mixture into a vat, adding more water. Then the vat man used a mold to form what would become a sheet of paper.

This mold—"mould" if you're British—is the key piece of equipment for traditional, old-fashioned, made-by-hand papermaking. It's a wooden frame designed with a detachable lip, or "deckle" fitted around its edge. A fine wire mesh, or "gauze" is stretched across the frame. Paper molds sort of resemble heavy-duty window screens.

The vat man dipped the mold into the solution, lifted it out, and sloshed the slurry back and forth as excess water drained through the mesh. This left a layer of pulp on the mesh's surface. It took some skill to make this pulp layer smooth and even, but it was essential, because it was this pulp that became paper.

The vat man then removed the deckle, let the sheet set for a moment, and passed the mold to the coucher, who gently laid the newly formed sheet onto a wet woven blanket, or "felt." The coucher passed the mold back to the vat man and laid another felt on top of the top of the sheet he had just couched.

With practice, a vat man and coucher could find a rhythm, passing molds back and forth, repeating the process, until they built a "post" of five or six layers of felts and sheets. When a post was complete, the assistants would put it in a screw press and squeeze out most of the water. They then hung the still-wet sheets in the mill's loft, a gallery with slotted walls that allowed the ever-present Northumberland breeze (in this case) to blow through. After the sheets dried, the sheet would be run through a glazing roller—similar to a rolling mill—compressing the pulp fibers even more tightly together.

The result: smooth sheets of paper that could be used for writing, drawing—or currency.

From start to finish it took several days to make a sheet. The craftsmanship required years to master. A boy might start as an assistant, advance to couching, and eventually work his way to vat man.

Meanwhile, the skills and equipment required to construct the all-important mold were just as specialized. The key apparatus was a loom the moldmaker used to weave the mesh from wire. After completing a section of mesh, the moldmaker built a wooden frame, secured the mesh into the frame, and, as a final touch, sewed a design into the mesh using thick wire to form lettering or symbols. This produced the paper's watermark—the distinctive, indelible signature that appeared in every sheet made from a particular mold.

In short, papermaking in the late 1700s was time-intensive and laborious. That's why paper was scarce and expensive. It was so scarce and expensive, in fact, that governments taxed individual sheets, according to their quality and what they'd be used for.

Getting paper was always a challenge for writers; they used the backs of broadsheets, old theater programs, or whatever else they could find for drafts. It's worth keeping in mind next time you buy that five hundred-sheet ream for a couple of bucks at the neighborhood convenience store to feed into your laser printer.

In the 1800s mechanization and chemistry changed everything. First, continuous-feed machines invented around the turn of the century made it possible to make paper in larger quantities. Then, in the 1830s, bleaching agents made it possible to make reasonably good white paper from wood. It was a classic disruptive technology; within a few years paper became as cheap and disposable as, well, Kleenex.

But that was in the future; we're interested in papermaking as practiced at the Haughton Castle mill in autumn 1793.

The mill was producing sheets yielding four bank notes, each about the size of a four-by-six-inch index card. If you held the notes to the light, you would see the watermark—the same watermark the French Republic put on its assignats:

LIBERTÉ ÉGALITÉ
NATION FRANÇAISE

French authorities changed their watermarks periodically. For a successful counterfeiting operation, you also needed an effective intelligence operation—agents to discover the latest watermark design in time to copy it, a clandestine network to get the blank notes to a printer, cutouts to transport the finished notes to the Continent and put them into circulation, someone to pay everyone involved, and so on. So a counterfeiting operation wasn't just forgery; it also required the arts of espionage, conspiracy, money laundering, and smuggling.

One thing we do know: it was a huge effort. The 90 reams of paper Sir John Edward Swinburne said the Haughton Castle mill shipped each week would have alone produced 180,000 notes (500 sheets per ream, 4 notes per sheet), and the British used additional mills in Warden and Kent. Buccaneer Smith probably subcontracted some production to other mills nearby, and that would have added even more to the total. By 1796, when the assignats were demonetized, more than half of the notes in circulation were fakes.[4]

To discover how it started, we need to go back to autumn 1792, when any Englishman with a lick of sense was trying to get out of Paris.

§ § §

For many years the Watt family perpetuated a legend that Junior fled Paris because he incurred the wrath of Robespierre.[5]

Junior, the legend went, happened to be present when Danton and Robespierre got into an argument. One was about to challenge the other to a duel; Junior stepped in, telling them France could not bear to lose either of its two greatest leaders. They should put the cause of liberty ahead of personal pique, he implored. The two settled down. But, it was said, Robespierre seethed.

A few weeks later, the legend continued, Robespierre began to give a speech at the Jacobin Club charging Junior and Cooper of being agents for Pitt (an odd accusation, considering Junior's politics). Nevertheless, the story went, Junior coolly took the floor, and rebutted Robespierre point by point in perfectly accented French. He carried the audience, which broke into a burst of applause. Robespierre skulked out the chamber.

When Junior returned to his hotel—so goes the legend—his sources inside Robespierre's entourage warned him his life was in imminent danger. Junior packed his bags and slipped out of Paris, taking his friend Cooper with him. Evading authorities, the two made their way south until they finally reached safety in Italy. That, at least, was the legend.[6]

Playfair was also trying to get out of France at the time, after young Brancas warned him that Barère was out for his hide. The problem was the authorities required a passport for anyone to leave Paris.[7]

The Thursday following the coup Playfair called on George Leveson-Gower, Duke of Sutherland and the British ambassador to France. Gower—a young man, serving in his first diplomatic assignment—was "quite alarmed" with the situation, Playfair said. But Gower couldn't even get a message out of the country; a passport for an entire party of British expats was out of the question.[8]

As they pondered, Playfair mused he might "apply to M. Brissot." Gower agreed it was worth a try.[9] With the king clearly on the way out and a republic on the way in, Brissot had become one of the most influential men in France.[10]

"I went next morning before 8 o'clock to Brissot's lodgings," Playfair recalled, and even at that hour "found several people waiting for audience of the great man." Brissot still lived in the sixth-floor flat Clavière had rented him back when he was broke. Now Brissot was holding court, dispensing favors. The line reached into the hall. Brissot's people admitted the petitioners in the order they arrived.[11]

Playfair waited his turn. He finally got to the head of the line. He went in. It must have been interesting when the two men faced each other; their lives had intersected often over the past five years: Jefferson, Barlow, Scioto, Duer, the pamphlet wars, and, of course, Clavière. But Playfair needed any help he could get.

Playfair began to explain that he was trying to leave the country and needed a passport. Brissot claimed he had no authority to issue one—technically true, since officially he was just another member of the Legislative Assembly. But, he allowed, he *could* write a letter for Playfair to give Pierre Henri Hélène Marie Lebrun-Tondu, the foreign minister. Perhaps *he* might give Playfair the exit visas.[12]

As Brissot began to write, it occurred to Playfair to "do the English a service" by convincing Brissot to allow *all* Britons out of the country. Playfair started to play Brissot, as he put it, fitting his "discourse to the man to whom it was addressed."

Playfair laid it on thick. "I know well, Sir, as Every Body does, your justice and philanthropy," he recalled telling Brissot. And, he said, "you understand the Rights of Man as well as you do the interests of nations." Playfair knew that Brissot thought himself a thinker and man of the world; he was a writer by trade and had had traveled across both Europe and America.

Playfair declared the British—*here's the wind-up*—"have nothing to do with your politics with which we have no Right to Interfere," so—*and there's the pitch!*—"do not you think it would be just & wise to pass a law to Enable all those to depart who wish to do so?"

While Brissot chewed on that, Playfair added the kicker: "It will show foreign nations that the present Rulers of France respect the rights of strangers," he said.[13]

Playfair scored. Brissot probably appreciated being called a "present Ruler of France."

"What you propose is very right," Brissot replied. The man who supposedly had no power said, "I shall have the decree passed this very day." According to Playfair, Brissot "was as good as his word and before five o'clock that evening the new law was proclaimed in the streets by the hawkers of newspapers, such was the rapidity with which public business was dispatched at that time."[14]

And that's how James Watt, Junior really got out of Paris.

There is absolutely no evidence that Junior broke up a duel between Danton and Robespierre, that he sparred with Robespierre in the Jacobin Club, that anyone put a price on his head, or that he and Cooper exfiltrated to Italy. The truth was that Junior's problem wasn't getting out of France; it was getting back into Britain.

Junior not only had no quarrels with Robespierre; he *admired* the man. Junior bought a portrait of Robespierre as a memento at the same time he bought pictures of Mirabeau and Pétion.[15] In a letter to his father in mid-September, Junior lumped Robespierre in with Priestley, Pétion, Thomas Paine, the Marquis de Condorcet and other reformers he said were "universally distinguished for their patriotism or their talents."[16]

Junior did lower his profile in the weeks before the coup. He had little choice; he was bedridden with "headache, sore throat, cough, fever, and other attendant symptoms" as the result of a bout of scarlet fever for much of July. "I am extremely debilitated of this disorder," he wrote his father.[17]

But even before he fell ill his father warned him of the risks he was running with his political activities. On 27 May 1792 Watt wrote Junior, "the eyes of the Ministry are upon you, and without you act cautiously, you may be found to have transgressed some of the laws of this country."[18]

Watt warned Junior again and again through the summer. The message finally got through. On 23 August Junior wrote his father that he was "much obliged to you for your observations on the Law. As you advise I shall suspend all thoughts upon the subject until I come to England."[19]

After that, Junior kept his assessments of Britain to himself. But he continued his commentary on France. It gives a flavor of the situation in the weeks before and after the coup.

Junior let his father know he was safe—thanks to the insurgents. "It is only the Guilty and the Traitors to their country who have anything to fear," he wrote. "I have the friendship of most of the Patriots here, so I am infinitely more safe than any Englishman in Paris."

He added that, "had the other party prevailed I probably should have been in the list of the proscribed," referring to the royalists. But, knowing his father's concern, he assured him, "However, I take no part in politics, farther than declaring freely my opinion."[20]

Junior watched events unfold following the coup. "The party of the People remains predominant, & the prisons are filled with their treacherous enemies," he wrote his father. Anticipating what lay ahead, he observed "the King has only saved his life to lose it on the scaffold." Meanwhile, the authorities had sealed the city, except for those leaving for the front to fight the Prussians.[21]

Junior was still in Paris when the September Massacre began. As the *sans-culottes* rampaged through the jails killing clergy and nobles, Junior wrote his father that "I am filled with involuntary horror at the scenes which pass before me and wish they would have been avoided, but at the same time I allow the absolute necessity of them."[22]

It was the beginning of the Reign of Terror. First the regime executed nobles and clergy from the old regime. During the next ten months, the factions comprising the new regime would turn on each other, rivals executing rivals.

Junior conceded, "In some instances the vengeance of the people has been savage & inhuman." That's how he described the murder of Princess de Lamballe, a friend of Marie Antoinette. He claimed the mob killed her, dragged her body through the streets, stuck her head on a pike, and "carried through Paris and shown to the King & Queen, who are in hourly expectation of the same fate."[23]

Junior and Cooper didn't have to sneak out of France. By the time they were ready, any Englishman could leave. If you believe Playfair, it was thanks to his deal with Brissot. At any rate, after the August insurrection and the September Massacres the two young men simply went on to their next stops as traveling salesmen and bill collectors: Nantes, Bordeaux, Marseille, and, by November, Naples.[24]

Clear of any danger, it was only then that Junior began to have second thoughts about the new regime, as the Reign of Terror proceeded beyond nobles, noncompliant clergy, and street rabble. Now many a thoughtful, distinguished *philosophe* was getting swept up for a one-way ride in a tumbrel. In other words, Junior's people.

"My friends in France, the friends of rational liberty," he wrote his father in December 1792 from Amsterdam, have "passed the fatal guillotine." Apparently forgetting the meetings he attended at the Jacobin Club, he claimed "the reigning party were always the objects of my hatred as well as of Mr Coopers."[25]

But it really didn't matter what Junior thought; his image was cast. In March 1793 Burke criticized Junior again in the House of Commons. He recalled how Junior carried a Union Jack in the Jacobin march the year before. Burke called the performance the "most infamous that ever disgraced the name of government." He described with disdain how the two men "went from the Hall of the Assembly to the Hall of the Jacobins, where they kissed the bloody cheek of Marat."[26]

It was more than a bit of hyperbole, and a stale charge to boot; it had been months since Junior participated in the march. But facts were facts: France and Britain were now at war and Junior had landed on the wrong side; associating with French Jacobins flirted with treason.

Junior began to wonder if he'd ever be able to go home. Cooper was making plans to emigrate for America. Burned out of his house in Birmingham, Joseph Priestley was close behind, as were his sons. When he got to Genoa, Junior wrote his father a long letter saying he was considering the same.[27]

The prospect of never seeing his son again must have shaken Watt. He wrote Junior on 9 October, offering an olive branch. "Do not suffer yourself to give way to a fruitless despondance, nor in the flames of your age cease to encourage hope," he wrote. But he had better shape up and get his life in order. It was that damned radicalism.

Watt told his son, "You ought to combat your own passions and consider coly whether many of your opinions are not founded on prejudice and false report." At the same time he softened the message with a note on the outside: "Friendly Advice." Watt wanted his son back.[28]

Junior complied. In November he wrote to the Walker brothers. "My father's last letters have given me great pleasures," he confessed, "as they breathe a warmth of affection I never before experienced from him." He could imagine life back in Soho, and that "with time and moderation on my side we shall live in that harmony I so much desire."[29]

Watt asked Matthew Boulton to help Junior to "make his peace" with the government by offering "a candid avowal" of his errors, and his "subsequent change of sentiment and renunciation of all correspondence with these trai-tors." It took more than a year for Boulton to pull the strings that would allow Junior to return.[30]

Watt, considering the available options, wrote Boulton that, "In the mean time, Junior had better make the best of his way to here, Liverpool, or Scot-land." To make the deal work, Junior needed to lie low for a while. Watt asked Boulton to query his government contacts to find out if they might prefer to sheep-dip Junior in Denmark, Hamburg, or Norway before his return home. America was an option, Watt thought, but British-American relations were still touchy; if the two nations went to war it wouldn't be good for James Watt's son to be in New York or Philadelphia.

Just in case Boulton discovered British officials had decided Junior too "obnoxious" to allow back under any conditions, Watt maneuvered to protect the company. If Junior had to remain an expat, Boulton should tell him his future letters "should be directed by another hand, and not signed."[31]

Watt needn't have worried. Junior was back in England by February 1794. He settled in with Boulton and turned to the family business.[32] "After all my rambles," he wrote a Dutch friend in April, "I probably shall never quit this country any more, particularly as I find all my friends, Dr. Priestley excepted, determined to remain here. Indeed, bad as this country may be, it is the best I know."[33]

And how did the story arise of Junior breaking up the confronta-tion between Danton and Robespierre and saving them from their worst inclinations?

James Muirhead first published the tale in the biography of Watt that he published in 1854. Muirhead said he got the story from a letter that the noted Scottish priest and essayist Archibald Allison had received in 1833. Allison said he got the letter from Robert Southey, a writer famous for his biographies of Nelson and Cromwell. And Southey, in turn, said he had been told the story by... James Watt, Junior.[34]

Junior might not have been the mechanical engineer his father was, but the paper trail says he was pretty good at engineering history—as Playfair would learn first-hand.

§ § §

Brissot's help came with strings attached.

"I had not returned above an hour when I received a note from Madame Brissot with her compliments and a request that I would call on her," Playfair recalled. "I did not much like the invitation, but went directly when she said that understanding from her husband that I was going to England with a friend she wished to ask a favour."[35]

According to Playfair, Madame Brissot "had two female relations in Paris who came from Boulogne and wished to return." The government was not allowing French citizens to leave Paris, but Madame Brissot thought, "as the wives of foreigners they will be allowed. My husband will get that put into the decree."

So that was the deal: Brissot lets Playfair return to England, and Playfair smuggles his wife's friends out of Paris. Playfair wasn't keen on the arrangement, but he couldn't let on. Brissot could easily write another note to Lebrun-Tendu, explaining that the situation had changed and thus it was now imperative for M. Playfair to remain in Paris—perhaps indefinitely.

Playfair told Madame Brissot *of course* he would escort her friends. She gave him a letter of introduction. He called on the two ladies. They were ready to travel.

Brissot was having Playfair run a huge risk. "I had acted from necessity," Playfair recalled, but "traveling with a woman as a wife who was not really so was punishable by six months imprisonment." And no one was saying what Playfair was supposed to do about Mary, his real wife—not to mention how to explain their kids—John, Elizabeth, and Andrew.

"I was determined one way or another to evade the performance," Playfair recalled. The next morning he called on Moore. He told him he had a letter to the Minister that would get the passports. Then he told him about the two ladies Madame Brissot was determined to get to Boulogne.

Moore had his priorities clear. "Are they handsome?" was his immediate question.

"No," Playfair said, "They are old maids as ugly as sin and as old as the hills."

Not worth the risk, Moore concluded. Playfair agreed. So he left a letter for Madame Brissot. He was sorry, he said, but instead of going through Boulogne to Calais, he had to go through Rouen to Dieppe—about 150 kilometers in the wrong direction. So, alas, he could not take the ladies.

Then he left instructions not to deliver the note until forty-eight hours after he was gone.

"On the Saturday evening I went to take a last sight of the Palais Royal," Playfair recalled, musing how "a resort for people in pursuit of pleasure" had "now become the center of cabal politics and intrigues of every sort."

As Playfair walked through the Palais, he ran into Jacques-Constantin Périer. The two had known each other since 1779, when Périer visited Boulton & Watt and Playfair was working in the counting house. After Playfair went to France, he sometimes competed with Périer on projects like the Machine de Marly. Périer was also known as something of a pirate at Boulton & Watt for using Watt's improvements without bothering to pay royalties.[36]

The two men walked together for a while. Périer said some of his people had been working that day at the Tuileries Gardens. They were breaking up the equestrian statue of Louis XV that had stood at the entrance opposite the palace. The plan was to melt down the metal and cast it into cannons. Playfair told Périer, that, being a man of taste, he must be sorry to destroy such a noble a piece of workmanship. "Not at all," Périer said. "Cannon are more useful than statues of kings."[37]

Playfair and the others set off in a post chaise to Dieppe on Sunday, 19 August.[38] Family lore says that he, Mary, and their kids fled Paris carrying only what they could fit into their son's bassinet. They had to travel light— Playfair had no time to lose.[39]

A source at police headquarters had told Playfair that afternoon that the authorities were about to seize his bank—and him. The *gendarmes* marched into his office next morning, inventoried the deposits on hand, sealed the premises, and detailed a couple of soldiers to look after the place. They had hoped to grab Playfair, too, but by that time he was on his way.[40]

Playfair got through Rouen just as the War of the First Coalition began. The combined Austrian-Prussian army was advancing from the Austrian-held Netherlands; within weeks they would be deep in France. Playfair and his party arrived in Dieppe on Tuesday, 21 August, the day after the declaration of war. But because "the wind was quite unfavourable," they had to wait. He told the rest of the party to take the next affordable boat to London. Playfair went to Holland.[41]

As for Jean-Jacques d'Eprémesnil: In August someone moved him from the Abbey of Saint-Germain to a more formidable prison across the river, the Grand Châtelet. Once account says that when the mobs swept through in the September Massacres, a National Guardsman from Bordeaux recognized him—and let him live. D'Eprémesnil found a sword and held off the mob.

That night, after his attackers had drunk themselves numb, he disguised himself as a *sans-culotte* and escaped, wading through ankle-deep gore. It took him over an hour to wash the blood from his boots and clothes in the nearby Fontaine Maubuée. He found friends who took him in. Then he headed north, home to Le Havre.[42]

§ § §

Playfair seemed to enjoy playing games with his readers. He was of two minds. Many of the activities he would carry out—counterfeiting, espionage, bribery, and conspiracy—were illegal or unsavory. At least they were not something one admitted to in proper society. Both he and his government sponsors would pay a price if they became known.

But Playfair also was a proud patriot. He seemed to want readers to know what he had done. So in both his publications and his private papers, he drops hints, mentions events, cites places, quotes acquaintances, and then leaves it to readers to figure out why.

Exhibit A: Playfair describes a French deception he witnessed in Paris in late 1790.

France's initial plan to pay off its debt with assignats rested on a critical assumption: the government would destroy the notes as they were exchanged for land. If the notes continued to circulate, it would be clear that there were no tangible assets backing them. Everyone would know they were nothing but fiat money and, once they figured out the government could print as many notes as it wished, inflation would soar.

French authorities decided to make a big show of destroying assignats that were supposedly cashed in. There's an eyewitness account of such a burning in an appendix to the edition of *Wealth of Nations* Playfair edited in 1805. It goes like this:[43]

> A person worthy of credit, and who is now in London, was acci- dentally present at the burning of the first million of assignats, by order of the assembly, in a garden belonging to a convent adjoining the hall where it sat, and under the inspection of three commissioners (members of the assembly). It was about one o'clock in the day, and four men with a vast quantity of assig- nats (tight bound up with cords, but not under covers), which they carried upon poles like two sedan chairs, arrived. They were

thrown into a fire, under a covered grate, which, for more security, was surrounded on all sides by a wire net, to prevent any of those Sybil's leaves from flying away.

The assignats at that time were all of 200, 500, and 2000 livres, and part were on coloured paper. Those burned appeared to have been very little in circulation, but though it did not occur to the person looking on at the time, he has since had occasion to see a million of assignats of nearly the same size, and they were not more bulky than four moderate octavo volumes of a book, and even if they had been all of the lowest sums, which by the colour he knows they were not, they would only have been the size of ten octavo volumes. The parcel burned, which was a load for four men, was at least fifty times the quantity. How this happened he never could conjecture, and did not think it prudent to enquire, after he did perceive the impossibility of their being only one million. The only certain conclusion is, that there was an intention to deceive the public.

The witness, of course, was Playfair, writing about himself. He had a way of "accidentally" seeing stuff he wasn't supposed to. Playfair "since had occasion to see a million of assignats" because he shipped them by the wagonload during his counterfeiting operation.

(Playfair also appreciated a good double entendre. He might have been a "person worthy of credit" as far as being a reliable eyewitness, but by 1805 his creditworthiness, financially speaking, was zero.)

After a while, you catch on, look for the telltale phrases that mean Playfair was up to something—usually espionage or subversion—and begin to read his accounts differently. Like Exhibit B, Playfair's story of how he obtained the plans for the French semaphore telegraph:[44]

I obtained, by accident, a description of the telegraph, when in Germany, at the time that there was no communication with France, and immediately set to work, composed an alphabet, and made two models, which worked and communicated across the street, at Frankfort on the Mayne. Lord Malmesbury's secretary, Mr. Ross, (who was lately Mr. Canning's private secretary), saw these telegraphs, which Major Ramsey, of the York Rangers, took with him to present to his Royal Highness the Duke of York.

France had the biggest army in Europe, but it couldn't be everywhere at once. So it had to shift its forces to wherever the current threat might be—quickly. Claude Chappe had the solution—the first digital information network. It consisted of a series of towers, each spaced twelve to fifteen miles apart. Each tower had four movable thirteen-foot "arms" operated through a system of pulleys and ropes, each arm ending in a three-foot long movable "hand."

To send a message, an operator would reposition his tower's arms and hands to represent a different character, word, or phrase; the process took about four seconds. Each tower operator would watch his neighboring towers through a telescope, and, when he saw a new signal, he would replicate it, sending it down the line in a domino-like process. Chappe called his invention the *télégraphe*, or "far writer."[45]

The French built their first semaphore telegraph line in 1793. It ran from the roof of the Louvre in Paris to the town of Lille, where their army was fighting the Austrians. Bernard Barère—Playfair's old nemesis—described the system to the National Convention on 15 August 1794 as "an artful contrivance to transmit thoughts, in a peculiar language, from one distance to another." With this invention, Barère said, "remoteness and distance almost disappear."[46]

Barère had it nailed. Lille was more than thirty leagues away—or the distance a man could walk (and thus carry a message) in thirty hours. The idea that a person in Paris and a person in Lille could share the same thought at almost the same instant was amazing. It had never happened before in the entire history of mankind.

The first English-language description of France's telegraph appeared less than a year later in Charles Hutton's *Mathematical and Philosophical Dictionary*. Hutton was a professor at the Royal Military Academy, Woolwich. He described the new invention in a section, "Explanation of the Machine (Telegraph) placed on the Mountain of Bellville, near Paris, for the purpose of communicating Intelligence."

The French, Hutton said, "have availed themselves of this contrivance to good purpose, in the present war." He understood the political potential, too: "The operations of Government can be very much facilitated by this contrivance, and the unity of the Republic can be the more consolidated by the speedy communication with all its parts." Communications equaled control.

Another key feature: "The greatest advantage which can be derived from this correspondence is, that, if one chooses, its object shall only be known to certain individuals, or to one individual alone." The system's alphabet—how each position of the arms represented a letter, number, or word—was, in effect, a code—what Barère had called a "peculiar language." Even if a spy could see the towers at work, he needed the alphabet to understand the message it was transmitting. The *télégraphe* was France's secure communications system.[47]

So where did Hutton get his information?

France was closed to foreigners—"at the time that there was no communication with France," as Playfair put it. But Playfair was making his own forays back to the Continent; he sometimes mentioned them in memos to British officials, and you can pick them up in his published work, too, if you read between the lines and understand the context.

The earliest trip Playfair made back to the Continent after fleeing Paris seems to be one in August 1793, when he apparently was at Dunkirk. Just a few weeks after France declared war, the Duke of York, commander in chief of the British army, tried to capture the port with a 28,000-man force comprising British, Hanoverian, Hessian, and Austrian units. The siege failed, and the Duke retreated northeast, up the coast to Flanders.

It wasn't pretty; take it from Playfair, he was there. You can find the giveaway in a footnote in *Political Portraits,* a book he published twenty years later. He recalled that "when the British army was repulsed," the Austrians acted "like savage enemies, not like allies; they smiled with a bitter, envious, and cruel joy, when they saw our fine fellows flying towards Fumes and Ostend."

Then comes the passage that reveals Playfair wasn't just retelling history; it was an eyewitness account. Playfair wrote he saw "that savage joy; and I ran the risk of my life for testifying, in very unequivocal terms, my anger; which indeed I was unable to disguise."[48]

Playfair was a busy man in those years. In his introduction to *Better Prospects to the Merchants and Manufacturers of Great Britain,* published in May 1793, he apologized for the brevity of the pamphlet, saying that he was "engaged at the present in a plan that promised considerable success and requires a great deal of attention"—an overt-but-oblique reference to the secret stuff he was doing for the British government.[49]

One problem the British had at Dunkirk, Playfair said, was a lack of intelligence. "The French began by paying spies and informers at an immoderate rate," Playfair recalled, but "the coalesced powers refused to pay any thing that was worth while for the ingenuity and risk of a spy."[50]

Apparently Playfair decided to fill the gap himself, and that explains how he "introduced" the telegraph to Britain.

From May to September 1794, Playfair was on a five-month "visit" to the Continent.[51] The war was proceeding at full tilt, when Playfair said he encountered "by accident" a former parlementaire from Bordeaux at an inn while passing through Frankfurt. Playfair chatted him up.

The parlementaire told Playfair about one of the towers he had seen on a mountain near Belleville in eastern France and described how it operated. Playfair then set to work, building two models of the telegraph tower and composing an alphabet, based on what he had learned. He tested the models, sending messages to an accomplice across the street. They worked.

The "Mr. Ross" in Playfair's account was James Ross, private secretary to James Harris—soon 1st Earl of Malmesbury and Pitt's representative to the German states. "Mr. Canning" was George Canning, an ambitious Tory writer-politician who would soon become under secretary at the Foreign Office; Ross would be his right hand man.[52]

"Major Ramsay" was actually Lieutenant Colonel George-William Ramsay, commander of the York Rangers, a 2,000-man cavalry regiment Ramsay raised for the Duke of York. Ross and Ramsay took the models to the Duke, who was commanding British forces in Flanders.[53]

The 1797 edition of the *Encyclopedia Britannica* blithely says in its entry for "TELEGRAPH" that "two working models" of "this instrument" were "sent by Mr W. Playfair to the Duke of York," and this was how "the plan and alphabet of the machine came to England." It doesn't mention the cloak-and-dagger aspects of Playfair's adventures in unilateral technology transfer.

But you get the picture: When Playfair says, "I obtained, by accident, a description of the telegraph," he really means he entered a war zone, recruited a source, pumped him for information, reverse-engineered the enemy's just-deployed communication system, and got the intelligence to the commander of the British army.[54]

Or consider Exhibit C: Playfair's account of a voyage he took down the Rhine in September on the last leg of his 1794 foray through Europe.

It's written on a single, frayed-edge sheet from his never-published memoirs.[55] Playfair said he was traveling with "a Prussian officer, Count d'Esternon, en route to join the York Rangers." In other words, d'Esternon was trying was trying to reach Ramsay to support the Duke of York.[56]

Playfair recalled, "I could get no post horses nor conveyance by land from Mainz." That was because the armies had commandeered all of them. "I went from Frankfort as the French were just then advancing and driving the allies beyond the Rhine," he continued, "and all horses and carriages were bespoke for ten or twelve days."

The French army had recovered the ground it had lost in 1793. Now it was counterattacking. Within a year, Austria would lose all of its lands in the Low Countries, and Britain would be forced to evacuate its forces from Holland. Playfair's immediate problem was that the French might cut him off from the Channel. So he hired a boat to get to Cologne; from there he could get to Flanders. It was perilous—the French were no more than a hundred miles away.

Then, as they were about to embark, a well-to-do French family approached him. Playfair described what happened next:[57]

> When we had got into the boat Colonel Vauban and his brother the marquis with his wife and a girl about eight or nine years of age came to ask us a favour to be permitted to have a place in the boat. The colonel who as he told me afterwards was in the Russian service said he and his brother were nephews of the famous Vauban and they were willing to pay their share and would be greatly obliged. I said I would receive them with pleasure if my fellow traveler had no objections.
>
> We accordingly came all down together. The count was a very intelligent knowing man with a great deal of anecdote respecting the court of St. Petersburg and I was very inquisitive particularly about the empress and Prince Potemkin under whom he had served in the war with Turkey.
>
> The marquis, the elder brother was a simple sort of gentleman and seamed to be completely kept under by his wife who was

rather handsome and his brother who seamed to be upon a most intimate footing.

It was the month of September and the rowing down the river was delightful with hills on both sides the base of the mountain being generally close to the river.

So who was this "Colonel Vauban?" And why might Playfair mention him in his memoirs?

The "famous Vauban" to whom Playfair referred was Sebastian Le Prestre de Vauban, perhaps the best-known military engineer Europe ever produced. Vauban specialized in massive, multi-tiered star-shaped fortifications; many survive, and a dozen are UNESCO World Heritage sites. Playfair had met his grandnephew, Colonel Jacques-Anne-Joseph Le Prestre de Vauban.[58]

Colonel Vauban had been an aide-de-camp to Comte de Rochambeau, commander of French forces in America during the War for Independence. Vauban fought at Yorktown and returned to France after the war. In 1791 he fled to Coblentz and fought with the émigrés against the republicans. He then left for Russia and accepted a commission from Catherine II. That's how he came to fight the Ottomans in the Russo-Turkish Wars.

What Playfair did *not* say in his memoirs was that he and Vauban shared a connection: William Windham. Vauban was corresponding secretly with Windham who, at that moment, was planning an invasion of France with Joseph-Geneviève de Puisaye.[59]

Puisaye was a tall, good-looking, persuasive forty-year-old army officer from Normandy. The fourth son of an old noble family, Puisaye had a remarkably unremarkable military career, never seeing combat and drifting from one nondemanding appointment to another. He settled into early de facto retirement at his Mortagne-au-Perche home, calling the next five years "the happiest of my life," with "all the delights of an agreeable and select society." He purchased a colonel's commission and married into wealth in 1788.[60]

Then the French Revolution began.

Puisaye's political ambitions were as modest as his military aspirations. Most likely it was his family's standing that led neighboring nobles to select him as their deputy to the Estates General. That got him into the Assembly after the storming of the Bastille. He aligned with the Girondins until the new constitution took effect in September 1791, and then went home, leaving politics behind.

The August 1792 coup sucked him back in. As a military officer—at least in principle—he was a natural choice to lead a unit in the Normandy militia when the Montagnards turned on the Girondins. That's how Puisaye found himself with about 3,000 Girondin soldiers facing about 1,200 Montagnards at the Château de Brécourt on 13 July 1793.

The Château would later be the site of the Battle of Brécourt Manor, a famous World War II action made even more famous when it was portrayed in the television series *Band of Brothers*. But that was 150 years in the future.

La Bataille de Brécourt is known as *la bataille sans larme*—no tears—because it was more Monty Python than Marshal Montgomery. As Thomas Carlyle put it, both sides "shrieked mutually, and took mutually to flight." The Montagnards came back later and sacked Puisaye's estate; Puisaye fled south to Brittany.[61]

He hooked up with the Chouans—Bretton counter-revolutionaries taking their name from Jean Chouan, the nom de guerre of their founder, Jean Cottereau. Puisaye may have seemed an unlikely insurgent, but he stuck with the Chouans and eventually made contact with British officials. In September 1794 he found himself in London with William Pitt planning to spark an insurgency via an invasion of France.[62]

Puisaye claimed Bretons—rural and deeply Catholic—would rise up against the republicans, now led by radical Parisian secularists. All the British had to do was land a small force, establish a beachhead, and Chouans across the countryside would join them. Once armed with British weapons, the insurgency would sweep across France.[63]

It seemed plausible. The British fleet assembled at Spithead in June 1795: nine warships and sixty transports commanded by Commodore Sir John Borlase Warren. The British planned to deploy about 4,000 soldiers—mainly French émigrés. Once ashore, they would expand their force with the Chouan locals. Their logistics reflected their expectations: they brought 23,000 uniforms, 27,000 muskets, and 600 barrels of powder.

Their target: Quiberon.

It seemed like a splendid spot for an invasion. Quiberon is at the end of a narrow peninsula that juts eight miles into the Atlantic from the Brittany coast—easy access from Britain, excellent anchorage. Its main defensive work, Fort Sans-Culotte (*née* Fort Penthièvre—designed, ironically enough, by

Sebastian de Vauban) was only half-manned. Quiberon had good karma, too; the British defeated a French fleet there in 1759 during the Seven Years War.

Records show Vauban arrived in London in 1794, so when Playfair encountered him on their trip down the Rhine he was probably en route. Vauban had heard Puisaye could connect him to the royalist army. He joined Puisaye, planning to command a column of Chouans once ashore.[64]

Everything was set.

It was a fiasco.

The fleet arrived on 25 June. The émigrés disembarked and began moving up the peninsula. As hoped, thousands of Chouans showed up. Soon the British were issuing so many weapons to the locals—15,000 muskets in under a week—that Warren sent a dispatch to London asking for more. It was going so well that Pitt considered having Comte d'Artois—younger brother of Louis XVI, living in exile in Edinburgh —join the émigrés to set up a government-in-waiting.[65]

For a brief moment it seemed the French Revolution might end right there. Then the operation tanked. The problem was simple: No one was in charge.

Puisaye's orders from the British Government gave him command of all forces in France. But Colonel Louis Charles d'Hervilly, commander of about half the émigré forces, had raised his regiments under a commission from the British army; he refused to turn them over to Puisaye.

It was a clash of personalities, politics, and tactics. Puisaye never saw combat; d'Hervilly fought in the American War and had defended the Tuileries Palace during the 10 August coup. Puisaye was a liberal, favoring a constitutional monarchy; d'Hervilly was a royalist wanting nothing less than a restoration of the *ancien régime*. Puisaye wanted to strike fast and spark an insurgency; d'Hervilly wanted a methodical, conventional offensive along a front.[66]

The invasion stalled as Puisaye and d'Hervilly squabbled. They lost the element of surprise. Then Louis Lazare Hoche arrived on the scene.

Hoche, twenty-seven, was a natural soldier; he had risen through the ranks from private to general in just nine years. Hoche had five thousand republican troops and raised five thousand more by commandeering units en route to Quiberon. He sealed off the peninsula; the battle turned into a rout. About 2,500 men made it back to the boats.

The troops remaining on the peninsula were doomed. They surrendered on 21 July. Some accounts claim Hoche promised quarter, but by then
Jean-Lambert Tallien had arrived, representing the National Convention.
Charged as traitors, commoners were allowed to join Hoche's army; nobles
faced trial by tribunal. Over fifteen days some 750 were executed.

It was a complete, unmitigated disaster. Years later, Playfair tried to make
sense of it. "Mr Windham," he recalled, his friend and patron now dead, "with
that eccentric impetuosity for which he was famous" managed the invasion.
Windham, Playfair claimed, delegated leadership in the field to "two emi-
grant intriguers, who had no knowledge of military affairs." Puisaye? D'Hervilly? Vauban? Playfair didn't say.[67]

The counter-revolution never recovered. Puisaye (who made it off the
beach) wrote a six-volume memoir, trying to exculpate himself. Vauban (he
got off the beach, too) also wrote a memoir. D'Hervilly never had the opportunity; he was shot in the chest two weeks into the invasion, and died in
London four months later.

You might ask, though, aside from that chance meeting with Vauban,
what was Playfair's connection with all of this?

The invasion of Quiberon was funded largely with forged assignats. The
émigrés brought trunkloads of the bogus notes with them, too, to buy sup-
plies and win over the locals.[68] Vauban himself received several hundred million.[69] After the invaders surrendered, Hoche reported to the Committee on
Public Safety that he was preparing to burn piles of counterfeit notes he had
confiscated.[70]

Playfair didn't say why he included that interlude with Vauban in his
memoir; it's just there. Most of the vignette describes Vauban hitting on his
sister-in-law, leading to a family squabble. But when you take in the whole
scene, you see it's a story of Playfair figuring out how to get back to British
lines, dodging the French army, and traveling with a émigré commander who
a year later would help lead an invasion funded with Playfair's counterfeit
money.

Perhaps that's why, thirty years later, just months before he died, Playfair could still remember a trip down the Rhine on a perfect September day
with an otherwise obscure French officer. His entire recollection fits on that
single, frayed-edge page. It might have just been the scribbling of an old man
wanting to touch a memory one more time. Or perhaps Playfair was leaving
breadcrumbs, hoping that, someday, somewhere, someone would unravel the

clues and people would realize how he had served his country. It's really hard to tell.[71]

FIGURE 14: Counterfeit 50-sol assignat confiscated at Quiberon. One give-away: The Scales of Justice that Themis is holding are incorrectly rendered; gen-uine notes had the vertical arm extending slightly below the horizontal beam. Source: *Catalogue general des assignat français.* Reproduced with permission.

§ § §

But that was in the future. Let's return to December 1792, as Playfair was making his way back to England after his escape from Paris.

A series of letters from that month preserved in the Austrian state archives begins with a proposal from Baron de Breteuil to Count Ludwig von Cobenzl. One of Austria's most experienced diplomats, Cobenzl would become its foreign minister the following year.

Breteuil had been a minister to Louis XVI with a broad portfolio—in effect, lord of public works and domestic policy. It was when Louis decided in July 1789 to give Necker's responsibilities for finance to Breteuil that rumors started about Louis giving up on reform. That led Parisians to stand up their militia, which led them to seize weapons from Les Invalides, which led them to seek powder, which led to the storming of the Bastille.

After the storming, Breteuil fled to Spa, in the Austrian Netherlands. He was part of the conspiracy behind the royal family's ill-fated attempt to escape France in June 1791. The following November, Louis, sensing he was in danger, gave Breteuil plenipotentiary powers—total authority to represent the regime abroad. Then came the coup of 10 August 1792. With Louis in Temple Prison, Breteuil effectively became head of France's government in exile.[72]

Now Breteuil was trying to bring down the revolutionary regime any way possible. He had first-hand knowledge of France's nonexistent tax base, so he also knew the Convention had to keep printing assignats to pay the nation's bills. Undermine the assignats, he said, and you will starve the Revolution.

Breteuil's proposal: a clandestine operation to cripple the economy of the new French regime. Austria and Prussia would print 150 million livres of counterfeit French assignats. They would then pay friendly banks to put the phony money into circulation.[73]

Cobenzl shared the proposal with Friedrich Wilhelm von der Schulenburg, his Prussian counterpart. Schulenburg was skeptical. His point-by-point critique listed everything that could go wrong: It would be impossible to find the special paper the forged notes required, the banks would not cooperate, France might retaliate in kind, and so on, and so on.[74]

As for the Emperor—he wanted no part of it. *So ein infames Project ist nicht anzunehmen*, Francis II wrote in regal, third person passive voice. Cobenzl agreed—with one caveat:

> *Gleichwohl könnte meines Erachtens dem Baron Breteuil zwar auf keine Art angerathen, jedoch lediglich überlassen werden, ob und wie er etwa von seinem Vorschlag in England einen Gebrauch zu machen erachten dürfte.*

Perhaps he might take his idea to the English?[75]

Playfair knew Breteuil well; he could recall waiting in the anteroom to Breteuil's office in Paris, along with Clavière and Jean Sylvain Bailly, astronomer, Assembly member, and mayor of Paris in the early years of the Revolution.[76] He called Breteuil "a plain-spoken, honest man, possessed of clear distinct perceptions, and good views."[77] Playfair even dedicated a book to him: *Tableaux d'Arithmetique lineaire*—the French translation of *Lineal Arithmetic.*[78]

Playfair believed Breteuil was "an exception to the general rule in France"—that is to say, "Not given to pleasure, loving business, and having good enlightened views." Playfair told his fellow Brits that "people who take him for one of their enemies, are under a great mistake." Playfair added that he was beholding to Breteuil and wanted to thank him for the "services he endeavored to render me." Breteuil set up the deal for Playfair's rolling mill.[79]

It's not clear whether Breteuil was borrowing an idea from Playfair to bring down France with bogus money or Playfair was borrowing an idea from Breteuil. Maybe it was two kindred minds arriving at the same idea at the same time. The evidence says they had ample opportunity to meet and plan.

Breteuil arrived in London in late January or early February 1793. He was there to lobby British officials to issue a statement demanding the new French regime spare the lives of Marie Antoinette and her children.[80]

Playfair returned to London around then, as well. He was publishing pamphlets again.[81]

A third potential conspirator was also in London in late January 1793: Baron de Batz.[82]

Breteuil and Batz were close, too.[83] Playfair would later recall how Breteuil gave Batz a privilege to set up the *Compagnie des assurances*—the insurance company in which Batz partnered with Étienne Clavière. (Playfair admitted it was a corrupt deal; he recalled when the company was founded "there were no fires in Paris," though, later, after it was in business, "many houses were insured and there were fires pretty regularly." Playfair observed, dryly, the *Compagnie* did "pretty well.")[84]

The traditional story is that Batz tried to intercept the carriage taking Louis to the guillotine on 21 January 1793. Batz, still supposedly helping the regime with its finances, had the passport from Clavière that let him in and out of France. He returned to Paris in early in the month and began organizing the rescue attempt.[85]

Batz thought he could count on four or five hundred supporters. He scouted out the route from the Temple to the scaffold at the Place de la Révolution. He thought he had a promising spot, on a knoll overlooking the route (today the spot, at 52 rue Beauregard, is marked with a plaque.)

But, the story goes, Paris was locked down tight. The authorities were determined to make sure nothing went awry. Some of his accomplices were warned the night before to get out of town. Others were members of the militia; authorities mustered everyone with a uniform and a weapon and lined them up along the procession path. Anyone inclined to aid Batz would be risking his life if he broke ranks.

So when Batz rushed down the knoll on his horse, calling out, "Follow me to save the king!" Batz found himself with just a handful of accomplices. Two were killed; one was captured and later executed. Batz managed to melt into the crowd and escape. A few days later he was back in England.[86]

Recall the slush fund Batz set up when he was engineering France's finances with Clavière. Breteuil mentioned a secret fund that had been set up for Louis for contingencies; he planned to use it to pay banks to circulate his bogus assignats. You can't prove it, but it sure sounds like the same.[87]

Breteuil family papers say Breteuil and Batz met in London in late January. Batz's own papers say that when he reached London he met with other royalist émigrés, Englishmen "of great position," and "persons he could confide in."[88]

Did Playfair meet with Breteuil in London? Did he meet with Batz? It's impossible to tell. There's a gap in Breteuil's papers; he may have destroyed compromising documents as he fled the Low Countries when France attacked in 1793.[89] That's often the problem in historical research. Gaps in archives, police records, and private papers, seem destined to occur at the most inopportune points. History is written around what's available.

But consider the contrary: How could Playfair *not* have met with Breteuil and Batz, two of his closest friends and associates, just arrived from France? At a minimum, they had information to exchange. And, if Batz was looking in London for a "person he could confide in," no one fit the bill better than Playfair—his business partner and "intimate friend."[90]

Here's what we do know: In early February Playfair floated the idea of economic warfare in public. His pamphlet, *A General View of the Actual Force and Resources of France in January 1793,* was designed to convince British readers that France was a hollow force, that it could not pay for its war, and that its morale was low.[91]

The assignats made France vulnerable, Playfair said. Playfair claimed he had argued for economic warfare against France for years, writing, "had some celebrated emigrants taken my advice in the year 1791, *in making war upon the credit of France instead of combating her troops*, we should not have had now to arm in England; so many brave men would not have bled in the field, nor so virtuous a monarch on the scaffold."[92]

Playfair did not identify the "celebrated emigrants." It didn't matter. Now, Playfair wrote, "let us undermine their credit* at the expence of their paper." The asterisk pointed the reader to the bottom of the page, where Playfair had added a footnote:

"It is evidently not here that the way of undermining their credit is to be discussed it is the expediency of the measures, not the manner of putting it into execution."[93]

So what *was* the "manner of putting it into execution," and where *was* Playfair planning to discuss it? Read the pamphlet closely, and you'll see the nub of the plan right there: Playfair observed that, "the necessity of manufacturing the assignats in great haste, prevents all those precautions which are necessary to avoid falsification." French currency was easy to forge.[94]

The conditions were in place: France was already inflating its currency; it just needed a nudge to push it over the edge. Its money was easy to counterfeit. The operation would even be self-financing, since Playfair planned to skim some of the proceeds to cover his expenses. All you had to do was get over any ethical qualms you might have; Playfair himself once called forgery "the most unpardonable of all crimes."[95]

But once you got over that moral hurdle, it was an easy call.

Playfair dated his plan 20 March 1793. It's as candid as you would expect a secret proposal for a clandestine operation to be, and resembles a "finding" that might authorize a covert operation in latter twentieth century.[96] And it offers some insights into Playfair's thinking and motivations. Read the transcript; it's in Appendix A.[97]

Playfair began by observing he'd recommended economic warfare in *A General View of the Actual Force and Resources of France*. He then gave the rationale behind his proposed operation. Playfair said destroying the value of the assignat would be like "snatching the pistol and the poignard from the hand of the wicked assassin." France's only revenue was from printing money. Make the money worthless, and France could not wage war.

Yes, Playfair conceded, most Britons considered counterfeiting despicable. "I know that malfeasance may impute to me a bad intention and that its failure may be attended with disagreeable consequences," he conceded. But, "I consider myself as a soldier who fights for his country," and whatever happened, he would "avow my enterprise and maintain my motives."

The plan was straightforward: "Fabricate one hundred millions of assignats and spread them in France by every means in my power." That would prove to be a low estimate, but Playfair was ready to produce more, and that's the important point. Forgers had been making bogus assignats for years. This was different. Playfair planned to produce volumes that would collapse the French currency system.

"On then I go," Playfair concluded, "let me proceed or fail. I commit myself frankly & fairly and protest against the interference of any law in this country while I hope one day to be lauded with should I succeed in executing what I propose."

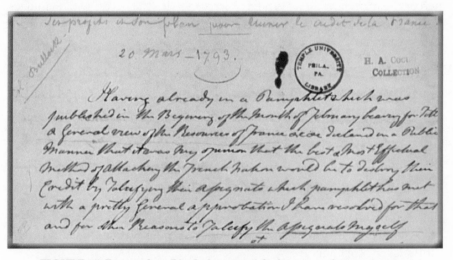

FIGURE 15: Excerpt from Playfair's proposal for his counterfeiting operation. Playfair signed each page of the six-page plan. See Appendix A for a transcription of the complete proposal. Source: The William Playfair Correspondence Collection, Special Collections Research Center, Temple University Libraries. Reproduced with permission.

"I must run my risqué and am prepared as every man should be who enters upon such undertakings," Playfair said, to himself as much to anyone. "Where there is no danger there is neither gain nor glory. Satisfied with my motives which I explain before I begin I hope that should I succeed my country shall gain, and my own will be the consequence, and that should I fail I can only blame myself."

Sometime during the life of the document someone wrote at the bottom: *Misérable Coquin!!!!* The unknown commentator may have thought Playfair a scoundrel, but today we'd call the memo the "smoking gun."

How did the secret proposal get out?

It first surfaced 1856 when French historian Louis Blanc described it in detail in the eighth volume of his epic *Histoire de la Révolution Française*. Blanc claimed he got the document from Alcide Donnadieu, a French ex-military officer living in London who collected autograph letters. However, Blanc's *Histoire* was never translated, so it has been available only in French, and his account of Playfair's proposal never caught much attention among English-speaking scholars.[98]

Donnadieu had sold Playfair's proposal in a lot advertised in 1851; the catalogue described it as a "melancholy instance of the perversion of a great man to do evil in an assumed good cause."[99] Eventually it landed in the collection of Harry A. Cochran, dean of the School of Business at Temple University. Cochran donated his collection to the university's library, and today Playfair's proposal is in its Special Collection Research Center.

Parts of the memo's circuitous history and chain of ownership may be lost, but the handwriting is unmistakably Playfair's (the elongated "c's" are one giveaway). It's genuine. The question is—who was the recipient?

The most likely candidate is Henry Dundas. The proposal was one of several documents in the Cochran collection. They may have been bought (or stolen) as a group before they made their way to Donnadieu. One of the other documents is a letter Playfair wrote to Dundas in 1804.[100]

So who was Henry Dundas?

Henry Dundas, later 1st Viscount Melville, was Pitt's friend and political ally, a hard-driving, plainspoken machine politician from Edinburgh— the alpha dog Pitt needed to knock heads in Scotland. Pitt made Dundas his Home Secretary in 1791. After France declared war on Britain in 1794, Dundas became Secretary of State for War.* Playfair's 1804 letter to Dundas

* At the time Britain divided oversight of the Army between the Secretary of State *for* War—Dundas—who was responsible for military policy, and the Secretary *at* War—

analyzes the future of British trade with America. The tone of the letter says Playfair and Dundas were no strangers.

And how would William Playfair, engineer, writer, and not-so-successful entrepreneur know Henry Dundas, Secretary of State for War?

It might have been Patrick Colquhoun. There was a track record; we know Colquhoun was friends with Playfair and introduced him to Sheffield. Colquhoun was in the Dundas camp (that's how he got his appointment as magistrate) and might have connected Playfair with Dundas, too.[101]

But there's an even simpler explanation: James Playfair built Henry Dundas' house.

Indeed, Dundas was one of James Playfair's most important clients. According to his journal, James began visiting Dundas at his home near Dalkeith in 1785. He designed Melville Castle for Dundas. It was a huge project—a three-story mansion. And James was doing all of this while he and William shared a house and a shop on Russell Place in London.[102]

That's the link. William Playfair knew Dundas through his brother James.

William thought the world of Dundas. He later called Dundas "a man of business, of political wisdom and sagacity, of industry, and boldness of character," who "perhaps never had an equal in this country, or in almost any other."[103]

Moreover, counterfeiting wasn't the only clandestine operation Playfair pitched Dundas. There's another proposal we know Playfair wrote around this time. It's from Britain's Home Office files, dated 24 April 1794—when Dundas was still Home Secretary—and describes a plan to set up a covert propaganda operation.[104]

Historian Arthur Aspinall found the proposal in the late 1940s. He included a transcript of it in *Politics and the Press*, his study of the British government's relations with the media.[105] Aspinall thought the proposal might have been sent to Sir Evan Nepean, a Home Office under secretary at the time. But if you retrieve the original and read the backside of page 2, you see it was addressed or routed to Dundas.[106]

Playfair wanted the Home Office to shape British public opinion; domestic audiences were considered fair game for propaganda, and the Pitt

---

Windham—who was responsible for military administration. It reflected Pitt's efforts to keep both Dundas and Windham in his coalition, along with William Henry Cavendish Cavendish-Bentinck, 3rd Duke of Portland, who led a faction of Whigs and became Home Secretary. In practice, personal influence was as important as formal rules; Dundas was personally closer to Pitt than was Windham. Playfair worked with both.

government often subsidized pamphlet writers who supported its policies. But this proposal is different; it has all the essential elements of a carefully planned, integrated information operation.

Playfair analyzed the target: "In every quarter of a large town, in every village, and in every place of habitual society and resort," he observed, "there are men who guide the opinion of others by superior information, impudence or talent for speaking." These men, Playfair said, usually rely on "some periodical publication or at least to some pamphlets that can easily be had."

So, the basic concept: Identify these opinion leaders and target them with pamphlets. Aspinall found no sign the Home Office did anything with Playfair's proposal. But forty years later James Sack, a University of Illinois historian, discovered evidence in the Windham papers at the British Library that suggest the Secretary at War picked up Playfair's idea.[107]

If you had any doubt Playfair was proposing a clandestine information operation, just read the side notes he included with the proposal. (Aspinall didn't cite these, and no one seems to have published them before, so I've included transcripts in Appendix B, along with the proposal itself.)[108]

To make sure the propaganda was convincing, Playfair wanted to use native French speakers to monitor the foreign press and pick up items to work into the product. "I would recommend Mr. Pettier a French writer who publishes a paper here, he has the sort of talents for it," Playfair wrote Dundas.

That would be Jean-Gabriel Peltier, who published several journals in London around then.[109] Peltier "could be employed by the medium of a bookseller," Playfair advised Dundas, "without knowing who he did it for & then it could be translated into English."

In other words, Playfair planned to use a cutout, an intermediary that would keep Peltier from knowing who was really paying him. That's not just government-sponsored journalism; that's a clandestine operation.

Playfair added a note: "Should it be wished to have any further communication upon the Subject" he advised, Dundas should send it "to Knightsbridge or to Mr Frazier No. 10 Little Bridge Street St. James," and "it will be forwarded to the Continent to the author who sets off in a few days." That was Playfair's mission to Flanders, Holland, and Germany, the one in which he made off with the plans for the French telegraph system and met with Vauban.

Meanwhile, the War of the First Coalition continued, and the Reign of Terror escalated.

In his political maneuvers in the Legislative Assembly, Brissot had allied with Charles-François Dumouriez, hero commander of the army that defeated the Prussians at Valmy six weeks after the 10 August coup. But Dumouriez turned out to be a closet monarchist and attempted a counter-coup in April 1793. When it failed, he defected to the Austrians. That made Brissot guilty by association.[110]

His enemies saw their opening. The Paris Commune charged Brissot and other top Girondins with treason—conspiring with foreigners to undermine the Republic. On 2 June gangs of *sans-culottes* and now-radicalized National Guard surrounded the National Convention, demanding their arrest. The deputies surrendered them.

Brissot, under house arrest, fled Paris but was caught en route to Normandy, hauled back to Paris, and executed on 31 October. His friend Clavière, whom Playfair had met seven years earlier at that dinner with Batz, refused to play along with the Revolutionary Tribunal. On 8 December, the day before his trial, the Genovese banker took his own life, putting a dagger into his heart.[111]

Nor was Le Havre distant enough to save the man who triggered everything. The arrest warrant was delivered in September. Seven months later, on Wednesday, 23 April 1794—even as William Playfair was preparing his propaganda proposal for Henry Dundas in London, and just a few weeks after James Playfair died at his brother John's home in Edinburgh—the revolutionary regime guillotined Jean-Jacques Duval d'Eprémesnil.[112]

§ § §

Did Playfair's plan succeed? Did it achieve its objectives? It's often hard to tell when a covert action works, especially when the target is big and complex, like a national economy. Too many factors are at play. But you can get a general sense of what happened.

One fact is clear: Assignats fell in value during the period the counterfeiting operation was underway. To see this, look at Figure 16, which plots their value from 1789 to 1796. (And, yes—we're using a graphic invented by Playfair to evaluate Playfair's covert operation.)

The chart shows the value of an assignat relative to an écu, a French gold coin that was widely used at the time. Two of the big dips in assignat values coincided with political convulsions: Louis' Flight to Varennes in June 1791, and the radicals' coup of August 1792. Yet there is a third big decline that does *not* follow a major political event: the steady drop after autumn 1793. By the end of 1795 assignats were worthless.[113]

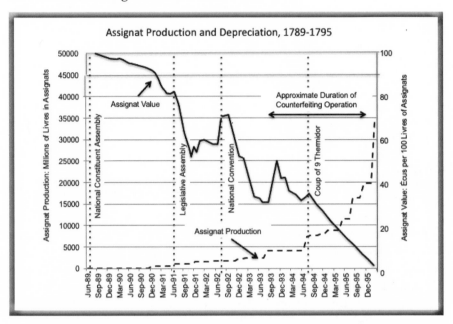

FIGURE 16: The Collapse of the Assignat*: This chart shows how the value of assignats fell over time. The left axis (solid line) tracks the value of assignats relative to the écu, a widely used French gold coin. The right axis (dashed line) traces the volume of assignats in production in French livres. Precipitous declines in value clearly coincide with major events that undermined confidence in the French regime; assignats also lost value during the flurry of production after 1793. Nevertheless, it's hard to miss the final plunge in value that took place during the counterfeiting operation.

---

*   Assignat depreciation is derived from Eugene Nelson White, "The French Revolution and the Politics of Government Finance, 1770–1815," *The Journal of Economic History*, Volume 55 (June 1995), 238. White cites Jean Bouchary, *Marché des changes de Paris à la fin du XVIIIe sicle* (1788–1800) Paris, 1937; and Antoine Bailleul, *Tableau complet de la valeur des Assignats, des Réscreptions et des Mandats* (Paris, 1797). Assignat production is derived from Elise S. Brezis and François Crouzet, "The Role of Assignats during the French Revolution: Evil or Rescuer?" *Journal of European Economic History* (April 1995), 7–40. Duration of the counterfeiting operation is estimated from John Edward Swinburne memorandum, Woodhorn Museum and Northumberland Archives at Ashington, Reference ZSW/590.

That decline happens to coincide with the counterfeiting operation. There is no official document (or at least none that's been found) recording the operation's precise start and finish. But recall the key dates:

Breteuil floated his proposal with the Austrians in December 1792. After they turned him down, Breteuil, Playfair, and Batz, had their opportunity to meet in London in early February 1793. That was just as Playfair published his pamphlet proposing economic warfare against France. Playfair drafted his secret plan for the counterfeiting operation one month later, in March.

§ § §

Sir John Edward Swinburne recalled in his memorandum that it was a few months after that, in autumn 1793, when he heard "French paper" was being made at Haughton Castle. It was also around this time feelers were out for craftsmen with the skills needed for a large-scale counterfeiting operation.

One of those feelers went to Thomas Bewick, a well-known Newcastle engraver. Obadiah Westwood, owner of a private mint in Birmingham, wrote to Bewick asking if he might make some specialized printing plates. Westwood was totally candid: he planned to use them to forge assignats.[114] Sir John also mentioned Bewick in his memorandum, saying that "a considerable person at Birmingham" had approached him.[115] Bewick turned down the request.[116]

Westwood likely knew Playfair. Birmingham wasn't that big—only about sixty thousand souls at the time. Also, the two men were in the same line of work—metalworking.[117]

Another feeler went out to a compositor working for newspaper publisher Samuel Swinton. Swinton, a former naval officer (and British agent during the American War) informed Home Office officials that one of his employees had been asked if "he could give Information of any Pressmen out of Employ," because some unidentified party was seeking "four Men to work on a Manufactory of French Assignats."[118]

In other words, evidence suggests the operation was ramping up in mid to late 1793—roughly the period when the assignats began their final plunge. A notation on Sir John's memo said that the Haughton Castle mill ceased production of assignat paper in 1795—about the time assignats had totally collapsed.

True, there were other factors at work. The chart shows how, in June 1794, French assignat production took off at a rate greater than ever before. The National Convention removed price controls in late December.[119] Either would have pushed assignat values down. Also, the British operation wasn't the only game in town; criminals and others—as we shall see—were forging assignats, too. Nevertheless, the assignat *did* collapse.

It had little impact on the battlefield, though; the French *won* the War of the First Coalition. Its army rallied in 1794, defeated the Austrians at Fleurus, and rolled into the Low Countries—the offensive Playfair was dodging as he made his way down the Rhine. By spring 1795 it turned into a rout, and the Duke of York evacuated his army via Bremen. Then the republicans defeated the émigrés at Quiberon.

It was on the political front that the counterfeiting operation seems to have had its greatest effect. This was part of Playfair's plan—though he could not anticipate how events would play out.

Even before Playfair proposed his operation, counterfeiting was creating chaos. Everyone knew there was forgery going on; there was too much bogus money in circulation to miss it. The regime, naturally, imposed draconian penalties, making assignat forgery a capital crime November 1790.[120] Soon the notes themselves even carried a warning:

LA LOI PUNIT DE MORT LE COUNTREFACTEUR

Nations choose the statements they put on their money. Their choice says something about the nature of their governance and their view of the world: *E Pluribus Unum*—Out of Many, One. Or *Dei Gratia Regina Fidei Defensatrix*—Defender of the Faith. The French motto, in effect, became "We'll Kill You If You Fake This."

You can just imagine a forger engraving a plate, meticulously inscribing, letter by letter, the penalty for the very act he was performing at that very moment: Death. Must have done wonders for the concentration. It didn't slow the counterfeiting, though. As the forgery got totally out of hand, the government began issuing pocket guides explaining to French citizens how to detect bogus bills—*LE VÉRIFICATEUR en chef des Assignats à ses Concitoyens.*[121]

Imagine you're a Frenchman. The government is printing unimaginable amounts of currency; inflation is, officially or not, national policy. Counterfeiting makes the currency depreciate even more. The law forces you to accept the script. Your savings lose value day and night, draining your wealth even as you sleep.

You suspect many of your fellow countrymen are playing the system. Can you trust your neighbor, who tries to pawn off his depreciating paper for your hard goods? Knowing that you may face death if you then happen to pass the notes yourself, and they prove *faux*? The counterfeiting operation wasn't just economic warfare; it was psychological warfare, too.

Yet the target wasn't just the mind of the average Frenchman trying to conduct his day-to-day business. The bigger prize, from early on, was the psyche of the French leadership.

By 1793 the republican radicals were in full control. As the Reign of Terror proceeded, regime leaders appeared to turn on each other. In April 1794 Danton was sent to the guillotine along with other leading Cordeliers.

The execution of Danton and the Cordeliers was a turning point, a major step in the eventual collapse of the French Republic. Today Danton is portrayed as a heroic victim, a foil to the scheming Robespierre, the orchestrator of the Terror. There's a statute honoring him in a square on Boulevard Saint-Germain, just off the Odéon Metro.

Was Danton's fall merely revolutionary power politics? Or did someone help the process along?

The formal charge against Danton was corruption. Supposedly he was part of a conspiracy hoping to make off with the assets of the French East India Company. The *Compagnie française pour le commerce des Indes orientales* had struggled for years, and the Convention decided to liquidate the crown-chartered corporation as a symbol of the Old Regime. Though troubled, the Compagnie still had valuable holdings; it was a fat target for graft.

Sure enough, in November 1793 François Chabot, a Montagnard deputy in the Convention, claimed he had been pitched a bribe at a dinner party three months earlier to engineer an untoward insider deal. It was a complex three-banked shot; suffice to say it would end with Compagnie directors signing over Compagnie assets to the members of the conspiracy, most of whom were well-connected insiders.

Chabot said he played along for a while, had second thoughts, and then reported the plot to Robespierre—naming Danton as one of the conspirators. He showed Robespierre 100,000 livres in assignats he'd received for the bribe. (No one knows if they were real or *faux*.)

Chabot's charges provided Robespierre the pretext he needed to purge Danton and his fellow Cordeliers. Danton and allies like Desmoulins and Fabre d'Eglantine were put on trial and guillotined on 5 April 1794. (So was Chabot, who failed to exculpate himself.) It raised the Terror to a new level, as the most radical leaders of the Revolution set upon each other.[122]

And who instigated the bribery scheme? Baron de Batz. At least, that's what the prosecutor for the revolutionary tribunal said.

Batz was at the dinner party. It was he, Chabot claimed, who orchestrated the pitch. Everyone knew Batz's reputation as a wheeler-dealer. He's worked on the Compagnie's account when he served on the Liquidation Committee. A few months after Danton and the alleged accomplices were executed, the Convention rolled up the rest of *la conspiration de Batz*—the "Batz Plot."

Élie Lacoste, the Convention deputy serving as prosecutor, reported to his colleagues on 14 June. Lacoste described the bribe, claiming, *"L'or et les assignats venaient d'Angleterre, Pitt et les émigrés avaient digéré le plan contre-révolution."* It was a foreign plot, Lacoste said, aimed at undermining the Revolution. Batz was the ringleader. The tribunal sent another fifty-four supposed conspirators to the guillotine, as "agents of Pitt."[123]

By then Batz was nowhere to be found.

The Reign of Terror ended on 17 July 1794 when the Convention—fearing for it own safety—turned on the Committee of Public Safety. Lacoste wrote the arrest order for Robespierre. After a brief skirmish, troops supporting the Convention seized Robespierre and his entourage. They were dead the next day.

Batz reappeared in the following October when royalists attempted a counter-coup on 13 Vendémiaire, only to be crushed by the French army—led by a forceful young general named Napoleon. Batz was arrested and held incommunicado for six days, interrogated, but managed to talk his way out.

He kept a low profile after that, until the monarchy returned to power in 1814. Then he received the Cross of Saint Louis and the rank of *maréchal de camp*, roughly equal to major general. Among the documents affirming his counter-revolutionary credentials: Élie Lacoste's report to the Convention.[124]

When Réné de Batz was writing his biography of Jean about a hundred years later, he found papers his ancestor had drafted sometime in 1793. If you believe the papers, Batz knew exactly what he was doing. Réné quoted Jean:[125]

The leadership of the regime is in a state of delirium, a state of convulsion...the laws of nature dictate that before long jealousies, suspicions, hatreds, and divisions will emerge and drag them into the abysses they themselves have opened. The only known means to accelerate these divisions and bring about a quicker collapse is to exacerbate those rivalries.

Now recall Playfair's March 1793 proposal for the counterfeiting operation. Playfair wrote:[126]

I shall also stir up divisions in the National Convention and bribe the Members, in short that every means in my power shall be taken to weaken France and thereby preserve to England a more cheap and a more humane victory than would be gained by sword and bayonet.

It could be a coincidence. Yet the fact remains that Playfair and Batz—two friends who had worked together for years—were in the same place at the same time in early 1793, and within months of each other proposed the same idea: Use bribery to turn the members of the Convention against one another.[127]

Look at their histories: every indicator says the bond between Playfair and Batz ran deep. Batz orchestrated Playfair's rolling mill deal. He introduced Playfair to the Brancas family. Luis Alberto de Brancas engineered Playfair's deal for the Machine de Marly. Antoine de Brancas warned Playfair to get out of Paris before Barré would have his hide. Batz was responsible for the connection between Playfair and Breteuil, too. There was their mutual connection with Jean-Jacques Duval d'Eprémesnil.

Is it really a surprise that, in the last months of his life, as Playfair wrote his memoirs, he felt compelled to mention Jean, Baron de Batz—just as he felt compelled to mention Jacques-Anne-Joseph le Prestre de Vauban? Batz was no more "just a French businessman" than Vauban was "just a French army officer."

But back to the main question: Was the counterfeiting operation a success?

About a year after Robespierre's fall, the Convention named a five-man committee, the Directory, as its executive. The Directory became synonymous with inflation, shortages, and corruption.

Combine feckless civilian leaders, a failing economy, continuing threats from abroad, and a successful military commander, and you have the recipe for a coup—like the one Napoleon staged in November 1799, ending the French First Republic. Napoleon, of course, went on to crown himself emperor and conquer Europe in a string of wars that killed more than three and half million people.

If the collapsing assignat had a role in any of this, and the counterfeiting operation contributed to the collapsing assignat, then it was an unintended consequence of truly epic proportions. That's covert action in the real world: often opportunistic in execution, frequently implemented by players with mixed motives, and shaped by uncontrolled and unanticipated events. The bigger the plan, the more ambitious the goals, the harder it is to anticipate what will lead to what.

But one thing cannot be denied: it sure was a Great Op.

§ § §

Perhaps the most intriguing thing about Playfair's forgery operation is that *he never told anyone about it*—remarkable, especially when you consider how officials today sell their memoirs for thousands or even millions of dollars. Yet, while Playfair's role remained hidden, the operation itself did not remain secret for long.

On 24 March 1794, Richard Sheridan took the floor to speak in Commons. The discussion underway was about the government's proposal to raise the tax on paper.

Sheridan said he thought it outrageous that the fancy paper "used by the higher ranks of life for their amusing and elegant correspondence" was taxed at a mere fourteen percent, while the paper used for newspapers, "the most useful and cheap communication of intelligence," was taxed at forty to fifty.

"This, if persisted in," Sheridan said, would amount to a "prohibition of almost all the cheap circulation of intelligence."

And then he veered off topic. The detour went all the way to Humshaugh.

Sheridan couldn't help but mention that, "There was a mill for the manufactory of paper to a great extent in this country, in which the French assignats was carried on." Sheridan had got wind of Sir John Edward Swinburne's letter to Charles Grey reporting the French paper made at Haughton Castle.

Sheridan had also heard about the ploy to have the notes stamped at the lower "fancy paper" rate. "The excise officer who attends this mill," Sheridan said, had complained because he had been given "authority for superintending this, as if it had been the regular and honest manufacture of paper in the way of trade."[128]

Pitt, from the front bench, dissembled. He said merely that information from forgers was not to be relied on. But now the counterfeiting operation was an open secret. With weeks the *Gazette Nationale ou Le Moniteur Universel* in Paris quoted Sheridan's comments in Commons.[129]

Word was out about the operation. Then Paul Lukyn blew its cover completely.

Lukyn, a stationer, was contracted to print some of the forged assignats. He approached an engraver, John Strongitharm, to make the printing plates. Strongitharm tried to beg off, but Lukyn persisted, saying that they were for the Duke of York. Strongitharm agreed to make the plates.

The two men agreed on a price—fifty pounds—and Strongitharm delivered the plates. Lukyn, according to testimony, "had immense numbers of these forged assignats printed off, and went abroad to sell them."[130]

Then Lukyn tried to stiff Strongitharm.

Lukyn thought he saw a loophole: Contracts depend on the government for enforcement. Forgery is a crime. So all agreements connected with a forgery operation are polluted with illegality. Lukyn claimed that, since the government could not enforce such a fouled agreement, his contract with Strongitharm was invalid and he had no obligation to pay.

Unfortunately Lukyn—apparently not a well man, who died suddenly four years later at the age of forty-three—chose the wrong engraver to play for a patsy.[131]

Strongitharm was ignorant of niceties when it came to dealing with customers. "Insolent & troublesome," one called him. That was never truer than when it came to deadbeats. He wasn't the least bit reluctant to take a debt-dodging stationer like Lukyn to court.[132]

The trial was convened on 18 November 1795. Strongitharm's witnesses testified that he took the job only after Lukyn convinced him the phony assignats were for the Duke of York—which is to say, the British army.

Strongitharm's lawyer argued that, since Government sanctioned the forgery, Government also sanctioned any agreement made to carry it out.[133]

The judge, Lloyd Kenyon, 1st Baron Kenyon, was a respected jurist—and a loyal member of Pitt's camp. He observed that the contract did not violate any statute, and he was not prepared to say whether "distressing the enemy" with bogus assignats was unlawful. (Playfair later observed Kenyon was known as "a very honest man"—except by "those who were afraid of his power.")[134]

With that ruling, the jury decided in favor of Strongitharm, and Lukyn had to pay up. He was out £264 for the plate in question, plus other plates Strongitharm had made for him. Strongitharm went on to become engraver to the Prince of Wales, brother of the Duke of York.[135]

British officials didn't want to leave Strongitharm in the lurch. But when they bailed out Strongitharm, they put a fact on the public record: the government had let out a contract to forge assignats.

So by 1794 it was generally known counterfeit assignats were circulating. And, after *Strongitharm v. Lukyn* was decided in 1795, it was tacitly assumed the Brits were behind a lot of it. A member of Commons, John Nichols, let the secret slip further in 1796, alluding to it in a floor speech. Yet no one confirmed the operation officially.[136]

When Puisaye published his account of Quiberon in 1804, he scoffed that "the sensible reader" would consider reports that "English ministers were making counterfeit assignats" as no more than a "rude calumny."[137] Then again, he was living in London at the pleasure of the British government.

No one blamed Puisaye for the Debacle on the Beach—probably because Pitt, Dundas, and especially Windham had to know knew they were as responsible as anyone. The less said, the better, and if Puisaye claimed the assignat counterfeiting was his idea, well, that was swell, too.[138]

So that was the official story: Yes, counterfeit assignats were appearing all over. Yes, we've heard the rumors. Yes, the republicans found huge numbers of bogus bills with the émigrés at Quiberon. But that was a *French* operation. *French*. Even Puisaye says so, and he's still tall, still good-looking, and still persuasive. Lukyn and Strongitharm? No comment.

It worked for a while; the counterfeiting reports faded from memory—until sixteen years later, when William Cobbett started writing about British monetary policy. In 1811 Cobbett's newspaper, the *Political Register*, began a series, "Paper Against Gold," railing against the Bank of England and the evils of paper money. It had already covered a litany of evils before Letter No. 24 pointed out one particular defect:

Currency, unlike gold, could be counterfeited.

In fact, Cobbett claimed, newspapers outside London were reporting at that very moment how Napoleon was smuggling bogus Bank of England notes into the country. "This is a war of finance with a vengeance!" he declared. But Britain could hardly object, Cobbett demurred, because it had done exactly the same, counterfeiting French notes. If anyone wanted proof, all they had to do was look up *Lukyn v. Strongitharm*.[139]

That resurfaced the counterfeiting operation. When members of Parliament began debating it in floor speeches, it became clear that some had known about it for years. One could also hear a split between supporters (generally Tories) and opponents (generally Whigs).

Earl Stanhope (who had broken with Pitt over the war with France) observed that Britain couldn't much object to French counterfeiting; the forgers "had an authority in the conduct of our own Government." Baron Holland (Whig) then weighed in, saying the forgery had been "disgraceful to this Government, and to the tribunals of the Government who approved it."[140]

Holland, incidentally, was the nephew of Charles James Fox—mentor to John Edward Swinburne.

Lord Liverpool—Robert Banks Jenkinson, Tory, soon to be Prime Minister and Playfair's would-be rescuer from Newgate—tried to walk back the cat. He dodged and weaved, observing "the alleged transaction" occurred at a time "when he could have no personal knowledge upon the subject." But, Jenkinson noted for the record, the question had once been put to "a member of the Government" and that the minister had "expressly and positively denied that that Government had ever sanctioned such a transaction."

It was a non-denial denial: Liverpool was saying *he* was not qualified to make any comment. But, if one *were* inclined, one *might* seek the view of a member who had been part of a government that was no longer in power. And *that* person—who was no longer present—would absolutely deny anything had occurred.

Cobbett had opened the proverbial can of worms.

So who was William Cobbett?

William Cobbett, born in Farnham in 1763, was, in succession, a farm laborer, gardener, soldier, journalist, publisher, convict, and (no comment intended on the logic of the progression) member of Parliament. He was a life-long gadfly. Many would say his politics drifted from right to left as he got older, but he really just had an uncontrollable instinct for questioning any and all authority.

So it wasn't surprising that in 1811 Cobbett was serving a two-year sentence for seditious libel. He had written a sarcastic piece objecting to the practice of flogging soldiers. When Cobbett went a bit too far and likened Britain's flogging policy to Napoleon's, Attorney General Vicary Gibbs—yes, *that* Vicary Gibbs—filed charges. Cobbett found himself writing his essays from a cell in Newgate.

But what would prompt Cobbett to dig up an obscure lawsuit referring to a government-sponsored counterfeiting operation in the first place? It just might have been that Cobbett and Playfair had a connection of their own.

Cobbett and Playfair had once shared a patron: William Windham. Windham had admired Cobbett—by almost all accounts, a gifted writer— and had funded the startup of the *Political Register* in 1802.[141] But Cobbett's congenital loathing of authority and "racy" style proved too much for the staid, deeply conservative Windham, and their friendship collapsed by 1806. By 1810 they were on polar ends of the political spectrum.[142] Playfair claimed he was amazed that Windham, "a scholar and a gentleman," had ever put up with what he called Cobbett's "low ribaldry."[143]

Only one problem: Playfair was forgetting how close he had been to Cobbett, too.

In 1792 Cobbett fled England for France to avoid a court martial, and then fled France for America a few weeks later when the radicals took over. He became a bookseller in Philadelphia, and one of the books he published in 1796 was…the American edition of *The History of Jacobinism, Its Crimes, Cruelties and Perfidies,* Playfair's account of the French Revolution.

Cobbett even included a dedication to Playfair in his edition of the book. He wrote, "I have seldom known a greater pleasure than I now feel, in rendering you my thanks, in a public manner, for your spirited efforts in the cause of order and *true* liberty."[144]

Did Playfair tell Cobbett about the forgery? Did Windham? As we've seen, it was an open secret among British leaders. Writing from Newgate, Cobbett likely relished making that sly reference to an operation his former allies were hoping to bury. Besides, there wasn't anything anyone could do to him. He was merely citing case law. And he was already in jail.

The story sat dormant again until 1852, when Newcastle author Thomas Doubleday took a fishing trip with friends on the River Tyne. The conversation happened to turn to the forgery of French assignats. One his hosts assured him the story was true, claiming the paper came from a nearby mill at Haughton Castle. He even offered to introduce Doubleday to the current owner, William Smith, son and namesake of the mill's builder.

When Doubleday returned a few weeks later, Smith recounted the story his father had told him: The mill's foreman, Magnay, had a son who moved to London to become a stationer. Smith said it was the son, Christopher Magnay, who had ordered the French paper. Smith even said he still possessed one of the molds from the operation. Doubleday included the tale in *Political Life of Sir Robert Peel*, his biography of the British statesman.[145]

Incidentally, as a young man Doubleday had been a friend and disciple of... William Cobbett.[146]

So now there was a published report claiming physical evidence of the counterfeiting operation existed—the paper mold. The topic surfaced again later that year when a reader posted a question in the journal *Notes and Queries*—sort of a nineteenth-century Internet forum or listserv.

"I have heard it asserted, that during the war with France," the reader wrote, "that Mr. Pitt's government landed on the French coast a large number of forged assignats, for the express purpose of weakening the national credit of the republican government."

"Can any of your readers say what ground there is for this anecdote?" The reader was aghast at the very notion, saying, "It would be well for the honour of England, and for the credit of modern warfare, if it were totally disproved."[147]

Several readers responded. Some said they had read the case history of *Strongitharm v. Lukyn*. Others said they know of existence of the forged bills. The final word came from Sir Walter Calverley Trevelyan—a geologist, naturalist and antiquarian. Trevelyan's story matched Doubleday's. He, too, reported the Smith family had kept one of the molds.[148]

The story sat yet again. Then, in 1882, Rev. George Rome Hall, an amateur Northumberland archeologist, brought a mold from the now-fabled operation to a meeting of the Society of Antiquaries of Newcastle-upon-Tyne for his colleagues to see. Hall said Buccaneer Smith's grandson had lent it to him (another generation had passed).

The Society of Antiquaries of Newcastle-upon-Tyne was founded in 1813. Its first president: John Edward Swinburne. Even from the grave, Sir John would not let go.

According to Rev. Hall, the mold had been tossed into a lumber room, where it had sat for years. He told the members the story of how Christopher Magnay had ordered the paper for an operation in which the Duke of York would distribute bogus currency to undermine the French economy.[149]

The Society accepted possession of the mold in 1938. Except, as it turned out, there were three molds, not one. The Society catalogued them: Archive Items 1938.6, 1938.7, and 1938.8.[150]

Another fifty years passed. Sometime around 1990 members of the Society decided to determine once and for all whether the molds really were used to make bogus assignats.

John Philipson, locally raised, lifelong historian of Northumberland, examined the molds. They were in good condition for their age. But the watermarks did not resemble those on any of the assignats the Society had on hand. So Philipson sought out a paper historian in London.

The historian confirmed that one mold, Item 1938.6, had a watermark resembling that of assignats issued under the decree of 29 September 1790. A second mold, Item 1938.7, had a watermark that matched assignats issued under the decree of 28 September 1793. The third mold, Item 1938.8, had an odd watermark that no one could identify—it read, "ORIGINAL SECURITY BANK." But the first two molds were enough to settle the matter: there had been counterfeiting going on at Haughton Castle.[151]

In addition, there was a paper trail. Around 1960 the county archivist had suggested to Sir John's descendants that they deposit their family papers in the Northumberland Record Office—including Sir John's memorandum recounting how he had discovered the counterfeiting operation.

Now Peter Isaac, civil engineer-turned-bibliophile, analyzed the memorandum. In the paragraph mentioning "Mr. Watson" as a participant along with Playfair, someone other than Swinburne had written in the margin, "quere Brook Watson." Then, after a space, someone (the second writer, or, possibly, a third) responded "yes."[152]

So who was Brook Watson?

Born in Plymouth in 1735 or 1736, Brook Watson was orphaned at the age of six. He was sent to America to live with his aunt and uncle in Boston. His uncle, a merchant trader, put him on the crew of one of his ships. He was fourteen. On one voyage, while he was swimming in Havana harbor, a shark attacked him; Watson walked the rest of his life with a peg leg.[153] (Years later John Singleton Copley captured the incident in a painting, "Watson and the Shark," which today hangs in the National Gallery of Art in Washington, D.C.)

Undeterred, Watson got connected with trading companies in Nova Scotia and mainland Lower Canada. By the early 1780s he was responsible for a quarter of all trade out of Quebec. Watson got rich. When the American Revolution broke out, he pretended to support the patriots; he was actually collecting intelligence for the British army.

After the war Watson helped evacuate loyalists from New York and set up charities for those emigrating to Britain. Watson's wealth got him into politics. He married a relative of William Pitt. He won a seat in Commons. That was about the time the Bank of England made him a director. From 1793 to 1796 he served as commissary general to the British army in Flanders, which explains a note attached to Sir John's memorandum:[154]

> The circumstances of the Troops in Flanders being paid in Assignats, that were found on examination on the frontier to be forged was subsequently made known to me by Col. Scott, Aide de Camp to Sir David Dundas serving there as well as that Brook Watson was the agent.

General David Dundas (a distant relative of Henry Dundas, if that) commanded a brigade under the Duke of York. Apparently Watson was paying British soldiers with bogus assignats. There is another note attached to Sir John's memo, apparently written by Henry Richmond, the gentleman he met in Humshaugh while investigating the mill at Haughton Castle. It makes Watson's link to the operation clear—and Playfair's:[155]

> Mr. Thelusson is the person who pays the Papermakers for the French paper & Mr. Playfair, the Author of several political Pamphlets, is the Agent who manages the Business and who lately went over to Ostend with Mr. Brook Watson—The assignat Paper is manufactured at two other Mills in the South of England.

Peter Isaac Thellusson, elected to Commons in 1795 and later created 1st Baron Rendlesham, was descended from a Geneva banking family that emigrated from France to England in the 1760s. He, too, was a director of the Bank of England—more evidence top British financial figures were in on the operation.[156]

The phony assignats were just one more item Commissary General Watson supplied the British army—but with a bonus effect. When the army paid a soldier in Flanders with a forged assignat, it was basically stealing from the French treasury. Later, when the soldier spent it, he diluted the value of all French money a little.

The note makes one thing clear, however: Playfair wasn't alone on those Continent tours. He was traveling with Watson, at least some of the time. William Windham was in Flanders, too.[157] So, of course, was the Duke of York. It helps explain what Playfair's five-month excursion through Holland, Flanders, and Germany that year was really about.

Swinburne's memo also implied Playfair was running an intelligence operation to watch for the periodic changes the French made in their watermarks. When he and the London partners learned the watermarks had changed, they would send new molds to the mills to match the new watermarks. Philipson and Isaac published their findings in *Archaeologia Aeliana*, the Society's journal.

And what about the third mold?

Item 1938.8 was a total cipher to Philipson. There was no record of an "Original Security Bank" in any catalogue of London financial institutions. Puzzling over the mold with the odd watermark, Philipson mused, "Whether there was likewise any especial story attached to mould 1938.8 to warrant its preservation remains to be discovered."[158]

It's a good thing the Society kept it. William Playfair set up the Original Security Bank the year after the forgery operation ended. He made the paper for his bank notes at the same mill he used for his bogus assignats. Finding all three molds in the same place provides the physical evidence that ties Playfair to the counterfeiting operation.

8 Back to Business

layfair had led three lives since returning from France in 1783: businessman, writer, and clandestine operator. There were no sharp lines between the three. The ideas Playfair wrote about became operations. The operations put Playfair in the offices of top officials. Officials got sucked into Playfair's business ventures—intentionally or not.

§ § §

John Stockdale's shop was one of a half-dozen bookstores on Piccadilly Street. Bookstores were the publishers of the time. Owners fronted the money to set a book in type after enough subscribers committed, and then had additional copies printed for sale "on spec." The author got a cut; advances were rare.

Stockdale sold Playfair's *History of Jacobinism* for 8 shillings as loose pages, a sixpence in boards. By comparison, he sold Jefferson's *Notes on the State of Virginia* for 7 shillings.[1] Playfair's pamphlets went for 1-2 shillings.

As today, it was hard to get rich with a pen. The sixty-four subscribers who signed up for *A History of Jacobinism* ordered a total of 132 copies.[2] So, assuming an author kept, say, an eighth of the list price, the first run of a book might earn him 100–150 shillings. At the time, a good mechanic made about 30 shillings a week.[3]

Little wonder Playfair called profits from writing "trifling."[4] When a cousin, James Rogers, came to London hoping for a journalism career in the Big City, Playfair talked him out of it, telling young Rogers, "you might make a decent livelihood; but you are at the mercy of your employer." He warned Rogers, "an ebullition of temper on his part, or an attack of illness on yours, might throw you helpless on the world."

Playfair must have been convincing. Rogers went home and became a minister.[5]

Bookstores were meeting places for the politically like-minded. Stockdale catered to Americans and readers interested in the new nation. He even rented a room to John Adams and his son John Quincy for a few months in 1783 when Adams arrived in London as U.S. ambassador.[6]

Playfair might easily have bumped into John Adams at Stockdale's shop; he lived less than a mile away. We do know Adams followed Playfair's work. When the Boston Public Library inherited Adams' book collection, someone ranked each volume by how many comments Adams wrote in the margins. Playfair's *History of Jacobinism* came in tenth. (Adams: "This writer traces things very well.")[7]

Adams had no comment on Playfair's style (or lack thereof). Others did. Commenting on his *Better Prospects to the Merchants and Manufacturers of Great Britain,* one reviewer wrote, "Mr. Playfair appears to be the regular agent of ministry, appointed to defend all their measures through thick and thin. We are astonished that they have not been able to *hire* a better writer or an abler advocate, as Mr. Playfair is scarcely able to write a sentence of Grammar. The treasury board surely gives poor salaries." And the final dig: "The paper and print of this pamphlet are about upon a par with its contents."[8]

Playfair never quite admitted, but never quite denied that the government paid him to write. He said that reviewers who accused him "writing from a certain quarter" were "rash." He insisted, "I have a sovereign contempt for those persons who make so free with the truth as to say that I am paid by government."[9]

Even if the government did not pay Playfair directly, ministers sometimes funded his travel and business ventures. In his 24 October 1795 letter to Windham, he described his original plan for the *Revolutionary Magazine,* a propaganda operation: print 20,000 copies of his proposed anti-Jacobin pamphlet and send a free copy to every parish in Britain. That would pump-prime sales. Recalling his earlier efforts, Playfair told Windham,[10]

> I gave up without ever publishing or distributing the prospectus;
> for tho' I am possessed of a great quantity of materials and can

get more through the best channels, yet I found on calculating that I must be <u>supported</u> otherwise I might get myself into a very embarrassed situation if it did not answer.

Playfair needed working capital; he hoped Windham could provide it. He scaled down his plan and asked Windham to fund printing two thousand copies and cover £250 in "general expenses," for a total of "5 or 600£."

Apparently Windham came through with the money. Playfair sent Windham another letter a week later. It's interesting because it not only implies Windham agreed to fund the project; it also suggests Windham had offered Playfair up-front compensation, but Playfair turned him down. Playfair wrote: [11]

> I have to thank you Sir in the most unfeigned terms for your question at the end of your letter. The way in which Government could be of great use to me and I flatter myself of service to the Public cause would be by Enabling me to Publish the Revolutionary Magazine, and if I do not make a favourable change in the minds of many people in this country before next Spring I should never pretend to any Judgement again. The Extent would depend wholey on those who favoured me with their support & my Exertions would always be so great as that support would enable me.

Six months later Playfair wrote Windham (in his ever-challenging grammar and syntax), accounting for expenditures:[12]

> The money that I have had is besides the first hundred guineas in past November £125 in 5 payments by two drafts on Messrs Randolph & Cooks, one for £50 and three of 25£ Each (say one hundred twenty five pounds).

Playfair later wrote that "ministers should have funds at their disposal" to reward men like him for ideas. If they "answered," to use the jargon of the time, "the proposer of a good plan" then "should be entitled to make a claim" that would "be settled fairly by an award or some easy and fair means." Secret service funds "ought only to go for services that require secrecy."[13]

Of course, this assumed everyone acted in good faith. It didn't always work out that way. Case in point: Playfair's plan to reform Britain's tax system.

No one—William Pitt included—really liked the existing tax system. It seemed arbitrary, opaque, and unfair. Even worse (at least in Pitt's view), it didn't produce enough revenue.[14]

In 1798 Playfair collaborated with William Cope on an alternative. Their plan would tax five categories of commercial transactions: interest, rent, retail sales, wholesale sales, and goods sold on commission. Individuals and businesses would pay the government the tax whenever completing a transaction, receiving a stamp as proof of payment.[15]

Cope used his entrée with Pitt, who "granted an audience," Playfair recalled, and listened "with great attention."

According to Playfair, Pitt said. "Yes, if it could be executed it would do." The Prime Minister rose from his seat, stirred the logs in the fireplace, sat again and continued to listen. He promised to pay £200,000 if the scheme were adopted and asked them to provide a detailed plan.

Playfair and Cope returned ten days later, detailed plan in hand. Pitt was just walking out his office. He seemed in a hurry.

"Will you trust me with your plan?" he asked—as though they had a choice with the Prime Minister of Great Britain. They handed it over. Pitt left, and neither heard a word about it again. Playfair was convinced the Exchequer used his idea a few years later, but by then Pitt was gone and no one would acknowledge any lineage.

Yet money wasn't his main motivation.

"I have lived in France, where I saw the evils of overturning a bad government," he wrote, "and I am doubly interested from feeling to do my little in supporting a good one. This was my motive when I wrote in France against the French, and it is still."[16]

§ § §

Playfair published around two-dozen books and pamphlets in the decade following his escape from France in 1792. The first was *Short Account of the Revolt and Massacre Which Took Place in Paris on the 10th of August 1792*— Playfair's first-person account of the insurrection that ousted Louis XVI.[17]

The author of *Short Account* was given only as "Persons Present At the Time." Playfair probably worried about compromising friends and accomplices who remained in Paris—like the source at police headquarters who told him Barère was after him. Playfair didn't reveal himself as the author until January 1794, when *Short Account* was advertised with several of his other publications.[18]

Playfair reached Dieppe on 21 August; he'd sent his family to Britain and detoured to Holland before returning home himself. *Short Account* was advertised in *The Times* on 12 September 1792 and several other papers. The timeline suggests Playfair was writing it on the run[19]

In February, Playfair published *A General View of the Actual Force and Resources of France*—the prescription for economic war he cited in his secret plan for the counterfeiting operation.[20] Later that year Playfair proposed partitioning France to keep it from ever launching another war; it had the straightforward, if not quite concise title, *Thoughts on the Present State of French Politics and the Necessity and Policy of Diminishing France for Her Internal Peace and to Secure the Tranquility of Europe.*

Playfair also wrote about politics, political reform, and democracy. A few weeks after his return from Paris he published *Inevitable Consequences of a Reform in Parliament.* Everyone knew Parliament wasn't apportioned fairly; the question was what to do about it, and that was really part of a bigger issue.[21]

Thinkers everywhere were grappling with how to embrace popular rule while keeping it from turning into...well, the French Revolution. Playfair's solution was constitutional monarchy. Kings and aristocrats would be a check and balance on elected legislators who might act rashly. It's unfashionable today, but Founding Fathers like John Adams toyed with the idea, too.[22]

Besides his books and pamphlets, Playfair launched a newspaper. Its quirky, never-explained name: *The Tomahawk! Or Censor General.* The first edition appeared on 27 October 1795. No names appeared on its masthead, just the address of J. Downes Bookseller ("Strand near Temple Bar"), where letters would be received.

The paper occasionally jested self-referentially about how readers were trying to discover its masterminds. No one knew who was responsible until Thomas Byerley confirmed in Playfair's obituary that he had been the editor and Samuel Arnold his partner. The partnership tells you something about the circles in which Playfair traveled.[23]

Arnold wasn't a politician or journalist; he was one of the best-known composers of the era. For nearly a century musicologists gave him credit for

To Anacreon in Heaven, the melody adopted for *The Star-Spangled Banner.* It was probably the same phenomenon of how quotations get misattributed to Winston Churchill or Mark Twain. (Today, experts are certain that John Stafford Smith, Arnold's much less-known contemporary, wrote the tune.)

Originally *The Tomahawk!* was to appear on Tuesdays, Thursdays, and Saturdays, selling for six pence. But just a week after the first issue it announced it would become a daily, four pages long, selling for two pence half.[24] A typical edition consisted of commentary on British–French relations (invariably anti-republican), political verse (embarrassingly high school quality), theater news (clearly Arnold's contribution), and what were alleged to be letters to the editor (about as genuine as those to *Dear Abby* or *The Playboy Advisor* in their heyday).

The Tomahawk! "was a daily paper without news or advertisements," just opinion and analysis, Playfair recalled, to avoid the stamp tax. Playfair later recalled it was "strongly in favour of government" and the masthead revealed its point of view: *Pro rege sæpe, pro patria semper* ("Often for the king, always for the nation").[25]

But news coverage regularly sneaked in; the revolution in France was always in the background. One early edition boasted:[26]

> By persons who arrived from Paris, about a month ago, we were informed of the state of men's minds in that capital with a precision and truth which we believe no persons, who go to acquire information, and are *strangers,* can be expected to possess.

(Notice how it echoes the note Playfair passed to William Windham five days earlier—Playfair planned to see "Mons. Messin," who can "give more information about Paris" than "any person who has resided there a stranger.")[27]

The Revolution could be hard on friendships. It tore apart Lansdowne's relationship with his old friend Barré. Lansdowne was skeptical of most wars; Barré thought it regrettable but necessary. He backed Pitt, and resigned the seat representing Calne that Lansdowne effectively owned. (Lansdowne gave it to Benjamin Vaughn. Jeremy Bentham had hoped for it; he sent Lansdowne a sixty-one page letter expressing his disappointment.)[28]

Playfair by this time was solidly in the Pitt camp. He remained fond of his one-time patron.[29] But politics was politics, which explains the skewering *The Tomahawk!* delivered in a November 1795 column. Taunting Lansdowne and two other members of Lords, it was a classic sarcastic hit on liberal hypocrisy, leavened with eighteenth-century formality. It gives a flavor of the paper's style:[30]

MOUTH PITY!

It is with much regret, that we see this sessions, as well as the last, a triumvirate in the UPPER HOUSE, *croaking* so very malignantly about the distresses of the poor, without any of these *Cræsuses* proposing seriously any measure to their relief!

The THREE NOBLEMEN alluded to are, perhaps, as *penurious* as any three men in the kingdom. Yet they are very prolific in MOUTH-PITY, without really having ever displayed any *solid* pity for the MOUTHS OF THEIR FELLOW-SUBJECTS!

...The Marquis of LANSDOWNE, skilled in the knowledge of the tricks of JACOBINISM, from his friend DUMONT, the *coadjutor* of MIRABEAU, came up from Wiltshire, crying about the distresses of his poor tenantry, who last year, he pretends, lived upon bread and water, and now they have no bread, he says, to eat! What an INDULGENT and CHARITABLE MASTER, with a PRINCELY fortune, to contribute himself *not one* SIXPENCE *towards their relief!* His IRISH tenantry, on the subject of THEIR LEASES, could tell even a *more* pitiable tale! Therefore we need not wonder at the impoverished state of his Wiltshire Cheese tenantry, when his Lordship is considered as their PHILANTHROPIC MASTER! This is quite *a la* MIRABEAU, to promote the mischief, and then blame the innocent victims of his own malignity!

The Tomahawk! occasionally echoed Playfair's clandestine operations; one column reported—sorry, analyzed—that "French paper is now one-third one percent or three hundred for one!"[31] It also anticipated some of Playfair's later publications; one issue had an article on "An Inquiry Into the Cause of the Decline and Fall of Nations."[32]

Yet, for all its support of the government, it was the government that killed *The Tomahawk!* Playfair later recalled how "the Stamp Office harassed us perpetually." The tax collectors wouldn't buy Playfair's dodge; they recognized news when they saw it. So, he said, "we resolved to give it up, which we did, disgusted with such treatment."[33] The paper bid farewell in its 7 March 1796 edition, bordered in black:[34]

Death of the Tomahawk.

THE PROPRIETORS OF THIS WORK, set up on *purpose* to support the LAW, would be the very last persons in the Kingdom to *infringe* upon that very LAW which they have all along endeavoured with so much *spirit* to SUPPORT.

They are sorry, however, not for THEMSELVES, but for their COUNTRY, and its FUTURE WELFARE, to inform the PUBLIC, that being prosecuted by some persons belonging to the STAMP-OF-FICE, and not wishing to stand the event of a LAW-SUIT, they think it proper to decline, in the future, THIS PUBLICATION.

While they mention this, they are the same time glory in having with so much acknowledged NERVE, contributed, for FIVE MONTHS, to the cause of the KING and the CONSTITUTION; and as they will very likely start, on a future occasion with a PLAN that will not be subject to any CROOKED molestation, they now respectfully, *for a time*, take FAREWELL OF THAT PUBLIC, which, on a *future occasion*, they shall again *endeavour* to ENTERTAIN with their *wonted* LOYALTY and SPIRIT.

Thus *The Tomahawk!* folded after a run of less than a year. Playfair moved on to the venture that would ruin him.

§ § §

As with the Scioto story, the tale of the Original Security Bank began with the arrival of ships from France.

Around noon on 22 February 1797 four French warships—two frigates, a schooner, and a lugger—were spotted along the coast of Pembrokeshire, Wales. They anchored that afternoon in Cardigan Bay, just off the village of Fishguard. Troops embarked in small boats and began to row to shore.

The "Last Invasion of Britain" was originally part of a larger French military operation originally scheduled for December 1796: the *Expédition d'Irlande*. The plan was to land 15,000 soldiers at Bantry Bay, on the far southwest corner of Ireland, hoping to spur a separatist uprising. Additional attacks targeted Bristol and Newcastle in England as diversions.[35]

The Expédition was the mirror image of the Quiberon operation: change the strategic equation by stoking a behind-the-lines insurgency. Fittingly, the French commander was Louis Lazare Hoche.

The plan failed when the Channel was swept by some of the worst storms in a century. The main invasion fleet struggled just to reach Bantry Bay, only to find the seas too rough to land the troops. Tossed by waves and beaten by winds for almost a week, the French staggered home. The Newcastle invasion fizzled, too; the new flat-bottomed assault boats the French planned to use proved completely unseaworthy.[36]

But Hoche went ahead with the Bristol attack anyway. He thought it might shake up British leaders in London. The thousand-man force planned to march north to Liverpool, burning, plundering, and generally creating mayhem along the way.[37]

Navigation was iffy in the eighteenth century, so instead of Bristol, the French wound up landing 150 miles to the west at Fishguard. Outmanned and cut off from resupply, they didn't have a chance. The local militia, volunteers, and yeomen rolled them up in two days. The military impact was nil.

The psychological effect, on the other hand, was enormous. Just the news that French troops were on British soil sent the markets into full-scale panic. Within days, fifty percent of the Bank of England's reserves went out the door as investors rushed to trade their notes for specie.[38]

The Bank's directors held an emergency meeting on Sunday at Mansion House, residence of the Lord Mayor of London.[39] The next edition of *The London Gazette* filled its front page with a letter they hoped would stop the bleeding:[40]

> We, whose Names are hereunto subscribed, being desirous to contribute, as far as we can, to the support of the Publick and Commercial Credit of the Kingdom at this important Crisis, do hereby agree and bind ourselves to receive the Notes of the Bank of England in all Payments as Money, and to support, as far as depends on us individually, their Circulation.

The names that followed were, in effect, the leadership of Great Britain: Pitt, Dundas, Grenville, Windham, Douglas, Portland, Kenyon, Addington, Malmesbury, Cornwallis, Liverpool, and so on. Then the Bank announced it was suspending redemptions; it wouldn't cash your notes for gold.[41]

That created a new problem. Most common trade was done with coin—gold and silver coin. Britons were already hoarding coin because they worried about the war. Coin became even scarcer when word got out there wasn't going to be any specie coming out of the Bank of England. Soon businesses had nothing to use for trade. Commerce, true to the cliché, was grinding to a halt.

Since Bank of England notes were now supposed to be the equivalent of money, the obvious solution was to issue notes in small denominations. But Britain's government and financial elite couldn't get their heads around the idea.

Why?

Blame a lot of it on mental inertia. Until the late eighteenth century bank notes were mainly used to transfer a big chunk of money from one bank to another. They were never intended for day-to-day purchases. Indeed, the typical Briton went through his or her entire lifetime without handling a piece of paper currency; they used coin.[42]

That's why until the early 1700s bank notes were literally notes, written by hand, like a business letter: "I promise to pay...." As trade grew, and banks transferred money more often, banks began preprinting notes with spaces allowing a clerk to simply fill an amount. From there it was a short step for British banks to issue notes in standard denominations.

By 1745 the Bank of England was printing notes ranging from £20 to £1,000. In 1793 it issued its first £5 note. Keep in mind, though, that £20 was more than most Britons earned in a year. Carrying around a £5 note was like carrying around a $500 bill today—not exactly easy to spend at the corner market.[43]

Sir John Sinclair—the farmer-statistician famous as "Agricultural Sir John"—thought the Bank of England could go even further. In 1796 he proposed issuing £2 and £3 notes.[44] Nothing came of his idea. The Bank's leadership just could not fathom millions of pounds sterling represented by nothing more than paper tickets, floating freely among the public, person to person. It was just too chancy.

Banking, printing currency, and taking chances. The British government might pass on the opportunity. But it was tailor-made for William Playfair.

Even before the Bank of England closed its gold window, Playfair had an idea to solve the scarcity of coin problem: the Original Security Bank. It was basically the same scheme Protot and Guillaume stumbled upon in setting up the *Maison de Secours*—and Playfair borrowed for his own Bank of Assignats: issue small IOU tickets to make change for large notes. The tickets would take the place of coin. The concept worked for assignats. It would work for pounds sterling, too.

Playfair got two partners to join him in the plan: Jan Casper Hartsinck and Julius Hutchinson. Hartsinck was a forty-one-year-old financier from an old Dutch family. In 1785 he had made partner in Hope & Company of Amsterdam, one of the largest commercial houses in Europe. Henry Hope's niece did not get along with Jan's wife, so he bought out Hartsinck, leaving him "a very considerable fortune," as relatives recalled.[45]

When the Batavian Revolution split the Netherlands, Hartsinck sided with the pro-British Orangist monarchists, who were vying for control with the pro-French republican patriots. That won him an appointment as minister plenipotentiary. After France invaded Holland in 1794, Hartsinck fled to England. By February 1795 he was a diplomat in exile, and people began referring to Jan as John.[46]

Reverend Julius Hutchinson was from an old family, too—an old English family. His grandfather, Colonel John Hutchinson, was a Roundhead hero, one of the nobles who signed the death warrant for Charles I in 1649, ending the English Civil War and absolute rule of kings. Julius had gone into the clergy, presiding over a manor house at Little Barford, north of London.[47]

The three partners published a prospectus on 28 December 1796. They observed how "men in trade have been reduced to great difficulties, on account of an evil generally known by the name of *scarcity of money.*" The problem: government securities were as sound as coin, but too large to trade conveniently. Their solution: the Original Security Bank would divide them into "convenient sums"—notes of 20p, 10p, 5p, and 2p. The bank opened an office on Norfolk Street, Strand.[48]

The small notes were a hit. The *Morning Chronicle* called them "ingenious." The *English Review*, with a bit more English reserve, acknowledged they offered "innumerable advantages."[49] Business got even better after the landing at Fishguard, when the Bank of England closed its gold window. On

28 February the Original Security Bank announced in *The Times* that customers could continue to exchange the now-unredeemable Bank of England notes for its own small denomination tickets.

The not-so-hidden message: The Bank of England left you in the lurch, but you can count on the Original Security Bank.

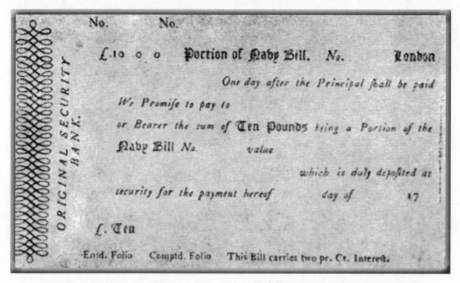

FIGURE 17: An early note from the Original Security Bank. Customers could deposit a large government-backed security and receive in exchange smaller notes like this one for £10. This note was itself probably too big to spend conveniently; the bank eventually issued notes in pence. Source: *The Times* (2 December 1796) and later published in S.R. Cope, "The Original Security Bank," *Economica* Volume 13 (February 1946), 53.

Then, early on Tuesday, 7 March, three men walked into the Original Security Bank. Two were dressed as gentlemen. One, Robert Astlett, was a clerk at the Bank of England. The other, Joseph Kaye, was the Bank's lawyer. The third man was in uniform—Thomas Carter, the Bank's doorkeeper, who doubled as a constable. They had come to arrest Playfair.[50]

The three claimed the Original Security Bank had committed forgery. A literal reading of the law said it was a crime to print a note—for that matter, any piece of paper—bearing the words "Bank of England." It was supposed to protect rubes who had never seen a bank note from getting duped, and give prosecutors running room to make cases against counterfeiters.

Playfair protested. Original Security Bank notes, he said, looked nothing like those of the Bank of England—by design, to avoid confusion (and, he might have added, to avoid prosecution). Yes, they bore the words "Bank of England"—but only because that's what they could be redeemed for.

Playfair's argument did no good. The three men escorted him out the door. They told him he was due to appear before the lord mayor of London. They said the lord mayor had been told of the crime. Even at that moment, the lord mayor was waiting to see Playfair in his chambers.

Astlett, Kaye and Carter marched Playfair to Mansion House, the lord mayor's residence. Sure enough, the lord mayor was waiting in the lord mayor's office, seated at the lord mayor's table. They looked at each other. The lord mayor, Playfair recalled, "told me with a most solemn countenance that I was accused of felony."[51]

It was Brook Watson. He had been elected lord mayor.

The entire time Playfair was being hustled to Mansion House, he knew exactly who would be waiting for him there. *The Tomahawk!* not only reported the election; it championed Watson and shamelessly promoted him after he won. On 9 November 1795, it had published a "letter" boosting Watson even before he officially took office:[52]

MR. TOMAHAWK,

Sir,

It is a great mistake of those who wish for things to go well, to endeavor to degrade public characters.

As such I see, with grief, the incendiary attempts made against the Lord Mayor elect and, as CENSOR GENERAL, I call upon you to pay some attention to this, and give us some of your good arguments and solid reasonings on the subject.

As far as I can understand, he is as good a man as is generally chosen to fill that station; and, therefore, I consider the attack upon his character as a political manœvre, and by no means any personal stain.

I am, Sir,
Yours, &c.
A CITIZEN OF LONDON

Even in his never-published memoirs Playfair didn't let on. He just described the scene. He recalled Watson—partner, co-conspirator, and traveling companion—addressing him with "farcical gravity." His account went like this:[53]

> _Lord Mayor_ Not only, Sir, are you accused of felony but in my opinion is that you are guilty and I am not apt to be mistaken.
>
> _Mr. P._ How can my notes be an imitation? They are narrow like a banker's check. Your notes are broad. I call them yours for you are a Bank director, I believe. Your notes are on thin papers mine are not besides do not they say on the face of them that they are payable in notes of the Bank of England which amounts to a declaration that they are not themselves Bank of England note? In addition to all that the engraver lives within three minutes walk of this place and I will tell you that his instruct were to make them as unlike Bank of England notes as possible.
>
> _Lord Mayor_ All that I dare say is true and I see that part of it namely that they promise to pay in notes of the Bank of England and here is the Act of Parliament which makes the felony consist in the very thing that you suppose clears you. The act makes it a felony to engrave the words Bank of England on a note and to use white letters on a black ground and you have engraved the words Bank of England.
>
> _Mr. P._ Yes I have owing to yours stopping payment after having the place of all the gold in the country. I have done the deed by the bank notes becoming the money of the country and still being not bona fide money it became necessary to state that the payment would be so made. This is one of the consequences of the stoppage of the Bank besides there are no white letter on a black ground.
>
> _Lord Mayor_ That does not alter the Act.
>
> _Mr. P._ If you take pieces of sentences I can say nothing but that it is unjust absurd and very unlike a man of the understanding known to be possessed by Mr. Brook Watson for it evidently no

imitation and the spirit of the act is prevent imitations or counterfeits which it mentions further on.

Lord Mayor I do nevertheless seriously believe it is an imitation and must go consult my brethren at Guildhall. You must stay here in the meantime.

I was conducted into a room on the same floor with the office and the mayor very civilly came in himself and gave me two newspapers to read till he returned.

Playfair didn't say whether Watson offered him a drink. Was Watson really ticked off with Playfair? Or was he going through the motions because he had to deal with his fellow Bank directors? It may have been both. Either way, Playfair wasn't going to surrender, and couldn't resist tweaking the Bank of England. He had an idea.

Playfair sent a messenger to Hartsinck, back at Norfolk Street. Playfair asked Hartsinck to send him a thousand pounds in Bank of England notes. "My Dear Friend, Do not be uneasy about this business," Playfair assured him. "The Plan of the Bank is to intimidate us & then get us to give over our Bank."

Playfair suspected that the Bank of England directors and staff flunkies like Aslett simply knew a good idea when they saw it and wanted the Original Security Bank's business for themselves. But, Playfair told Hartsinck, "The Law is in our Favour & against them they will be very happy to compromise the matter—I beg you will not be uneasy."[54]

The messenger returned with the notes, whereupon Playfair presented them to the Bank officers—and asked for payment in gold. They followed the emergency policy and refused—just as Playfair knew they would.

Playfair's ploy put the Bank in an impossible position. They had proven, right there in Mansion House, the Original Security Bank's raison d'être: The Bank of England couldn't make change for its own notes, but Playfair could.

Moreover, as he told Hartsinck, "the Law is in our Favour."

The Bank of England operated under an Act of Parliament. Its charter _demanded_ that it redeem its notes—in specie. The directors could print all the signatures they wanted on the front page of _The Gazette_, but it didn't change the statute. They could not change their charter simply because markets had taken an inconvenient turn. They were breaking the law; Playfair said he was ready to file charges.[55]

Brook Watson returned sometime around four o'clock. He had consulted his fellow directors. They agreed privately no jury was going to convict Playfair. But they couldn't just let him leave; that would make the Bank look foolish. So they insisted he post bail.

It took some scrambling to find the money—no one in the city wanted to get on the wrong side of the Bank of England. But Playfair finally got home at seven that evening. He immediately started writing.

He drafted a pamphlet containing three letters—one to the public, one to the Bank directors, and one to Watson. Playfair planned to get popular opinion on his side by kicking up as much brouhaha as possible, using, as he put it, "both reason and ridicule."[56]

"My heart bleeds to ask what is become of English honour, or English faith," he wrote in his letter to the public. "I have often gloried in contrasting our conduct in matters of finance with that of our rivals the French." He was comparing Bank of England's directors to the *French*. Playfair knew that, to a British banker, would be a low blow.

Yet, he said, "since the fatal 27th of February I can do that no more." That was when the Bank of England stopped redeeming its notes for gold.[57]

Then Playfair recounted the day: summoning, accusing, counter-accusing, making bail. He described how officials of the mighty Bank of England were hassling an honest businessman using an absurd legal argument—saying that a note promising to pay its bearer in Bank of England notes was a forgery of a Bank of England note.

Playfair balanced persuasion and threats: "We have had the best advice, and are perfectly easy, as to the result of Trial," Playfair told the directors. "We know that, though a large and respectable body, the Bank of England must ultimately obey the laws of the country, as well as we."

Moreover, Playfair wrote, "exposing this business in full form will at this time be productive of very disagreeable sensations to you, and that many things will be touched upon that it is not in the general interest to have brought before the Public."[58]

Was Playfair threatening to expose the counterfeiting operation? Would he reveal that he and Watson were co-conspirators in a cross-Channel felony? Probably not. More likely it was one of Playfair's double entendres—telling the directors that he would take the Original Security Bank story public, while reminding Watson about the secrets they shared.

Playfair said that, "till Monday at twelve o'clock, we shall be ready to hear any propositions that may be made to us on your part."[59] So, "if any mode can be thought of by you to accommodate this matter, we are prepared to give up something to the interests of the nation at large, by a private and honourable accommodation."[60]

Then Playfair had 500 copies printed. He recalled later "only two or three were given out and contrived to be shown to the Bank directors." He marked one with the legend, "Not to be Distributed"—meaning, "Gentlemen, you can be sure this will be distributed if we don't fix this."[61]

Watson must have straightened things out, because by Friday everyone reached the inevitable conclusion. The Bank dropped its charges against Playfair; Playfair dropped his suit against the Bank. They haggled over who would cover the legal fees; in the end, the Bank of England agreed to pay.

On the way out, a septuagenarian director confessed to Playfair that the Bank's board knew Astlett was off base. But they had to back their employee; it was that reputation thing. (Five years later Astlett was convicted of embezzling seven hundred thousand pounds. The court gave him death; he lucked out when the King had him transported instead.)[62]

Playfair burned the pamphlets he had printed; he "did not even keep a copy of the pamphlet to myself," he later recalled in his memoirs. Yet somehow at least one of the copies he gave the Bank directors as part of his veiled threat survived—which is how we know the account he wrote a quarter-century later is true.

One thing is for certain: There are not many records of Playfair's bank; John Philipson couldn't even find a listing for it when he tried to identify the paper mold with the bank's watermark. In all the literature about money and finance, the only account of the Original Security Bank seems to be an article Sydney Cope published in *Economica* in 1946.[63]

Cope wasn't a historian or an economist; he was a banker. He started at Guinness Mahon, served in World War II as a telecommunications specialist, and returned to Guinness before joining the World Bank as a loan officer in 1947, where he remained for the next twenty-five years.[64]

In Cope's account, after the Bank of England closed its gold window, a member of Commons, Sir William Pulteney—a longtime critic of the Bank—floated the idea of creating a second public bank. If the Bank of

England wasn't prepared to cash its notes, Pulteney said, perhaps another would. Cope mentioned in passing that another member, Sheridan, spoke in support of Pulteney's motion, and even touted the Original Security Bank as a candidate for the second public bank.

But, Cope wrote, "Baring, Thornton, and others spoke against the motion, which was defeated." According to Cope, "faced with the open hostility of the Bank of England and indifference on the part of the Government, the Original Security Bank was bound to fail." A few months later "the bankruptcy of Hartsinck & Co. was announced."[65]

This didn't upset Cope at all; he thought Britain was better off with the Bank of England's monopoly. It was efficient, and usually reliable. So, he concluded, "the inglorious failure of the Original Security Bank is not wholly to be deplored." For Cope, Playfair was just an "inventor, company promoter, and pamphleteer," who tried to sell Ohio lands "which, for all he knew, might never have existed."[66]

§ § §

The Original Security Bank was indeed kaput by November 1797. But it wasn't the Bank of England that put it out of business. It was a classic cash crunch, combined with bad management—and a disagreement among the partners about what kind of business they were running.

Naturally, since it involved Playfair, it was complicated. And, naturally, since it involved Playfair, it was linked to the counterfeiting operation.

Playfair's account can be found in a file in the Guildhall records at the London Metropolitan Archives. Most of the file is correspondence between Playfair and his lawyers, but there's also an undated memorandum titled, "A Statement by W Playfair."[67]

"I have long owed to the Public to the Creditors of the Estate & to myself a true statement of the Original Security Bank's transactions and to insolvency," Playfair begins. "Recent circumstances have determined me to delay no longer."

The memorandum ends somewhat abruptly after nine pages, but there's enough there to get a gist of what was going on. Playfair recalled that the bank's original plan—the one they printed and circulated—was to issue small denomination notes, using large government notes as collateral. It was a proven moneymaking idea from his Paris days.

Unfortunately, "Mr. Hartsinck," Playfair said, "thought it would be well to lend on Pledges of other sorts such goods, land, houses, and any real value." That is, Hartsinck changed the business plan. He turned a retail bank into an investment bank—like Hope and Company. Playfair wasn't pleased, but Hartsinck was the "monied partner"—the one putting up the working capital—so there was nothing he could do about it.[68]

Then, Playfair continued, Hartsinck withdrew £11,600 of the £16,600 he originally put up, leaving just £5,000 in reserves. The bank had loaned a total of £40,000. "With such scanty means," Playfair said, "it is very easy to see that the bank might fail without any real loss, only through delay in payments."[69]

In other words, the Original Security Bank could easily wind up solvent, but illiquid. If just a few borrowers missed making their payments, the bank would have assets on its books, but would be unable to pay its investors because it would be cash short.

Even worse, Playfair said, just three of those loans totaled £26,000—more than half of all the money the bank had lent. One loan was for £8,000 to some "Irish adventurers" setting up their own bank in Bath. Another £9,000 went to an Edward May, who now was residing in debtor's prison. And a third loan—also for £9,000—went to a Mr. Sheridan, who ran a theater.[70]

At this point you're probably saying—wait a minute. Who is this "Sheridan" guy who keeps popping up?

Richard Brinsley Sheridan—poet, playwright, and impresario—is best known for *The School for Scandal*, the classic comedy of manners. Sheridan owned the Theater Royal in Drury Lane. In 1794 he replaced the existing 117-year-old building with a state-of-the-art facility costing £160,000—double the original construction estimate. Revenues never met expectations, which helps explain why he couldn't keep up with his payments to the Original Security Bank.[71]

Sheridan presented a special problem as a debtor because when he wasn't running the Drury Lane Theater, he was representing the constituency of Stafford in the House of Commons. Members of Parliament enjoyed protection from bill collectors. (For example, you couldn't send a member to debtor's prison, which was the main enforcement mechanism at the time.)

Sheridan was well liked on both sides of Commons. Everyone appreciated his sense of humor. And in an age that prized oratory, no one could beat him; he was, after all, a professional when came to staging theatrics. He made his reputation with a five-hour speech in 1788 on a topic that was controversial then, albeit forgotten today. The performance was more memorable than the substance in any case. When he finished, Sheridan gasped, "My Lords, I am done!" and did a stage-faint into the arms of Edmund Burke.[72]

Sheridan had opposed the American War. He opposed the war with France. He opposed subsidizing Austria, Prussia, and the other German states to fight France. He opposed using émigrés to fight France.[73]

And, when he heard about it, he opposed government counterfeiting to fight France, too.

That's right. Richard Brinsley Sheridan was the "Mr Sheridan" who first blew the cover on Playfair's counterfeiting operation in Commons back in 1793. Yet he was also the "Sheridan" who promoted the Original Security Bank when Pulteney proposed authorizing a second public bank.

Playfair and Sheridan were bound by a unique mix of personal friendship, professional differences, and mutual respect, all held together with a bit of quid pro quo.

In 1797 Britain's war with France was going badly—very, very badly. The Duke of York had withdrawn his forces from the Continent after the French overran the Low Countries in 1795. Prussia had quit the war in 1796; Austria was on the ropes and would quit the following year. It seemed the only things preventing a French invasion of Britain was bad weather and the Royal Navy.

Which made it a national crisis when the crews of the Channel Fleet at Portsmouth, mutinied on Easter Day.[74]

The sailors had valid grievances. Their food was terrible. Their pay hadn't been raised in a hundred years. Sailors—many "recruited" by a press gang—might serve for years without shore leave. They petitioned for relief; the Admiralty did nothing. So the crews secretly organized and, en masse, refused to sail. Essentially, they went on strike. The Royal Navy was immobilized.

Sheridan was a frequent critic of the Navy; he had opposed raising its budget just six months earlier. He had been a skeptic when it came to the French invasion threat before Bantry Bay and Fishguard. But now he understood the peril and used his most potent weapon to fix the situation: acting.[75]

On 9 May 1797 Sheridan gave a speech in Commons like no one else could. He made three arguments at once: The sailors should go back to their posts; that was their duty. His fellow Whigs should boost Navy funding; that was *their* duty. And Pitt's ministers should get on the ball and make life tolerable for the crews.[76]

It was the performance of a thespian. By saying everyone shared in the blame, Sheridan gave everyone a stake in a solution. All sides were now determined to make Britain safe. Add a King's pardon, and the mutiny was settled. Sheridan was a hero.

But then, on 12 May, there was another mutiny—this time in the North Sea Fleet anchored in the Nore, at the mouth of the Thames, just forty miles east of London. This one was different; the mutineers were political—radicals, in fact. They demanded that the Government resign. They demanded peace with France. They announced a blockade of the city.

When Sheridan spoke in Commons on 2 June, he was playing an entirely different role—hard-nosed tough guy. The government, he said, had but one choice: crush the mutineers, crush them ruthlessly, and crush them now. It was the difference between a grievance and an insurrection. The government refused to negotiate. In days the mutiny collapsed. The ringleaders were hanged, flogged, jailed, or transported.[77]

Playfair thought Sheridan was a stand-up guy who put his nation before politics—unlike "the Foxes, Bedfords, and Greys," Whigs who "looked idly on" during the mutinies.[78] By Playfair's measure, Sheridan was "one of the best public men" of his day.[79]

Moreover, Playfair knew that Sheridan's speech was just part of the story of how the mutiny was put down. There was more going on more behind the scenes—much more. The situation was sensitive; few officials wanted to discuss it publicly.

When the sailors of the North Sea Fleet mutinied, it was as though a hostile navy had suddenly materialized at the doorstep of London. Usually you need a navy to defeat a navy, and even on the ships that had not mutinied, sailors were unlikely to fire on their fellow sailors.

British leaders had to improvise. Fortunately, improvisation is precisely what actors do. Some say it was Sheridan's idea to take up the buoys and beacons that marked the bends and shoals of the Thames. Handling any sailing vessel is challenging, and for the typical Jack Tar with little experience at the helm, it's almost impossible if the channel markers have disappeared. The mutineers were trapped.[80]

Playfair was working behind the scenes, too. He recruited an armed vessel manned by Dutch sailors—in effect, a privateer—to take on the mutineers. It may have been the perspective of two landlubbers, but Playfair and Sheridan could be forgiven if they felt they had been through battle together.[81]

On the evening Sheridan gave his speech urging the government to put down the mutineers, he met Playfair and a few unnamed associates at a tavern to conduct, as Playfair put it, "some business."[82]

Playfair and Sheridan first met around 1787, before Playfair left for Paris. Both were reform-minded Whigs at the time.[83] More than a decade had passed since they last met. When the Whigs split over the French Revolution, Playfair and Sheridan landed on opposite sides. Playfair (like Windham and Burke) feared Jacobin radicalism. Sheridan (like Fox) hoped the French Revolution would set an example for political reform in Britain.[84]

Playfair recalled he felt a need to clear the air. "No doubt, Sir, as I had the honour of being known to you about ten or twelve years ago," Playfair said, "and was then what they call a whig, and am now called an aristocrat, you may think me a turn-coat."

The fact was, Playfair said, "My father was a clergyman, and my grand-father a farmer," he told Sheridan, and "as for riches, I am not possessed." He explained to Sheridan, "I have lived in France, where, during the three first years of the revolution, I saw so many wild and wicked transactions." They left him with "a complete disgust to the violent Political Reformers."[85]

Playfair said was "an enemy to violent reforms." He was "a friend to those smaller reforms, which, without touching the main principles of the constitution, keep it pure." If that meant a less than perfect government, so be it. Playfair confessed he had "a sort of indifference with respect to smaller abuses." Indeed, he believed those minor abuses would eventually "bring on a general change of things."[86]

Sheridan understood. Had he been caught in France, the impresario conceded, he might have left with the same feelings, too.[87]

Playfair was becoming more conservative all the time. He admitted this to Charles Kirkpatrick Sharpe, the eccentric, but well-connected Edinburgh writer who was one of his occasional information sources. "I am," Playfair confessed, "in point of religion and politics, a very old-fashioned man."[88]

What about Sheridan's exposing the counterfeiting operation? Playfair didn't say. Sheridan might not have known Playfair had a role in it; Swinburne had discovered Playfair was managing the operation only *after* he had written his letter to Charles Grey—the letter that spurred Sheridan object to Commons.

Besides, the op was over. Now Playfair was using the Haughton Castle mill to make notes for the Original Security Bank—which Sheridan was promoting in Commons.

That was the quid pro quo.

When Sheridan spoke in behalf of Pulteney's proposal endorsing a second public bank, he touted the Original Security Bank—even mentioning Hartsinck by name; it was within a day or two of when Sheridan, Playfair, and a "few others" met at that tavern to do "some business."[89]

That "business" might have been the £9,000 unsecured loan the Original Security Bank gave Sheridan. And that wasn't Sheridan's only stake in the Original Security Bank. Sheridan sold shares in his theatre to "renters"—who financed those shares through the Original Security Bank.[90]

Sheridan's finances had as many twists and turns as his scripts. He was finally ruined in 1809 when the Drury Lane Theater burned down. By then he had lost his seat in Commons—along with his immunity. His creditors laid into him.[91] Years later his debt was one of the assets the Original Security Bank assignees were dickering over.[92]

Playfair devoted a chapter to Sheridan in *Political Portraits* in 1814. He wrote with disdain how Sheridan's political enemies—and many of his allies—had turned on him like sharks. The government should establish sinecures, Playfair said, to ensure talented men like Sheridan could at least participate in Parliament's sessions.

Then he went on: "We have nothing to do with Mr. Sheridan's private affairs; but we must observe, that while numbers, without either industry or talents, have been robbing their country to enrich themselves, Mr. Sheridan has neglected his own interest, and never let pass a single occasion of serving his country."[93]

The first part of that statement is a lie. If a man owes you £9,000, you know a *lot* about his private affairs. And Sheridan *had* tried to enrich himself. He was head and shoulders into the public trough as much as anyone.

The last part, though, was true; Sheridan was indeed a patriot. That was probably the strongest bond between the two. Playfair said Sheridan "neglected his own interest" and "never let pass a single occasion of serving his country"—nearly verbatim what Byerley would declare in the obituary he would write for Playfair.

How strong was the bond? Playfair recalled how Sheridan broke with his Whig colleagues to defeat the mutiny. "Richard moved from their ranks," he wrote, "and extinguished the flames that were about to consume the country."[94]

Richard.

You can read hundreds of pages of Playfair's published works, and scores of his letters—and you might never find another instance in which he called another man by his Christian name.

§ § §

When the Original Security Bank failed, depositors sought compensation; the government sought culpability. It brought the case to the Court of King's Bench and a "Special Jury." *The Times* reported Hartsinck "admitted that his failure was owing to losses he had experienced in consequence of stock-jobbing transactions." Apparently he was playing the market with the cash flow.[95]

Hutchinson, Playfair said, was not part of the plot, and "made every effort to prevent bankruptcy."[96]

Hartsinck, on the other hand, hid his personal funds to limit his losses. "I did not know that Mr. Hartsinck had determined on becoming a bankrupt," Playfair testified, "and committed an act of bankruptcy expressly for the purpose, having previously secured most part of his money and other property."[97] Playfair accepted a judgment by default.

Whatever the details, the simple fact was that the Original Security Bank failed, and its owners were personally liable for its losses. The *Morning Chronicle* broke the news on 2 November 1797: the Original Security Bank announced it was seeking new arrangements with its creditors.[98] By March Playfair, Hartsinck, and Hutchinson were scheduled to surrender themselves and make a full disclosure of their effects.[99]

The specific debt (or at least one of them) that landed Playfair in prison was the 46 pounds, 2 shillings, and 6 pence he owed to Isaac Bernal the younger.[100] In May Playfair told his lawyers that he was preparing to move into Fleet Prison.[101]

Playfair knew exactly what he was getting into. He had written about Britain's bankruptcy laws many years before in *Increase of Manufacturers,* his pamphlet about entrepreneurship. Playfair argued that when governments capped the upside of successful ventures, they discouraged risk taking; investment suffered. Yet he also argued the inverse: when government allows an unlimited downside for failed ventures, investment also suffers.

He had asked what was the sense that "an unfortunate, or even an impru-dent man, a father, perhaps of a family, should languish in a prison, shut up from every comfort, from the means of relief, and without a possibility of earning bread for the support of innocent children?" That was the penalty for an investment "failing to answer," to use the expression of the time.[102]

It was now the penalty he faced. Indeed, Playfair would become some-thing of a connoisseur of prisons during the last third of his life, spending suf-ficient time in a sufficiently broad sample—Fleet, Whitecross Street, perhaps King's Bench, and, of course, Newgate—to facilitate comparisons.

The Prison of the Fleet had nothing to do with the Royal Navy; like Fleet Street, it was named for River Fleet, a smallish stream that ran nearby before emptying into the Thames. (Today it's a covered sewer.) As prisons went, Fleet wasn't so bad. It had made significant improvements since it was founded in the eleventh century, when inmates were routinely pilloried and often had their ears removed... before they were branded.[103]

Still, Fleet *was* a prison—and thus a symbol of government. That made it a target in the 1780 Gordon Riots, an anti-Catholic protest that mutated into general mayhem. Some demonstrators decided to implement their own approach to prison reform: They notified the staff and gave the inmates a day to pack. Then they leveled the building. City authorities quickly built a replacement, so Playfair was actually moving into a nearly new facility.

In practice, debtor's prison in the late 1700s was as much compulsory boarding house as it was incarceration; the commissioners liquidated all your assets, so you needed a place to stay. Edward Hutton's *A New View of London* provided a *Fodor's*-like review. It reported that Fleet was so much "preferred before most other Prisons" that would-be inmates jockeyed to get in. And that was before the teardown and rebuild.[104]

Rooms were allotted by ability to pay and seniority; stay longer, and you could request a lower floor room with fewer steps to climb. The best rooms on the first floor rented for 4 to 8 shillings a week. An inmate who could swear that his net worth was less than five pounds received begging rights and could solicit alms from passers-by through a grate on the Common Side. One could even venture into the surrounding neighborhood to do business within the "boundary of the Rules." Records show Playfair left Fleet seven times between August and September 1799.[105]

Meanwhile, bankruptcy commissioners tried to sort out the wreckage of the Original Security Bank.

It's too bad they never had a chance to meet Benjamin Walker or William Duer; they'd have told them what it was like trying to untangle a financial edifice Playfair designed. Calling the Bank's organization byzantine would be unfair to Byzantium. The *Evening Mail* observed, "no bankruptcy of late years attended with so much mysterious circumstances."[106] The commissioners (or, rather, their successors) were still meeting in 1827.[107]

Playfair served several months in the Fleet, perhaps even a year or two.[108] Apparently he never did receive a certificate, and was released instead under the provisions of the Insolvent Act. It got him out of prison, but didn't erase his debts. By March 1802 he was free, but still broke.[109]

As for Julius Hutchinson: the Special Jury decided he wasn't witting to Hartsinck's scheme and let his certificate stand. But that just meant bankruptcy as normally practiced.

Little Barford Manor went on the block in July 1798.[110] The commissioners finished liquidating Hutchinson's assets in December 1800; his wife recalled it put the family "in strait circumstances"—a polite way to say they had to work for a living.[111] Hutchinson turned to editing his grandfather's memoirs for publication. One of the subscribers was Richard Brinsley Sheridan.[112]

It's harder to tell how Hartsinck fared. At first he seemed to get off the hook; the commissioners initially granted him his certificate on 6 November 1798, freeing him from his debts. Playfair believed Hartsinck's father-in-law, the well-known financier John Julius Angerstein, pulled strings on his behalf.[113] But then the Special Jury, Playfair said, "saw how the matter stood," and disallowed Hartsinck's certificate.[114] Playfair believed Hartsinck hurt his case by acting "with great obstinacy and duplicity."[115]

Hartsinck's wife was bitter; a relative said "a frightful reverse of fortune has plunged her into depths of misery." The family was so ashamed they would not even risk writing about it in a letter.[116] She blamed it all on Playfair—a "worthless man" whom her husband should have known better than to deal with.[117]

§ § §

Were it not for Peter Bower, the molds linking Playfair to the counterfeiting operation might have disappeared.

The Society of Antiquaries of Newcastle upon Tyne moved from venue to venue over its 200-year history. Its first home was the Keep, part of the fortress that gives Newcastle its name—the "new castle" the son of William the Conqueror built. Then the Society moved to the Bigg Market; then to the Lit and Phil; then back to the Keep; then to Black Gate, a different part of the Castle; and, finally, after 1930, to the Mining Institute. As the Society moved, so did its collection.

The molds from Haughton Castle were forgotten when John Philipson and Peter Isaac passed away. Soon after that, the Society's collection was absorbed into the newly created Tyne & Wear Archives & Museums (TWAM), a North Country consortium. That buried the trail further. Now anyone wanting to find the molds had to look through nine different organizations.[118]

I got interested in the molds around 2007, when I began to suspect William Playfair was more than your run of the mill statistician with a roguish reputation. I came upon the Philipson and Isaac articles, and the transcript of Sir John Edward Swinburne's memorandum. It linked Playfair to the counterfeiting. But by then no one could find the molds.

Eventually I caught up with Antony Braithwaite, the current owner of Haughton Castle. Braithwaite introduced me to his neighbor at nearby Capheaton: John Browne-Swinburne, Sir John's grandson six times removed. He steered me to his family's papers, now at the Northumberland Museum and Archives at Woodhorn. (Like Sir John, Browne-Swinburne is devoted to North Country history; he's a Woodhorn trustee.)

Though I had read Isaac's transcript in *Archaeologia Aeliana*, I wanted to see Sir John's original memorandum. Transcripts usually don't include marginal notes, scribbles on the backs of documents, addresses, and postal markings, all of which can sometimes provide clues to piecing together a story. Besides, there's nothing like handling an actual artifact. It's a physical connection between you and the man you're trying to figure out.

The Woodhorn archive is just like a county records office in the United States, except that its records go back five centuries. You can even request the original title for Haughton Castle, and the ever-helpful staff will bring the parchment scroll to your table in the reading room.

So I filled out a slip for file ZSW/590. And there it was: Sir John's original account, in his own hand. Henry Richmond's list of players was in the folder, too: Playfair, Watson, Thellusson, the Duke of York, and so on. If you know the characters, the outlines of the operation fall into place.[119]

That was documentary evidence. However, for positive proof of Playfair's operation—hard, physical evidence—you needed the molds. Yet no one could find them. It was like the last scene of *Indiana Jones and Raiders of the Lost Ark*: warehouse workers box the Ark of the Covenant, slot it into a vast sea of crates, and the credits roll as the artifact vanishes into the maw of a bureaucracy.[120]

Newcastle University has connections to TWAM—some of its museums are adjacent to its campus—so I began to ask faculty members if any of them had heard of the molds. The problem was that no one was studying paper currency, let alone counterfeit paper currency. But everyone seemed ready to assist an American with an unusual interest in an obscure "British economist." (That seemed like the easiest way to identify Playfair and explain why he might be involved with paper molds.)

Over the years Andrew Parkin (museum collection keeper) led to Stafford Linsley (industrial archeologist). That led to Rob Collins (Roman archeology). Collins specialized in "small finds" and "material culture" at TWAM's Great North Museum. That meant he followed Roman coins, which was close enough to early French currency to make it worth taking a trip to Newcastle.

Collins and I kicked around ideas about where the molds might have landed. Collins asked his colleagues; perhaps they landed at Woodhorn with the Swinburne memo. But the staff confirmed Woodhorn keeps only documents, not objects.

Collins kept searching, dismayed that an artifact could simply disappear from the Museum's collection. Perhaps the owner had reclaimed it, he mused, or a member of the Society had taken it home to study. Then I recalled the *Archaeologia Aeliana* article; it named the paper historian in London that Philipson had consulted: Peter Bower.

"Paper historian" is a term with a double meaning—the history of paper, and the use of paper to track history. Sometimes you can tell as much about events by the characteristics and composition of a sheet of paper a what's written on it. The link between paper and history persists even in today's Digital Age. Bower likes to show his picture of British astronaut Tim Peake, preparing for launch to the International Space Station in a Soyuz capsule. Amidst all the electronics, there's a rack of loose-leaf tech manuals. And Peake is holding a notepad.

"Even spacemen need paper," Bower says.

Bower offers his expertise to auction houses and banks to prove—or disprove—documents are what they claim to be. For years, he had a special interest in assignats; he had heard the stories of a British counterfeiting operation. His contacts at the Bank of England denied knowing anything about it; certainly the Bank wasn't involved, they said. Probably never happened. Just folklore. Nothing to see here; move along.

Then, around 1990, Bower was in Newcastle to give a lecture at Northumbria University. That's when he met Philipson and Isaac. They asked him if he might help them with their project. Bower was the one who matched the mold watermarks to bona fide assignats.

No matter what the Bank of England said, if you put the molds, specimens, and the Swinburne memo all together, it was clear: the counterfeiting was fact, not fable. Bower wrote up his findings, and moved on to other things.[121]

Two decades later I found Bower, still in London, and we began to correspond. He said he didn't know what happened to the molds. But he *had* kept images of them—both the two for counterfeiting assignats, and the one for making Original Security Bank notes.

At least we had proof the molds existed. But where did they go?

Bower started pulling on his own leads. In October 2015 the trail led to Nick Hodgson, principal keeper of archaeology—and honorary secretary of the Society. Hodgson began asking members if they knew anything about the molds.

Eventually Bower got steered to John Clayson at Newcastle's Discovery Museum—the science museum in the TWAM consortium, about a half a mile from the Great North, where Collins had been looking. Apparently sometime in the late 1990s or early 2000s someone decided the molds were technology, not archeology. Kylea Little went searching; she found two cartons in the storerooms. I caught another flight to Newcastle.

On 16 May 2016—almost 10 years after the search began, and 221 years after Playfair proposed his counterfeiting operation—the trail ended at Rack 55, Shelf E, with Boxes 159 and 160. The two cardboard cartons were marked "MEDICAL." The museum recycles its archival boxes.

Inside, the tags describing the objects simply said: "MOULDS." How apt.

FIGURE 18: Proof of the counterfeiting operation and William Playfair's role in it: two of the paper molds found together at the Haughton Castle Mill. The mold in the back produces paper with a watermark matching French assignats. The mold in front produces bank notes with the watermark "Original Security Bank"—Playfair's bank. Playfair used the same mill to make paper for both. Source: Discovery Museum, Newcastle upon Tyne, reproduced with permission.

Until Bower asked, the museum staff had lost track of what the moulds were; they just seemed like three heavy frames with old wire mesh. That's one of the quirks of curating. Unless someone is using an artifact in his or her research, the significance of an object can get lost. Interests change; records can fall through the cracks. Cataloguing systems change as collections are merged.

We laid the molds on a table in one of the museum's back rooms. There were gaps and tears in the gauze of all three; the wires had corroded badly over two centuries. Bower told me later that they are likely the oldest paper molds of any kind in Britain.

FIGURE 19: Close-up of Item 1938.6, the paper mold designed to produce paper with the watermark for a French assignat issued under a 1790 decree; notice the date. Source: Discovery Museum, Newcastle upon Tyne, reproduced with permission.

But despite the wear and tear, enough of the gauze remained to make a match. The first two molds would produce paper with watermarks for counterfeit assignats. The third mold would produce a watermark for Original Security Bank notes—the notes that got Playfair dragged in to face Lord Mayor Brook Watson.

FIGURE 20: Close-up of Item 1938.8, the paper mold designed to produce paper with the watermark for a note issued by the Original Security Bank. Source: Discovery Museum, Newcastle upon Tyne, reproduced with permission.

Toward the end of his life, Playfair wrote that if forgers could "get all the assistance that money could command, there is no doubt but that they might make perfect imitations." If so, "then it would be fair to say, that what one man can do, another will be found to imitate." Playfair, well read, was familiar with Samuel Johnson's aphorism about counterfeiting.

But, "the true question is this," Playfair continued. "Can men be found, who are willing to risk their lives, and are of sufficient ability to execute secretly what a wealthy company with money at command can procure artists to execute publicly?"[122]

Playfair answered his own question. The molds for the counterfeiting and the mold for his bank notes were found in the same place at the same time. They shared the same provenance and history. It proved the case. Playfair had run the risks and had obtained, as he put it, the "expensive and bulky machinery" needed for the forgery, and brought together the required "reunion of men of different talents and professions."

He ran the Great Op.

9 Inventing Political Economy

I n September 1805 Playfair sent a package to R.S. Wadeson, one of the solicitors sorting out the wreckage of the Original Security Bank. It had been years since the bank failed, but the proceedings were still…proceeding. It was the kind of case a lawyer could make a career out of. They were still proceeding more than twenty years later.[1]

Playfair got along well with Wadeson. Five months earlier he had told him, "When you came to be solicitor to the bankruptcy all was confusion," and "falsities had been invented." Hartsinck, Playfair said, was out "to save his reputation at my expense."[2] Wadeson had made the chaos a little more orderly.

Playfair was grateful; the package was a gift to Wadeson's daughter. "Sir," Playfair wrote with his usual stream-of-consciousness grammar, "Give me leave to request your acceptance of the Statistical Breviary sent with this for the use of your young ladies who will find it aid them considerably in their study of geography and modern history."[3]

Playfair was trying to write his way out of debt. The result: some of the most important works in statistics, economics, and strategic analysis were written in London's Fleet Prison.[4]

The Statistical Breviary began to take shape in 1799, just as the Original Security Bank began its final plunge. John Stockdale was planning a sort of encyclopedia: *A Geographical Historical, and Political Description of the Empire of Germany, Holland, the Netherlands, Switzerland, Prussia, Italy, Sicily, Corsica, and Sardinia.*[5] The book was as expansive as its title—390 pages—and expensive—six pounds, the equivalent of four or five weeks' labor by a mechanic, or two-thirds the price of a cow.[6]

Pricey or not, it was a huge success. About a thousand subscribers were listed. The King, the Queen, and the Prince of Wales all appear, along with assorted nobles, military units, and government ministries and offices. The Duke of York endorsed it.[7]

The book's main attraction was its maps; good maps were hard to find, and the book had some new ones. It also had a bonus feature: an eighty-seven-page annex, *Statistical Tables Exhibiting a View of All the States of Europe*. That's where Playfair came in.[8]

Jakob Gottlieb Boetticher, a statistician from the German port city of Königsberg, originally compiled the tables in 1789 and published them as *Statistische Uebersichts-Tabellen aller Europäischen Staaten*.[9] Stockdale had the tables translated. The he had Playfair draft an update, keeping the same format, which Stockdale inserted at the end of the book.[10]

Playfair wasn't satisfied with the result. The "tables" were really just a hodgepodge of facts about each country. They lacked context, and it was nearly impossible to compare one country with another. So he planned his own book, easier to use and easier to understand.[11]

First, Playfair limited his book to just sixty-four pages. He reorganized the data into a series of chapters, each summarizing a single country. The chapters all followed an identical format. Each provided a summary of recent developments, along with a table that included *just* the variables for comparing one country to another: numbers of people, size of budget, volume of trade, numbers of soldiers and ships, and so on.

Playfair had come upon one of the most important rules of analysis: an analyst's job is *not* to collect and present facts, let alone every fact. Quite the opposite; an analyst's job is to *select, distill, and integrate* facts so the reader can see how they fit together—hopefully, in a form the reader finds useful, memorable, and easy to comprehend.

It's one of the hardest rules for analysts to learn. Analysts get immersed in their subjects. Cutting out any detail in the final product often feels like *Sophie's Choice*—leaving one of your children behind for the good of the other. But ignore that rule, and analysis isn't analysis; it's just self-indulgent claptrap, spewing data without thinking about the needs of the user.

In pioneering analytic triage, Playfair was pioneering analytic tradecraft.

Then Playfair used graphics to make it easier to compare one country to another. He returned to a device he used in *The Commercial and Political Atlas* to show relative size—the bar chart—and then introduced a new kind of graphic that showed relative composition—the pie chart, a circular display to express fractions.

Playfair compared the size and composition of the countries in his survey with "bars" and "pies" of different sizes. This use of graphics was a breakthrough. To see why, first look at how Stockdale presented his translation of Boetticher's table on Turkey. There's a lot of information in there—somewhere—but it's a mess. There's no way to understand the significance of anything.

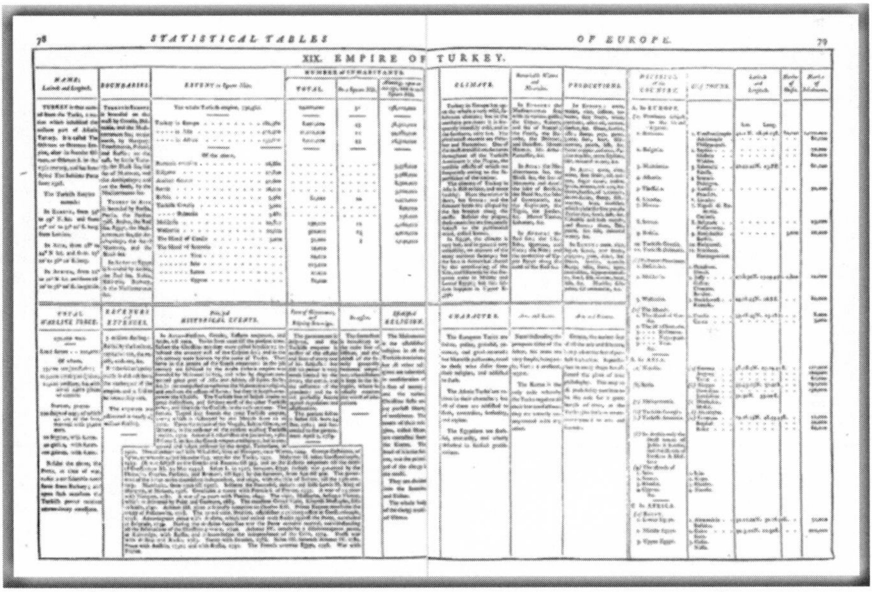
78 STATISTICAL TABLES OF EUROPE. 79

XIX. EMPIRE OF TURKEY.

FIGURE 21: Sample page of J.G. Boetticher, *Statistical Tables Exhibiting a View of All the States of Europe* (London: John Stockdale, 1800). Source: Bavarian State Library, Munich. Reproduced with permission.

Now look at how Playfair presented the size, populations, and revenues of the "principal nations of Europe." In the chart:

The size of each circle is proportionate to each nation's land area. Light shading (red in the original) signifies land powers; the darker shading (blue in the original, now faded to light green) signifies sea powers.

The line to the left of each circle indicates a nation's population in millions of people; the line to the right of each circle indicates the size of its budget in millions of pound sterling.

The dotted line connecting the two vertical lines relates a nation's revenues to its population; a slope down, left to right, indicates a heavy per capita burden, a slope up indicates a lighter burden.

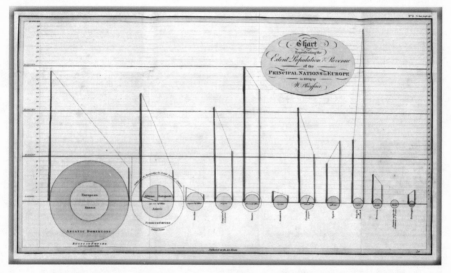

FIGURE 22: Sample page of William Playfair, *The Statistical Breviary* (London: J. Wallis et al., 1801); Source: Thomas Fisher Rare Book Library, University of Toronto. Reproduced with permission.

It takes some upfront effort to learn how to read the chart, but it's not that hard, and once you know the key, comparisons are easy—and indelible. It's instantly apparent Russia is about twice as big as Turkey in area, but only has maybe a million more people. Meanwhile, Britain (fourth from the right) is tiny, geographically speaking, and has far fewer people than either Russia or Turkey. But the bar indicating British revenues dwarfs that of every other country; only France comes close.

Other comparisons: Germany and France are small geographically, but match Russia and Turkey in population. Spain—once a dominant power in Europe—is now a geographic, demographic, and financial welterweight. Per capita, Britain, Spain, Portugal, and the United Provinces have light tax burdens, while everyone else has a heavy burden.

Any minister or military officer could see some implications: Russia or Turkey can put hordes of soldiers on the battlefield, but Britain can buy more ships, muskets, and cannon. As Playfair put it in the *Breviary*, "making an appeal to the eye when proportion and magnitude are concerned, is the best and readiest method of conveying a distinct idea."[12]

One could even imagine how wars might play out: Russian troops attack in human waves; the well-equipped French army rakes them with artillery fire. Or Swedish and Danish armies fight as near-mirror images of each other. One could also better understand grand strategy: Britain concentrates on maintaining its good credit, so it can bankroll allies and proxies while ensuring the Royal Navy's expensive ships are everywhere, ready to tilt the strategic balance one way or another.

It's easy to miss an equally important invention in *The Statistical Breviary* simply because it is so obvious: The book provides a concise, country-by-country summary of capabilities for every nation in the world. It resembles the *World Factbook* that the United States began to produce in World War II and continues to publish online today.[13]

Even when Playfair presented raw numbers, he did it in a way that was easy to digest. He used a consistent format that made the relevant parameters stand out and facilitated comparisons between one nation and another. Playfair was showing the way to the modern database.

It was a remarkable effort, especially considering how little reliable data Playfair had to work with. Britain didn't conduct its first national census until 1801, and other nations would take years or even decades to follow. Playfair used "persons who have lived in the different countries at a late period" and extracted and extrapolated from previously published numbers, like Boetticher's tables.

How accurate was he? Playfair estimated Great Britain's land area (including Ireland) at 104,000 square miles; today, using space-age technology, the combined area of the United Kingdom and the Republic of Ireland is calculated to be 113,418 square miles. So Playfair was 9 percent low. His estimates for Spain and Portugal—two countries whose borders have remained constant for over 350 years—were 22–24 percent low.

BRITAIN AND IRELAND.   37

Extent in fquare miles 104,000
Number of inhabitants 14,000,000
Number of perfons to a fquare mile 136
Extent in Englifh acres 67,000,000
Number of acres to each perfon 4¾
Number of acres in cultivation 40,000,000
Revenues in pounds fterling 27,000,000
Amount of public debt, ... 400,000,000
Land forces in time of peace , ... 45,000
Ditto regulars and militia of all forts this war .. 350,000
Seamen in time of peace 18,000
Ditto in time of war 112,000
Ships of the line 187
Frigates, floops, &c. 441
Extent of feacoaft in leagues 1,200
Tonnage of merchant fhips 1,800,000
Number of inhabitants in the capital 1,100,000
Number of parifhes, 9,000 in England and 1000 in
    Scotland (not including Ireland) 10,000
Exports to all parts, average 30,000,000
Imports from all parts, ditto 25,000,000
Expence of maintaining the poor 3,000,000
Expence of the clergy 7,000,000
Great divifions of the country, England, Scotland, Wales,
    Ireland 4
Smaller divifions, counties .... , 117
Chief towns, London, Dublin, Edinburgh, York, Liver-
    pool, Briftol, Newcaftle.
Longitude of central point 1° 3′ weft.
Latitude of ditto 53° 40′ north.
Longitude of the capital city 0° 0′, this and moft Englifh
    books calculate from the meridian of London.
Latitude of ditto 51° 31′ north.
Amount of taxes on each perfon 1l. 18s. 3d.
Rate of intereft of money, 5 per cent. in England and
    Scotland, 6 per cent. in Ireland.
Religion, Proteftant, Lutheran and Calvinift ; all fects
    tolerated.

C 3

FIGURE 23: One of the earliest databases—sample page from *The Statistical Breviary* (London: J. Wallis et al., 1801). Source: Internet Archive/European Libraries collection.

As to population, Playfair estimated Great Britain (including Ireland) was home to 14 million people. Extrapolating backward from the first census covering England, Scotland, and Ireland (taken in 1821), one would estimate their actual population was around 15.4 million, suggesting that Playfair was about 10 percent low. In all, not a bad effort, or at least a starting point to build on.

The Statistical Breviary was the book Playfair envisioned in *Joseph and Benjamin*—the imaginary "political bible" his imaginary Benjamin Franklin claimed France kept in an imaginary sanctum sanctorum with "all due care and secrecy." No country ever actually had such a book; Playfair created it in his mind, and fifteen years later made it real—to work his way out of debt.

§ § §

The Statistical Breviary was just what the King of France might appreciate—or the daughter of the lawyer trying to make heads or tails of the Original Security Bank. Playfair hoped graphics would make statistics easier to understand, especially for youngsters. He knew that "no study is less alluring or more dry and tedious than statistics, unless the mind and imagination are set free to work."[14]

So how was it that Playfair got his idea for statistical graphics?[15]

Playfair credited his brother, John, the amateur meteorologist. William would later recall how John "made me keep a register of a thermometer, expressing the variations by lines on a divided scale." William said it was his brother who "taught me to know that whatever can be expressed in numbers, may be represented by lines.[16]

It also helped that Playfair worked at Boulton & Watt. "Suppose," he asked, "the money received by a man in trade were all in guineas, and that every evening he made a single pile of all the guineas received during the day." If he did, then "each pile would represent a day, and its height would be proportioned to the receipts of that day; so that by this plain operation, *time, proportion,* and *amount,* would all be physically combined."[17]

Stacks of received money arranged in a row across a table: That's what Playfair likely saw as he was working each day in the Boulton & Watt countinghouse. It's the image of a bar chart.

There's more. Whenever Playfair worked on installing a steam engine, he was thinking about spatial relationships—cylinder diameters, rod lengths, lever ratios, and the like. If you design mechanisms for Mr. Watt during the day, thinking spatially becomes second nature if you write about economics at night.

It may help explain why, for instance, the pie chart Playfair would introduce in *The Statistical Breviary* looks like the face of a watch—or, more precisely, a pedometer.

Boulton & Watt charged customers by how much work an engine performed—literally, the number of strokes it completed. Boulton came up with the idea for a self-contained, high-capacity, tamper-proof stroke-tallying machine in May 1777; Logan Henderson helped.[18]

Boulton's design borrowed ideas from a pedometer that Liverpool watchmaker Wyke and Green sold at the time. Unlike earlier pedometers, which were triggered by a cord attached to a walker's boot, the Wyke and Green device was self-contained. A miniature pendulum inside oscillated with each step its bearer took; the pendulum worked a pawl, which ratcheted a wheel, which recorded the steps on a dial.[19]

Boulton proposed what was essentially a pedometer for steam engines. It linked several ratchet wheels in series, each counting to ten, and each advancing the next wheel one notch when it completed a revolution. So the first wheel counted strokes by 1s, the second by 10s, the third by 100s and so on to the seventh wheel, which counted by millions. The entire apparatus was sealed in a box with a locking glass door to prevent anyone from fiddling with the tally.

Since the device was self-contained, you could mount it on the main beam of any engine, and it would diligently keep track of each stroke; Boulton sent Watt a rough sketch, boasting it "goes true & can't committ a mistake for 30 Years."[20] With impeccable British precision, they assigned a name to their counting device: "The Counter."

You can probably see where this is going. There were numbers on the dial, yes. But when you looked at a Counter—like a pedometer, a watch, a speedometer, or a fuel gauge—your first reaction is to the *spatial* representation. Has the engine performed a lot of work? Or has it been sitting idle?

The Counter tells you the essential situation before you even have a chance to focus and read the numbers. So does the pie chart Playfair published in the *Breviary*: More than half of all Turkish Empire subjects live in Asia, roughly a quarter live in Europe, and the rest live in Africa.

Imagine you're watching the population of Turkey march by, recording each on a Counter-like device. When the last European passes, the dial on the Counter reads roughly 6 million, with the hand of the Counter pointing to the three o'clock position. Then you count subjects from Asia; when the last one passes, the Counter reads roughly 20 million, and the dial has advanced to the ten o'clock position.

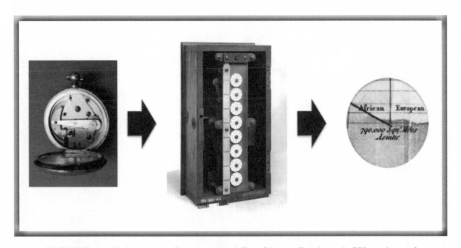

FIGURE 24: Pedometers, Counters, and Pie Charts. Boulton & Watt charged customers by strokes each of its licensed engines completed. Borrowing the mechanism for a self-contained pedometer (left), Matthew Bolton linked several dials to record strokes into a single unit, creating The Counter (center). The dials gave a visual representation of how much work an engine performed. These bear a remarkable resemblance to the pie chart Playfair later drew to show the proportion of Africans, Europeans, and Asian in Turkey (right). Sources: Pedometer image courtesy of and copyright by David M. Riches, www.mathsinstruments. me.uk. Boulton & Watt Counter image courtesy of Science & Society Picture Library. Reproduced with permission. Pie chart from Wikimedia Commons.

Or consider another idea from the engineering minds at Boulton & Watt. It's almost always overlooked in books about statistics, which is a pity, because it's likely the source of the first statistical graph ever generated by a machine.

Engineers need to know how the pressure inside an engine cylinder varies throughout its stroke; it offers insight into the engine's power and efficiency. Sometime around 1790 Watt designed a simple pressure-measuring device, consisting of a tube leading from an engine's cylinder to a mechanical barometer.

One could watch the barometer's needle as the engine completed a stroke. Did it reach the maximum pressure expected? Did it fall off early in the stroke? A discerning eye could catch an abnormality.

Again with impeccable British precision, Watt assigned a name to the device indicating cylinder pressure changes: he called it, "The Indicator."

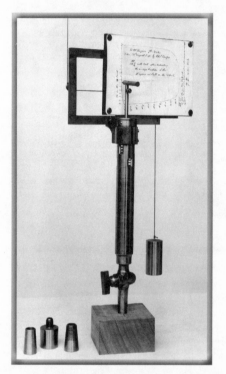 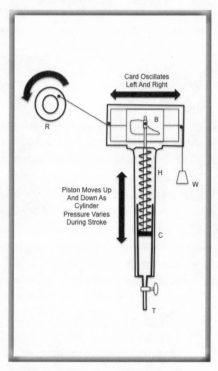

FIGURE 25: The Indicator—John Southern worked with James Watt to develop their company's secret for analyzing engine performance. The Indicator is screwed into turncock T, which is connected to the engine's cylinder. A cord is attached to the arm or flywheel R, which pulls card carrier B horizontally left as it rotates, completing the first half of a revolution. Weight W returns the carrier right in the second half. The pressure within the engine cylinder pushes piston C up; spring H forces it back to the bottom of its range as cylinder pressure decreases. A pencil attached to the piston draws a trace on the card. The result: A record of pressure variation in the engine cylinder through the completion of a revolution. Source (left): Science & Society Picture Library, reproduced with permission; Source (right): Adapted from Cecil H. Peabody, *Manual of the Steam-Engine Indicator* (New York: John Wiley, 1900), 2.

Not everyone has a discerning eye, however, and that led to the next step. John Southern added a pencil to the needle so it marked a paper card. The card, mounted in a holder linked by a cord to the engine's main beam or piston rod (flywheel or crank in later models), moved left during the down stroke and returned right with the up stroke. As the engine completed a cycle, the pencil drew a curve from one edge of the card to the opposite edge and back, recording the rise and fall in cylinder pressure.

The result: a mechanically generated line graph. It's called a pressure-volume or "PV" curve. The vertical axis measures cylinder pressure; the horizontal axis indicates cylinder volume, which is determined by where the piston is on its stroke.[21]

Look at the example in Figure 26. A–B–C–D is the curve traced during the downstroke. B–C shows the maximum pressure the steam exerts, as the stroke begins; C–D shows the drop in pressure as the piston descends down the cylinder; D–E shows pressure bottoming out as the exhaust valve opens. E–F–A is the return of the piston to the top of the cylinder.

Deviations from an ideal trace indicate problems. If B–C peaks low or drops off midway, there may be a leak; better check for a worn piston or cylinder. If D–E doesn't fall completely to zero, then the engine is wasting energy; there's still steam under pressure in the cylinder that could be providing power, though the piston is beginning its return stroke. Need to check that valve timing.

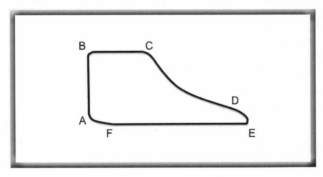

FIGURE 26: Steam Indicator Plot. A closer look at what is likely the earliest machine-generated chart. The concept hasn't changed in more than two centuries: a variable plotted on a vertical scale, measured over a constant rate of time plotted on a horizontal scale. Source: Adapted from Cecil H. Peabody, *Manual of the Steam-Engine Indicator* (New York: John Wiley, 1900), 3.

Squint your eyes and use a little imagination, and a PV curve might remind you of Playfair's graphs of trade balances or government spending—which makes sense, because they all depict a time series: a variable measured on a vertical axis, plotted against time, measured on a horizontal axis.

It's hard to tell just what led to what. Boulton & Watt was adopting Boulton's Counter at about the time Playfair arrived; it might have stuck in his head years later when he invented the pie chart. Playfair sent Watt and Boulton copies of his *Atlas* with its graphs; it might have inspired Southern to invent the recording Indicator a few years later. Yet you can't help but notice how many opportunities there were for cross-pollination between steam engines and statistical graphics.[22]

§ § §

The Statistical Breviary did have one major gap: It didn't include the United States. Three years later Playfair fixed that.

Thanks to his friend and dinner-partner Vandermonde, Playfair occasionally sat in on meetings of the Academy of Sciences.[23] That's likely how Playfair got to know statistician Denis-François Donnant, the Academy secretary. Donnant translated the *Breviary* into French—and added data for the United States. Playfair, in turn, translated Donnant's added material; this became his *Statistical Account of the United States of America.*[24]

The small pie charts Playfair used in *The Statistical Breviary* were just a first step. In *Statistical Account of the United States of America*, Playfair made a large, detailed pie chart the centerpiece of his analysis—or, more precisely, the frontispiece of his book, before the title page. He called the chart a "Divided Circle." It depicted the total U.S. land mass as it existed in 1805, indicating the share held by each state and territory.[25]

Pie charts often suffer a bad reputation among graphics mavens; they complain the round displays don't express quantities as clearly as, say, a bar chart. If you put two bars next to each other, it's easy to see which is taller, and if you add hash marks across the chart, you can determine their exact value. You can't do that with pie charts. Some go so far as to say pie charts *never* should be used [26]

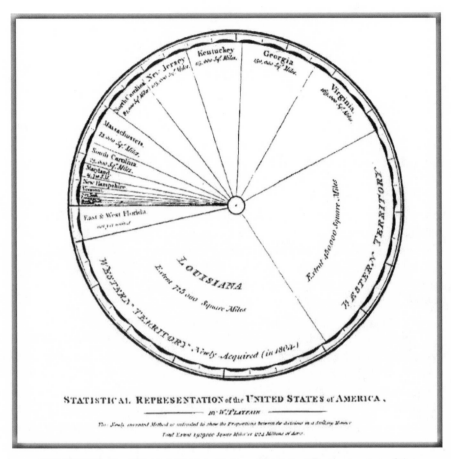

FIGURE 27: The "Divided Circle" offering a "Statistical Representation of the United States of America" that Playfair provided for D.F. Donnant's *Statistical Account of the United States of America* (London: J.J. Whiting, 1805). Playfair translated the book and sent copies to Thomas Jefferson. Source: reproduced in Willard Cope Brinton, *Graphic Presentation* (New York: Brinton Associates, 1939), 81, via the Prelinger Library.

Not so fast; look again at Playfair's Divided Circle (which resembles a clock, a Wyke and Green pedometer, or one of Boulton & Watt's Counters). The (implied) headline hits you square in the face:

THE LOUISIANA PURCHASE GREATLY EXPANDED U.S. TERRITORY.

It's Huge.

The important thing wasn't whether the Louisiana Purchase increased the area of the United States by 28 percent or 32 percent or 31.64 percent. No one really knew for sure, anyway; in 1805 Lewis and Clark were still trekking along the Upper Missouri just trying to figure out what was *in* the territory, never mind how big it was.

What really mattered was simply *proportion, grossly expressed.* You have to squint to make out Maryland, South Carolina, and all those other small existing states. But you can't miss the Louisiana Purchase, and that's the point Playfair was making. It was the Purchase's magnitude, suddenness, and geopolitical impact that were important. In this case, the *lack* of graphic detail, numbers, and metrics actually enhanced the message by stripping it to its essentials. Remember: effective analysis is often triage.

Or, as Robert Browning put it, sometimes less is more.

Unless you're launching a satellite and need to know the precise second to fire the upper stage engine for an orbital adjustment, you're not apt to say anything like, "seventeen minutes, thirty-two-point-four seconds remaining" before an event. In daily life you're more likely on your way to a meeting and just want to glance at a clock to see whether it's "half past" or a "quarter 'till" to get a sense of whether you'll be on time or need to start improvising excuses. In the scale of most human activities, much precision is often irrelevant.[27]

That's why, even in the most electronics-laden automobile, drivers still appreciate that analogue speedometer; for its purpose, it's an ideal graphic. A driver knows roughly where the needle should be. He probably doesn't even "see" the numbers, and doesn't care. If the needle wonders way past the familiar range for very long, he feels in his gut there's a speeding ticket in his future, and that's what really wants to know. The round pie chart/speedometer puts reality squarely in his face.

Another thing: pie charts might not be best for measuring *how much*, but they can't be beat for expressing *what share*, and often that's the relevant question. In the French Revolution, it wasn't just that members of the Third Estate paid *high* taxes and had *low* incomes; the issue was that they paid *most* of the nation's taxes and enjoyed *little* of the nation's total income—just a sliver of the pie, so to speak.

Playfair dedicated *Statistical Account of the United States of America* to Thomas Jefferson—now President—and sent him twenty-five copies. He even included blank pages in the books so Jefferson could add notes if he wished.

Playfair also offered Jefferson a suggestion.

"To render statistical accounts accurate and complete," he argued in *The Statistical Breviary*, a "habitual and regular practice of collecting information, both generally and locally, is necessary."[28] Perhaps, Playfair wrote Jefferson, the President might direct "the government of the United States towards collecting and perfecting statistical knowledge." It was too difficult and too expensive for individuals, but "every government in the ordinary exercise of its functions becomes possessed of many precious materials." He was planting the seed for today's *Statistical Abstract*.[29]

Playfair was bullish on the United States. America, he believed, was destined to grow; that's why the break with Britain was inevitable. Americans were bound to demand representation in Parliament, but if the colonies got the same deal as say, Scotland or Ireland, someday they would have a majority of seats in Westminster. No way England would accept *that*. He just wished the break had been managed better.

Like Shelburne, Playfair believed Britain didn't need to *own* America; it just needed the opportunity to trade with it. After all, he said, the United States would never match Britain in manufacturing; its strong suit was as a source for timber and livestock and corn. Britain and the United States were a natural match, natural allies. Forget the recently unpleasantness; by Playfair's measure George Washington was "one of the best and greatest of men."[30]

As for Jefferson—he still respected Playfair even after the Scioto debacle. Or at least he still respected his scholarship. Jefferson bought a copy of the third edition of the *Commercial and Political Atlas* when it was published in 1801 (he paid $7.50), and his copy of *Tableaux a'Arithmetique lineaire*—bound in calf leather with gilt back, pale blue endpapers, and a red silk bookmark—was still in his collection when he sold his library to the government in 1815.[31]

Jefferson thought enough of Playfair's work that he gave a copy of one of Playfair's books to Friedrich Wilhelm Heinrich Alexander von Humboldt, a young, ambitious Prussian officer, later famous as a founder of modern geography. Jefferson admired Humboldt, though it's not clear exactly which book Jefferson gave him; Humboldt simply thanked Jefferson for the "copy of Playfair" he sent. He only wished the President had autographed it.[32]

Still, accolades or not, Playfair remained a bankrupt living in poverty with Mary and the children. To make matters worse, when the Pitt government fell, Playfair lost his two most important patrons—William Windham and Henry Dundas.

Pitt resigned in March 1801 when George III balked at granting Catholics full political rights. Pitt hoped "emancipation" would keep Ireland in the kingdom. But if it hadn't been the Catholic issue, it likely would have been something else. The economy was dragging. The wars continued to go badly. Domestic unrest simmered.

Windham was already out the door, a month ahead of Pitt. Dundas left, too; he had wanted to retire for years. He often told Pitt he was exhausted and unable to sleep.[33] Henry Addington stepped in, determined to make peace with France. The Treaty of Amiens was signed a year later.

Playfair's career as an (overt) propagandist and (covert) intelligence officer depended a lot on his personal relationships with Dundas and Windham. Playfair sent Dundas his analysis of the British East India Company's legal monopoly; the cover letter suggests Dundas had given Playfair comments on an earlier draft. Playfair said that if Dundas (who considered the Company his personal preserve) had any problems with his paper, he was "without any hesitation determined to suppress it."[34]

Playfair said that, even if Dundas didn't want him to publish his book, he would still be glad to give the Company's Secret Committee his unexpurgated views through a back channel. He later offered Dundas a strategy for dealing with America: Encourage British exports to maintain Britain's influence—and discourage the Americans from developing their own industry.[35]

It's interesting that Paris records show Playfair visiting France around this time, when the 1802 Treaty of Amiens provided a break in the fighting. Bankrupts were allowed to travel, but that does not explain who paid for the trip. And Playfair was most assuredly broke.[36]

§ § §

In February 1802, Sir Richard Phillips sent a letter to Dr. Thomas Dale, a London physician. Sir Richard published *The Monthly Magazine* and was thoroughly plugged in the British literary scene. He had heard about Playfair's money problems and hoped the Literary Fund might consider him for assistance.[37]

The Fund was the brainchild of Rev. David Williams. When Floyer Sydenham, a well-liked Greek classicist, died in debtor's prison, Williams, Dale, and others used the tragedy to spur London literary luminaries to underwrite the Fund. Grants were never very large, but for a down-and-out author they could sometimes mean the difference between surviving as a writer and, perhaps, not surviving at all. Joseph Conrad, James Joyce, and Dylan Thomas all received aid from the Fund at one time or another.[38]

Playfair "has been involved in great difficulties," Phillips wrote Dale, after "an unfortunate connection with the House of Hartsinck office in Cornhill." Phillips had heard about the Original Security Bank debacle. As a result, Playfair "has spent some time in the Fleet."

Phillips described Playfair as "the inventor of Linear Arithmetic & the author of many well known works on Financial, Statistical, & Commercial Subjects." That made Playfair an established writer. That qualified him for support.

The Fund directors voted on 18 March to sponsor Playfair. Five days later Playfair signed a receipt for "a gratuity of ten pounds by the hands of Doctor Dale." Playfair became Case No. 121 in the Fund's records.[39] He began working on a book about Britain's future.

Playfair reached back to some unsigned columns he'd published in *The Tomahawk!* and compiled them into a book titled *An Inquiry into the Permanent Causes of the Decline and Fall of Powerful and Wealthy Nations.* Adam Smith had asked in *The Wealth of Nations*: "How does a country grow rich?" Playfair now proposed the follow-up question: "How do countries become poor?"[40]

Playfair originally thought Dugald Stewart should write such a book. Stewart had written a brief biography of Smith for the Royal Society of Edinburgh in 1793, three years after Smith's death.[41] Playfair believed he was "more likely to succeed in philosophy, elegance, and deep research, in the manner of his deceased friend, than any other author that we know of in this country."[42]

Stewart, however, was now more interested in philosophy than in political economy. Besides, Playfair needed the money. So he got to work.

Inquiry speaks at two levels. At one level, it's a book about economics. At another level, it's a book about Playfair.

The economic argument in *Inquiry* explains the big, enduring factors—the "permanent causes," to use Playfair's term—that caused nations to decline over history. Playfair claimed wealth moved from nation to nation, and provided a "Chart of Universal Commercial History" to demonstrate the point.

Playfair said took his idea for the chart from Joseph Priestley's "Chart of Universal History," a timeline correlating the life spans of famous men; he created a chart correlating the "life spans" of famous nations. Then, on top of each nation's life span, Playfair added a mini-graph depicting the rise and fall of its wealth over time—akin to the line graphs he used in the *Commercial and Political Atlas.*

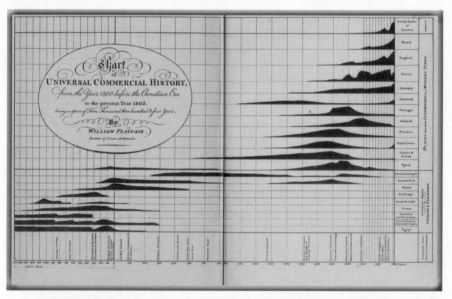

FIGURE 28: Playfair's depiction of the rise and fall of nations; the data for the power of later nations (at top) is real, that for earlier civilizations (at bottom) is Playfair's estimate. Source: William Playfair, *An Inquiry Into the Permanent Causes of the Decline and Fall of Powerful and Wealthy Nations* (London: Greenland and Norris, 1805) via Wikimedia Commons.

Nation after nation—Egypt, Assyria, Babylon, Palmyra, Sidon, Tyre, and others—had emerged, prospered, and declined. Playfair observed, "wealth and power have never been long permanent in any place," but instead "travel over the face of the earth, something like a caravan of merchants." More ominously, he also observed that wealth and power "never have been renewed when once destroyed."[43]

Yet the opening paragraph is more telling of what the book was really about.

Playfair was now forty-five. He had been married twenty-four years. He had barely got out of France alive; many of his friends did not. For good or bad, he was known—if inconspicuously—by British leaders for his adventures and misadventures.

Playfair had fathered six children; one died as an infant in France; Zenobia, born soon after Mary and William returned to London, was blind and required constant attention. His businesses—and his money—were gone. He had been stuck in the Fleet until the Literary Fund bailed him out.

What was most on Playfair's mind?

It was his brother, John, back in Edinburgh. Taking dip pen in hand, William began his book:[44]

> I think it well to embrace this opportunity, the best I have had, and, perhaps, the last I ever shall have, of making some return, (as far as acknowledgment is a return) for an obligation, of a nature never to be repaid, by acknowledging publicly, that, to the best and most affectionate of brothers, I owe the invention of those Charts.

Inquiry provides 120,000 or so words—about the length of this book—written in longhand, revealing Playfair's values and his view of life. It's this view that is the foundation of his theory explaining why nations rise and decline.

Like many such theories since, *Inquiry* likened nations to people: They start out full of energy and prepared to take risks. But, for a variety of reasons, they—nations as well as people—slow as they get older. Many—nations and people—never rise at all.

Playfair admitted his title was designed to evoke two of the most famous books of the era: Gibbon's *The History of the Decline and Fall of the Roman Empire* and Smith's *An Inquiry into the Nature and Causes of the Wealth of Nations*, both published in 1776. Gibbon, Lord Sheffield's friend, wrote about the decline of a particular nation. Smith, John Playfair's mentor, wrote about general principles. Combine the two approaches, and you get an inquiry into the decline of nations in general.[45]

Reviews of *Inquiry* were mixed; they ranged from lukewarm to abysmal. Some reviewers liked the diagrams; no one liked the prose.

The London-based *Critical Review* skewered the book.[46] "Mr. Playfair," the reviewer said, is one of those writers "who boast of the advantages of connection and arrangement only in the index and table of contents." The book, he said, "is evidently the production of one who thinks, though not of one who thinks with clearness or precision."[47]

Exercising double and triple negatives in ways that only nineteenth-century British literati have ever truly mastered, he continued: "In this respect our author has certainly an advantage over his commentators, as his oracular obscurity not infrequently serves as a protection to arguments, which might possibly not prove impregnable if the access to them could be easily discovered."[48]

(The reviewer—apparently without irony—was trying to say Playfair did not write clearly and was thus hard to critique.)

The Anti-Jacobin Review—which one would expect to be friendly—said Playfair's reasoning "is generally sound, and his conclusions, on the whole, are just and important." But Playfair's "diction sometimes becomes either wholly unintelligible, or not to be understood without difficulty."[49]

The reviewer liked the pictures, though: This "mode of conveying ideas, which is very ingenious" show "the migrations, the rise, the duration, and the decline and fall of the wealth and power of nations, in a manner wonderfully easy and impressive." He said they "require no exertion of thought, besides that of attention to the explanations."[50]

The Monthly Review disparaged Playfair for disagreeing with Adam Smith—except for those points on which *The Monthly Review* also disagreed with Adam Smith. (Smith thought apprenticeships amounted to slavery; Playfair thought they promoted self-discipline; the *Review* agreed with Playfair.) But—it's unanimous!—the *Review* said Playfair's "composition also admits of much polish and correction."[51]

§ § §

True, Playfair's prose was often turgid as the River Fleet. But, if you suffer through it, you will find at least four big ideas that economists depend on today.

The first big idea was simply that one could even make a theory about the rise and fall of nations. There weren't many theories about *anything* in the early nineteenth century, or at least not as we understand theories today: logical explanations based on assumptions, supported by observation. Keep in mind James Watt improved the steam engine without really even knowing what steam was—or water, or thermodynamics. He used terms like "strong steam" and "weak steam."[52]

Playfair said he was driven to write *Inquiry* partly because Edmund Burke said such a theory was impossible. Burke doubted, as Playfair put it, "the history of mankind was complete enough, or if ever it could be so, to furnish the grounds for a sure theory." There were too many details that were too hard to measure.[53]

Playfair's insight was that these details don't matter for understanding big events shaped by, as he put it, "permanent" causes. This is a fundamental principle of all science today, and especially social science. We know there's a lot of small-scale stuff we'll never measure. But we assume the significant factors are so weighty that they'll stand out from the noise. That assumption is what allows explanation and prediction.

Playfair's theory about national decline was straightforward: Some enduring factors, internal and external, promote growth; other enduring factors, internal and external, impede growth. When the latter factors outweigh the former, nations stop growing and decline.

The main internal factor that causes nations to grow wealthier is individual entrepreneurship, combined with technology. The main internal factor that cause decline is the accretion of self-serving special interests, combined with sloth. The main external factor that causes growth is international trade; the external factors that cause decline are conflicts over trade, the costs of war, and the costs of controlling foreign lands.

The second big idea in Playfair's *Inquiry* is "comparative advantage." It's a key concept behind the modern rationale for free trade.

Adam Smith argued in *Wealth of Nations* that a nation should buy a good from abroad whenever another country can produce it for less—that is, whenever the other country enjoys an "absolute advantage." That will make nations wealthier, Smith said, because their people will be able to buy stuff for less, and then have more money to spend on more stuff—or to invest, which will make them wealthier still.[54]

Comparative advantage takes the idea a step further and adds a twist. Economists say the world *as a whole* creates more wealth when every country concentrates on producing those things it does best (or "least bad"). It's an argument for lowering tariffs and trade barriers worldwide, not just here and there.

Free traders say capital and labor will allocate themselves optimally among all countries. With more wealth to go around, all countries are likely to benefit. What's more, they will all have a shared interest in the system. Trading partners will build deeper ties, and gradually everyone will become fat and happy—and more interested in making money than, say, making war.

London financier David Ricardo usually gets credit for the idea of comparative advantage. Ricardo made a fortune playing the markets prior to Waterloo; fortune made, he turned to writing about economics.[55] He explained comparative advantage this way in his 1817 book, *On the Principles of Political Economy and Taxation*:[56]

> Under a system of perfectly free commerce, each country naturally devotes its capital and labour to such employments as are most beneficial to each. This pursuit of individual advantage is admirably connected with the universal good of the whole. By stimulating industry, by rewarding ingenuity, and by using most efficaciously the peculiar powers bestowed by nature, it distributes labour most effectively and most economically; while, by increasing the general mass of productions, it diffuses general benefit, and binds together, on one common tie of interest and intercourse, the universal society of nations throughout the civilized world. It is this principle which determines that wine shall be made in France and Portugal, that corn shall be grown in America and Poland, and that hardware and other goods shall be manufactured in England.

But Ricardo might not have been first, after all. Here's a passage from Playfair writing more than ten years earlier in *Inquiry*:[57]

Some nations are situated by nature so as to be commercial, just as others are to raise grapes and fine fruits; therefore, though one nation has more than what appears to be an equal share of commerce, it ought not to be a reason for envy, much less for enmity.

Some nations also find it their interest to attend chiefly to agriculture, others may find it necessary to attend more to manufactures; but that ought to be no cause of enmity or rivalship....

Britain, the wealthiest of nations, at this time, sells little of the produce of her soil, and a great deal of the produce of her industry; but she purchases a great deal of the produce of the soil of other countries, though not much of their industry: in this there is great mutual conveniency and no rivalship. In fact, her wealth arises nearly altogether from internal industry, and, by no means from that commerce that is the envy of other nations; for it is clear, that whoever produces a great deal may consume a great deal, without any exchange of commodities, and without commerce....

If France would cultivate her soil with the same care that we attend to manufactures...she would be a much richer country than England, without having a single manufacture for exportation. Her wines, brandies, fruits, &c. &c. would procure her amply whatever she might want from other nations....

It does look as though Ricardo was looking over Playfair's shoulder; they even use similar examples. Playfair was more skeptical that trade would make the world richer as a whole; his concern was Britain. But both agree: nations left to their own devices will naturally specialize, most will benefit economically, and trading partners are less likely to go to war.[58]

Sure, it could be coincidence. But it probably isn't. Recall William Petty, Earl of Shelburne, Later Marquess of Lansdowne—and the Bowood Circle.

Ricardo knew Jeremy Bentham—knew him well, in fact. They met through the historian-philosopher James Mill. Together, these thinkers provided the intellectual ammunition that helped transform the Whigs into the Liberals, one of the two parties that dominated British politics through the early twentieth century. As they all became famous, Bentham liked to tell people, "I was the spiritual father of Mill, and Mill was the spiritual father of Ricardo, so that Ricardo was my spiritual grandson."[59]

It was the kind of "X begat Y" that begins the Book of Genesis, and just the kind of self-indulgent rodomontade one might expect from Bentham—who we know read Playfair's work. The Whig-turned-Tory Playfair shaped the thinking of Whig-turned-Liberal Bentham, who shaped the thinking of the speculator-turned-economist Ricardo.

Most economists don't know about Playfair—probably because they don't know about the Lansdowne link. Playfair visited Bowood, corresponded with Lansdowne, and dedicated a book to him. Lansdowne promoted Bentham, who knew Playfair's work. From Bentham it was just another step to Mill, and then to Ricardo.[60]

Playfair was thinking about comparative advantage years before he wrote *Inquiry*. Recall *Joseph and Benjamin*, where Playfair had "Franklin" telling "Joseph II" how he was always trying to persuade Americans to focus on husbandry, breeding cattle, and manufacturing those "coarse materials" the lower classes needed.

"Our luxuries," his Franklin said, "we should purchase with the overplus of this sort of labour." It was the optimal allocation of effort—and America's comparative advantage.[61]

So, if today's arguments for the efficiencies of free trade have a lineage to Playfair, what shaped Playfair's thinking? Be forewarned: when you trace the idea to its roots, what you find is not pretty.

Playfair was prone to hair-trigger generalizations when it came to nations. "All men, ideots excepted, shew certain tastes and propensities as soon as they come of an age," Playfair wrote in his 1793 analysis of the French economy. "On the great scale the same is the case with nations."

The French, said Playfair, excelled in "gaiety, dress, and gallantry." However, they "never were capable of shining in politics," because "their national character is unfavourable to the discussions and details which a well-poised government requires."[62]

Playfair was prone to generalizations when it came their economies, too. "Everything in France is incomplete, either from want of time, or through length of time," he would write. He claimed the situation in France "is worse than Scotland, not so bad as Ireland, and has not the least resemblance to England."[63]

In other words, Playfair got his idea of different nations having different strengths and weaknesses from experience, his disdain of France, and a good bit of eighteenth century ethnocentric pseudoscientific hokum. Nevertheless, the idea of nations differing in character, temperament, and abilities does get you closer to the concept of comparative advantage. Playfair's thinking was typical of the time, and, to be fair, he didn't think these differences were *born* in a person. Rather, he wrote how this or that man had been *bred*—brought up, educated, and shaped by his culture.

That, in turn, led to Playfair's third big idea: the psychological dimension of economics—attitudes toward risk taking, investing, and buying things—and how they can change, and be changed, over time.[64]

Playfair observed how young nations were full of daring, energetic entrepreneurs. But, he said, as nations get older, their people tend to get soft. Businesses lobby for laws to protect their markets and cripple competitors. Just about everyone seeks favors—subsidies, pensions, or some other transfer payment. As time goes on, more people figure out how to get protection and benefits; fewer people take risks or work hard. Those who do are stymied.

The result: nations, like people, pass through phases of "infancy, manhood, and decrepitude."[65] Some modern economists have argued the same—Mancur Olson is probably best known.[66] The question Playfair posed, though, is whether a nation—like Britain—can do anything to extend the ascent and defer the decline.

It all depended, he said, on a nation's attitudes. Today we call such attitudes part of "behavioral economics," a field that emerged in the 1960s and 1970s when psychologists and economists began to appreciate what marketing experts knew instinctively: People in the real world don't always make simple, cold-blooded rational decisions. There are other things at work, like perception, upbringing, and environmental cues.

How to shape those perceptions and cues and keep the entrepreneurial drive alive in next-generation Britons? Playfair believed much would depend on teachers. As he put it, "education and the manners of a people are so closely connected that it is difficult, from observation, to know which is the cause, and which the effect." This was why educating women was so important, he said; they had the greatest impact on the kids.[67]

Playfair's attitude toward work and risk was where his objective analysis began to blur into his personal beliefs. If there was anything Playfair believed in, it was hard work. You see it throughout his life; no matter how badly things went, he never gave up, never stopped trying. There was always the hope for an upside.

Which brings us to Playfair's fourth big idea: *the importance of the middle class to the rise of a nation.* Playfair was one of the first writers to see the linkage between a big, hard-working middle class and economic growth.[68] Playfair thought an aristocracy made a country stable, but it was the tradesman, shop-keepers, and entrepreneurs who made it wealthy—and, over time, wealthier.

That's because it's the members of the middle class who are most apt to be looking for that upside. "In order to become the object of desire, there must be a hope founded on a reasonable expectation of obtaining the object," Playfair wrote. "This can be but very small in the lower classes, when they look at the overgrown rich, and have no intermediate rank to envy or emulate."[69]

Playfair thought that few aspiring merchants or tradesmen could ratio-nally expect to be a Matthew Boulton, Henry Ford, Bill Gates, or Mark Zuckerberg; the odds are too small. But, in a well-governed, well-functioning nation, the average Joe *can* aspire to "intermediate rank," landing solidly in the middle class. If they do, Playfair believed, they would all work hard, and that would keep their nation—Britain—wealthy.

§ § §

Besides *Inquiry* and editing a new release of *Wealth of Nations* that included Dugald Stewart' s biography of Adam Smith, Playfair published another book sometime around 1805: *The Creditor and Bankrupt's Assistant,* a practical guide for anyone who found himself participating in a bankruptcy process: officiators, creditors, lawyers, and, of course, bankrupts.[70] (He hadn't lost his sense of irony.) The book listed Joshua Montefiore as its author, but Playfair was the ghostwriter.[71]

So who was Joshua Montefiore?

Born in 1763 into a successful London merchant family, Joshua Monte-fiore graduated from Oxford and published several well-regarded books on business and law. He and Playfair were made for each other; both were incur-able risk-takers. In 1791 Montefiore organized an expedition to colonize the island of Bolam off the western coast of Africa. The Bolamans, however, didn't care to be colonized; Montefiore was one of only a handful of survivors.[72]

Family records say Montefiore made it back to Britain, wrote a book about his travels, and joined the British Army, reportedly becoming the first Jewish officer in the service. Playfair had just returned from France and—in addition to organizing the forgery operation—was writing his own book, *History of Jacobinism*. Playfair and Montefiore may have met on the authors' circuit.[73]

Then again, they may have met in Fleet Prison.

The *Gazette* lists Montefiore on the same page as Playfair as a resident of Fleet: same place, same time, and, presumably, same reason.[74] Playfair plugged *Law of Copyright*, the 1802 book Montefiore apparently wrote while in prison, and he was listed as a subscriber to *Commercial Dictionary*, which Montefiore published the following year.[75`]

Montefiore was getting back on his feet when he and Playfair collaborated. Montefiore (or, more likely, his family) bought a commission—that's how it was done at the time—and he entered the army as an ensign.[76] Montefiore eventually went on to a distinguished law career in America, ultimately fathering nine kids with two wives before passing away at the age of eighty-one in Vermont.

In any case, in *The Creditor and Bankrupt's Assistant*, Montefiore—that is, Playfair—offers guidance on how to navigate bankruptcy. One continual reminder to bankrupts: be honest. It's kind of ironic, considering how often Playfair's portrayed as a flimflam artist today.

The law, says the *Assistant*, offers some important protections. You can, for example, propose your assignees (the people who will sell off your belongings) and you can choose where to declare bankruptcy (some jurisdictions are friendlier than others). But remember the law is there mainly to protect the creditors you've left in the lurch. So don't abuse the process by, say, concealing wealth. (That's Playfair's taunting Jan Casper Hartsinck).

Yet even after publishing a half-dozen books, Playfair was still broke. His health was beginning to falter, too; this is when his letters begin to say he's having trouble walking. Playfair thought it was gout; his description suggests it might have been peripheral arterial disease or rheumatoid arthritis. Whatever it was, it would leave him crippled; in the end it would kill him.[77]

Playfair turned to Lord Sheffield for help. More than twenty years had passed since James Watt had suggested to Playfair that Sheffield might be interested in his *Commercial and Political Atlas*, and Patrick Colquhoun arranged an introduction.

And who was Lord Sheffield?

Playfair would later write, "A volume might be written about this nobleman; but it frequently happens that where the most might be said, the least is necessary." Most well-read Britons knew Colonel John Baker-Holroyd had saved the Bank of England.[78]

During the Gordon Riots in June 1780, approximately fifty thousand Londoners bent on mayhem took to the streets. Authorities had to call out the army, deploying 15,000 regulars along with gentleman volunteers. Between three hundred and seven hundred persons were killed or wounded. Fleet Prison was just one casualty; the main targets were the Houses of Parliament, Newgate, Catholic chapels, embassies—and the Bank of England.[79]

Rioters surrounded the Bank on 7 June. Holroyd commanded a detachment of Northumberland militiamen defending the building. Waves of rioters rushed the entrance. Holroyd's troops fired volley after volley, stopping them at the doorstep. No one knows how many died in the fighting; both sides removed their bodies during the night. The king rewarded Holroyd with a peerage.[80]

Watt had directed Playfair to Sheffield because he thought they might share interests in economics. Now Playfair needed help. "It is not without much pain to myself that I take the liberty of troubling your Lordship," Playfair wrote Sheffield, "but tho' I should with less pain give ten other persons there is none to whom I would so willingly give an obligation as your Lordship."

He told Sheffield that for months he had been "unable to write & now only walking a little with the help of crutches." He went on to plea that "this & having a family of 4 children at home the eldest of whom a girl is blind has reduced me to some difficulties."

Playfair closed by telling Sheffield that "many have written better but few more than I have done in an equal time," and none "with a more steady attachment to the Established Government & Religion of England."[81]

John Baker-Holroyd, 1st Earl of Sheffield, was one of early funders of the Literary Fund.[82]

You have to wonder what was going through the mind of David Williams when Sheffield asked him to present Playfair's letters to the Literary Fund's board. Playfair was more and more a defender of the Crown, the Tory government, and the Church of England. Rev. Williams was a Dissenter, had been friendly with republicans like Brissot, and—like Joel Barlow and Jeremy Bentham—was an honorary citizen of France.[83]

It says something about how Britain worked. A week later Playfair signed a receipt for ten guineas, and a week after that he sent a list of publications and a copy of *Inquiry* to the Fund so the directors "may judge to whom it has given relief."[84]

§ § §

Mere bankruptcy could not keep Playfair from new ventures. On 12 December 1800 he received Patent No. 2455, for "improvements in naval architecture" that enabled vessels "to sail faster than they now do, particularly in a heavy sea." His partner listed on the patent, Nicholas le Farre, was a Dubliner who appears to have managed to get through life without leaving a trace other than his patent with Playfair.[85]

British ships were known for their stiffness; they used diagonal cross members along the lengths of their hulls, bracing them like a cantilever bridge. The bracing prevented "hogging" and "sagging." Stiff hulls normally sail better and last longer, but in heavy seas flexible ships—like those from France—often seemed to have an advantage. When an inopportune swell hit a French ship, it "gave" a little. Many thought that made them easier to handle.

So Playfair and Le Farre designed a hinged, sprung shield to be fastened to a ship's hull. In rough seas, it would absorb the energy of waves, enabling the ship to maintain its heading.[86]

Ingenious. Elegant. Nothing ever came of it. But at least it didn't land Playfair in jail—which is more than could be said of his other ventures at the time.

At some point Playfair entered into a partnership to make gun carriages with Robert Kennett, an unemployed Bond Street upholsterer. They were targeting the British East India Company as their main customer. (The Company operated its own fleet of armed vessels.)

Kennett seemed to come from a respectable family; his uncle was a magistrate and one of his sons was an army officer.[87] Yet that's not what you would conclude after reading the case brief the government's attorney, George Wood, filed on 21 July 1805 for *Rex v. Kennett, Kennett, Kennett, and Playfair*.

Wood called Kennett a "quack doctor" and a "man of great Depravity." He said Lord Kenyon believed Kennett "ought to have been marked on the forehead with the letter **R** that all mankind might at once know him to be a Rogue."[88] Kennett once tried to bribe the Duke of York, proffering the perpetually indebted son of George III a huge "loan" in exchange for an appointment as customs collector for Surinam.[89]

Now Kennett had designed a swindle that was, criminality aside, truly a work of art. Indeed, *Rex v. Kennett, Kennett, Kennett, and Playfair* was a criminal trial so remarkable and so interesting that it is actually cited in *A Collection of Remarkable and Interesting Criminal Trials*, a casebook for lawyers.[90]

When Kennett went bankrupt in 1801, he had his brother, Brackley Kennett, appointed as his assignee. (Recall from the *Bankrupt's Assistant* that bankrupts have some say in the selection.) Robert received his certificate, absolving him of further responsibility, and he went back into the world, debts forgiven.

Since one usually lost everything in bankruptcy, Kennett's thirty-odd creditors were dumbstruck when he took out a long-term lease on a house in March 1802. They were even more surprised when he started making renovations. The creditors complained to the Lord Chancellor, who revoked Robert's certificate.[91]

As Robert Kennett's newly unleashed creditors came after him, he transferred the lease to his not-yet-adult son, Henry. Then he filed for bankruptcy again. That's where Playfair came in.

Playfair agreed to serve as Robert's new assignee. Later Playfair said he did it out of friendship; it might have also been because Robert owed Playfair twenty-five pounds. Keep in mind Playfair was himself still bankrupt. The judges sorting out the case later would say this made Playfair ineligible, but they also observed Kennett's creditors were present when Playfair was selected, so everyone involved knew what they were getting into.[92]

Playfair's qualifications may have seemed questionable, but those of Robert's other new assignee, John Parlby, were mind-boggling. The commissioners had to track him down. When they did they discovered Parlby lived 60 miles away...in Portsmouth...in the custody of a parish.

Wood referred to Parlby as an "imbecile;" today we would say he suffered from dementia. Robert somehow got Parlby to certify a debt against him (making him eligible to serve as an assignee), and then somehow got him to sign a power of attorney allowing Kennett's brother Henry to act for him.

Playfair swore he didn't know about the Kennetts' scheme. He vowed that he alerted the authorities when he discovered it.[93] Creditors claimed Playfair turned in his partner only after the two quarreled over the gun carriage business. Whatever the truth, the government took them all to court, charging abuse of the bankruptcy law. The Lord Chancellor, John Scott, 1st Earl of

Eldon, heard the case. He sent the case to the lord chief justice and a Special Jury to hear.[94]

You might expect Playfair would resent Eldon for pursuing the case. Not so. Playfair would later write admiringly of Eldon's "remarkable talent for distinguishing between points of importance, and points of no importance," cutting to the nub quickly.[95]

The Lord Chief Justice now hearing the case was the aptly named Edward Law, 1st Baron Ellenborough. You might think Playfair would have ill feelings toward him, too. Not so. Playfair praised Ellenborough, calling him "as unbiased a judge as Lord Kenyon"—the same Lord Kenyon who "was not prepared to say" whether it was unlawful to make bogus assignats "for the purpose of distressing the enemy."[96]

Clearly there was something going on. It also didn't hurt that Ellenborough was responsible for the Insolvents Act—"Lord Ellenborough's Act"— the statute that sprung Playfair out of the Fleet. Ellenborough also was a leading advocate for reforming libel laws; keep this in mind, you will see why later.[97]

In any event, on 21 December 1805 the Special Jury found Robert Kennett, Henry Kennett, and William Playfair guilty. Yet the reporter covering the trial for *The Times* went out of his way to note Playfair was "a good man."[98] And, guilty or not, there is no record showing that Playfair went to jail—at least not yet. It was as though someone were protecting him.[99]

§ § §

Playfair moved on to another writing venture with William Windham's support—a newspaper available at "every Bookseller and Newsman in the United Kingdom," Its title: *Anticipation in Politics, Commerce, and Finance During the Present Crisis*. The "present crisis" was the domestic unrest in Britain, Napoleon's conquest of Europe, and the trade embargo he imposed—the so-called "Continental System"—which was severely stressing the British economy. The first issue appeared on 12 March 1808; publication lasted four months.[100]

The rationale for *Anticipation*: Public opinion was now so important, Playfair claimed (repeating the argument he gave Dundas ten years earlier) that the government had an obligation to influence it. As the new periodical put it put it:[101]

Among the doctrines of those who employ the liberty of the press to embarrass government and to render the people discontented, one is, *that the government of a country, should not interfere even in guiding the press, or instructing the people in their true interest*; and what is not a little astonishing is their sophistry has so far succeeded, as to make government itself incline to the same opinion, so that when it does interfere, it is in a concealed manner.

Playfair could even "see the day approaching when to DIRECT PUBLIC OPINION, will be one of the BUSINESSES of government, as it has always been one of its DUTIES." And that was the mission of *Anticipation*. Playfair was providing a public service by assisting the government in telling people what to think.[102]

One of Playfair's favorite literary devices in *Anticipation* was a "letter" from an older figure "in the shades"—British, foreign, or mythical—advising a current-generation counterpart "in the sunshine." William Pitt might write to Spencer Perceval, for example, or Peter the Great might advise Alexander I, or Hamlet might advise the Crown Prince of Denmark. It was *Joseph and Benjamin*, déjà vu: Playfair putting his words in the mouths of famous figures.

The rest of *Anticipation* was filled with think pieces, such as a proposal to improve army recruiting by offering land grants to retirees.[103] Some material was recycled straight from *Inquiry* and Playfair's earlier works. Much was new, however, and he would use it in later publications—like his analysis of rising bread prices, using data he got from the clerk's office at Guildhall.[104]

Playfair occasionally drew on personal experience, though you would have to know him to realize it—like the column profiling the Literary Fund's worthy efforts.[105] Or the one supporting bankruptcy reforms that released insolvents from prison to work off their debts.[106] Or the proposed asylum for female servants who fell on hard times. Zenobia—his youngest daughter, blind, and on a path for life as a governess—was often on his mind.[107]

§ § §

Around this time Playfair produced another innovation: Using statistics to develop strategy. The idea—a breakthrough, really—evolved out of *The Statistical Breviary*.

After leading the coup that toppled the Directory in 1799, Napoleon consolidated power under the Consulate, the three-man junta that followed. In

1804 he squeezed out his Consulate partners and crowned himself emperor. Over the next decade he conquered most of Europe, and seemed unstoppable—that is, until 1812, when he invaded Russia.

It was a disaster. As the Russians retreated into their Motherland, they destroyed their crops, their livestock, their houses—everything. They left nothing behind. Napoleon's army fed itself by living off the land. The Russians sucked them into a desolate wasteland where they would starve.

When Napoleon reached Moscow on 14 September (the Russians burned that, too), the French were effectively marooned, hundreds of miles from Paris. They had scanty provisions. Winter began to close in. Realizing the situation, Napoleon began the long trek home. The Russians harried them the entire way. The Grande Armée lost around half a million soldiers. Russian losses were somewhat lower, but nearly as harrowing.[108]

There was an American casualty, too: Joel Barlow.

After lying low in England, Barlow returned to France, making money by buying lands émigrés lost when they fled the country. Then he became a trade agent offering access to and from the United States; he charged up to ten percent of the value of a cargo.[109]

A few years later Barlow parlayed his connections into a diplomatic appointment, and made more money shipping pirated goods from Algiers. He'd come a long way from the young poet hoping to tour Europe by selling preemption rights of questionable provenance. This kind of side dealing was common practice for diplomats at the time, who often paid their own expenses. The graft was just a return on an investment—much like William Fullarton's commission.[110]

Barlow eventually made enough money to buy a tract of land in the District of Columbia. It's a particularly scenic point where Rock Creek cuts a gorge through the hills marking the end of the Piedmont plateau and the beginning of the Atlantic coastal plain. Jefferson recommended it to him. Barlow named the estate "Calorama," Greek for "beautiful view." Today it's Washington's toney Kalorama district, home to many an official who made good or cashed out.[111]

In December 1812 Barlow was on another diplomatic mission, trying to meet up with Napoleon. It was the middle of the French retreat. Trapped in the chaos and the winter, he caught pneumonia, and died somewhere near Żarnowiec, about 150 miles south of Warsaw—winning the mark in history he sought for so long by becoming the first American envoy to die on duty.[112]

A year later the Russian-led coalition defeated the French at the Battle of Leipzig and its armies were marching on Paris. France was on its way to defeat and European leaders began to look ahead. That's where Playfair and his statistics came in.

Playfair floated an outline for a peace plan in a sixty-four-page pamphlet, *Outlines of a Plan for a New and Solid Balance of Power in Europe.* The idea was to arrange alliances in Europe so war was less likely. Playfair had toyed with similar ideas back in 1793 in *Thoughts on the Present State of French Politics.* The difference was that this time his proposal was based on hard data.

The "balance of power" concept had been around since at least 1741, when David Hume described how nations could form alliances so no one country dominated the others. (Hume acknowledged the concept dated from ancient times.)[113] Playfair understood the idea, too; the *Commercial and Political Atlas* observed how "a balance of power among nations" is "a law something like that to which fluids are subject," an equilibrium where no nation had the confidence to attack another.[114]

The problem, Playfair said, was that the "old Balance of Power in Europe was a political combination," built "without any regular plan." He likened it to "the manner that old irregular cities were built."[115] A successful balance of power needed a design, Playfair said, and now was the time for "employing this crisis to reconstruct the equilibrium of Europe."[116]

Russia and Britain were the cornerstones of his plan. The "Russian Empire, as a continental power, and Britain as a maritime and mercantile one," Playfair wrote, "are both interested in the peace of the world, and in the prosperity of each other."[117]

Any design for a balance of power required a measurable unit of power, and Playfair acknowledged that troop numbers are "the nearest measure of power for hostile attack." But *national* power, Playfair said, "is a compound of armed force, revenue, and population."[118] He showed how to create a balance using this more complex concept of power by using a "Statistical Table, Shewing the most important Circumstances that relate to the Power of the different Nations of Europe." The table gave fourteen components of national capabilities and influence: geographic size, population, revenue, numbers of troops, and so on.[119]

STATISTICAL TABLE,

Shewing the most important Circumstances that relate to the Power of the different Nations of Europe.

	1	2	3	4	5	6	7	8	9	10	11	12	13	14
COUNTRIES.	Extent in Square Miles.	Population.	Persons in a sq. mile	Total Revenue in Pounds Sterling. £	Free Revenue.	Free Revenue according to the Value of Money. £	Tax on each Person in s. & d.	Army in Peace.	Army in War.	Disposable Army.	Seamen in Peace.	Seamen in War.	Leagues of Sea-Coast.	Proportional value of Money.
Russia . . .	4,720,000	40,000,000	8	7,500,000	7,000,000	23,500,000	3,9	380,000	530,000	250,000	20,000	40,000	1550	3,5 : 1
Turkey . . .	700,000	24,000,000	34	7,200,000	7,200,000	18,000,000	6,0	120,000	300,000	150,000	30,000	60,000	1300	2,5 : 1
Sweden . . .	209,000	3,000,000	14	1,500,000	1,150,000	5,250,000	10,0	50,000	140,000	80,000	15,000	35,000	380	3,5 : 1
Germanic States	204,000	25,000,000	122	14,000,000	unknown	28,000,000	11,2	120,000	260,000	120,000	———	———	—	2 : 1
Austria . . .	180,000	19,000,000	105	11,000,000	9,000,000	18,000,000	11,7	365,000	450,000	200,000	———	———	18	2 : 1
France . . .	182,000	25,000,000	138	28,000,000	25,000,000	37,500,000	22,4	300,000	600,000	400,000	24,000	120,000	470	1,5 : 1
Denmark . .	170,000	2,300,000	13	1,200,000	1,075,000	3,225,000	10,5	75,000	130,000	50,000	18,000	40,000	578	3 : 1
Poland before 1793	160,000	9,000,000	56	450,000	450,000	1,800,000	1,0	18,000	100,000	60,000	———	———	—	4 : 1
Spain . . .	148,000	11,000,000	74	14,000,000	11,600,000	17,400,000	25,5	104,000	250,000	100,000	28,000	104,000	466	1,5 : 1
Britain & Ireland	105,000	15,000,000	142	66,000,000	45,000,000	45,000,000	88,0	45,000	350,000	75,000	18,000	130,000	1200	Standard
Prussia . . .	56,000	5,500,000	89	4,200,000	4,200,000	10,500,000	15,3	224,000	350,000	150,000	———	150,000	50	2,5 : 1
Naples & Sicily	30,000	6,000,000	200	1,400,000	1,400,000	4,200,000	4,8	34,000	80,000	30,000	5,000	8,000	586	3 : 1
Portugal . .	27,000	2,000,000	74	2,150,000	1,950,000	2,925,000	21,6	36,000	60,000	30,000	12,000	22,000	166	1,5 : 1
Sardinia & Savoy	20,000	3,253,000	162	1,820,000	1,820,000	5,460,000	11,2	38,000	100,000	50,000	6,000	10,000	*	3 : 1
Holland . .	10,000	2,758,000	275	3,500,005	2,950,000	4,425,000	25,4	36,000	75,000	40,000	16,000	40,000	216	1,5 : 1

FIGURE 29: Playfair analyzes national capabilities to calculate a European Balance of Power in 1813. Source: William Playfair, *Outlines of a Plan for a New and Solid Balance of Power in Europe* (London: J, Stockdale, 1813). This one is from my own collection.

Much of the data had already appeared in *The Statistical Breviary*, but by presenting it side-by-side on a single page, Playfair showed how various combinations of allies might constitute a balance. His own proposal was an alliance between Britain (providing money and arms) and Russia (providing soldiers and geographic depth). States like Turkey, Spain, Sweden, Holland, Prussia, and Poland fine-tuned the balance with their location, motivation, or unique capabilities.[120]

Playfair could have presented the data as a stacked bar chart; that would have revealed the point when the composite capabilities of Britain, Russia, and their lesser allies offset those of France, indicating a balance was reached. But in this case raw numbers were better.

Graphic displays simplify *comparison*. Tables simplify *calculation* and *integration*. Aligning data vertically and horizontally makes addition and subtraction easier—indeed, invites it. Playfair let readers do their own numerical manipulations, using whatever combination of nations and capabilities they might envision in an alliance.

James Watt would have smiled, were he prone to smiling.

Playfair dedicated the booklet to Czar Alexander I. Like Napoleon, Alexander was a warrior king, commander as well as ruler. The Treaty of Orebro made Russia and Britain allies, and Alexander was a hero for defeating Napoleon. The Czar sent Playfair a note of approval via his ambassador in London, Christopher Lieven.[121] Playfair thought highly of Lieven; he claimed the ambassador was "more like a member of the British cabinet, than a foreign minister."[122]

Playfair is often acknowledged for inventing statistical graphics. But this was different: this is statistical *analysis*—using numbers to estimate the correlation of forces among nations and coalitions.

Once you know how to measure the balance of power, you can try to engineer it. Today this kind of quantified analysis is used in everything from planning U.S. military force structure to negotiating international arms control treaties—all employing databases that bear a remarkable resemblance to Playfair's Statistical Table. If anyone attempted this before Playfair, I have not found it. Playfair probably was first, if only because no one previously had the data.

William Playfair invented modern strategic studies.

10 Return to France, Back to Britain

Suppose you want historians to portray you as an off-kilter, slightly eccentric, blowhard writer from the early 1800s. Short of claiming that you *are* Napoleon, it's hard to think of a more effective strategy than claiming you unsuccessfully tried to warn of Napoleon's escape from Elba. It has all the needed elements of Cassandrian grandiosity combined with an inherent lack of verifiability, and just a hint that you might be hearing voices.

Naturally, William Playfair claimed he tried, unsuccessfully, to warn the British government about Napoleon's plans to escape from Elba.

§ § §

It took two years for the Sixth Coalition to drive the Grande Armée all the way back to Paris. In April 1814 Napoleon's generals made him accept a comfortable but power-free exile to Elba, a sunny-but-barren island off the coast of Tuscany. Then the Allies convened the Congress of Vienna to redraw the map of Europe.

They failed to understand Napoleon had never accepted defeat. He knew support for Louis XVIII—the king the Allies installed in France under the Restoration—was thin. He knew his popularity among many Frenchmen was still strong.

So Napoleon set sail in the *Inconstant* from Elba on 26 February 1815, landing near Cannes. As he marched to Paris, officer after officer disavowed his new king and recommitted to his old emperor. By May Napoleon had raised an army of almost 200,000 soldiers.

The Allies were caught flatfooted. Napoleon's strategy was to strike fast. He planned first to split the British and Prussian armies by attacking north, and then destroying them piecemeal. After that he would turn east and defeat the Austrians, and finally the Russians. Then he would offer terms for peace. The Empire would be restored.

The French began their advance toward Brussels on 15 June 1815, triggering the War of the Seventh Coalition. They met Wellington's army at Waterloo on 18 June. The Prussians arrived in the nick of time, and Wellington won, as he put it, the "nearest run thing." The Allies got rid of Napoleon for good this time, marooning him on St. Helena, a desolate rock in the South Atlantic as far removed from anything as anything.

Waterloo was a historic military victory for Britain, but Napoleon's escape from Elba was a huge intelligence failure. The Allies came close to losing everything they had gained since the Russian defense of Moscow in1812. Why hadn't anyone warned that Napoleon was planning an escape?

Playfair said he did.

On 25 March 1815, even as the Allies were scrambling to redeploy their armies, Playfair published: *A statement, which was made in October, to Earl Bathurst, one of His Majesty's Principal Secretaries of State, and in November, 1814, to the comte de La Chatre, the French ambassador, of Buonaparte's plot to re-usurp the Crown of France.*[1] Its story can best be characterized as "odd."

"Earl Bathurst" was Henry Bathurst, 3rd Earl Bathurst; he was Secretary of State for War and the Colonies, akin to Henry Dundas' old post. "Comte de la Châtre" was Claude-Louis de La Châtre, veteran of Quiberon, Louis XVIII's ambassador in London—and one of a handful of correspondents Jean de Batz kept in touch with in London.[2]

Playfair claimed that he "accidentally became acquainted" with a dark-skinned, middle-aged Italian named Caraman six months earlier. (Remember, that's Playfair's euphemism for "recruited a source.") Caraman said he was a veteran of Napoleon's army and, after that, a member of Napoleon's guard at Elba. He told Playfair he left Napoleon for "private reasons."

Playfair said he met Caraman on 10 September 1814 for dinner on at Pagliano's, a restaurant on London's Martin Street. Thomas Byerley joined them as a witness. Playfair pretended to be an admirer of Napoleon, and chatted up Caraman, a talkative man.

As Playfair goaded him on, Caraman let drop what he claimed was Napoleon's plan for a comeback. Caraman said conspirators were planning to assassinate Louis XVIII; after they accomplished that, Napoleon would leave Elba for Italy and announce a French government in exile.

Caraman—still thinking Playfair was a Napoleon sympathizer—shared with him a map of Elba, an encrypted message, and a cipher table to decrypt it. Napoleon, Caraman said, was just waiting for the Congress of Vienna to end; once that happened, he would strike.

The encrypted message was a call to arms Napoleon planned to release at the right moment, spreading it among his followers. Playfair later decrypted and translated it; it read: [3]

> Frenchmen! Your country was betrayed; your Emperor alone can replace you in the splendid state suitable for France. Give your entire confidence to him who has always led you to glory. His eagles will again soar on high, and strike the nations with astonishment.

Sure sounds like Napoleon. Playfair claimed he then contacted Bathurst, who replied with "his compliments." Bathurst invited Playfair to call at the Foreign Office the following week and ask for "Mr. Morier." That was most likely John Philip "Jack" Morier, a long-time, well-traveled British diplomat. [4]

When they met four days later, Playfair offered a proposal: He would go to France and "bring proofs" that would convince the Allies Napoleon planned to escape from Elba. That, Playfair said, would compel them to pre-empt the deposed emperor and move him to a more secure location where he could do no further mischief.

Morier, Playfair recalled, would have none of it. He said Morier received him "*coolly,—coldly*, nay most FORBIDDINGLY." Sitting by the fire, Morier puzzled over the encrypted message and the cypher table Playfair had brought. "What is the meaning of this *conundrum?*" he mused. Morier said he had no knowledge of ciphers—and no interest.

"Dundas and Wyndham did not treat me so," Playfair recalled. [5] But Henry Dundas and William Windham were gone. Playfair then approached Châtre—but fared no better. That's when Playfair published his pamphlet, along with shorter versions in *The Times* and various foreign papers. [6] He backed up his story with copies of some—but not all—of his correspondence and an affidavit by Byerley corroborating his account.

The public's reaction? Virtually nil. One London writer said Playfair had been making himself "conspicuous" in alleging he warned British ministers. "Little notice, however, was taken of what he imparted to government," it said, and "the public appeared to regard it with equal indifference."[7] Today, historians treat Playfair's story as bizarre—assuming they are even aware of it.

Did Playfair really try to warn British officials? The answer is yes. There's proof.

In 1923, after a decades-long project, the British government published the final tranche of Bathurst's collected papers. There are summaries and excerpts from three letters by Playfair in his files, dated 31 October, 3 November, and 5 November 1814—roughly corresponding to letters he described in his pamphlet.

It's the last letter —which Playfair alluded to, but did not reproduce in his pamphlet—that's most interesting. One section read:[8]

> When I had the honor of writing to your Lordship respecting the conspiracy in France, it did not occur to me that as Government has often been deceived by pretended communications and money obtained, it would be necessary for me to say that I will do what is necessary at my own expense, but I must have protection such that the French Government may not suspect me, for I shall have to go into some very disaffected societies. I can make no farther offer, and certainly if I succeed, of which I have little doubt, trust to be rewarded, for unless good cause is shown for placing Bonaparte in a state of security there will appear much injustice in doing so. What I simply and unequivocally propose is to furnish those proofs.

Playfair was never this explicit in public. He didn't say in his pamphlet that he had offered to fund the mission himself. (Given his finances, one has to wonder how. But let that pass for now.)

The most revealing—and sensitive—part, however, was Playfair's request for "protection," so that "the French Government"—that is, Napoleon's government, back in place for the time being—"may not suspect me," and so that he could "go into some very disaffected societies."

Playfair was asking the government to provide him cover.

What kind of cover? Playfair might have simply wanted a passport, requesting foreign authorities to let him "pass without delay or hindrance," as the standard language goes. Or, he may have wanted Bathurst to backstop a "legend," so Playfair could pose as, say, a writer poking around France on a five-month tour that might end with, say, a voyage down the Rhine back to friendlier territory.

In 1814 Playfair was fifty-five, and he was an old fifty-five. The problems with his legs, whatever it was, made it harder and harder to get around. But he wanted to get back in the saddle. His sources told him that Napoleon was about to escape. Playfair had, as they say, special skills: He was fluent in the local language, he had years of on-the ground experience, and he knew how to set up an operation—fast.

Unfortunately for Playfair, a new generation of British leaders had come to power, and they turned him down. That's when he went public. The challenge he issued at the end of his pamphlet made sense only if you knew what he had been doing all those years:[9]

> If it can be shewn that, in any one instance, I ever gave wrong information, or evinced a disposition to impose on any of the members of Government, or that I ever attempted to gain advantage to myself at the public expense, I think it will be a vindication for the incredulity complained of—but if, on the contrary, it can be made appear that I have often given useful information, and never asked any reward, and that, for more than twenty years, I have employed such abilities as I am possessed of, in support of the cause in which the country fought, without asking any reward from Government;—then I do think that there is an obligation somewhere of giving an explanation of the cause for treating my information with neglect.

After Waterloo, the wars were truly over; Napoleon was on far-away St. Helena. The French Revolution had burned itself out. Playfair needed a job and saw a new opportunity.

§ § §

Another day, another duel. They were becoming common in Paris in 1817. But this wasn't like Shelburne and Fullarton facing off in Hyde Park because of a misunderstanding over some ill-chosen words. This was serious, unsettled business—a legacy of the war just past.

One of the duelists was Guillaume-Michel Barbier Dufay. A loud, strapping brawler, Dufay had marched with Napoleon. He had been on half pay since the Grande Armée stood down, although he had done well for himself during the war, having acquired the chateau of a noble who had fled the country.

That chateau belonged to his opponent, Charles-Étienne de Bourgevin de Vialart, comte de Saint-Morys, a slight, slope-shouldered man who wrote about politics and travel. At least it *would* have belonged to him if Saint-Morys had not left with his father in 1791 to join the émigrés at Coblentz. The republicans declared their estate abandoned and seized it, which is how it wound up with Dufay.

But Saint-Morys' mother had remained behind, and when the regime took the chateau, she moved into the barnyard. So, technically, it had never been abandoned. After the Restoration, young Saint-Morys returned and was able to recuperate about half the family estate. Making the best of the situation, he settled in the stable with his mother and his wife, Marie-Anne, whom he had met and married in Coblentz.

This left Dufay in a slow burn. Having the effete, wellborn aristocrat parked outside his front door was more than the grizzled republican veteran could stand. Dufay tried to buy out his unwanted neighbor; Saint-Morys wouldn't sell. Indeed, Saint-Morys ran for local office—and won, becoming mayor of nearby Housainville.

Dufay vowed either he or Saint-Morys had to die. And he apparently didn't much care which. So he conjured up a plot to draw Saint-Morys into a duel. All he had to do was post a letter so insulting that Saint-Morys could not possibly ignore it and keep his honor. Saint-Morys would be obliged to issue a challenge. Then Dufay would have his opportunity to kill or be killed.[10]

Saint-Morys was an officer in the Garde du Corps—the ancient, prestigious, and largely ceremonial cavalry unit nominally responsible for protecting King Louis XVIII. Dufay published his letter. It must have been some letter; the captains of the Garde thought it so insulting that it was an affront to the entire unit.

Dueling with Napoleon's ex-officers was part of the Garde's lifestyle. Café Tortoni, the hangout for celebrities and wannabes on the Boulevard des Italiens, even had a backroom set aside for the exchange of challenges and responses.[11]

That lifestyle wasn't Saint-Morys, though; he was in the Garde for the political connections and pension. He had absolutely no appetite for a duel—none. But his captains insisted he cleanse his honor.

When Saint-Morys finally responded, Dufay—technically, the challenged party—had the prerogative to choose the form of the duel. He proposed what was essentially Russian roulette. Saint-Morys was to choose from two pistols in a sack—one loaded, one empty. The men would be bound together, aim at each other at point-blank range, and simultaneously pull their triggers.

Dufay really *was* indifferent about whether he lived or died. He just wanted to be rid of Saint-Morys, one way or another.

Saint-Morys pleaded to the Guarde captains; he was dealing with a lunatic. This was far, far beyond any officer's duty. The captains wouldn't budge. By now Marie-Anne was frantic.

The captains finally conceded that Saint-Morys was entitled to demand a more conventional contest. More negotiations followed. The two men finally agreed: a traditional duel, with pistols, followed, if necessary, by swords.

They met in the early evening of Tuesday, 22 July, on the Champs-Élysées. A crowd gathered. Dueling was illegal—on paper, if not in practice—so they moved to a field behind a nearby building. After expending two braces of pistols—reports don't say whether the duelists missed or the pistols misfired—they turned to their swords.

Yet, as arduous as the negotiations had been, no one had settled one critical detail: how the outcome would be decided. As the swords flailed, Saint-Morys nicked Dufay. Or he thought he did. Believing—or hoping—the duel was to be to "first blood," Saint-Morys called out, "*Monsieur, vous êtes blessé!*" He dropped his guard, leaving himself open.

"*Non, monsieur,*" Dufay replied. "*Mais vous êtes mort!*" Dufay ran him through, plunging his sword into Saint-Morys, twisting the blade inside his opponent with a turn of his wrist to ensure the strike was fatal. Saint-Morys hit the ground, dead.[12]

The duel made page four of *Galignani's Messenger* two days later. The report dashed out the names of Saint-Morys and Dufay, though anyone who cared knew who they were. The account went:[13]

A fatal duel which took place on Tuesday evening, furnishes another cogent reason for abolishing a custom barbarous and disgraceful to civilized nations, when it is considered that a valuable life has been lost to his country on the path of false honour. The Marshal de Camp Count de...was killed in the field behind the establishment of the Montagues Rasses, about half past eight o'clock in the evening by Colonel....The parties went to the Bois de Boulogne, accompanied by three witnesses on each side, but there being a number of persons walking in every direction and a crowd having followed them, they were sometime in getting clear from observation, and finally found themselves so in the spot behind the mentioned place. Having discharged four pistol shots without effect, they attacked each other with their swords, and the Count de...received a thrust through the body, which killed him on the spot.

Galignani's Messenger was the English-language daily published in Paris. William Playfair was its editor. He seems to have landed the job sometime in 1815 or 1816.[14]

Giovanni Antonio Galignani came from long line of booksellers. Born in Brescia sometime around 1752, he emigrated to Paris around 1790, and left for London when the Revolution heated up. He moved back to Paris in 1800 and opened a shop offering books in French, Italian, German, Spanish—and, especially, English. It reflected his hope for peace and cooperation in Europe.

It also reflected the fact that it was nearly impossible to enforce a foreign copyright in France. The pirated edition of *The Complete Works of Lord Byron* alone had made Galignani a wealthy man. He would reprint a book hot off the press in London, and sell it at a fraction of its list price in Paris. Or he would rent it to his subscribers at his circulating library at 18 rue Vivienne where, for just a few francs a month, one could relax in Galignani's tearoom and browse his collection.[15]

That's where the *Messenger* came in—Galignani made copies available in the tearoom, aiming at boosting foot traffic. The first edition appeared on 2 July 1814. It quickly developed a broader readership, with subscriptions selling for nine francs per month, eighty-eight francs for a year.[16]

Playfair was a natural choice for editor, with all his connections in France and fluency in the local language and culture. The early issues of the *Messenger* were, let us say, thin. But it hit its stride about the time Playfair arrived, becoming sharper and more focused, with more hard news.

Published as a four-page, two-column broadsheet, the *Messenger* consisted largely of excerpts from British papers. It made no apologies for being a cut-and-paste job. To the contrary, the *Messenger* boasted of the "immense advantage of reproducing, in a single journal, the Leaders and Intelligence given by the London daily and weekly newspapers."[17]

Today we'd call the *Messenger* a news aggregator, and for a tiny operation, the line of distinguished writers who spent time working there is remarkable. Victorian-era chronicler Cyrus Redding was one; he wrote the account of the duel between Dufay and Saint-Morys.[18] W.M. Thackeray, famous later for *Vanity Fair*, wrote for the *Messenger*, too; he recalled making ten francs a day.[19] Playfair—compiler of *The Statistical Breviary*, traveler, and sometime British secret agent—fit right in.

Read a copy of the *Messenger* and you get a snapshot of early nineteenth-century world affairs. It's clear that whoever was putting together the paper was plugged in.

The front-page news in mid-1817: Pro-British insurgents had seized Amelia Island from Spain.[20] Back pages provided market reports, official announcements, ship arrivals, and weather. There was also a brief section with original Paris reporting; that's where the account of the duel appeared. And there were advertisements. (Example: "Rue des Martyrs, No. 62—Several Apartments to Let, Furnished, with the facility of Board or separate meals. After dinner French and Italian conversation.")[21]

The *Messenger* also occasionally reviewed recent books, which is what got Playfair kicked out of France. But to understand what really happened, you need to know about the counterfeiting operation.

§ § §

One year later, a middle-aged woman sat in the Tribunal of the Correctional Police. It was summer, but she was dressed all in black. It was Marie-Anne Charlotte de Valicourt—the widow Saint-Morys. She was still in mourning. Her husband was dead. Someone had to be to blame; someone had to pay.

A few weeks after the duel Marie-Anne published a pamphlet to rally public outrage at Dufay: *Dénonciation contre Guillaume-Michel-Étienne Barbier, dit Dufaÿ*. All that came out of that was Dufay filing a case against *her*—for slander.[22] Then Marie-Anne pressed charges against the Guarde officers who pressured her husband into the duel. The king appointed a panel of nobles to try the case; in January it ruled the officers had followed the code of honor precisely.[23]

Then Playfair stepped in—or, one might say, stepped in it.

"Madame la Comtesse de St. Morys has published a Memoir of twenty-seven sheets," Playfair reported, referring to *Dénonciation* in an unsigned-but-later-attributed column in the *Messenger* of 27 March 1818. "We conceive this Lady," Playfair wrote, "to be extremely ill-advised." He said, "The Public are acquainted with the real facts of the case." Just about everyone had heard about the challenge, the evasions, the negotiations, the contest, and the outcome.

"We confess," Playfair wrote, that "it is a great misfortune for Madame de St. Morys to have lost her husband in a duel." But—here its comes—it is a greater misfortune "that he should die with the universal impression of being less brave than his sword." Marie-Anne should let the matter drop, Playfair suggested, "rather than seek to keep alive sentiments and recollections which do his memory no honor."[24]

It was really just a fleeting, unintentionally provocative, and excessively accurate comment—one might even call it Shelburnesque—buried in the bottom corner of Page Three on a slow news day. It followed a blurb about the Dutchess of Angoulême dispensing soup to the poor in Saint-Germain l'Auxerrois parish, and preceded a mention of the recent fire at the Odéon Theater.[25]

Nevertheless, those five words—*less brave than his sword*—were among the most costly Playfair would ever write. They were right up there with the pamphlets that ticked off Bertrand Barère and anything he might have signed facilitating the Original Security Bank.

Under French law a man's honor was sacrosanct—even a dead man's honor. Marie-Anne filed libel charges against *Galignani's Messenger*—specifically, its publisher and editor.[26]

The trial stretched out over a month. Playfair described it later: There are three judges. The president sits in the middle. The two on each side seem never to say anything as the president carries out "a sort of conversation with witnesses." Then everyone adjourns for eight days. Then the other side is heard, "and after some more delay, judgment is given."[27]

It was barely four years since Waterloo. No French court was going to acquit an Englishman on a matter concerning a Frenchman's honor, dead or not. Of course, it might have helped if Playfair had behaved himself. Not a chance. Playfair was, as reports put it, "ironic," "sarcastic," and "venturing into advocacy."[28]

The results were predictable.

Giovanni Galignani, Italian-born and popular in Paris, got off completely.[29]

Marie-Anne, the grieving widow of a well-liked noble, was found guilty of slandering Dufay, but got just the proverbial slap on the wrist: she had to print, at her expense, fifty copies of a retraction. (It says something about what the judges thought of Dufay, an unsympathetic anti-royalist bully who had had more than one run-in with the police.)[30]

And as for Playfair: The cocky, unrepentant Brit felt the full force of the French legal system. He was sentenced to three months in jail and a fine of 6,000 francs. The court ordered him to print two hundred copies of a retraction and pay Marie-Anne a thousand francs in damages. Playfair also forfeited his civil rights for five years. That's why he fled France. (It's not clear if he served the sentence.)[31]

Back in Britain, Playfair would later publish *France As It Is*, a sort of travel guide combined with political commentary. He offered this advice to any of his countrymen considering France as a destination: "Attention to the courts as they are now constituted, and as they now practise, is earnestly recommended to those who visit Paris for any length of time."[32]

True that.

§ § §

A casual observer might think that Playfair just stumbled into another mess, carelessly slandering a French noble. But of course there's more to the story, and of course it all goes back to the counterfeiting operation.

Marie-Anne's husband, Charles-Étienne, comte de Saint-Morys wasn't just some random French noble. Recall the ninety reams of "French Paper" Sir John Edward Swinburne said the Haughton Castle mill was sending each week to London by mail coach. Here's a message Playfair sent William Windham on 31 October 1795:[33]

> In answer to the note which you did me the Honor of writing
> yesterday I have to inform you that the Person who has the claim

on M. de St Morie is John Lightly on No. 178 Upper Thames Street. I only meddled in that business to bring it to an amicable End & shall be Extremely happy to contribute in doing so. The paper it is certain never was delivered on Sloan Street because it was the custom of them to give the order to be delivered in Thames Street & remain there ready when demanded. The last word that M. de St. Morie said (as Lightly tells me) to him was, demanding a delay of three months for paying that & probably he Expected to be returned from the Expedition by that time.

John Lightly was a London stationer; he was the "clerk to the warehouse in London" that Swinburne mentioned in the attachment to his memorandum describing the counterfeiting operation at Haughton Castle. "M. de St Morie" was Playfair's butchered rendering of "Charles-Paul-Jean-Baptiste de Bourgevin Vialart, compte de Saint-Morys." He was one of the main players in the counterfeiting operation.[34]

He was also Charles-Étienne's father.

From Playfair's letter, it sounds like the usual routine was to ship French paper to Lightly, who then distributed it to Saint-Morys, who paid him. It also sounds like there were some complications with the payment from Charles-Paul, and Playfair was trying to straighten things out.

The main complication was that Charles-Paul was dead.

Charles-Paul Saint-Morys didn't "return from Expedition;" he was killed at Quiberon. Today Saint-Morys is best known for his art collection; much of it hangs in the Louvre. That's because the republicans confiscated it when Charles-Paul fled to Coblentz with his son Charles-Étienne, leaving behind the wealthy heiress he had married, Eléonore-Angélique de Beauterre—the wife who remained behind, living in the stable after the republicans seized their chateau.

The thing you need to know about Charles-Paul is that, before he married Eléonore, he was by training...an engraver.[35]

In late 1791 the Council of Princes, the royal court of France in exile, authorized Saint-Morys to set up a factory to produce assignats.[36] By December, Paris newspapers were reporting one busy at work in Coblentz.[37]

So when Joseph de Puisaye arrived in London from Brittany in September 1794, he knew there was already a lot of assignat counterfeiting going on. Reports said that royalist émigrés were behind at least some of it. He suspected that Britain might be harboring or aiding some of them. (It was one of the justifications France gave when it declared war on Britain in February 1793.)

Puisaye had no problem with the counterfeiting; his concern was quality control. The early forgeries were hard for the average Frenchman to spot, but easy for authorities to identify. That was a lethal combination, because it didn't matter whether you were deliberately passing a bogus bill or just took one in payment while selling your goat; getting caught with a forged assignat was a life-abbreviating experience. Puisaye called the forged bills *lettres de change de mort*—"death notes."[38]

Indeed, Puisaye was thinking along the same lines as Playfair. He wanted to "establish an immense manufacture" of high quality assignats, and crank them out "in a proportion still more considerable than that of the Convention." That is, he wanted to flood the market. He also wanted to include a secret mark on his notes, so the monarchy could redeem them once it was restored.[39]

It took Puisaye some effort to work his way into the émigré community; they suspected the new arrival from Brittany might be a mole. But eventually he found Abbé Calonne, who introduced Puisaye to his friend and collaborator: Charles-Paul de Saint-Morys.[40]

"It is regrettable," Saint-Morys said when Puisaye met him and floated the idea of secret mark, "that when a similar operation was proposed, the ideas you have communicated to me were not suggested at the same time." In other words, the counterfeiting operation was already underway; they just hadn't thought of marking the bills.[41]

Still, there was room for more printers and distributors. Saint-Morys and Abbé Calonne signed an agreement with Puisaye on 20 September 1794 to establish a "manufactory of assignats" that were "in all respects similar to those which have been issued, or which will be issued thereafter, by the so-called Convention of the Rebels." Their assignats would "bear a secret character of recognition."[42]

Saint-Morys meshed well with Abbé de Calonne. The two men had complementary skills, complementary interests—and, as it transpired, complementary offspring. Charles-Paul's son, Charles-Étienne, and the Abbé's daughter, Marie-Anne, married in Coblentz in November 1791. So Charles-Paul Saint-Morys and Abbé de Calonne were more than friends and co-conspirators. They were brothers-in-law.

Calonne and Saint-Morys had their own operation for forging assignats even before the British entered the war. Puisaye offers part of the story, but most of what we know comes from the correspondence of Colonel John Gordon Sinclair.

And who was John Gordon Sinclair?

Bred to be a soldier, Sinclair fought the Americans at Bunker Hill, where he was wounded and taken prisoner.[43] He became friends with Lafayette; evidently the two soldiers let bygones be bygones. After the storming of the Bastille, Lafayette invited him to France to help reform its army.[44]

According to Sinclair, after King Louis's Flight to Varennes and the Revolution turned radical, he carried out a secret mission to assist opponents of the republicans, with the knowledge of "a certain great personage."[45] Then a friend persuaded him that he would be of more use with the émigrés at Coblentz.[46]

Sinclair raised a regiment, received a commission from the French royalists—that's how he came to be "Colonel Sinclair"—and deployed to the Low Countries. Funded by a note for unlimited credit by the house of Charles Herries (father of John Charles Herries), Sinclair returned to Britain in late 1791 to buy arms.[47]

He returned to Coblentz in January 1792. There he was shocked to find the French officers in "all engaged in an illicit manufactory of assignats" at a factory in Neuwied, ten miles down the Rhine. The Calonne brothers and Saint-Morys were directing it.[48]

As far as Sinclair was concerned, forgery was forgery and he ordered the officers arrested. But the officers appealed to their troops, who decided to support their fellow Frenchmen. Thus, it was Sinclair who was arrested. Charles-Étienne took over Sinclair's regiment—to guard the assignat factory. The French eventually released Sinclair, but there would always be bad blood between him and the Saint-Morys and the Calonnes.[49]

Playfair's letter to Windham about the screwed-up delivery of French paper to Charles-Paul says that the émigrés merged their counterfeiting efforts with the British operation soon after Playfair prepared his forgery plan in March 1793. Puisaye recalled that by the time arrived in London in the following year there were seventeen or eighteen assignat "manufactories," in addition to those in Germany and Switzerland.[50]

There's another sign of collaboration in Puisaye's papers: a letter from Charles-Étienne's sister. She was apparently involved in the operation, too; she requested forty pounds of ink from Windham for printing notes.[51]

Sometime in 1794 Charles-Paul went to London to serve in the Quiberon invasion as quartermaster general for the émigré army.[52] Records show him on the frigate HMS *Pomone* when the invasion force embarked in July 1795—the same ship transporting Jacques-Anne-Joseph Le Prestre de Vauban, Playfair's companion on his sojourn down the Rhine the year before.[53]

Charles-Paul Saint-Morys never returned. He died when an epidemic swept through the troops during the voyage back to Britain, killing one out of every eight soldiers who had survived the invasion itself. (In the 1700s disease was as deadly as combat in a typical campaign.) Charles-Étienne thus inherited his father's title.

And, as you have no doubt figured out, the Marie-Anne that Charles-Étienne married in Coblentz—who pleaded to get her husband out of his duel with Dufay—was the widow who filed libel charges against Playfair.

Marie-Anne had to know who Playfair was and his connection to the counterfeiting operation. Her father, father-in-law, and sister-in-law all took part in it. Playfair was one of the key players, and dealt with Charles-Paul. Her husband, Charles-Étienne, got his commission when the émigrés squeezed out Sinclair—a result of the flap over counterfeiting. Under the agreement with Puisaye, Charles-Paul was to share any assets left over from counterfeiting operation; that went to Charles-Étienne—and, thus, Marie-Anne—after Charles-Paul died. (Charles-Étienne also inherited monies that Abbé Calonne owed his father.)[54]

But back to Sinclair. He presented a delicate problem for Playfair and Windham. When Sinclair discovered Calonne and Saint-Morys churning out bogus assignats, he did what one would expect an officer to do: report it and shut it down. He had no way to know his own government was not only about to join in, but would expand the operation on a scale the émigrés could have imagined only in their dreams.

Once the British and the émigré counterfeiting were linked, compromising one could compromise the other. Here's a letter Playfair sent to Windham on 26 March 1796. He wrote, cryptically:[55]

> I shall have the honour of waiting on you in a few days having something to mention about a Col. Sinclair whom I took the liberty to mention thence months ago as being a troublesome man. He has the intention of being troublesome to one of your colleagues & as by a means of a third person I have not lost sight of what he is about if to be apprised of his intentions his means will be of any use I can offer that without betraying any thing or any one. If it will not then I hope you will consider this offer only as meant to serve a gentleman to whom I am much obliged if I can do it.

Why would Playfair call Sinclair "troublesome?" Perhaps it was because Sinclair had tried to shut down the émigré counterfeiting effort. Or Playfair may have feared Sinclair would try to get even with Calonne and Saint-Morys for seizing his regiment. Either could compromise the operation.

Then again, Sinclair might have been less "troublesome" if Playfair hadn't borrowed £397 from him.

Three days after Playfair wrote Windham, he wrote Sinclair, thanking him for covering a debt he owed another officer. If Sinclair had not known the officer and "killed the matter," Playfair said, he would "know not how I should have got over it." It would explain why Playfair said he felt "much obliged" to him.[56]

Sinclair was the colonel Playfair was confiding in when he warned Windham was "misinformed & misled by the emigrants." In a postscript that winds its way around the back, across the bottom, and up the sides of the page, Playfair advised Sinclair he could trust Windham, who, "however much he may be mistaken certainly acts from good principles."[57]

Playfair's relationships, to put it mildly, were complicated. He was working with Saint-Morys, but he disdained the Coblentz émigrés—by his measure, dupes "decoyed out by Monsieur de Calonne."[58] He was warning Windham that Sinclair was "troublesome," even as he borrowed money from the colonel—and advising him in his own relations with Windham.

One final twist: One of the "friends" who suggested to Sinclair that he go to Coblentz to assist the émigrés was... Reverend Julius Hutchinson.

As it turns out, Hutchinson wasn't just a parish priest hoping to make some extra money as a silent partner in the Original Security Bank. He was bankrolling the counter-revolutionaries.

§ § §

Hutchinson's "political principles and attachment to me," Sinclair recalled, "induced him to assist me with large sums not only to accelerate my mission for the Princes, but also to complete my regiment."[59] They met when they were both visiting royalist forces organizing near Calais. Hutchinson warned Sinclair to be wary of Calonne and Saint-Morys. Apparently Sinclair wasn't wary enough.[60]

A few years later Sinclair got ensnared in another dispute with the Calonnes, this time with Charles-Alexander, the Abbé's brother, former finance minister to Louis XVI, and would-be sponsor to Boulton & Watt's proposal to replace the Machine de Marly with a steam engine.

Charles-Alexander received (or confiscated) a horse from Sinclair when they quarreled over the assignat factory. Sinclair claimed he was never paid. Calonne produced a receipt. Sinclair claimed it was a forgery. Calonne filed a charge of perjury against Sinclair. The court found Sinclair culpable.[61]

The judge was Lord Kenyon—yes, *that* Lord Kenyon. Sinclair's lawyer was Vicary Gibbs—yes, *that* Vicary Gibbs. Sinclair had over a dozen affidavits to attest to his military record and honor. Affiants included the Duke of York, Henry Dundas, the comte d'Artois—and Julius Hutchinson.[62]

Another affidavit came from John Lightly of Thames Street—the stationer receiving French paper for Saint-Morys.

Lightly testified as an expert witness, able to "distinguish paper of English manufactory from foreign paper." Lightly swore the paper for the receipt Sinclair supposedly signed came from England. Since Calonne said the receipt came from the Continent, it was, just as Sinclair claimed, a forgery. That meant Sinclair was innocent, no matter what the court had ruled.[63] Sinclair spent time in prison, but considering who was vouching for him, it seems he was on his way to a royal pardon.[64]

And to complete the circle: Sinclair was involved in the Original Security Bank, too. His name appears on a letter from Playfair indicating Sinclair either deposited £460, or tried to fix one of the bank's shortfalls.[65] The link makes even more sense once you know Hutchinson and Sinclair were connected.

After his release, Sinclair took his dispute with the Calonne brothers and their entourage to Comte d'Artois. That, of course, could thoroughly complicate matters, and Playfair tried to warn Windham as "a duty I owe you for

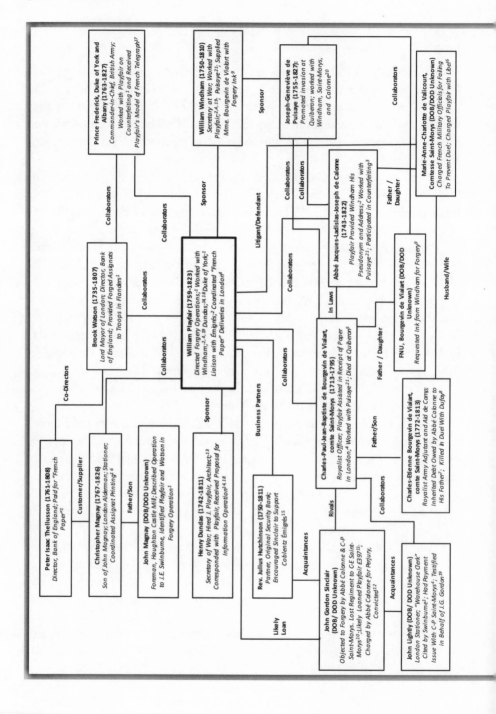

FIGURE 30: Playfair's Counterfeiting Network

The organizational chart at left presents a network analysis of Playfair's secret operation to counterfeit French assignats, documenting the key players and their relationships with each other. It includes senior British government officials, titans of industry, accomplices (both witting and unwitting), and a variety of foreign contacts—all comprising the network that carried out the world's first clandestine operation to collapse a nation's economy.

Sources: **1.** Sir J. E. Swinburne Memorandum (c1793–1794) Northumberland Archives, ZSW/590; **2.** W. Playfair to W. Windham (24 Oct 1795) BL ADD 37875, fol. 227; **3.** A. de Lestapis, "Emigration et faux assignats II," *La revue des Deux Mondes,* (Oct 1955), 457; **4.** W. Playfair to W. Windham (London, 31 Oct 1795, 8 Nov 1795) BL ADD 37875, fols. 232 and 254; **5.** Joseph de Puisaye, *Mémoires du comte Joseph de Puisaye* Vol. 6 (Londres: De L'imprimerie de Harper et Co., 1807), 530; **6.** "Countess Saint-Morys," *Public Characters of All Nations,* Vol. 3 (London: Sir Richard Phillips and Co., 1823), 314; **7.** S. Burrows, *French Exile Journalism and European Politics, 1792–1814* (Woodbridge, Suffolk: Boydell Press, 2000), 55. Burrows cites Archives nationales, 297AP/2. pièce 85, 'Contrat relative au Courier de l'Europe, 1805' [draft]' pièce 89, J.-L.-J. de Calonne to Blondel, Trois-Revières, 2 Sep. 1816; and Courier de Londres xlv/36 (3 May 1799); **8.** *The Gentleman's Magazine* (July–December, 1817), 116–119; and J.G. Millingen, *The History of Dueling* (London: Richard Bentley, 1841), 242; **9.** L. Blanc, *Histoire de la Revolution Française* Volume 14 (Paris: Librairie Internationale, 1878), 188–189. Blanc cites *Papiers de Puisaye,* British Library, Volume C1; **10.** J.G. Sinclair, "Brief Copy of Colonel Sinclair's Affidavit," (28 July 1798) NA HO 42/45, fol. 185, 16; **11.** W. Playfair to J.G. Sinclair (Lambeth Marsh, 29 Mar 1796) NAGL ADD MS 403; **12.** "The King versus John Gordon Sinclair," *The Sporting Magazine* (Jun 1798), 146-148; **13.** James Playfair, "Journal of Architecture 1783, 4, 5, 6, 7, 8,—1789–90—91 of James Playfair, Architect" National Library of Scotland, Adv. MS.33.5.25; **14.** W. Playfair to H. Dundas, (Old Brompton, 9 Oct 1804), Temple University Libraries, Special Collections Research Center, (SPC) MSS BH 118 COCH; **15.** "Declaration of the Rev. Julius Hutchinson," in John Gordon Sinclair Brief Copy of Colonel Sinclair's Affidavit, Filed in Court (28 July 1798) NA, HO 42/45 fol. 191–192; **16.** T. Doubleday, *The Political Life of Sir Robert Peel,* Volume 1 (London: Smith, Elder, and Co., 1856), 41–42; **17.** W. Playfair, *Political Portraits in this New Æra,* Volume 2 (London: C. Chapple, 1814), 220; **18.** W. Playfair to H. Dundas, (Knightsbridge, 24 April 1794) NA HO 42/29, fol 474–482; **19.** W. Playfair to W. Windham (Fitzroy Square, 21 Jan 1801) BL ADD 37868 fols. 17–18.; **20.** William Staddon Blake and John Lightly, "Extract of Affidavit," in John Gordon Sinclair, Brief Copy of Colonel Sinclair's Affidavit, Filed in Court (18 May 1798) NA HO 42/45 fol. 193, 30; **21.** Joseph de Puisaye, *Mémoires du comte Joseph de Puisaye,* Volume 3 (London: Harper and Co., 1804), 320–321, 373–396.

favours I have received." He wanted Windham to know "before any serious obligations are entered into that you may have to inform yourself of the real circumstances."[66]

Playfair, Hutchinson, Hartsinck, the elder and younger Saint-Morys, the widow Marie-Anne, the Calonne brothers, and Sinclair—and, by extension, the Original Security Bank, Brook Watson, the Duke of York, and Playfair's libel conviction in France—were all links in a network of relationships impossible to understand fully unless you also understand the counterfeiting operation and Playfair's secret relationships as a British agent.

§ § §

There's a epilogue to the Saint-Morys episode: it's the last piece of evidence linking Playfair to the counterfeiting operation. It shows Playfair not only planned and managed the operation; he helped orchestrate the cover-up, too.

On 8 July 1811, William Wyndham Grenville, 1st Baron Grenville, took the floor to speak in the House of Lords. From his prison cell, William Cobbett had been resurrecting the old stories of British counterfeiting French currency during the Revolution. By now Pitt was dead; so was Dundas. William Windham, Playfair's friend and patron, had passed a month earlier. Of the senior ministers who led Britain during the War of the First Coalition, only Grenville remained.

Grenville had been Pitt's Home Secretary and, later, Foreign Secretary. He feared radicalism spilling over into Britain as much as anyone. He supported the war against France—even suspending habeas corpus to control protesters. But he had the heart of a Whig when it came to domestic reform.

Grenville resigned with Pitt in 1801. After that his bent for reform—especially abolition of the slave trade—drew him closer to Fox and Grey. When Pitt returned to power in 1804, Grenville declined to join his government, partly because the King would not tolerate Fox in the cabinet.

Pitt died in January 1806. Napoleon dominated the Continent. The British economy was lifeless. Demands for political reform remained. It all created a sense of urgency—or desperation.

The king turned to Grenville. His "Ministry of All the Talents" was a unity government. It lasted just a year and accomplished little. Since Grenville had burnt his bridges with the Tories, he remained in the opposition for the rest of his career.[67]

Even so, Grenville felt compelled to respond to the counterfeiting accusations. He told his fellow Lords the charge was "grossly calumnious." He called it "one of the most unfounded aspersions that was ever advanced," adding that he had "never once harboured a thought, or participated in any one act, which could implicate him in the smallest degree in such an accusation."

Grenville was drawing a fine line; recall the network of informants his diplomats had run across Europe; besides Wickham in Berne, there was Francis Drake in Genoa, Sidney Smith in Toulon, and others. Perhaps Grenville felt espionage was less odious than subterfuge. Secret correspondence? No problem. Forgery? Heaven forbid.[68]

Grenville continued—digging himself in even deeper. He insisted that, "nothing of such a nature could have been done by the King's ministers without his being privy to it." Then he solemnly swore, "in the name of Almighty God that he was innocent himself of the charge which had been so brought forward."[69]

There are no reports of lightning strikes landing nearby as he uttered those words.

Playfair respected Grenville—by his reckoning, one of the "political characters who acted a remarkable part at the beginning of the present revolutionary war." Playfair appreciated a Whig who did not allow his devotion to domestic reform get in the way of fighting the French. But apparently the Secretary for War—Dundas—and the Secretary at War—Windom—never told the Foreign Secretary—Grenville—that Britain was cranking out bogus assignats.[70]

It explains the private note Playfair sent Grenville two days after his speech in Lords. He hoped to keep Grenville from telling an outright lie—especially a lie that might be exposed, discrediting Grenville and tainting anyone and everyone connected with the counterfeiting operation.[71]

"On reading the report of your speech on Monday, the 8th, in which your lordship is made to disclaim all knowledge on the part of his Majesty's Ministers of *assignats* fabricated in England," Playfair wrote, and, "knowing at the same time your strict honour and veracity, I am induced to enclose a paper that will undeceive your lordship on that subject."

Playfair continued: "It is to my efforts at the time (for the honour of the country and from friendship for Mr. Wyndham) that the Administration of which your lordship formed a part owes its not being exposed in a Court of Justice as paying for the fabrication of those very *assignats*."

It was typical Playfair: a candid letter combined with an unaddressed, unsigned memorandum, offering a fig leaf of deniability. The memorandum was a flashback to October 1795 and the outstanding bill for the French paper.

Playfair recalled how "a manufactory of assignats in imitation of those made in France was established at the back of Sloane Street," and that "Abbé de Calonne (brother to the minister), Mr. de Puisay and St. Morrice" ran it. Playfair still couldn't get the spelling of "Saint-Morys" straight.

The émigrés "had no money," Playfair continued. So when they sailed for Quiberon, they left unpaid a "large quantity of paper with the watermark" with the warehouseman on Upper Thames Street, "to the value of about 700L."

The stationer—John Lightly—had told Playfair that he was suing Calonne. He planned to prove Calonne was working in behalf of His Majesty's government, which, he claimed, was now responsible for the debt.

Shades of *Lukyn v. Strongitharm*. Except this flap had the potential to expose the operation far beyond a single engraver. John Lightly wasn't just trying to recover his own costs; he was representing everyone up and down his supply chain, and was under pressure to deliver.

Playfair had told Windham at the time, "Lightly acts for himself & others with full Powers as he did when he gave the credit." "Therefore," he would "forfeit all confidence were he to accept of too small a sum" in settling the debt. Who were the other creditors?

"Part of the Claimants live in Northumberland," wrote Playfair in his letter to Windham. In other words, Buccaneer Smith.[72]

Playfair went on to tell Grenville, "I was then in habits of seeing Mr. Wyndham, and informed him how Government was likely to be exposed." William Windham—Playfair often used the traditional spelling, though Windham didn't—"made light of it at first." But as the trial approached, he realized that the "man sent out to Quiberon with the assignats by Government would be proved to have fabricated them at an expense probably of 40,000L."

That sum—£40,000—provides a sense of the scale of the operation, and that would have been just the part the British were conducting with the French émigrés under Puisaye. Recall that Sir John Edward Swinburne had said production from Haughton Castle Mill was going to the Duke of York in Flanders, an entirely separate affair on the other side of France.

Since the émigrés "had no money," as Playfair put it, the British government had to cover the outstanding bill. "Mr. Wyndham desired me to settle it
so, if I could," Playfair said. So he did. Lightly "agreed to deduct twenty-five
per cent from the selling price and to allow 30L for the material left." That
meant the government owed Lightly £490, "which Mr. Wyndham promised
should be paid next day at 2 o'clock."

"I never saw any of the Frenchmen," Playfair told Grenville, "nor did I
know Calonne or anyone concerned." But, "I know that Lightly had plenty of
proof that Government paid, and this transaction, in which I was concerned
as stated."

Playfair's memorandum tracks with the reports he gave William Windham sixteen years earlier. It also suggests additional details about the operation: When the British manufactured paper for the bogus notes, at least part
of it went to the French émigrés for printing. Once they delivered the paper
to the émigrés, they had little knowledge or control of where it went.

It helps explain how Puisaye could deny so forcefully that British were
"making counterfeit assignats in London." From his perspective, the British weren't making *assignats*; they were merely making *paper*. It was Puisaye,
and Calonne, and Saint-Morys—duly authorized by the French monarchy
in exile—who were printing currency. If additional forgery were going on,
Puisaye had nothing to say, and likely would not know.

"I advised Mr. Wyndham," Playfair continued, that he should pay Lightly
and tacitly confirm the operation because, while "denial would only add to the
disgrace," the operation could be justified on the grounds that "the original
French assignats were themselves forged mortgages on the estates of emigrants issued by a Government of usurpers, and that the emigrants had at
least as good a right to issue assignate."

"Mr. Wyndham smiled," Playfair recalled, "and said that was true, and
might satisfy the mind of those concerned, but would not satisfy the public."
Playfair was an operator; Wyndham was a politician, and understood his
constituents.

"When the expedition sailed," Playfair claimed, "the manufactory ceased."
He wasn't clear on whether he meant all manufacturing ceased, or just the
part the French émigrés were doing. It *is* clear is that Playfair wasn't telling
Grenville the whole story.

Playfair said nothing about travel to the Continent. He skipped over his
meetings with Brook Watson, or Peter Isaac Thellusson's acting as paymaster,

or Obadiah Westwood soliciting engravers, or the Duke of York paying troops with *faux* assignats. Playfair gave Grenville just enough information to steer him clear of trouble without implicating more people than necessary.

"I should suppose that it would be better in return, neither to own or disown the transaction," Playfair advised him, "for there are people still living who can prove it."

Playfair assured Grenville that "indeed if I did not know positively that though your lordship was not privy to the business, others of Administration were." Grenville needed to know all this for own good, Playfair said, "as undoubtedly it would be very painful to have a formal assertion contradicted in an authentic way."

"I write this," Playfair closed, "in order that his lordship may confine the disavowal to his own knowledge, but not extend it to the whole Administration." And that was how Playfair informed the former Prime Minister about the British covert operation to collapse the French economy with counterfeit money.

When he received Playfair's letter, Grenville wrote a memorandum to himself; it was apparently in the same files as Playfair's note. Grenville said that *if* Playfair's message were true, then *perhaps* his cousin William knew of the "transaction" *after the fact*.

Not so; William Windham was completely knowing, totally witting, and utterly sanguine.

Grenville nevertheless wanted the record—even if it was his just own private record—to show that his hands were clean. "On the best recollection that I can give to it," Grenville wrote, "I cannot call to mind any the smallest knowledge of this fact, and I feel persuaded that it was never communicated to me."

The memorandum (reproduced in Appendix C) remained buried in the Grenville family archives until 1892, when the British Historical Manuscripts Commission began a project to publish Grenville's official papers. It was a massive effort, ultimately filling ten volumes.

Playfair's letter to Grenville was probably in the last files, which did not appear until the final volume, which was not published until 1927. By then the original editor of the project was dead. His successors simply put out the materials that remained, without analysis. The letter went unnoticed—and no one was the wiser of how William Playfair conceived, orchestrated, and, in the end, preserved the secret of the Great Op.[73]

11 An Unconventional Business Model

In September 1816, Archibald James Edward Douglas, 1st Baron Douglas, received a letter from one William Playfair. It was posted from Union Court, a middle-class London neighborhood favored by stockbrokers.[1]

The name would have instantly rung a bell with Archibald. In 1788 James Playfair designed Bothwell House, the Douglas mansion in Lanarkshire, about ten miles east of Glasgow on the River Clyde. In his journal James noted meeting Archibald several times while building the 30,000-square-foot dwelling.[2]

"Having had occasion to send to Paris to recover some papers that have been under a sort of sequestration ever since December 1792," the letter began, "some curious papers fell into the hands of the friend who went over for me." The papers, the letter said, were "relative to the succession of the noble Family of Douglas."[3]

You occasionally read that William Playfair become an extortionist in his later years. It's not true. Or at least it's not entirely true. Playfair was no extortionist. He was merely a struggling journalist with an unconventional business model.

The letter continued: It appeared the papers "were sought for but kept back when the great cause was pleaded." It added, "They can now be obtained on easy terms."[4]

The "great cause" was the Douglas Cause, the proverbial "trial of the century"—in this case, eighteenth-century Britain. It began when, in July 1748, Colonel John Stewart and his wife Lady Jane Douglas visited Paris. Stewart was sixty; Lady Jane was forty-nine. When they returned from France, they brought with them infant twins, Archibald and Sholto.[5]

The Douglas Cause rested on a simple question: Were the twins really the sons of Colonel Stewart and Lady Jane? Or did the couple buy the children when they were in Paris?[6]

Lady Jane was in line to inherit the Douglas fortune—perhaps the largest in Britain—from her childless brother, the Duke of Douglas. If the babies were truly hers, they would receive the fortune when the Duke died. If not, it would go to another family, related by marriage, the Hamiltons—specifically, the Duke of Hamilton.

The couple returned to England in 1749 with the two boys. Sholto, long sickly, died of a fever in May 1753. Jane died the following November, after months of stomach pains. No one knows what it was; medicine was primitive at the time. The Duke of Douglas died in 1761. The following year Hamilton filed papers in Edinburgh claiming Archibald Douglas was an impostor. The case went to the House of Lords.

The proceedings combined the scandal of the Sam Sheppard case with the sensationalism of the O.J. Simpson trial. Investigators and interviewers scoured France for evidence. Newspapers, just becoming popular, discovered the concept of "continuous coverage." Conjugal relations and biological functions were discussed in never-before detail.

Everyone had an opinion. Thomas Boswell supported Douglas. David Hume backed Hamilton. Naturally, William Petty had his view, too: "If ever I saw a Frenchman he is one," Lord Shelburne said of Archibald.[7] But the Lords found in favor of Douglas.

Now, five decades later, Playfair claimed he had documents proving the decision was wrong. He was offering to arrange their sale to Archibald for a mere five hundred pounds—presumably so Archibald could make them disappear. Archibald consulted his lawyer, David Wemyss. After a three-month back-and-forth, he told Playfair to bug off.

Today the correspondence among Playfair, Archibald, Wemyss, and Charles Douglas, Archibald's son, is preserved in a file in the Douglas-Home family archives. In articles about Playfair you occasionally see a line from one of the letters, where Wemyss refers to Playfair as "a daring worthless fellow." The tag stuck.[8]

Yet there's more to the story. Playfair was trying to get money out of Archibald Douglas, no doubt about that. But you need to read the file—the entire file—and carefully. When you do, you find three items that reveal what was really going on, and what Playfair was really up to.

The first is a letter from Charles, writing his father from Oxford on 20 December 1816. Archibald had sent his son copies of the correspondence to review. Charles proposed taking the case to the Attorney General. Charles wrote (cross outs and underlining as in the originals): [9]

> ...you wish, if possible, to <u>punish</u> Mr Playfair for attempting by threats & ~~tru~~ made up stories to extort money from you, under pretence of keeping something a secret, which, if true & published, might be prejudicial to you; as for his producing anything which could unsettle the Question already disposed of by the House of Lords in the Douglas Cause, I take it to be totally illegal & impractical; still however a little good management and cautious sound advice may be necessary.

So Charles thought Playfair might indeed have something "which, if true & published," could "unsettle" the case. His objection to whatever materials Playfair had wasn't that they were fabrications; it was that producing them now would be "illegal & impractical."

In a second letter, written on Christmas Day, Archibald replied. He wrote Charles:[10]

> I never saw Playfair to my knowledge in my life, nor do I remember that his brother the architect who built this house ever mentioned his existence to me.

But then, in the very next sentence, he wrote:

> I have seen political pamphlets about the beginning of the French Revolution written by a person of this name, and I always have supposed this man was the author. If I am right in ~~my~~ this conjecture it may give a colour in some degree for his supposed finding the papers he proposes now to publish, tho I suspect the whole to be a ~~forgery~~ tale invented and manufactured by himself.

So Archibald *did* know who Playfair was and knew of his French connections. He thought Playfair might have had *some* kind of documents, though he was not sure what they might be, nor how convincing. He started to write "forgery"—but changed his mind.[11]

One thing *is* clear; Archibald Douglas was a very angry man. You can imagine him heatedly crossing out and then inserting words. He loathed even having to deal with Playfair. He wanted to strike back. He told Charles,[12]

> It is quite immaterial to me whether you take the Attorney General, or Solicitor General's ~~opinion~~ advise upon this occasion, all I want is, that if possible, such an infamous attempt to imposition should not be allowed to pass unpunished."

Note that Archibald said *imposition*—not *lie*. In any case, Charles took the matter to the Attorney General, William Garrow, where...Charles was advised not to press the issue. That's the third overlooked item in the file: a transcript of a two-sentence memo Garrow wrote on 2 January 1817. Garrow said,[13]

> I am of opinion that at present it is not advisable to take any notice of Mr. Playfair or his proposed publications. Let care be taken of any further Communications he may be pleased to make but let no Answer be sent to them.

In a follow-up letter the next day, Charles told his father that Garrow had said he was seeing more of these kinds of "attacks to obtain money." Nevertheless, Garrow advised Archibald and Charles to stand pat. Charles satisfied himself saying he thought Playfair would not go further.[14]

So who was William Garrow?

Sir William Garrow is a legend in legal circles. Many credit him with the idea of the adversarial trial, where a defendant has equal standing with the prosecution. It's a concept crucial to Anglo-American jurisprudence.

Garrow is also famous for making courtroom cross-examination an art form. It's fair to say he created the persona of the methodical, relentless defense attorney who dissects prosecution witnesses unfortunate enough to face him—in other words, Perry Mason. (The BBC series *Garrow's Law*, produced from 2009 to 2011, was based on real trials from the Old Bailey, but its portrayal of Garrow was wholly fictional.)[15]

Garrow first gained attention as a reform-minded, Fox-aligned Whig defense attorney, but evolved into a conservative, Pitt-supporting Tory prosecutor. Garrow was appointed King's counsel in 1793, elected to Commons in 1805, and appointed solicitor general during Lord Liverpool's ministry in 1812. Liverpool then named Garrow Attorney General in 1813. It was four years later that Charles brought the Playfair matter to him.[16]

And Playfair's take on Garrow?

"No lawyer in the kingdom," Playfair said, "is better qualified, either by legal abilities or by unwearied industry, to fill the place of his Majesty's attorney-general."[17] Playfair thought Garrow was a fine fellow. One reason, he said, was that no one was "more fit or capable of assisting in bringing the law, in cases of libel, to some fixed principle."[18]

Archibald and Charles Douglas weren't aiming to have Playfair prosecuted for *blackmail*. That's because blackmail wasn't a crime in 1816.[19]

They wanted him prosecuted for *libel*.

Archibald suspected Playfair's documents were forgeries. Then again, he also allowed they just might be real. It didn't matter, and he really didn't care. He and Charles thought they had grounds simply because Playfair had the gall to publish something "prejudicial," on a matter the House of Lords had "already disposed of."

In short, they believed there were some things Playfair simply should not be allowed to put in print. If he did, he ought to be *punished*.

In 1816 libel laws were evolving. Newspapers, pamphlets, postal systems—even the semaphore telegraph—were making it possible to spread words further and faster. And mass-produced, printed words had a persistence that words spoken in the village square did not.

Traditionally, the law had likened words to weapons—they could threaten the government. (Early libel law focused on seditious libel.) Words could injure individuals, too, and now the damage to a man's reputation or a woman's honor could be fast, far-reaching, and permanent. That was the case for tough libel laws—the relief Archibald and Charles were seeking.

But the benefits of the new technology were clear, too. Writers—like Playfair— obviously wanted to make the most of it. But so did their readers, and anyone who communicated with pen and ink.

In this environment even legal thinkers disagreed on what "libel" might be. Think about twenty-first century arguments over whether and how to control Internet trolling, and you get a sense of what was at stake: freedom and opportunity versus protection and security. As Playfair said, libel lacked a "fixed principle," and he thought Garrow was the man to find one.[20]

As it happened, Playfair himself often wrote about libel law.[21] Presumably, he thought Garrow would arrive at a "fixed principle" to his liking. The now-accepted principle that truth is always a defense against libel was still years in the future. For the time being, Playfair was prepared to argue simply that, "truth spoken, when one is concerned with the business, is not a libel."[22]

In other words, Playfair didn't think anyone could just scurrilously spout off scandalous statements about an individual. But, if a statement were true, and served some public purpose—"concerned with the business," as he put it—Playfair believed he was free to publish it.

And, if for some reason someone didn't want him to publish it—well, he was prepared to negotiate.

That was Playfair's "unconventional" business model: Find a fact, write an article—and then see if someone would pay him *not* to publish it. Or at least modify it. If he were lucky, he'd cash in on both ends of the deal: for the article and for, let us say, the "modification."

Even today legal scholars struggle with the very concept of blackmail. The problem is so well known that it's often called the "paradox of blackmail." The paradox is that it's not clear why blackmail should be a crime.[23]

Reduced to basics, blackmail is simply a transaction two parties both desire: One party discovers a fact and proposes to publish it. The other party prefers it not to be published. The two parties agree to suppress it at an agreed price. That's the deal Playfair was offering Archibald.

In any case, the ever-analytical Garrow could see how things would play out: If Archibald declined to pay to suppress the documents—real or not—then it would be pointless for Playfair to publish them; he would get no money, and it could cause him considerable trouble. So Garrow knew Playfair would drop the matter. Which he did.

Of course, not everyone has the analytical mind of a William Garrow; some failed to see the logic. Case in point: John Rennie.

Like Playfair, Rennie went to work for Boulton & Watt after apprenticing with Andrew Meikle. Like Playfair, he left to go into business for himself. Unlike Playfair, he was hugely successful. As a civil engineer, Rennie literally built Great Britain. He directed the construction of bridges, canals, and other public projects across the nation.

Two months before Playfair put the squeeze on Douglas, he tried an almost identical ploy on Rennie. Thomas Byerley joined in on this one.

Byerley dummied up a prospectus for an article he supposedly planned to publish. It resembled the one Playfair later sent to Archibald—except, instead of describing recently unearthed papers that would question the Douglas claim, Byerley described a proposed article that would expose civil engineers who low-balled bids on public works projects and gouged the government with price adjustments after construction began.[24]

Playfair sent the prospectus to Rennie on 17 July 1816, saying that he was "sorry to see some severe allegations against you which appear to be supported."[25] Rennie wrote back almost immediately in a letter he labeled "Private." He insisted he did no wrong. Any overruns were just honest errors, inevitable on big projects.[26] Playfair suggested they meet at the Museum Tavern.[27] A back-and-forth ensued.

The two met again around 26 July, this time at the London Coffee House. They agreed: Playfair would ensure that whatever Byerley published made clear that Rennie wasn't among the miscreants.[28] They put the agreement in writing.[29] Playfair then hit up Rennie for a twenty-five pound "loan," documenting in their exchange that it was only a favor between two friends who had once worked for the same master.[30]

It does sound like extortion. But if Rennie were guiltless, why did he pay? If he had nothing to hide, why did he mark his letters to Playfair "Private"? Byerley insisted—in writing—that he had proof.[31] One could almost even say that the fearless, muckraking journalist William Playfair, willing to speak truth to power, was performing a public service. Well, almost.

Playfair's adventures in coercive journalism were directly tied to another ill-fated project he tried after debtor's prison. It combined philosophy, politics, and a pragmatic need to pay the bills. The result: Playfair became an expert on British nobility—the good, the bad, and the scandalous.

After publishing *Inquiry* and editing the re-release of *Wealth of Nations*, Playfair hooked up with two publishers, Thomas Reynolds and Harvey Grace. The plan was to produce a series they called *British Family Antiquity* detailing the lineage of British nobles. Playfair contributed research and charts depicting family lineages.

It was a spinoff of his statistical graphics, and he was apparently quite proud of the product; he sent a copy to James Watt, "as a mark of the esteem Playfair has ever had for Mr. Watt."[32] Reynolds and Grace set up a company to sell the books—which cost from 45 to 75 guineas, or more than most workingmen would see in a year.[33] At that price, there were few buyers; Reynolds and Grace went bankrupt in January 1812, losing everything.[34]

The project, however, did provide Playfair an opportunity to present his views about how to design a government: *A Fair and Candid Address to the Nobility and Baronets of the United Kingdom Accompanied with Illustrations and Proofs of the Advantage of Hereditary Rank and Title in a Free Country.* The pamphlet was the intellectual argument behind *British Family Antiquity.*[35]

Playfair felt Britain needed a "body of nobility" for stability, "to support the rights both of the crown and of the people." The way he saw it, *someone* had to be in charge of the nation; it might as well be a hereditary aristocracy. Playfair had, let us say, a casual attitude to fairness.

Sure, Old Sarum's representation in Commons made no sense. But *any* districting plan was bound to have errors. (Keep in mind that Britain didn't have census yet.) [36] Playfair would argue a little misrepresentation was to be preferred to what he had seen in France under either the Republic or the Empire: rioting, insurrection, mass executions, dictatorship, and wars across the length and breadth of Europe that killed millions.[37]

One thing is for sure: he had no illusions that aristocrats were unusually qualified to rule. To the contrary: "Hereditary nobility is like a lottery," he said, "in which the prizes are already drawn."[38] By now he was totally cynical and pragmatic at the same time. He recalled his old friend Batz—who finagled his own title with d'Eprémesnil's help—told him how "few noble families could be traced farther back than the tenth century."[39]

Even after Reynolds and Grace went bust, Playfair continued as an expert on nobles and the noteworthy. To compile his data, Playfair targeted politicians, nobles, and other notables as subjects, sources, and customers. Sometimes this backfired, as when Playfair sought George Canning's comments on a draft of some kind in March 1813. Canning sent the draft back, his reply dripping with umbrage.

"A publick man must of course make up his mind to the seeing his character torne to pieces by any writer who may be disposed to seek reputation or profit at his expense," Canning wrote. "But I am not aware that he is under any obligation to entertain the private communication of the abuse or calumny which it may be intended to publish against him, or to enter into a controversy with his revilers."

Canning harrumphed in a postscript, "Perhaps I ought to add that your Note is false in fact; but the suppression or publication of it is to me matter of indifference."[40]

Playfair was likely collecting information for *Political Portraits*, which he launched after *British Family Antiquity* went belly up. It's easy to see why Canning might have a beef with Playfair.

Playfair started by called Canning "solid and brilliant" as well as "assiduous and attentive" in *Political Portraits*. He added that he "regretted" that Canning wasn't holding office. Then Playfair inserted the stiletto into the side of his neck, recounting how Canning had been snookered into buying bogus documents from a French spy. Canning, after serving as Under-Secretary for Foreign Affairs, went on to become Foreign Secretary, and served as Prime Minister for a few months in 1827.[41]

§ § §

There may have been another reason that would make a British minister pause before prosecuting Playfair for trying to extract five hundred pounds from Archibald Douglas using excavated gossip, innuendo, and old documents: Playfair was providing the government the same services.

On 6 August 1808 Playfair sent a note from Covent Garden to then-Home Secretary Spencer Perceval:[42]

> Sir
>
> A manuscript of which the enclosed is the Title was yesterday brought to me with a request to correct it & make it ready for the Group.
>
> Tho' after reading it I determined not to do anything in it I said I would take it in hand if I had time in a day or two. I can therefore have it back and tho' I think it most probably is a Fabrication I determined to let you know as it seemed to concern you in some parts and if I can render any service it is ready.

I have the honor to be

Sir

Your most obt
& very humble Servant
William Playfair

Correspondence suggests Playfair was assisting the commissioners appointed
to conduct "An Inquiry of Delicate Investigation into the Conduct of Her
Royal Highness the Princess of Wales." Besides the correspondence between
Playfair and Perceval, there's at least one memo—marked "Secret," with
double underlining—that appears to be John Charles Herries advising Perceval on the purchase of materials from Playfair.[43]

Even as Playfair was making his way down the Rhine with Vauban in
1794, Lord Malmesbury was engineering the final touches on a marriage
between the Prince of Wales and Caroline of Brunswick. The connubial
diplomacy was aimed at firming up Britain's German alliances; Malmesbury's
job was to fetch Caroline and get her to Britain safely, avoiding the advancing
French army.[44]

Unfortunately, the Prince of Wales and Caroline could not stand each
other. The marriage was a disaster. A decade later they were living apart,
though legally married. Caroline fashioned a sort of parallel court at Montague House, attracting an entourage of émigré nobles, socialites, and politicians. Most conservatives aligned with the Prince, most reformers with the
Princess. (The parallels with the twentieth-century Prince and Princess of
Wales are thoroughly familiar to devotees of British royalty.)

Rumors started that wild things were going on inside Montague House;
the word was that guests were acting "indecently." Even worse, Caroline was
prone to hysterics. So when one of her ladies in waiting announced in 1802
that she was pregnant, so did Caroline. And Caroline, who apparently loved
children, had some youngsters wandering around Montague House that she
had taken in as informal adoptees.

That presented a delicate question: Had Caroline really been with child?
If so, was it possible one of the children roaming Montague House had been
born out of wedlock to the future Queen Mother? Caroline was still married
to the Prince. Recall Ann Boleyn. Recall Catherine Howard. It was a mess,

and that was the delicate question that led to what came to be called The Delicate Investigation of 1805.

King George III appointed the top officials of Great Britain to a commission tasked with The Delicate Investigation. It included, among others, the Prime Minister, the Lord Chancellor, and the Lord Chief Justice. Spencer Perceval was its chairman.[45]

Before DNA testing, the only way to resolve such a question was with interviews, testimony, and detective work—just like the Douglas Cause. This was a job tailor-made for Playfair, known for having the inside scoop on the behavior and misbehavior of aristocrats; hence the material and advice he was providing Perceval. Caroline was acquitted of adultery, but banished from official functions.

Today *Political Portraits* is mainly forgotten and even aristocracy aficionados rarely cite *British Family Antiquity*. But Playfair's connections were genuine. The dedication of *A Fair and Candid Address* read, "To His Majesty, By Permission."

Playfair attempted his "unconventional business model" on at least one other occasion. It would bring him full circle, crossing paths again with James Watt, Junior.

It turned out that Playfair and Junior both had a knack for espionage—in Junior's case, industrial espionage. As Playfair was making his way through Flanders, Holland, and Germany, in summer 1794, Junior was laying low waiting for any lingering recriminations over his radical days to blow over.[46]

Sometime that year Junior joined his father's company. One of his responsibilities was to ferret out anyone with the temerity to think they could install a condenser on a steam engine without paying a royalty to Boulton & Watt. Junior performed his Sam Spade duties with gusto.

In February 1796 Junior wrote tongue-in-check to Matthew Robinson Boulton that he had settled a case with the Bowling Ironworks for an unlicensed steam-powered blast furnace. Junior sent young Boulton "a copy of the treaty of peace, not amity, concluded at Leeds, on Saturday last, between me, Minister Plenipotentiary to your Highnesses on the one part, and the Bowling Pirates in person on the other part."[47]

It was cops-and-robbers and cat-and-mouse in the Midlands. Junior had around a half-dozen men working for him at one time or another. But his master spy was James Lawson.

Lawson, a longtime Boulton & Watt engineer, roamed from town to town, posing as a jockey looking for challenge races. He asked the locals about any mines or mills in the area; the laborers might want to place a wager. Lawson would chat them up, asking about their work—and whether there was a steam engine involved. Lawson passed the information to Junior. Then, as Junior put it, the law, "like the exterminating angel, swoops down upon them, and Mercy they shall have none."[48]

On 24 March Lawson wrote Junior, "I intend riding tomorrow to see Sir G. Warren's engine." Lawson knew what to look for. The next day he wrote from Stockport, "I have now finished my espionage, having just seen the engine on a coal mine near Bullock's Smithy, which has an air pump and condenser exactly similar to Boulton and Watt's, only, like all the rest, well concealed."[49]

Once Junior made the case, negotiations began. Offenders had a choice: Pay royalties or dismantle their engine, removing the patented parts. Either way, offenders were liable for back payments.[50]

Matthew Boulton and James Watt wanted to turn their company over to their sons and position it for when their steam engine patent expired in 1800. Where Boulton & Watt sold licenses and key engine parts, Boulton, Watt & Sons would manufacture complete engines.[51]

Boulton designed a new industrial complex, the Soho Foundry, about a mile from his manufactory. It opened in 1796; Junior ran the day-to-day operations.[52] As Junior's social standing rose, his radical past faded from everyone's memory. In 1818 he took out a lease on Aston Hall, an enormous two-hundred-year-old mansion near Birmingham. He would live there for the next thirty years.[53]

James Watt died the following year at the age of eighty-three. Junior was devastated. He and his father had buried their old conflicts and grown ever closer after Junior returned from France. Junior became obsessed with preserving—and controlling—his father's legacy. He wrote Rennie, "It is my intention to devote all my spare hours to the collecting and managing materials for a history of my father, as soon as I can set about it."[54]

Junior envisioned a massive, multi-year project. Watt—the man who had told his son to "keep your letters, and other loose paper, regularly folded up and docketed"—had rooms full of accumulated records and correspondence. For now, though, magazine editors just wanted a memoir, short and fast.

Six weeks after Watt's passing, *The Monthly Magazine* published a ten-page article, "The late James Watt, Esq., F.R.S. &c. &c.," communicated by "Mr. Wm. Playfair." It recalled the early history of steam engines, Watt's condenser breakthrough, his years of struggle, and, later, his success with Boulton.[55]

Then, in December, another journal, the *New Monthly Magazine,* published its own eight-page "Memoir of James Watt, Esq., F.R.S." It had a curious introductory statement:[56]

> "The following Memoir was expressly written for the proprietors of this Magazine by Mr. Playfair, who received a handsome remuneration, for the same; while however, it was in the hands of a friend of the late Mr. Watt, for revision, the writer thought proper to dispose of a copy of the same to the old Monthly Magazine. The Editor has felt compelled to make this statement, to account for its having already appeared in that journal, and leaves the public to form their own opinion of Mr. Playfair."

The *Monthly Magazine* and the *New Monthly Magazine* were commercial competitors and political rivals (the former leaned left, the latter leaned right).[57] It sounds as though Playfair swindled the *New Monthly Magazine* into paying for an article he'd already published in the *Monthly Magazine.*

Not quite—remember, this is William Playfair. Nothing is simple.

Henry Colburn, publisher of the *New Monthly Magazine,* had written Junior on 11 September 1819. He was planning to publish "a correct memoir & portrait of your late father." Colburn had received a draft and, at John Rennie's suggestion, he was sending it to Junior for his review.

"It is written by Mr. Playfair," he said, adding that Playfair would be "happy to attend to any corrections you may propose."[58]

Rennie happened to write Junior the same day. He said Colburn "was a very respectable young man," but "little acquainted" with Playfair. Colburn had given Playfair the assignment, Rennie said, because he seemed to know things about Watt that others did not. Rennie also told Junior that Colburn was prepared to delay publishing the memoir until November to make sure it was accurate.[59]

Two weeks later, on 25 September, Playfair wrote Junior. He sent him "a memoir of your Excellent Father which I volunteered to write." But it wasn't the memoir that Colburn had sent Junior; it was the page proofs for a memoir that Playfair had written for the *Monthly Magazine* and was about to appear in press. In his letter to Junior he wrote:[60]

> I have written another memoir to the same effect but varied in the manner for the <u>New</u> Monthly Magazine that I have not yet received the proof tho' I expect it before this day. I suppose from some accident it will not appear this month.

In other words, Playfair was telling Junior he had written *two* articles. The one Playfair sent him was for the *Monthly Magazine*. He wasn't asking for Junior to comment on it; he was hoping Junior would endorse it. (From what Junior wrote Rennie, that's what Junior thought, too). Playfair also asked Junior for money. His letter continued: [61]

> My eldest brother died very lately and as he and I were always on good terms unfortunately for me it is thought he left me money which was not the case (for he did not have much & that very properly to his two sisters) some people to whom I owe money have put me to expense already owing to that mistake. I shall be able to pay all I owe when December comes but in the mean time the time being especially I am troubled for a trifling sum something between 10 and 20£. I am very sorry & feel ashamed to say that a lend of that for three or four months would be of especial service to me. If you have the goodness to assist me I hope it will be soon. If not I hope that you will not [allude?] to the disagreeable circumstance that I mention my having taken liberty to mention this subject.

Junior was annoyed, but not because Playfair leaned on him for a loan. For that matter, he didn't seem to care that Playfair was selling two similar articles to two different journals. His problem was that he didn't like what Playfair was writing—and thought Playfair should have let him see his article before it was put into proofs, and could no longer be changed.

The *Monthly Magazine* article Playfair sent Junior in proofs reflected Playfair's admiration for his old master. It also offered some candid tidbits— apparently too candid, by Junior's thinking.

For example, because "Mr. Watt had married a lady without any fortune, by whom he had two children," he was obliged "to attend to his means of existence." His invention thus "was on the point of being left in embryo."

Playfair was implying Junior's mother was a poor catch and as a result Watt had to work night and day. It stalled the development of his transformative engine, almost fatally.

And, Playfair wrote, Watt's "modesty was even carried on to bashfulness." Not exactly a comment a son wants to hear about his father.

And, Watt "never attempted to assist in making models." Was Playfair implying James Watt was less than fully engaged in the design of his engines? Patently unacceptable (so to speak).

And, Watt, who mainly worked in his home, "seldom went in above once a week." to the office "to see what was doing, and sometimes not so often." Sounds as though Watt was a slacker.

On 14 October Junior wrote Rennie, saying that he had seen Playfair's article "in the last *Monthly Magazine*." He told Rennie it "contains many mistakes" and he thought it "is in other important respects very objectionable."[62]

Now Junior was sitting on Playfair's *New Monthly Magazine* article; he was the "friend of the late Mr Watt" to whom Colburn sent the article for revision. Playfair heard nothing from Junior for three weeks. That can be tough for a man living hand to mouth. It explains the scam he used to prod Junior along.

"If I was wrong in expecting that you would do me any act of friendship," Playfair wrote Junior on 12 October, referring to the loan, "I did at least have a right to expect that from your civility you would have acknowledged the receipt of the memoir."

Then he added, "I enclose an abridged copy of a letter received."[63]

Playfair claimed it was a prospectus for an article that he'd prevented from being published. It had the neat, uniform—and anonymous—handwriting of an engrosser. The author—inevitably, "J. Smith"— trashed Matthew Boulton.

It wasn't libelous, just discomforting. Its "revelations" were well known to the Birmingham crowd: Boulton inherited wealth, married into more wealth by wedding a cousin, and when she died, married into yet more wealth by wedding her sister.

"J. Smith" provided a few lines about Watt at the end of his piece: Watt was stingy with Murdoch (true) and was not entirely responsible for the steam engine (also true). But that was about it. William Playfair wouldn't write anything really bad about James Watt; he was too devoted to the man. He was just letting Junior know how unfavorable an article *might* be if one chose to write it that way.

It could not have been more ironic. Forty years earlier Playfair schemed with Keir to get Junior and Matthew Robinson into his counting house to teach them how to "reckon and draw." Now Playfair, the patriotic failed entrepreneur, was trying to squeeze money from Junior to stay out of debtor's prison. Junior, the pseudo-radical who inherited his wealth, was sitting on Playfair's article because it was less than perfectly respectful of the father he had once rebelled against.

On 25 October Rennie wrote Junior recalling how Playfair tried a similar ploy with him; Rennie hadn't forgiven or forgotten. "He made an attempt some years since to extort money from me in the same way," Rennie wrote, "by fabricating a letter under the name of Thomas Byerley." Rennie apparently thought "Thomas Byerley" was just another "J. Smith" who didn't even exist. Rennie didn't tell Junior he fell for the ruse.[64]

Junior finally sent the manuscript back to Playfair with his edits. Playfair replied on 22 October. He quibbled on a few historical details, apparently accepted the changes, but defended the frankness of his original. He told Junior, "I wished to tell the matters as they were. Flattery to your Father was not necessary."[65]

Another week passed. Rennie wrote Junior on 1 November to say he "would fair hope" Playfair "will not venture further," adding that "If I am rightly informed he will be more cautious than he has hitherto been, as I understand he was driven out of France & dare not return." Rennie had heard about the Saint-Morys trial.

Because of "the Death of his brother, he has no recourse left but his own Brains," Rennie continued, so Playfair would need to "apply himself to a more honest calling than he has hitherto done or starve." But, Rennie added, "I say more honest because I am certain he is incapable of being truly so."[66]

Line up Playfair's two articles side by side, and you'll see they cover much of the same ground, but clearly are two different works. Junior's edits in the *New Monthly Magazine* article stand out like added-on commentary designed to mitigate anything critical Playfair said: Watt suffered headaches—but they did not affect his good nature. Watt was not only an inventor—he was an "uncommonly great" man of business. And as for his partnership with

Boulton, "nothing could equal their patience and continued attention to the business."

There's no sign Playfair extracted money out of Junior. But he did get that "handsome" remuneration from Colburn, who was probably the only dissatisfied party in the whole affair. Colburn thought he had an exclusive. Playfair was selling two different articles; they just weren't different enough for Colburn. Playfair told Junior what he was doing. Apparently he didn't tell Colburn.

So who was Henry Colburn?

Today Colburn is best known as a publisher of "Silver Fork" novels, utterly forgettable period pieces portraying British high society. They were quite popular in the 1820s and 1830s; dandies pored over them the way urban metrosexuals ate up *Details* in the 1990s for pointers on style and dress. Colburn also published fluffy works by Benjamin Disraeli (a dandy in his early years), as well as many serious books.[67]

Despite what Rennie told Junior, Colburn did know Playfair; Colburn was the dismissive reviewer of *A statement, which was made in October, to Earl Bathurst...* who wrote that Playfair's warning of the return of Napoleon received "little notice" by the government and "equal indifference" by the public.[68] Also, Colburn had a reputation as prickly. It's no surprise he would stick it to Playfair when he saw his *Monthly Magazine* article.[69]

Of course, there's a postscript.

One of Colburn's first jobs was at a circulating library owned by Thomas Charles Morgan, an English bibliophile. Morgan was knighted in 1811, becoming Sir Charles. The following year he married Sydney Owenson, one of the best-selling authors of her era.[70]

The library gave Colburn his start in publishing; one of his first books was a volume by his boss's wife that he published in 1817: *France,* a current, pro-Revolution guide to the country. It sold well; indeed, it was Colburn's very first publishing success. It became known as "Lady Morgan's France"—after its author, who used her titled name after marrying.[71]

Less than a year after Colburn tagged him in print as a double-dealing rake, Playfair published *France As It Is.* Playfair touted it as a firsthand guide from someone who truly knew the country, rather than the musings of someone "who evidently spoke from a very slight knowledge of the people." The subtitle: *Not Lady Morgan's France.*[72]

§ § §

Playfair scraped by as a writer in his final years. After his memoir(s) of Watt, he published his last major work: *A Letter on Our Agricultural Distresses* in early 1821, a pamphlet "Addressed to the Lords and Commons." And, like just about everything else in Playfair's life, to fully understand it, you need to know about the counterfeiting operation.[73]

It seemed British farmers simply could not make a profit in the post-war economy. Playfair said that middlemen—dealers and speculators—were to blame; they were hoarding grain, buying it when cheap, and borrowing money to keep it off the market until prices rose. Since well over half of Britain's population worked on farms—the Industrial Revolution was just starting—if farms were stretched, the entire economy was going to be bad off.

To demonstrate his point, Playfair plotted wheat prices from 1565 to 1820 (he used data from *Wealth of Nations*, with adjustments and updates from the 1805 edition he edited). Playfair then compared wheat prices to bread prices, using the Guildhall data he originally published in *Anticipation*.[74] The difference between the price of wheat and bread indicated the middlemen's take; as it grew, the farmers were squeezed. The solution, Playfair said, was to limit middlemen to two-month loans, so they had less money to play the market.

Playfair even drafted the legislation; if they desired, the Lords and Commons could simply tear a few pages from his pamphlet and vote them into law. Yet Playfair was on to something more important than just the current "distresses" Britain was experiencing.

It was impossible, Playfair observed, to estimate the middlemen's share without a metric that could compare prices and wages in different eras. For example, the price of bread was higher in 1820 than when Elizabeth ruled, but, then again, so were wages. Playfair's solution: lineal arithmetic.

"I have adopted," he wrote, "the method I invented nearly forty years ago, of representing, by charts and diagrams, the progress and proportional amounts of prices."[75] Playfair titled his chart "CHART Shewing the Value of the Quarter of Wheat in Shillings & in Days Wages OF A GOOD MECHANIC from 1565 to 1821." It showed how the market price of wheat had been soaring—even as the number of day's wages a mechanic needed to buy a quarter of wheat had been plummeting.

Where was the money going? Playfair claimed "the farmer in former times got for his wheat as much as the public or the consumers paid for the bread, allowing a fair price for baking, carriage and other unavoidable expenses; but that of late this is not the case, and that about one-third or 33 percent is, by some means or other, added to the price of the material before it gets into the hands of the baker." In other words, middlemen costs.[76]

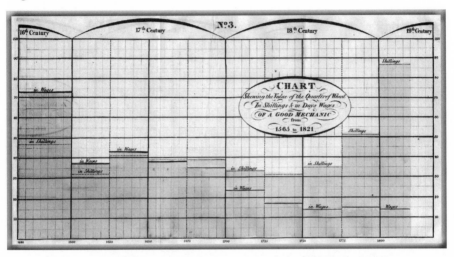

FIGURE 31: Playfair's comparison of wheat prices and wages. The number of days a "good mechanic" required to earn wages sufficient to buy a quarter of wheat had plummeted, but the price of wheat measured in shillings had soared. Inflation accounted for some of the price growth; middlemen costs accounted for most of the rest. Source: William Playfair, *A Letter on Our Agricultural Distresses* (London: William Sams, 1821) via Wikimedia Commons.

Competing interests of farmers, mechanics, and middlemen aside, Playfair was groping his way toward an important concept in economics: adjusting prices for inflation. Today we call the adjustment an "index number," a statistic calculated to adjust other statistics—the Consumer Price Index (CPI), which aggregates price changes within a standardized "basket of goods" probably the most familiar. You can use the CPI to convince your boss to give you a cost-of-living raise, or to draft a long term contract in a way that makes sure inflation doesn't eat you up you in the out years.[77]

There was one other innovation in Playfair's last pamphlet. Like the way he organized data nation-by-nation in *The Statistical Breviary*, it was so obvious it was easy to overlook.

Playfair titled another figure in *Agricultural Distresses* "CHART Shewing in One View The Price of The Quarter of Wheat & Wages of Labour by the Weeks, The Year 1565 to 1821." The key phrase was, "in one view." Playfair put three variables on a single horizontal metric measuring time: wages, prices, and the monarch who was reigning at the time.[78]

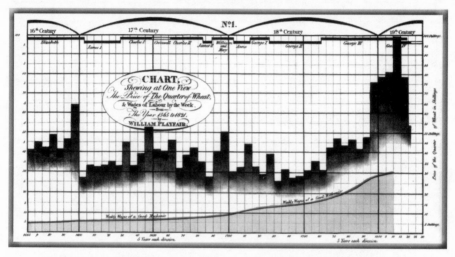

FIGURE 32: Playfair's analysis of cost of living trends, plotting the prices of wheat and wages. Prices were lower in Elizabeth's reign, but, when you considered the growth in the wage of a "good mechanic," it was clear Englishmen were better off under George III, at least until prices spiked around 1795. Source: William Playfair, *A Letter on Our Agricultural Distresses* (London: William Sams, 1821) via Wikimedia Commons.

Later that year Playfair took the idea one step further when he contributed a chart to an utterly obscure reference book, *Chronology of Public Events and Remarkable Occurrences within the Last Fifty Years; or from 1771 to 1821*. The book was simply an 832-page list of events arranged by date. The publisher said he would update and issue it annually; there is no indication he got past 1824. In any case, its editor called Playfair's chart a "linear chronology."[79]

The chart looked like a handful of spaghetti thrown against a wall. Readers had certainly never seen anything like it before. It depicted annual values for seven variables, each in a different color: government revenue (dark orange in the original); government expenditures (green); public borrowing (pink, labeled "debt" in the chart); exports (purple); price of bread (yellow); price of wheat (light orange), and price of government bonds (blue, labeled "stocks" in the chart). It also marked the years of the American War, the War Against the French Republic, and the War Against Napoleon.

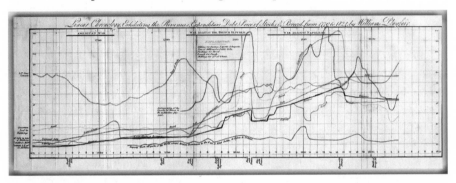

FIGURE 33: Playfair combines his data into one mega-chart. The book it accompanied was a "chronology" of events so it was natural to call the chart a "lineal chronology." This particular figure came from an updated edition published the year after Playfair died. Source: *Chronology of Public Events and Remarkable Occurrences within the Last Fifty Years; or from 1774 to 1824* (London: G. and W. B. Whittaker, 1824) via Wikimedia Commons.

Putting several variables on a single horizontal time line might seem like no big deal—just a way to conserve paper, or make for a more compact publication. But it was a major breakthrough. Playfair's earlier charts revealed *trends*, like rising or falling trade balances, or *comparisons*, such as the size of Britain's population versus that of France. By superimposing several variables in one view, the charts revealed *covariation* and *correlation*.

For example: Did the price of government bonds increase when Britain exported more goods, and fall when it exported less? Did bond prices rise during the periods when Britain's deficit grew? Did wages grow more during Elizabeth's reign, or under George III? Did the answer to any of these questions depend on a third variable, such as whether Britain was at war?

Correlation is important because it helps answer "if/then/when" questions—*if* we do this, *then* we should expect that to happen, perhaps *when* other conditions hold. Decades later Francis Galton, Karl Pearson, and others would invent regression analysis to estimate these relationships mathematically; for the time being, you couldn't do better than Playfair's visual displays.

§§§

But back to wheat prices and wages for a moment: Where did Playfair get the idea of an index number? That's where the counterfeiting operation comes in.

It was late 1792. Playfair had just returned to Britain, after fleeing France with Mary and the children. He began working on a problem he had been pondering for more than a year: If the French increase the quantity of assignats in circulation, what will be the decrease in their value? And how quickly might they decline to zero?

Playfair showed how one could calculate an answer: First, start with the value of the assignats France had authorized; official reports said it was equal to about £112 million. Second, divide it by actual amount of specie—gold and silver—held by the French government; Playfair estimated it was £50 million, meaning they had already devalued their paper by a little more than half. Third, since France had no working tax system, assume it would have to print £4 million each month to pay its government expenses. And, fourth, assume individuals in France would have to liquidate £1 million monthly to cover their own expenses.

Playfair admitted these were crude estimates, but close enough. He then repeated the process to estimate the month-by-month dilution in the value of assignats. Playfair summarized the results of his projection in a table, which he tacked onto the end of pamphlet he was writing at the time—*A General View of the Actual Force and Resources of France*, the one advocating economic war.

Notice the table's far right column: It indicates the month-by-month exchange rate between pounds and assignats. At the beginning of the exercise it would be 1 to 13.2; by December 1794 Playfair calculated it would be 1 to 0.83. In other words, inflation would take more than nine-tenths of an assignat's original value.

They're index numbers.

TABLE ſhewing the monthly Increaſe in Quantity, and Diminution in Value, of the French Aſſignâts, calculated after
the foregoing Data, which, though certainly not Exact, are
not very far from it.

Months from this Time 1793.	Total Quantity of Aſſignats created.	Real Value repreſented by the Aſſignats.	Value of Paper which is equal to 1 Million in Specie.	Monthly Sum in Specie	Sum Neceſſary for Ex- pences per Month.	Rate of Exchange as it ought to be.
February	112,000,000	50,000,000	2,250,000	4	8,900,000	13,2
March	120,900,000	49,000,000	2,467,000	4	9,868,000	12,2
April	130,768,000	48,000,000	2,724,000	4	10,896,000	11,0
May	141,164,000	47,000,000	3,003,000	4	12,012,000	9,99
June	153,492,000	46,000,000	3,329,000	4	13,316,000	9,01
July	166,288,000	45,000,000	3,699,000	4	14,796,000	8,11
Auguſt	181,768,000	44,000,000	4,120,000	4	16,480,000	7,28
September	197,164,000	43,000,000	4,599,000	4	18,396,000	6,52
October	216,748,000	42,000,000	5,146,000	4	20,584,000	5,82
November	236,844,000	41,000,000	5,774,000	4	23,096,000	5,19
December	259,826,000	40,000,000	6,496,000	4	25,982,000	4,61
Janua. 1794	285,138,000	39,000,000	7,328,000	4	29,312,000	4,09
February	315,310,000	38,000,000	8,293,000	4	33,172,000	3,61
March	348,962,000	37,000,000	9,413,000	4	37,652,000	3,18
April	385,846,000	36,000,000	10,721,000	4	42,884,000	2,79
May	428,854,000	35,000,000	12,252,000	4	49,008,000	2,44
June	477,070,000	34,000,000	14,054,000	4	56,216,000	2,13
July	534,802,000	33,000,000	16,183,000	4	64,732,000	1,85
Auguſt	598,662,000	32,000,000	18,715,000	4	74,860,000	1,60
September	673,586,000	31,000,000	21,731,000	4	86,924,000	1,38
October	760,586,000	30,000,000	25,352,000	4	100,408,000	1,20
November	860,994,000	29,000,000	29,689,000	4	118,756,000	1,01
December	970,750,000	28,000,000	34,990,000	4	139,960,000	0,83

FIGURE 34: Playfair's table for calculating index numbers projecting the decline in the value of assignats. Playfair was trying to figure out when France's policy of freely printing assignats would render the currency worthless—and what Britain would need to do to keep it on schedule. Source: William Playfair, *A General View of the Actual Force and Resources of France* (London: John Stockdale, 1793), 53. Courtesy University of California Libraries, via The Internet Archive.

Now, look at the edition of *Wealth of Nations* Playfair edited in 1805. Not far from his account of the French authorities burning assignats, he recalled, "A calculation was made in the end of 1792, in London of the probable depreciation of assignats monthly," and that "a table of depreciation was made out and printed, which was very near what actually took place."[80] Playfair was referring to that table.

The "end of 1792" was when Playfair was planning the counterfeiting operation—just before he, Breteuil, and Batz had their opportunity to meet in London. Playfair drafted his article; calculated the table; published the pamphlet; and then drafted his proposal for the counterfeiting operation.

Playfair's index numbers showed how quickly the French would drive the value of their money to zero—and how much currency the British would need to print to keep the French on pace. Or push them a bit faster.

Playfair conceded, "as my data are not very exact, so neither can be my results." Since "collateral causes are continually operating, which are totally incalculable, I shall never find my table verified by experience with any degree of nearness." He was being disingenuous, failing to mention that one of the "collateral causes" might be coachloads of bogus bills shipped from the mill at Haughton Castle.

Even so, Playfair continued, "I do consider it as a matter both of curious and important inquiry, to calculate how quickly the assignat has a tendency to sink in value from its own nature only." It was important because that was the planning baseline. Playfair's calculations guided the operation.[81]

Playfair had anticipated that, "Until it costs a million to make a million in assignats, they will still have a value."[82] And, sure enough, he recalled years later, "At last the paper money fell nearly to one eighth per cent of its nominal value. It cost almost as much to make the assignats, as they would pass for with the public."[83]

"Then," Playfair said, "the nature of things put an end to the operation." It was another double entendre.

The "nature of things" put an end to the *French* operation—printing assignats to support the French government. When their value reached near zero, French officials had to stop. But the "nature of things" also put an end to the *British* operation—printing assignats to collapse the French government. The Great Op was supposed to be self-financing. So when assignats cost more to print than they could fetch in exchange, the British shut it down.

But before they did, Playfair presented what just may be the world's first price index—born from the need to estimate how much bogus currency Britain had to print in order to collapse the French economy.

12 Endings

The case is clear: William Playfair—writer, engineer, economist—proposed, planned, and executed a covert operation in 1793 to collapse the French economy by printing vast amounts of counterfeit assignats, the paper currency France had adopted to pay for their government and wars. The material evidence includes:

- Playfair's plan for the counterfeiting operation. Lost until now, it is written in his hand, dated March 1793, and was found among other correspondence from Playfair to British Secretary of State for War Henry Dundas.[1]

- Three paper molds found at the Haughton Castle mill. Two are for counterfeiting assignats, while the third is for making notes for Playfair's Original Security Bank. This indicates Playfair used the same paper mill to make notes for his bank that he used for the covert operation.[2]

- The first-hand report of Sir John Edward Swinburne, who witnessed the papermaking. Sir John recounted that the foreman of the mill said Playfair was conducting the operation, working with the Duke of York, who was commander of the British army; and Brook Watson, director of the Bank of England.[3]

- Documents showing Playfair managing the operation in London in behalf of Secretary at War William Windham in 1795, resolving issues with suppliers and known French royalists.[4]

- A private letter from Playfair to former Prime Minister William Wyndham Grenville, written in 1811, confirming the government's role in the operation and advising him how to respond to inquiries so as not to incriminate himself.[5]

Additional documents show Playfair worked directly with Dundas and Windham in other clandestine activities. These included intelligence collection, secret diplomacy, and information operations.

Also, circumstantial evidence shows Playfair had the opportunity to meet two long-time acquaintances (and potential co-conspirators) in London in early 1793:

- Jean, Baron de Batz, who had been Playfair's friend and business partner in France, who had played a key role in setting up the French system of assignats, and who would go on to carry out clandestine operations against the republicans; and

- Louis Auguste Le Tonnelier de Breteuil, exiled minister plenipotentiary for Louis XVI; documents show Breteuil had proposed a counterfeiting operation to Austrian leaders, who turned him down, but floated the idea of taking the proposal to the British.

This picture of Playfair is completely contrary to the one depicted by most scholars. They portray Playfair as a lightweight flimflam artist. In reality, he was (in addition to all his other pursuits) an ingenious, risk-taking intelligence officer who pioneered many basic concepts of tradecraft used for collection, analysis, and operations. And he was a patriot, frequently putting the interests of his country ahead of his own.

One might say Playfair is the most famous man you have never heard of. He appears everywhere; he knows everyone. Time and again, he's at the hinge point of history: the Industrial Revolution, the French Revolution, the founding of the United States, the birth of modern economics, the Age of Napoleon. Documents and artifacts link him to influential ideas and famous men. He's the Forrest Gump of his era—except, unlike Gump, he's brilliant, and, unlike Gump, he's not just an accidental witness stumbling on the scene—he's shaping and driving events.

How could so many experts have been so wrong?

§ § §

The Royal Literary Fund opened its archives to researchers in 1933. It became a unique information source on all the writers the Fund had helped—some famous, some infamous, and some… not so much. The one thing they had in common was that they were all established authors and they were all more or less broke.

William Playfair was one of them. There were no guarantees in Playfair's line of work. After decades of adventure and assisting top British officials, Playfair was abandoned and destitute. He depended solely on his writing to survive, and his health was failing.

You can get a copy of Playfair's file from the Royal Literary Fund through the British Library. Case No. 121 totals forty-five scanned pages, which break roughly into two strings of letters and supporting notes.

The first string runs from March 1802 to June 1807. Playfair applied to the Literary Fund after the collapse of the Original Security Bank ruined him. The Fund gave Playfair ten guineas in 1802 to help him when he got out of Fleet Prison.[6] The records show the Fund gave him another ten guineas in May 1807, after Lord Sheffield wrote on his behalf.[7]

The second string of letters and notes starts in April 1820, after he published his memoirs of James Watt and *France As It Is*. Playfair went back to the Fund, saying he is "now Past the Age of Sixty," in "Bad Health, & confined (in the infirmary) of White Cross Street Prison for debt." He received a ten-pound grant in May.[8]

Playfair wrote to the Fund again in July. He appreciated their assistance. But, he said, an emergency grant of ten pounds was not enough to relieve an "unfortunate man of letters." Might the Fund, he asked, establish a program to provide small, but continuing stipends of seven or eight pence a week to writers in need?[9]

Playfair told the directors he had been in debtors' prison since March. Its grant had not been sufficient to secure his release. And, he asked, if it were not possible to provide relief, could the Fund please send him a formal denial as soon as possible so he could make other arrangements for his family?[10]

On the last week of August someone wrote a notation at the top of Playfair's July letter: "Request cannot be granted."[11] Whatever the "other arrangements" might have been, his letters were now addressed from 43 Bedford Street.[12]

In December Playfair wrote to Henry Addington, 1st Viscount Sidmouth, now Home Secretary. It seems to have been Playfair's last letter to a minister. He claimed he had information exposing an army plot against the government.

An army plot? It sounds far-fetched; some said Playfair suffered from "anxiety of mind" in his last years.[13] Only an insider would know he had provided ministers intelligence for decades. Few outside the Admiralty would know about that Dutch-manned privateer he volunteered for crushing the navy mutineers back in 1797.

"I appeal to your Lordship's justice and candor," he wrote. He asked, plaintively, "whether I ever gave False Intelligence?" or "even asked for any reward?"

It was the same challenge Playfair offered when he tried to warn the Foreign Office of Napoleon's return from Elba—and raises the question again: Was he ever paid? Playfair closed, apologizing, "I am confined with the Rheumatism otherwise I should wait on your Lordship & could tell you more than I chuse to write."[14]

A week later Addington's clerk replied: "Sir: I am instructed by Lord Sidmouth to thank you for your communication of the 11 Instant, & to express his hope that you will speedily recover from the painful complaint under which you labour."[15] And that, apparently, was the end of Playfair's service to the British government.

This would have been about the time Playfair was writing *Agricultural Distresses*. Guildhall is almost two miles from Bedford Street, and Playfair could hardly walk. He recycled the data on bread prices he compiled fifteen years earlier for the article he published in *Anticipation*.

This was also about the time Playfair began drafting his memoirs.

After a fire destroyed the theater on Drury Lane in 1809, Richard Sheridan turned the business over to his friend Samuel Whitbread, a fellow Whig who had led the movement to turn out Henry Dundas in 1805. Whitbread's theater, completed in 1812, was built on the same site, just a few blocks from Bedford Street, across the Covent Garden piazza.[16]

Most paper was still made from rag and was still expensive. Playfair wrote his memoirs, section by section, on the backs of old broadsides from the

Theatre. He pasted the sections into a booklet to arrange the narrative—sort of an early form of word processing.

The next letter in the Fund's files was written a little more than two years later. Playfair was desperate. He wasn't seeking a grant; he was begging for charity:[17]

21 January 1823

My Lords & Gentleman,

In the course of 30 years I have been three times assisted by the Literary Fund; Privation, Debility, and Sickness Induce me to supplicate your aid for tho my mind is unimpaired in its Faculties yet I have not the Strength Sufficient to write to any Great Purpose.

My condition may be seen by taking the trouble to send some person here.

I have known to be with great respect

My Lords & Gentleman
                        Your much obliged
                & most obedient humble servant
                            William Playfair

A notation at the top of the letter instructed the clerk to refer it to a Committee of Inquiry.

It takes about two hours to read through the forty-five items in Playfair's file. The letters for the most part are from Playfair; a few are letters and various notes by Fund officials. Then you get to the last item.

When you open it, the image of a letter written nearly two hundred years ago appears on your screen. It's different from the others. Unlike William's hopeless scrawl, it's neat, clear, and precise. Then you realize—it's from Mary:[18]

19th March 1823

43 Bedford Street

Gentleman,

Accept my most grateful and humble thanks for the twenty pounds which you have so liberally subscribed for my relief.

For this and all other favours during my husbands lifetime believe me to be most truly sensible.

I am Gentleman,

With due respect,

Your most humble servant,
Mary Playfair

If you go back and look again at Playfair's 21 January letter, you'll see someone had added a note in the margin: "Mr. P died in St Geo's Hospital." It says the committee voted to send twenty pounds to Mary and her family on 12 March. The writer added, as though to justify the grant, "Mr. P. was the author of *British Family Antiquity, Political Portraits, France As It Is,* and *A Vindication of the King,* to be published by Sams." Rounding out Playfair's life, it notes that "Two of his publications in the Library of Paris."[19]

Robert Stuart's memoir, published six years later, fills in the details. "In the autumn of 1822," Stuart wrote, "Playfair was released from the prison in which he had been confined many months for a debt (for which he had been a surety for a friend) of a few guineas." Then "a disease in his legs, which had made him a cripple for years, took an unfavourable turn, and showing symptoms of mortification, poor unfortunate Playfair was carried to an hospital for the purpose of undergoing an operation."[20]

"Mortification" is gangrene; the "operation" would have been amputation. A skilled surgeon at the time could remove a leg in about a minute. The survival rate was about eighty percent. Anesthesia was still a few decades away.[21] But it didn't matter. Playfair, Stuart recalled, "expired on the 11th of February, 1823."[22]

William Playfair's funeral was held at St. George's Church at Hanover Square; parishioners were usually buried in its Bayswater cemetery. Today St. George's is just off Savile Row, London's center for bespoke men's suiting. Bayswater is two miles west, in Kensington, not far from the Science Museum—and James Watt's engines.[23]

Thomas Byerley's obituary appeared in *The Literary Chronicle* a few weeks after his passing. By then Byerley had worked with Playfair for almost ten years. He would have been able to speak with Mary and might have seen whatever notes Playfair had managed to save as he was periodically taken into custody and released.[24]

As anyone who has read the *Bankrupt's Assistant* knows, those bound for debtors' prison must surrender any papers they possess to their commissioners. It's remarkable the thirty-six pages of Playfair's memoir survived.

Byerley conceded his list of Playfair's works might not be complete, but he did add into the public record several books that Playfair had listed as "no name" anonymous publications when he applied to the Literary Fund—such as *Joseph and Benjamin*, perhaps the first book to describe what a modern intelligence estimate would look like.

Byerley recalled Playfair apprenticed alongside "John Rennie, the celebrated engineer, who has superintended the construction of the Waterloo Bridge, and several other of our most splendid national works." He did not say whether the celebrated Rennie low-balled his bid on any of those splendid national works, or if they were among the projects he and Playfair had threatened to expose.

The obituary paints the picture of an amiable, if somewhat erratic man. You get the impression Playfair worked hard, occasionally cut corners, and never really seemed to live up to his potential. Yet if you read the obit carefully and know the true story, you can spot the gaps that, if filled in, would reveal his secret life.

After Playfair's writings "provoked the enmity of Barrere, who obtained an order for his arrest," the obituary says he learned he was in danger and "succeeded in making his escape." It doesn't identify Brancas, the Jacobin army lieutenant who warned him as a family favor.

The memoir continues: "On his return to London, Mr. Playfair projected a bank." It skips over the subversion, espionage, and propaganda operations for William Windham and Henry Dundas.

"This bank was opened in Cornhill; its object was to lend money on such securities as were valuable, but not easy to borrow money upon." No mention of Brook Watson's collusion. "Unfortunately, however, sufficient attention was not paid to the nature of the security, and bankruptcy ensued." Those damned loans to Sheridan. Did Playfair let friendship and patriotism cloud his judgment? Or was he just an opportunist?

The obituary says that whatever services Playfair performed were often "unrewarded and unrecognized," and that he "often incurred expenses which his circumstances would very ill bear." So Playfair may indeed have paid for the mission to Flanders with his own money. Then again, he probably printed the money himself.

"Mr Playfair has left two daughters, one of whom is blind," it closes. "As the daughter of a person whose life was devoted to the service of the British government, she has strong claims on its bounty, and we trust they will not be overlooked."

A reader of the obit might reasonably ask in what sense anyone could say the life of a marginally-employed writer like Playfair had been "devoted to the service of the British government." In any case, *The Gentleman's Magazine* and *The Annual Biography and Obituary* published near-identical versions over the following months.[25]

London grew throughout the nineteenth century and St. George's closed its Bayswater cemetery in 1854. Sometime in the early 1900s the church removed most of the gravestones and turned the grounds into a garden and archery range. In 1964 St. George's petitioned Parliament for permission to sell the tract to developers. After a forty-five-minute discussion, the question was put and agreed to. Whatever remained in the ground at Bayswater was dug up, cremated, and reinterred at West Norwood Cemetery, eight miles to the south.[26]

§ § §

"Robert Stuart" was a pseudonym; his real name was Robert Stuart Meikleham. Even his biographers did not know much about him other than he came from Scotland and was an engineer before becoming a writer. Stuart knew the inventors and businessmen who built the steam engine industry, so in the early 1800s he was one of the field's top experts.[27]

The three-page bio Stuart wrote of Playfair in 1829 was actually just a long footnote in his book, *Historical and Descriptive Anecdotes of Steam-Engines*. Stuart credited Byerley's obituary as a starting point, and added information that seemed to come from other friends and acquaintances. Its conclusions mainly followed Byerley's: Playfair was smart, industrious, but never as successful as he might have been. Stuart added that his family didn't object to the poverty because, like Playfair, they relished the adventure.[28]

And that was the accepted wisdom about William Playfair—if anyone cared, and, to be blunt, few did. Just another minor player in the maelstrom of history. Then something odd happened.

Usually a man's reputation, good or bad, is determined during his lifetime. Dead men commit no sins, and few make new friends. Playfair's reputation plunged from mundane to bad to rotten—beginning about fifty years after his death. It occurred in steps.

As the centennial of the French Revolution approached, John Goldworth Alger became interested in the British angle. *The Times* of London had hired Alger in 1869 to cover Parliament. Eight years later it sent him to Paris. He reported from France for the next twenty-eight years.[29]

Besides his newspaper reporting, Alger wrote several books about France, the Revolution, and the Empire under Napoleon. Alger identified Playfair as one of the "Englishmen" on the scene. For some reason, Alger had a miserable opinion of the man. In his 1904 book, *Napoleon's British Visitors and Captives, 1801–1815*, he described Playfair as an "erratic journalist" and "an adventurer and a weathercock."[30] And that wasn't the worst part.

Alger was the author of that entry in the 1896 edition of the *Dictionary of National Biography*.[31]

In today's Information Age, it's hard to appreciate how much influence the *Dictionary* had. Alger started with the basic facts from Byerley's obituary. Then he moved on to reconstruct the Scioto affair, using as his source... Gouverneur Morris.

Anne Cary Morris had just published her grandfather's diaries in 1888. Alger quoted her to sum up the project: "Some hundreds of unfortunate families were lured to destruction by the picture of a salubrious climate and fertile soil."[32] Thus was Playfair—in Alger's account, the Scioto Company's "agent"—tagged as a reckless swindler.

Alger was also the one who gratuitously asserted that Richard Lovell Edgeworth, not Playfair, was responsible for the "invention and adoption" of the semaphore telegraph—implying Playfair stole the idea. (Which he did, but not in the sense Alger meant; it was espionage, not puffery.) Alger suggested Playfair fled France under a cloud in 1793 (true) and then did little but write "vehemently" against the Revolution (most definitely not true).

Playfair, Alger said, returned to Paris post-Waterloo to edit *Galignani's Messenger* (apparently a trifle in his view) until fleeing France again to escape that libel charge. After that Playfair earned a "precarious livelihood" by writing. Listing his publications, Alger conflated *The Statistical Breviary* and the *Commercial and Political Atlas* into a single book, the "*Statistical Breviary and Atlas*" and never mentioned anything about graphics—which means he never read them.

To be fair: Alger was writing from France. It was fifty years after Playfair's passing. He had only second-hand access to the British side of the story. And Playfair's secret correspondence with British officials was still filed away.

The *Dictionary of National Biography* was concise. It was authoritative. And it was the first source a young scholar with a newly minted master's degree from Harvard might turn to if he were writing a history of the Scioto affair while on a Colonial Dames fellowship at the University of Cincinnati. After Theodore Belote got finished, one might think the reputation of a slick-talking Englishman "eager to fill his pockets with that French gold" would have hit rock bottom. Not so.

James Watt, Junior never did write that biography of his father. Instead, he gave the project to John Patrick Muirhead, a cousin. After Muirhead published *The Life of James Watt* in 1858, Watt's descendants gave other writers access to the family papers. Samuel Smiles, a popular biographer, published *Lives of Boulton and Watt* in 1865. None of these made more than a passing mention of Playfair, a minor character who worked at the firm for just a few years.[33]

After Junior died, James Watt & Co. kept the papers until 1895, when W.T. Avery, Ltd. acquired the firm. Philanthropist-engineer George Tangye bought the collection and preserved it in a small "Watt museum." He donated the papers to the City of Birmingham in 1915, which opened them to researchers through the Birmingham Reference Library (later the Birmingham Central Library, and today the Library of Birmingham).[34]

That happened to be about the time when statisticians got interested in the history of the visual display of data—infographics.

The earliest English-language article that credits Playfair as the inventor of statistical graphics seems to be an unsigned piece in the September 1926 *Bulletin of the Business Historical Society*.[35] The author apparently also used the *Dictionary of National Biography*. Its comments that Playfair "lacked business judgment," and "failed at every serious undertaking which he attempted" track with Alger's.[36]

It was the Boulton & Watt archives and the new interest in statistical graphics that finished wrecking whatever was left of Playfair's reputation. He became not just a schemer, but a dunderhead as well. No one planned it, but that was the result.

First, Edward Tufte, a Yale political science professor, became fascinated with the connection between how people reasoned and how they expressed their reasoning in pictures. His 1983 book, *The Visual Display of Quantitative Information,* was a multi-edition hit. Tufte called Playfair one of the "great inventors of modern graphical design," and credited him with the "first time series using economic data."[37]

Then in 1990 two statisticians, Patricia Costigan-Eaves and Michael Macdonald-Ross published an article about Playfair in *Statistical Sciences*. When others describe Playfair's contributions, they're usually drawing from this article—whether they realize it or not, as in the case of Byerley's obit. The article captured the historical influences, the evolution of Playfair's charts, and Playfair's own commentary about his method, taken from his books. Neither wrote further about Playfair; Costigan-Eaves became an education consultant, and Macdonald-Ross a top chess expert.[38]

The article also contained a booby trap.

In their article, Costigan-Eaves and Macdonald-Ross mused that Playfair's experience as a draftsman for Boulton & Watt might have shaped his thinking about charts and graphs. Trying to fill out Playfair's character, they quoted Watt: "I must warn you, Playfair is a blunderer."

Where did that line come from? It often appears in articles about Playfair.

It takes some digging to discover the full story. Costigan-Eaves and Macdonald-Ross took their quotation verbatim from *James Watt and the Steam Engine*, a zeppelin anchor of a book that Henry William Dickinson and Rhys Jenkins published in 1927. You can't fault the two statisticians for their selection of a reference; it's the most complete, authoritative study of Boulton and Watt you'll find.

Dickinson and Jenkins were giving an overview of Boulton & Watt staff with thumbnail sketches of personnel who appeared in company documents; Playfair was just one of several employees. To explain how Playfair came to be Watt's assistant, on page 285 they quoted a passage from a letter Watt wrote to Boulton:[39]

> I would recall Playfair who can do part of the business and I think now that you are at home you can contrive to give him proper assistance. I must warn you that Playfair is a blunderer.

Sounds damning, indeed. But if you dig a bit deeper, you discover the quote is just a snippet of a longer passage, and further, that it's misleading.

Dickinson, a British Science Museum associate, was quoting from a selection of Watt's letters he had published twelve years earlier in *The Institution of Mechanical Engineers Proceedings*. The Watt papers had just become available; Dickinson was providing readers a sample.[40]

One letter was from Watt to Boulton saying he wanted to sack John Hall, one of their erectors, and replace him with Playfair, making him his personal assistant. Watt was livid; Hall had been pilfering.[41]

The letter starts with Watt railing about Hall. It ends with a discussion of various production problems. In the middle of the letter there are two sentences—just two—concerning Playfair: [42]

> I would recall Playfair who can do part of the business, & I think now you are at home you can contrive to gett him proper assistance—I must warn you that Playfair is a blunderer but I dare say he will be assiduous and obedient and plain direction must be given him.

"Blunder," "blunders," and "blunderer" were among Watt's favorite epithets; he cited Hall's "blunders, delays, and omissions" in the very same letter Dickinson quoted. Watt was even apt to turn the appellation on himself when he made mistakes. To wit: Watt told Boulton at roughly the same time that, "The blunder lies with myself," acknowledging when had given unclear directions.[43]

But all of this misses the whole point of the letter: Watt wasn't writing to *criticize* Playfair; he was giving him a *promotion*. Watt thought Playfair could assume more responsibilities; the twenty-one-year-old just needed some clear direction.

And Boulton agreed. Seven days later he wrote Watt, "I believe we had better take some pains to make Playfair a better writer and accountant and then he may do pretty well."[44] They wanted Playfair to replace Hall as soon as possible.[45]

If there is one thing that we don't lack, it's documentation of James Watt's opinion of William Playfair. It emerges and becomes clear in pages and pages of documents at the Library of Birmingham.

Watt made Playfair his personal assistant. Each day, Playfair went to Watt's workshop.[46] Watt put Playfair in his counting house; he trusted him with his money. He trusted him to act as a witness for his patent applications, too—a very big deal, considering how often patents were contested, not to mention Watt's penchant for secrecy.[47] When Watt started a new company to manufacture copying machines, he hired Playfair to handle accounting and correspondence with customers.[48]

Some writers claim Watt did not think much of Playfair's drawings—forgetting, apparently, Robert Small's on-the-record judgment that they were "remarkably good." They cite a couple of letters Watt sent Boulton in January 1782 complaining about drawings Playfair did for a specific job. But there does not seem to be another example of such a complaint.[49]

Moreover, when their company needed to hire a new draftsman, Watt and Boulton turned to…yes, Playfair. Boulton asked Playfair to ask his brother James for a recommendation. James found a candidate; William later thanked Boulton for his hospitality when James visited Birmingham.[50]

(Criticism of Playfair's drawing abilities is ironic because the problem wasn't his straightedge drafting; it was his freehand penmanship. To truly appreciate the man's utter lack of eye-hand coordination and mid-sentence mind skips one must read the hundreds of pages required for a biography. It is the stuff of ophthalmology legend. Playfair knew this; he hired an engrosser for some of his early reports to Boulton.[51] He once even had a professional transcribe a letter to his lawyer, adding a note at the bottom in his own hand, "I have had this copied as my writing is not very good to read."[52])

In short, Playfair and Watt and were about as close as a twenty-something employee and his forty-something employer might be in the ultra-structured society of eighteenth-century England. Day in, day out, they worked together. When Playfair arrived at Boulton & Watt, Watt believed he was getting a good man. Somehow, Robert Small's glowing description of Playfair's character—the "goodness of his heart" and "honourableness of his principles"—fell through the cracks of history, along with the assessment of his drawing abilities.

Once the ball got rolling, the misquotations and passages taken out of context accumulated and took on a life of their own. Playfair's adventures, misadventures, and shenanigans—fabricated, exaggerated, and true—all became lore. One scholar cited another, and the academic errors seeped into popular media—like *The Economist*. It continues to this day.

§ § §

Those keeping score will have figured out by now that Playfair got a bum rap. Watt did *not* consider Playfair a blunderer. Playfair did *not* steal ideas from Keir. Playfair did *not* embezzle money from the Scioto settlers. British authorities did *not* shut down the Original Security Bank. And, at least in the opinion of the Attorney General, Playfair may have been at the ragged edge of legality when he grifted Archibald Douglas—but *not* beyond it.

Playfair got that bum rap partly because his life was so outsized. You need to combine the skills of a historian, economist, mechanical engineer, strategic analyst, and statistician to really appreciate all his work. A degree in cognitive psychology doesn't hurt, and it helps to know both English and French. Playfair came from a world of Renaissance Men; we live in a world of credentialed specialists.[53]

But Playfair's reputation is mainly Playfair's own doing. He was so determined to keep his secret relationship with the British government secret that, were it not for a few scraps of paper scattered across continents that somehow survived for two hundred years, and three paper molds that periodically disappeared and reappeared, we would have no evidence—none—of Playfair's most ambitious project, the one that puts him into an entirely different light.

It would have simply been impossible to uncover this story ten or even five years ago. John Marshall Newton worked at the speed of the U.S. Mail; today the Internet makes it possible to piece together data from libraries and archives on the other side of the world. Theodore Belote's year in Cincinnati was a once-in-a-lifetime adventure; now jet airliners, ubiquitous rental cars, and Eurostar make it possible to travel to Toronto, Birmingham, Paris, Edinburgh, or a castle in northern England all on the spur of the moment, and repeatedly.

Yet though technology makes better analysis possible, it doesn't happen unless analysts are disciplined—and curious. Errors codified in "standard texts" and "authoritative references," echoed and recycled, distorted Playfair's character and biography.

As I said at the beginning, often the hardest task for any analyst is challenging the conventional wisdom, especially when it's been codified—like, "Playfair is a scoundrel." There is no such thing as "settled science." If it's settled, it's not science. It's just dogma, and cant.

Playfair was no scoundrel. He was an ambitious, audacious, and woefully imperfect British patriot—and a pioneer. His plan to collapse the French economy was probably the biggest, most complex covert operation anyone had ever conceived. It required all of the basic intelligence disciplines familiar today: espionage, operations, technology, and analysis.

Playfair was ideally suited to the task. The history of intelligence is full of unusually talented men and women who are often poor fits for any other kind of organization, who do their bit, make a contribution, and then go about their lives. Sometime they take their experience with them, and sometimes it benefits society, often in unpredictable ways.

Julia Child was an intelligence officer carrying out information operations in Ceylon for the Office of Strategic Services (OSS) in World War II. She went on to write *Mastering the Art of French Cooking*. It changed how people eat. Playfair carried out his counterfeiting operation for Britain in the War of the First Coalition. He went on to publish *The Statistical Breviary*. It changed how people think.[54]

Historically, intelligence programs are ephemeral. Careers are often brief. Wall Street lawyer William Donovan headed the OSS for only thirty months—the organization's entire life span.[55] Playfair served the British government off and on for decades, but the counterfeiting operation was spun up and wound down in just two years.

Part of this reflects the realities of politics. Donovan was dismissed because his patron, Franklin Roosevelt, died and his successor, Harry Truman did not want him or the OSS. Playfair continued serving the British government after Dundas and Windham left the scene. But he never had the opportunities he previously enjoyed. He never had another chance at a Great Op.

Much of the churn you find in intelligence organizations is the flip side of the opportunistic, ad hoc nature that enables them to do things and go places other organizations cannot. If they couldn't wind down an operation quickly, they probably couldn't spin one up quickly, either. The organization would be as incremental and moribund as any other bureaucracy, and the op would never happen—and the buccaneers looking for adventure serving their country would look elsewhere in any case.

No known portrait of William Playfair exists; he was too poor ever to have one painted. Neither is there is a monument to him—at least none besides the charts and graphs that appear in books, journals, briefing slides, government reports, financial statements, and computer displays everywhere in world, everyday, all the time.

Playfair might have preferred it that way, and if his ghost objects to being exposed, I apologize. He truly was the man who kept the secrets—and changed the way we see the world.

 Appendix A: Playfair's Proposal for his Counterfeiting Operation

Source: The William Playfair Correspondence Collection, Special Collections Research Center, Temple University Libraries, Philadelphia, PA

Having already in a Pamphlet which was published in the beginning of the month of February bearing for title, A General View of the Resources of France etc etc I declared in a Public Manner that it was my opinion that the best & most effectual method of attacking the French Nation would be to destroy their credit by falsifying their Assignats, which pamphlet has met with a pretty general approbation, I have resolved for that and for other reasons <u>to falsify the Assignats myself</u>.

1st

As we are at war with France I think that it becomes every British subject to destroy the force of the enemy in the way that he thinks the most effectual and that is the most practical for himself.

2d

That to me it appears that in the present war shortening its duration is shortening the duration of robery and murder and that even in the interest of France and to the French themselves it is an advantage and an act of mercy to cut short the present scene of misery and murder.

3d

That the Assignats are the force of all the crimes committed in France and that to destroy the Assignats will be in great measure snatching the pistol and the poignard from the hand of the wicked assassin.

4th

That as it relates to France it is therefore clear that this fictitious price of crimes cannot be too soon reduced to nothing, and that as to her enemies which at present comprehend almost all the civilized nations of Europe, it is of the highest importance to destroy a paper which has served the ends of the wicked persons to destroy their happiness and disturb their repose.

5

That there are two ways of combatting the French nation the forces of which are measured by men and money. Their assignats are their money and it is better to destroy this paper founded upon an iniquitous extortion and a villainous deception than to shed the blood of men; therefore I think it is meritorious to destroy the assignats, that it is patriotic as an Englishman and humane as a man who wishes to spare the blood of other men.

To this end I have formed the following plan, I know that it is attended with difficulty, I know that malfeasance may impute to me a bad intention and that its failure may be attended with disagreeable consequences, but I have taken my resolution and do not blush to explain my plan. My reasons I have already as they regards the public and I will now give them as regards myself. I consider myself as a soldier who fights for his country and into whatever disagreeable dilemma I may be led, or whatever good fortune may attend me, my language I shall never be found to change. I shall avow my enterprise and maintain my motives.

Plan

To fabricate one hundred millions of assignats and spread them in France by every means in my power reserving to the exiled clergy of France now in England on whose possessions the assignats are mortgaged one fifth of all the sum that may accrue from the operation after the expenses are paid and which sums shall be subscribed to the fund for supporting them under initials such as used by persons who desire to remain unknown.

That all the enemies of France shall be supplied with as great a quantity of that paper as they can disperse by means of their respective armies and that at a very low rate.

That after recovery for myself and those who assist me a sum sufficient to be above want the expenses of the British Army on the Continent shall be defrayed by this means; that part of the sums received shall also be destined to the discrediting of the Assignats, that I shall sell letters of Change upon Paris at an under price upon the Change of London and thereby ruin the Assignats; that I shall also stir up divisions in the National Convention and bribe the Members, in short that every means in my power shall be taken to weaken France and thereby preserve to England a more cheap and a more humane victory than would be gained by sword and bayonet.

After all I know the clause of personal profit will with the selfish and those who have no public spirit themselves go against me, to such persons I answer that both soldiers and sailors defend their country with an intention to be advanced and well paid, and that I do the same.

Would any person through ignorance say that counterfeiting Assignats is a crime in this country I would answer no. That they are not to be regarded in this country as that is forbidden by an express Act of Parliament even for the true Assignats that therefore none of his Majesty's subjects can be defrauded by a treacherous paper which this King, Lords, and Commons have declared unlawful in this country and therefor there can be no law against making them here for the use of any other country.

That on the other hand those who create the Assignats have extorted by force from its lawful owners the property upon which they are mortgaged and that I or any one else has the same right to make Assignats that they have. That is I have the power and the will and they have nothing more.

Should it be said by the ignorant that this may lead to the counterfeiting of Bills, Bonds, or Bank Notes I observe that the Assignats are none of these—where are they payable? To whom are they payable? Or by whom? or have they any intrinsic value? No the Assignats resembles no more our Bank Note than a bit of oak bark resembles a guinea, and I must observe that it is not the difficulty of making a Bank of England note that prevents forgery but that checks and probability from its being payable at sight of being soon discovered, This is indeed the case with all paper ever created except the American paper and the Assignats the former of which was counterfeited in General Howe's Army with that ever being accounted a crime.

On then I go, let me proceed or fail, I commit myself frankly & fairly and protest against the interference of any law in this country while I hope one day to be lauded with should I succeed in executing what I propose.

As to the eventual dangers I must run my risqué and am prepared as every man should be who enters upon such undertakings, Where there is no danger there is neither gain nor glory. Satisfied with my motives which I explain before I begin I hope that should I succeed my country shall gain, and my own will be the consequence, and that should I fail I can only blame myself.

London this 20th March 1793
William Playfair

Each Page is Signed with my paraphe thus
W

(Notation in a hand other than Playfair's):

Misérable Coquin!!! (A. deD)

B Appendix B: Playfair's Proposal for an Information Operation to Guide Public Opinion

Source: William Playfair to Henry Dundas (Knightsbridge, 24 April 1794), The National Archives, HO 42/29, fols. 474–482.

I have now the honour of sending inclosed the ideas which have occurred to me on the subject of guiding public opinion and in consequence of which I took the liberty of writing to you already.

I can but add to that an offer of any services that I can render as a volunteer in the cause, should it meet with approbation, taking the liberty to suggest that a trial would be easily made and could cost little. The effects would be seen in a few months and measures taken accordingly by an individual of no fortune is always supposed to have personal motives for his zeal in the public cause & I think a man never loses any thing by avowing them frankly. My motives are plainly these, that whether right or wrong I know not I am fully convinced in my own mind that should discontents augment it will before many years produce some changes in this country and that if they begin America is the only refuge for a Peaceable Man for I have witnessed it that there is <u>no moderation in Reformers and neither liberty Peace nor Safety in Revolutions</u> for tho' I do not believe they are so wrong headed in this country as in France yet they must not be much depended upon for in France there were tolerably reasonable at first & got more & more worse as they went on.

I shall be highly flattered if my ideas are honoured with your approbation & shall [1-2 words unintelligible] if upon a trial they may be found to be of any use.

I have the honour to be

with respect
your most obdnt
& most humble svnt
William Playfair

Knightsbridge 24th April 1794

Of the Necessity & Manner of Guiding Public Opinion

It is certainly a very fortunate circumstance for this country that the French Revolution, like certain venomous animals, carries an antidote for its poison along with it.

Altho' Sedition and Insurrection have Reared their heads victoriously there, and an Example has been set by which factious & discontented men are Rendered Bold, and instructed in the way to reduce disorder to a sort of System, yet it has been attended with so much Real Mischief & Misery that it has furnished answers to all those Reasonings upon which the thing itself is founded. The Fact is, that the Reasonable & well meaning man, who five years ago, was less afraid of the anarchy of a Democratic Government, than of monarchical despotism, is not so now, and the faults which might he found with a mixt Government like ours are greatly diminished if not intirely done away. Perfection in Government has been aimed at in France, but that philanthropy & philosophy which were taken as guides served to lead to a system of the most horrid Tyranny & confusion that was ever known in the annals of mankind.

It is therefore I say fortunate far us that as these Principles So Specious at first Light but really so dangerous have been so completely proved by experience to be so, that moderate men may refute with facility all those innovators, who by way of Reform seek the destruction of the Present Government.

This merits great attention, because it furnishes the Executive Government with a new means of protecting the present order of things.

Until lately, Reform, as it is called appeared in an amiable light, its arguments were strong & seemed intended for public happiness; it was not then any wonder that the Executive Government wished rather to avoid the discussion of questions where the odds seemed so much against it; but now the tables are turned, discussions are nevertheless perpetually begun, it is therefore in vain to shrink from them, & it is not wise to do it because these Reformers can he answered so victoriously.

The attacks made upon peace and order by levellers are systematically followed up, they are supported by the money of many persons who do not choose themselves to appear openly, and their efforts have that energy & boldness which have all along been the leading features of the Jacobins and their emissaries.

Public opinion in a free country must in the end be the guide in public affairs, it is therefore of the utmost importance that that public opinion should not take a wrong direction.

With the Democratic Energy on one side, and the Aristocratic Coolness, or, rather apathy on the other there is little doubt which way the public opinion must in the end be led. The democrats, with an appearance of reason on their side, say that punishments for propagating opinion are not answers, so that tho' punishments & severe punishments are necessary, it would be necessary also in order to impress the common mind with the justice of such punishment to have the principles of which the propagation is a crime fully refuted, as, for instance, those innovators who are going to Botany Bay have got leave to tell their own story, & it is a fact that many people seem to think them hardly treated, whereas a few observations might clear up the public mind at once.[*]

The country is divided into three classes of men, the friends of present order, its opposers, & the great number of inhabitants who ~~desire~~ wish all to he done for the best, but who are therefore liable to follow that party which is at the most pains to Reason them into a belief that they are Right. This great third class of people turns the scale for or against Government, it is the most important class & is the object of Jacobin attack, of that <u>systematic attack</u> which it is so necessary to counteract.

In every quarter of a large town in every village and in every place of habitual society & resort, there are men who guide the opinion of others by superior information, impudence or talent for speaking, & those men are generally themselves obliged to apply either to some periodical publication or at least to some pamphlets that can easily be had. Paine's Book on the Rights of Man, as he called it, was just adapted to this class, and it was artfully put into their hands, ~~& have~~ as all other seditious things are, and tho' there are generally in all places of public resort other orators who would be very glad and very ready to refute these, yet they, not ~~having~~ possessing the advantage of having arguments put into their mouths, cannot stand their ground.[**] Thus it happens that everywhere political opinions are discussed there is scarce a tavern coffeehouse or alehouse in England where there is not an advantageous contest carried on by the democrats in this way.

---

[*] As imprisonment at home is converted into triumph by their seditious companions it ceased to be a Punishments, therefor Banishment was adopted from Necessity as for Royal Chancery <u>was it ever employed upon men found guilty by their Peers & who persist and glory in their crime?</u>

[**] The impossibility of furnishing these persons with arguments unless Government supports such an undertaking is clear from this fact that 500 or 1000 are the most that are ever sold of any Government Pamphlet, as it does not pay for advertisements to make it enough known & booksellers cannot be guided but by profit & loss the Democratic works on the contrary are circulated ~~by~~ in immense numbers.

If those who support the other side of the question were furnished with arguments then the triumph of the other would be very short lived but this cannot be done ~~by~~ but by support in money.

I would therefore take the liberty to suggest that as all Governments are in the habit of keeping up a force for defence against open attack ~~it would~~ and that at very Great Expense, that as the present order is in danger from opinion more than from open Force it would not be unwise to employ a sum comparatively very small for defence against this sort of attack.

Such a sum would Require to be put into the hands of some person of Rank & Fortune who has [1 word unintelligible] method & the talents & activity necessary, and upon whom confidence might be placed, for the wise and Faithful Employment of the money but this ought to be done in a ~~much~~ way very different from the pamphlets circulated gratis in a public manner for here it must be observed that to' gratis pamphlets, as they are circulated by men who have no ostensible nor public fund for that purpose are considered as being circulated through the zeal of individuals in the democratic cause ~~but~~ those in support of Government are suppose to be paid for. The difficulty of overcoming this obstacle is considerable nevertheless it ~~would~~ is by no means impossible & should the idea in general be approved the means of putting it in Execution will easily be communicated.

As the price that a thing may cost is always an object that ought to be ingrained into whatever value may be, after considering the Regular Periodical Channels by which people in all parts of the country are influenced, and also the assisting in ~~propagating~~ extending by advertisements the sale of such works as deserve it, probably a sum of from 8 to twelve thousand pounds a year would do & it is probable that it might not be necessary after one year.

It is plain that such a thing if done would require to be done calmly & quietly, without any Bustle and even without being perceived as any person of known fortune who set the things to work might be supposed by those whom he immediately Employed to do it at his own Expense out of a love of order & the Present Government.

I would beg leave to recommend the Employing Some person to compile as short history of the <u>crimes & cruelties of the Revolution in France,</u> as details of that sort are read with Great Avidity (this is proved by the sale of Books of Martyrs and all relations that excite horror) a book called Crimes of Kings & Queens of France did great service to the Democratic cause in the beginning of the Revolution. The horror of the French Government is by no means known by the general body of the people have in its time Extent & a very cheap book of this kind would certainly do great good because it would be circulated without any difficulty or as least without much as for other Publications there are many that would be useful & for Every particular sort of working a man should be employed who has a reasonable moderate way of expressing himself & who. As to the working part for three hundred a year they could get that done by men of sufficient abilities, the great expense would be advertisements but part of that comes back into the Treasury and perhaps is the thing is done very judiciously it will cost scarcely any thing but for advertisements.

Note 1: Should the Crimes of the Revolution be written I would recommend Mr. Peltier a French writer who publishes a paper here, he has the sort of talents for it & proposes the materials is himself he is I believe a Loyal Man & could be employed by the medium of a bookseller without knowing who he did it for & then it could be translated into English. No Englishman is fit to do this work which would open peoples Eyes amazingly as Facts are stubborn things & being interesting would take deep root in the Mind.

Note 2: Should it be wished to have any further communication upon the Subject of this [material?] paper if it is sent to Knightsbridge or to Mr Frazier No. 10 Little Bridge Street St. James it will be forwarded to the Continent to the author who sets off in a few days.

(Notation on the reverse of Page 2 of Playfair's proposal, in a hand other than Playfair's and catalogued under fol 478):

This seems to be page 2 of a Manuscript sent to the Right Honorable Henry Dundas two days ago by Mr Playfair wich M.S. therefore incomplete without it.

Appendix C: Playfair's Letter to Grenville Recalling Counterfeiting Operations in London

Source: William Playfair to William Wyndham Grenville (High Holborn, 10 July 1811), Historical Manuscripts Commission, The Manuscripts of J. B. Fortscue, Esq., Preserved at Dropmore Volume 10. (London: HMSO, 1927), 155–157. Italics are rendered as in the published version.

On reading the report of your speech on Monday, the 8th, in which your lordship is made to disclaim all knowledge on the part of his Majesty's Ministers of *assignats* fabricated in England, and knowing at the same time your strict honour and veracity, I am induced to enclose a paper that will undeceive your lordship on that subject.

It is to my efforts at the time (for the honour of the country and from friendship for Mr. Wyndham [Windham])* that the Administration of which your lordship formed a part owes its not being exposed in a Court of Justice as paying for the fabrication of those very *assignats*. I should suppose that it would be better in return, neither to own or disown the transaction, for there are people still living who can prove it; and indeed if I did not know positively that though your lordship was not privy to the business, others of Administration were, after what your lordship said I could not believe that Government was concerned; but knowing positively that it was so, I think it right to inform your lordship, as undoubtedly it would be very painful to have a formal assertion contradicted in an authentic way.

---

* The corrections in brackets were made by the editors of the *Manuscripts*. "Wyndham" was the older spelling that Playfair used; the editors were noting William Windham's preferred form.

Enclosure:

Statement relative to false *assignats* fabricated by French emigrants patronised by some of his Majesty's Ministers and sent out to Quiberon.

In 1794 and 95 a manufactory of *assignats* in imitation of those made in France was established at the back of Sloane Street, conducted by the Abbé de Calonne (brother to the Minister), Mr. de Puisay and St. Morrice, the same persons who were sent to Quiberon when France was invaded, where they had a principal command and took with them the *assignats* so manufactured, in great quantities and at a vast expense.

Independent of the open and expensive manner in which the manufactory was carried on by emigrants who had no money and who did not offer the *assignats* for sale as private persons did, the following fact puts the connection with Government beyond all doubt.

When the expedition sailed to Quiberon, the manufactory ceased, and the managers all went off except Calonne. A large quantity of paper with the water-mark made on purpose was left on hand of a paper warehouseman in Upper Thames Street to the value of about 700l.* This man brought an action against Calonne and retained Mr. Mackintosh (now Sir James) to plead his cause and prove that the credit was given on account of Government, and that Calonne was a principal agent.

This came to my knowledge from the paper maker, who was determined to proceed. I was then in habits of seeing Mr. Wyndham [Windham], and informed him how Government was likely to be exposed. He made light of it at first, but when the time of trial approached, considering that the very man sent out to Quiberon with the *assignats* by Government would

---

* At the time, correspondents frequently wrote, e.g., "£700" as "700l," using either an uppercase or lowercase "L."

be proved to have fabricated them at an expense probably of 40,000l, he (Mr. Wyndham [Windham]) desired me to see if I could stop the business, asking what I thought would be fair. I said I thought the man ought to be contented with prime cost for the paper and allow a fair value for it to manufacture over again. Mr. Windham desired me to settle it so, if I could. I did settle it so; the maker, John Lightly (Hill Livery), agreed to deduct twenty-five per cent. from the selling price and to allow 30L for the material left. The amount then remaining was about 490l., which Mr. Wyndham promised should be paid next day at 2 o'clock.

At 2 o'clock on that next day two Frenchmen called on Lightly, paid him the money and took a receipt in full.

I never saw any of the Frenchmen, nor did I know Calonne or anyone concerned; but I know that Lightly had plenty of proof that Government paid, and this transaction, in which I was concerned as stated, is a proof of it.

I should farther state that I advised Mr. Wyndham [Windham] if he would not pay, rather to vindicate than to deny the fabrication, for that the denial would only add to the disgrace, whereas it might be vindicated on this footing: that the original French *assignats* were themselves forged mortgages on the estates of emigrants issued by a Government of usurpers, and that the emigrants had at least as good a right to issue *assignats*, and certainly had a right completely to try to bring them to discredit. Mr. Wyndham smiled, and said that was true, and might satisfy the mind of those concerned, but would not satisfy the public.

I write this in consequence of Lord Grenville's speech in the House of Commons [Lords] on the 8th July, 1811, in order that his lordship may confine the disavowal to his own knowledge, but not extend it to the whole Administration.

—London, 10th July, 1811

Note by Lord Grenville

1811, July 12—I have this day received the enclosed. It seems to prove (if the statement be correct) that Mr. Windham certainly had some knowledge after the fact of the transaction in question, and that he took measures to prevent its exposure by the payment of money.

On the best recollection that I can give to it, I cannot call to mind any the smallest knowledge of this fact, and I feel persuaded that it was never communicated to me.

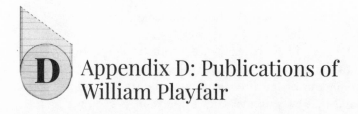

Appendix D: Publications of William Playfair

Year	Title	Publisher
1785	The Increase of Manufactures, Commerce, and Finance, with the Extension of Civil Liberty, Proposed in Regulations for the Interest of Money.	Robinson
1785	Commercial and Political Atlas, prelim edition	(Self-published)
1786	Commercial and Political Atlas, 1st edition	Debrett
1787	An essay on the national debt, with copper plate charts, for comparing annuities with perpetual loans	Robinson
1787	Commercial and Political Atlas, 2nd edition	J. Stockdale
1787	Joseph and Benjamin, A Conversation	J. Murray
1787	The Letters of Alliance in Defense of Governor Hastings	Debrett
1789	Tableaux d'arithmétique linéaire, du commerce, des finances, et de la dette nationale de l'Angleterre	Chez Barrois l'aine
1790	Quèst-ce que le papier-monnaie?	(None given)
1790	Lettre II. d'un Anglais a un Francais sur les assignats	(None given)
1792	A Letter to the People of England on the Revolution in France.	Debrett
1792	Inevitable Consequences of Parliamentary Reform	J. Stockdale

Year	Title	Publisher
1792	Short Account of the Revolt and Massacre Which Took Place in Paris, on the 10th of August 1791	J. Stockdale
1793	A General View of the Actual Force and Resources of France	J. Stockdale
1793	Better Prospects to the Merchants and Manufacturers of Great Britain	J. Stockdale
1793	Thoughts on the Present State of French Politics, and the Necessity and Policy of Diminishing France, for her Internal Peace	J. Stockdale
1794	Democracy More Dangerous Than Royal Prerogative	J. Stockdale
1794	Peace with the Jacobins impossible	J. Stockdale
1795	Electioneering and Parliamentary Review	Proprietors of the Review
1795	Letter to the Right Honorable Earl Fitzwilliam, Occasioned by His Two Letter to the Earl of Carlisle	Byrne, Wogan, Jones & Pots
1795	Proposal for History of Jacobinism	J. Stockdale
1795–1796	The Tomahawk! (first issue is 27 October 1795; last issue is 7 March 1796)	(None given)
1795	The History of Jacobinism, its Crimes, Cruelties and Perfidies	Stockdale (Cobbett in US)
1796	Playfair's Answer to Thomas Paine's Decline and Fall of the English System of Finance	Oracle and Public Advertiser
1796	For the Use of the Enemies of England: A Real Statement of the Finances and Resources of Great Britain	J. Stockdale
1797	A Fair Statement of the Proceedings of the Bank of England, Against the Original Security Bank on Tuesday the Seventh of March, 1797	(Self-published)

Year	Title	Publisher
1797	Letter to Sir W. Pulteney... on the establishment of another public bank in London	Crosby
1798	Lineal Arithmetic	A. Paris
1799	Strictures on the Asiatic establishments of Great Britain	Carpenter & Co.; Murray and Highley
1800	A Geographical, Historical, and Political Description of the Empire of Germany, Holland, the Netherlands, Switzerland, Prussia, Italy, Sicily	J. Stockdale
1800	Statistical Tables Exhibiting a View of All the States of Europe (by Jakob Gottlieb Boetticher, with supplementary table by Playfair)	J. Stockdale
1801	Commercial & Political Atlas, 3rd edition	Wallis et al.
1801	The Statistical Breviary	Wallis et al.
1802	Statistical Account of the United States of America (by D.F. Donnant, trans. w/notes by Playfair)	Greenland & Norris
1802	Élémens de statistique	Batilloit et Genets
1804	Proofs Relative to the Falsification, by the French, of the Intercepted Letter Found on Board the Admiral Aplin East Indiaman	Glendinning
1805	An Inquiry into the Permanent Causes of the Decline and Fall of Powerful and Wealthy Nations	Greenland & Norris
1805	An Inquiry into the Nature and Causes of the Wealth of Nations (by Adam Smith, edited and with commentary by Playfair)*	Cadell and Davies

*   Playfair's edition of Adam Smith's Wealth of Nations was first published in 1805; there were several later releases , with numerous differences in Playfair's commentary, and even differences between the British and American releases of the same edition. The citations in this book refere to the specific edition used for each reference.

Year	Title	Publisher
1806	The Creditor and Bankrupt's Assistant: Being the Spirit of the Bankrupt Laws, with Observations (published under the name of Joshua Montefiore, authored by Playfair)	W. Clarke and Sons
1807	An Inquiry into the Permanent Causes of the Decline and Fall of Powerful and Wealthy Nations, 2nd edition	Greenland & Norris
1807	European Commerce, Shewing New and Secure Channels of Trade with the Continent of Europe (published under the name of J.J. Oddy, authored by Playfair)	Humphreys
1808	Anticipation (weekly, approximately 30 issues)	(Printed by Glindon, sold by "Booksellers throughout the UK")
1809	Fair & Candid Address to Nobility & Baronet of the UK	Proprietors of Family Antiquity
1809	British Family Antiquity, Vol. 1	T. Reynolds and H. Grace
1810	A Sketch for the Improvement of the Political, Commercial, and Local Interests of Britain, As Exemplified by the Inland Navigations of Europe	J.J. Stockdale
1809	A Fair and Candid Address to the Nobility and Baronets of the United Kingdom: Accompanied with Illustrations and Proofs on the Advantage of Hereditary Rank and Title in a Free Country	Proprietors of Family Antiquity
1810	Second Address to the British Nobility Accompanied with Illustrations and Proofs on the Advantage of Hereditary Rank and File in a Free Country	Proprietors of Family Antiquity

Year	Title	Publisher
1811	British Baronetage; Illustrative of the Origin and Progress of the Rank, Hounours, and Personal Merit of the Baronets of the United Kingdom	T. Reynolds and H. Grace
1811	A Vindication of the Reign of His Present Majesty, King George III (published under the name William Hunter, authored by Playfair)	J.J. Stockdale
1812	Early Friends of the Prince Regent	J.J. Stockdale
1812	A Letter to His Royal Highness the Prince Regent on the Ultimate tendency of the Roman Catholic Claims (published under the name William Hunter, possibly authored by Playfair)	(Not known)
1813	Bonaparte's Journey to Moscow In the Manner of John Gilpin	By the Author
1813	Outlines of a Plan for a New and Solid Balance of Power in Europe	Stockdale
1814	A Letter from William Pitt in the Shades to the Allied Sovereigns in the Sun-shine	Blacklock
1814	A Letter to the Right Honourable and Honourable the Lords and Commons of Great Britain on the Advantages of Apprenticeships	Sherwood, Neely, and Jones
1814	Political Portraits in this New Era, Volume 2	Chapple
1815	An Answer to the Calumniators of Louis XVIII	J. Stockdale

Year	Title	Publisher
1815	A statement, which was made in October, to Earl Bathurst, one of His Majesty's Principal Secretaries of State, and in November, 1814, to the comte de La Chatre, the French ambassador, of Buonaparte's plot to re-usurp the Crown of France	J.J. Stockdale
1816	Supplementary Volume to Political Portraits in this New Era	Chapple
1819	France As It Is, Not Lady Morgan's France, Volume 1	Chapple
1819	Memoir of the late James Watt, Esq., F.R.S. & etc. (New Monthly Magazine, pp. 230-239)	New Monthly Magazine
1819	Memoir of James Watt, Esq., F.R.S. (Monthly Magazine, pp. 576-584)	Monthly Magazine
1820	France As It Is, Not Lady Morgan's France, Volume 2	Chapple
1820	Advantages of Emigration to France	Souter
1821	A Letter on Our Agricultural Distresses	Sams
1822	Can This Continue?	Sams

Notes on References

In addition to telling William Playfair's story, my editor, John W. Warren, and I wanted to try some new approaches to scholarship and academic publishing.

Part of our approach was related to style. There's no reason why original, thoroughly documented research can't be engaging—even entertaining. Besides, it would be hard to do justice to a character like Playfair any other way.

Another part of our approach was how we presented all of that original, thoroughly-documented research.

Analysis should be substantiated, documented, and replicable, with no fudging about the level of confidence one has in an inference or conclusion. That's why I tried to tie each statement of fact in this book to a source, along with the information needed to retrieve it. Where possible, original source material used in the cited reference is also cited. We want to make it possible for anyone to replicate and verify the work.

Analysis should also be cumulative. Everyone builds on others' work, adding information and insight along the way. (And, when necessary, making corrections.) It's all part of the process of creating knowledge. By making the source material easier to obtain, we hope to encourage others to follow up with their own research.

One important source for this book was a heretofore-unpublished memoir Playfair wrote during the last two years of his life. It consists of thirty-six pages and was passed down through successive generations to John Playfair, William's great-great-great-great grandson, who now holds it. Each page is preserved in a separate, numbered plastic jacket.

To create an archival document that others can use, we created a transcript of the memoir and have posted it—along with scans of the original—on the Internet Archive website. In the mid-1990s, Ian Spence prepared an annotated version of the memoir for John Playfair; I retained Spence's chronological organization, checking the original to verify the text, and making corrections where warranted.

A few other remarks: The Boulton and Watt archives at the Library of Birmingham were especially useful in piecing together Playfair's life before his first journey to France. The collection is massive, and it's evolved over the years as material was added. But there's a challenge in using it.

The papers came from several different collections, and the early biographers did not keep the papers in their original state as they used them. In addition, there was no cataloguing system. So Birmingham's archivists have often had to reconstruct their organization.

There is also considerable inconsistency in how scholars have cited the papers over the years. Books written during the early to mid-1900s refer to the Birmingham Reference Library, which was later the Birmingham Central Library, and now the Library of Birmingham. They catagorized documents as "Muirhead" (papers sorted by James Patrick Muirhead, Watt's first biographer), "Doldowlod" (papers that were kept at the Watt family estate), or "Tangye," (the Boulton & Watt company papers George Tangye bought and preserved). Some authors referred simply to "James Watt Papers" or "Matthew Boulton Papers."

When an original document was important to my analysis, I tracked it down and have provided the current MSS number the Library of Birmingham uses. When that wasn't practical, I've provided the reference as rendered in the book or article to make the documents as retrievable as possible.

Finally, about those secondary sources: Most of the books I used were published before the early 1900s and are out of copyright, so you can find them on archive.org, hathitrust.org, or gallica.bnf.fr. Those that are not can usually be bought from commercial sites.

With all this in mind, abbreviations for collections cited in the references are as follows:

- AAS: American Antiquarian Society
- AN: Archives nationales
- BCL: Birmingham Central Library
- BL: British Library
- BRL: Birmingham Reference Library
- GP: Gallipolis Papers, Cincinnati History Library and Archives at the Cincinnati Museum Center
- LB: Library of Birmingham

- LOC: Library of Congress
- NA: The National Archives (UK)
- NW: Northumberland Archives at Woodhorn (previously the Northumberland Collections Service and Northumberland County Record Office)
- NAGL: National Archives (UK), Guildhall Library Manuscripts Section
- NAS: National Archives of Scotland
- NRAS: National Register of Archives for Scotland
- NLS: National Library of Scotland
- OHC: Ohio History Connection
- TU/SRC: Temple University Libraries, Special Collections Research Center

Notes

Introduction: The Castle in Northumberland

1   Philip Dixon, "From Hall to Tower: The Change in Seigneurial Houses on the An-glo-Scottish Border after c. 1250," in P.R. Coss and S.D. Lloyd, eds., *Thirteenth Century England IV: Proceedings of the Newcastle Upon Tyne Conference 1991* (Woodbridge, Suffolk, UK: Boydell Press, 1992), 94–96.

2   "Sir John Edward Swinburne, Bart." *The Gentleman's Magazine* (November 1860), 551–552.

3   George Otto Trevelyan, *The Early History of Charles James Fox* (London: Longmans, Green, and Co., 1881), 87–93. Fox's lifestyle wasn't that unusual for the time and in some quarters enhanced his stature.

4   The most exhaustive biography of Pitt is probably the three-volume series by John Ehr-man, *The Younger Pitt* (London: Constable, 1969, 1983, 1996) but also see William Hague, *Pitt the Younger* (New York: Alfred A. Knopf, 2005) and Jennifer Mori, *William Pitt and the French Revolution: 1785–1795* (New York: St. Martin's Press, 1997).

5   See Charles Dickens, "One Pound Note, Guineas, etc.," *All the Year Round* Volume 7 (January 2, 1892–June 25, 1892), 42.

6   For Swinburne's account see "Memorandum by Sir John E. Swinburne About Manufac-ture at Paper Mill near Capheaton of Paper to Make Assignats," (Caphaeton, c 1793–1794) NW ZSW/590. Swinburne identified the man confirming the forgery rumors only as "Richmond." He's likely Henry Richmond of the village of Humshaugh, who Eneas Mackenzie describes in *An Historical, Topographical, and Descriptive View of the County of Northumberland*, Volume 2 (Newcastle Upon Tyne: McKenzie and Dent, 1825), 242. For further information on Humshaugh, see Jen Ogle, "Notes on Humshaugh Past," in *Humshaugh Handbook 2016*, published by the Humshaugh Parish Council.

7   Northumberland County Committee, "Humshaugh Parish," *A History of Northumberland*, Volume 15 (London: A. Reid, 1940), 208–210.

8   Swinburne, NWZSW/590. Swinburne said that he spoke with the "foreman." Peter Isaac identified the foreman as "Magnay," father of Christopher Magnay, later alderman of Vinty Ward and Lord Mayor of London; see his "Sir John Swinburne and the Forged Assignats from Haughton Mill," *Archaeologia Aeliana* (Fifth Series, Volume 18) 162. Christopher's father is, in turn, identified as "John Magnay, of Williamswick Tower, Nor-thumberland" in Bernard Burke, *A Genealogical and Heraldic Dictionary of the Peerage and Baronetage of the British Empire*, 13th edition (London: Harrison, 1868), 722.

9   Historian Arthur Aspinall offers a discussion of Pitt's "hirelings" in *Politics and the Press, c. 1780–1850* (London: Home & Van Thal, 1949), 163–164.

10 John Fielding's quotation is from *A Brief Description of the Cities of London and Westminster*. London: J. Wilkie, 1776), xxviii. You might also recognize Covent Garden as the workplace of Eliza Doolittle, famous first as the flower girl in Shaw's *Pygmalion*, and, later, in Lerner and Loewe's *My Fair Lady*.

11 For a snapshot of Covent Garden in the eighteen century, see Reginal Jacobs, *Covent Garden: Its Romance and History* (London: Simpkin, Marshall, Hamilton, Kent & Co., 1913).

12 That's the assessment rendered in "Worth a Thousand Words," *The Economist* (December 19, 2007). Available at http://www.economist.com/node/10278643 (accessed 3 February 2017).

13 John Goldworth Alger, "Playfair, William (1759–1823)" in Sidney Lee, ed., *Dictionary of National Biography*, Volume 45 (London: Smith, Elder, & Co., 1896), 415.

Chapter 1: Inventing William Playfair

1 Playfair's physical appearance is described in "PLAYFAIR, Mr. William," *The Annual Biography and Obituary for the Year 1824*, Volume 8 (London: Longman, Hurst, Rees, Orme, Brown, and Green, 1824), 460. It's also in his prison records; see HO 26/PRIS 10, Piece 6, 82, via Ancestor.com, "England & Wales, Criminal Registers 1791–1892."

2 Hugh Playfair, *The Playfair Family* (Blackford, Somerset, self-published 1999), 1.

3 John G. Playfair, ed., *The Works of John Playfair, Esq.* (Edinburgh: Archibald Constable & Co., 1822), xiv–xv. John G. Playfair was John Playfair's nephew.

4 Samuel Smiles, *Lives of the Engineers. Harbours-Lighthouses-Bridges. Smeaton and Rennie.* (London: John Murray, 1874), 199–212. Hugh Playfair (35) says that William "was sent" to apprentice with Meikle, suggesting it was John, his guardian, who sent him.

5 William Playfair, *A Letter to the Right Honourable and Honourable the Lords and Commons of Great Britain on the Advantages of Apprenticeships* (London: Sherwood, Neely, and Jones, 1814), 8.

6 Herbert L. Ganter in "William Small, Jefferson's Beloved Teacher," *William and Mary Quarterly* (October 1947), 506.

7 Gillian Hull, "William Small 1734–1775: No Publications, Much Influence," *Journal of the Royal Society of Medicine*, Volume 90 (February 1997), 103; Hull cites G.W. Ewing, "Early Teaching of Science at the College of William and Mary," *Journal of Chemical Education*, Volume 13 (January 1938), 3–13.

8 Ibid.

9 This is the traditional etymology; H.W. Dickinson, in his biography of Boulton, was skeptical; see his *Matthew Boulton* (Cambridge: Cambridge University Press, 1937), 44–45.

10 Samuel Smiles, *Lives of Boulton and Watt* (London: John Murray, 1865), 106–108.

11 See Eric Roll, *An Early Experiment in Industrial Organization, Being History of the Firm of Boulton & Watt, 1775–1805* (London: Frank Cass & Co., 1930), 13.

12 For details on the patent, see James Muirhead, *Origin and Progress of the Mechanical Inventions of James Watt*, Volume 3 (London: John Murray, 1854), 10–16.

13 Watt previously partnered with John Roebuck. The two made little progress, and when Roebuck hit the financial skids, Boulton bought him out and used his political connections to extend Watt's patent. See Eric Robinson, "Matthew Boulton and the Art of Parliamentary Lobbying," *The Historical Journal*, Volume 7, No. 2 (1964), 209–229.

14 Dickinson, *Boulton*, 197.

15 See Mary Anne Schimmelpenninck, C.C. Hankin, ed., *Life of Mary Anne Schimmelpen-ninck* Volume 1 (London: Longman, Brown, Green, Longmans, and Roberts, 1858), 40. Schimmelpenninck was a writer and a member of Birmingham's intellectual circles.

16 James Keir to Matthew Boulton (c. 1777, no location given), LB MS 3782/12/65. Keir quoted from Small's letter. One sometimes sees this letter cited. For a while, Adam Matthew Publications provided an excerpt as a sample of its microfilm edition of the Boulton & Watt Archives and Matthew Boulton Papers. The Adam Matthew collection was based on a catalogue entry by the Archives of Soho Project at the Library of Birmingham. The excerpt, however, does not include the last passage in which Keir, quoting Small, describes Playfair's character, and so it's rarely included when the letter is quoted.

17 See Roll, *An Early Experiment*, 24. Also see Robert Williams, "Management Accounting Practice and Price Calculation at Boulton and Watt's Soho Foundry: A Late 18th Century Example." *The Accounting Historians Journal*, Volume 26, No. 2 (December 1999), 65–88.

18 Quoted in John Lord, *Capital and Steam-Power* (London: P.S. King & Son, 1923), 203. Lord cites Law to Playfair (10 June 1781) in "Tangye MSS," referring to the Boulton & Watt Papers now at Library of Birmingham. Impressment was a fact of life and Law was reporting his first-hand experience, though the threat of press gangs is often exaggerated (the Royal Navy preferred experienced hands). James Watt had his own experience dodging the gangs as a young man in London; see James Watt to James Watt of Greenock (London, 31 March 1756). MS 3219/3/93, letter 27; reproduced at http://www.libraryof-birmingham.com/article/archivesofsohofigures/jameswatt (accessed 8 February 2017).

19 Paul Andrew Luter, "The Hornblower Saga," *Broseley Local History Society*, No. 26 (2004), 29; Luter said he based his article on the Boulton & Watt Papers at the Birmingham Reference Library (now the Library of Birmingham), but did not cite a specific item.

20 William Playfair to Logan Henderson (Soho, 16 September 1780), LB MS 3782/12/25/9.

21 Playfair served as a clerk and handled customer relations; see his letters to various customers (Soho, 25 September–10 Decembers 1781), LB MS 3147/19/1 fols. 92–108.

22 James Keir to James Watt (Winson Green, 12 November 1781), LB MS 3219/4/90/1

23 Matthew Boulton to James Watt (London, 9 October 1781), LB James Watt Papers, Box 20/23: excerpt from Biography Section of the archives catalogue, provided by Library staff (26 June 2006).

24 Matthew Boulton to James Watt (Soho, 23 October 1781), LB MS 3782/12/4.

25 James Watt to Matthew Boulton (Birmingham, 5 November 1785), reproduced in H.W. Dickinson, "Some Unpublished Letters of James Watt," *The Institution of Mechanical Engineers Proceedings* (October–December 1915), 515. From the date of the letter, this appears to be LB MS 3782/12/79/38.

26 William Playfair, "Original Memoirs of Eminent Persons: The Late James Watt," *The Monthly Magazine*, Volume 48 (1819), 236.

27 H.W. Dickinson and R. Jenkins, *James Watt and the Steam Engine*, reprint of 1927 edition (London: Encore Editions, 1989), 285–286.

28 See, for example, John Griffiths, *The Third Man: The Life and Times of William Murdoch, Inventor of Gaslight* (London: Andre Deutsch, 1992).

29 Quoted in Dickinson and Jenkins, *Watt and the Steam Engine*, 291.

30 Smiles, *Lives of Boulton and Watt*, 256–257; and Griffths, *The Third Man*, 92–93.

31 Dickinson and Jenkins, *Watt and the Steam Engine*, 260, *fn* 2.

32 For examples of Watt's determination to dominate both his competitors and his employees, see Griffths, *The Third Man*, 196–197.

33 Dickinson and Jenkins, *Watt and the Steam Engine*, 296–297.

34 Griffths, *The Third Man*, 332–333.

35 See Cyril T. G. Boucher, *John Rennie 1761–1821: The Life and Work of a Great Engineer* (Manchester: University of Manchester Press, 1963), 9–10.

36 William Playfair to Matthew Boulton (Soho, 30 September 1780), LB MS 3782/12/25/63.

37 William Playfair to Matthew Boulton (London, 15 October 1781), LB MS 3782/12/26/106.

38 Ibid.

39 Ibid.

40 Keir to Watt,(12 November 1781), LB MS 3219/4/90/1.

41 Bennet Woodcroft, *Subject-Matter Index of Patents of Invention From March 2, 1617 (14 James I), to October 1, 1852 (16 Victoria)* Part I (London: Great Seal Patent Office, 1857), 263, 816.

42 *Rolling Mills, Rolls, and Roll Making: A Brief Historical Account of their Development from the Fifteenth Century to the Present Day.* (Pittsburgh: Mackintosh-Hemphill Co., 1953), 18.

43 Ibid., 23. The authors refer to Playfair as "Playfield," but the patent they reference is Playfair's.

44 See, for example, J.R. Adams, "Hardened and Ground Rolls," in *Year Book of the American Iron and Steel Institute, 1924* (New York: American Iron and Steel Institute, 1925), 118; and Francis Palgrave, "Calendar of Specifications of Patents of Inventions," *The Mechanics' Magazine* (6 February 1847), 165.

45 See *The Repertory of Arts and Manufactures: Consisting of Original Communications, Specification of Patent Inventions, and Selections of Useful and Practical Papers from the Transactions of the Philosophical Societies of All Nations, &c. &c*, Volume VIII (London: H. Lowndes, 1798), 158–167.

46 Woodcroft, *Subject-Matter Index of Patents*, 509. Also see the original application with the report of the Solicitor General; Stephen Stigler, at the University of Chicago provided it from his personal collection.

47 See H. I. Dutton, *The Patent System and Inventive Activity During the Industrial Revolution, 1750–1852* (Manchester, UK: Manchester University Press, 1984), 35. The actual cost to the applicant depended on how much protection he wanted; Dutton says a patent applicable to England cost £100–120.

48 Arthur Grimwade, *London Goldsmiths 1697–1837: Their Marks and Lives from the Original Registers at Goldsmiths' Hall and Other Sources* New York: Faber & Faber, 1990), 628.

49 William Playfair to Matthew Boulton (London, 9 March 1782), LB MS 3782/12/27/9.

50 Matthew Boulton to James Watt (Soho, 12 March 1782), LB James Watt Papers, D/4, excerpted in an communication from the Library staff (26 June 2006).

51 Playfair to Boulton (London, 9 March 1782), LB MS 3782/12/27/9.

52 William Playfair to Matthew Boulton (London, 23 January 1783), LB MS 3782/12/28/8.

53 James Keir to Matthew Boulton (Winson Green, 4 March 1781), LB MS 3782/12/65/56 fol. 64.

54 See *Sketch of the Life of James Keir, Esq.*(London: Robert Edmund Taylor, 1868), 63–64. Most of Keir's papers were lost in a fire; his daughter assembled this collection from what she could find.

55 Roll, *Early Experiment in Industrial Organization*, 130.

56 Kristen M. Schranz, "The Tipton Chemical Works of Mr James Keir: Networks of Conversants, Chemicals, Canals and Coal Mines," *International Journal for the History of Engineering & Technology* Volume 84, Issue 2 (2014). Available at http://www.tandfonline.com/doi/full/10.1179/1758120614Z.00000000049 (accessed 20 September 2016).

57 See the advertisement in *The Times* (14 April 1785), 1. Also see Grimwade, *London Goldsmiths*, 628, cited by the *Online Encyclopedia of Silver Marks, Hallmarks & Maker's Marks*. Available at http://www.925-1000.com/forum/viewtopic.php?t=23553 (accessed 7 January 2017). The evidence that Keir and Blair were legally linked to Playfair is the announcement of their company's dissolution; they specifically described it as a "partnership." See *London Gazette* (26 April 1785), 209.

58 Jenny Uglow, *The Lunar Men: The Friends Who Made the Future* (London: Faber and Faber, 2002), 291; Uglaw associates "Eldorado" with Boulton and Keir; as will be seen, Boulton worked with Keir in some of Keir's development projects.

59 Woodcroft, *Subject-Matter Index of Patents*, 509.

60 Ibid.

61 "Petition of Willm. Playfair for an Invention" (26 January 1785), from Stephen Stigler's collection.

62 Woodcroft, *Subject-Matter Index of Patents*, 132, 439.

63 Anslen Kuhn, "The Uses of Gold and its Technology as Recorded in Early British Patents," *Gold Bulletin*, Volume 32, No. 1 (1999), 63–64.

64 *Journal of the Institute of Metals* (Volume 44, no, 2) 1930, 180.

65 See Frederick A. Lowenheim, ed., *Modern Electroplating* (New York: John Wiley & Sons, 1974).

66 *The Times* (1 April 1785), 1.

67 *London Gazette* (25 June 1785), 313.

68 Grimwade, *London Goldsmiths*, 628.

69 *London Gazette* (26 April 1785), 209.

70 Alger, "Playfair," *Dictionary of National Biography*, 415.

71 See Ian Spence, "Playfair, William (1759–1823)," *Oxford Dictionary of National Biography*, Volume 44 (Oxford: Oxford University Press, 2004), 562–563. Available at http://www.oxforddnb.com/index/22/101022370/, and at http://psych.utoronto.ca/users/spence/Spence_2004.pdf (accessed 3 January 2017). This requires some discussion. Spence writes:

> Playfair and Keir were associates in the company formed to market Watt's copying machine, but this venture had little success. Between 1781 and 1785 Playfair applied for and obtained four patents for working metals, elaborations of the methods previously developed at the Soho manufactory of Boulton and Watt. Keir disputed the originality, believing that his own ideas had been appropriated, and there was an acrimonious breach.

Spence cites R. B. Prosser, *Birmingham Inventors and Inventions,* a book published as a fifty-copy run for private circulation in 1881. Richard Bissell Prosser was a British patent examiner who later in his life wrote about technology development and penned some fifty-odd entries for the *Dictionary of National Biography* under the initials "R.B.P." Prosser's book was reissued in 1970 by S.R. Publishers, a small house that listed its address in the 1960s and 1970s as East Ardsley, Yorkshire, near Leeds (There are other publishers using similar names today; they appear to be unrelated).

But if you track down the book, you find there's no mention by Prosser of a conflict between Keir and Playfair. In the first section that makes reference to Playfair, Prosser says Playfair served as witness for Watt's copying machine patent. Prosser then writes (50–51):

> Playfair proposed to prepare the metal for making buckles by rolling it in the form of rods through rolls having grooves of the required section, either engraved wih ornaments or plain, according to the circumstances. The ornament may also be impressed by stamping or swaging. For plain buckles the metal is drawn through dies. A sufficient length is then cut off, bent to the outline of the buckle, and soldered. Buckles and other articles are plated by interposing a thin layer of fusible silver-alloy between the surface to be coated and the plate of silver, for the purposes of facilitating the junction of the two.

That is all Prosser has to say at this point about Playfair. Later, in the only other section of the book that deals with Playfair, Prosser writes (143–144):

> In common with many of his countrymen he seems to have possessed an instinctive partiality for the south, and he accordingly found his way to Soho, where he was employed as a draughtsman for some years. In 1781 he patented "a method of making tongs, spoons, knives, forks, and medals out of solid silver or other metal, which will tend greatly to reduce the price of those articles." The idea of sinking impressions on rolls instead of dies has been patented repeatedly, as we have already shown, and Playfair's method does not differ materially from any of the others, except that he proposes, under certain circumstances, to use a sector in place of a complete roll, which is to oscillate backwards and forwards, suitable precautions being observed to ensure the correspondence of the two impressions. In 1783 he had removed to London, taking up his residence in Howland Street, Fitzroy Square. He took out two patents in that year for rolling and drawing sash bars, metal mouldings, and beading of all kinds, ornamental metal borders for trays, bottle stands, &c. One of his patents included a method of rolling blanks for horse shoes and for bending the blanks into shape. He used for his sash bars an alloy he called "El Dorado metal," consisting of copper, zinc, and iron, which we believe to have been identical with "Keir's metal." A large trade was done in articles of the kind by one J. Cruckshanks, of Gerrard Street, Soho, two of whose pattern books are preserved in the library of Sir John Soanne's Museum in Lincoln's Inn Fields. These sashes and mouldings were, in all probability, made by Keir at Tipton, where, as we have shown in the fourth article of this series, he had established a manufactory of rolled window sashes of his patent alloy of copper, zinc, and iron, which was capable of being worked at a red heat."

The article then goes on to describe Playfair's plating patent. So, though Prosser says others had also patented rolling mills that stamped out metal goods, and that Keir apparently was producing metal goods at his own mill at Tipton, there is no mention of a dispute between Keir and Playfair, and no suggestion that Playfair stole ideas from Boulton & Watt or from Keir.

When contacted, Spence said his source was not Prosser after all, but that there were letters, apparently not cited in his article, substantiating the events he described. Spence—who had completed the research for the ODNB entry more than ten years earlier and had since retired—later reported with some chagrin that he was unable to find the letters in his files (Communications September–December 2016).

In my own search of the Library of Birmingham archives, I found several letters describing various disagreements between Playfair and Keir (discussed shortly) but none that fit the description in the ODNB. In sum, unless and until definitive proof turns up, there is no basis for the notion of a dispute between Keir and Playfair over intellectual property, nor that Playfair appropriated Keir's ideas.

72 James Keir to Matthew Boulton (c 1777, no location given), LB MS 3782/12/65.
73 As noted earlier, see Keir to Watt (12 November 1781), LB MS 3219/4/90/1; and *London Gazette* (26 April 1785), 209.
74 William Playfair to James Watt (London, 20 September 1785), LBMS 3219/4/94; Playfair's description of his dispute with Keir is in the second half of the cover letter he sent Watt with the first copy of *The Commercial and Political Atlas* (more on this later). As will be seen, shortly after receiving this letter Watt did indeed tell his wife that Playfair threatened to retaliate in kind; see James Watt to Anne Watt (Birmingham, 25 September 1785), LB MS 3219/4/123 (Letter Book).
75 James Watt to Anne Watt, LB MS 3219/4/123. The verbatim quotation from Watt reads as:

> I had a letter from Playfair lately with a present of the first number of his Commercial Atlas which is mere plummery. He complains much of injurious and unjust treatment from Mr. K and imputes it in part to K's being chagrined by constant want of success in all his schemes, and impending ruin staring him the face & hints that the carriage was set up to support his credit & says he thinks of imitating him in that, by way of fighting him with his own weapons—What a rascal!

At the time a "carriage" referred to a financial arrangement. Ten additional words follow that are impossible to read, even with magnification and image correction; from the context, Watt may be asking Anne to keep his comments confidential, or he may be alluding to a comment by Keir.

76 James Watt to William Playfair (Birmingham, 10 October 1785), LB MS 3219/4/123.
77 Mark Saniforth, "The Introduction and Use of Copper Sheathing—A History," *Bulletin of the Australian Institute for Maritime Archaeology*, Volume 9, No. 1/2 (1985) 21–48; and Michael McCarthy, *Ships' Fastenings: From Sewn Boat to Steamship* (College Station: Texas A&M University Press, 2005), 103–109. Barbara M.D. Smith and J.L. Moilliet, "James Keir of the Lunar Society," *Notes and Records of the Royal Society of London*, Volume 22, No. 1/2 (September 1967), 147.

78   "PLAYFAIR," *Annual Biography 1824*, 458.

79   See H. J. Louw, "The Rise of the Metal Window in the Early Industrial Period in Britain, c. 1750–1830." *Construction History*, Volume 3 (1987), 31–54. Louw credits Keir for the Eldorado alloy on 41, and, as noted earlier, includes the drawings from Playfair's rolling mill patent on 36. This pairing is another indicator suggesting how Keir's and Playfair's inventions intermingled.

80   See Keir to Boulton, LB MS 3782/12/65/56 fol. 64. This letter includes a revealing passage in which Keir quotes to Boulton a note Keir says he wrote to himself weighing the wisdom of continuing with the company. The letter goes on to list services Keir says he rendered and the professional risks he took in joining Boulton & Watt. Keir complains of having "lost two years of my lifetime" waiting for Boulton to make him a partner with a share in profits. The Library of Birmingham put the letter online; it's available at   http://calmview.birmingham.gov.uk/CalmView/Record.aspx?src=CalmView.Catalog&id=MS+3782%2f12%2f65%2f56&pos=1 (accessed 3 January 2017).

81   Ibid. After listing his grievances over his terms of employment, Keir turned to a disagreement he had over intellectual property—but not with Playfair; rather, with Boulton. Keir wrote, "As to what you say concerning the bolt-metal, I always understood that it was first discovered in our joint experiments upon chinese copper. I never knew that you had made it before, nor ever heard of any goods having been made of it. Nevertheless I am perfectly convinced that it is so since you say it. I admitted that you had an equal right but I did not know that you had a better. I wish I had known it sooner."

82   Robert Stuart, *Historical and Descriptive Anecdotes of Steam-Engines, and of Their Inventors and Improvers* (London: Wightman and Cramp, 1829), 547.

83   William Playfair, *The Increase of Manufactures, Commerce, and Finance, with the Extension of Civil Liberty, Proposed in the Regulations for the Interest of Money* (London: G.G.J. and J. Robinson, 1787).

84   Playfair, *Increase of Manufactures*, 26.

85   Jeremy Bentham to George Wilson (Chichoff, 4–15 May 1787), reproduced in John Bowring, ed., *The Works of Jeremy Bentham*, Volume 10 (Edinburgh, William Tait, 1843), 174.

86   Quarto books are printed with four pages, or leaves, printed on the both the front and back of a sheet; the bookbinder folds the sheet and cuts the outer ends to form eight pages. "Octovo" binding yields starts with an eight pages on the front and back of each sheet, albeit in a smaller format, yielding sixteen pages total. A folio is made up of one or more full sheets of paper, four pages of text are printed on each, two on each side; each sheet is then folded once to produce two leaves. Folio binding produces the largest format and is most expensive.

87   Playfair, *Increase of Manufactures*, 109–110. Capitalization as in the original.

88   Emmett J. Vaughan and Therese M. Vaughan *Fundamentals of Risk and Insurance*, 11th Edition (New York: John Wiley & Sons, 2014), 1–11.

89   Howard Raiffa, *The Art and Science of Negotiation* (Cambridge, Massachusetts: Harvard University Press, 1982).

90   Daniel Ellsberg, "The Crude Analysis of Strategy Choices," *The American Economic Review*, Volume 51 (May 1961), 472–478.

91   Bruce Bueno de Mesquita, *The War Trap* (New Haven: Yale University Press, 1981).

92   See James Watt to Matthew Boulton (Glasgow, 5 July 1775), reproduced in Dickinson and Jenkins, *Watt and the Steam Engine*, 43–44.

Chapter 2: A Dundee Scot In King Louis' Court

1   This account draws on J.G. Milligen, *The History of Dueling*, Volume 2 (London: Richard Bentley, 1841), 108–110.

2   See *Parliamentary History*, Volume 21, Lords, 6 March 1780 (London: Longman, Hurst, Rees, Orme, & Brown, *et al*, 1814), 217–219.

3   Ibid., 224.

4   See *The Westminster Review* Volume 48 (July–October 1875), 312–314; Lord Edmond Fitzmaurice, *William, Earl of Shelburne, With Extracts from His Papers and Correspondence*. Volume 2 (London: Macmillan, 1912), 52–53.

5   For Shelburne's relationship with Franklin, see Fitzmaurice, *Life of William, Earl of Shelburne*, Volume 1, 221; and "List of Fossils Sent by George Croghan to the Earl of Shelburne and Benjamin Franklin," *Philosophical Transactions*, Volume 57 (New Haven: Yale University Press, 1970), 25–29. Available at http://founders.archives.gov/documents/Franklin/01-14-02-0019 (accessed 8 February 2017).

6   See, for example, Samuel Renshaw, "The Visual Perception and Reproduction of Forms by Tachistoscopic Methods," *The Journal of Psychology*, Volume 20 (1945), 217–232; V. Ramachandran and S. Cobb, "Visual Attention Modulates Metacontrast Masking, *Nature* (January 1995, 66–68; and John Shelley-Tremblay and Arien Mack, "Metacontrast Masking and Attention," *Psychological Science*, Volume 10 (November, 1999), 508–515.

7   See, for example, C.P. Whaley, "Word-Nonword Classification Time," *Journal of Memory and Language*, Volume 17 (1978), 143–154; and J. Grainger, "Word Frequency and Neighborhood Frequency Effects in Lexical Decision and Naming," *Journal of Memory and Language*, Volume 29 (1990), 228–244. Also see Stephen E. Palmer, *Vision Science: Photons to Phenomenology* (Cambridge, Mass: MIT Press, 1999).

8   The meme appears to have originated in a dissertation by G.E. Rawlinson that examined the phenomenon, "The Significance of Letter Position in Word Recognition." Ph.D. Thesis (Nottingham, UK: Psychology Department, University of Nottingham, 1976). Matt Davis, a program leader at the Medical Research Council's Cognition and Brain Sciences Unit attempted to sort out the meme; see http://www.mrc-cbu.cam.ac.uk/people/matt.davis/cmabridge/ (accessed 30 January 2015).

9   Leo X. McCusker, Phillip B. Gough, and Randolph G. Bias, "Word Recognition Inside Out and Outside In," *Journal of Experimental Psychology: Human Perception and Performance*, Volume 77 (June 1981), 538–551; and Alice F. Healy, "Detection Errors on the Word *the:* Evidence for Reading Units Larger than Letters," *Journal of Experimental Psychology*, Volume 2 (May 1976), 235–242.

10   See Ulric Neisser, *Cognitive Psychology: Classic Edition* (New York: Psychology Press, 2014), a reprint of the 1967 text that some believe first captured the core principles of the field.

11   William Playfair, *The Commercial and Political Atlas*, Second Edition (London: John Stockdale, 1787), 5.

12   Ibid., 6.

13   Review of "The Commercial and Political Atlas; representing by means of stained Cop-per-plate Charts, the Exports, Imports, and general Trade of England; the National Debt, and other public Accounts; with Observations and Remarks. By William Playfair," in *The Monthly Review or Literary Journal*, Volume 78 (January–June, 1788), 505–509. Also see the review of "An Essay on the National Debt, with Copper-plate Charts, for comparing Annuities with perpetual Loans, By William Playfair," in *Monthly Review*, Volume 77 (January–June, 1789), 414. Playfair credited Priestly for the idea of a chronological metric arrayed along a horizontal axis; see William Playfair, *An Inquiry into the Permanent Causes of the Decline and Fall of Powerful and Wealthy Nations* (London: Greenland and Norris, 1805), 78.

14   Playfair, *Atlas*, Second Edition, 114.

15   See Edward R. Tufte, *The Visual Display of Quantitative Information* (Cheshire, Connecti-cut: Graphics Press, 1983), 53–77; and Howard Wainer, *Graphic Discovery: A Trout in the Milk and Other Visual Adventures* (Princeton, N.J.: Princeton University Press, 2005), 28–38. Wainer offers a literature review, crediting the earliest discussion of distortion in graphics to Willard C. Brinton, *Graphic Methods for Presenting Facts* (New York: Mc-Graw-Hill, 1914). Wainer also cites Calvin F. Schmid, *Statistical Graphics: Design Prin-ciples and Practices* (New York: John Wiley & Sons, 1983) and William S. Cleveland, *The Elements of Graphing Data* (Summit, N.J.: Hobart Press, 1994).

16   Playfair to Watt (Howland Street, 20 September 1785), LB MS 3219/4/94.

17   James Watt to William Playfair (10 October 1785), LB MS 3219/4/123 (Letter Book).

18   William Playfair, *A Real Statement of the Finances and Resources of Great Britain* (London: C. Whittingham, 1796), 19.

19   James Williams, "Holroyd, John Baker, First Earl Sheffield (1735–1821)" in Sidney Lee, ed., *Dictionary of National Biography*, Volume 27 (New York: Macmillan, 1891), 200–202.

20   The copy I used is from the University of London library, and imaged by Gale/Cengage Learning. The inscription in on the first page and is in Playfair's handwriting.

21   Patrick Colquhoun to William Playfair (16 October 1786). UG Patrick Colquhoun Copy Letter Book; MS Murray 551. (Underlining in original.)

22   Ἰατρος. (pseudonym), *A Biographical Sketch of the Life and Writings of Patrick Colquhoun, Esq., LL.D.* (London: G. Smeeton, 1818), 5–10.

23   To get a sense of the interconnections and interactions, take a look at the correspon-dence among Jeremy Bentham, Charles Abbot, and William Wickham in June 1799, reproduced in John Bowring, ed., *The Works of Jeremy Bentham*, Volume 10, 329–333. Col-quhoun went on to write *Treatise on the Police of the Metropolis*. It became a guide for cities worldwide, going through seven printings in ten years.

24   Colquhoun to Playfair (16 October 1786), UG MS Murray 551. Colquhoun might have written "proves" rather than "provides." The reference to Sheffield occurs at the beginning of the letter.

25   Fitzmaurice, *Life of William, Earl of Shelburne*, Volume 1, 96–97.

26   See John Rae, *Life of Adam Smith* (London: Macmillan, 1895), 153. Rae, who gets credit for the "Road to Damascas" metaphor, refers to Dugald Stewart, "Account of the Life and Writings of Adam Smith, LL.D.," in *Transactions of the Royal Society of Edinburgh*, read 21 Jan 1793 and 18 Mar 1793, reproduced in Sir William Hamilton, ed., *The Collected Works of Dugald Stewart*, Volume 10 (Edinburgh: Thomas Constable and Company, 1858).

27 Fitzmaurice describes the negotiations and maneuvers leading to Shelburne's creation as Marquis of Lansdowne in *Life of William, Earl of Shelburne,* Volume 2, 290–294; he describes Bentham's role in the Bowood Circle, 315–316.

28 For his account of these sessions, see William Playfair, *France As It Is, Not Lady Morgan's France,* Volume 2 (London: C. Chapple, 1820), 314–315.

29 Stewart and John Playfair joined the already-established Oyster Club and later formed their own Friday Club. See Gordon Macintyre, *Dugald Stewart: The Pride and Ornament of Scotland* (Brighton, UK: Sussex Academic Press, 2003), 122.

30 Dugald Stewart to Benjamin Vaughan (c. 1786), NLS, MS 2521, fol.171–2. Stewart says in the letter that he met William Playfair "last winter." Though the letter has no date, Macintyre places it chronologically in the context of other events; see his *Dugald Stewart,* 46–53. The letter thus implies Playfair was in Edinburgh in late 1785 or early 1786, and met Stewart. As wil be seen, Stewart was effusive in his praise for Playfair.

31 Fitzmaurice, *Life of William, Earl of Shelburne,* Volume 2, 165.

32 See George S. Rowell, "Benjamin Vaughan—Patriot, Scholar, Diplomat," *The Magazine of History with Notes and Queries* (March 1916), 43–57. The reference to strawberries is on 44.

33 Stewart to Vaughan (c. 1786), NLS, MS 2521, fol.171–2.

34 In particular, see Jean-François Dunyach's analysis in "William Playfair (1759–1823), Scottish Enlightenment from Below?" in Allan I. Macinnes and Douglas J. Hamilton, eds., *Jacobitism, Enlightenment and Empire, 1680–1820* (New York: Pickering & Chatto, 2014), 167–168.

35 Edward A. Ross, "Sinking Funds," *Publications of the American Economic Association,* Volume 7 (July–September, 1892), 1–20.

36 For background on Barré and the Lansdowne-Barré relationship, see "BARRE, Isaac (1726–1802), of Manchester Buildings, Westminster," in R. G. Thorne, *The History of Parliament: the House of Commons 1790–1820* (London: Boydell & Brewer, 1964).Available at http://www.historyofparliamentonline.org/volume/1754-1790/member/barrea-cute-isaac-1726-1802 (accessed 17 February 2016).

37 Playfair, *France As It Is,* Volume 2, 314.

38 William Playfair, *An Essay on the National Debt, with Copper Plate Charts, for Comparing Annuities with Perpetual Loans* (London: J. Debrett and G.G.J and J. Robinson, 1787), iii–iv. Landowne also had Playfair meet with Richard Price—an expert on demography and finance, and another member of Lansdowne's network—when he returned to London; see Dunyach, "Scottish Enlightenment from Below?" 168

39 Playfair, *Atlas,* Second Edition, 28. Playfair writes that he "received a letter" from "a noble Lord, once high in administration" about a section he was drafting on taxes. That was Lansdowne. For Lansdowne's opposition to war with France, see William B. Willcox, "Lord Lansdowne on the French Revolution and the Irish Rebellion," *Journal of Modern History* Volume 17 (March 1945), 29–36. Willcox reproduced twenty-three letters Lansdowne wrote to banker Thomas Coutts between 1793 and 1798. Lansdowne was skeptical of any war; once underway, he would make the darkest prenogstications of its outcome. As Lansdowne put it to Coutts, the conflict with France was "a war of opinion, and must be met by opinion and not by force."

40 William Playfair, *Joseph and Benjamin in Conversation* (London: J. Murray, 1787). Two decades later Playfair listed it as a "no name" publication (that is, anonymous) in a letter to the Literary Fund, so it would have been known among that limited circle. See William Playfair to David Williams (Old Brompton, 13 May 1807), BL © The British Library Board (BLB). Loan 96 RLF 1/121

41 Playfair, *Joseph and Benjamin*, 38.

42 *The Critical Review* Volume 65 (1788), 395.

43 *The Monthly Review* Volume 78 (January 1788), 257.

44 See "A Look Back...Benjamin Franklin: Founding Father of Covert Action," available at https://www.cia.gov/news-information/featured-story-archive/benjamin-franklin.html (accessed 2 January 2015).

45 William Temple Franklin, *Memoirs of the Life and Writings of Benjamin Franklin, LL.D.* (London: Henry Colburn, 1818), 318.

46 "Memorandum of Dr. Franklin," (de petit Luxembourg, 26 May 1777), reproduced in John Bigelow, ed., *The Complete Works of Benjamin Franklin*, Volume 10 (New York: G.P. Putnam's Sons, 1888), 343–344.

47 Playfair, *Joseph and Benjamin*, 38, 83–86.

48 For Morellet's role in the Treaty of Paris and Shelburne's gratitude, see Playfair memoirs, fol. 1.; and Fitzmaurice, *Life of William, Earl of Shelburne*, Volume 2, 264. Also see "Morellet (L'Abbé André)," *Musée des variétés littéraires*, Volume 5 (London: Samuel Leigh, 1824), 102.

49 Playfair recalled the encounter in Playfair memoirs, fols. 1–2. For Morellet's version, see Abbé Morellet to Lansdowne (27 June 1787), reproduced in Lord Edmond Fitzmaurice, ed., *Lettres de l'Abbé Morellet de L'académie Francaise to Lord Shelburne Depuis Marquis de Lansdowne, 1772–1813.* (Paris: Librairie Plon, 1898), 240–244.

50 W.O. Henderson, "The Anglo-French Commercial Treaty of 1786," *The Economic History Review* Volume 10, No. 1 (1957), 108. The treaty is also known as the Eden Agreement, after Britain's chief negotiator, William Eden, 1st Baron Auckland.

51 Playfair wrote that he arrived in Paris "two months" after the Commercial Treaty went into force; see Playfair memoirs, fol. 30. In a letter to Lansdowne shortly after the event, Morellet said he met Playfair in late June; see Morellet to Lansdowne (27 June 1787) in Fitzmaurice, *Lettres de L'Abbé Morellet*, 240.

52 Munro Price, *Preserving the Monarchy: The Comte de Vergennes, 1774–1787* (Cambridge: Cambridge University Press, 1995), 228. Price cites F. Métra, *Correspondence Secréte, Politique et Littéraire*, Volume 2 (18 vols., London: 1787–90), 108.

53 Playfair memoirs, fol. 30.

54 This section is based on Playfair memoirs, fol. 3. Playfair recalled these events took place when he "had not been two months in Paris." Playfair seems to identify his French interlocutor as "d'Ajeux," although I've found no other record of such a person, and deciphering Playfair's inscrutable handwriting is more art than science. The context suggests the "Mr. Cecil" to whom Playfair referred was Henry Cecil, later 1st Earl of Exeter and 1st Marquess of Exeter.

55 This section is also based on Playfair memoirs, fol 3. The Frenchman, "M. Gérentet," would be Playfair's partner in the Société de Gérentet et Playfair; he's mentioned in Fernand Evrard, *Collection de Documents Inédits Relatifs a l'Histoire Économique de la Révolu-*

tion (Paris: Ernest Le Roux, 1935), 197; J. Bouchary, "Les Compagnies financieres a Paris a la fin du XVIII siècle," *Annales historiques de le Révolution Française* (May–June 1940), 129; and Fernand Évrard, *Versailles, ville du roi (1770–1789)* (Paris: Librairie Ernest Le-roux, 1935), 197. In his memoirs, Playfair recalled Gérentet, "whom I had known in Bir-mingham as a maker of coloured foil and who had a manufactory of ballons in Paris." Playfair was referring to piloted balloons—not the toy kind—which had just begun to appear in Birmingham in 1785; see Robert K. Dent, *The Making of Birmingham: Being a History of the Rise & Growth of the Midland Metropolis* (London: J.L. Allday, 1894), 180. Jean-François Dunyach writes that Gérentet had been in Birmingham to set up a busi-ness to make paper for balloons; see his "Les réaux d'un excentrique: vies et parcours de William Playfair (1759–1823)," in Ann Thomson, Simon Burrows, and Edmond Dziem-bowski, eds, *Cultural Transfers: France and Britain in the Long Eighteenth Century* (Oxford, UK: Voltaire Foundation, 2010), 121.

56 Playfair memoirs, fol. 4. Playfair described his interlocutor as "the author of a Voyage to Italy and Malta which had been published with views at the price of 1200 livres or 504.6 a copy." That's likely Jean-Claude Richard, Abbé St. Non, a painter and engraver, who self-published a lavish book of travel drawings, *Voyage Pittoresque à Naples et en Sicile* (Paris: 1781)

57 Playfair identified Breteuil as "Minister of the Interior" in his memoirs, fol. 4. Breteuil had a wide range of responsibilities and Playfair, as will be seen, knew Breteuil well, but when writing thirty years later apparently misremembered his title or didn't make a distinction.

58 Emma Orczy, *El Dorado: An Adventure of the Scarlet Pimpernel* (New York: Hodder & Stoughton, 1913). A fictional de Batz also appears in Rafael Sabatini, *Scaramouche the Kingmaker* (New York: Houghton Mifflin, 1931); Willa Gibbs, *Seed of Mischief* (New York: Farrar, Straus, and Young, 1953); and other novels. To keep all of this perspective, remember that, when Playfair was writing his memoirs, Batz was well-known as a count-er-revolutionary but had not gained action-hero status.

59 Orczy, *El Dorado*, viii.

60 See G. Lenôtre, *Un Conspirateur Royaliste pendant le Terreur: le Baron de Batz 1792–1795* (Paris: Perrin et s., 1896), 387–391. This appears to be the earliest book-length biography of Batz. "G. Lenôtre" was the pen name of Louis Léon Théodore Gosselin, the author of popular, scholarly books using primary sources; he is generally respected by historians, and often cited. "Mrs. Rodolph Stawell" (Maud Margaret Key Stawell) published a very readable English translation, *A Gascon Royalist in Revolutionary Paris, the Baron de Batz, 1792–1795* (London: William Heinemann, 1910).

René, Baron de Batz (1865–1928, descedent and heir of Jean), said he used Lenôtre's work, official documents, and family papers for his two-volume biography, *La vie et les conspirations de Jean, baron de Batz 1754–1793* (Paris: Calmann-Lévy, 1908); and *Les con-spirations et la fin de Jean, Baron de Batz, 1793–1822* (Paris: Calmann-Lévy, 1911). René also used accounts that had been passed down word of mouth, but which he asserted were substantiated by circumstances or by the authority of the people offering them (See René's comments, *La vie et les conspirations de Jean, baron de Batz 1754–1793*, xii.)

Also see Meade Minnigerode, *Marie Antoinette's Henchman: The Career of Jean, Baron de Batz in the French Revolution* (New York: Farrar & Rinehart, 1936), 300–303. Minnigerode's book does not provide references, but the author said it is based on French histories and Batz family papers, including the afore-mentioned biographies by René.

61   Playfair memoirs, fol. 4.

62   Ibid., fols. 4–5.

63   Ibid.

64   William Playfair, *A Fair and Candid Address to the Nobility and Baronets of the United Kingdom... of the Advantages of Hereditary Rank and Title in a Free Country* (London: Proprietors of Family Antiquity, 1809), 25.

65   Ibid.

66   See Bouchary, "Les Compagnies financières," 129. Bouchary reports that, "William Playfair, installé dans la capitale plusieurs années avant la Revolution, avait obtenu le 5 avril 1788 des lettres patentes du roi l' autorisant a constituer une société pour l'établissement d'un moulin a laminer et polir les métaux en France, entreprise qui avait vu le jour le 5 juin suivant sous le nom de Société de Gérentet et Playfair," which translates as "William Playfair, who arrived in the capital several years before the Revolution, had obtained from the King on 5 April 1788 letters patent authorizing him to form a company to establish a rolling mill and metal finishing facility in France; the business was established on 5 June under the name Société of Gérentet and Playfair." Bouchary cites Archives de la Seine, D Q 10, carton 1443, dossier 3.128. Also see William Playfair, *Lineal Arithmetic: Applied to Shew the Progress of the Commerce and Revenue of England During the Present Century* (London: A. Paris, 1798), 6; and Playfair memoirs, fol. 4–5.

Chapter 3: Accidental Revolutionaries

1   François Guizot and Henriette Guizot de Witt, *History of France*, Volume 5 (New York: P.F. Collier & Son, 1902), 359; and Henri Martin, *History of France, from the Most Remote Period to 1789* Volume 2 (Boston: Walker, Fuller, and Company, 1866), 542.

2   No one seems to have published a biography of Jean-Jacques d'Eprémesnil in English, though Jeremy Popkin discusses his political activities at some length in "The *Gazette de Leyde* and French Politics Under Louis XVI," in Jack R. Censer and Jeremy D. Popkin, eds., *Press and Politics in Pre-Revolutionary France* (Berkeley, CA: University of California Press, 1987), 75–132. Henri Carré published a profile in French, depicting d'Eprémesnil as a defender of tradition and the prerogatives of magistrates: see his "Un précurseur inconscient de la revolution, Le Counseiller du val d'Eprémesnil," in F.A. Aulard, ed., *La Révolution française: revue d'histoire moderne et contemporaine* (Paris: Société de L'histoire de La Révolution Française, 1897), 349–373 and 405–437.

3   See Price, *Preserving the Monarchy*, 124 for d'Eprémesnil's critique of his colleagues. Also see Robert Choate Darnton, "Trends in Radical Propaganda on the Eve of the French Revolution (1782–1788), Ph.D. thesis, Nuffield College, Oxford (Trinity Term 1964), 303–314.

4   This section draws from Robert Darnton, *Mesmerism and the End of the Enlightenment in France* (Cambridge, Massachusetts: Harvard University Press, 1968), 48–62; and Darnton, "Trends in Radical Propaganda," 1–8.

5   James R. Gaines, *For Liberty and Glory: Washington, Lafayette, and Their Revolutions* (New York: W.W. Norton, 2007), 225.

6   Eloise Ellery, *Brissot de Warville: A Study in the History of the French Revolution* (Boston: Houghton Mifflin Company, 1915), 216–302.

7   Darnton, *Mesmerism,* 79.

8   See Eugene Nelson White, "Was There a Solution to the *Ancien Régime's* Financial Dilemma?" *The Journal of Economic History* Volume 49 (September 1989), 545–568. According to White, France's situation, while dire, could have been salvaged with some modest measures.

9   These are commonly accepted estimates; take them with a grain of salt, as recordkeeping was spotty at best.

10 J.H. Shennan, *The Parlement of Paris* (Ithaca, New York: Cornell University Press, 1968), 9–49.

11 Ibid., 312. Also see William Doyle, "The Parlements of France and the Breakdown of the Old Regime 1771–1788," *French Historical Studies,* Volume 6 (Autumn, 1970), 415–458

12 Martin, *History of France,* Volume 16, 544.

13 Thomas Carlyle seems to be responsible for the legend that d'Eprémesnil and Goeslard exfiltrated via the shingles of Paris; see *The French Revolution: The Bastille,* Volume 1 (London: George Bell and Sons, 1902), 120. The site of the Palais de la Cité is now home to the Palais de justice.

14 Bailey S. Stone, *The French Parlements and the Crisis of the Old Regime* (Chapel Hill: University of North Carolina Press, 2011), 10–11; Martin, *History of France,* Volume 2, 546–547. For d'Agoult's side of the story, Carré cites his *Histoire du siege du palais* (1788), which is available at http://gallica.bnf.fr/ark:/12148/bpt6k471044.r=Histoire%20du%20 siege%20du%20PalaisHistoire%20du%20siege%20du%20Palais%20par%20le%20Cap-itaine%20d%27Agoult%2C%20Histoire%20du%20siege%20du%20Palais%20par%20 le%20Capitaine%20d%27Agoult%2C?rk=21459;2 (accessed 10 April 2017).

15 William Doyle, *The Origins of the French Revolution* (Oxford, UK: Oxford University Press, 1999), 113–114.

16 See Carré, "Un précurseur inconscient de la revolution," 426–430.

17 See Playfair, *The Playfair Family,* 43. It lists the birthdate for Zenobia as 1792, but official records from ancestry.co.uk indicate 1795.

18 Playfair, *Real Statement,* iv–v; and Playfair, *Lineal Arithmatic,* 6. Also see William Playfair, *A Letter to the People of England on the Revolution in France* (London: J. Debrett, 1792), 23; Playfair identified his friend here only as a "member of the academy of sciences who thinks himself a great man in knowledge of governments," but the context says it's Vandermonde.

19 Quotations regarding Vandermonde are from Playfair memoirs, fol. 8.

20 Playfair, *Letter to the People of England,* 8.

21 Fernand Évrard, *Versailles, ville du roi (1770–1789)* (Paris: Librairie Ernest Leroux, 1935), 196–197.

22 Dickinson and Jenkins, *Watt and the Steam Engine,* 66.

23 Playfair memoirs, fol. 35; Batz, *La vie et les conspirations 1754–1793,* 52–53; and Minnigerode, *Marie Antoinette's Henchman,* 7. And to complete the circle: Louis-Léon was a committed Anglophile. He spent much of his time in Britain, where he developed a close relationship with…Lord Shelburne. See C.H. Lockitt, *The Relations of French and English Society, 1763–1793* (London: Longmans, Green and Co., 190), 13.

24 William Playfair, *The History of Jacobinism, Its Crimes, Cruelties, and Perfidies* (London: John Stockdale, 1795), 214.

25 For some insight into Réveillon's background, see Leonard N. Rosenband, "Jean-Baptiste Réveillon: A Man on the Make in Old Regime France," *Historical Studies*, Volume 20 (Summer 1997), 481–510; and William Doyle, *The Oxford History of the French Revolution* (Oxford, UK: Oxford University Press, 1989), 98.

26 For a discussion of the development of the faubourgs and the demography of Paris in the late 1700s, see George Rudé, *The Crowd in the French Revolution* (New York: Oxford University Press, 1959), 10–20.

27 The first census of Paris was conducted in 1801, but the 1789 population can be roughly approximated by extrapolating backward. For a sense of living conditions, see David Garrioch, *The Making of Revolutionary Paris* (Los Angeles: University of California Press, 2002).

28 For Réveillon's remark and employment practices, see Hippolyte Adolphe Taine, *The French Revolution* (New York: Henry Holt and Company, 1878), 27–28. For wages in Paris, see Daniel Roche, *The People of Paris: An Essay in Popular Culture in the 18th Century* (Berkeley: University of California Press, 1987), 108.

29 Body counts varied because of chaos or because the various parties had an interest in exaggerating or understating how much violence took place—or simply because no one was really responsible for collecting valid data. In any event, see Rudé, *Crowd in the French Revolution*, 35–39; Taine, *French Revolution*, Volume 1, 28–30; Marquis de Ferrières, *Correspondence inédite, 1789, 1790, 1791* (Paris: Librairie Armand Colin, 1932), 37–41; and Doyle, *Oxford History*, 98.

30 Theodore A. Zunder, "Joel Barlow and Seasickness," *Yale Journal of Biology and Medicine*, Volume 1 (July 1929) 385–390. The original passage from his journal can be found in the Barlow papers, Diary; MS Am 1448(9). Houghton Library (seq. 4). Available at http://nrs.harvard.edu/urn-3:FHCL.HOUGH:20292330?n=4 (accessed 28 August 2015).

31 Barlow papers, Diary; MS Am 1448(9). Houghton Library (seq. 5). Available at http://nrs.harvard.edu/urn-3:FHCL.HOUGH:20292330?n=5 (accessed 28 August 2015).

32 William Parker Cutler and Julia Perkins Cutler, *Life Journals and Correspondence of Rev. Manasseh Cutler, LLD*. Volume 1(Cincinnati: Robert Clarke & Co., 1888), 224–229.

33 William Frederick Poole, *The Ordinance of 1787 and Dr. Manasseh Cutler as an Agent in Its Formation* (Cambridge, Massachusetts: Welch, Bigelow, and Company, 1876), 20–24; and Joseph Stancliffe Davis, *Essays in the Earlier History of American Corporations*, Nos. 1–3 (Cambridge, Massachusetts: Harvard University Press, 1917), 132.

34 Davis, *Essays in American Corporations*, 126.

35 See Robert F. Jones, "William Duer and the Business of Government in the Era of the American Revolution," *William and Mary Quarterly* Vo. 32 (July 1975), 395–396.

36 Cutler and Cutler, *Manasseh Cutler*, Volume 1, 240–241. They cite Cutler's journal entry of 20 July 1787.

37 To wit: Economic historian Joseph Stancliffe Davis wrote that, "There is good reason to believe that by the close of the war he [Duer] was a wealthy man;" see his *Essays in American Corporations* 122. On the other hand, Robert F. Jones, Duer's biographer, thinks he may have inherited and earned a good deal of money, but lost a lot of it by deals gone bad

and debt; see his *The King of the Alley: William Duer: Politician, Entrepreneur, and Speculator 1768–1799* (Philadelphia: American Philosophical Society, 1992), 86–88.

38 See "Articles of Agreement of the Scioto Company," (New York, 29 October 1787) AAS Craigie Papers, Box 13, f. 3.; and Davis, *Essays in American Corporations*, 133–134.

39 Duer agreed to advance Cutler $100,000, but he wound up loaning him $143,000. See "Agreement Between Manasseh Cutler, Winthrop Sargent, and William Duer." (New York, 29 October 1787), GP, Volume 1, 99; and Davis, *Essays in American Corporations*, 139.

40 Cutler and Cutler, *Manasseh Cutler*, Volume 1, 494. They cite Cutler's journal entry of July 20, 1787.

41 Archer Butler Hulbert, "The Methods and Operations of the Scioto Group of Speculators," *The Mississippi Valley Historical Review*, Volume 1, No. 4 (March 1915), 502.

42 See Royal Flint to George Washington (Camp Rariton, New Jersey, 10 May 1779), reproduced in *Papers of George Washington*, Volume 20 (Charlottesville: University of Virginia Press), 419–421. Available at http://founders.archives.gov/documents/Washington/03-20-02-0362 (accessed 6 August 2015).

43 Anthony J. Connors, "Andrew Craigie: Brief Life of a Patriot and Scoundrel: 1754–1819," *Harvard Magazine* (November–December 2011), available at http://harvardmagazine.com/2011/11/andrew-craigie (accessed 6 August 2015).

44 Hulbert, "Methods and Operations" (March, 1915), 506.

45 See "Articles of Agreement of the Scioto Company," (New York, 29 October 1787) AAS Craigie Papers, Box 13, f. 3. There are three signatories to the agreement: Duer, Cutler, and Winthrop Sargent, another partner in the Ohio Company. Richard Platt (Ohio Company treasurer) and Royal Flint (Duer's associate) signed as witnesses. Neither Duer nor Flint gave an affiliation.

46 See, for example, "Commission of Benjamin Walker," Wm. Duer, Royal Flint, and Wm. Craigie to Benjamin Walker (New York, 11 September 1790), GP, Volume 1, 149.

47 See Peter Hill, *Joel Barlow: American Diplomat and Nation Builder* (Dulles, Virginia: Potomac Books, Inc. 2012), 14.

48 Cutler and Cutler, *Manasseh Cutler*, Volume 1, 381–382.

49 Joel Barlow, *The Vision of Columbus: A Poem in Nine Books* (Hartford: Printed for the Author by Hudson and Goodwin, 1787). Available at https://archive.org/details/visioncolumbusa00barlgoog (accessed 5 January 2017). Also see .James Woodress, *A Yankee's Odyssey: The Life of Joel Barlow* (Philadelphia: J.B. Lippincott Company, 1958), 85.

50 See, for example, Joel Barlow to Ruth (Baldwin) Barlow (Near Paramus, 11 September 1780). Barlow Papers, MS Am 1448(126) http://nrs.harvard.edu/urn-3:FHCL.HOUGH:23521649 (accessed 28 August 2016).

51 Charles Burr Todd, *Life and Letters of Joel Barlow, LL.D.: Poet, Statesman, Philosopher* (New York: G.P. Putnam's Sons, 1886), 36–37.

52 Theodore A. Zunder, "Joel Barlow and George Washington," *Modern Language Notes* (April 1929), 255.

53 Woodress, *Yankee's Odyssey*, 58–59. Barlow, Humphreys and others would later form a humor society, the Hartford Wits.

54 George Washington to Marquis de Lafayette (Mt. Vernon, 28 May 1788), reproduced in John C Fitzpatrick, ed., *The Writings of George Washington from the Original Manuscript*

Sources, 1745–1799, Volume 29 (Washington, DC: U.S. Government Printing Office, 1939), 506.

55   Barlow papers, Diary; MS Am 1448(9). Houghton Library (seq. 34). Available at http://nrs.harvard.edu/urn-3:FHCL.HOUGH:20292330?n=34 (accessed 29 August 2015).

56   Todd, *Life and Letters of Joel Barlow*, 74. Barlow was delivering George Washington Greene, son of Revolutionary War hero General Nathanael Greene, to Jefferson and Lafayette, for schooling in Europe.

57   Jones, *King of the Alley*, 80, 98–100.

58   Todd, *Life and Letters of Joel Barlow*, 70.

59   Barlow papers, Diary; MS Am 1448(9). Houghton Library (seq. 77). Available at http://nrs.harvard.edu/urn-3:FHCL.HOUGH:20292330?n=77 (accessed 28 August 2015).

60   Barlow papers, Diary; MS Am 1448(9). Houghton Library (seq. 73). Available at http://nrs.harvard.edu/urn-3:FHCL.HOUGH:20292330?n=73 (accessed 28 August 2015).

61   Barlow papers, Diary; MS Am 1448(9). Houghton Library (seq. 103–105). Available at https://iiif.lib.harvard.edu/manifests/view/drs:51762155$103i (accessed 22 September 2016).

62   See Gregg L. Lint et al, eds., *The Adams Papers* Volume 13 (Cambridge, Massachusetts: The Belknap Press of Harvard University Press, 2006), x–xi, xv–xix.

63   Henry M. Wriston, "The Special Envoy," *Foreign Affairs* (January 1960). Available at https://www.foreignaffairs.com/articles/1960-01-01/special-envoy (accessed 26 November 2015).

64   Gouverneur Morris, *The Diary and Letters of Gouverneur Morris* Volume 1 (New York: Charles Scribner's Sons, 1888), 18.

65   Playfair memoirs, fol. 1.

66   Thomas Byerley, "An Account of the French Settlements on the Sioto," *The Colonial Journal*, Volume 3 (March 1817), 376.

67   Playfair memoirs, fol. 8. Playfair does not identify his dinner host beyond his last name, but the context makes clear it was Étienne Delessert, one of the most respected bankers in France. Delessert specialized in commercial and industrial investments, so it was natural for the two to hit it off. See *Encyclopedia Britannica*, Volume 7 (Cambridge, UK: Cambridge University Press, 1910) 953–954. Available at https://archive.org/details/encyclopaediabrit07chisrich (accessed 3 June 2015)

68   See "Académie des Sciences. Eloge historique de Benjamin Delessert, par M. Flourens, secrétaire perpetual," *Le Semeur, Journal Philosophique et Litteraire*, Volume 19 (1 January–31 August 1850), 79–80. Also see the website for the Institut Benjamin Delessert, available at http://www.institut-benjamin-delessert.net/fr/institut/qui-etait-benjamin-delessert/index.html. For Benjamin Delessert's acquaintance with John Playfair, see *Biographie Univerelle (Michaud) Ancienne et Moderne* Volume 10 (Paris: Chez Madame C. Desplaces, 1855), 319, available at http://gallicalabs.bnf.fr/ark:/12148/bpt6k51650f (accessed 2 June 2015).

69   See J. Marc McDonald, "Crossroads of Enlightenment 1685–1850: Exploring Education, Science, and Industry Across the Delessert Network," Ph.D. Dissertation, Department of History, University of Saskatchewan (March 2015), 18. McDonald drew on the Delessert family papers. For the Boulton-Delessert connection, see Peter M. Jones, "Living the Enlightenment and the French Revolution: James Watt, Matthew Boulton, and Their Sons,"

The Historical Journal), Volume 42, No. 1 (1999), 167; Jones cites an undated draft letter from Matthew Boulton to Madame Delessert, BCL Matthew Boulton Papers 242 Letter Box L1. For the Delessert geneology, see "DELESSERT famille - Cimetières de France et d'ailleurs" available at https://www.landrucimetieres.fr/spip/spip.php?article2840 (accessed 5 January 2017). Benjamin Delessert would become one of France's most famous industrialists and, later, one of its most famous philanthropists.

70   Robert Darnton, *George Washington's False Teeth: An Unconventional Guide to the Eighteenth Century* (New York: Norton, 2003), 144.

71   Owen Connelly, *The French Revolution and Napoleonic Era* (Boston: Wadsworth, 2000), 70.

72   Stockdale published an English edition of Berquin's most famous work, *L'Ami des Enfans.* See Eric Stockdale, *'Tis Treason, My Good Man! Four Revolutionary Presidents and a Piccadilly Bookshop* (London: Oak Knoll Press, 2005), 213–214.

73   This section is based on Playfair memoirs, fol. 8.

74   The scene was captured in a widely reproduced engraving, *L'Ouverture des États Généraux à Versailles le 5 Mai 1789* by Isidore-Stanislaus Helman, which was based on a drawing by Charles Monnet. See the website of Bibliothèque nationale de France: http://gallica.bnf.fr/ark:/12148/btv1b69426650/ (accessed 17 June 2015).

75   Playfair, *History of Jacobinism,* 82.

76   Ibid., 63–64.

77   Carré, "Un précurseur inconscient de la revolution," 435–437; and Shennan, *Parlement of Paris,* 322–324.

78   Playfair, *History of Jacobinism,* 742.

79   R.B. Rose, *The Making of the Sans-Culottes* (Manchester, UK: Manchester University Press, 1983), 47.

80   Playfair, *History of Jacobinism,* 140.

81   Frantz Funck-Bretano, George Maidment, trans. *Legends of the Bastille* (London: Downey & Co., 1899) 246.

82   Rose, *The Making of the Sans-Culottes,* 51. Rose ascertained that twenty-seven of sixty districts raised a militia.

83   William Playfair, *Letter to the People of England,* 47–48.

84   Quoted in Funck-Brentano, *Legends of the Bastille,* 253.

85   Playfair, *History of Jacobinism,* 141–155.

86   Ibid., 145.

87   Ibid., 147.

88   Thomas Jefferson to John Jay (Paris, 19 July 1789), reproduced in *The Papers of Thomas Jefferson,* Volume 15 (Princeton: Princeton University Press, 1958), 284–291. Available at http://founders.archives.gov/documents/Jefferson/01-15-02-0277 (accessed 20 June 2015).

89   *London Gazette* (18–22 July 1795), 501.

90   Playfair, *History of Jacobinism,* 148.

91   *London Gazette* (18–22 July 1795), 501.

92   Heinrich vn Sybel, *History of the French Revolution* English edition, Volume 1 (London: John Murray, 1867), 75.

93   Playfair, *History of Jacobinism,* 148–149.

94 Ibid., 148–149.
95 Ibid., 149–150.
96 Ibid., 150–151.
97 Ibid., 151.
98 Ibid., 743–745.
99 Georges Lecocq, *La prise de la Bastille et ses anniversaires d'après des documents inédits* (Paris: Charavay Freres Editeurs, 1881), 270. Also see Rose, *The Making of the Sans-Culottes* (Manchester, UK: Manchester University Press, 1983), 51. Rose independently analyzed the rosters and found Playfair among those reporting to Petit Sainte-Antoine. Rose cited AN C 134 Dossier 1. John G. Alger also placed Playfair in the storming in *Englishmen in the French Revolution* (London: Sampson Low, Marston, Dearle & Rivington, 1889), 10–11.
100 Playfair, *Letter to the People of England*, 5.
101 Playfair, *History of Jacobinism*, 214.
102 See Georges Lefebvre, *The Great Fear of 1789: Rural Panic in Revolutionary France* (Princeton, NJ: Princeton University Press, 1972). This is a translation of Lefebvre's 1932 study.
103 James Watt, Jr. to Matthew Boulton (Manchester, 4 December 1789), reproduced in Dickinson and Jenkins, *Watt and the Steam Engine*, 71.
104 James Keir to Matthew Boulton (Chacewater, near Truro, Cornwall 11 December 1779), LB MS 3782/12/65/44.
105 A.E. Musson and Eric Robinson, "Training Captains of Industry: The Education of Matthew Robinson Boulton (1770–1842) and James Watt, Junior (1769–1848)," in A.E. Musson and Eric Robinson, eds., *Science and Technology in the Industrial Revolution* (Manchester: University of Manchester Press, 1969), 202. They cite a letter from James Watt to an unnamed schoolmaster (Birmingham, 5 August 1780) Doldowlod Papers.Junior did not go to the Shifnal school, though Watt may have enrolled him elsewhere.
106 Musson and Robinson, "Training Captains of Industry", 203. They cite a letter from James Watt to Rev. Mr. Dean (Birmingham, 2 November 1780) Doldowlod Papers.
107 Musson and Robinson, "Training Captains of Industry," 206–207. They cite BRL James Watt to James Watt, Jr. (17 July 1785).
108 Musson and Robinson, "Training Captains of Industry," 203–205.
109 Jones, "Living the Enlightenment," 155–167. Jones cites James Watt to James Watt, Jr. (Birmingham, 15 October 1786), BCL Muirhead IV, Box 15.
110 Musson and Robinson, "Training Captains of Industry," 206–207. They cite BRL James Watt to James Watt, Jr. (13 March 1785).
111 Quoted in Jones, "Living the Enlightenment," 167. Jones cites James Watt to James Watt, Junior (Birmingham, 15 Oct 1786) BCL James Watt Papers, Muirhead IV Box 13.
112 See Jones, "Living the Enlightenment," 166; Jones quotes Anne Watt to James Watt, Jr. (Birmingham, 15 March 1786), BCL Muirhead IV, Box 15.
113 For Junior's barber fetish, see Richard Hills, "Dalton's Manchester: The First Industrial City" (Presented at the Manchester Association of Engineers, 154th Session Transaction (24 November 2009), 19.
114 See Jones, "Living the Enlightenment," 167; Jones quotes James Watt to James Watt, Jr. (Birmingham, 4 December 1785), BCL Muirhead IV, Box 15.

115 Edward J. Wood, *Curiosities of Clocks and Watches from the Earliest Times* (London: Richard Bentley, 1866), 342–343; and Roger Boutet de Monvel, *Beu Brummell and his Times* (London: Eveleigh Nash, 1908). Note in particular the chapter by Mary Craven on "Dress and the Dandies," 18–19.

116 William Playfair, *France as It Is, Not Lady Morgan's France,* Volume 1 (London: C Chapple, 1819), 96–97.

117 Jones, "Living the Enlightenment," 168. Jones quotes James Watt to James Watt, Jr., (Birmingham, 24 September 1788), BCL Muirhead IV, Box 15.

118 Jones, "Living the Enlightenment," 168. Jones quotes Matthew Robinson Boulton to Matthew Boulton (Stadtfeld, 18 November 1788), BCL Matthew Boulton Papers, 280.

119 See Richard Hills, "Dalton's Manchester: The First Industrial City," Paper presented at the 154th Session of the Transactions of the Manchester Association of Engineers (24 November 2009). Available at http://www.mae.uk.com/Daltons%20Manchester.PDF (accessed 8 August 2016). Hills quotes Charles Taylor to James Watt (Manchester, 7 October 1788), BCL James Watt Papers. James Watt Papers, W7.2.8.

120 For the return of James Watt, Junior, to Birmingham, see Jones, "Living the Enlightenment," 168. For his apprenticeship to Maxwell, Taylor, and Company, see A.E. Musson, "Chemical Developments in Dyeing," in Musson and Robinson, eds., *Science and Technology in the Industrial Revolution,* 344–345. Musson cites a letter from Thomas Henry to James Watt (23 October 1788), BCL Doldowlod Papers.

121 James Watt to James Watt, Junior (Birmingham, 31 December 1788), LB MS 3219/4/123. (Letter Book).

122 See Eric Robinson, "An English Jacobin: James Watt, Junior, 1769–1848," *Cambridge Historical Journal* Volume 11, No. 3 (1955), 350; and Jones, "Living the Enlightenment," 170.

123 For this summary judgment, see the usually restrained H. W. Dickinson and his co-author Arthur Titley, *Richard Trevithick: The Engineer and the Man* (Cambridge, UK: Cambridge University Press, 1934), 24. They were referring in this particular case to Junior's management style in his later years, but the quotation reflects their overall assessment of the man.

124 Robinson, "An English Jacobin," 350.

125 Unattributed, *Biographical Memoirs of Thomas Walker, Esq. of Manchester* (London: William Hone: Oxford University, 1820).

126 William Playfair gave his assessment of the *sans-culottes* in *A Short Account of the Revolt and Massacre Which Took Place in Paris on the 10th of August 1792* (London: John Stockdale, 1792), 10–11. Published anonymously in September 1792, Playfair identified himself as the author in a 1794 publication. Albert Soboul claimed that the term *sans-culotte* was actually coined many years after the Revolution by historians; see his *The Sans-Culottes* (New York: Doubleday & Company, 1972), xxi. Also see Rose, *The Making of the Sans-culottes,* passim.

Chapter 4: Feudal France on the Banks of the Ohio

1   For weather conditions in Alexandria, see Edward Naret, *History of the French Settlers at Gallipolis, Ohio, in 1790* (Cincinnati: Keating and Company, 1890), 8. Reprinted by the Ohio Valley Bank Co., 1990.

2   Beth Haney, trans., "Passenger List for the Ship *Patriot.*" Posted by the Gallia County Genealogical Society OGS Chapter, available at http://www.galliagenealogy.org/

French500/patriot.htm (accessed 19 June 2015); she lists 149 passengers. However, also see Lawrence J. Kenny, "The Gallipolis Colony (1790), *The Catholic Historical Review* Volume 4 (April 1918–January 1919), 430; he puts the number of passengers at 218.

3   Naret, *French Settlers at Gallipolis*, 8–9.

4   Beth Haney, trans., "Passenger List for the Ship *Liberty.*" Posted by the Gallia County Genealogical Society OGS Chapter, available at http://www.galliagenealogy.org/French500/Liberty.htm (accessed 19 June 2015).

5   *Virginia Gazette and Alexandria Advertiser* (13 May 1790), reproduced in Wesley E. Pippenger and James D. Munson, eds. (Westster MD.: Willow Bend Books, 2002), 69.

6   Kenny, "The Gallipolis Colony," 429. Also see *Virginia Gazette* (13 May 1790), in Pippenger and Munson, 69.

7   Henrietta C. Evans, "Introduction to 1790 Passenger Lists" Posted by the Gallia County Genealogical Society OGS Chapter, available at http://www.galliagenealogy.org/French500/french500.htm (accessed 28 August 2015).

8   *Prospectus pour l'etablissement sur les rivieres d'Ohio et de Scioto, en Amerique*, available at: https://archive.org/details/prospectuspourle00inscio (accessed 28 August 2015). At least one traveler brought a copy of the Prospectus (the document is in the Gallipolis Papers), though it is not clear on which ship he or she arrived.

9   The holder of the deed was on the first ship to arrive in Alexandria; see "Passenger List for the Ship *Patriot,*" available at http://www.galliagenealogy.org/French500/patriot.htm (accessed 24 August 2015). The manifest includes Jean Baptist Parmentier.

10   Daniel J. Ryan, "The Scioto Company and its Purchase," *The Centennial Anniversary of the City of Gallipolis, Ohio* Volume 3 (October 16–19, 1890), 123–125. Also see Bette W. Oliver, *Surviving the French Revolution: A Bridge Across Time* (Lanham, MD: Lexington Books, 2013), 36.

11   Library of Congress, *The Debates and Proceedings of the Congress of the United States* (Washington, DC: Gales and Seaton, 1849), 868–870; Available at https://memory.loc.gov/ammem/amlaw/lwaclink.html (accessed 8 August 2016); Library of Congress, *Journal of the House of Representatives of the United States, 1789–1793* (20 February 1793); Available at https://memory.loc.gov/ammem/amlaw/lwhjlink.html (accessed 8 August 2016); and Albion Morris Dyer, *First Ownership of Ohio Lands* (Boston : New England Historic Genealogical Society, 1911), 84–85.

12   John Rome to George Washington (Philadelphia, 6 March 1793), reproduced in *Papers of George Washington*, Volume 12. 272–274. Available at http://founders.archives.gov/documents/Washington/05-12-02-0211 (accessed 1 September 2015).

13   These quotations are from the petition, which is reproduced in Clarence Edwin Carter et al., eds., *The Territorial Papers of the United States*. Volume 2 (Washington, D.C: U.S. Government Printing Office, 1934), 422–28.

14   Jocelyne Moreau-Zanelli, *Gallipolis: L'histoire d'un mirage américain au XVIIIe siècle* (Paris: L'Harmattan, 2000), 294.

15   William Bradford, "French Settlers at Galliopolis [sic]" *American State Papers* "Public Lands, "Volume 1, 29–30. Available at http://memory.loc.gov/cgi-bin/ampage?collId=llsp&fileName=028/llsp028.db&recNum=32 (accessed 24 Aug 2015).

16   William E. Peters, *Ohio Lands and Their Subdivision* (Athens, Ohio: W.E. Peters, 1918), 180–183.

17   Richard Buel, Jr., *Joel Barlow: American Citizen in a Revolutionary World* (Baltimore, MD: Johns Hopkins University Press, 2011), 186.

18   John Bach McMaster, *A History of the People of the United States* Volume 2 (New York: A. Appleton and Company, 1885), 146–151.

19   Margaret Rives King, *Rufus King in the Development of Cincinnati During the Last Fifty Years* (Cincinnati: Robert Clarke & Company, 1891), 1–54.

20   Rufus King, *Ohio: First Fruits of the Ordinance of 1787* (Boston: Houghton, Mifflin, and Company, 1891), 215–224, and 429.

21   Ibid., 220–223.

22   E.C. Dawes, "The Scioto Purchase in 1787," *Magazine of American History*, Volume 22 (June–December 1889), 470–482.

23   See "Biography of Ephraim C. Dawes," on the Newberry Library website. Available at https://mms.newberry.org/xml/xml_files/Dawes.xml#bio1 (accessed 24 July 2017).

24   Dawes, "The Scioto Purchase," 470. Dawes and Newton knew each other through the Ohio Sons of the Revolution; see *Year Book of the Ohio Society Sons Of The Revolution (*1895), 77, 89.

25   See *Society of Mayflower Descendants of the State of Ohio*, 61. Available at https://archive. org/stream/societyofmayflow00gen#page/n7/mode/2up (accessed 14 August 2015); and Mary Jane Seymour, *Lineage Book*, Volume 8 (Washington, DC: Daughters of the American Revolution, 1895), 101; and Paul E. Johnson and Sean Wilentz, *The Kingdom of Matthias: A Story of Sex and Salvation in 19th-Century America* (Oxford, UK: Oxford University Press, 1994), 196.

26   George Eastman patented roll film in 1888; Eastman Kodak introduced its Brownie camera, the first mass-produced personal imaging device, in 1900. For an example of Newton's efforts to collect papers on the Scioto affair, see John M Newton to Wm. A. Whitehead, Esq. (Cincinnati, 6 June 1873), reproduced in *Proceedings of the New Jersey Historical Society* Second Series, Volume 3 (Newark, N.J., 1874), 147. At the time Newton said that he was, at that time, "profoundly ignorant" of the composition, organization, and records of the Scioto Company and was seeking help from historians elsewhere in the United States.

27   Bob McKay, "An Extended Lease on Life," *Cincinnati Magazine* (October 1978), 110–111.

28   The Gallipolis Papers also include materials about the Scioto Affair from the 1800s, and two smaller volumes with materials that appear to have been added to the collection later.

29   Dawes, "The Scioto Purchase," 471.

30   Ibid., 472.

31   Ibid., 473. As part of this deal the Ohio Company gave up its part of the speculation.

32   Ibid., 475.

33   Ibid., 476.

34   E.C. Dawes, "Major John Burnham and His Company," *The Centennial Anniversary of the City of Gallipolis, Ohio*, Volume 3 (Columbus, Ohio: Ohio Archeological and Historical Society, 1891), 40–45.

35   Dawes, "The Scioto Purchase," 476–477.

36   Ibid., 477.

37   Dawes, "The Scioto Purchase," 478. The letter is William Duer to Joel Barlow (New York, 4 November 1790), GP, Volume 1, 149; we'll come back to it shortly.

38 Dawes, "The Scioto Purchase," 477.
39 Ibid., 478.
40 For Barlow's "exoneration," see Cutler and Cutler, *Manasseh Cutler,* Volume 1, 517, which is a section that Dawes contributed.
41 Ibid., 479.
42 Ibid.
43 See Belote's obituary, "Theo. Belote: Was Curator of History," in *The Washington Post* (4 December 1953), 30. Between the time Dawes published his article and Belote published his monograph, Edward Naret published *French Settlers at Gallipolis.* Naret, born in 1800, was the nephew of one of the French settlers, Jean-Pierre Romain Bureau. He was sent to Gallipolis to live with his uncle around 1815. After he died in 1875, his daughters published a booklet with a short memoir he had written, *History of the French Settlers at Gallipolis in 1790* (Cincinnati, Keating and Co., c. 1890). It did not contradict the prevailing wisdom of it time and does not affect the story here.
44 *Annual Report of the American Historical Association for the Year 1911,* Volume 1 (Washington, D.C., American Historical Association, 1913), 269. Belote seems to have received his funding from the Ohio Society of the National Society of Colonial Dames under a fellowship the Dames established at the University of Cincinnati. See *University of Cincinnati Record: Annual Reports 1905* (Cincinnati: University of Cincinnati Press, 1905), 29.
45 Theodore Thomas Belote, "The Scioto Speculation and the French Settlement at Gallipolis," *University Studies,* Volume III (Cincinnati: University of Cincinnati Press, Sept.–Oct. 1907), 1–82. At about the same time Belote published his monograph, he also published a collection of fifteen items transcribed from Newton's collection in "Selections from the Gallipolis Papers," *Quarterly Publication of the Historical and Philosophical Society of Ohio* Volume 2 (April–June 1907), 39–92. Some, but not all, of the papers had been reproduced in Belote's monograph.
46 Belote, "The Scioto Speculation," 24.
47 Ibid.
48 Ibid., 25.
49 Ibid., 24.
50 Belote, "Selections from the Gallipolis Papers," 67. Similarly, in "The Scioto Speculation" (38) trying to explain why Barlow would not pay the drafts he told Duer to submit, Belote concluded—again, with no evidence—that the "most natural explanation would be that Playfair and Soissons had made way with the money Barlow supposed was in the coffers of the Scioto Company in Paris."
51 Belote, "The Scioto Speculation," 43.
52 Dawes, "The Scioto Purchase," 477.
53 See, for example, the LOC website commentary to Louis Le Bègue de Presle Duportail to George Washington (Paris, 10 February 1790). Available at http://founders.archives.gov/?q=playfair&s=1511311111&r=5 (accessed 6 September 2015).
54 See Ohio History Connection, "Scioto Company," *Ohio History Central.* Available at http://www.ohiohistorycentral.org/w/Scioto_Company (accessed 6 September 2015). It concisely says "Land agent William Playfair kept the company's money for himself, and the investors were not able to pay Congress for the land."
55 Woodress, *Yankee's Odyssey,* 315; Buel, *Joel Barlow,* 414.

56 See Davis, *Essays in American Corporations*, 213, 244; and Shaw Livermore, *Early American Land Companies: Their Influence on Corporate Development* (New York: The Commonwealth Fund, 1939), 139.

57 Jonathan Sachs, "1786/1801: William Playfair, Statistical Graphics, and the Meaning of an Event." BRANCH: Britain, Representation and Nineteenth-Century History. ed., Dino Franco Felluga. Extension of Romanticism and Victorianism on the Net. Available at http://www.branchcollective.org/?ps_articles=jonathan-sachs-17861801-william-playfair-statistical-graphics-and-the-meaning-of-an-event (accessed 10 April 2017). Sach says Playfair "became involved in the notorious Scioto land swindle."

58 Theodore T. Belote, *American and European Swords in the Historical Collections of the United States National Museum*, Smithsonian Institution United States National Museum Bulletin 163 (Washington, D.C.: U.S. Government Printing Office, 1932).

59 See William L. Bird, *Souvenir Nation: Relics, Keepsakes, and Curios from the Smithsonian's National Museum of American History* (Princeton, N.J.: Princeton Architectural Press, 2013), 40–44. The Museum was dedicated in 1964, eleven years after Belote died.

60 The price of *Political Portraits* was advertised in the back of Edward Hanking, *Political Reflections* (London: C. Chapple, 1815), 45.

61 William Playfair, *Political Portraits in this New Æra*, Volume 1 (London: C. Chapple, 1813) 137–140.

62 Joel Barlow to Benjamin Walker (Paris, 21 December 1790), GP, Volume 1, 139. Note that either in Barlow's original or Newton's transcript the date was miswritten as "1799;" someone corrected it in the Library's current copy. Belote also gave the date as "1799" when he presented the document in his "Selections from the Gallipolis Papers" (possibly trying to provide a literal reproduction of what he saw), but used the correct date in his description. Given Barlow's later activities, the letter could not possibly have been written in 1799.

63 Joel Barlow to Benjamin Walker (Paris, 3 May 1791), GP, Volume 1, 141.

64 Playfair, *Political Portraits*, Volume 1, 137–140.

65 See "Preface," *The Colonial Journal*, Volume 1 (January–July 1816), ix–xvii.

66 Byerley, "An Account of the French Settlements on the Sioto," 375–380.

67 Thompson Cooper, "Byerley, Thomas (d. 1826)," *Dictionary of National Biography, 1885–1900*, Leslie Stephen, ed., Volume 8 (New York: Macmillan and Co., 1886), 110; and Laurel Brake and Marysa Demoor, eds., *Dictionary of Nineteenth-Century Journalism in Great Britain and Ireland* (Gent: Academia Press, 2009), 365.

68 See "Mr. William Playfair," *The Literary Chronicle and Weekly Review* (15 March 1823), 171–172. The obit was unsigned, but Robert Stuart, writing six years after its publication, identified Byerley as the author in his biographic sketch of Playfair; in *Steam-Engines*, 550.

69 William Sibley, *The French Five Hundred and Other Papers* (Gallipolis, Ohio: The Tribune Press, 1901).

70 For the background of the Slack Collection, see Hortense Foglesong, "The Charles G. Slack Collection of Manuscripts, Marietta College," in *Annual Report of the Ohio Valley Historical Association*, Volume 2 (Columbus, Ohio: Press of Fred J. Heer, 1909), 20–25. An associate at the college's Special Collections told me that most of the Slack Collection was auctioned off at a time of financial need, and those letters are now likely scattered

in private hands. (Communication, 6 October 2015; also see the catalogue for Sotheby's Fine Manuscript and Printed Americana auction in New York, 12 December 1992; it highlights the Charles Goddard Slack Collection.) But, on investigation, the associate also found that there is no record in the catalogue that Playfair's November 20 letter was ever in the collection. It's possible that Slack—who mainly collected letters by famous Americans—did not feel compelled to catalogue a letter by a relatively unknown Englishman. Or perhaps he did not include it in the papers he donated to Marietta. Or, he might have loaned it to Sibley and Sibley kept it. In any case, the circumstantial evidence indicates that the letter did exist and its contents indicates it was authentic. Since it makes no reference of Walker, it was probably written before he arrived; in his later December 27 letter to Duer, Playfair did mention Walker's arrival, saying that he thought it a good thing as it would improve communication between the American and European sides of the project.

71   William Playfair to William Duer (Paris, 27 December 1790), GP, Volume 1, 177.

72   William Playfair to William Duer (Paris, 20 November 1790), reproduced in Sibley, *The French Five Hundred,* 39–48.

73   Belote, "The Scioto Speculation," 60.

74   Henri Carré used the d'Eprémesnil Papers when he examined the Scioto Affair in the late 1890s, but he had the opposite problem—he did not have American sources, so he missed the American side of the story. For example, he the said that Playfair worked for Duer as his "agent" and didn't mention Barlow. See Henri Carré, "Les émigrés français en Amérique, 1789–1793," *Revue de Paris* (May 15, 1898). Reprinted by Imprimerie Chaix, and available at http://nrs.harvard.edu/urn-3:FHCL:929130 (accessed 2 November 2015).

75   Jocelyne Moreau-Zanelli, "L'affaire du Scioto," thesis submitted for the degree of Doctorate in North American Studies, Université d'Orléans under the direction of Bernard Vicent, 1996.

76   Moreau-Zanelli, *Gallipolis.* A handful of American scholars, who are also bilingual and have a special interest in viewing French history from the grass roots have referenced Moreau-Zanelli and added additional perspective; in particular, see Suzanne Desan, "Transatlantic Space of Revolution: The French Revolution, *Sciotomanie,* and American Lands, *Journal of Early Modern History,* Volume 12 (2008), 467–505; and Oliver, *Surviving the French Revolution.*

77   Joel Barlow to Ruth (Baldwin) Barlow (Paris, 1 January 1790). Barlow Papers, MS Am 1448(178) http://nrs.harvard.edu/urn-3:FHCL.HOUGH:23521701 (accessed 21 May 2015).

78   See Woodress, *Yankee's Odyssey,* passim 49–82.

79   Joel Barlow to William Duer (Paris, 29 November 1789), GP, Volume 1, 133.

80   One early exception is Archer Butler Hulbert, "The Methods and Operations of the Scioto Group of Speculators," *The Mississippi Valley Historical Review,* Volume 2, No. 1 (June 1915), 66. Hulbert observes that in all the known correspondence of the Scioto associates that there is not a single mention of improving a property. He also suggests that "Barlow probably had as little idea of his real mission when he crossed the Atlantic as he had real knowledge of how to accomplish what he thought was his mission." Also see Hulbert's "Andrew Craigie and the Scioto Associates," *Proceedings of the American Antiquarian So-*

ciety (October 1913), 222–236. Moreau-Zanelli later put this fact at the center of her analysis. As she puts it, "Imagine the amazement and dismay of Duer in receiving this news. Remember that he and his associates never imagined, in sending Barlow in Europe, that he would establish his own company to sell their land in small increments." See Moreau-Zanelli, *Gallipois*, 120.

81   George Washington to Samuel Blackden (Valley Forge, 30 December 1777), reproduced in *Papers of George Washington*, Volume 13. 58–59. Available at http://founders.archives. gov/documents/Washington/03-13-02-0055 (accessed 8 October 2015).

82   George Washington, "General Orders, 10 October 1778" (Fredericksburg, 10 October 1778), available at http://founders.archives.gov/documents/Washington/03-17-02-0349 (accessed 21 May 2015).

83   Samuel Blackden to George Washington (Paris, 28 May 1789) reproduced in *Papers of George Washington*, Volume 2, 398. Available at http://founders.archives.gov/documents/ Washington/05-02-02-0289 (accessed 27 May 2015).

84   Samuel Blackden to Henry Knox, London, 20 August 1786, Gilder Lehrman Collection #: GLC02437.03294. Summary available at http://www.gilderlehrman.org/collections/ 5c3102ea-daef-4b61-8076-355932181587 (accessed 27 May 2015).

85   One example: Samuel Blackden to Thomas Jefferson (Richmond, 9 November 1794), reproduced in *Papers of Thomas Jefferson*, Volume 28, 187–189. Available at http://found-ers.archives.gov/documents/Jefferson/01-28-02-0138(accessed 27 May 2015). Another: Samuel Blackden to Thomas Jefferson (Brussells, 25 December 1790," reproduced in *Papers of Thomas Jefferson*, Volume 16, 247–251. Available at https://founders.archives.gov/ documents/Jefferson/01-16-02-0138-0002 (accessed 10 February 2017).

86   Horace Porter and Franklin Sanborn, eds., *Letters of John Paul Jones* (Boston: The Biblio-phile Society, 1905), 61–62; and *Papers Relating to the Foreign Relations of the United States* (Washington: U.S. Government Printing Office, 1906), 421–422.

87   See, for example, Moncure D. Conway, "Newly Discovered Writings of Thomas Paine," *The Athenæum* No. 3696 (27 August 1898), 291; Blackden and Barlow were neighbors, lodged in the same hotel.

88   See "The Paris Agreement," (29 November 1789), GP, Volume 3, Book A, 40. Belote cited this document, but did not appreciate its context or implications. Playfair was being compensated, in advance, both for finding partners and for establishing the Compagnie precisely because he had the contacts and business experience that Barlow did not. One of Barlow's biographers, Richard Buel Jr., suggests that Barlow was responsible for con-necting the Compagnie with the Society of the Twenty-Four when he says "twenty-three prominent Frenchmen joined with Barlow in forming a 'Company of Twenty-Four,' known as the *Vingt-quatre.*" See his *Joel Barlow*, 121. But there is no evidence that Barlow did anything more than join, and it is illogical to believe that Barlow could have organized it. Buel cited Carré's "Les émigrés français en Amérique" as his source. Yet the article doesn't suggest Barlow was responsible for founding the group; indeed, it does not even mention Barlow. Carré was focused on d'Eprémesnil and Lezay-Marnésia, describing their efforts to set up the Society. When contacted to clarify the reference, Buel said that he would not dispute that Playfair was the "primary agency" behind the establishment of the Society (Communication, 25 July 2016).

402 NOTES PAGES 100–101

90 See Batz, *La vie et les conspirations 1754–1793*, 92; he refers to Baroud as "banquiers agents du baron, le nommé Baroud;" also see Lawrence Barnell Phillips, *The Dictionary of Biographical Reference* (London: Sampson, Low, Son, & Marston, 1871), 102; he calls Baroud a "jurist and writer on finance." For Baroud's participation in the insurance company, see Batz, *La vie et les conspirations 1754–1793*, 251. For Baroud's meeting d'Eprémesnil after his return to Paris, see Carré, "Un précurseur inconscient de la revolution," 425.

91 Playfair gave his opinion of Clavière in, *History of Jacobinism*, 472.

92 For an account of one such meeting, see William Playfair, *Thoughts on the Present State of French Politics* (London: John Stockdale, 1793), 43–44.

93 Darnton, *False Teeth*. 143–144 and passim.

94 Desan, "Transatlantic Space of Revolution" 500–501. Desan quoted Brissot's paper *Patriote français*, supplément au numéro 258, 23 avril 1790.

95 Brissot de Warville to William Duer (Paris, 31 January 1789), GP, Volume 1, 145. The original is in the Scioto Papers at the American Historical Society, quoted in Ellery, *Brissot de Warville*, 436–437. Ellery also quotes correspondence between Craigie and Duer. Also see Moreau-Zanelli, *Gallipolis*, 15.

96 Ellery, *Brissot de Warville*, 66. To be precise, Parker wrote to Craigie, who, in turn, made the connection to his partner Duer.

97 William Duer to George Washington (New York, 4 November 1788), reproduced in *Papers of George Washington*. Volume 1, 90–91. Available at: http://founders.archives.gov/documents/Washington/05-01-02-0070 (accessed 23 March 2015).

98 J.P. Brissot Warville, *Nouveau voyage dans les États-Unis de l'amérique septernroinale*. Second edition (Paris: Chex Buisson, April 1791), 424–426. Also see Ellery, *Brissot de Warville*, 69. For a recent study of Brissot's travels through America, see Bette W. Oliver, *Jacques Pierre Brissot in America and France, 1788–1793: In Search of Better Worlds* (Lanham, MD: Lexington Books, 2016).

99 Zanelli communication (30 September 2015).

100 The address appears on many documents in the Gallipolis Papers. Rue Neuve des Petits Champs was bisected by Avenue de l'Opera during Haussmann's renovation of Paris. The block that included No. 164 was later renamed as rue Danielle Casanova, after the French Resistance fighter.

101 There's some ambiguity in exactly what Jefferson wrote and allowed to be posted. Dawes referred to a "certificate" attesting to "Barlow's high character and the wealth of Colonel Duer." But Dawes never actually saw the document; it's not in the Gallipolis Papers. Rather, he had to be describing it on the basis of second-hand reports; see the chapter he contributed to Cutler and Cutler, *Manasseh Cutler*, Volume 1, 503. Thomas Byerley—who also did not see the document and was relying on Playfair's recollections—alluded to Jefferson's endorsement of the project and his official approval of the mortgage scheme in his *Colonial Journal* article. It's possible that the descriptions of both were accurate, but partial.

102 *Prospectus pour l'établissement sur les rivières d'Ohio et de Scioto en Amérique* (No date or publisher given). Available at https://ia801403.us.archive.org/28/items/prospectuspour-le00scio/prospectuspourle00scio.pdf (accessed 24 June 2015).

103 See, for example, Todd, *Life and Letters of Joel Barlow,* 69. Todd published the first biography of Barlow, working from Barlow family letters. To describe the *Prospectus,* Todd provided this passage:

> A climate wholesome and delightful, frost even in winter almost entirely unknown, and a river called, by way of eminence, The Beautiful, and abounding in excellent fish of a vast size. Noble forests, consisting of trees that spontaneously produce sugar (the sugar maple) and a plant that yields ready-made candles (myrica cerifera). Venison in plenty, the pursuit of which is uninterrupted by wolves, foxes, lions or tigers. A couple of swine will multiply themselves hundredfold in two or three years, without taking any care of them. No taxes to pay, no military services to be performed.

Todd acknowledged the passage is actually a translation of a paraphrase. It originally appeared in C.F. Volney, *The Soil and Climate of the United States of America* (Philadelphia: J. Conrad & Co., 1804), as translated by C.B. Brown. Nevertheless, it is occasionally represented as an exact quotation when others use it. It is not; the *Prospectus* is written in a business style and is rather dry.

104 Menassah Cutler, *An Explanation of the Map Which Delineates that Part of the Federal Lands, Comprehended Between Pennsylvania West Line, the Rivers Ohio and Sioto, and Lake Erie: Confirmed to the United States by Sundry Tribes of Indians, in the Treaties of 1784 and 1786, and Now Ready for Settlement* (Salem, Massachusetts: Printed by Dabney & Cushing, 1797). Available at https://archive.org/stream/explanationofmap00cutl#page/n5/mode/2up (accessed 6 January 2017).

105 Cutler and Cutler, *Manasseh Cutler,* Volume 1, 499.

106 As Moreau-Zanelli put it, "The author of the Prospectus seems to have a perfect knowledge of the psychology of its customers and his arguments to convince them." See her *Gallipolis,* 80.

107 See Desan, "Transatlantic Space of Revolution," 467–505; and Moreau-Zanelli, *Gallipolis,* 80.

108 D'Allemagne (pseudonym), *Nouvelles du Scioto, ou Relation Fidele du voyage et des infortunes d'un parisien qui arrive de ces pays-la, ou il etoit alle pour s'etablir* (Paris, Chez Lenoir et Leboucher, Imprimeurs, 1790), quoted in Henry J. Yeager, ed., "Nouvelles du Scioto—The Story of a Fraud," *Ohio History Journal,* Volume 78 (Autumn 1969), 267.

109 Gauloise cigarettes did not arrive until 1910; this is an anachronistic metaphor used for the sake of color.

110 Moreau-Zanelli, *Gallipolis,* 138–139, 149–150.

111 Timothy Tackett, *Becoming a Revolutionary: The Deputies of the French National Assembly and the Emergence of a Revolutionary Culture (1789–1790)* (University Park, Pa.: Penn State Press, 2006) 168. Tackett believes, based on his reading of journals and diaries of the time, that Foullon's murder made a greater impression on the deputies than the storming of the Bastille.

112 Zanelli communication (30 September 2015).

113 Carré, "Un précurseur inconscient de la revolution," 433.

114 Bailey Stone, "Conservatism and Radicalism in the Paris Parlement, 1774–1789," *The Journal of Modern History* Vol 49 (September 1977), D1326.

115 Tackett, *Becoming a Revolutionary,* 93.

116 Tackett, *Becoming a Revolutionary,* 188.

117 Moreau-Zanelli, *Gallipolis,* 167–169.

118 For a sense of Lezay-Marnésia's personality, see Claude-François de Lezay-Marnésia, *Letters Written from the Banks of the Ohio,* Benjamin Hoffmann, ed., and Alan J. Singerman, trans. (University Park, Pennsylvania: Penn State Press, 2017). Also see Emile-Auguste Begin, ed., "Claude-François de Lezay-Marnésia," in *Biographie de la Moselle ou Histoire,* Volume 2 (Paris: Metz, 1829), 539–542; and Moreau-Zanelli, *Gallipolis,* 174–175.

119 Belote, "The Scioto Speculation," 63–64.

120 Moreau-Zanelli, *Gallipolis,* 184–195. A list of the members is provided in De Maubranche (Paris, 10 February 1790) reproduced in "Papers Relating to the French Settlement at Gallipolis," *United States Catholic Historical Magazine* Volume 3 (New York: Press of the United States Catholic Historical Society, 1890), 395.

121 "Papers Relating to the French Settlement at Gallipolis," 395–396. Each member was obliged to buy 1,000 acres; d'Eprémesnil, Lezay-Marnésia, and a few others bought additional plots. Carré puts the total at 24,000 acres; see his, "Les émigrés français en Amérique, 1789–1793." Carré was probably only calculating the land the nobles bought through the Society; several bought more on their own.

122 Batz, *La vie et les conspirations 1754–1793,* 52–56.

123 Ibid., 47–51.

124 Desan, "Transatlantic Space of Revolution," 484. She cites Claude Adrien de Lezay-Marnésia, *Lettres écrites des rives de l'Ohio,* 12, and Gallipolis Papers, Volume 1, 155, "Lettre de Barlow à Boulogne," (1 January 1790), both as cited in Roland Guy Bonnel, *Ethique et esthétique du retour à la campagne* (New York: Peter Lang Publishing Inc, 1995), 366–367.

125 Kenny, "The Gallipolis Colony," 434. Kenny cites Gallipolis Papers, Volume 3, Book A., 176.

126 Moreau-Zanelli, *Gallipolis,* 188. She cites copies of the minutes of meetings of the Society of the Twenty-Four, available in the departmental archives of the Seine-Maritie Le Havre and in the Gallipolis Papers.

127 See Carré, "Les émigrés français en Amérique, 1789–1793," 8. In fact, d'Eprémesnil bought 1,000 acres in conjunction with the Société, and an additional 10,000 acres independently. See Bernard U. Campbell, "Papers Related to the French Settlement at Gallipolis," *United States Catholic Historical Magazine,* Volume 3 (New York: United States Catholic Historical Society Press, 1890), 395–396.

128 Kenny, "The Gallipolis Colony," 434. Kenny cites Gallipolis Papers, Volume 3, Book A., 176.

129 William Playfair to Jean-Jacques d'Eprémesnil (Paris, 10 June 1790) d'Eprémesnil Papers, AN 158/AP12, Dossier 4. Also see Moreau-Zanelli, *Gallipolis,* 212.

130 Ibid.

131 See Sylvia Harris, "Search for Eden: An Eighteenth Century Disaster-Memoires of Count de Lezay-Marnésia," *The Franco-American Review,* Volume 2 (1937), 50–60; and Phillip J. Wolfe and Warren J. Wolfe, "Prospects for the Gallipolis Settlement: French Diplomatic

Dispatches, *Ohio History Journal* Volume 103 (1994) 53. They cite d'Eprémesnil Papers, AN 158 AP, carton 12, dossier 2, item 35, "Letter to M Guerom (4 October 1790), and another letter, item 46, which states 600 colonists were in Gallipolis and 200 in Marietta as of 19 October 1790. They also cite Albert-Magdelaine-Claude de Lezay-Marnésia, the 18-year-old son who wrote his memoirs, *Mes Souvenirs*. Hoffmann credits the elder Lezay-Marnésia with the name "Aigle-Lys" in his comments to *Letters Written from the Banks of the Ohio* (University Park, Pennsylvania: Penn State Press, 2017). Hoffmann disagrees that d'Eprémesnil and Lezay-Marnésia intended to recreate French feudalism, saying that they envisioned more social mobility.

132 See the entry on James Playfair in the Dictionary of Scottish Architects, available at http://www.scottisharchitects.org.uk/architect_full.php?id=201988 (accessed 2 July 2015). The author mentions the American City, but says its plans cannot be found.

133 See James Playfair, "Journal of Architecture 1783, 4, 5, 6, 7, 8,—1789–90—91 of James Playfair," NLS, Adv. MS.33.5.25. [Editor's note: this reference appears odd, the m-dashes don't seem to make sense, but this is actually the way James Playfair titled his journal, by hand; he kept adding years to the journal's cover in an inconsistent fashion.] James kept daily records of his architectural practice. The entries for 8 August and 15–18 August 1790 have him working on "plans of W. Playfair's American City." James recorded that he completed the plans on 17 August, though he logged work on the project the following day. James generally recorded fees received; he apparently did not charge his brother.

134 Moreau-Zanelli, *Gallipolis*, 221; she cites *Annales de France* (6 February 1790).

135 See Hoffmann's comments in his introduction to *Letters Written from the Banks of the Ohio*, Kindle edition.

136 Moreau-Zanelli, *Gallipolis*, 221; she cites *le Fouet national* (9 February 1790).

137 Moreau-Zanelli, *Gallipolis*, passim; she surveyed the letters, cataloguing the backgrounds of the correspondents. Also see Oliver, *Surviving the French Revolution*), 36. Both cite the d'Eprémesnil Papers, AN 158 AP, carton 12.

138 Moreau-Zanelli, *Gallipolis*, 142.

139 Lezay-Marnésia's thinking in planning Gallipolis (or at least his thinking about it before leaving for America) reflected his philosophy about basing a society on agrarian principles. See Roland Bonnel, "Sur les rives de l'Ohio: la cité utopique de Lezay-Marnésia," *Lumen: travaux choisis de la Société canadienne d'étude du dix-huitième siècle*, Volume 13 (1994), 43–59.

Chapter 5: The First Great Scandal of American Politics

1   Joel Barlow to William Duer (Paris, 8 December 1789), GP Volume 1, 135.

2   Joel Barlow to William Duer (Paris, 29 December 1789), GP, Volume 1, 135.

3   Joel Barlow to George Washington (Paris, 24 April 1790), reproduced in *Papers of George Washington*, Volume 5, 340–342. Available at http://founders.archives.gov/documents/Washington/05-05-02-0224 (accessed 23 March 2015).

4   Louis Le Bègue de Presle Duportail to George Washington (Paris, 10 February 1790), reproduced in *Papers of George Washington*, Volume 5, 126–128. Available at http://founders.archives.gov/documents/Washington/05-05-02-0067 (accessed 24 August 2015).

5   Ibid. Duportail apologized for his grammar, saying that he had been studying German and Italian, which "made forget the english," though he remained attached to the United States.

6   See the series of letters, including the memorandum by (Louis Lebègue) Duportail and (Étienne Nicolas Marie Béchet, Sieur de) Rochefontaine (Paris, 11 February 1790) reproduced in "Papers Relating to the French Settlement at Gallipolis," 392–394. Like Duportail, Rochefontaine bought 2,000 acres.

7   John Edward Ferling, *The First of Men: A Life of George Washington* (Oxford: Oxford University Press, 1988), 378.

8   John Joseph de Barth and Mr. Thiebaud to George Washington (New York, 19 May 1790), reproduced in *Papers of George Washington*, Volume 5, 405–406. Available at http://founders.archives.gov/documents/Washington/05-05-02-0257 (accessed 23 March 2015).

9   Beth Haney, trans., "Passenger List for the Ship *Patriot*," posted by the Gallia County Genealogical Society OGS Chapter. Available at http://www.galliagenealogy.org/French500/patriot.htm (accessed 19 June 2015). Also see *Virginia Gazette* (6 May 1790) in Pippenger and Munson, 64.

10   Joel Achenbach described Washington's plans and travels to the region in *The Grand Idea: George Washington's Potomac and the Race to the West* (New York: Simon and Schuster, 2004).

11   Washington's land on the Ohio was in the present locations of Wood and Jackson Counties. His land on the Great Kanawha was in the vicinity of the Coal River, near present-day Charleston, West Virginia. See LOC, "Eight Survey Tracts Along the Kanawha River, W.Va. Showing Land Granted to George Washington and Others." Available at https://www.loc.gov/resource/g3892k.ct000363/ (accessed 15 June 2017). Also see W.W. Abbot, "George Washington, the West, and the Union," *Indiana Magazine of History*, Volume 84 (March 1988), 3–14.

12   See George Washington, "Account of Expenditures for Trip to the Great Kanawha, 6 October–30 November 1770," reproduced in *Papers of George Washington*, Volume 8, 393–395. Available at http://founders.archives.gov/documents/Washington/02-08-02-0262 (accessed 11 October 2015). Also see Achenbach, *The Grand Idea*, 59.

13   In addition, Washington's half-brothers, Lawrence and Augustine, were partners in an earlier "Ohio Company" (similar name, different organization) that had tried to settle the territory. See Emilius Oviatt Randall, *History of Ohio: The Rise and Progress of an American State*, Volume 1 (New York: The Century History Company, 1912), 465–466.

14   George Washington to George Clendinen (Philadelphia?, 31 March 1791?), reproduced in *Papers of George Washington*, 609–610. Available at http://founders.archives.gov/documents/Washington/05-07-02-0346 (accessed 8 June 2017). The editor says the copyist mistyped the date, and that the letter was "clearly written on 21 Mar 1791," and that Washington had left Philadelphia, presumably for Mount Vernon. He cites (fn 2) a bond Barth signed for the land. George Clendinen was a Scottish-born Virginian who had settled on a tract along the Kanawha, and agreed to assist Washington in selling the land. See Delia A McCullock, "The Clendinens," *The West Virginia Historical Quarteerly* (July 1904), 192. Barth had previously sought to buy 108 acres of Ohio Company land from

Putnam for $400, financed by Duer; see Putnam memorandum (Marietta, 26 November 1790), reproduced in "Papers Relating to the French Settlement at Gallipolis," 400.

15 See George Washington to Presley Nevill (Philadelphia, 16 June 1794), reproduced in *Papers of George Washington*, Volume 16, 236–240. Available at http://founders.archives. gov/documents/Washington/05-16-02-0192 (accessed 20 October 2015).

16 George Washington to George Clendinen (New York, 25 June 1790), reproduced in *Papers of George Washington*, Volume 5, 552–553. Available at http://founders.archives. gov/documents/Washington/05-05-02-0361 (accessed 8 June 2017). Also see George Clendinen to George Washington (Philadelphia, 25 June 1791), reproduced in *Papers of George Washington*, Volume 8, 299. Available at http://founders.archives.gov/documents/ Washington/05-08-02-0202 (accessed 4 November 2015). Washington's sale eventually fell through; the Revolution ruined Barth's finances and he couldn't make payments; see Tobias Lear to George Washington (Philadelphia, 3 April 1793), reproduced in *Papers of George Washington*, Volume 12, 402–408. Available at http://founders.archives. gov/documents/Washington/05-12-02-0325 (accessed 11 Aug 2015). Also see George Washingtonto Tobias Lear (Mt. Vernon, 3 April 1793), reproduced in *Papers of George Washington*,Volume 12, 402–408. Available at http://founders.archives.gov/documents/ Washington/05-12-02-0325 (accessed 11 August 2015). Washington let him out of the deal without recriminations; see Tobias Lear to John J. de Barth (Philadelphia, 2 May 1793) George Washington Papers, Library of Congress, 1741–1799: Series 2 Letterbooks. He never did find another buyer for his land on the Ohio and Great Kanawha; it was still part of his estate when he died in 1799.

17 Louis-Guillaume Otto to Armand Marc, comte de Montmorin (New York, 21 January 1790), reproduced in Wolfe and Wolfe, "Prospects," 41–56. Montmorin was foreign minister.

18 Louis-Guillaume Otto to Armand Marc, comte de Montmorin (New York, 10 June 1790), reproduced in Wolfe and Wolfe, "Prospects," 41–56.

19 Alexander Hamilton to William Duer (New York, 4–7 April 1790), reproduced in *Papers of Alexander Hamilton*, Volume 6, 346–347. Available at http://founders.archives.gov/documents/Hamilton/01-06-02-0219 (accessed 23 March 2015).

20 For example, see Alexander Hamilton to William Duer (Philadelphia, 17 August 1791), reproduced in *Papers of Alexander Hamilton*, Volume 9, 74–75. Available at http://founders.archives.gov/documents/Hamilton/01-09-02-0055 (accessed 25 Aug 2015). Hamilton mentioned in passing that he had heard one of the member of the Society of the Twenty-Four might be planning to embark for Scioto.

21 Alexander Hamilton to Arthur St. Clair (New York, 19 May 1790), reproduced in *Papers of Alexander Hamilton*, Volume 6, 421–422. Available at http://founders.archives.gov/documents/Hamilton/01-06-02-0298 (accessed 23 March 2015).

22 See, for example, Alexander Hamilton to George Washington (New York, 21 September 1790), reproduced in *Papers of George Washington*, Volume 6, 491–493. Available at http:// founders.archives.gov/documents/Washington/05-06-02-0227 (accessed 25 August 2015).

23 William Short to Alexander Hamilton (Paris, 4 April 1790) reproduced in *Papers of Alexander Hamilton*, Volume 6, 349–352. Available at http://founders.archives.gov/documents/Hamilton/01-06-02-0222 (accessed 22 September 2016).

24 See, for example, the memorandum Parker provided Jefferson in October 1788, "Shipping Between Boston and Le Harve," LOC, available at http://hdl.loc.gov/loc.mss/mtj. mtjbib003880 (accessed 8 June 2017); and Thomas Jefferson to Daniel Parker (Cowes, 20 October 1789), reproduced in *Papers of Thomas Jefferson*, Volume 15 (Princeton: Princeton University Press, 1958), 526. Available at http://founders.archives.gov/documents/Jefferson/01-15-02-0507 (accessed 8 June 2017). Also see John Brown Cutting to Thomas Jefferson (London, 16 September 1788), reproduced in *Papers of Thomas Jefferson*, Volume 13, 608–613. Available at http://founders.archives.gov/documents/Jefferson/01-13-02-0487 (accessed 26 September 2015). Cutting served in the Hospital Department during the American Revolution and, like Parker, became a network-weaving businessman in Europe. Barlow was in route when Cutting wrote Jefferson mentioning Barlow's interest in "Muskingum"—that is, Scioto—and that Parker would deliver notes and newspapers which, "taken collectively contain the most recent information of american affairs that can be furnish'd from England."

25 For example, see Todd, *Life and Letters of Joel Barlow*, 70, 82–83.

26 Byerley, "An Account of the French Settlements on the Sioto," 377.

27 Marquis Lafayette to Thomas Jefferson (Paris, 1 February 1790), reproduced in *Papers of Thomas Jefferson*, Volume 27, 772. Available at http://founders.archives.gov/documents/Jefferson/01-27-02-0713 (accessed 25 August 2015).

28 Gouverneur Morris to Thomas Jefferson (London, 24 December 1790), reproduced in *Papers of Thomas Jefferson*, Volume 18, 363–365. Available at http://founders.archives.gov/documents/Jefferson/01-18-02-0134 (accessed 23 March 2015).

29 For example, see (FNU) Causin to Thomas Jefferson (Paris, 3 May 1791), reproduced in *Papers of Thomas Jefferson*, Volume 20, 352. Available at http://founders.archives.gov/documents/Jefferson/01-20-02-0104 (accessed 24 November 2015).

30 Thomas Jefferson to John Joseph de Barth (Philadelphia, 17 March 1792), reproduced in *Papers of Thomas Jefferson* Volume 23, 289. Available at http://founders.archives.gov/documents/Jefferson/01-23-02-0250 (accessed 11 June 2017). Jefferson described his land, observing "The climate and country would particularly suit the islanders, who may have slaves of their own," apparently referring to Frenchmen who might move from Saint-Domingue. Slavery was a major issue in Revolutionary France, partly because it genuinely resonated with *liberté, égalité, fraternité*, and partly because the republicans (who generally favored abolition) used it as an issue to marginalize the monarchists (who often supported it, as they had large holdings in Saint-Domingue). Brissot, Clavière, and Robespierre were all members of the Société des amis des Noirs or Amis des noirs, or Society of Friends of Blacks. As noted, it wasn't clear yet whether the Northwest Territories would be slave or free, and many Southerners sensed Cutler was an abolitionist.

31 See William Playfair to Thomas Jefferson (Paris, 13 March 1789), reproduced in *Papers of Thomas Jefferson* Volume 14, 654. Available at http://founders.archives.gov/documents/Jefferson/01-14-02-0404 (accessed 17 October 2015); and John Trumbull to Thomas Jefferson (London, 10 March 1789), reproduced in *Papers of Thomas Jefferson*, Volume 14, 634–635. Available at http://founders.archives.gov/documents/Jefferson/01-14-02-0383 (accessed 17 October 2015).

32 Stephen Rochefontaine to Claude-François de Lezay-Marnésia (Paris, August 1790), quoted in Cutler and Cutler, *Manasseh Cutler*, Volume 1, 515.

33 Dawes, "The Scioto Purchase," 474.

34 Davis, *Essays in American Corporations,* 233. Davis cites the Craigie Papers, Cambridge Historical Society, Volume 2, 151-153.

35 Byerley, "An Account of the French Settlements on the Sioto," 378.

36 Ryan, "The Scioto Company and its Purchase," 120.

37 Barlow to Walker (21 December 1790), GP, Volume 1, 139.

38 Joel Barlow to William Duer (Paris, 29 November 1789), GP, Volume 1, 133.

39 D'Allemagne *Nouvelles du Scioto*, quoted in Yeager, 269.

40 Ibid., 267.

41 *Virginia Gazette* (27 May 1790), in Pippenger and Munson, 78. Also see D'Allemagne, *Nouvelles du Scioto*, quoted in Yeager, 271, where d'Allemagne describes his return. The dates and the ships in the two accounts match, which puts d'Allemagne at the scene.

42 This is literary license, using another anachronistic metaphor; Robert Whitehead invented the topedo in 1866.

43 William Playfair to William Duer (Paris, 27 December 1790), GP, Volume 1, 177.

44 For details on the deal, see Moreau-Zanelli, *Gallipolis,* 240. For Belote's comment, see "The Scioto Speculation," 39.

45 Barlow to Walker (21 December 1790), GP, Volume 1, 139.

46 Ibid.

47 Gouverneur Morris, *A Diary of the French Revolution*, Volume 1 (Boston, Houghton Mifflin Company, 1939), 536.

48 Ibid., Volume 1, 558.

49 Ibid., Volume 1, 581.

50 Ibid.

51 Ibid., Volume 2, 60.

52 Stephen Rochefontaine to William Duer (Paris, 15 August 1790), GP, Volume 1, 181. Davis quoted this letter in *Essays in American Corporations*, 241, mistakenly dating it 17 August and leaving out the last part of the sentence referring to Playfair, making it seem as though Rochefontaine only wanted to replace Barlow. As will be seen later, Rochefontaine respected the effort that Playfair had committed up to then, and valued his knowledge of Paris and France.

53 Archives de la Préfecture de la Police, Paris, A/A/ 85, fol. 51–54 (Provided in Suzanne Desan communication, 10 July 2015). To be clear, some of the altercations likely involved business matters other than the Compangnie; as will be seen, Playfair was deeply involved in many ventures, any number of which might make a disgruntled Frenchman reach for a stick. But it definitely seems like a lot of shoving was going on, someone was taking a swing at someone—and Playfair was developing a reputation with the authorities.

54 Archives de la Préfecture de la Police, Paris, A/A/ 86, fol. 1 (Desan communication, 10 July 2015).

55 Gerald Edward Kahler, "Gentlemen of the Family: General George Washington's Aides-de-Camp and Military Secretaries," (1997), Master's Thesis, Department of History, University of Richmond, Paper 618. See especially 162.

56 "Notes and Querries," *Magazine of American History* (Philadelphia, August 1886), 199.

57 Alexander Hamilton to George Washington (28 August 1790), reproduced in *Papers of Alexander Hamilton*, Volume 6, 577–578. Available at http://founders.archives.gov/doc-

uments/Hamilton/01-06-02-0485 (accessed 23 March 2015); and Tobias Lear to Alexander Hamilton (United States, 28 August 1790), reproduced in *Papers of Alexander Hamilton*, Volume 6, 575. Available at http://founders.archives.gov/documents/Hamilton/01-06-02-0481 (accessed 23 March 2015).

58   Alexander Hamilton to Benjamin Walker (Treasury Department, 10 September 1790), reproduced in *Papers of Alexander Hamilton*, Volume 7, 30–31. Available at http://founders.archives.gov/documents/Hamilton/01-07-02-0024 (accessed 23 March 2015).

59   Duer to Barlow (New York, 4 November 1790), GP, Volume 1, 149. For Duer's earlier demands to Barlow, see his letters of 8 April 1789 and 21 April 1790, GP, Volume 1, 148–149.

60   This estimate of Walker's time of arrival is based on sailing time and known correspondence; in principle, he might have arrived anytime between late-October to the latter weeks of December. He could not have left before 11 September, when he received his letters from the Scioto associates authorizing him to take action; he might have left as late as 4 November if Walker took Duer's letter to Barlow with him to deliver in person. No known correspondence from the parties in Paris—Playfair, Barlow, Morris, or Jefferson—mentions Walker's being there in November. Travel across the Atlantic, west to east, required 25–30 days.

61   See Belote, "The Scioto Speculation," 43.

62   William Playfair to William Duer (Paris, 27 December 1790), GP, Volume 1, 177.

63   William Playfair to Thomas Jefferson (Paris, 20 March 1791), reproduced in *Papers of Thomas Jefferson*, Volume 19, 592–596. Available at http://founders.archives.gov/documents/Jefferson/01-19-02-0155 (accessed 2 November 2015).

64   William Playfair to Alexander Hamilton (Paris, 30 March 1791), reproduced in *Papers of Alexander Hamilton*, Volume 8, 227–233. Available at http://founders.archives.gov/documents/Hamilton/01-08-02-0165 (accessed 1 July 2015).

65   These were the letters authorizing Walker to inspect the Paris operation's books, work with Barlow, or relieve Barlow, as he saw fit. See "Commission of Benjamin Walker," GP, Volume 1, 149.

66   "Walker to Hamilton (Paris, 28 December 1790).

67   Ibid.

68   Gouverneur Morris wrote in his diary on 30 January 1791 that "Mr. Walker and Mr. Richard come together. The Object seems to be at first how to manage with Barlow and Playfair against whom there us a Judgment in the Consulate and the different Summonses have been issued." See Morris, *Diary of the French Revolution*, Volume 2, 111.

69   Ibid., Volume 1, 376.

70   Ibid., Volume 1, 340–341.

71   Ibid., Volume 1, 284. Also note that Morris said that that on 6 January 1790 he had received a copy of the "Plan of the Scioto Company," from a potential buyer of land he was himself trying to sell; see 359.

72   William Playfair to Benjamin Walker (Paris, 18 March 1791), OHC William Playfair Papers, VFM 2110

73   Ibid.

74   "William Playfair to Thomas Jefferson (Paris, 20 March 1791), reproduced in Julian Boyd, ed., *The Papers of Thomas Jefferson*, Volume 19 (Princeton: Princeton University Press, 1974),

592. Available at: http://founders.archives.gov/documents/Jefferson/01-19-02-0155 (accessed 22 September 2016); Playfair to Hamilton (30 March 1791), in *Papers of Alexander Hamilton*; Playfair told Hamilton that "Mr Barlow who was here has Run away in debt without informing me or any other Person;" and Stephen Rochefontaine to William Duer (Paris, 15 August 1790), GP, Volume 1, 182. Rouchefontaine said in his letter that, in addition to Barlow meeting with potential funders Rouchefontaine could not vouch for, Barlow was also meeting with Bourogne and trying to to keep it a secret. It may have been part of the deal Barlow ultimately made with Barth.

75 Joel Barlow to Benjamin Walker (10 April 1791) MS Am 1448(529), Seq. 36–37. Houghton Library, Harvard University. Available at https://iiif.lib.harvard.edu/manifests/view/drs:52504785$36i (accessed 28 September 2016). The letter is a copy and the transcriber may have simply made a mistake, but every other letter in the file has a return address, and few of Barlow's other letters are missing one. The letter begins, "Yours of the 31 March came safe...." It's an odd remark, if both men were in the same city at the time. This letter may also explain why Dawes and Belote thought Playfair left Paris. Barlow said that he had only that he had *heard* that Playfair had announced in a handbill that, *if* he were in the country, he would charge Walker with libel—sugesting he had left. But Barlow also said in his letter that he had not actually *seen* Playfair's handbill—nor Walker's. This also implies that Barlow was laying low. As will be seen, Playfair's other business activities place him in the city at this time.

76 Rochefontaine to Walker (15 August 1790),GP, Volume 1, 182; Barlow to Walker (Paris, 3 May 1791), GP, Volume 1, 141; Playfair to Duer (Paris, 20 November 1790), in Sibley, *The French Five Hundred.*

77 Joel Barlow to Abraham Baldwin (Paris, 3 May 1791), MS Am 1448(65). Houghton Library, Harvard University. Available at http://nrs.harvard.edu/urn-3:FHCL.HOUGH:23521588 (accessed 30 April 2016).

78 Joel Barlow to Abraham Baldwin (London, 17 October 1791), MS Am 1448(66). Houghton Library, Harvard University. Available at http://nrs.harvard.edu/urn-3:FH-CL.HOUGH:23521589 (accessed 24 November 2015).

79 See Dawes, "The Scioto Purchase," 478, and the chapter Dawes contributed to Cutler and Cutler, *Manasseh Cutler,* Volume 1, 517, which Belote cited in "The Scioto Speculation," 43. Dawes did not provide a citation, but, as noted, his claim is substantiated by Barlow's letter of 10 April to Walker, where Barlow says he had heard about Walker's handbill; see Barlow to Walker (10 April 1791), MS Am 1448(529), Seq. 36–37

80 William Duer to Benjamin Walker (Philadelphia, 26 March 1791), GP, Volume 1, 167. This letter is occasionally cited, e.g., Davis, *Essays,* 242, but there are some issues with it. It's a transcript, and though it's attributed to Duer, the transcript does not indicate a signature. There is a note at the bottom that appears to be Bliss's or (less likely) Newton's, saying, "I don't know who the original writer of the above is. It is in a fine handwriting." The content and context indicates it's Duer's.

81 See Playfair to Hamilton (30 March 1791), in *Papers of Alexander Hamilton*, where Playfair says he has responded to Walker; and Barlow to Walker (10 April 1791) MS Am 1448(529), Seq. 36–37, where Barlow says he has heard about Playfair's postings. Neither Dawes nor Belote mentioned that Playfair responded to Walker's postings.

82 Playfair to Hamilton (30 March 1791), in *Papers of Alexander Hamilton.*

83 Barlow to Walker (21 December 1790), GP, Volume 1, 139 (emphasis in original).

84 Playfair to Hamilton (30 March 1791), in *Papers of Alexander Hamilton*. Playfair wrote, "I have titles to deliver & quittances for money paid, which, deduction being made of the Percentage that was allowed to me by the original agreement do more than Balance the account for Lands Sold" (emphasis in original).

85 Jones believed Duer's out-of-pocket expenses from the Scioto affair were small, and attributed his bankruptcy to his other ventures; see *King of the Alley*, 151. Davis had a more measured view, arguing that Duer's expenses in the venture were substantial, although he managed to push many of them off on the friends and associates he stiffed; see *Essays in American Corporations*, 252–253.

86 William Duer to Alexander Hamilton (New York, 11? March 1792), reproduced in *Papers of Alexander Hamilton,* Volume 11, 126–127). Available at http://founders.archives.gov/documents/Hamilton/01-11-02-0099 (accessed 23 March 2015).

87 Andrew Craigie to Benjamin Walker (New York, 3 November 1790), reproduced in Davis, *Essays in American Corporations*, 243. Davis quotes from a copy of the letter dated 4 November, and cites the Craigie Papers at the American Antiquarian Society.

88 Davis, *Essays in American Corporations*, 290–291. Davis cites a 12 March letter from Walcott to Duer in the Wolcott Papers at the Connecticut Historical Society.

89 Duer to Hamilton (11? March 1792), *Papers of Alexander Hamilton*, Volume 11, 126–127.

90 William Duer to Alexander Hamilton (New York: 21 March 1792), reproduced in *Papers of Alexander Hamilton*, Volume 26, 652–654. Available at http://founders.archives.gov/documents/Hamilton/01-26-02-0002-0321 (accessed 23 March 2015).

91 Ibid.

92 William Duer to Alexander Hamilton (New York, 30 May 1792), reproduced in *Papers of Alexander Hamilton*, Volume 26, 671–673. Available at http://founders.archives.gov/documents/Hamilton/01-26-02-0002-0336 (accessed 24 November 2015).

93 Tobias Lear to Thomas Jefferson (6 March 1793), reproduced in *Papers of Thomas Jefferson*, Volume 25, 320. Available at http://founders.archives.gov/documents/Jefferson/01-25-02-0288 (accessed 23 Mar 2015).

94 Thomas Jefferson to James Madison (Philadelphia, 7 April 1793), reproduced in Thomas A. Mason, Robert A. Rutland, and Jeanne K. Sisson, ed., *The Papers of James Madison*, Volume 15 (Charlottesville: University Press of Virginia, 1985), 5. Available at http://founders.archives.gov/documents/Madison/01-15-02-0008 (accessed 23 Mar 2015).

95 Barlow to Baldwin (17 October 1791) MS Am 1448(66). Houghton Library.

96 Samuel Blackden to Thomas Jefferson (20 May 1791), reproduced in *Papers of Thomas Jefferson*, Volume 20, 430–432. Available at http://founders.archives.gov/documents/Jefferson/01-20-02-0171 (accessed 12 February 2015).

97 Samuel Blackden to Thomas Jefferson (20 May 1791), reproduced in *Papers of Thomas Jefferson*, Volume 20, 430–432. Available at http://founders.archives.gov/documents/Jefferson/01-20-02-0171 (accessed 12 Feb 2015).

98 Barlow to Baldwin (17 October 1791) MS Am 1448(66). Houghton Library. Available at http://nrs.harvard.edu/urn-3:FHCL.HOUGH:23521589 (accessed 24 November 2015).

99 See Stuart, *Steam-Engines*, 548.

100 Belote, "The Scioto Speculation," 24.

101 Archives nationales 158AP/12.
102 Moreau-Zanelli,*Gallipolis,* 211; she cites the d'Eprémesnil Papers.

Chapter 6: Turning Point

1   See Dora Wiebenson, "L'Architecture Terrible" and the "Jardin Anglo-Chinois," *Journal of the Society of Architectural Historians* Volume 27, No. 2 (May, 1968), 136–139.

2   William Playfair to John Charles Herries (Warwick Court, 10 April 1809) NA TS 11/318/1/33 fol 120. Available by order at http://discovery.nationalarchives.gov.uk/details/r/C7864688.

3   William Playfair, *Political Portraits in this New Æra*, Volume 2 (London: C. Chapple, 1814), 104.

4   John Charles Herries to William Playfair (Downing Street, 11 April 1809), NA TS 11/106/318/1/35 fol 13a. Available by order at http://discovery.nationalarchives.gov.uk/details/r/C7864690.

5   William Playfair to Spencer Perceval (Newgate; 31 April 1809 [sic]), NA TS 11/106/31/1/39, fol. 38a; available by order at http://discovery.nationalarchives.gov.uk/details/r/C7864694; Playfair, writing after the sentencing, refers in this letter to Gibbs and Litchfield intervening in his behalf.; for Playfair's opinion of Gibbs, see Playfair, *Political Portraits,* Volume 2, 14.

6   William Playfair to John Charles Herries (Warwick Court, Holborn, 26 Apr 1809), NA TS 11/106/318/1/38 fol. 8a. Available by order at http://discovery.nationalarchives.gov.uk/details/r/C7864693.

7   See *Rex v. Kennett, Kennett, Kennett, and Playfair* (London, 27 April 1809), NA TS 11/457/1520. Available for order at http://discovery.nationalarchives.gov.uk/details/r/C7866830.

8   William Playfair to Spencer Perceval (Newgate; 31 April 1809 [sic]), NA TS 11/106/31/1/39, fols. 37a, 38a; available by order at http://discovery.nationalarchives.gov.uk/details/r/C7864694. The date on the letter is "April 31st." Playfair probably meant "April 30;" under the circumstances, he might not have had ready access to a calendar.

9   See "JENKINSON, Hon. Robert Banks (1770–1828), of Coombe Wood, nr. Kingston, Surr." in R. G. Thorne, *The History of Parliament: the House of Commons 1790–1820* (London: Boydell & Brewer, 1986). Available at http://www.historyofparliamentonline.org/volume/1790-1820/member/jenkinson-hon-robert-banks-1770-1828 (accessed 16 October 2016).

10   William Playfair to John Charles Herries (Newgate, 31 April 1809 [sic]), NA TS 11/106/318/1/39 fol. 37a, 38a; available by order at http://discovery.nationalarchives.gov.uk/details/r/C7864694. Playfair misdated his letter to Herries as well.

11   William Playfair to John Charles Herries (Newgate 4 May 1809), NA TS 11/106/318/1/40 fol. 39a; available by order at http://discovery.nationalarchives.gov.uk/details/r/C7864695. Playfair was still having trouble figuring out what day it was; he started writing a "3" for the date, and then overwrote it with a "4".

12   William Playfair to John Charles Herries and Spencer Perceval (Newgate, 6 May 1809), NA TS 11/106/318/1/42 fol. 10a; available by order at http://discovery.nationalarchives.gov.uk/details/r/C7864697.

13 William Playfair to John Charles Herries and Spencer Perceval (Newgate, 13 May 1809), NA TS 11/106/318/1/46, fol. 11; available by order at http://discovery.nationalarchives.gov.uk/details/r/C7864701.

14 William Playfair to John Ring (Old Brompton, 28 October 1805), NA; HO 42/81/113 fol. 195; available by order at http://discovery.nationalarchives.gov.uk/details/r/C14732987.

15 Enclosure attached to 28 October 1805 letter from William Playfair to John Ring (26 October 1805) NA HO 42/81/113 fol. 196; available by order at http://discovery.nationalarchives.gov.uk/details/r/C14732987.

16 Enclosure attached to letter from William Playfair to William Windham (Bow Lane, 31 October 1795), BL ©BLB ADD 37875 fol. 233–235. Italics and capitalization as in the original.

17 William Playfair to William Windham (Bow Lane, 24 October 1795), BL ©BLB ADD 37875, fol. 228.

18 William Playfair to William Windham (Bow Lane, 24 October 1795), BL ©BLB ADD 37875, fol. 227.

19 See Pierre de Nouvion and, Émile Liez, *Mademoiselle Bertin, Marchande de Modes de la Reine, 1747–1813* (Paris: Henri Leclerc, 1911), 166–167, and the English adaptation, Emile Langlade, *Rose Bertin: The Creator of Fashion at the Court of Marie-Antoinette* (New York: Charles Scribner's Sons, 1913), 263–265. Messin was one of nine citizens who signed Bertin's certificate confirming she left the country for business, not political reasons; that indicated the regimes considered Messin loyal, and thus he would be allowed to travel, too.

20 Arnaud de Lestapis, "Émigration et faux assignats, II," *Revue des Deux Mondes* (October 1955), 457. Also see Simon Burrows, *French Exile Journalism and European Politics, 1792–1814* (London: The Boydell Press, 2000), 36 and 95–142; Burrows cites from the Windham Papers, Calonne to Windham (c. 28 July 1795), ADD 37859.

21 William Playfair to William Windham (22 January 1796), BL ©BLB ADD 37876, fol. 3.

22 William Playfair to William Windham (Lambeth, 26 March 1796), BL ©BLB ADD 37876, fol. 38.

23 Ibid; and William Playfair to Col. Sinclair (Lambeth, 29 March 1796), NAGL ADD MS 403.

24 Batz, *La vie et les conspirations 1754–1793*, 317–321; and Augustin Challamel, *Les clubs contre-révolutionnaires : cercles, comités, sociétés, salons, réunions, cafés, restaurants et librairies* (Paris: L. Cerf, Charles Noblet, Maison Quantin, 1895), 417.

25 See "Cazalès, Jacques Antoine Marie de," *Encyclopædia Britannica* Eleventh Edition, Volume 5 (New York: Encyclopædia Britannica, Inc., 1910), 590; and Tackett, *Becoming a Revolutionary*, 187, 248–251. For the relationships among Cazalès, Edmund Burke, and Richard Burke, see Thomas Macknight, *History of the Life and Times of Edmund Burke* (London: Chapman and Hall, 1860), 439–441.

26 Playfair to Sinclair (Lambeth, 29 March 1796), NAGL ADD MS 403.

27 See Christopher Andrew, *Defend the Realm: The Authorized History of MI5* (New York: Vintage Books, 2009), 3–28. Also see the history pages on the official MI5 website, available at https://www.mi5.gov.uk/who-we-are (accessed 8 January 2017). MI5 refers to Andrew's book using its British title, *Defence of the Realm*. The official name of Britain's

foreign intelligence organization is "Secret Intelligence Service." The monicker "MI6," commonly used by writers and journalists, dates from World War II when it was used as as a flag of convenience. See the SIS website, available at https://www.sis.gov.uk/our-history. html (accessed 8 January 2017).

28   For example, see Elizabeth Sparrow, "Secret Service under Pitt's Administrations, 1792–1806" *Journal of the Historical Association* Volume 83 (April 1998) 280–294; and Michael Durey, "The British Secret Service and the Escape of Sir Sidney Smith from Paris in 1798," *History,* Volume 84 (July 1999), 437–457.

29   For a concise summary of how Britain conducted intelligence operations during this period, see Steven E. Maffeo, *Most Secret and Confidential: Intelligence in the Age of Nelson* (Annapolis, MD: Naval Institute Press, 2000), 1–34.

30   See "History of Intelligence—Revolutionary Ideas" on the CIA website. Available at https://www.cia.gov/kids-page/6-12th-grade/operation-history/history-of-american-in-telligence.html (accessed 26 Nov 2015). For the operation William Easton led against Tripoli, see Robert F. Turner, *President Thomas Jefferson and the Barbary Pirates,* Newport Papers 35 (Naval War College, 2010), 157–171.

31   Michael Durey, "William Wickham, the Christ Church Connection and the Rise and Fall of the Security Service in Britain, 1793–1801," *The English Historical Review,* Volume 121 (June 2006), 714–745.

32   Michael Durey, *William Wickham, Master Spy* (London: Pickering & Chatto, 2009), 47–49. Durey cites Grenville to George III (St. James Square, 5 October 1794), and George III to Grenville (Windsor, 6 October 1794), reproduced in *The Manuscripts of J.B. Fortescue, Esq, Preserved at Dropmore* Volume 2 (London: HMSO, 1894), 637–638.

33   Durey, *William Wickham, Master Spy,* passim; and John Andrew Hamilton, "Wickham, William (1761–1840)," in Sidney Lee, ed., *Dictionary of National Biography,* Volume 61 (London: Smith, Elder, & Co. 1900), 177–178.

34   Durey, *William Wickham, Master Spy,* 191. Durey cites William Wickham to Charles Abbot (23 May 1804) NA PRO 30/9/15.

35   Ibid., 189. Durey cites William Wickham to Portland (12 October 1800) Wickham Papers, Hampshire Record Office.

36   Ibid., 191–195.

37   Playfair memoirs, fol. 31.

38   James Gordon, *History of the Rebellion in Ireland in the Year 1798* (London: T. Hurst, 1803), 60–61.

39   See W.J. Fitzpatrick, *Secret Service Under Pitt* (London: Longmans, Green, and Co., 1892) 301–306; and Fitzpatrick's earlier study, *The Sham Squire and the Informers of 1798* (Boston: Patrick Monroe, 1866). For Cope's background, see Joseph W. Hammond, "Mr. William Cope's Petition, 1804," *Dublin Historical Record,* Volume 6 (September–November 1943), 25–38. For Reynolds' side of the story, see the memoir by Thomas Reynolds (his son), *The Life of Thomas Reynolds, Esq.* Volume 1 (London: Longman, Orme, Brown, and Longman, 1838). Also see Charles Ross, ed., *Correspondence of Charles, First Marquis Cornwallis* (London: John Murray, 1859), 373.

40   Playfair memoirs, fol. 31–32.

41   Converting Playfair's money into today's money is a challenge because inflation rates, exchange rates, and purchasing power all complicate the calculation. For rough but rea-

sonable estimates here and elsewhere in the book, I used the online converter posted by The National Archives, available at this writing (2017) at http://www.nationalarchives. gov.uk/currency/default0.asp#mid, and then used the exchange rate of 1:1.25 pounds for dollars.

42   Charles Maurice de Talleyrand-Périgord, *Memoirs of the Prince de Talleyrand*, Volume 1 (London: Griffith, Farran, Okenden, and Welsh, 1891), 4–5, 102–103.

43   Tackett, *Becoming a Revolutionary*, 204. Tackett notes that though Talleyrand made the formal motion to confiscate Church lands, it had been proposed on a number of occasions. Also see E. Levasseur, "The Assignats: A Study in the Finances of the French Revolution," *The Journal of Political Economy*, Volume 2 (March 1894), 180. This decree applied specifically to ecclesiastical property; national lands had been taken earlier.

44   See Levasseur, "The Assignats" *Journal of Political Economy*; R.G. Hawtrey, "The Collapse of the French Assignats," *The Economic Journal*, Volume 28 (September 1918), 300–318; Elise S Brezis and Francios M Crouzet, "The Role of Assignats during the French Revolution: Evil or Rescuer?" *Journal of European Economic History* (April 1995), 8; and a recent study, Jeff Horn, "Lasting Economic Structures: Successes, Failures, and Revolutionary Political Economy," in David Andress, ed., *The Oxford Handbook of the French Revolution* (Oxford, U.K.: Oxford University Press, 2015), 611. For a comprehensive overview of the notes themselves, see John E. Sandrock, *Bank Notes of the French Revolution: Part I—The Royal Assignats*. Available at http://www.thecurrencycollector.com/pdfs/BankNotesoftheFrenchRevolutionPartI.pdf and John E. Sandrock, *Bank Notes of the French Revolution, Part II—The Assignats of the First Republic* http://www.thecurrencycollector.com/pdfs/BankNotesoftheFrenchRevolutionPartII.pdf (both accessed 28 March 2017).

45   See A. de Lestapis and A. de Lestagnes, "Batz et la liquidation de la créance Guichon," *Annales historiques de la Révolution française* (September–October 1952), 377–399; and Minnigerode, *Marie Antoinette's Henchman*, 27–29. For Clavière's role, see Michael Sonenscher, *Sans-culottes: An Eighteenth-century Emblem in the French Revolution* (Princeton: Princeton University Press, 2008), pp 319–320. Sonenscher cites two articles Clavière published at the time, "Letter aux rédacteurs du Courier de Provence," *Courier de Provence* Volume 48 (29 September–1 October 1789), 18–24; and "Sur les rapports de provinces et de Paris, relativement à la dette publique," *Courier de Provence* Volume 61 (2–3 November 1789), 34–43. Batz was a member of the Assembly's Finance Committee; the Liquidation Committee was, effectively, a subcomittee or an ad hoc supporting body with assigned responsibilities.

46   F.A. Aulard *Les orateurs de l'assemblée constituante* (Paris: Librairie Hachette, 1882) 289. In this example Batz sparred with Cazalès.

47   Pierre de Vaissière, "Baron de Batz: d'après des documents inédits," *Le Correspondant* Volume 196 (1899); 747– 770.

48   Batz, *La vie et les conspirations 1754–1793*, 277–281; and Minnigerode, *Marie Antoinette's Henchman*, 33–35. Also David Andress, *The Terror: The Merciless War for Freedom in Revolutionary France* (New York: Farrar Straus & Giroux, 2007), 146, who reports Batz skimmed funds when individuals were compensated after their offices were abolished in the process of political reform.

49   René assessed the Batz-Clavier relationship in *La vie et les conspirations 1754–1793*, 67–81.

50   For a citation putting Clavière's signature on the death warrant, see *The Political State of Europe for the Year 1793* (London: J.S. Joran, 1793), 145; for a citation of the use of his carriage, see Edmond Biré, *The Diary of a Citizen of Paris During the Terror*, Volume 1 (London: Chatto & Windus, 1896), 278; it, in turn, cites AN AF ii 3: Conseil Exécutif Provisoire.

51   William Playfair, *Qu'est-ce que le papier-monnoie?* (Paris, 1790). Available at https://archive.org/details/questcequelepapi00play (accessed 2 June 2015). The booklet is dated only as "1790," but Playfair wrote later in *Lettre II. d'un Anglais a un Français sur les assignats* (Paris, 1790) that this first pamphlet was published in January.

52   Levasseur, "The Assignats", 182–184; and R. G. Hawtrey, "The Collapse of the French Assignats," *The Economic Journal*, Volume 28 (September 1918), 300–301.

53   Playfair, *Lettre II*, 5.

54   Playfair, *Lettre II*, 19. The passage reads as: "Je crois devoir saisir cette occasion pour dire un mot sur ler petits billets de 25, de 50, et de 100 liv qu'on propose de créer. Une telle émission seroit sans doute infiniment utile, mair il faut convenir en meme temps qu'elle est tres-delicate, et même très-dangérous; parce que, au cas que les ouvriere et la classe la plus indigente du peuple vint à perdre sur ce papiner, le mécontentement qui en resulteroit prendroit une tournure bien sérieuse," which translates as "I ought to take this opportunity to say a word about the small notes of 25, 50, and 100 livres that have been proposed. Such an issuance would undoubtedly be infinitely useful, but at the same time one must concede it would be very delicate, and even very dangerous because, if workers and the most destitute of the people lost out while using these notes, the resulting discontent would be very serious."

55   This episode, except where noted, is based on Playfair memoirs, fol 10–13. Jean-Antoine Chais de Soissons appears in many documents related to Scioto; writers variously refer to him as Playfair's sub-agent, partner, lawyer, or associate. In his memoir, Playfair called Soissons his "chief clerk."

56   Ellery, *Brissot de Warville*, 244–245.

57   I've inferred the date from Playfair's comment in his memoirs (fol. 12) when, in describing events of May 1792, he says the establishment was set up "little more than a year" earlier.

58   When Playfair said he would loan Protot "100 Louis," he was referring to a Louis d'or, a French gold coin of the time, worth twenty-four livre. Livres traded for pounds at a ratio of roughly 10 or 15 to 1, so Playfair was loaning Protot around £2,400–£3,600 pounds. That's about $150,000–$200,000 in today's money (as always, keeping in mind the vagaries of converting between nation and eras). Another way of looking at the deal is to use the current price for a Louis d'or, which reflects both its metallic and neumistic value; a really ratty specimen can be had for around $800; you'll pay $2,500 for one that looks fresh from the mint. This method of estimation would put Playfair's investment at $80,000–$250,000.

59   Delcampe offered the note for auction in 2012; see https://www.delcampe.net/fr/collections/monnaies-billets/billets-france-assignats-mandats-territoriaux/billet-de-40-sols-de-la-maison-de-secours-1791-169938777.html (accessed 27 February 2017). There are also several examples on the Paris Museum's website: http://parismuseescollections.paris.fr/fr/musee-carnavalet/oeuvres/billet-de-30-sols-maison-de-secours-rue-des-filles-

saint-thomas-18-7bre (accessed 30 August 2016); the website mistakenly renders "Protot" as "Drotot."

60   See A.F. Bertrand de Moleville, *Histoire de la Révolution de France, pendant les dernières annnées du règne de Louis XVI,* Volume 2 (Paris: Chez Giguet et Michaud, 1802), 251–253. Also see the 1791 case involving Guillaume and Pretot cited in M. Monceaux, ed., *Historique du Departement de L'yonne, Recueil de Documents Authentiques Destinés a Former la Statistique Départementale 57° Année Septième 1893,* Volume 7 "Arrêté du Conseil municipal pour l'échange des billets de la Maison de secours, signés Guillaume et Protot." (Paris: Ch. Milon, 1892), 318; and the November 1792 proceedings in Ch. Milon, ed., *Annuaire historique du département de l'Yonne,* Volume 57 (Auxerre, France: Department of Yonne, 1892), 318–319.

61   "What is the Maison de Secours on rue des Filles St. Thomas, and who established it?" The poster appeared 18 October. See Sigismond Lacroix, *Actes de la Commune de Paris pendant la Révolution,* Volume 6 (Paris: L. Cerf 1908), 369.

62   "Fifth Column" was the term General Emilio Mola used during the Spanish Civil War in 1936 to describe Nationalist supporters within Madrid who would support his four columns attacking the city from outside; it's is one more anachronistic metaphor, knowingly employed. French scholars in the early 1900s appeared to know about Protot, Guillaume, and the *Maison de Secours,* referring to reports alleging Danton cooperated with Guillaume; see, for example, Albert Mathiez, "Danton et Guillaume," *Annales historiques de la Révolution française* (November–December 1929), 577–588. In his article, Mathiez argued that these reports were based on a confusion, but referred to the story of the bank and the fact Guillaume escaped to Britain as though it were accepted fact—corroborating Playfair's account.

63   Little documentation survived the Bank of Assignats. As noted in the text, Playfair referred to it in his memoirs (fols. 18–19), and Robert Stuart described it in *Steam-Engines* (548). There is also a passing mention of it in Isaac Parrish, *An Examination of the Principles of the Independent Treasury Bills, the Objections Urged Against It, and the Antagonist or Bank System of the Opposition* (Washington: The Globe Office, 1840), 6. Playfair also described the basic scheme of a bank that issued small denomination script in exchange for large denomination assignats later as part his commentary in the re-issue of *Wealth of Nations* that he edited in 1805; the description could have applied to either his bank, the one Protot and Guillaume founded, or others that seem to have been operating at the time. See Adam Smith *Wealth of Nations,* Volume 2 (Hartford, Ct.: Oliver D. Cooke, 1811), 355–358.

64   Playfair, *Letter to the People of England,* Appendix, 8.

65   Ibid., 8–9.

66   Ibid., 9

67   Thomas Cooper, *A Reply to Mr. Burke's Invective Against Mr. Cooper and Mr. Watt in the House of Commons* (London: J. Johnson, 1792), 86.

68   See James Watt, Junior, account book 1792–1793, 37, LB MS 3219/6/29.

69   Cooper, *Reply to Mr. Burke's Invective,* 7.

70   See D.V. Erdman, *Commerce de lumieres: John Oswald and the British in Paris 1790–1793* (New York: Columbia University Press, 1986), 153.

71   James Watt, Junior, to James Watt (Paris, 5 May 1792), LB MS 3219/4/13/32.

72 Edmund Burke, *The Speeches of Edmund Burke in the Hose of Commons and in Westminster-Hall*, Volume 4 (London: Longman, Hurst, Rees, Orme, and Brown, 1816), 48.

73 James Watt, Junior, to James Watt (Paris, 19 May 1792), LB MS 3219/4/13/33.

74 James Watt, Junior, to Watt (5 May 1792), LB MS 3219/4/13/32. Also see Jones, "Living the Enlightenment," 176.

75 Herbert Joyce, *The History of the Post Office from Its Establishment Down to 1835* (London: Richard Bentley & Son, 1893), 170, 269; Rowland Hill and George Birkbeck Hill, *The Life of Sir Rowland Hill and the History of Penny Postage*, Volume 2 (London: Thos. De La Rue & Co., 1880), 28; and the discussion in Kenneth Ellis, *The Post Office in the Eighteenth Century: A Study in Administrative History* (Oxford: Oxford University Press, 1958), 60–70.

76 Playfair, *History of Jacobinism*, 170–171.

77 Playfair, *Letter to the People of England*, 5.

78 Ibid., 26.

79 Ibid., 17.

80 Ibid., 26.

81 Ibid., 31.

82 Ibid., 40.

83 Ibid., 43. Italics in original.

84 For Lafayette's role in designing the *tricolor*, see his *Memoirs: Correspondence and Manuscripts of General Lafayette*, Volume 2 (London: Saunders and Otley, 1837), 252.

85 Doyle, *Oxford History*, 154.

86 See Albert Soboul (Rémy Inglis Hall, trans.) *The Sans-Culottes* (New York: Doubleday & Company, 1972), 3–14.

87 This account is based on Playfair, *Thoughts on the Present State of French Politics*, 23–25; William Playfair, *Anticipation on Politics, Commerce and Finance During the Present Crisis* (18 June 1808), 298–299; Playfair, *France as It Is*, Volume 1, xxxviii; and William Playfair, memoirs, fol. 16–17. Some details come from other sources, as cited. There are a few minor inconsistencies in Playfair's accounts—specifically on how many Guardsman arrived, and when—but they don't have much effect on the basic story, which changed little in his telling over the years.

88 Playfair, *Thoughts on the Present State of French Politics*, 25.

89 Fifteen hundred troops are a lot of soldiers—larger than a modern battalion. Nevertheless, that is the estimate Playfair gave eight months after the event in *Thoughts on the Present State of French Politics*, 24.

90 Thomas Carlyle, *The French Revolution: The Constitution*, Volume 2 (London: George Bell and Sons, 1902), 159. The reference giving Pétion credit is fleeting, and can be hard to find in the various editions; search for the sentence, "In the midst of which, however, let the reader discern clearly one figure running for its life: Crispin-Catline d'Espréménil."

91 Playfair had a low opinion of Pétion by the time he wrote his account in 1793 and was apt to paint him in unflattering colors; he thought Pétion failed to protect the king, and was no kinder in his memoirs three decades later. Even so, Sergent-Marceau, later a member of the Convention, corroborated Playfair; see M.C.M. Simpson, *Reminiscences of a Regicide* (London: Chapman and Hall, 1899), 196. For an example of Pétion getting credit for the rescue, see Alphonse de Lamartine, *History of the Girondists: Personal Memoirs of the*

Patriots of the French Revolution, Volume 2 (London: George Bell and Sons, 1888), 29. For an example of how some writers tried to correct the record, see Justin H. McCarthy, *The French Revolution,* Volume 2, London: Chatto & Windus, 1890), 368. For the version that says Pétion fled the scene, fearing he would be compromised, see Pierre Clément, *Portraits historiques* (Paris: Diderm Libraire-Éditeur, 1855), 421. Taken together, one gets a sense of the difficultes of capturing an event even in real time, and how it can morph over the years.

92   See Playfair memoirs, fol. 18. Also see the obituary "Mr. W. Playfair," *New Monthly Magazine* (1 June 1823), 282—not the one drafted by Byerley—which says Playfair "projected a bank of small assignats, which, giving rise to others, the whole were closed by a decree of the [French] government;" and that "Playfair, even contrary to his intentions, was obliged to retain the money which he had received for his small tickets."

93   This account is mainly from Playfair memoirs, fol. 18–23. Robert Stuart says that Playfair got word from "a friend at headquarters" that the authorities were planning to raid his bank in retaliation for his criticism of the government; see Stuart, *Steam-Engines,* 548. To be precise, Playfair actually wrote that Moore "took out his pistols and laid them on the table," so it seems he was carrying more than one, but few men packed more than two.

94   Playfair does not identify the partners, other than to say one was named "Moore." This almost certainly was *not* Dr. John Moore, who was present in Paris during the insurrection and later published a popular book based on his personal experiences, *Journal During a Residence in France;* he arrived just a few days before the insurrection, and well after the Bank of Assignats was up and doing business, so it is unlikely he would be a partner.

95   Assume that by 1792 assignats had lost about a third their value; that a Louis d'or today is worth between $800 and $2,5000, depending on its numismatic premium; that livres traded for pounds at a rate between 10:1 to 15:1; that a pound from 1792 is worth about £50 today; and that today a pound is worth 1.25 dollars. If so, the bank had between $2.4 and $4.6 million on hand in today's dollars, and each partner's parcel was worth between $600,000 and $1.15 million. It's a very rough approximation, but it gives an idea of the amounts of money Playfair was handling.

96   See William Hunter (William Playfair), *A Vindication of the Reign of His Present Majesty, King George III* (London, J.J. Stockdale, 1811), 5. Playfair identified himself as the author of this pamphlet when he listed his previous publications on the cover of *A statement, which was made in October, to Earl Bathurst....of Buonaparte's plot to re-usurp the Crown of France* (London: J.J. Stockdale, 1815). Also, in a footnote on the same page "Hunter" says he wrote about the Revolution "in May 1792, in a pamphlet printed in Paris;" that coincides with Playfair's *A Letter to the People of England on the Revolution in France.*

97   This account comes from Playfair, *France as It Is,* Volume 1, xxxix. For Playfair's views of French political culture, see *Thoughts on the Present States of French Politics,* 30–32.

98   Playfair, *Short Account of the Revolt and Massacre,* 10–11; and Playfair, *History of Jacobinism,* 416.

99   Playfair, *Short Account of the Revolt and Massacre,* 17–18.

100 Playfair memoirs, fol. 19.

101 Ibid.

102 Playfair, *Short Account of the Revolt and Massacre,* 20.

103 Ibid., 21–22.

104 Playfair memoirs, fol. 19.

105 A few weeks after the battle, Playfair estimated that no more than six hundred Swiss guards were present. See Playfair, *Short Account of the Revolt and Massacre*, 13. Today scholars estimate nine hundred were present, and about six hundred perished; see Doyle, *Oxford History*, 189.

106 Playfair, *Short Account of the Revolt and Massacre*, 30.

107 Playfair memoirs, fols. 19–20; and William Playfair, *Short Account of the Revolt and Massacre Which Took Place in Paris, on the 10th of August 1792* (London: John Stockdale, 1792), 1–2.

108 Playfair, *Short Account of the Revolt and Massacre*, 26.

109 See Rudé, *Crowd in the French Revolution*, 95–111.

110 Playfair memoirs, fol. 20. Playfair renders Lauragais as "Lorigais," but the context makes clear to whom he was referring. For a genealogy of the father and sons, see http://www.geni.com/people/Louis-Léon-Félicité-de-Brancas-duc-de-Villars-Brancas/6000000015703966949; http://www.geni.com/people/Antoine-Constant-de-Brancas/6000000022692641533; and http://www.geni.com/people/Luis-de-Brancas-y-Newkirchen/6000000026873257950 (accessed 19 January 2016). For the association of the son with the Jacobin Club, see F.A. Aulard, *La Society des Jacobins: Recueil de documents pour l'histoire du Club des Jacobins de Paris*, Volume 1 (Paris: Librairie Jouaust, Librairie Noblet, Maison Quantin, 1889), xxxix.

111 See Aulard, *Les orateurs de l'assemblée constituante*, 18–19. Barère later was one of the deputies who wanted to commission David to paint an even more epic depiction of the event; David never completed it, managing only to finish the faces of Mirabeau, Barnave, Dubois-Crancé, and Gérard.

112 Playfair explained how *Letter to the People of England* was "printed in Paris and published in London" in *A General View of the Actual Force and Resources of France in January 1793*. (London: John Stockdale, 1793), 5.

113 Playfair, *Letter to the People of England*. The "reproach" quotation is on 29; the financial analysis is in the appendix.

114 Playfair memoirs, fol 8.

115 Playfair, *Force and Resources of France*, 15.

116 Playfair, *Letter to the People of England*, Appendix, 21.

117 Playfair, *History of Jacobinism*, 20.

Chapter 7: The British Agent

1 See Peter Bower, "Economic Warfare: Banknote Forgery as a Deliberate Weapon," in Virginia Hewitt, ed., *The Banker's Art: Studies in Paper Money* (London: British Museum Press, 1995), 46–60.

2 B.N. Turner, "Johnsonian Letter the Third," *The New Monthly Magazine* Volume 12 (1 December 1819), 554.

3 See P.T.W., "History and Manufacture of Writing Paper," *The Mirror of Literature, Amusement and Instruction* (24 May 1823), 3–4. Also see R. B. Griffin and A.D. Little, *The Chemistry of Paper-Making* (New York: Howard Lockwood & Co., 1894).

4   Information on production rates, the involvement of other mills, and printing in London comes from several communications from Bower, drawing from his personal records. He reports that by 1796 there were an estimated 147,000 million notes in circulation, half of which were fake, meaning that counterfeiters (British and others) produced abut 73 million notes. Also see Alan Crocker, "The Paper Mills of Surrey," *IPH Yearbook* (International Association of Paper Historians, 1988), 17–18, and Alan Crocker, *Paper Mills of the Tillingbourne* (Surrey, England: Oxshott, Tabard Private Press, 1988), 37–39. For a video of a modern version of the process, see "Papermaking by hand at Hayle Mill, England in 1976," available at https://www.youtube.com/watch?v=Xs3PfwOItto (accessed 13 August 2016).

5   Robinson, "An English Jacobin," 353. As he put it, "There is a legend preserved in the Watt family."

6   The story first began to appear as part of the Watt literature in Muirhead's 1854 authorized biography, *Origin and Progress*, ccix–ccixiii. Muirhead repeated it four years later in his *Life of James Watt with Selections from His Correspondence* (London: John Murray, 1858), 478–480. Samuel Smiles duly included it in *Lives of the Engineers. The Steam–Engine. Boulton and Watt* (London: John Murray, 1874), 336. Charles F. Himes repeated the story in his biography of Cooper, including the part of Junior breaking up a duel between Danton and Robespierre; see his *Life and Times of Judge Thomas Cooper* (Carlisle, PA: Dickinson School of Law, 1918), 10–11. Even H.W. Dickinson included the tale in *James Watt: Craftsman & Engineer* (Cambridge: Cambridge University Press, 1936), 164. More on all of this in a moment.

7   Playfair said in his memoirs he sought a "passport," but today we would more likely call it an "exit visa." In 1792, the passport we find familiar today—a reusable, standard-issue booklet with the bearer's photo and sophisticated devices to prevent counterfeiting—had not yet arrived. Passports then were individualized hand-written letters, usually with limited terms and conditions, and perhaps with a seal to prove their authenticity. For the situation in France at the time, see John Torpey, *The Invention of the Passport: Surveillance, Citizenship and the State* (Cambridge: Cambridge University Press, 2000), in particular 42–43; and Doyle, *Oxford History*, 190.

8   Playfair, *A Vindication of the Reign of George III*, 28–29.

9   For Gower's assessment of the situation, see Oscar Browning, ed., *The Dispatches of Earl Gower, English Ambassador at Paris from June 1790 to August 1792* (Cambridge, UK: Cambridge University Press, 1885), 204–215.

10   Ellery, *Brissot de Warville*, 303–305.

11   This account and quotations are from Playfair memoirs, fol. 21–22.

12   Playfair's memory was off when he wrote this part of his memoirs. He recalled that Brissot said that "he could not give one but he would give me a letter to M. le Brun, Minister of the Interior, desiring him to give me what I wanted"; the context makes clear when he was referring to LeBrun, the foreign minister.

13   Playfair memoirs, fol 22. He seems most likely to have written "present Rulers of France," but it may have been "present Rules of France."

14   See Torpey, *The Invention of the Passport*, 42–43. Torpey reports that the Assembly voted in early 1792 to restrict movement, but in early September of that year voted to reduce restrictions. This would be consistent with Playfair's account of his encounter with Bris-

sot. The embassy's charge d'affaires received his passport to leave France on 4 September; Gower remained in Paris through January 1793, when France declared war on Britain. See Browning, *Dispatches of Earl Gower*, 235, 279, 282.

15 James Watt, Junior, account book 1792–1793, 15, LB MS 3219/6/29. Also see Jones, "Living the Enlightenment," 174.

16 Robinson, "An English Jacobin," 353. Robinson cites James Watt, Junior, to James Watt (Paris, 12 September 1792) Doldowlod Papers.

17 James Watt, Junior, to James Watt (Paris, 19 July 1792), LB MS 3219/4/13/34.

18 Jones, "Living the Enlightenment," 176; Jones cites James Watt to James Watt, Junior, (Heathfield, 27 May 1792) LB James Watt Private Letter Book 2.

19 James Watt, Junior, to James Watt (Paris, 23 August 1792), LB MS 3219/4/13/39.

20 Ibid.

21 James Watt, Junior, to James Watt (Paris, 15 August 1792), LB MS 3219/4/13/38.

22 James Watt, Junior, to James Watt (Paris, 4 September 1792), LB MS 3219/4/13/40.

23 Ibid. Lamballe's murder became a cause celebre—Playfair cited it, too, see *History of Jacobanism*, 159. Even so, Andress in *The Terror* (93–95) quotes official reports that indicate Lamballe's murder, while violent, was less macabre than commonly portrayed.

24 Robinson seems to have been the first to describe Junior's drama-free departure from France; see his "An English Jacobin," 353. Jones filled in details in "Living the Enlightenment", 175. Jones cites James Watt, Jr., to S. Delessert (Soho: 10 September 1794) BCL James Watt Papers, Private Letter Book 7. For Junior's itinerary, see James Watt, Junior, account book 1792–1793, 39–85, LB MS 3219/6/29.

25 Robinson, "An English Jacobin," 354. Robinson quotes James Watt, Junior, to James Watt (Amsterdam, 2 December 1792), Doldowlod Collection.

26 See *Parliamentary History*, Volume 30 (London: Longman, Hurst, Rees, Orme, & Brown, et al, 1817), 552–555. Also see Erdman, *Commerce de lumiere*, 151.

27 Robinson, "An English Jacobin," 355. Robinson quotes James Watt, Junior, to James Watt (Genoa, 6 September 1793), Doldowlod Collection.

28 Jones, "Living the Enlightenment," 178. Jones quotes James Watt to James Watt, Junior, (Birmingham, 9 October 1793), BCL Muirhead IV Box 15.

29 Jones, "Living the Enlightenment," 178. Jones quotes James Watt, Junior, to Thomas and Robert Walker (Frankfurt, 5 November 1793), BCL Muirhead 1 7/1.

30 Smiles, *Lives of Boulton and Watt* , 416. Smiles quotes James Watt to Matthew Boulton (19 May 1796), Boulton Papers.

31 Ibid.

32 Jones, "Living the Enlightenment," 179.

33 Ibid., 182. Jones quotes James Watt, Junior, to L.D. Huichelbos van Liender (5 April 1794), BCL James Watt Papers, private letter book.

34 As noted, the story of the quarrel first appeared in Muirhead, *Origin and Progress*, ccxi–ccxiv. Muirhead described the path from Junior to Southey to Allison to himself, citing a letter from Southey to Allison (Keswick, 17 April 1833) and a passage in Charles Cuthbert Southey, ed., *Life and Correspondence of Robert Southey*, Volume 6 (London: Longman, Brown, Green, and Longmans, 1850), 209. So the trail of Junior's deception was there from the beginning; the only thing that was missing was the fact that it was a deception.

35 This interlude with Madame Brissot is from Playfair memoirs, fol. 22.
36 See Playfair, *France As It Is*, Volume 2, 292. Also see James Watt to Abbé Colonne (10 February 1787), reproduced in Dickinson, "Some Unpublished Letters of James Watt," 520–525.
37 Playfair memoirs, fol. 22.
38 Ibid.
39 Playfair, *Playfair Family*, 36.
40 Stuart, *Steam-Engines*, 548.
41 Playfair memoirs, fol. 23. Specifically, he wrote, "I wished to pass by Rouen and see the home on the island of which I had taken a lease which I did leaving strict injunctions to embark with each ship bound for London as much as it would take at a certain limited price." This implies Playfair left instructions (and a budget cap) with the others in his party, and then went off on his own.
42 Alphonse de Lamartine, *History of the Girondists*, Volume 2 (New York: Harper & Brothers, 1848), 148.
43 Adam Smith, *An Inquiry Into the Nature and Causes of the Wealth of Nations*, edited with comments by William Playfair, Volume 3 (London: T. Cadell and W. Davies, 1805), 497–498. This was probably the burning carried out at the end of 1790, which the Chairman of the Finance Committee reported to the Assembly. See Levasseur, "The Assignats," 184–185.
44 Playfair, *Political Portraits*, Volume 2, 220.
45 See J.-M. Dilhac, "The Telegraph of Claude Chappe—An Optical Telecommunication Network for the XVIIIth Century." Available on theEngineering and Technology Wiki, at http://www.ieeeghn.org/wiki/images/1/17/Dilhac.pdf (accessed 9 January 2017). A group of enthusiasts built a replica; for a 2013 video demonstrating its operation, see https://www.youtube.com/watch?v=uzZJr2OnAzM (accessed 9 January 2017).
46 Charles Hutton, *A Mathematical and Philosophical Dictionary* Volume 2 (London: J. Johnson and I Robinson, 1795), 564–566.
47 Ibid.
48 Playfair, *Political Portraits*, Volume 1, 73–74.
49 William Playfair, *Better Prospects to the Merchants and Manufacturers of Great Britain* (London: John Stockdale, 1793), ix–x.
50 Playfair, *History of Jacobinism*, 636.
51 One piece of evidence that documents and dates this trip: In his 24 April 1794 cover letter to the Home Office accompanying his proposal for a propaganda operation, Playfair he said that he would be leaving for the Continent "in a few days." See William Playfair to Henry Dundas (Knightsbridge, 24 April 1794), NA HO 42/29, fols. 475–482. More on this later. Another piece of evidence appears in the four-page flyer, "Proposals [sic] for Publishing by Subscription the History of Jacobinism: Its Crimes, Cruelties, and Perfidies." On page 2 of the flyer, dated 19 March 1795, Playfair recalled that he had recently spent "five months travelling in Holland, Flanders, and Germany."
52 For Playfair's account, see his *Political Portraits in this New Æra*, Volume 2 (London: C. Chapple, 1814) 220, where Playfair identifies Lieutenant Colonel Ramsay as "Major Ramsay." For the background of the man Playfair identifies only as "Mr. Ross," see James Harris, Third Earl of Malmesbury, ed., *Diaries and Correspondence of James Harris, First*

Earl of Malmesbury, Volume 3 (London: Richard Bentley, 1844); James Ross is mentioned throughout.

53 John Burke and John Bernard Burke provide background on George-William Ramsay and the York Rangers in *A Genealogical and Heraldic Dictionary of the Landed Gentry of Great Britain & Ireland*, Volume 2 (London: Henry Colburn, Publisher, 1847), 1098. J.W. Fortescue mentions them in *British Campaigns in Flanders 1690–1794* (London: Macmillan and Co., 1918), 278, 370. (Sometimes Ramsay's York Rangers are confused with the Queen's York Rangers, a Canadian Forces regiment that traces its lineage to 1775 and distinguished itself in the American Revolution, the War of 1812 and, especially, World War I.)

54 See *Encyclopedia Britannica*, Volume 18 (Edinburgh: A. Bell and C. Macfarquhar, 1797), 336. The quotation also appears in various later editions, and in encyclopedias printed outside Britain; for example, see the 1798 edition of the *Encyclopedia: Dictionary of Arts, Sciences ad Miscellaneous Literature*, Volume 18 (Philadelphia: Thomas Dobson, printer, 1798), 336. The telegraph was also described in an article in *The English Review* (June, 1796). Playfair's 1823 obituary in *The Literary Chronicle* quotes the *Encyclopedia Britannica* passage, suggesting that Byerley was using it to substantiate Playfair's contribution.

55 Playfair memoirs, fol. 24. The page in Playfair's memoirs is marked with the number "94," suggesting that he writing about travels he made in 1794.

56 Some explanation and equivocation is needed here. The officer' name, rendered in Playfair's scrawl, looks like "Count Esternon," but a search through records yields no "Count Esternon" for Prussia or any other nation at that time. There was, however, a young French officer who fits Playfair's profile: Comte Ange-Philippe-Honoré d'Esterno, the son of a French diplomat who had served in Prussia under the Old Regime and died in 1790. The younger d'Esterno later gave up his military career because of ill health and became a member of the National Assembly after the Restoration. See *Annales du Comité flamand de France*, Volume 9 (Paris: V. Didron, 1868), 228, for a family biography, available at http://gallica.bnf.fr/ark:/12148/bpt6k5505343j/f228.item.r=d'esterno (accessed 9 February 2017); and his entry on the National Assembly website, available at www2.assemblee-nationale.fr/sycomore/fiche/%28num_dept%29/14256 (accessed 10 February 2016).

57 Playfair memoirs, fol. 24.

58 See M-d.j (Michaud jeune, pseud. for Louis Gabriel Michaud), "VAUBAN, Anne Joseph Le Prestre," *Biographie universelle ancienne et moderne*, Volume 48 (Paris: Chez L.G. Michaud, 1827), 14–15; and Asa Bird Gardiner, *The Order of the Cincinnati in France* (Providence: Rhode Island State Society of the Cincinnati, 1905), 97.

59 Le Comte de * * * (Jacques Anne Joseph Le Prestre de Vauban), *Mémoires pour servir a l'histoire de la guerre de la vendé* (Paris: Maison de Commission en Librairie, 1806), 57–60. In one of his letters, Puisaye cautions Vauban in a postscript, "Le billet doit entre tenu secret" (it really *was* a secret operation).

60 For a biography of Puisaye, see Peter N. Moogk, "Puisaye, Joseph-Geneviève de Puisaye," in *Dictionary of Canadian Biography*, Volume 6. Available at http://www.biographi.ca/en/bio/puisaye_joseph_genevieve_de_6E.html (accessed 17 December 2016). Puisaye later became important to Canadian history when he led a group of settlers to Ontario.

61 Thomas Carlyle, *The French Revolution: The Guillotine*, Volume 3 (London: George Bell and Sons, 1902), 203.

62   Earl Stanhope, *Life of the Right Honourable William Pitt*, Volume 2 (London: John Murray, 1861), 334–335.

63   This account is based mainly on Maurice Hutt, *Chouannerie and Counter-revolution: Puisaye, the Princes and the British Government in the 1790s* Volume 2 (Cambridge: Cambridge University Press, 1983), 270–356, a well-documented analysis of the Quiberon invasion. Hutt drew on original documents and memoirs by Puisaye, Vauban, and others. For an earlier, quasi-official version, see Stanhope, *Life of William Pitt*, Volume 2, 333–343.

64   Vauban, *Mémoires pour servir*, 48.

65   See Hutt, *Chouannerie and Counter-revolution*, 278. Hutt cites letters from Warren to Earl Spencer, from Spencer to George III, and from Pitt to Lord Grenville.

66   See Maurice Hutt, "The British Government's Responsibility for the 'Divided Command' of the Expedition to Quiberon, 1795" *The English Historical Review*, Volume 76 (July 1961), 481–482.

67   Playfair, *Political Portraits*, Volume 2, 276–277.

68   See "Arreté relatif a la fabrication de faux assignats," (Order Relating to the Manufacture of Counterfeit Assignats), (20 September 1794), reproduced in A.D. Lanne, *Le mystère de Quiberon: 1794–1795* (Paris: Dujarric & Cie., 1904), 129–130, *fn*; and 386–389. Also see Prince de Bouillon to William Windham (2 March 1795) NA FO 95/605/7, fol. 30, in which he includes assignats in the materials being prepared for the invasion. Prince de Bouillon (Philippe d'Auvergne) was the adopted son of Godefroy de La Tour d'Auvergne, Duke of Bouillon, and ran clandestine operations for the British during the French Revolution, including the distribution of counterfeit assignats. Most, but not all of the assignats found with the émigrés were counterfeit.

69   Augustin Rouille, *Assignats et Papiers-Monnaie: Guerres de Vendée & Chouannerie 1793–1796* (La Roche-sur-von: Ivonnet, 1891), 46.

70   A. Rousselin, *Vie de Lazare Hoche, General des Armées de la republique*, Volume 2 (Paris: Desne, 1845), 200. Hoche reported that he was propearing to burn "ten billion" forged assignats, but presumably ten billion livre, not individual notes.

71   Playfair memoirs, fol. 24.

72   Munro Price, *The Road from Versailles* (New York: St. Martin's Press, 2003), 115.

73   "Bréteuil's Mémoir, Prägung falscher Assignaten," reproduced in Alfred Vivenot, ed., No. 728. *Quellen zur Geschichte der Deutschen Kaiserpolitik Österreichs während der französischen Revolutionskriege* (1793–1797) (Vienna: Wilhelm Braumüller, 1874), 440–444. Available at https://archive.org/stream/quellenzurgesch08vivegoog#page/n457/mode/2up (accessed 20 December 2015). The proposal was published as an attachment to a 15 December 1793 letter from Schulenburg to Cobenzl (see below). Also see Price, *The Road from Versailles*, 349–350.

74   Schulenburg to Cobenzl (Berlin, 15 December 1792), reproduced in Alfred Vivenot, ed., No. 727. *Quellen zur Geschichte der Deutschen Kaiserpolitik Österreichs während der französischen Revolutionskriege* (1793–1797) (Vienna: Wilhelm Braumüller, 1874), 437–440. Available at https://archive.org/stream/quellenzurgesch08vivegoog#page/n453/mode/2up (accessed 20 December 2015). The name of the Prussian minister, usually referred to simply as "Count Schulenburg," is provided in the commentary for the letter, B. Franklin and Silas Dean to Schulenberg "American Commissioners to Baron Schulenburg," (14 February 1777), reproduced in William B. Willcox, ed., *The Papers of Benjamin*

Franklin, Volume 23 (New Haven: Yale University Press, 1983), 327–328. Available at http://founders.archives.gov/documents/Franklin/01-23-02-0205 (accessed 25 December 2015).

75   PH. Cobenzl an den Kaiser (27 December 1792), reproduced in Alfred Vivenot, ed., No. 726, *Quellen zur Geschichte der Deutschen Kaiserpolitik Österreichs während der französischen Revolutionskriege* (1793–1797) (Vienna: Wilhelm Braumüller, 1874), 437. The Emperor's decision and comment, "Kaiserliche Resolution," is appended to the bottom and translates as, "Such an infamous project is not to be considered." Available at https://archive.org/stream/quellenzurgesch08vivegoog#page/n453/mode/2up (accessed 20 December 2015). Cobenzl's comment is idiomatic, but roughly translates as, "I find the opinion of the Prussian Minister so compelling" that to take part in Breteuil's proposal would be "quite unthinkable." However, Cobenzl continues, "I think Baron Breteuil cannot be advised in any way, but should be left alone to decide whether and how he might make use of his proposal in England."

76   Playfair, *Thoughts on the Present State of French Politics*, 34.

77   Playfair, *Real Statement*, iv.

78   William Playfair, *Tableaux d'Arithmétique linéaire, du commerce, des finances, et de la dette nationale de l'Angleterre* (Paris: Chez Barrois l'aîné, 1789), v–vi.

79   William Playfair, *Letter to the People of England*, 8–9.

80   Munro Price, *The Road from Versailles* (New York: St. Martin's Press, 2003), 329–334.

81   Playfair was almost certainly in Britain by 1 December, when his *Inevitable Consequences of a Reform in Parliament* (London: John Stockdale, 1792) was published; the publication date can be inferred from an advertisement on the last page of the pamphlet.

82   See Batz, *La conspirations...*, 1–2; Minnigerode, *Marie Antoinette's Henchman*, 49; and Vaissière, "Baron de Batz: d'après des documents inédits," 751–752.

83   Batz, *La conspirations et la fin de Jean, baron de Batz 1793–1822*, 10, *fn*.

84   Playfair memoirs, fol. 34. Also see Batz, *La vie et les conspirations 1754–1793*, 83.

85   Batz, *La vie et les conspirations 1754–1793*, 437–442.

86   This is the often-quoted account. It appears in Lenôtre, *Un Conspirateur Royaliste*, 10–11, and Batz, *La vie et les conspirations 1754–1793*, 443. They may have borrowed from a similar description of events that appeared earlier in M.A. de Beauchesne, *Louis XVII, sa vie, son agonie, sa mort captivité de la famille royale au temple*, Volume 1 (Paris: Henri Plon, 1861), 446, and there were fragments of the tale that appeared even before that. Also see the account by Price, *The Road from Versailles*, 326–327. David Andress offers a variant of the traditional story, recounting that Batz was in communication with minister-in-exile Breteuil via Swedish general Axel von Fersen, former aide to Rochambeau and confident of Marie Antoinette; Breteuil, desperate for options as time ran out, approved the attempt. See his *The Terror*, 146–147.

87   See Price, *Road from Versailles*, 349. Price, who used Breteuil family papers in his research, argued on the basis of circumstantial evidence that Baron de Batz and the Bishop of Pamiers contributed to Breteuil's proposal.

88   See Price, *Road from Versailles*, 334; and *Les conspirations et la fin 1793–1822*, 10.

89   Munro Price communication, 24 February 2016; also see the forward to his *Road from Versailles*, xiv–xv.

90   René recounted, "Jean trouva donc, à Londres, des personnes auxquelles il pouvait se con-
fier;" see Batz, *Les conspirations et la fin 1793–1822*, 8. René then mentions comte de la
Châtre was one of the individuals Jean met; Playfair and Châtre would later have their
own interaction.

91   Playfair, *Force and Resources of France*, 22–24. Its date of publication—9 February 1793—
appears in a pamphlet Playfair published one year later, *Peace with the Jacobins Impossible*
(London: John Stockdale, 1794), which listed on page "E" several of his previous works
for sale.

92   Ibid., 24; italics in the original.

93   Ibid., 26.

94   Ibid., 16.

95   Playfair, *Increase of Manufactures,* p. 35.

96   For an example, see the memorandum and finding that were declassified and released by
the White House in 1987, available at http://www.nytimes.com/1987/01/10/world/texts-
of-order-by-reagan-and-memo.html?pagewanted=all (accessed 7 August 2016).

97   William Playfair memorandum (London, 20 March 1793). TU SRC MSS BH 118
COCH. The date on the portion of the original reproduced here was added by someone
else; Playfair dated the proposal in his own hand when he signed the last page.

98   Louis Blanc, *Histoire de la Révolution Française* Volume 8 (Brussels: Meline, Cans and Co.,
1856), 386–387; Blanc wrote while in England from 1847 to 1862. Annie Besant cited
Blanc and Playfair's excerpted proposal in her *History of the Great French Revolution* (London: Freethought Publishing Company, 1883), 167–168. Also, though he does not cite a
source, Eugène Bonnemère may have been referring to Blanc's account when he alluded
to Playfair carrying out counterfeiting along with Puisaye in his *La Vendée en 1793* (Paris:
Librairie Internationle, 1866), 84. Finally, Arnaud de Lestapis cited Blanc's paraphrased
version of Playfair's proposal in "Emigration et faux assignats II," 453. For Donnadieu's
background, see the British Museum catalogue, "Alcide Donnadieu," available at http://
collection.britishmuseum.org/resource?uri=http://collection.britishmuseum.org/id/per-
son-institution/25480, and the profile at the Fondation Custodia website, available at
http://www.marquesdecollections.fr/detail.cfm/marque/5387 (both accessed 30 January
2016).

99   *Catalogue of Highly Interesting and Valuable Autograph Letters and Historical Manuscripts
Being the Well Known Collection of Monsr. A. Donnadieu*, Catalogue compiled by Messrs.
Puttick and Simpson, auctioneers for private distribution (London, 1851), 126. It is possible Donnadieu was responsible for the inscription at the bottom; the initials "A de D"
are nearby (see Appendix A).

100 William Playfair to Henry Dundas (Old Brompton, 9 October 1804) TU SRC MSS BH
118 COCH. The third document is an analysis written on New Years Day, 1823 (two
months before Playfair's death) comparing a steam carriage patented by Bramah Engineers in Pimlico with steamboats.

101 As noted earlier, Colquhoun and Playfair were close enough for Colquhoun to send his
wife's regards; see Colquhoun to Playfair (16 October 1786) UG MS Murray 551. For
Colquhoun's links to Dundas, see, for example, Robert Chambers, ed., *Lives of Illustrious
and Distinguished Scotsman*, Volume 1 (Glasgow: Backie and Son, 1841), 548; and "Col-

quhoun, Patrick (1745–1820)," in Gerald Newman, ed., *Britain in the Hanoverian Age, 1714–1837: An Encyclopedia* (New York: Garland Publishing, 1997), 151.

102 James Playfair, "Journal of Architecture 1783, 4, 5, 6, 7, 8,—1789–90—91 of James Playfair," NLS, Adv. MS.33.5.25. James did not number the pages in his journal, but three pages in there is a list of jobs for 1785; the eleventh line is an entry for "Attended at Melvill," which would likely be the earliest work he performed for Dundas. There are other entries indicating work for Dundas as well.

103 Playfair, *Political Portraits*, Volume 2, 217.

104 William Playfair to Henry Dundas (Knightbridge, 24 April 1794) NA HO 42/29, fol 474–482.

105 Aspinall, *Politics and the Press*, 152–153; 436–438.

106 Playfair thought highly of Nepean, too—as he put it, "one of those excellent characters who do their duty without noise, or making their own private ambition, or private interest, run in a direction contrary to the duty they owe their country;" see Playfair, *Political Portraits*, Volume 2, 270. After serving as a naval officer, Nepean moved to the Home Office. One of his responsibilities was intelligence; see "Sir Evan Nepean" on the Musée de Nepean Museum website. Available at http://www.nepeanmuseum.ca/content/sir-evan-nepean (accessed 30 July 2026).

107 James J. Sack, *From Jacobite to Conservative: Reaction and Orthodoxy in Britain, c. 1760–1832* (Cambridge: Cambridge University Press, 1993), 93. Sack found a proposal and page proofs for a journal, *The Revolutionary Magazine,* aimed at stirring up anti-revolutionary support in Britain by reporting the lurid abuses by the French regime. See William Playfair to William Windham (Bow Lane, 24 October; Bow Lane, 31 October; London, 4 November; and 10 November 1795), ADD MS 37875, fols. 227–233, 247–250; 253–256; and William Playfair to William Windham (London, 26 March 1796) BL ©BLB ADD MS 37876, fol. 38. It's not clear if *The Revolutionary* was produced, but, as will be seen, Windham supported at least one other periodical by Playfair that was published.

108 Jennifer Mori identified Dundas as the recipient in "Languages of Loyalism: Patriotism, Nationhood, and the State in the 1790s," *English Historical Review* (February 2003), 35, fn 8, but did not refer to the supporting notes, which suggest the covert nature of Playfair's proposed operation.

109 Simon Burrows, *French Exile Journalism and European Politics, 1792–1814* (London: The Boydell Press, 2000), 21–22.

110 Ellery, *Brissot de Warville*, 332–335.

111 For Brissot's temporary escape, see Andress, *The Terror*, 180. As for Clavière, the common account is that killed himself with a dagger to the heart; see, for example, Richard Whatmore, *Against War and Empire: Geneva, Britain, and France in the Eighteenth Century* (New Haven, Ct.: Yale University Press, 2012), 255. Playfair said he cut his throat; see *History of Jacobinism*, 472. Either way, the effect would have been the same.

112 Eduard Maria Oettinger, *Bibliographie biographique universelle*, Volume 1 (Paris: A. Lacroix & Co., 1866), 485; Edinburgh *Evening Courant* (24 February 1794).

113 See Edward Nelson White, "The French Revolution and the Politics of Government Finance, 1770–1815," *The Journal of Economic History*, Volume 55 (June 1995), 238. Nelson cites *Marché des changes de Paris à la fin du XVIIIe sicle (1788–1800)* (Paris, 1937) and

Antoine Bailleul, *Tableau complet de la valeur des Assignats, des Réscreptions et des Mandats* (Paris, 1797).

114 Joseph Hill, *The Book Makers of Old Birmingham* (Birmingham: Cornish Brothers, Ltd., 1907), 119; and D.W. Dykes, "John Gregory Hancock and the Westwood Brothers: An Eighteenth-Century Token Consortium," *British Numismatics Journal*, Volume 69 (1999), 173–86.

115 Isaac, "Sir John Swinburne and the Forged Assignats," 162.

116 Thomas Bewick to Obadiah Westwood (Newcastle, 30 October 1793), reproduced in Bayne Robert, *Historical Sketch of Rickmansworth and the Surrounding Parishes* (London: Printed by Watson and Hazell, 1870), 21.

117 Woodcroft, *Subject-Matter Index of Patents*, 498.

118 Samuel Swinton to Home Office (Sloan Street, 21 December 1793) NA HO 44/41 fol. 87. For Swinton's activities as an agent, see Burrows, *French Exile Journalism and European Politics, 1792–1814*, 19; Burrows cites Hélène Maspero Clerc, "Samuel Swinton, éditeur du Courier de l'Europe à Boulogne-sur-Mer (1778–1783) et agent secret du Gouvernement britannique," *Annales de la Révolution française* (October–December 1985), 527–531. Swinton wasn't sure the matter was "of any consequence that the Government should know," though his compositor said "French gentlemen" headed the manufactory. As will be seen, the British and royalist counterfeiting efforts were linked.

119 R.G. Hawtrey, "The Collapse of the French Assignats," *The Economic Journal*, Volume 28 (Sept 1918), 303.

120 See "Loi Concernant la fabrication des Assignats (10 November 1790), reproduced on-the website "Catalogue général des assignats français." Available at http://assignat.fr/3-loi/loi-1790-11-04?PHPSESSID=g0q259dm808vu4lt7r9dd97vm7 (accessed 3 March 2017).

121 See the copy at on the website "Catalogue général des assignats français," available at http://assignat.fr/4-faux/doc-002?PHPSESSID=g0q259dm808vu4lt7r9dd97vm7 (accessed 19 February 2017).

122 See N. Hampson, "Francois Chabot and His Plot," *Transactions of the Royal Historical Society*, Volume 26 (7 February 1976), 1–14. Also see Andress, *The Terror*, 273–276.

123 Lacoste claimed in his *Rapport fait à la Convention sur la conspiration de Batz*, "The gold and assignats came from England; Pitt and the émigrés formulated the counterrevolutionary plan." See the coverage of the report by the *Gazette nationale, ou Le moniteur universel* (15 June 1794). A reprint is available in *Reimpression of L'ancien Monireut* Volume 20, May 1789–November 1799 (Paris: Au Bureau Central, 1841); the quotation is on 726. For a discussion of the Plot and how it turned Jacobin leaders against one another, see Norman Hampson, "Robespierre and the Terror," in William Doyle and Colin Haydon, eds., *Robespierre* (Cambridge: Cambridge University Press, 2006), 167–169.

124 It took some effort for Batz to make his case, though in the end he succeeded and was recognized. The rank he received—a paid position—was, in effect, a reward for his services in the counter-revolution. See Batz, *Les conspirations et la fin 1793–1822*, 440–444.

125 Ibid., 22–31. In explaining the background of the documents, René says that Jean, while preparing his case for compensation to submit to the restored monarchy sometime around 1818, came upon papers that he had written "before the fall of Robespierre." That would suggest Jean wrote them in the latter half of 1793, or the first half of 1794. Réné said that

he had found the papers while researching Jean's life almost a hundred years later. René quoted the papers on pages 30–31. In them, Jean rhetorically asks how the Convention can be brought down, and then provides his answer—by sowing discord among the members. The original reads as:

Me demande-t-on comment pouvait finir une puissance aussi formidable, sous laquelle toutes les têtes se courbaient en silence? Je réponds qu'un tel régime est dans ses chefs un délire, un état de convulsion; et que toute action violente, est par cela même, de peu de durée selon les lois irrésistibles de la nature, que toujours les jalousies, les défiances, les haines, les divisions se mettent entre eux et les entraînent à leur tour dans les abîmes qu'eux-mêmes ont ouverts; que préparer ces divisions, que les hâter en semant les défiances, en irritant les rivalités, est, à défaut des armes, l'unique manière bien entendue de conspirer contre un tel gouvernement et d'en amener la plus prompte chute.

In a footnote on 25–26, René concedes that his family archives were often in fragments that could be difficult to disentangle. In some cases, René said he used material from the National Convention's investigation of Jean to help make sense of them. ("Les manuscrits du baron sont tellement difficiles à débrouiller et à classer que j'avais attribué l'extrait dont je parle à un projet de tra vail sur la Convention nationale.") The government's files, in turn, René said, had their own gaps and errors, which he tried to correct by correlating them with the family papers he possessed.

Also see the discussion of this material by Price in *The Road from Versailles*, 347–348.

126 Playfair memorandum (London, 20 March 1793), TU SRC MSS BH 118 COCH; see 5.

127 See Lestapis, "Emigration et faux assignats II", 454; Lestapis was unwilling to go so far as to say there was "connivance" between Playfair and Batz, but could not help but note the "synchronization of their thinking."

128 "A Constitutional Friend," ed. (pseudonym), *The Speeches of the Right Honourable Richard Brinsley Sheridan*, Volume 4 (London: Patrick Martin, 1816), 274-275.

129 *Gazette National ou Le Moniteur Universel* No. 203 (12 April 1794), cited in Blanc, *Histoire de la Révolution*, Volume 14, 386.

130 The details of the trial are provided in Isaac Espinasse, *Reports of Cases Argues and Ruled at Nisi Prius. In the Courts of King's Bench and Common Pleas, from Easter Term 33 George III 1793 to Hilary Term, 36 George III, 1796* (London: Butterworth, 1801), 388–391. Also see Sampson Perry, "Register of Occurrences: False Assignat Making," *The Argus* (London: H.D. Symonds, 1796), 246–247; Perry's account also appeared in several other publications.

131 See Lukyn's obituary in *Gentleman's Magazine and Historical Chronicle for the Year MDC-CXCIX*, Volume 64, Part 2 (1799), 821.

132 For customer feedback on Strongitharm, see the website maintained by Larry J. Schaff, "The Correspondence of William Henry Fox Talbot," available at http://foxtalbot. dmu.ac.uk/letters/transcriptFreetext.php?keystring=cole&keystring2=&keystring3=&-year1=1826&year2=1877&pageNumber=108&pageTotal=342&referringPage=5 (accessed 21 February 2016). He cites Elisabeth Theresa Fielding, née Fox Strangways to William Henry Fox Talbot (London, 30 July 1836), BL, LA 36–51, fol. 3346.

133 Lewis Goldsmith, *The Crimes of Cabinets, or A Review of their Plans and Aggressions for the Annihilation of the Liberties of France and the Dismemberment of Her Territories* (London: J.S. Jordan, 1801), 258.

134 Smith, *Wealth of Nations* (London, 1805), Volume 2, 354

135 See "John Strongitharm" on the British Museum website, available at http://www.britishmuseum.org/research/search_the_collection_database/term_details.aspx?bioId=201 (accessed 9 January 2017).

136 See floor speech by John Nichols, 5 December 1796, reported in *Parliamentary Register* 5th Session, 18th Parliament (London: J. Debrett, 1801), 413.

137 The passage reads as:

> ... Car quoique on ait publié, parmi les royalistes comme parmi les républicains, que les ministres Anglois faisoient fabriquer de faux assignats à Londres, je dois déclarer que cela est faux, et le lecteur sensé rangera cette fable, au nombre des calomnies grossières qui ont assez dû prouver, qu'avec du génie, du courage, et surtout de la persévérance, il n'est pas d'ennemi qu'on ne réduise à l'impossibilité de nuire. Car dans les querelles publiques, comme dans les discussions particulières, les injures sont l'aveu de l'impuissance.
>
> Les Princes François avoient le droit de faire circuler un papier monnoie en France, en en ga- rantissant le remboursement, sur la propriété de l'état: le gouvernement Britannique ne i'avoit pas: et ce qui étoit légitime pour les uns, n'eût été qu'une bassesse criminelle chez les autres.

See Joseph de Puisaye, *Mémoires du comte Joseph de Puisaye*, Volume 3 (London: Harper and Co., 1804), 384–386. The gist of the passage is: Claims (by both royalists and republicans) that "English ministers" made counterfeit assignats are untrue—merely the libelous accusations to which a desperate enemy might resort. The British government did not have a legal right to make French currency. However, the French government in exile did, and Puisaye had received its authorization. Therefore, whatever currency he might have produced was not counterfeit; it was simply currency.

138 Puisaye went on to his next project in 1798, a British-backed effort to settle some of the French émigrés in Upper Canada. It suggests he remained in good standing with at least some ministers. That project failed, too. See Rev. Brother Alfred [Dooner], "The Windham or "Oak Ridges" Settlement of French Royalist Refugees in York County, Upper Canada, 1798," *Canadian Catholic Historical Association Report*, Volume 7 (1939–1940), 11–26.

139 William Cobbett, "Paper Against Gold," *Cobbett's Weekly Political Register*, Volume 19 (18 May 1811), 1217–1228. The letters were collected and published as a single volume; see William Cobbett, *Paper Against Gold* (New York: John Doyle, 1834); Letter XXIV is on 301–313.

140 These are quotations of paraphrases published in *The Parliamentary Register* (14 April 1812), 417–418. For Stanhope's political evolution, see Ghita Stanhope and G.P. Gooch, *The Life of Charles, Third Earl Stanhope* (London: Longmans, Green, and Co. 1914), 110–141.

141 For Windham's initial support of Cobbett, see J.A. Hamilton, "Windham, William (1750–1810)," in Sidney Lee, ed., *Dictionary of National Biography*, Volume 21 (New York:

The Macmillan Company, 1900), 174; and G.D.H. Cole, *The Life of William Cobbett* (New York: W. Collins Sons, 1925), 73–74.

142 See James Grande, *William Cobbett, the Press, and Rural England* (London: Palgrave Macmillan, 2014), 38–59; Grande cites extensively from the Windham Papers. John W. Osburne gets credit for the "racy" sobriquet; see his entry in *Encyclopedia Britannica*, available at https://www.britannica.com/biography/William-Cobbett-British-journalist (accessed 15 August 2016).

143 Playfair, *Political Portraits*, Volume 2, 105–106.

144 William Cobbett, "Dedication to Mr. William Playfair," in the American edition of William Playfair, *The History of Jacobinism, Its Crimes, Cruelties and Perfidies*, Volume 2 (Philadelphia, William Cobbett, November 1796), 5–6. Italics in the original.

145 Thomas Doubleday, *The Political Life of Sir Robert Peel* (London: Smith, Elder, and Co., 1856), 41–42. Doubleday had alluded to British counterfeiting in an earlier book, although his account then was fragmentary; see Thomas Doubleday, *A Financial, Monetary, and Statistical History of England: From the Revolution of 1688 to the Present Time.* (London: Effingham Wilson, Royal Exchange, 1847), 133–134.

Even though their responsibility for the operation was thoroughly exposed, British leaders maintained the official fiction that the operation was conducted wholly by French émigrés. When Philip Stanhope, 5th Earl Stanhope, published his *Life of the Right Honourable William Pitt*, Volume 2 (London: John Murray, 1861), 335, he described the counterfeiting this way:

> The English Government, in addition to its earlier advances, supplied ten thousand guineas in gold for the military chest, and there had been fabricated by order of M. de Puisaye a large number of Assignats, distinguished by a private mark and designed for a ready circulation.

146 For Cobbett's influence, see Doubleday's obituary by W.E. Adams, *Notes and Queries*, Fifth Series, Volume 6 (12 August 1876) 131; and Matthe Roberts, "The Feast of the Gridiron is at Hand: Chartism, Cobbett, and Currency," in James Grande and John Stevenson, eds., *William Cobbett, Romanticism and the Enlightenment* 9 Abingdon, UK: Routledge, 2016), 108.

147 "E.C.R.," "Forged Assignats," *Notes and Queries* (24 July 1858), 70.

148 W.C. Trevelyan "Forged Assignats," *Notes and Queries* (25 September 1858), 255–256.

149 "Newcastle Society of Antiquaries—Jan. 25—Sixty-Ninth Annual Meeting," *The Antiquary*, Volume 5 (January–June 1882), 129–130.

150 John Philipson, "A Case of Economic Warfare in the Late Eighteen Century," *Archaeologia Aeliana* (Fifth Series, Volume XVIII, 1990), 151.

151 Ibid., 153–154.

152 Ibid., 162.

153 Clarence Ward, "The Story of Brook Watson," *New Brunswick Magazine*, Volume 1 (July–December, 1898), 96–103; and Francess G. Halpenny and Jean Hamelin, eds., "Sir Brook Watson," *Dictionary of Canadian Biography*, Volume 5 (Toronto: University of Toronto Press, 1983), 842–844.

154 Swinburne, NW ZSW/590. The note is unsigned, and not labeled.

155 Ibid. The note is unsigned, and labeled just as "No. 1." In the body of his memo, however, Sir John says, "I applied to a Gentleman that lives at Humshaugh by the name of Rich-

mond, who informed me that it was true, & that it was the paper with the French water mark that was made at this place, his note no. 1 indicates the paymaster, & the agents for the distribution of these notes."This implies Richmond wrote the note, and possibly provided it to Sir John to include as part of the package. In his article, Peter Isaac described this note after describing the unlabeled, unsigned note referring to General Dundas and Col. Scott; I've reversed the presentation for clarity. Bear in mind that all these items are loose in the same folder, and have been shuffled over the years.

156 The two other mills would have corresponded to John Finch in Kent, and Charles Bell in Surrey, which were also produced paper for counterfeit assignats. Bower (communication, 15 December 2015) says Finch produced assignat paper for the British Government and was involved in the distribution of the printed notes through Flanders, and Ball made assignat paper for the Comte d'Artois (later Charles X of France after the Restoration); Bower covers some of this ground in his article, "What One Man Can Make, Another Man Can Copy," *Bond & Banknote News* (October/November 1988). Also see Isaac, "Sir John Swinburne and the Forged Assignats;" he cites Alan Crocker, *Paper Mills of the Tillingbourne: a history of paper making in a Surrey Valley 1704–1875* (Oxshott, 1988), 37–39; and Jean Lafaurie, *Les Assignats et les papiers-monnaies émis par l'État au XVIIIe siècle* (Paris: Le Léopard d'or, 1981).

It is possible that the "Mr Thelusson" mentioned in the note was Peter Thellusson, Peter Isaac Thellusson's father. He had been a director of the Bank of England, too. Many customers of the elder Thellusson were émigrés, and he had been Necker's banking partner in Paris; see the anonymously authored *Tales of the Bank of England: With Anecdotes of London Bankers* (London: James Hogg, 1882), 42. However, this is less likely; by 1794 the younger Thellusson was listed as a Bank of England director at the time of the forgery operation, while his father was not. See "Directors' Annual Lists 1694–1908," 99–100, available from the Bank at its website, http://www.bankofengland.co.uk/archive/Pages/digitalcontent/archivedocs/directorsannuallists.aspx (accessed 13 May 2017). Also, Peter Isaac Thellusson was politically active and known as a Pitt supporter; see "THELLUSSON, Peter Isaac (1761–1808), of Rendlesham House, nr. Woodbridge, Suff.," *The History of Parliament: the House of Commons 1790–1820* (London: Boydell & Brewer, 1986). Available at http://www.historyofparliamentonline.org/volume/1790-1820/member/thellusson-peter-isaac-1761-1808 (accessed 13 May 2017). The Thellussons later gained notoriety for the exceptionally complex will that Peter Thellusson left and the legal proceedings it generated.

157 J.A. Hamilton, "Windham, William (1750–1810)," in Sidney Lee, ed., *Dictionary of National Biography*, Volume 21 (New York: The Macmillan Company, 1900), 174.

158 Philipson, "Case of Economic Warfare," 156.

Chapter 8: Back to Business

1   Prices for Playfair's publications appear, for example, in the advertisement in the back of *Thoughts on the Present State of French Politics*, 188; and *Peace with the Jacobins Impossible* (London: John Stockdale, 1794). By the time Playfair died in in 1823, the price for his pamphlets had gone up to 5 shillings. The price of *History of Jacobinism* (London: John

Stockdale, 1795) appears on its cover. For Stockdale's price for *Notes on Virginia*, see Stockdale, *'Tis Treason*, 182.

2   Playfair, *History of Jacobinism*, 14–17.

3   For a mechanic's typical wage, see William Playfair, *A Letter on Our Agricultural Distresses* (London: William Sams, 1822), chart 1.

4   William Playfair, *Letter to the Right Honourable The Earl Fitzwilliam, Occasioned by His Two Letters to the Earl of Carlisle* (London: John Stockdale, 1795), 3.

5   Charles Roger, *A Century of Scottish Life: Memorials and Recollections of Historical and Remarkable Persons* (London: Charles Griffin & Co., 1872), 22.

6   Stockdale, *'Tis Treason My Good Man*, 148. Stockdale was preparing Adams' book, *A Defence of the Constitution of Government of the United States*, for publication.

7   See John Adam's copy of *A History of Jacobinism* in the Boston Public Library, 307. Adams owned a copy of the edition William Cobbett published in Philadelphia. Most of his marginalia simply noted names or ideas that Adams might have wanted to return to later.

8   Review of "Better Prospects to the Merchants and Manufacturers of Great Britain," *The Critical Review*, Volume 8 (1793), 457.

9   Playfair, *Better Prospects*, x; and Playfair, *History of Jacobinism*, 17.

10   William Playfair to William Windham (Bow Lane, 24 October 1795), BL ©BLB ADD 37875, fol. 229.

11   William Playfair to William Windham (Bow Lane, 31 October 1795), BL ©BLB ADD 37875, fol. 232–233.

12   William Playfair to William Windham (London, 26 March 1796), BL ©BLB ADD 37876, fol. 38.

13   J. Jepson Oddy (William Playfair), *European Commerce, Shewing New and Secure Channels of Trade with the Continent of Europe* (London: W.J. and J. Richardson, 1805), 621–622. Oddy was a British merchant; Byerley's obituary attributed the book to Playfair.

14   Edwin Robert Anderson Seligman, *The Income Tax: A Study of the History, Theory, and Practice of Income Taxation at Home and Abroad* (New York: Macmillan, 1914), 71–82. Pitt eventually gravitated toward an income tax, adopted in 1799.

15   This account is based on Playfair memoirs, fol. 31. There was also a third partner who worked with Playfair and Cope, but Playfair did not identify him.

16   Playfair, *Better Prospects*, xi–xii.

17   Playfair, *Short Account*.

18   See William Playfair, *Peace with the Jacobins Impossible* (London: John Stockdale, 1794). The advertisement follows page 32 and is titled "The following Works, by WILLIAM PLAYFAIR, are printed for JOHN STOCKDALE;" it includes "*Account of the Revolt and Massacre which took Place in PARIS on the 10th of Augus 1792;*" the price is one shilling.

19   *Short Account* does not indicate a date of publication; it was advertised in *The Times* on 12 September 1792, and William Pressly reports it was also advertised in at least seven other papers; see his *The French Revolution as Blasphemy* (Berkeley: University of California Press, 1999), 193. As noted previously, Robert Stuart, who based his biographical essay of Playfair on Thomas Byerley's obituary and, most likely, personal acquaintances, said that Playfair went to Holland after fleeing France; see Stuart, *Steam-Engines*, 548. As also previously noted, Playfair's memoirs suggest he sent his family to England separately.

20   Playfair, *General View of the Actual Force and Resources of France*.

21 Playfair, *Inevitable Consequences of a Reform in Parliament*.

22 For an analysis of Adams' views, which evolved over time, see Richard Alan Ryerson, "Like a Hare before the Hunters: John Adams and the Idea of Republican Monarchy," *Proceedings of the Massachusetts Historical Society*, Volume 107 (1995), 16–29.

23 For Samuel Arnold's participation in *The Tomahawk!*, see the obituary by Byerley, "Mr. William Playfair," *Literary Chronicle* (15 March 1823), 171–172.

24 Arthur Warren *The Charles Whittinghams Printers* (New York: The Growler Club of New York, 1896), 24–26.

25 Playfair memoirs, fol. 25.

26 *The Tomahawk!* (29 October 1795), 1–2. *The Tomahawk!* numbered its pages consecutively and continuously across issues, beginning with 1 in this first issue, and ending with 454 in its final edition of 7 March 1796.

27 Playfair to Windham (24 October 1795), BL ©BLB ADD37875, fol. 227.

28 For Lansdowne's opposition to the war (and just about any war), see Fitzmaurice, *Life of William, Earl of Shelburne*, Volume 2, 368–401; for Bentham's letter (summarized, with Lansdowne's diplomatic response), see 399.

29 See, for example, Playfair, *Political Portraits*, Volume 2, 143; Playfair compared the current Marquis, Henry Petty, unfavorably to his father, who Playfair called "one of the best-informed men of his time."

30 *The Tomahawk!* (4 November 1795), 30.

31 *The Tomahawk!* (10 November 1795), 50.

32 *The Tomahawk!* (11 November 1795), 53.

33 Playfair memoirs, fol. 25.

34 *The Tomahawk!* (7 March 1796), 452.

35 J.E. Thomas, *Britain's Last Invasion: Fishguard 1797* (Stroud, Gloucestershire: Tempus, 2007), 53–54.

36 Donald R. Come, "French Threat to British Shores, 1793–1798," *Military Affairs* (Winter 1952), 16 (4): 174–88.

37 Thomas, *Britain's Last Invasion*, 62–66; Thomas cites Hoche's instructions to William Tate, the invasion force commander, which he said were reproduced in David Salmon, "The French Invasion of Fishguard in 1797; Official Documents, Contemporary Letters, and Early Narratives," in *West Wales Historical Records*, Volume 14 (Carmarthen, Wales: William Spurrell, 1929). 38   F.A. Hayek and William Warren Bartley, *The Collected Works of F.A. Hayek. Volume III: Trend of Economic Thinking: Essays on Political Economists and Economic History* (Chicago: University of Chicago Press, 1991), 187–188.

39 Joseph Hume Francis, *History of the Bank of England* (Chicago: Euclid Publishing Company, 1888), 89–90.

40 *London Gazette* (28 February–4 March 1797), 215.

41 Bartley and Kresge, *The Collected Works of F.A. Hayek. Volume III*, 186–188.

42 See the Bank of England's website, "A Brief History of Banknotes." Available at http://www.bankofengland.co.uk/banknotes/pages/about/history.aspx (accessed 2 March 2016). Today, of course, the opposite is true: a Briton might go through a lifetime without handling a gold or silver coin.

43 Again, this uses the currency converter provided by The National Archives. To be precise, £5 in 1790s Britain would $380 at the time this is being written, but the point is that the five-pound note the Bank of England was issuing at the time was inconvenient for trade.

44 Sir John Sinclair, *Letters Written to the Governor and Directors of the Bank of England, in September, 1796 on the Pecuniary Distresses of the Country, and the Means of Preventing Them* (London: G. Nicole, 1797), 15.

45 See Samuel H. Day, ed., *Family Papers* (London: privately published, 1911), Documents 436–440, reproduced by HardPress Publishing. The Hartsinck and Day families were related by marriage.

46 See Arthur Francis Day, *John C.F.S. Day: His Forbears and Himself. A Biographical Study by One of His Sons* (London: Heath, Cranton, Ltd., 1916), 41–43. Also see Hartsinck to the Prince of Orange (10 and 26 February 1795), items 2–3 in Day, *Family Papers*.

47 See William Page, ed., "Parishes: Little Barford," *A History of the County of Bedford: Volume 2* (1908), 206–209. Available at http://www.british-history.ac.uk/vch/beds/vol2/pp206-209 (accessed 3 March 2016).

48 Playfair memoirs, fol. 26. There is also an undated "Plan of the Original Security Bank" in NAGL ADD MS 403. It refers to Playfair's pamphlet, *A Letter to Sir William Pultney*, which has a 23 May 1797 publication date. This would this indicate the Plan was published sometime after that date. The Bank's office was in Strand, near Playfair's residence on Howland Street; the district is now part of the Metropolitan Borough of Westminster.

49 William E. Thompson, "New Species of Bank Notes," *The English Review* (December 1796), 589; and S.R. Cope, "The Original Security Bank," *Economica* Volume 13 (February 1946), 51, citing *The Times* (2 December 1796); Cope cites the *Morning Chronicle* (23 September, 5 October, and 21 October 1796).

50 See Playfair memoirs, fol. 26, and William Playfair, *A Fair Statement of the Proceedings of the Bank of England, Against the Original Security Bank on Tuesday the Seventh of March 1797* (London: Printed for the Author, 8 March 1797), 9–10, where Playfair identifies Astlett, Kaye, and Carter. Kaye is further identified in Randall McGowen, "Managing the Gallows: The Bank of England and the Death Penalty, 1797–1821," *Law and History Review*, Volume 25 (Summer, 2007), 241–282.

51 Playfair memoirs, fol. 27. Playfair indicates the location of the meeting in his letter to Jan Casper Hartsinck (Mansion House, 3 o'clock), NAGL ADD MS 403. Playfair did not date this letter, but it matches the description of the note that he recalled in his memoirs sending Hartsinck.

52 See *The Tomahawk!* (7 November 1795), 40; and *The Tomahawk!* (9 November, 1795), 46.

53 Playfair memoirs, fol. 27. Playfair described Watson's demeanor in *Fair Statement*, 17.

54 William Playfair to Jan Casper Hartsinck (Mansion House, 3 o'clock), NAGL ADD MS 403.

55 Larry Allen, *The Encyclopedia of Money* (Santa Barbara, CA: ABC-CLIO, LLC, Greenwood Publishing Group, 2009), 38. Parliament would amend the law in May.

56 Playfair memoirs, fols. 27–28.

57 Playfair, *Fair Statement*, 4.

58 Ibid., 8–9.

59 Ibid.

60 Ibid.

61   This inscription appeared on the cover of the copy I used; it matches Playfair's handwriting—nearly indecipherable, as usual.

62   Andrew Knapp and William Baldwin, *The Newgate Calendar: Comprising Interesting Memoirs of the Most Notorious Characters Who Have Been Convicted of Outrages on the Laws of England*, Volume 3 (London: J. Robins and Co., 1825), 367–376. Some accounts indicate Aslett was acquitted on a technicality; these appear to overlook that he was tried again on related, but different charges.

63   Cope, "Original Security Bank," 50–55.

64   Robert Oliver, "Transcript of Interview with Sydney Cope," Oral History Research Office, Columbia University (August 9, 1961), 1–2. The interview is part of the World Bank/IFC Archives Oral History Program. Cope is misidentified as "Sydney H. Cope" in the transcript, but Oliver's summary has Cope's correct name.

65   Cope, "Original Security Bank," 54–55. Cope was referring to either Henry Thornton, Member for Southwark; or his brother Robert Thornton, Member for Colchester; and either Francis Baring, Member for Chipping Wycombe and Calne; or his brother John Baring, Member for Exeter. John and Francis founded what eventually became Barings Bank.

66   Cope, "Original Security Bank," 51. Cope was quoting from Playfair's obituary in *Gentleman's Magazine*, Volume 43, Part 1 (January–June 1823), 564; the speculation that Playfair might have been indifferent as to whether or not the Ohio lands existed is his own.

67   William Playfair, "A Statement by W. Playfair," NAGL ADD MS 403. The document heading actually seems to read "A Statement se by W Playfair" or (less likely) "A Statement re by W Playfair." But it's not clear what the "se" or "re" might refer to. This could be "the statement I made on Tuesday" that Playfair mentioned in his 26 May 1798 note to William Hutchins, as there are no other documents in the file that fit the description. Playfair numbered the pages, but there is no date or signature on the last page, so it's possible there were additional pages. The file can be ordered from the London Metropolitan Archive through http://discovery.nationalarchives.gov.uk/details/rd/N13974147 (accessed 4 April 2017).

68   Playfair, "A Statement by W. Playfair," 1 NAGL ADD MS 403.

69   Playfair, "A Statement by W. Playfair," 2 NAGL ADD MS 403.

70   Playfair, "A Statement by W. Playfair," 2 NAGL ADD MS 403. For Edward May's bankruptcy, see *London Gazette* (17 February 1798), 159; and *London Gazette* (19–23 February 1799), 184.

71   Mark S. Auburn, "Theatre in the Age of Garrick and Sheridan," in James Morwood and David Crane, eds., *Sheridan Studies* (Cambridge: Cambridge University Press, 1995), 36–45.

72   The subject was the impeachment of Warren Hastings, governor-general of India, for corruption. See "Sheridan: The Trial of Warren Hastings," 1789), in Williams Jenning Bryan and Francis W. Halsey, eds., *The World's Famous Orations* Volume 6 (New York: Funk and Wagnalls Company, 1906), 77–98.

73   For Sheridan's legislative record and reputation, see "SHERIDAN, Richard Brinsley (1751–1816), of no fixed address," in R. G. Thorne, *The History of Parliament: the House of Commons 1790–1820* (London: Boydell & Brewer, 1986). Available at http://www.historyofparliamentonline.org/volume/1790-1820/member/sheridan-richard-brins-

ley-1751-1816 (accessed 7 October 2016). Also see Fraser Rae, "Sheridan, Richard Brinsley (1751–1816)," in Sidney Lee, ed., *Dictionary of National Biography*, Volume 18 (New York: The Macmillan Company, 1909), 78–85.

74 Specifics of the mutinies are taken from Conrad Gill, *The Naval Mutinies of 1797* (Manchester: Manchester University Press, 1913). Also see Ann Veronia Coats and Philip MacDougall, eds., *The Naval Mutinies of 1797: Unity and Perseverance* (Woodbridge, Suffolk: The Boydell Press, 2011).

75 Constitutional Friend, *Speeches of Sheridan*, Volume 4, 276–281.

76 Ibid., 397–405.

77 Ibid., 405–410.

78 Playfair, *Political Portraits*, Volume 2, 348.

79 Ibid., Volume 1, 327.

80 See Thomas Moore, *Memoirs of the Life of the Right Honorable Richard Brinsley Sheridan* Volume 1 (Philadelphia: A Sherman, 1826), 171; and W.J. Fitzpatrickm *Secret Service Under Pitt* (London: Longmans, Green, and Co. 1892), 113. Also see William Johnson Neale, *Narrative of the Mutiny at the Nore* (London: William Tegg, 1861), 225. Neale served in the Royal Navy early in his life, and then became a lawyer and novelist. Conrad Gill (see below), who wrote the most frequently referenced history of the mutinies, considered Neale inaccurate but nevertheless occasionally cited him. Gill discusses the removal of the buoys on 195–196, but says nothing about involvement by Sheridan.

81 Conrad Gill, *The Naval Mutinies of 1797* (Manchester: Manchester University Press, 1913), 202–203. Gill cites the *Admiralty Digest* 7 June 1797, 150.

82 Playfair, *A Fair and Candid Address*, 94. Playfair says the dinner occurred "on the same day that Mr. Sheridan acted so noble a part in the House of Commons," referring to the speech Sheridan delivered on 2 June, urging a united front against the mutineers; see "Constitutional Friend," *Speeches of Sheridan*, Volume 4, 405–410.

83 Playfair, *Political Portraits*, Volume 2, 105–106.

84 F. O'Gorman, *The Whig Party and the French Revolution* (London: Macmillan, 1967), 70–90. O'Gorman argued that the French Revolution was a catalyst that triggered or accelerated the impact of a number of fault lines among the Whigs.

85 Playfair, *A Fair and Candid Address*, 94–95.

86 Playfair, *History of Jacobinism*, 20.

87 Playfair, *A Fair and Candid Address*, 94–95.

88 William Playfair to C. Kirkpatrick Sharpe (Thavies Inn, 2 December 1809), reproduced in Alexander Allardyce, ed., *Letters From and To Charles Kirkpatrick Sharpe, Esq.* (Edinburgh and London: William Blackwood and Sons, 1888), 393. Playfair went on to say, "and consequently the Edinburgh Reviewers, and those who follow the new fashions, have long declared deadly war against me."

89 Cope, "Original Security Bank," 55. Cope cites *Commons Journals*, Volume 52, 623. Also see *Annual Register*, 1797, "History of Europe," 204. Constitutional Friend, *Speeches of Sheridan*, Volume 4,1816), 420.

90 See the complaint by two renters who filed charges after the Bank's collapse, Charles Durnford and Edward Hyde East, "Haussoullier Against Hartsinck and Others," in *Reports of Cases Argued and Determined in the Court of King's Bench*, Michaelmas Term, 37th

George III, 1796 to Trinity Term, 38th George III, 1798. Volume 7 (Dublin: L. White, Byrne, J. Moore, and J. Rice, 1799), 733–735.

91 Fraser Rae insisted that Sheridan's financial problems were exaggerated; see his "Sheridan, Richard Brinsley (1751–1816)," in Sidney Lee, ed., *Dictionary of National Biography*, Volume 18 (New York: The Macmillan Company, 1909), 78–85. But Rae was writing almost a hundred years after the fact, and provides no hard evidence other than the extravagance of Sheridan's funeral. Playfair, who knew Sheridan personally and was sympathetic, described Sheridan's difficulties in his profile in *Politcal Portraits*.

92 *London Gazette* (2–5 January 1813), 40; and *London Gazette* (9 January 1813), 61.

93 Playfair, *Political Portraits*, Volume 2, 351.

94 Ibid., 348.

95 *The Times*, 18 April 1802, 3; William Playfair to William Curtis (Newgate, 23 May 1798) and William Playfair to W. Wadeson (25 May 1798), NAGL ADD MS 403.

96 Playfair, "A Statement by W. Playfair," 4, NAGL ADD MS 403.

97 Ibid., 3.

98 Cope, "Original Security Bank," 55.

99 *London Gazette* (17 February 1798), 159.

100 William Playfair to William Curtis (Newgate, 30 June 1798), NAGL ADD MS 403; Playfair wrote his solicitor that he had been served with a subpoena by Bernal and assignees. The amounts he owed to Bernal are given in NA PRIS 10 Records of the Fleet Prison; accessed via Ancestry.com under "Piece 156: London, England, King's Bench and Fleet Prison Discharge Books and Prisoner Lists, 1734–1862," Image 432.

101 William Playfair to William Curtis (Newgate, 23 May 1798) and William Playfair to W. Wadeson (25 May 1798) NAGL ADD MS 403. Playfair also spent eleven days in Newgate Prison before being released on bail. See HO 26, Piece 6, Page 82; accessed via Ancestry.com "England & Wales, Criminal Registers, 1791–1892."

102 Playfair, *Increase of Manufactures*, 65–66.

103 See Walter Thornbury, "The Fleet Prison," in *Old and New London*, Volume 2 (London: Cassell & Company, 1878), 404–416. Also see John Ashton, *The Fleet: Its River, Prison, and Marriages* (London: T. Fisher Unwin, 1888).

104 Edward Hutton, *A New View of London: or an Ample Account of that City in Eight Sections*, Volume 2 (London: John Nicholson, 1708), 745.

105 NA PRIS 10 Records of the Fleet Prison; accessed via Ancestory.com under "Piece 052: Fleet Prison: Entry Books for Discharges (1793–1805), Image 252.

106 *The Evening Mail* (30 March 1798), 4.

107 *London Gazette* (13 April 1827), 857. Criticisms of Byzantium are possibly unjustified; see Judith Herrin, *Byzantium: The Surprising Life of a Medieval Empire* (Princeton, NJ: Princeton University Press, 2008).

108 Notices in *London Gazette* from July to August 1801 list Playfair's residence as Fleet Prison. See *London Gazette* (4 July 1801), 764; (11 July 1801), 832; (18 August 1801), 1027; and (22 August 1801), 1043. Additional notices appear in the editions of (13 October 1801), 1261; (22 December 1801), 1526; 16 January 1802), p 65; (6 February 1802), 65; (22 February 1800), 193; (27 February 1802), 225; and (31 July 1802), 813; these do not list him as living in Fleet, but indicate the duration of his bankruptcy proceedings. There was some confusion in the notices appearing in the *Gazette*. The 4 July edition lists a "first

notice," the 18 August edition lists a "second notice" and the edition of 22 August lists a "third notice." But the 11 July edition lists a "third notice," as well.

109 See the government's brief in *Rex v. Kennett, Kennett, Kennett, and Playfair* (21 July 1805), NA TS 11/457, which describes Playfair as a bankrupt, although he was apparently free to do business. Also see *The Times* (23 December 1805), 3–4; it says that because of the bankruptcy of the "well known banking-house of Playfair, Hartsinck, Playfair, and Co." *[sic]* at that time Playfair "not having obtained his certificate, he remained a prisoner in the Fleet, but was subsequently discharged under the Insovent Act."

110 See *London Gazette* (21 July 1798), 694–695; and William Page, ed., *A History of the County of Bedford,* Volume 2 (London, 1908). Available at http://www.british-history.ac.uk/vch/beds/vol2/pp206-209 (accessed 30 March 2016).

111 *London Gazette* (23 December 1800), 1450; Lucy Hutchinson, *Memoirs of the Life of Colonel Hutchinson,* Seventh Edition (London: Henry G. Bohn, 1848), xi.

112 Rev. Julius Hutchinson and Lucy Hutchinson, *Memoirs of Colonel Hutchinson* (London: Longman, Hurst, Rees, and Orme, 1806), frontmatter.

113 *London Gazette* (31 October 1798), 974; Memorandum by William Playfair, 6, NAGL ADD MS 403. Playfair was familiar with Angerstein and respected him; see Playfair, *Political Portraits,* Volume 1, 121–124.

114 *The Times,* 18 April 1802, 3. The commissioners may have only disallowed parts of the certificate, but the effect was the same: Hartsinck was toast.

115 Memorandum by William Playfair, 9, NAGL ADD MS 403.

116 Aubrey Le Blond, *Charlotte Sophie Countess Bentinck: Her Life and Times, 1715–1800* Volume 2 (London: Hutchinson & Co.), 161.

117 A.F. Twist, *Widening Circles in Finance, Philanthropy, and the Arts: A Study of the Life of John Julius Angerstein, 1735–1823,* Ph.D. thesis, University of Amsterdam, Instituut voor Cultuur en Geschiedenis, 2002, Chapter 5.

118 David J. Breeze, ed., *The Society of Antiquaries of Newcastle upon Tyne, 1813–2013* (Newcastle: The Society of Antiquaries of Newcastle upon Tyne, 2013), 1–14.

119 I published the broad outlines of the story as I understood it at the time in "An Agent of Influence," *The American Interest,* October/November 2009), 102–109, working from transcrips of Sir John's memorandum and photographs of the molds.

120 See https://www.youtube.com/watch?v=Fdjf4lMmiiI (accessed 14 January 2017). For those with an interest, the Ark is in Crate No. 990673.

121 Bower, "Economic Warfare, 46–63.

122 These are Playfair's words, from *France As It Is,* Volume 2, 243.

Chapter 9: Inventing Political Economy

1 Stuart, *Steam-Engines,* 549.

2 William Playfair to R.S. Wadeson (18 April 1805), NAGL ADD MS 403.

3 William Playfair to R.S. Wadeson (18 September 1805), NAGL ADD MS 403.

4 A notice ("Advertisement") on 64 of the first edition of the *Statistical Breviary,* in which Playfair solicits readers for information to be used in a future publication, is dated 30 July 1801. The *London Gazette* lists him as a prisoner in Fleet in notices of 4 July 1801, 11 July

1801, 18 August 1801, and 22 August 1801—meaning Playfair almost certainly wrote *The Statistical Breviary* while residing there.

5   John Stockdale, ed., *A Geographical Historical, and Political Description of the Empire of Germany, Holland, the Netherlands, Switzerland, Prussia, Italy, Sicily, Corsica, and Sardinia* (London: John Stockdale, 1800).

6   According to the compendium by James Thorold Rogers, *A History of Agriculture and Prices in England* (Oxford: Oxford University Press, 1866), during the latter eighteenth century a cow cost roughly four pounds; see 362–375.

7   Stockdale, *Geographical Historical, and Political Description...*, 9.

8   John Stockdale, ed., *Statistical Tables Exhibiting a View of All the States of Europe* (London: John Stockdale, 1800).

9   Jakob Gottlieb Boetticher, *Statistische Uebersichts-Tabellen aller Europäischen Staaten* (Königsberg, 1790). Boetticher's book is cited often, but there's little information available about him. For his dates of birth and death, see the Deutsche Digitale Bibliothek enty at https://www.deutsche-digitale-bibliothek.de/item/66V3F4BCQOKKQCEANED-NTMSCVSWPF62Q (accessed 23 June 2016). The only other work by Boetticher that comes up in searches is *Winke für Eltern, Erzieher und Jünglinge die Selbstbefleckung betreffend*, published in 1791. Few cities have had as tumultuous a history as Königsberg (currently, Kaliningrad); once the home of Immanuel Kant, at has been attacked, at various times, by Russian, French, Prussian, and German armies; bombed by the Royal Air Force in 1944; and overrun, depopulated, and annexed by the Soviet Union in 1945–1946. It may be expected that its archives and libraries are in less than pristine condition.

10 William Playfair, *The Statistical Breviary* (London: J. Wallis, et al, 1801), 3.

11 Ibid., A1.

12 Ibid., 4.

13 See "The World Factbook," available at https://www.cia.gov/library/publications/resources/the-world-factbook/ (accessed 19 April 2017).

14 Playfair, *Statistical Breviary*, 16.

15 Wainer, *Graphic Discovery*, 9; Wainer credits the question, "Why Playfair?" to social scientist Albert Biderman and a community of statisticians, including Patricia Costigan-Eaves and Michael Macdonald-Ross, who rediscovered Playfair in the late 1980s.

16 Playfair, *Inquiry*, xvi.

17 William Playfair, *The Commercial and Political Atlas*, Third Edition (London: J. Wallis, Carpenter & Co, Verner and Hood, and Black and Parry, 1801), xi. Italics in the original.

18 See Dickinson, *James Watt: Craftsman & Engineer*, 108; and Dickinson and Jenkins, *Watt and the Steam Engine*, 226–227. They say Watt came up with the basic idea of a mechanical counter in 1775, and Boulton's improvements made it tamper-proof and expanded its capacity.

19 The British Science Museum has such a cord-operated "step counter" that Augsburg watchmaker Johann Willebrand crafted sometime before his death in 1727. See "Pedometer, Gilded Brass and Silver, Cord Operated." Available at http://collection.sciencemuseum.org.uk/objects/co53024/pedometer-gilded-brass-and-silver-cord-operated-pedometer (accessed 1 March 2017). Pendulum-powered pedometers began to appear at about the same time as self-winding watches; the mechanisms are similar. Abraham-Louis Perrelet usually gets credit for the basic idea behind both, along with Abraham-Louis

Bréguet and Louis Recordon. See John Jewkes, David Sawers, and Richard Stillerman, *The Sources of Invention*, Second Edition (New York: Macmillan and Company, 1969), 293–294. The pedometer mechanism used in the illustration near this note is actually from the 1830s or 1840s, but it's nearly identical to the one patented by Perrelet.

20 Matthew Boulton to James Watt (12 May 1777), reproduced in Dickinson and Jenkins, *Watt and the Steam Engine*, 227.

21 See Dickinson and Jenkins, *Watt and the Steam Engine*, 228–233.

22 See Dionysius Lardner, *The Steam Engine Explained and Illustrated* (London: Taylor and Walton, 1840), 274–277.

As if to prove a totally different approach can lead to a similar result, see Michael S. Reidy, "Gauging Science and Technology in the Early Victorian Era," in Helen M. Rozwadowski and David K. van Keuren, eds., *The Machine in Neptune's Garden: Historical Perspectives on Technology and the Marine Environment* (Sagamore Beach, MA: Science History Publications, 2004), 1–38. Reidy looked at the development of recording tidal guages in the early 1800s. He notes how they produced their own form of statistical graphics—and points out that that the idea came not academics or philosophers, but from harbormasters and naval surveyors needing a practical solution to a problem (3–4). Playfair and Watt would have both been pleased.

David Philip Miller traced the development of the Indicator (and a possible attempt by James Watt, Junior, to fake the true date of its invention to enhance the stature of his father) in "The Mysterious Case of James Watt's '1785' Steam Indicator: Forgery or Folklore in the History of an Instrument?" *International Journal for the History of Engineering and Technology*, Volume 81 (January 2011), 132–134. Miller cites W. J. M. Rankine, "On the Geometrical Representation of the Expansive Action of Heat, and the Theory of Thermodynamic Engines," *Philosophical Transactions* (1854), 115–76, in which Rankine credited Watt for the "first application of a geometric diagram depicting engine performance."

23 See Playfair, *A Fair and Candid Address*, 93–94.

24 For Donnant's background, see "Denis-François Donnant," in A.V. Arnault, A. Jay, E. Jouy, and J. Norvins, *Biographie nouvelle des Contemporains*, Volume 6 (Paris: La Librairie Historiquem 1822), 49–50. For Donnant's link to the Academy and publications, see Joseph Marie Quérard, *Les supercheries littéraires dévoilées*, Volume 3 (Paris: Librairie de Féchoz et Letouzey, 1850), 5–6.

25 See D.F. Donnant, *Statistical Account of the United States of America* (London: Greenland and Norris, 1805).

26 See Tufte, *Visual Display of Quantitative Information*, 178.

27 Robert Browning, "Andrea del Sarto," in Basil Worsford, ed., *Men and Women* Volume 2 (London: Alesander Moring, 1904), 5. The aphorism is also often attributed to Ludwig Mies Van Der Rohe, with Philip Johnson publicizing it; see Tom Wolfe, *From Bauhaus to Our House* (New York: Farrar, Straus and Giroux, 1981), 57.

28 Playfair, *Statistical Breviary*, 9.

29 William Playfair to Thomas Jefferson (Old Brompton, 17 April 1805). Available at http://founders.archives.gov/documents/Jefferson/99-01-02-1534 (accessed 29 May 2016).

30 Playfair, *Political Portraits*, Volume 2, 191. In this portait of James Madison, Playfair praised Washington in passing, and blamed Madison for botching British-American relations.

31   See "Sowerby Catalogue Volume III" in *Thomas Jefferson's Libraries*, available at http://
tjlibraries.monticello.org/transcripts/sowerby/III 27.html (accessed 21 December 2015).
Three of Playfair's books were in the collection Jefferson sold to the government and now
in the Library of Congress: *The Commercial and Political Atlas, Tableaux a'Arithmetique lineaire*, and *The Statistical Breviary*. But the *Statistical Account of the United States of America*
was not among them, so he may have regifted his copy. At least one of Jefferson's correspondents cited Playfair's *Commercial and Political Atlas*; see "Tench Coxe's Notes on the
American Fisheries," [ca. 23 November 1790], Available at: http://founders.archives.gov/
documents/Jefferson/01-19-02-0013-0005 (accessed 24 November 2015), reproduced in
Papers of Thomas Jefferson, Volume 19, 182–195.

32   Alexander von Humboldt to Thomas Jefferson (Paris, 12 June 1809), reproduced in *Papers
of Thomas Jefferson*, Volume 1, 264–267; available at http://founders.archives.gov/docu-
ments/Jefferson/03-01-02-0215 (accessed 18 Aug 2015). Also see Helmut de Terra, "Alexander von Humbolt's Correspondence with Jefferson, Madison, and Gallatin," *Proceedings of the American Philosophical Society*, Volume 103, Studies of Historical Documents in
the Library of the American Philosophical Society (15 December 1959), 790. Jefferson
might have sent him copies of either *Lineal Arithmetic* or *The Statistical Breviary*, both of
which Hulboldt cited later in his own book; see Alexander de Humboldt, *Political Essay on
the Kingdom of New Spain*, Volume 4 (London: Longman, Hurst, Rees, Orme, and Brown,
1822), 246, 320, and 352.

33   James Alexander Lovat-Fraser *Henry Dundas, Viscount Melville* (London: Cambridge
University Press, 1916), 69–75.

34   William Playfair to Henry Dundas (Ludgate Hill, 3 August 1799), NAS GD51/3/646/1;
and William Playfair to Henry Dundas (Ludgate Hill, 7 September 1799) NAS
GD51/3/646/2. The draft was likely Playfair's *Strictures on the Asiatic Establishments of
Great Britain* (London: Carpenter and Co.; and Murray and Highly, 1799).

35   William Playfair to Henry Dundas (Old Brompton, 9 October 1804). Temple University
Libraries, Special Collections Research Center (SPC), MSS BH 118 COCH. Dundas
returned to the government with Pitt in 1804 to become First Lord of the Admiralty, but
was impeached for financial mismanagement in 1806—the same year Pitt died. He was
acquitted, but never returned to politics.

36   See J.G. Alger, "British Visitors to Paris, 1802–03," *The English Historical Review*, Volume
14 (October 1899), 740. Alger writes, "National Archives at Paris contain a register (F 7*,
2231) of the principal foreign visitors from February to November 1802," and provides a
list of names, which includes Playfair. Alger says the list also includes Jeremy Bentham.

37   Sir Richard Phillips to Thomas Dale (London, 25 February 1802), BL ©BLB, Loan 96
RLF 1/121/1. The Royal Literary Fund files from between 1790 to the mid twentieth
century are available through the British Library. Playfair's file is catalogued under Loan
96 RLF 1/121. The correspondence from from Phillips is signed only as "R. Phillips," but
the return address was given as "71 St. Paul's," which was Sir Richard's residence.

38   The Fund became the Royal Literary Fund after Prince Albert took an interest in it
during the 1840s and served as its president, though it has always been privately financed.
See "The Literary Fund," *The Literary Gazette* (14 May 1842), 330; *The Royal Literary
Fund*, Annual Report (London, 1866), 3–15; and Janet Adam Smith, "A Short History,"
available on the Fund's website at https://www.rlf.org.uk/wp-content/uploads/2013/10/

RLFShortHistory.pdf (accessed 27 May 2016). Also see David Williams' own account in the book he co-authored with William Boscawen, *The Claims of Literature* (London: W. Miller, 1802).

39   See the summary record for "Registered Case, No. 121, Vol. 3," BL © Loan 96 RLF 1/121; Sir Richard Phillips to Thomas Dale (London, 15 March 1802), BL © Loan 96 RLF 1/121/2; and the receipt from William Playfair (Old Brompton, 23 March 1802), BL © Loan 96 RLF 1/121/3.

40   "An Inquiry into the Causes of the Decline and Fall of Nations," *The Tomahawk!* (11 November 1795), 53.

41   Dugald Stewart, "Account of the Life and Writings of Adam Smith LL.D.," *Transactions of the Royal Society of Edinburgh* (21 January and 18 March 1793); reprinted in Sir William Hamilton, ed., *The Collected Works of Dugald Stewart*, Volume 10 (Edinburgh: Thomas Constable and Company, 1858), 5–98.

42   "Inquiry," *Tomahawk!* (11 November 1795), 53. Playfair was apparently unable to complete this serial before the newspaper ceased publication.

43   Playfair, *Inquiry*, 79.

44   Playfair, *Inquiry*, xvi.

45   For Playfair's encounter with Smith, see Rae, *Life of Adam Smith*, 334–337 and 404.

46   For the political leanings of *The Critical Review*, see Maurice Cross, *Selections from the Edinburgh Review*, Volume 1 (Paris: Baudry's European Library, 1835), 8–91 and Sack, *From Jacobite to Conservative*, 63–64.

47   *The Critical Review* (June 1806), 1–2, 170.

48   Ibid., 166.

49   *The Anti-Jacobin Review* Volume 22 (September–December 1806), 245.

50   Ibid., 259.

51   *The Monthly Review* (July 1807), 224–238.

52   Watt went on to fill much of that knowledge gap; see David Philip Miller, *Discovering Water: James Watt, Henry Cavendish, and the Nineteenth Century 'Water Controversy'* (Aldershot, UK: Ashgate Publishing, 2004).

53   Playfair, *Inquiry*, vii.

54   In effect, Playfair said, Smith was applying his idea about the efficiencies from the division of labor to nations. See Playfair, *France As It Is*, Volume 1, xxxii–xxxiii.

55   David Weatherall, *David Ricardo: A Biography* (The Hague: Martinus Nijhoff, 1976), 70–71. The popular story has Ricardo using early news of the British victory to gull counterparts into dumping stock which he then bought at a bargain price; in Weatherall's account, Ricardo was simply daring, and put all his money on a bet he was confident he would win.

56   David Ricardo, *On the Principles of Political Economy and Taxation* (London: John Murray, 1817), 156–157.

57   Playfair, *Inquiry*, 290–291.

58   For readers who track down original sources, some clarifications: First, just before the passage quoted you will find Playfair saying:

> Variety of soil and climate, difference of taste, of manners, and an infinity of other causes, have rendered commerce necessary, though it does not increase

the aggregate wealth of mankind: but nations are in an error when they set a greater value on commerce than on productive industry. (*Inquiry*, 289)

Playfair was saying that trade ("commerce") only results in an exchange of goods; it doesn't create additional goods ("wealth"); he says only "productive industry" will achieve that. Ricardo, on the other hand, believed that under free trade each nation will find its optmal niche and capital will find its best use, and that will indeed increase the world's wealth, and, moreover, all nations would benefit. That disagreement—whether free trade creates more wealth, or simply makes some wealthier at the expense of others—is at the nub of many arguments about free trade even today, even among those (like Playfair and Ricardo) who favor free trade.

Second, at the end of the quoted passage, Playfair goes on to say:

Let France make good laws to favour industry; and, above all, render property secure, and she will have no occasion to envy England. (*Inquiry*, 291)

Playfair was not suggesting France adopt a policy to encourage *industrialization*; quite the opposite, he believed France should concentrate on agriculture. He was arguing for property laws encouraging Frenchmen to be *industrious*.

59   Piero Sraffa, ed., with M.H. Dobb, *The Works and Correspondence of David Ricardo* Volume 6 (Cambridge: Cambridg University Press, 1973), xxviii. Also see John Bowring, ed., *The Works of Jeremy Bentham, Part XX* (Edinburgh: William Tait, 1842), 498.

60   For Ricardo's account of the Bentham-Ricardo-Mill relationship, see James Bonar, ed., *Letters of David Ricardo to Thomas Robert Malthus, 1810–1823* (Oxford: Clarendon Press, 1887), passim.

61   Playfair, *Joseph and Benjamin*, 38, 37–38. The full quotation from Playfair "Franklin" is, "Our luxuries, which should be few, we should purchase with the overplus of of this sort of labour." Playfair was familiar with Franklin's prescriptions for austerity and making a man healthy, wealthy, and wise.

62   Playfair, *Thoughts on the Present State of French Politics*, 31–32.

63   Playfair, *France As It Is*, Volume 1, 6.

64   David Levy and Sandra Peart have tracked the evolution in thinking about group differences and economic behavior; see David M. Levy and Sandra J. Peart, "Group Analytics in Adam Smith's Work," *Eastern Economic Journal* (September 2016), 514–527; and Sandra J. Peart and David M. Levy, "Attitudes Toward Race, Hierarchy and Transformation in the 19th Century," *History of Economic Thought* Volume 47 (December 2005), 15–31.

65   Playfair, *Inquiry*, v and 90–91.

66   Mancur Olson, *The Rise and Decline of Nations: Economic Growth, Stagflation, and Social Rigidities* (New Haven: Yale University Press, 1982).

67   Playfair, *Inquiry*, 99–101.

68   Henry William Spiegel, "Theories of Economic Development: History and Classification," *Journal of the History of Ideas*, Volume 16 (October 1955), 530.

69   Playfair, *Inquiry*, 132.

70   Joshua Montefiore, *The Creditor and Bankrupt's Assistant: Being the Spirit of the Bankrupt Laws, With Observations* (London: W. Clarke and Sons, 1806).

71 See Byerley, "Mr. William Playfair," *Literary Chronicle* (15 March 1823), 172. Also see T. J. Carty, ed., *A Dictionary of Literary Pseudonyms in the English Language,* Second Edition (New York: Routledge, 2004).

72 J. Montefiore, *An Authentic Account of the Late Expedition to Bulam on the Coast of Africa* (London: J. Johnson, 1794).

73 Lucien Wolf, *Sir Moses Montefiore: A Centennial Biography Wih Extracts from Letters and Journals* (New York: Harper & Brothers, 1885), 7–9.

74 *London Gazette* (11–14 July 1801), 832, posts Monetefiore's first notice and Playfair's third notice; they are both listed as "Prisoners in His Majesty's Prison of the Fleet." An earlier notice indicates Monetefiore was ordered to surrender himself to commissioners and make a declaration of his possessions, the step preceding their liquidation; see *London Gazette* (5 February 1799), 133. A later notice indicates he received his certificate; see *London Gazette* (9 April 1799), 346. Montefiore's third notice appears in *London Gazette* (18 July 1801), 885. According to a communication from his fourth-great-granddaughter, citing his discharge papers, Montefiore was committed to debtor's prison on 20 January 1801 and discharged 6 August 1802.

75 See Joshua Montefiore, *Commercial Dictionary: Containing the Present State of Mercantile Law* (London: Printed for the Author, 1803), xxxvii. For Playfair's endorsement of *Law of Copyright,* see *American Jewish Historical Quarterly,* Volume 40 (1950), 133.

76 For Montefiore's commission as an ensign in the York Light Infantry Volunteers, see *London Gazette* (21 February 1807), 226. An earlier notice lists him as quartermaster for the London Loyal Volunteers; see *London Gazette* (23 July 1805), 956.

77 Diagnoses two centuries after the fact are always risky, especially by nonprofessionals, but gout would not leave a man bedridden for months or unable to write, as Playfair said he sometimes was. Peripheral arterial disease or an advanced case of or rheumatoid arthritis could, and would also be more likely to lead to the other health problems Playfair faced in has later years.

78 Playfair, *Political Portraits,* Volume 2, 344.

79 For a concise summary of the riots, see the introduction by Ian Haywood and John Seed, eds., in *The Gordon Riots: Politics, Culture and Insurrection in Late Eighteenth Britain* (Cambridge, UK: Cambridge University Press, 2012), 1–9.

80 See the account in the letter from Edward Gibbon to his stepmother (London, 8 June 1780), reproduced in Rowland E. Prothero, ed., *Private Letters of Edward Gibbon (1753–1794)* Volume 1 (London: John Murray, 1896). 393. For a description of the battle at the Bank of England, see (unattributed) *Tales of the Bank of England: With Anecdotes of London Bankers* (London: James Hogg, 1882), 72; and James Williams, "Holroyd, John Baker, first Earl of Sheffield (1785–1821)," in Sidney Lee, ed., *Dictionary of National Biography,* Volume 27 (London: Smith, Elder, & Co, 1891), 200–202.

81 William Playfair to John Baker-Holroyd (11 April 1807), BL © Loan 96 RLF 1/121/4. This letter raises a few questions. Playfair said his eldest daughter was blind; his eldest daughter was Elizabeth. But Elizabeth went on to marry, emigrated to Canada, and was mother to at least one daughter, born in 1818; in all, a challenging, but not insurmountable series of challenges for a blind woman. Zenobia, the youngest daughter, never married, and went on to live a long life in England as a servant and governess—a frequent

profession for educated blind single women—reflected in the establishment of an annuity for Deaf and Blind Governesses in 1836 by Rev. David Laing.

82 See the Fund's report, *An Account of the Institution of the Society for the Establishment of the Literary Fund* (London: 1804), 44.

83 See Rachel Rogers, "Vectors of Revolution: The British Radical Community in Early Republican Paris, 1792–1794."Ph.D. Dissertation, Department of History. Université Toulouse le Mirail, 2012, 11. Available at https://halshs.archives-ouvertes.fr/tel-00797967/document (accessed 2 September 2016).

84 William Playfair to David Williams; (Old Brompton, 9 May 1807; 13 May 1807; 16 May 1807; 6 June 1807; 12 June 1807); and BL © BLB, Loan 96 RLF 1/121/5, 6, 8, 9, 10; and "List of Works by William Playfair," BL © BLB, Loan 96 RLF 1/121/7.

85 Saying "there are no records" is a chancy assertion, but, other than the patent he shared with Playfair, le Farre simply does not seem to turn up no matter the archival catalogue, database, or search engine one uses. For the patent he and Playfair shared, see Woodcroft, *Subject-Matter Index of Patents*, 515; and *The Annual Register or a View of the History, Politics, and Literature for the Year 1800* (London: W. Otridge and Son, etc. 1801), 385.

86 Andrew Wilson, *Appendix to the Naval History of the United Kingdom* (London: John Murray et al., 1807), 13–14.

87 Andrew Knapp and William Baldwin, *The Newgate Calendar,* Volume 4 (London: J. Robins and Co., 1828), 117.

88 Case Brief, *Rex v. Kennett, Kennett, Kennett, and Playfair* (21 July 1805), NA TS 11/457/1520.

89 Knapp and Baldwin, *The Newgate Calendar,* Volume 4, 115–116.

90 W.M. Medland and Charles Weobly, *A Collection of Remarkable and Interesting Criminal Trials, Actions at Law, and Other Legal Decisions,* Volume 2 (London: John Badcock, 1804), 33–35; 422–430.

91 John Morgan and Thomas Walter William, *The Law Journal for Hilary and Easter Terms 1803* (London: Richard Phillips, 1803), 218–223.

92 Medland and Weobly, *Collection,* 427.

93 William Playfair to Spencer Perceval (Newgate, 31 April 1809 *sic*), NA TS 11/106, fol. 38a.

94 Medland and Weobly, *Collection,* 422–430; and *London Gazette* (22 May 1804), 658.

95 Playfair, *Political Portraits,* Volume 1, 280.

96 Isaac Espinasse, *Reports of Cases Argues and Ruled at Nisi Prius. In the Courts of King's Bench and Common Pleas, from Easter Term 33 George III 1793 to Hilary Term, 36 George III, 1796* (London: Butterworth, 1801), 391.

97 Playfair, *Political Portraits,* Volume 1, 293–306; and Playfair, *Political Portraits,* Volume 2, 10.

98 *The Times* (23 December 1805), 3–4.

99 *Rex v. Kennett, Kennett, Kennett, and Playfair* (27 April 1809), NA TS 11/457/1520. This court order refers to the Kennett case, even though it has Playfair being remanded to Newgate in response to a writ of habeous corpus four years after the trial.

100 See *Anticipation on Politics, Commerce and Finance During the Present Crisis* (12 March 1808), front cover. The first issue said the publication would consist of twenty-two "letters" issued weekly, so it was more like a serialized book than a newspaper. The last article in the

last edition ends with the words, "To be continued," but also it also says, "End of Vol. 1," so even Playfair might have been unsure. A collection of *Anticipation* issues is available at https://archive.org/details/anticipationonp00unkngoog (accessed 25 August 2026). This is a compilation Playfair apparently gave to Robert Clifford, an author who at the time wrote about the Jacobins and the French Revolution; Playfair autographed the title page. See the entry for Clifford in *A Biographical Dictionary of the Living Authors of Great Britain and Ireland* (London: Henry Colburn, 1816), 67. Windham's sponsorship is cited in some of Playfair's obituaries; see "Mr. William Playfair," *Gentleman's Magazine*, Volume 43, Part 1 (January–June 1823), 566.

101 *Anticipation* (12 March 1808), iv. Italics in the original.

102 Ibid. (12 March 1808), vi.

103 Ibid. (19 March 1808), 38–39.

104 Ibid. (12 March 1808), 14–16.

105 Ibid. (23 April 1808), 132–134.

106 Ibid. (9 April 1808), 94–95.

107 Ibid. (19 March 1808), 30–31.

108 People often ask if Playfair was responsible for the famous graphic depicting the invasion of Russia and the attrition of Napoleon's forces. It's a masterpiece of design, but Playfair wasn't the author; it was French civil engineer Charles Joseph Minard, who published it in 1869 as *Carte figurative des pertes successives en hommes de l'Armée Française dans la campagne de Russie 1812–1813*. Just as with Playfair's graphics, it wasn't fully appreciated until the twentieth century. See Tufte, *Visual Display of Quantitative Information*, 40–41: and John Corbett, "Charles Joseph Minard: Mapping Napoleon's March, 1861," *CSISS Classics* (Center for Spatially Integrated Social Science, 2001). Available at http://escholarship.org/uc/item/4qj8h064 (accessed 16 June 2016).

109 Woodress, *Yankee's Odyssey*, 144–149.

110 Joel Barlow to Capt. Chapin Sampson (Algiers, 1 Feb, 1797) Joel Barlow Papers, Letter Book 3, 6 September 1796–12 January 1797, 8 –10 and 20–22 Houghton Library, Harvard University; and Joel Barlow to R & J Montgomery (Algiers, 1 February 1797. Available at https://iiif.lib.harvard.edu/manifests/view/drs:51670551$12i Seq. 22–23 (accessed 12 September 2016). Also see Buel, *Joel Barlow*, 211–212.

111 Buel, *Joel Barlow*, 303.

112 According to the American Foreign Service Association, William Palfrey, a former aide to Washington and a commissioner appointed by the Continental Congress, was lost at sea in 1780. Barlow was the first diplomat to die after the Constitution was adopted. See "AFSA Memorial Plaque List," which lists the names on the memorial in the lobby of the State Department. Available at http://www.afsa.org/afsa-memorial-plaque-list (accessed 2 October 2015).

113 David Hume, "Essay VII: Of the Balance of Power," in *Essays and Treatises on Several Subjects* (Edinburgh: T. Cadell and W. Davies, 1809), 353–362.

114 Playfair, *Atlas*, Second Edition, 4.

115 William Playfair, *Outlines of a Plan for a New and Solid Balance of Power in Europe* (London: J, Stockdale, 1813), 15.

116 Ibid., 13.

117 Ibid., 22.

118 Ibid., 31.
119 Ibid., between 33 and 34.
120 Ibid., 48.
121 Playfair, *France As It Is*, Volume 2, 178.
122 Playfair, *Political Portraits*, Volume 2, 162; for Playfair's opinion of Alexander, see Playfair, *Political Portraits*, Volume 1, xi–xii and 111–121.

Chapter 10: Return to France, Back to Britain

1   William Playfair, *A statement, which was made in October, to Earl Bathurst, one of His Majesty's Principal Secretaries of State, and in November, 1814, to the comte de La Chatre, the French ambassador, of Buonaparte's plot to re-usurp the Crown of France* (London: J.J. Stockdale, 1815).
2   Batz, *Les conspirations et la fin 1793–1822*, 440–444, 7–8 and passim.
3   Playfair, *A Statement to Earl Bathurst...*, 23. One might wonder whether this cipher is related to the Playfair Cipher, well known in cryptographic circles. It is unlikely. The Playfair Cipher, promoted in the mid-nineteenth century by Lyon Playfair, 1st Baron Playfair, was invented by the scientist and inventor Charles Wheatstone. Even if Wheatstone was aware of William's 1815 pamphlet, the link to Baron Playfair (and thus the name) would have been a coincidence. See David Kahn, *The Codebreakers: The Story of Secret Writing* (New York: Scribner, 1967), 198–202.
4   Stanley Lane-Poole, "Morier, John Philip," *Dictionary of National Biography*, Sidney Lee, ed., Volume 34 (New York: Macmillan and Co, 1894), 52.
5   Playfair sometimes spelled "Windham" as "Wyndham."
6   See Playfair, *A Statement to Earl Bathurst...* It was also reprinted in foreign languages, e.g., Dutch, as *Waarschuwend Verslag, Reeds Gedaan in de Maand October 1814, aan den Engelschen Staats-Secretarrts Lord Bathurst, en Vervolgens in November Deszelven Jaars aan den Franschen Ambassadeur, den graaf de la Châtre, Wegens het Beraamd Ontwerp van Bounaparte, ter Ontsnapping van het Eiland Elba en Weder Overweldiging van den Franschen Troon* (Amsterdam: A. Vinnk en N. Budde, 1815). The cipher appeared later in collections of puzzles, amusements, and math challenges, e.g., *Curiosities for the Ingenious* (London: Thomas Boys, 1821), 50; and, in French, *Nouveau manuel de physique et de chimie amusantes...* (Paris: B. Renault, 1858), 299. Also see *The Times* (1 April 1815), 2.
7   *A Biographical Dictionary of the Living Authors of Great Britain and Ireland* (London: Henry Colburn, 1816), 276.
8   William Playfair to Earl Bathurst (Poland Street, 31 October 1814); William Playfair to Earl Bathurst (Finsbury Square, 3 November 1814); and William Playfair to Earl Bathurst (Finsbury Square, 5 November 1814), reproduced in Francis Bickley, ed., *Report on the Manuscripts of Earl Bathurst, Preserved at Cirencester Park* (London: HMSO, 1923), 220, 303, 304. The editors dated the first letter "3 November 1812," but this seems to be a mistake, as Napoleon would have been in the midst of his Moscow campaign at the time.
9   Playfair, *A Statement to Earl Bathurst*, iv.
10 For the events leading to the duel, see J. Mavidal and E. Laurent, eds., *Archives Parlementaires de 1787 a 1860*, Volume 20 (Paris: Librairie Administrative de Paul Dupont, 1870), 560–569.

11   See Rees Howell Gronow, *The Reminiscences and Recollections of Captain Gronow*, Volume 1 (London: John C. Nimmo, 1900), 104–105.

12   There are several accounts of the duel between Saint-Morys and Dufay; this composite relies mainly on a letter, "E. to Sylvanus Urban" (Paris, 25 July 1817), reproduced in *Gentleman's Magazine* (August, 1817), 117–119; and the section describing the duel in A.M. Stirling, *The Letter-Bag of Lady Elizabeth Spencer-Stanhope*, Volume 1 (London: John Lane, 1913), 260–263.

13   *Galignani's Messenger* (24 July 1817), 4. Issues are available through the Bibliothèque nationale de France (BnF) website, available at http://gallica.bnf.fr/ark:/12148/cb32779538j/date1817 (accessed 2 April 2016).

14   Many accounts say that Playfair became editor "after Waterloo," or mid-1815, but, as will be seen, numerous letters place him in London from July to December 1816. It would have been possible for Playfair to travel between London and Paris; as will also be seen, this would have been plausible and would have fit into his work at the *Messenger*, as well as other activities. But someone would have had to cover his travel costs, and there does not seem to be a mention anywhere that he was a regular commuter.

15   "English Literature in France," *The Monthly Magazine* (July–December 1837), 278–280.

16   See Diana Cooper-Richet and Emily Borgeaud; English version by Iain Watson, *Galignani* (Paris: Galignani, 1999), 4. The publication cites two M.A. theses: Nicholas Bernard-Dastaras, University of Versailles, *The Galignani Messenger: Nasissance et évolution d'un quotidien anglais à Pris (1814–1852)*, supervised by Diana Cooper-Richet and Emily Borgeaud, 1999; and Daniele Pluvinage, Faculté des Lettres et Sciences humaines de Paris, *Galignani's Messenger: an English Newspaper issued in Paris* supervised by Professor Pierre Nordon, 1968. Also see Giles Barber, "Galignani's and the Publication of English Books in France from 1800 to 1852," *The Library* 5th Series, Edition 16 (1961), 267–286.

17   W. Roberts, "Galignani's Messenger," *The Athenæum* No. 4007 (13 August 1904), 210. Technically, though laid out like a broadsheet, the *Messenger* was closer in size to a modern tabloid; broadsheets are much larger—usually 56 cm vertically and various widths.

18   Cyrus Redding says in his memoirs that "I agreed to become editor of Galignani's paper" at this time. See Charles Redding, *Fifty Years' Recollections, Literary and Personal*, Volume 2 (London: C.J. Skeet, 1858), 36. "Editors" at the *Messenger* seem to have doubled as reporters, so there were likely several, and Playfair and Redding may have had similar and overlapping responsibilities. In this connection, also see W. Roberts, "Galignani's Messenger," *The Athenæum* No. 4007 (13 August 1904), 210. Roberts observed that Redding was sometimes mistakenly cited as the first editor of the *Messenger*, noting that Redding arrived after the *Messenger* started publication. But Roberts was apparently unaware of Playfair; he surmised that Galignani edited the early editions himself.

Redding claimed that he was responsible for the account of the duel that appeared in the *Messenger*, writing in his memoirs that, "I gave as impartial an account of the duel as I was able." He recalled Dufay came to the office two days later, complaining the article was unfair. Redding assured him it was not, and that any misunderstanding was a result of Dufay's imperfect understanding of English (*Recollections*, 40–41).

19   W.M. Thackeray, *A Collection of Letters of W.M. Thackeray, 1847–1855* (London: Smith, Elder & Co., 1887).

20   *Galignani's Messenger* (2 September 1817), 1. Available at http://gallica.bnf.fr/ark:/12148/ bpt6k6775243t.item (accessed 21 April 2017).

21   *Galignani's Messenger* (1 September 1817), 4. Available at http://gallica.bnf.fr/ark:/12148/ bpt6k6775242d/f4.item (accessed 21 April 2017).

22   Marie-Anne-Charlotte de Valicourt Saint-Morys, *Dénonciation contre Guillaume-Michel-Étienne Barbier, dit Dufaÿ* (10 August 1817). WorldCat shows several available copies.

23   *Chambre des Pairs, Constituée en cour de justice* (Saturday, 31 January 1818). Also see J. Mavidal and E. Laurent, eds., *Archives Parlementaires de 1787 a 1860*, Volume 20 (Paris: Librairie Administrative de Paul Dupont, 1870), 560–569.

24   *Galignani's Messenger* (27 March 1818), 3; emphasis added. Available at http://gallica. bnf.fr/ark:/12148/bpt6k6775413c/f3.item (accessed 21 April 2017). Reports of the trial cited this phrase as the grounds for libel; see *Journal des débats politiques et littéraires* (8 July 1818), 4. Specifically: "Avant de lire le passage où l'on reproche à M. de Saint-Morys d'avoir été moins brave que son épée, et à sa veuve de réveiller, par une procédure criminelle, une affaire qu'elle auroit dû laisser tomber dans l'oubli, M. Couture a présenté les témoignages honorables de plusieurs maréchaux de France sur la conduite qu'il a tenue et dû tenir avant le duel." Part of Saint-Mory's case against Playfair was that French peers had testified to her husband's bravery.

25   *Galignani's Messenger* (27 March 1818), 4. There was also a "letter to the editor" nearby complaining how the small denomination notes issued by the Bank of England until recently were so crudely designed that they they could be forged "by any engraver's apprentice-boy who has been six month's at the trade." The supposed letter-writer closes saying of the Bank's directors, "I would not advise them to enter Charon's boat with the sades of their victims, lest they should be worse treated than the despotic King who passed the river with Telemachus." The language is pure Playfair.

26   For a summary of applicable French law at the time, see Alfred Le Poittevin, "Criminal Procedure," in S.J. Barrows, ed., *Penal Codes of France, Germany, Belgium and Japan: Reports Prepared for the International Prison Commission*, U.S. House of Representatives, Committee on the Judiciary (Washington, D.C.: U.S. Government Printing Office, 1901), 50–51. Under the French code, an infraction of the law may also injure an individual, in which case two suits result—one to impose punishment, the other to recover damages.

27   Playfair, *France As It Is*, Volume 2, 177. Playfair insisted he was only offering Marie-Anne advice for her own good; some of the witnesses at the trial suggested Playfair was shilling for Dufay to support the colonel's libel case against Marie-Anne. The trial received ample coverage (which is how we know Marie-Ann was wearing black in the middle of the summer); in addition to the citations from *Journal des débats politiques et littéraires*, see *Le moniteur universel*, Volume 61 (30 July 1818), 908.

28   *Journal des débats politiques et littéraires* (15 July 1818), 3–4. Specifically: "Que ledit Playfair ne rapporte pas la preunve légale desdits faits, et que ses torts se seroient plutôt aggravés qu'affoiblis par les ironies et les sarcasmes employés dans sa défense;" and "Quelques faits étrangers au procès, et des é'oges ironiques hasardés dans la plaidoirie ont donné lieu, ainsi qu'on va le voir, à une plus grat de séverité. Voiri le jugement qui a été prononcé aujourd hui à ' l'ouverture de l'audience."

29 *Journal des débats politiques et littéraires* (8 July 1818), 4. It reported, "Le ministère public a conclu à l'absolution de M. Galignani, et à la condemnation de M. Playfair."

30 *Journal des débats politiques et littéraires* (14 August 1818), 4. Dufay and his encounters with the law were described in *La police dévoilée depuis la Restauration: et notamment sous messieurs franchet et delavau* Volume 1 (Paris: Lemonnier, editeur, 1829), 202–208; *Journal de Palais: jurisprudence administrative* Volume 2, 1814–1819 (Paris: Bureaux de L'administration, c. 1820) 561–562; and, drawing on French sources, in "A Horrible Duel," *Sacramento Daily Union*, Volume 11 (19 March 1880).

31 *Journal des débats politiques et littéraires* (29 July 1818), 4.

32 Playfair, *France As It Is*, Volume 2, 186.

33 William Playfair to William Windham (London, 31 October 1795) BL ©BLB ADD 37875, fol. 232.

34 John Lightly was a partner with George Atkinson in Lightly and Atkinson, listed as doing business at 178 Upper Thames Street. See "Exeter Working Papers in Book History," available at http://bookhistory.blogspot.com/2007/01/london-1775-1800-l.html (accessed 18 March 2016). A notice indicated Lightly had been doing business at that address when he dissolved his partnership with Atkinson; see *London Gazette* (10 July 1802), 738. Lightly went bankrupt shortly thereafter; see *London Gazette* (10 May 1803), 560 and London Gazette (3 January 1804), 30.

35 See Jacqueline Labbé, "Saint-Morys, Charles Paul Jean-Baptiste de Bourgevin Vialart de (1743–1795), collector, amateur draughtsman, engraver," *Grove Index Online*, summary available at http://oxfordindex.oup.com/view/10.1093/gao/9781884446054.article. T075146 (accessed 6 April 2016).

36 Arnaud de Lestapis, "Emigration et faux assignats I," *La revue des Deux Mondes* (September 1955), 242; de Lestapis noted that, while he did not find the specific document authorizing Saint-Morys, he found original correspondence from the Council, acting under the authority of the prince regent, referring to the authorization. The Council order that later authorized Puisaye to print assignats, cited in A.D. Lanne's *Le mystère de Quiberon*, would have corroborated his analysis, though Lestapis did not mention it.

37 Lestapis, "Emigration et faux assignats I), 239; de Lestapis cites *Annales patriotiques et litteraraires* of 19 December 1791.

38 Puisaye *Mémoires*. Volume 3, 380–381.

39 Ibid., 382–384.

40 Ibid., 381.

41 Ibid., 384. Puisaye recalled the conversation with Saint-Morys as, "Il est à regretter, me dit-il, que lorsqu'on a proposé une opération semblable, on n'ait pas suggéré en même temps, les idées que vous mecommuniquez: mais aujour d'hui il est trop tard." By "too late," Puisaye seems to have been referring to the secret mark he wanted to add.

42 Agreement by le comte Joseph de Puisaye with l'abbé de Calonne, de Saint-Morys (London? 20 September 1794) reproduced in Saint-Albin Berville, François Barrière, eds., *Collection des mémoires relatifs a la revolution française*, Volume 4 (Paris: Baudouin Frères, 1825), 133–135. The relevant passage, in Article 1 of the agreement, reads "Il sera établi une manufacture d'assignats en tout semblables à ceux qui ont été émis ou qui le seront, par la suite, par la soi-disant Convention des rebelles; ces assignats porteront un caractère secret de reconnaissance."

43   John Gordon Sinclair, "Brief Copy of Colonel Sinclair's Affidavit, Filed in Court." (28 July 1798); attachment to the published letter, *To His Royal Highness Monsieur, Brother to Louis XVIII, King of France, &c, &c, &c.* (King's Bench, 12 August 1798), NA HO 42/45, fol. 184.

44   John Gordon Sinclair, *Colonel Sinclair's Letters to His Enemies* (Surry [sic]: Self-published, 1796), 11–14.

45   Sinclair, *Colonel Sinclair's Letters*, 16.

46   Sinclair, "Brief Copy of Colonel Sinclair's Affidavit," NA HO 42/45, fol. 191.

47   Sinclair, "Brief Copy of Colonel Sinclair's Affidavit," NA HO 42/45, fols. 178, 184–185.

48   Sinclair identified the location of the manufactury in his self-published book, *The Effects of Delusion* (London? 1796?), xi.

49   Sinclair, "Brief Copy of Colonel Sinclair's Affidavit," NA HO 42/45, fols. 184–185. Also see William Playfair to William Windham (Fitzroy Square, 21 January 1801), BL ©BLB ADD 37868, fols. 17–23.

50   Puisaye *Mémoires*. Volume 3, 378.

51   Louis Blanc, *Histoire de la Révolution Française* Volume 12 (Paris: Pagnerre, 1862), 110. Blanc cites a letter in *Papiers de Puisaye*, Volume C1 at the British Museum in which Saint-Morys' daughter requested Marquis Dumesnil to approach Windham for the ink.

52   Eugène de la Gournerie, *Les débris de Quiberon: souvenirs du désastre de 1795, suivis de la liste des victims* (Nantes: Librairie Catholique Libaros, 1875), 161. Also see Spencer Pickering, *Memoirs of Anna Maria Wilhelmina Pickering* (London: Hodder and Stoughton, 1903), 478–480.

53   Puisaye, *Mémoires,* Volume 6 (London: Harper and Co., 1807 and 1808), 526. Records show the HMS *Pomone* was a 40-gun French vessel the British captured in 1794 and incorporated into their own fleet.

54   For Puisaye's account of the death of Saint-Morys, see Puisaye *Mémoires*. Volume 6, 614–615. According to Playfair, a "French gentleman" had told him that, when Saint-Morys was on his deathbed he had told his friends to be sure to pay for the paper; see Playfair to Windham (Bows Lane, 8 November 1795), BL ©BLB, ADD 37875 fols. 253–254. For a discussion of the younger Saint-Morys inheriting monies owed his father, see Burrows, *French Exile Journalism*, 55

55   William Playfair to William Windham (Lambeth Marsh, 26 March 1796) ,BL ©BLB, ADD 37876 fol. 38. This was the letter quoted earlier in which Playfair said, "I confess your conduct towards me has been such that I am inclined to let no occasion slip of shewing my gratitude."

56   William Playfair to Col. Sinclair (Lambeth Marsh, 29 March 1796), NAGL ADD MS 403. This is the letter mentioned earlier that is addressed simply to "Col. Sinclair." It's John Gordon Sinclair. There is no one named "Sinclair" on the British Army's Officer List of the period who would fit the description; John Gordon Sinclair received his commission from the French Princes after raising his regiment. In his 22 December 1795 letter to Windham (see BL © BLB, ADD 37875 fol. 285), Playfair said he believed Sinclair to be "an Extraordinary Character."

57   Playfair to Sinclair (29 March 1796), NAGL ADD MS 403. In the postscript Playfair also advised Sinclair not to get drunk when meeting with a third person, Leachmore,

closing, "it is dangerous to you and therefore try to avoid that if you can – WP." Playfair either genuinely liked Sinclair, or he was working him like a dray horse.

58   William Playfair, *Political Portraits in this New Æra*, Supplementary Volume (London: C. Chapple, 1816), 169.

59   Sinclair, *Colonel Sinclair's Letters*, 48.

60   "Declaration of the Rev. Julius Hutchinson," (28 July 1798); attachment to the published letter, *To His Royal Highness Monsieur, Brother to Louis XVIII, King of France, &c, &c, &c.* (King's Bench, 12 August 1798), NA HO 42/45 fol. 191–192; Hutchison recalled he first met Sinclair at "the Camp of St. Omers, commanded by the Prince of Condé," which was near Calais. After that Sinclair was invited to Paris and met with Lafayette and considered supporting the "constitutionalists" before some friends persuaded him to join the "King's Brothers"—that is, the royalists—at Coblentz, against Hutchinson's advice.

61   "Case of John Gordon Sinclair," attachment to *To His Brother to Louis XVIII, King of France, &c, &c, &c.* NA HO 42/45 fol. 177.

62   "Declaration of the Rev. Julius Hutchinson," (28 July 1798 attachment to *To His Brother to Louis XVIII, King of France, &c, &c, &c,* NA HO 42/45 fol. 191–192. Also see the summary of the trial in "The King versus John Gordon Sinclair," *The Sporting Magazine* (June 1798). 146–148. Despite its name, *The Sporting Magazine* carried news of general interest.

63   William Staddon Blake and John Lightly, "Extract of Affidavit," (1 May 1798), attachment to *To His Brother to Louis XVIII, King of France, &c, &c, &c.* NA HO 42/45, unnumbered, follows fol. 192.

64   Petition by Colonel John Gordon Sinclair to King George III (King's Bench, 20 December 1798) NA HO 42/45, fols. 199–200; the supporting affidavits are in the published letter, *To His Royal Highness Monsieur, Brother to Louis XVIII, King of France, &c, &c, &c,* (King's Bench, 12 August 1798), NA HO 42/45, fols. 186–198.

65   William Playfair to unknown recipient (23 August 1797), NAGL ADD MS 403. The passage reads as:

> I thought he had informed you that Vertaul had secreted or kept back a portion of the notes which were given to him to discount for the Bath Bank & that the 460 L was a part of the restitution. This infidelity of the part of Vertaul was kept a secret that shame might prompt him to come to the Bath people from coming all upon us to be paid without any renewals (which I can prove was the Plan) & so commensing our business very unfortunately…

Playfair was likely referring to Peter Vertaul, who wrote on economic matters and was listed as bankrupt shortly after the Original Security Bank failure; see *London Gazette* (27 February–3 March 1798), 192. For a reference to his writing, see *La Nation Angloise ne peut etre ruinee par ses Emprunts* ("The English Nation Cannot be Ruined by Loans"), 1798; *Catalogue of the library of the Athenæum, Liverpool* (Printed for the Athenæum by Cheswick Press, 1864) 573.

66   Playfair to Windham (Fitzroy Square, 21 January 1801).

67   See A.D. Harvey, "The Ministry of all the Talent: The Whigs in Office, February 1806 to March 1807," *The Historical Journal* Volume 15, No. 4 (1972), 619–648. Harvey agreed the "Ministry of All the Talents was a set-back rather than an advance for the Whig party," but believed it deserved more credit than it usually received. Grenville did succeed

in abolishing the British slave trade, which, in retrospect, may have been as important as anything.

68   For Wickham's espionage services, see Michael Durey, *William Wickham* as cited previously. For Smith, see Durey, "Escape of Sir Sidney Smith," 438–439. To get a sense of Drake's activities, see the "Bulletins" he provided the Ministry, reproduced in *The Manuscripts of J. B. Fortescue, esq., Preserved at Dropmore*, Volume 2 (London: HMSO, 1894), iv and passim.

69   *Hansard*, Volume 20, Col. 867, HL Debate (8 July 1811). The Grenville quotations are as published in the Hansard, so they are likely paraphrases. Available at http://hansard. millbanksystems.com/lords/1811/jul/08/gold-coin-and-bank-note-bill#column_867 (accessed 23 December 2016).

70   Playfair, *Political Portraits*, Volume 2, 66–71.

71   William Playfair to William Wyndham Grenville (10 July 1811), reproduced in *The Manuscripts of J. B. Fortescue, esq., Preserved at Dropmore*, Volume 10 (London: HMSO, 1927), 155–156.

72   Playfair to Windham (Bows Lane, 8 November 1795).

73   See "Introduction," *Manuscripts of J. B. Fortescue*, Volume 10 (London: HMSO, 1927), vii.

Chapter 11: An Unconventional Business Model

1   Walter Thornbury, *Old and New London: A Narrative of its People and Its Places* (London: Cassell, Petter & Galpin, 1873), 202, 526.

2   See James Playfair, "Journal of Architecture 1783, 4, 5, 6, 7, 8,—1789–90—91 of James Playfair," NLS, Adv. MS.33.5.25. James listed several meetings with Douglas and work on "Bothwell Castle" in July 1788. Bothwell House, also known as New Bothwell Castle, was demolished in 1926; see Alastair McNeill, "Historians Look for Help in Uncovering Story of Demolished Bothwell Mansion," (Glasgow) *Daily Record and Sunday Mail (*28 July 2011); available at http://www.dailyrecord.co.uk/news/local-news/historians-look-help-uncovering-story-2416152#ZlbZTJDEgMRjxsyh.99 (accessed 19 June 2016); and "Bothwell House," in *The Douglas Archives* available at http://www.douglashistory.co.uk/history/Places/bothwell-house.htm (accessed 22 January 2017).

3   William Playfair to Archibald Douglas (London, 23 September 1816) NRAS859/Box 44/Bundle 10. The primary source for the exchanges between among Playfair, Douglas, and others involved in the affair are the papers preserved in the Douglas-Home family archives. (Douglas and Home, two of the oldest Border families, were joined when Cospatrick Alexander Home married Jane Margaret Douglas, the only daughter of Archibald Douglas in 1875.) The papers are privately held, but catalogued by the National Records of Scotland, which made them available at the National Library of Scotland.

4   For an example of Playfair being described as an extortionist, see Ian Spence, "Playfair, William," 562–563. Spence doubted the papers Playfair offered for sale existed.

5   The Duke of Douglas was also named Archibald—he was Archibald Douglas, 1st Duke of Douglas. The son of Lady Jane and Colonel Stewart ultimately became Archibald Douglas, 1st Baron Douglas. For brevity and clarity, we'll call the elder Archibald "the Duke of Douglas," and the younger Archibald "Archibald."

6   This is how the question was phrased by Karl Sabbagh, in *The Trials of Lady Jane Douglas: The Scandal that Divided 18th Century Britain* (Newbold on Stour, Warwickshire: Skyscraper Publications, Ltd., 2014), the most recent and probably the most detailed analysis of the Douglas Cause.

7   Fitzmaurice, *Life of William, Earl of Shelburne*, Volume 1, 7.

8   Ian Spence and Howard Wainer, William Playfair: A Daring Worthless Fellow," *Chance*, Volume 10, Issue 1 (1997), 31–34. Also see Sabbagh, *The Trials of Lady Jane Douglas*, 362.

9   Charles Douglas to Archibald Douglas (All Souls College, 20 December 1816); Douglas-Home family, Earls of Home: NRAS859/Box 44/Bundle 10.

10   Archibald Douglas to Charles Douglas (Bothwell Castle, 25 December 1816); Douglas-Home family, Earls of Home: NRAS859/Box 44/Bundle 10.

11   See Sabbagh, *The Trials of Lady Jane Douglas*, 361, 378. Sabbagh thought Playfair might have had "documents someone tried to sell him," but is generally dismissive. Sabbagh also thought, however, that Archibald might indeed have been purchased as a child; he found what appeared to be a prayer note in the Douglas-Home archives that Lady Jane may have written as she was facing death. In the note, she seemed to ask forgiveness for an unspeakable sin.

12   Archibald Douglas to Charles Douglas (Bothwell Castle, 25 December 1816); Douglas-Home family, Earls of Home: NRAS859/ Box 44/Bundle 10.

13   William Garrow to David Wemyss (Lincoln's Inn, 2 January 1817), Douglas-Home family, Earls of Home: NRAS859/ Box 44/Bundle 10. The memorandum is is in the copybook that Wemyss appears to have prepared for Archibald. It is possible that Garrow sent the original to Wemyss, or to one of the other lawyers involved in the case, or to Charles himself after their conversation. In any case, Garrow is providing his opinion about how to deal with Playfair.

14   Charles Douglas to Archibald Douglas (Bruton Street, 3 January 1817); Douglas-Home family, Earls of Home: NRAS859/ Box 44/Bundle 10.

15   For a factual account of Garrow's career, see John Hostettler and Richard Braby, *Sir William Garrow: His Life, Times and Fight for Justice* (Sheffield Gable, UK: Waterside Press, 2009).

16   G.F. Russell Barker, "Garrow, Sir William (1760–1840)," *Dictionary of National Biography*, Volume 21 (New York: Macmillan and Co., 1890), 28–29.

17   Playfair, *Political Portraits* Volume 2, 1.

18   Ibid., 10.

19   See James Lindgren, "Unraveling the Paradox of Blackmail," *Columbia Law Review* Volume 84 (April 1984). Lindgren observes Parliament did not pass an anti-blackmail statue until 1843. He notes (675) that a 1757 act made it illegal to "expose a capital offense or an infamous crime," but applying it here would have been a stretch. The only potential "crime" Playfair would have exposed would have been acts of Colonel Stewart and Lady Jane, which, as Archibald said, was long settled. Playfair was merely seeking money by threatening to publicize facts Archibald would find inconvenient.

20   See Van Vechten Veeder, "The History and Theory of the Law of Defamation, Part I," *Columbia Law Review*, Volume 3 (December 1903), 546–573; and Van Vechten Veeder, "The History and Theory of the Law of Defamation, Part II," *Columbia Law Review*, Volume 4 (January 1904), 33–56.

21 See, for example, Playfair, *Letter to the Right Honourable the Earl Fitzwilliam*, 8–10; Playfair, *Political Portraits*, Volume 2, 10–13 and 16–17; Playfair, *France As It Is*, Volume 1, 244–247 and 252–254; and Volume 2, 175–186.

22 Playfair, *Political Portraits*, Volume 2, 17.

23 The term "paradox of blackmail" is credited to Glanville Williams; see his "Blackmail," *The Criminal Law Review* (1954) 163. The paradox is that "two rights make a wrong," or as Williams put it, "two things that taken separately are moral and legal whites together make a moral and legal black." Others argue that the prospective acts may be legal, but if they interfere in the law or make the government a party to an act deemed illegal, then they are illegal, too; see Michael Clark "There Is No Paradox of Blackmail," *Analysis*, Volume 54 (January 1994), 54–61.

24 Thomas Byerley to William Playfair (41 Long Acre, 11 July 1816), NLS MS 19829, fol. 13; and "A Warning Address to The Monied Interest concerning the Abuses and Frauds committed by the making of False Estimates of Canals, Bridges, Mills, Machinery & Buildings by Civil Engineers with a variety of Curious Facts," (undated), NLS MS 19829, fols. 15–16.

25 William Playfair to John Rennie (Holborn Hill, 17 July 1816), NLS MS 19829, fol. 14.

26 John Rennie to William Playfair (Stamford Street, 22 July 1816), NLS MS 19829, fol. 21–22. There is also a copy of the letter at fols. 23, 26.

27 William Playfair to John Rennie (Holborn Hill, 23 July 1816), NLS MS 19829, fol. 25.

28 William Playfair to John Rennie (Holborn Hill, 26 July 1816), NLS MS 19829, fol. 29; John Rennie to William Playfair (Stamford Street, 27 July 1816), NLS MS 19829, fol. 31.

29 William Playfair to John Rennie (Holborn Hill, 29 July 1816), NLS MS 19829, fol. 33; Thomas Byerley to William Playfair (41 Long Acre, 1 August 1816), NLS MS 19829, fol. 37; and William Playfair, "Memorandum" (London, 23 August 1816), NLS, MS 19829, fol. 49.

30 William Playfair to John Rennie (Holborn Hill, 23 August 1816), NLS MS 19829, fol. 46–48.

31 Thomas Byerley to William Playfair (41 Long Acre, 12 August 1816), NLS MS 19829, fol. 40.

32 Willliam Playfair to James Watt (Tavis Inn, Holborn 13 April 1810), LB MS 3219/4/50.

33 Byerley, "Mr. William Playfair," *Literary Chronicle* (15 March 1823), 172.

34 *London Gazette* (7 January 1815), 32. Also see *London Gazette* (6 May 1815), 864, which reports Grace losing his house, shop, and nursery.

35 Playfair, *A Fair and Candid Address*.

36 See Playfair, *Inevitable Consequences of a Reform in Parliament*, 7.

37 Playfair, *A Fair and Candid Address*, 35.

38 Ibid., 6.

39 Ibid., 25.

40 George Canning to William Playfair (Glouster Lodge, 19 March 1813), NLS SC-085-15, Acc.13236/49.

41 Playfair, *Political Portraits*, Volume 1, 218.

42 William Playfair to Spencer Perceval (Covent Garden, 6 August 1808), NA TS 11/106/318/1/1, fol 40a. The last words in the first sentence seem most likely to read as "the Group" but they might be "Mr [indistinguishable]." Also, it is not clear what the

manuscript was. John Charles Herries drafted a reply to a 19 November letter from Playfair suggesting there was a disagreement over the terms of his engagement. The National
Archives filed this series of letters with the Treasury Solicitor's materials on the Delicate
Investigation, though the last part of the file consists of letters related to Playfair's efforts
to get out of Newgate.

43   John Charles Herries to Spencer Perceval (Downing Street, 6 November 1808), NA TS
11/106, fol. 17. The letter appears to read, "I cannot better explain the object of my present application to you than by sending you enclosed letters from Mr. Huskisson [most
likely William Huskisson, Under-Secretary of the Treasury] as you will perceive that it
is relative to the purchase of another copy of the book of which one was redeemed from
the hands of Playfair some time since." Huskisson, like Playfair, was a protégé of Dundas
and, while in France, was interested in assignats. The book might have been about finance,
but was found in the archives in the files pertaining to the Delicate Investigation. On the
surface, Playfair's letter resembles those he used to extort money from targets like Douglas and Rennie, but subsequent letters in the file suggest that he was on good terms with
Herries and Perceval.

44   Jane Robins chronicled Caroline's marriage and the Delicate Investigation in *Rebel Queen:
How the Trial of Caroline Brought England to the Brink of Revolution* (London: Pocket
Books, 2007).

45   For the Commission's report, see Spencer Perceval, *The Genuine Book: An Inquiry or Delicate Investigation into the Conduct of Her Royal Highness the Princess of Wales* (London: M.
Jones, 1813).

46   Jones, "Living the Enlightenment," 179.

47   Quoted in Samuel Smiles, *Lives of Boulton and Watt* (London, J. Murray, 1865), 418.

48   A.E. Musson and E. Robinson, "The Early Growth of Steam Power," *The Economic History Review*, Volume 11, no. 3 (1958), 431. They cite James Watt, Junior, to James Lawson
(Soho, 17 March 1796), BCL Letter Book A.

49   W.H. Chaloner, "The Cheshire Activities of Matthew Boulton and James Watt of Soho
near Birmingham 1776–1817," *Transactions of the Lancashire and Cheshire Antiquarian
Society*, Volume LXI (1951) 130. Emphasis in original.

50   Chaloner, "The Cheshire Activities," 131.

51   H.W. Dickinson, *James Watt: Craftsmn & Engineer* (Cambridge: Cambridge University
Press, 1936), 165–167.

52   Dickinson and Jenkins, *Watt and the Steam Engine*, 347.

53   Oliver Fairclough, "Aston Hall," in Andy Foster, ed., *Birmingham* (New Haven: Yale University Press, 2005), 274; and Alfred Davidson, *A History of the Holtes of Aston* (Birmingham: E. Evritt, 1854), 55.

54   James Watt, Junior to John Rennie (London, 14 October 1819), LB James Watt Papers
C6/10. David Philip Miller originally identified this exchange of letters for his book, *Discovering Water*. The Library of Birmingham changed its cataloguing system since Miller
did his research, but the Library staff were able to retrieve copies using his references.
Because they come from Junior's papers, the Library has clear copies of only Playfair's and
Rennie's side of the exchange. Junior's letters are press copies and thus difficult to read in
their entirety.

55   Playfair, "The Late James Watt," *Monthly Magazine*, 230–239.

56   William Playfair, "Memoir of James Watt, Esq., F.R.S," *The New Monthly Magazine* Volume 12 (1 December 1819), 576.

57   See David Higgins, "The New Monthly Magazine," in *The Literary Encyclopedia* (22 October 2006. Available at http://www.litencyc.com/php/stopics.php?rec=true&UID=1682 (accessed 15 July 2016); and Sack, *From Jacobite to Conservative*, 18. The politics of the two magazines later flip-flopped, with the *Monthly Magazine* becoming the more conservative and the *New Monthly Magazine* more liberal.

58   Henry Colburn to James Watt, Junior (London: 11 September 1819), LB James Watt Papers C6/10.

59   John Rennie to James Watt, Junior (London, 11 September 1819), LB James Watt Papers C6/10.

60   William Playfair to James Watt, Junior (Holborn, 25 September 1819), LB James Watt Papers C6/10. Playfair's underlining.

61   William Playfair to James Watt, Junior (Holborn, 25 September 1819), LB James Watt Papers C6/10.

62   James Watt, Junior to John Rennie (Soho, 14 October 1819), LB James Watt Papers C6/10.

63   William Playfair to James Watt, Junior (Holborn, 12 October 1819), LB James Watt Papers C6/10.

64   John Rennie to James Watt, Junior (London, 25 October 1819), LB James Watt Papers C6/10.

65   William Playfair to James Watt, Junior (Holborn, 22 October 1819), LB James Watt Papers C6/10.

66   John Rennie to James Watt, Junior (London, 1 November 1819), LB James Watt Papers, C6/10.

67   See Matthew Whiting Rosa, *The Silver-Fork School: Novels of Fashion Preceding Vanity Fair* (New York : Columbia University Press, 1936).

68   *A Biographical Dictionary of the Living Authors of Great Britain and Ireland* (London: Henry Colburn, 1816), 276.

69   See, for example, Veronica Melnyk, "Half Fashion and Half Passion: The Life of Publisher Henry Colburn," Doctoral Thesis, Department of English, University of Birmingham (September 2002). Melnyk acknowledges Colburn's reputation as "troublesome" with competitors, partners, and authors, but argues it may be unfair.

70   Henry Richard Tedder, "Colburn, Henry," in Leslie Stephen, *Dictionary of National Biography, 1885-1900*, Volume 11 (New York: Macmillan and Company, 1887), 254.

71   Lady Morgan (Sydney Owenson), *France* (New York: James Eastburn & Co., 1817).

72   Playfair, *France as It Is*, Volume 1, xxxvi.

73   Playfair, *Agricultural Distresses*. Playfair would also publish a four-page pamphlet showing that interest on Britain's national debt was exceeding its income: *Can This Continue?* (London: William Sams, 1822). The pamphlet is not dated, but the chart includes data through 1821, implying it was published the following year.

74   *Anticipation* (12 March 1808), 15–16.

75   Playfair, *Agricultural Distresses* , iv.

76   Ibid., 13.

77 Playfair, *A General View of the Actual Force and Resources of France*, 51–54. William Fleetwood usually gets credit for inventing the idea of an inflation adjustment index a hundred
years earlier. In 1706, a student asked Fleetwood, a fellow at King's College at Cambridge,
for help with a moral question: The college's 1438 charter said no student could be admitted whose family had an estate worth more than five pounds. Could, the student asked
Fleetwood, swear that his family's estate, nominally valued at six pounds, met the charter's
criteria "under the presumption that six pounds now is not worth what five pounds was
when that statute was made?" Fleetwood, who had collected historical price data, told the
student he could indeed swear the oath, since the purchasing power of his money had
fallen. Nevertheless Playfair gets credit for first illustrating the idea with real data and
applying it to a time series. See E.H. Phelps Brown and Sheila V. Hopkins, "Seven Centuries of Wages and Prices: Some Earlier Estimates," *Economica*, Volume 28 (February
1961), 30–36; and W. A. Chance, "A Note on the Origins of Index Numbers" *The Review
of Economics and Statistics*, Volume 48 (February 1966), 108–110.
78 Playfair, *Letter on Our Agricultural Distresses*, 31.
79 *Chronology of Public Events and Remarkable Occurrences within the Last Fifty Years; or from
1774 to 1824* (London: G. and W. B. Whittaker, 1824).
80 Smith, *Wealth of Nations* (Hartford, 1811) Volume 2, 358.
81 Ibid., 359.
82 Playfair, *History of Jacobinism*, 229–230.
83 Smith, *Wealth of Nations* (Hartford, 1811) Volume 2, 359.

Chapter 12: Endings

1 William Playfair memorandum (London, 20 March 1793), TU/SRC MSS BH 118
COCH.
2 Philipson, "Case of Economic Warfare," 151–157. Also see the images presented in
Chapter Eight.
3 Swinburne, NWZSW/590.
4 William Playfair to William Windham (Bow Lane, 8, 10 November 1795), BL ©BLB
ADD 37875, fols. 253–256.
5 William Playfair to William Wyndham Grenville (10 July 1811), reproduced in *The Manuscripts of J. B. Fortescue, esq., Preserved at Dropmore*, Volume 10 (London: HMSO, 1927),
155–156.
6 Sir. R. (Richard) Philips to Dr. (Thomas) Dale (25 February 1802), BL ©BLB, Loan 96
RLF 1/121, fol. 1–2; and receipt from Playfair to Dale (Old Brompton, 9 May 1802), BL
©BLB, Loan 96 RLF 1/121, fol. 3.
7 William Playfair to David William (Old Brompton, 9 May 1807), BL ©BLB, Loan
96 RLF 1/121, fol. 5; and William Playfair to David William (Old Brompton, 13 May
1807), BL ©BLB, Loan 96 RLF 1/121, fols. 6–7.
8 William Playfair to Literary Fund (Infirmary, White Cross Street, 8 April 1820), BL
©BLB, Loan 96 RLF 1/121, fol. 11. After waiting almost two weeks for a reply, Playfair
wrote again, asking for an answer; see William Playfair to Literary Fund (White Cross
Street Prison, 29 April 1820), BL ©BLB, Loan 96 RLF 1/121, fol. 12. He sent a receipt for ten pounds to the Fund five weeks later; see William Playfair to Literary Fund

(White Cross Street Prison, 25 May 1820), BL ©BLB,Loan 96 RLF 1/121, fol. 13; and a follow-up letter, William Playfair to Literary Fund (White Cross Street Prison, 29 May 1820), BL ©BLB,Loan 96 RLF 1/121, fol. 14.

9   William Playfair to Literary Fund (2 July 1820), BL ©BLB, Loan 96 RLF 1/121, fol. 15.

10   William Playfair to Literary Fund (22 August 1820), BL ©BLB, Loan 96 RLF 1/121, fol. 17.

11   William Playfair to Literary Fund (In the hand of the Prison, White Cross Street, 31 July 1820), BL ©BLB, Loan 96 RLF 1/121, fol. 16. The rejection notice is Literary Fund to William Playfair (69 Great Queens St., 23 August 1820), BL ©BLB, Loan 96 RLF 1/121, fol. 18.

12   William Playfair to Literary Fund (15 December 1820), BL ©BLB, Loan 96 RLF 1/121, fol. 19. An internal memorandum dated 21 December suggests the Board did consider the plan; see fol. 20. In 1999, the Royal Literary Fund adopted a scheme similar to what Playfair proposed, basing established authors in universities where they could assist students.

13   "Playfair," *The New Monthly Magazine,* 282.

14   William Playfair to Henry Addington, 1st Viscount Sidmouth (London, 11 December 1820) NA HO 44/3, fol. 184.

15   H. Hobhouse to William Playfair (Whitehall, 18 December 1820), NA HO 44/3. fol. 184b.

16   Mark S. Auburn, "Theatre in the Age of Garrick and Sheridan," in James Morwood and David Crane, eds., *Sheridan Studies* (Cambridge: Cambridge University Press, 1995), 44–45.

17   William Playfair to Literary Fund (21 January 1823), BL ©BLB, Loan 96 RLF 1/121, fol. 21.

18   Mary Playfair to Literary Fund (19 March 1823), BL ©BLB, Loan 96 RLF 1/121, fol. 22.

19   William Playfair to Literary Fund (21 January 1823), BL ©BLB, Loan 96 RLF 1/121, fol. 21.

20   Stuart, *Steam-Engines,* 549.

21   See, for example, George Hayward, "Statistics of the Amputations of the Large Limbs That Have Been Performed at the Massachusetts General Hospital," in *The Boston Medical and Surgical Journal* (Boston: David Clapp, Printer, 1850).

22   Stuart, *Steam-Engines,* 550.

23   There is a discussion of burials of parishioners of St. George's at Hanover Square and its Bayswater burial ground (used between 1762 and 1854) at http://www.regencyhistory.net/2015/09/st-georges-hanover-square.html; also see the discussion by relatives and others at http://www.rootschat.com/forum/index.php?topic=518641.0 (accessed 19 August 2016).

24   Byerley, "Mr. William Playfair," *Literary Chronicle* (15 March 1823), 172. As noted earlier, Robert Stuart credited Byerley for the obituary in *Historical and Descriptive Anecdotes of Steam-Engines, and of Their Inventors and Improvers* (London: Wightman and Cramp, 1829), 547–350. Byerley's obituary appeared first and that, plus his association with Playfair, says that he was the one who originally gathered the facts.

25   See "Mr. William Playfair," *The Gentleman's Magazine: and Historical Chronicle* from January to June 1823 (London: John Nichole and Son, 1923) 564–566; and "PLAYFAIR,"

Annual Biography 1824, 458–460. The *Gentleman's Magazine* credited the *Literary Chronicle*.

26 "Saint George Hanover Square Burial Ground Bill," *Hansard*, Volume 689, HC Debates (11 February 1964), 300–314.

27 See H.W. Dickinson and A.A. Gomme, "Robert Stuart Meikleham," paper read at the Institution of Structural Engineers, London (11 March 1942).

28 Stuart, *Steam-Engines*, 550.

29 S.E. Fryer, "John Goldworth Alger," *Dictionary of National Biography, Second Supplement*, Vol. 1 (New York: The Macmillan Company, 1912) 32–33.

30 John Goldworth Alger, *Napoleon's Visitors and Captives 1801–1815* (London: Archibald Constable and Company, Ltd., 1904), 108–109. Alger's *Englishmen in the French Revolution* appeared in 1889—just eight years after Lecocq published the roster of the Petit Sainte-Antoine militia in *La prise de la Bastille*. He wrote that Playfair "must have assisted in the capture of the Bastille" because he was on the roster (10–11).

31 Alger, "Playfair," *Dictionary of National Biography*, 415.

32 Anne Cary Morris, ed., *The Diary and Letters of Gouverneur Morris* Volume 1 (New York: Charles Scribner's Sons, 1888), 261.

33 James Patrick Muirhead, *The Life of James Watt* (London: John Murray, 1858). James Watt, Junior, did write an anonymous article on his father for the *Encyclopedia Britannica* in 1824. Also see Samuel Smiles, *Lives of Boulton and Watt* (London: John Murray, 1865). Smiles cited Playfair's *New Monthly Magazine* memoir as a source in passing; see 483.

34 I.W. Chubb, "Museum of Watt Developments," *Power and the Engineer* (21 June 1910), 1109–1112; also see I. William Chubb, "Watt Centenary Celebration in England," *Power* (22 November 1919), 597. In addition to the company files, the Boulton family donated their papers in 1974. The City of Birmingham purchased the papers of Watt and family in 1994. See Mike Lockley, "Archives of Soho lift the lid on the genius of James Watt and Matthew Boulton," *Birmingham Mail* 14 October 2012), available at http://www.birminghammail.co.uk/news/local-news/archives-of-soho-lift-the-lid-on-the-genius-3297 (accessed 29 July 2016).

35 Two German scholars had mentioned Playfair: August Ferdinand Lueder, *Kritische Geschichte der Statistik* (Gottingen, Johan Friederich Rowe, 1817), 118–119; and A. Meitzen, *History, Theory and Techniques of Statistics* (Philadelphia: American Academy of Political and Social Science, 1891); see Patricia Costigan-Eaves and Michael Macdonald-Ross, "William Playfair (1759–1823)," *Statistical Science*, Volume 5, No. 5 (1990), 318. Also, Fernand Faure cited *Tableaux a'Arithmetique lineaire* in his Éléments de Statistique (Paris: Larose & Tenin, 1906), 74; Faure noted that the French translation had fewer graphics than the original English *Lineal Arithmetic*, indicating he was familiar with both.

36 "The Inventor of Graphic Statistics," *Bulletin of the Business Historical Society* Volume 1 (September 1926), 13–16.

37 See Tufte, *Visual Display of Quantitative Information*, 31: for the backstory of how Tufte came to write the book and founded a successful business of products and seminars around it, see Mark Zachry and Charlotte Thrall, "An Interview with Edward R. Tufte," *Technical Communication Quarterly*, Volume 13, Number 4 (2004), 452.

38 Patricia Costigan-Eaves and Michael Macdonald-Ross, "William Playfair (1759–1823)," *Statistical* Science Volume 5 (August 1990), 318–326. Costigan-Eaves and Macdon-

ald-Ross, like Tufte and many of their contemporaries, drew on H.G. Funkhouser, who had written about Playfair's graphics earlier. See his "Historical Development of the Graphical Representation of Data," *Osiris,* Volume 3 (1937), 269–404. At about the same time, Willard Cope Brinton published an update of the book he had written in 1914 on statistical graphics, *Graphic Methods for Presenting Facts,* saying, with much regret, that he had been unaware of Playfair at the time of first publication; he provided his own brief memoir in *Graphic Presentation* (New York: Brinton Associates, 1939), which he dedicated to Playfair, "First Exponent of Graphic Charts for General Use."

39   Dickinson and Jenkins, *Watt and the Steam Engine,* 285.

40   Dickinson, "Some Unpublished Letters of James Watt," 487–534.

41   James Watt to Matthew Boulton (Redruth, 27 June 1778), reproduced in Dickenson,"Some Unpublished Letters of James Watt," 497. The original letter is now listed in the Library of Birmingham as MS 3782/12/76/37. The letter refers to "Mr Hall," but fits the description of John Hall, the foreman Boulton & Watt appointed in 1778. For examples of Hall's activities (and therefore some of the responsibilities Playfair assumed), see John Hall to Matthew Boulton (Soho, 8 February 1778), LB MS 3782/12/24/158; and John Hall to Matthew Boulton (Soho, 15 February 1778), LB MS 3782/12/24/160. Watt also previously expressed his ire with Hall—and to a slightly less degree with Playfair—in James Watt to Matthew Boulton (Redruth, 19 June 1778), LB MS 3782/12/76, fol. 35.

42   James Watt to Matthew Boulton, in Dickenson, 497.

43   James Watt to Matthew Boulton, LB MS 3782/12/76.

44   Matthew Boulton to James Watt (4 July 1778); cited as Box 20/5 in the LB Archives Catalogue, provided by Library staff (26 June 2006), however, as of July 2017 this appears to be part of MS 3147/3/3.

45   On 29 July Boulton told Watt that Playfair was on the road with Logan Henderson, a former Marine officer who came to work at Boulton & Watt a few years before Playfair. "Although I am convinced that we must take another in Hall's place," Boulton wrote, "in the confused State we are in at present I think it better for him to stay until Henderson sends Playfare back." See Matthew Boulton to James Watt (Soho, 29 July 1778), LB MS 3147/3/2.

46   William Playfair to Logan Henderson (Soho, 16 September 1780), LB MS 3782/12/25/9.

47   James Keir to Matthew Boulton (Soho. 11 December 1779), LB MS 3782/12/76/37; Muirhead, *Origin and Progress,* 27–35.

48   William Playfair to various individuals, LB MS 3147/19/1 fols. 92–108.

49   James Watt to Matthew Boulton (Cosgarne, 21 and 23 January 1782), reproduced in James Patrick Muirhead, *The Origins and Progress of the Mechanical Inventions of James Watt* (London: John Murray, 1854), 138–139.

50   John Buchanan to James Watt (Soho, 6 November 1781), LB MS 53147/3/246. James recommended the candidate, though frankly telling Buchanan that his man was "not very bright" and not "a good hand at finished drawings, but you are to judge whether that he will be wanted." Emphasis in the original.

51   William Playfair to Matthew Boulton (Soho, 7 February 1778), LB MS 3782/12/24/157.

52   William Playfair to William Hutchins (London, 17 June 1798), NA ADD MS 403.

53   Kudos for this observation goes to Adam Garfinkle, who made it while editing my article, "An Agent of Influence," *The American Interest* (October/November 2009), 102–109.

54 See Jennet Conant, *A Covert Affair: When Julia and Paul Child Joined the OSS* (New York: Simon and Schuster, 2011).

55 See Douglas C. Waller, *Wild Bill Donovan: The Spymaster Who Created the OSS and Modern American Espionage* (New York: Free Press, 2011).

Index

A Note on the Type

The text of this book is set in Adobe Caslon Pro. This typeface, designed by Carol Twombly, is based on specimen pages printed by London-based engraver William Caslon (1692–1766) between 1734 and 1770.

Chapter titles, headers, page numbers, and drop caps are set in Playfair Display—also used on the book's jacket cover—created by typeface designer Claus Eggers Sørensen. Assuredly it doesn't have anything to do with our William Playfair, but we like to think he would have been pleased by the design's efficient appearance and the symmetry of the name. According to the designer, "Playfair is a transitional design. From the time of enlightenment in the late 18th century, the broad nib quills were replaced by pointed steel pens. This influenced typographical letterforms to become increasingly detached from the written ones. Developments in printing technology, ink and paper making, made it possible to print letterforms of high contrast and delicate hairlines." See also http://www.forthehearts.net/playfair-display.